# François Rabelais

*a reference guide*
*1950–1990*

*A*
*Reference*
*Guide*
*to*
*Literature*

*David O'Connell*
*Editor*

# François Rabelais

*a reference guide*
*1950–1990*

BRUNO BRAUNROT

G.K. Hall & Co.
An Imprint of Macmillan Publishing Company
*New York*

Maxwell Macmillan Canada
*Toronto*

Maxwell Macmillan International
*New York    Oxford    Singapore    Sydney*

G. K. Hall & Co.
An Imprint of Macmillan Publishing Company
866 Third Avenue
New York, NY 10022

Library of Congress Catalog Card Number: 93–48314

Printed in the United States of America

Printing number
1  2  3  4  5  6  7  8  9  10

**Library of Congress Cataloging-in-Publication Data**

Braunrot, Bruno.
    François Rabelais : a reference guide 1950–1990 / Bruno Braunrot.
      p. cm. — (A Reference guide to literature)
    Includes bibliographical references and index.
    ISBN 0-8161-9079-8
    1. Rabelais, François, ca. 1490–1553?—Bibliography.   I Title.
  II. Series.
    Z8730.B79   1994
[PQ1693]
016.843'3—dc20                          93-48314
                                              CIP

*Pauca meis*

# Contents

# The Author

Born in Warsaw and educated in Paris and Montreal, Bruno Braunrot holds a B.A. (in philosophy) and an M.A. (in French literature) from McGill University. He received his Ph.D. in French literature from Yale University in 1970.

After two years as a teaching assistant at Yale, he taught at McGill University, the University of Virginia, Wayne State University, and Georgia State University, where he presently chairs the Department of Modern and Classical Languages.

Bruno Braunrot is the author of *L'Imagination poétique chez du Bartas*, and a number of articles on the poet of *La Création du Monde*. He is also one of the contributors to the two volumes on the Renaissance in the *Cabeen Bibliography*, published by Syracuse University Press in 1986.

# Preface

Founded in 1903 by Abel Lefranc, *La Revue des Études Rabelaisiennes* ceased publication under that title a mere nine years later, allegedly because nothing remained to be said on the specific topic for which it had been created. The reader of the present volume, to say nothing of its author, can probably be forgiven for finding such an assessment to have been decidedly premature. If the progress of Rabelais studies was relatively slow in the period immediately following the decision to turn *La Revue des Études Rabelaisiennes* into the somewhat less specialized *Revue du Seizième Siècle*, the subsequent pace of research on Rabelais between the two world wars, and especially in the last forty years, has made it an increasingly daunting prospect for scholars and students to keep abreast of the significant work done in the field. Despite the ready availability of conventional bibliographical listings, the intensity of critical activity surrounding Rabelais' novels has made the task of establishing a meaningful preliminary *état présent* in any given area of Rabelais studies an ever more difficult undertaking. It is with this difficulty in mind that this annotated bibliography has been written.

The decision to cover in this reference guide the relatively long span of forty years makes it possible for the reader to follow the evolution of critical attitudes toward Rabelais during a particularly innovative period in the history of literary criticism. The opportunity to observe the full spectrum of critical approaches as they are brought to bear on a body of writings is perhaps particularly to be welcomed in this case, if one is to believe—with some justification, it seems to me—Leo Spitzer's celebrated denunciation of his "Rabelaisant" colleagues for having allowed Rabelais criticism to lag by at least half a century behind critical activity in other areas of Western literature.

Admittedly, these benefits could not have been achieved without some small compromise. For the ten years preceding 1980, Otto Klapp's bibliography lists more than 800 entries on Rabelais. Judging by the number of entries in the present study, Rabelais research seems to have accelerated even more dramatically in the following decade. Under these circumstances, some degree of selectivity has proved inevitable, since a truly comprehensive annotated bibliography, however sketchy the annotations, was clearly out of the question if it were to appear within the confines of one volume of manageable proportions. Thus items of strictly local or ephemeral nature, or written in a language other than French, English, German, Italian, Spanish, Dutch, or Polish, have haᴅ to be excluded. Nor have the occasional newspaper articles found a place in the present survey; of obvious potential interest in the case of contemporary authors, in the case of Rabelais they were thought unlikely to contain any significant information which the writer did not share elsewhere, in a more scholarly setting.

For the rest, every effort has been made to include not only the major books and articles devoted to Rabelais during the period covered here, but every note, however brief—in one case, a *notule*—which advances to the slightest extent our knowledge of Rabelais or his work, especially if it has found some echo in the work of another scholar. Also included is a significant number of studies whose scope transcends in one way or another the limits of our subject, but whose authors have been led by the nature of their topic to treat—sometimes in passing, sometimes at greater length—a particular aspect of Rabelais' work. The inclusion of these general studies should prove particularly useful, since recourse to standard bibliographies is most unlikely to attract the reader's attention to their existence.

Doctoral dissertations presented to American universities are listed and annotated on the basis of information provided in *Dissertation Abstracts International*. In the absence of a similar source for European dissertations, the latter are mentioned only if they were subsequently published. In that event, they are treated like any other publication.

The nature of the annotations is directly related to their purpose: to help the readers determine, given their own objectives, whether any particular entry warrants further investigation. In strict conformity to the guidelines pertaining to the *Reference Guide to Literature* series, the annotations are meant to be informative and objective rather than critical. The relative length of an entry should not be seen as reflecting in any way the relative importance of the item in the annotator's opinion. Some texts were merely found to lend themselves more easily than others, by their very nature, to a succinct summary of their content.

Rabelais scholars are notoriously inconsistent in their references to nouns and places in Rabelais' novels. Bridoye is thus likely to change into Bridlegoose under the pen of an Anglo-Saxon critic; one and the same character will appear in turn as Friar John, Frère Jean, Frère Jehan, frere Jean, Frere Jan, or any other combination of the two terms. *Theleme*, as it is spelled in Pierre Jourda's authoritative edition, is most often endowed with two accents, whereas *Thalamege*, the ship upon which the Pantagruelists embark on their quest for the Oracle of the Dive Bouteille (or, for some, the Divine Bottle) is not extended the same typographical courtesy. I have taken it upon myself to correct this small injustice, and to adorn it with the *accent grave* which I have long felt to be its due. For the rest, the variations in the spelling of proper nouns and in the mode of reference to the various episodes in Rabelais' work largely reflect the usage of the author whose critical text is under discussion.

One last series of preliminary remarks. Instead of supplying the customary list of first editions of Rabelais' texts, I thought it more useful to draw attention to the numerous editions, both critical and otherwise, that have appeared during the period covered by this survey. The reader will also find a short list of reprints of important studies on Rabelais first published before the *terminus a quo* of this investigation. The latter covers critical writings on Rabelais since 1950. For an overview of Rabelais criticism in the ten years immediately previous to this survey, the reader may wish to consult V. L. Saulnier, "Dix années d'études rabelaisiennes," *Bibliothèque d'Humanisme et Renaissance* 9 (1949):104–28, and Carlo Cordié, "Recenti studi sulla vita e sulle opere di François Rabelais, 1939–1950," *Letterature Moderne I* (1950):107–20. For the preceding period, Jean Plattard's *Etat présent des études sur Rabelais* (1927) may prove of use. Lastly, Mikhail Bakhtin's *Rabelais and His World* contains a discussion of significant works on Rabelais by Russian critics. Some of these works fall within the chronological parameters of the present study.

# Acknowledgments

First and foremost, I am happy for this opportunity to express my appreciation to Mrs. Marjorie Patterson of the Inter-Library Loan Office at Georgia State University for her unfailingly cheerful and efficient help in locating the innumerable books and articles I was unable to consult during my all-too-brief and all-too-infrequent visits to the British Library and the Bibliothèque Nationale. I would also like to thank a group of colleagues: David O'Connell for suggesting the project, Marion L. Kuntz and Georges Perla for checking a number of references, and John Austin and Jerry Pendrick for guiding me through the meanders of German syntax. Finally, both the author and the reader owe a debt of gratitude to my wife, Christabel Pendrill Braunrot, for urging me periodically to bring at long last to completion what had threatened, on more than one occasion, to become quite literally an endless task.

# François Rabelais

*a reference guide*

*1950–1990*

# Introduction

Any attempt to discern the ideological intentions behind the comic surface of Rabelais' novels is as controversial and fraught with difficulty today as it was commonplace and relatively simple forty years ago. In his introduction to the first volume of *Études Rabelaisiennes* in 1956, Robert Marichal was able to single out, as the most obvious link between the otherwise very different studies comprising the volume, an overriding preoccupation with the serious thinker whom Abel Lefranc had discovered at the turn of the century behind the mask of the entertainer. No such claim could be made for any collection of articles published today, be it in the most traditionally-oriented literary journals. Formal analysis, bearing in turn upon Rabelais' narrative technique, his arsenal of comic devices, his creative use of language, and the structural principles underlying his seemingly fragmented text, has tended to replace the more conventional study of Rabelais' thought—without making it lose ground altogether. Insofar as it remains at all concerned with content rather than form, recent criticism has been inclined to view Rabelais' work as above all a meditation on the nature of language and the meaning of literary creation, interpreting his innumerable references to the political, religious, and other serious concerns of his day as mere literary themes, as interchangeable building blocks in an intellectual and verbal game rather than an earnest expression of a coherent ideology.

To follow step by step this change in attitude towards Rabelais' fiction in the second half of this century is to be struck by both the overwhelming amount of scholarly and critical activity engendered by the text, and by the surprisingly polemical nature of much of Rabelais criticism during that period. The story does indeed sometimes read like a series of endless *Querelles*: between those for whom Rabelais' text is essentially a historical or biographical document, to be understood primarily in the light of a particular historical moment, and those for whom it is above all a literary expression of an original artistic sensibility; between those who detect behind the facetious tone of the narrative a core of high moral seriousness and those who deny the presence of any deeper purpose than that of eliciting the reader's laughter; between those who seek the work's *sustantificque mouelle* through symbolic interpretation and those for whom the marrow of which Rabelais speaks is laughter itself; those for whom the tenor of Rabelais' work is patently humanistic and those for whom the work embodies, on the contrary, the spirit of carnivalesque counter-culture; between those for whom the text's meanings are many and those who would reduce it to a single, univocal message. These contradictory claims have been voiced on occasion with such vehemence and such *parti pris* that they are likely to conjure up in the the mind of the irreverent reader the memorable debates "dont furent faictes grosses guerres" in the mock-heroic episode of the Picrocholine War. But for all their reluctance to "interpréter à bien" in that spirit of tolerance—to say nothing of evangelical charity—which lies at the very heart of Rabelais' notion of *Pantagruélisme*, these controversies have undoubtedly generated as much light as heat. By focusing in turn on the many facets of Rabelais' fictional work, the scholarly and the hermeneutic studies surveyed in the following pages have at last drawn attention to its full stature as an incomparable comic masterpiece as well as an ideological text echoing some of the major preoccupations of the Renaissance and foreshadowing, especially in its reflection on language and literary interpretation, some of the most seminal and most controversial concerns of our own time.

As in the case of any enterprise of this kind, the *terminus a quo* of the present survey may seem arbitrary and thus requires a brief explanation. Admittedly the year 1950 in itself does not mark any significant turning point in the history of Rabelais criticism. In the early years of the second half of the century, however, two important events had a determining effect on its development. In quick succession the death of Abel Lefranc in 1952 and the fourth centenary of Rabelais' death a year later provided the opportunity, if not to change the course of Rabelais studies, at least to accelerate its evolution in the direction indicated by Abel Lefranc, fifty years earlier, when he launched the Société des Études Rabelaisiennes in 1903. Without treating the matter in excessive detail, it may be helpful to recall that for Lefranc the importance of Rabelais' work lay mainly in its documentary value. Documentary first of all in its realism, since Lefranc believed he could discern, behind Rabelais' fantasy and the flights of his imagination, the elements of a geographical and cultural reality from which Rabelais' work, like any other work of literature, in his eyes drew its most serious claim to attention. But documentary also in that the work allowed access into the author's very thought, through pages such as Gargantua's letter to his son, the chapters on the Giants' education or the Abbaye de Thélème episode—in short the pages whose seriousness provides a striking contrast with the rest of the chronicles, and points to the *sustantificque mouelle* promised to the assiduous reader by the Prologue to *Gargantua*. In the wake of Lefranc, French academic criticism of the 1950s, most notably the team of contributors to *Études Rabelaisiennes* led by Robert Marichal, continued to study Rabelais' work from the double perspective of realism and historicity. Behind every fictive character, scholars strove to identify a historic model, behind every episode the echo of an actual event, behind every geographical notation an allusion to an existing site. Admittedly, problems of a literary and linguistic nature did not meet with total neglect. The nature and coherence of Rabelais' characters were occasionally, sometimes brilliantly explored, most memorably perhaps by Mario Roques in the case of Panurge. Elements of parody and satire were dutifully identi-

2

fied and related to classical or medieval antecedents. Notes on vocabulary and syntax were carefully collected for future use in projected critical editions which Lefranc and his colleagues had been unable to complete. But it was above all the thinker, and not the artist, whom critics sought to unmask behind the frivolous façade of his fiction. What did Rabelais think of women, of monks, of war? What was his conception of the past, the present, and the future? How broad and how sound was his erudition, how extensive his debt to the philosophers and writers of the past and of his own day? Rejecting Lefranc's thesis of a free-thinking Rabelais, but without attempting to question his critical method, scholars sought to define what they saw as Rabelais' evangelism: militant at first, then progressively more cautious according to L.-V. Saulnier; Erasmian and somewhat tinged with stoicism, if one was to believe M. A. Screech among others. Even critics of a Marxist persuasion tended to view Rabelais' work from an essentially similar angle. Although their conception of the Renaissance is often poles apart from that of Lefranc, their belief in historical determinism leads them to limit their view of Rabelais' work to its ideological dimension. Neither Henri Lefèvre, in his *Rabelais*, nor the group of critics responsible for the 1954 special edition of *Europe* devoted exclusively to the writer, are able to see much beyond what they proclaim to be the populist message of his work, a message hitherto ignored by bourgeois critics intent upon minimizing its revolutionary significance.

Whatever their differences, both academic and Marxist criticism can thus be seen to perpetuate, each in its own way, an essentially historical interpretation of Rabelais' work. They share the conviction that its main importance lies above all in an ideological undercurrent purportedly detected in a number of pages highlighted for the occasion and considered as embodying, despite their satirical or burlesque context, a genuine *profession de foi*. But this historicist attitude is not shared by all. In the midst of the flood of historico-ideological studies generated by the anniversary of Rabelais' death, the *Cahiers du Collège de Pataphysique* discover in Rabelais a kindred spirit, a *pataphysicien avant la lettre*, and proceed to question, with a characteristic mixture of impertinence and erudition, not only the traditional theses but also the methodological principles upon which they were based. In a celebrated early study, Lefranc had noted that the series of episodes making up the Picrocholine War at the heart of *Pantagruel*, however whimsical and burlesque they might appear on the surface, could in fact be followed, in minutest detail, on a map of the region surrounding the town of Chinon. In order to discredit the "thèse réaliste" propounded by Lefranc on the strength of this discovery, the anonymous author of one of the articles published in the *Cahiers* devoted to *Rabelais pataphysicien* had only to recall that for most of Rabelais' contemporaries, just as for the modern reader, the names of the various villages mentioned in the episode were nothing but names, of no significance other than the resonance they might have in the reader's imagination. With equal ease, René Étiemble—an occasional *pataphysicien* of uncommon stature—is able to catch official criticism in *flagrant délit* of self-contradiction when it claims to discover in the text the genuine "pensée profonde" of its author. To make his case, Étiemble need only draw out (admittedly with a grain of mischief) the logical consequences of the historic-realist position: if Rabelais' text is indeed the reflection of contemprary reality that critics of historicorealistic persuasion believe it to be, nothing allows them to hear in the so-called serious pages of the Rabelaisian chronicles anything other than an echo of the ideological struggle dividing contemporary public opinion. From the critics' particular perspective, nothing justifies the implication that Rabelais himself was seriously committed to the ideological debates of his day.

The two-volume *Cahiers de Pataphysique* devoted to Rabelais probably deserves more attention than it subsequently received. It seems to have gone equally unnoticed at the time, lying as it did well outside the mainstream of *la critique universitaire*. The decisive blow to tradition, a blow whose far-reaching repercussions can to a certain extent still be felt today, came from abroad. Having previously wreaked havoc among medievalists with his celebrated ahistorical reading of Villon's *Ballade des Dames du Temps Jadis*, Leo Spitzer proceeded, just before the beginning of World War II, to provide Renaissance scholars with an equally unsettling experience by denouncing Rabelais' so-called realism ("le prétendu réalisme de Rabelais"), whose sole function, according to the controversial German philologist, was to lend an appearance of reality to a work belonging, in its essence, to the order of myth. Twenty years later, the publication of a volume of articles in the *Travaux d'Humanisme et Renaissance* series on the occasion of the fourth centenary of Rabelais' death provided Spitzer with an opportunity to renew his assault on the traditional approach to Rabelais' work. With the now-familiar contempt that the intervening years had done nothing to tone down, he proceeded to take to task, in his famous article on "Rabelais et les 'rabelaisants'," those of his colleagues who persisted in dwelling on the work's documentary significance at the expense of its artistic value, in stifling the poetic quality of the text under the weight of an erudition at best misplaced, at worst suspicious or downright unfounded. To the Rabelais specialists complacently wallowing in academic isolation, the critic proposed that they abandon their antiquated approach ("les faux problèmes d'un historicisme et d'un réalisme désuets") and that they acknowledge at long last the work's specifically literary nature.

This time the appeal did not go unheard. In both England and the United States, if not yet in France, some of the most significant studies on Rabelais published in the 1960s fall squarely within the perspective advocated by Spitzer. If most critics still hesitated to follow Spitzer to the letter and to view Rabelais above all as a poet, they seemed ready nonetheless to forget at least momentarily the thinker in favor of the prose writer and novelist. In the work of Abraham Keller, Marcel Tetel, Floyd Gray, Dorothy Coleman and Raymond LaCharité, a little later in that of Edwin Duval and Barbara Bowen, critical attention was brought to bear on those aspects of the Rabelaisian text which define it primarily as a work of fiction. The critics now sought to bring out the originality of Rabelais' narrative techniques, to analyze with ever increasing precision the nature of Rabelaisian comedy. Behind an appearance of disorder, critics strove to discern a unifying principle of composition, and began to envisage the possibilty of a conjuncture between form and meaning. The question of the work's ambiguity began to be studied with ever greater urgency at the hand of critics more and more aware of the need to ground their analyses on sound methodological foundations. Even the prologues, treated until then as typical prefatory texts wherein the author unveils more or less clearly, with more or less sincerity, the nature of his intentions, were now subjected to an examination wherein questions of rhetoric tended to predominate over matters of content. In this light, it soon became apparent that the liminary text is as thoroughly ambiguous as the text it is meant to explain. It became clear in particular that in contrast with so many apparently similar texts, the Rabelaisian prologues are uttered by a narrator whom we are not meant to identify with the author himself; that they are addressed to a carefully characterized body of *narrataires* who are not meant to be equated with the work's actual readers; that they are situated well within the fictional universe they claim to introduce; and that by that very fact they stood, like the rest of Rabelais' text, in urgent need of interpretation. In short, Rabelaisian criticism could at long last be said to acknowledge textual analysis as the indispensible tool that literary criticism in general had recognized it to be a full half-century earlier.

Next to the polemic occasioned by Spitzer's article on the antiquated ways of the "rabelaisants", the most significant event of the 1960s was without doubt the publication of Mikhail Bakhtin's *Rabelais and His World*. In view of the notoriety the book has enjoyed in literary circles since its publication in English translation in 1968, little need be said about the work itself, except perhaps to suggest in a few words the direction in which the joint influence of Spitzer and Bakhtin seems to have inflected the course of critical reflection upon Rabelais' text. In the last few years, studies such as those of Richard Berrong, and more recently, of Walter Stephens, have tended to question the validity of Bakhtin's theses and their pertinence to Rabelais' work as a whole. The initial reaction had been significantly more favorable. By its insistence upon what Rabelais' work owed to popular culture and folklore, Bakhtin proposed an ideological reading that Marxist criticism in the West—that of Jean Paris in his *Rabelais au futur*, for example—was quick to claim as its own and adapt to its own purposes. Other readers, less prone to interpretations of a political nature, used Bakhtin's attempt to devalue Rabelais' humanistic message as an occasion to minimize the importance of any message, of whatever kind, in favor of what Michel Beaujour was to call "le jeu de Rabelais." Reducing the text's humanistic message to a mere rejection of conventional views of knowledge and culture, seeing its subversive role as operating on the plane of literary aesthetics rather than that of ideology, Beaujour went so far as to claim that Rabelais' text was devoid of all meaning, or at least of any intention to signify—"Rabelais *ne veut rien dire*"—and to interpret Rabelais' treatment of words, images, and ideas in strictly poetic terms.

The excessive nature of such otherwise attractive claims was bound to stir up yet another heated debate. In an eloquent defense of scholarly interpretation, Gérard Defaux proceeded to revive the post-Spitzerian polemic between historicists and aestheticians, by championing the cause of historical criticism as an indispensable *garde-fou* against misreadings of texts of the past, if not necessarily as the sole key to the recovery of their meaning: "pour comprendre ce que Rabelais a voulu dire, pour restituer à l'oeuvre sa richesse originelle de signification, pour éviter les contresens, les anachronismes, les interprétations aventureuses ou injustifiées, la documentation historique, si elle n'est pas un but en soi, reste cependant...la condition *sine qua non* de toute autre spéculation." (See 1977.13, p. 726.) For such scholars as Defaux and Screech, who staunchly refuse to see Rabelais' oeuvre solely as a product of creative imagination without regard for the significance of its ideological message, erudition—"pertinente et bien comprise," to quote Gérard Defaux once again—provides with the force of indisputable evidence the necessary first step towards a proper understanding of a text whose roots so obviously reach down into the social and intellectual life of the author's time.

But what meaning was it, precisely, that critics had in mind when debating the most effective means for its detection? Was it univocal, fixed once and for all, buried by the author in the fictional texture of his work and recoverable with relative ease by the attentive reader? Or was it ambiguous and polyvalent, perpetually changing under the gaze of the perplexed reader, a meaning which the reader must recreate at each successive reading, and for which he, rather than the author, must ultimately bear the responsibility? For in the meantime, the *mise en question* to which language had been subjected at the hands of the post-structuralists, in the wake of Jacques Derrida, had finally caught up with Rabelais criticism, providing the most recent opportunity to indulge in the series of polemics which periodically quicken the pulse of Rabelais specialists. More important, however, than the clash of points of view in this latest debate and the vehemence with which it was waged in the academic press, is the fact that this most recent *querelle* helped focus attention on a body of texts that bear witness to a reflection on language and on literary creation, foreshadowing on many points the preoccupations of contemporary theorists. In his book *Les Langages de Rabelais* (1972), François Rigolot had seen in Rabelais' concern with the problems of language "la grande aventure intérieure" of his novel. The numerous studies which appeared in the wake of that seminal work have sought to clarify, particularly with reference to the fascinating episode of the Frozen Words, Rabelais' ideas on the relationship between words and things. In addition, such episodes as the gestural debate between Thaumaste and Panurge have acquired a new claim to the reader's attention insofar as they too seem to call into question the privileged status of the linguistic sign by implying a superiority of gesture over verbal discourse in the act of communication.

This relatively new concern with the so-called *problématique du langage* has led a number of critics to deny the presence in Rabelais' work of any specific, immutable, univocal meaning. Invoking the authority of post-structuralist theorists as well as that of Rabelais himself, such critics refuse to deprive his text of its rightful polyvalence, of its plurality, of its essential ambiguity. The peculiarities of a text in which signifiers fail to signify—or do so with mystifying reluctance—where symbols call for a decoding whose success is constantly jeopardized by innumerable risks of error, have even prompted the most extreme wing of the critical avant-garde to question the possibility of *any* interpretation, of a meaningful reading of *any* kind.

Not surprisingly, none of these theoretical dilemmas have prevented Rabelais studies from running their course. In the aftermath of post-structuralist quarrels, many of the old questions have come back under critical scrutiny, although the reader's fear of *déjà lu* is likely to prove groundless, since these traditional topics tend to be treated this time with a significantly sharpened consciousness of their inherent complexity. Such articles as T. M. Greene's on the theme of thirst in *Rabelais' Incomparable Book*, those by Michel Jeanneret on the function of food, of Françoise Charpentier and Carla Freccero on women in Rabelais' novel, as well as the recent work by Samuel Kaiser and Walter Stephens on Rabelais' giants come to mind as examples of what Rabelais criticism stands to gain by rethinking perennial themes from a new, often interdisciplinary perspective, enriched by its debt to such diverse fields as economics, anthropology, folklore, and women's studies. A number of intertextual readings (those of Terence Cave among them) have successfully treated the old questions of source and influence with a new awareness of their implications. Linguistic and stylistic investigations of Rabelais' work, most notably by Mireille Huchon in her *Rabelais grammairien*, have been carried out with a new and welcome methodological rigor and made it not only possible to assess with greater precision the exact extent of Rabelais' originality on this score, but also, in the case of Huchon, to provide what may well turn out to be a definitive solution to the nagging problem of authorship of the *Cinquiesme Livre*. The continued relevance of contextual studies and historical scholarship is clearly attested by such works as M. A. Screech's monumental *Rabelais*, published some fifteen years ago, or by the Colloquium on *Rabelais in Context* held at Vanderbilt University in 1991.

Where, it might well be asked at this point, do we stand today? Although a full-scale answer could not possibly be undertaken within the scope of this introduction, one might tentatively suggest that on balance an impartial assessment of Rabelais criticism in the last forty years would not be entirely positive. One might deplore, for instance, the ever widening distance created between the general reader and Rabelais' text by certain scholars' emphasis on erudition (often of an exceedingly specialized nature) as an absolute prerequisite for an adequate appreciation of his work. One might find equally regrettable a tendency on the part of such scholars to confuse the text with its historical context, to equate them for reasons which might be valid in the case of a second-rate author, but which must be held to be at the very least debatable when one is dealing with an author of genius, whose genius lies precisely in his ability to safeguard his independence in relation to the aesthetic and intellectual currents of his time. Lastly, one may deplore as well the occasional excesses of certain avant-garde critics more prone to follow prevailing fashion than to read Rabelais' work with the attention it deserves. On the whole, however, it seems safe to say that no responsible observer could fail to acknowledge that contemporary criticism has succeeded—often brilliantly—in illuminating the full stature of Rabelais' novel: that of a teasingly ambiguous comic masterpiece, enriched by an undercurrent of theoretical insights into the problems of language and literary creation whose relevance does not cease to astound. As for the possible direction that Rabelais studies might take in the years to come, such books as Jerome Schwartz's *Irony and Ideology in Rabelais* and Edwin Duval's *Pantagruel* (1991) lead one to hope that we have left behind the era of theoretical debate and ushered in a more constructive spirit of synthesis and conciliation. Beyond that, the future of Rabelais criticism will no doubt be marked by the emergence of new interpretive approaches, although in the absence of any reliable oracular predictions it would be less than prudent to speculate on their possible nature, except perhaps to suggest that they too are likely to have already been anticipated, in some as yet unsuspected way, by Rabelais' inexhaustibly seminal work.

# Editions of Rabelais' Works Published
# between 1950 and 1990

## CRITICAL EDITIONS

*Pantagruel: Première publication critique sur le texte original.* Par V.-L. Saulnier. Nouvelle édition augmentée. Geneva: Librairie Droz, 1965. liv + 265 pp.

*Gargantua: Première édition critique faite sur "l'Editio princeps".* Texte établi par R. Calder. Avec introduction, commentaires, tables et glossaires par M. A. Screech. Préface par V.-L. Saulnier. Textes Littéraires Français, no. 163. Geneva: Librairie Droz; Paris: Minard, 1970. lxviii + 457 pp.

*Le Tiers Livre.* Édition critique commentée par M. A. Screech. Textes Littéraires Français, no. 102. Geneva: Librairie Droz; Paris: Minard, 1964. xxix + 467 pp.

*Oeuvres de François Rabelais. Édition critique publiée sous la direction de Abel Lefranc. Tome VIe, Le Quart Livre, chapitres I–XVII.* Introduction, texte et notes par Dr. Paul Delaunay, Antoinette Huon, Robert Marichal, Charles Perrat et V.-L. Saulnier. Travaux d'Humanisme et Renaissance XIX. Geneva: Librairie Droz; Lille: Librairie Giard, 1955. 215 pp.

*Pantagrueline Prognostication pour l'an 1533. Avec les Almanachs pour les ans 1533, 1535 et 1541. La grande et vraye Pronostication nouvelle de 1544.* Textes établis, avec introduction, commentaires, appendices et glossaires par M. A. Screech, assisté par Gwyneth Tootill, Anne Reeve, Martine Morin, Sally North, Stephen Bamforth. Textes Littéraires Français, no. 215. Geneva: Librairie Droz, 1974. xxxvii + 179 pp.

## OTHER EDITIONS

*Oeuvres complètes.* Texte établi et annoté par J. Boulenger, revu et complété par L. Scheler. 1955. Reprint. Paris: Gallimard, Bibliothèque de la Pléiade, 1970. xxiii + 1033 pp.

*Oeuvres complètes*. Introduction, notes, bibliographie et relevé de variantes par P. Jourda. 2 vols. Paris: Classiques Garnier, 1962. lxii + 632 and 613 pp.

*Oeuvres complètes de Maître François Rabelais*. Texte établi et annoté par Marcel Guilbaud, de la Bibliothèque Nationale, avec la collaboration de Robert Baudry, de l'Imprimerie Nationale. Bibliothèque Française. 5 vols. Paris: Nouvelle Librairie de France, 1968–69. 1670 pp.

*Oeuvres complètes*. Edition établie, préfacée et annotée par Guy Demerson, avec une translation en français moderne due à un groupe d'étudiants. Paris: Editions du Seuil, L'Intégrale, 1973. 1024 pp.

*Oeuvres complètes*. Edited by Albert Demazière. Editions de Saint-Clair, 1975.

*Pantagruel*. Introduction et notes de Louis Desgraves. Bordeaux: Delmas, 1952. 205 pp.

*Pantagruel. Publié sur le texte définitif.* Introduction et présentation de V.-L. Saulnier. Texte établi et annoté par Pierre Michel. Club du Meilleur Livre, 1962. xliii + 242 pp.

*Pantagruel*. Chronologie et avant-propos par V.-L. Saulnier. Introduction et lexique par Jean-Yves Pouilloux. Paris: Garnier-Flammarion, 1969. 189 pp.

*Pantagruel*. Présenté par Nicole Cazauran. Illustrations de Jacques-Charles Delahaye. Paris: Imprimerie Nationale, 1989. 340 pp.

*Gargantua: Publié sur le texte définitif.* Etabli et annoté par Pierre Michel. Paris: Livre de Poche, 1965. 447 pp.

*La Vie très horrificque du grand Gargantua*. Chronologie et avant-propos par V.-L. Saulnier. Introduction et lexique par Jean-Yves Pouilloux. Paris: Garnier-Flammarion, 1968. 248 pp.

*Gargantua: Fac-similé de l'édition François Juste, 1542*. Texte établi et présenté par Claude Gaignebet. Alfortville: Quatre Feuilles, 1971. xlii pp. + 155 folios.

*Le Tiers Livre: Publié sur le texte définitif.* Établi et annoté par Pierre Michel. Préface d'Alain. Paris: Livre de Poche, 1966. 540 pp.

*Le Tiers Livre des faicts et dicts héroïques du bon Pantagruel*. Chronologie par V.-L. Saulnier. Introduction et lexique par Jean-Yves Pouilloux. Paris: Garnier-Flammarion, 1970. 252 pp.

*Le Quart Livre des faicts et dicts héroïques du bon Pantagruel*. Introduction et lexique par Jean-Yves Pouilloux. Paris: Garnier-Flammarion, 1971. 256 pp.

*Le Quart Livre des faicts et dicts heroïques du bon Pantagruel*. Publié par Michael Heath. Egham, Surrey: Runnymede Books, 1990. 309 pp.

## RELATED WORKS

*Les Croniques Admirables du puissant roy Gargantua.* Réimprimées avec une introduction et des notes par Marcel Françon. Rochecorbon, Indre-et-Loire: Edit. Ch. Gay, 1956. lxxxiii + 151 pp.

*Les Songes drôlatiques de Pantagruel.* Reproduits en fac-similé avec une Introduction par Jean Porcher. Paris: Lucien Mazenod, 1959. 64 leaves + 29 pp.

Horry, Nicolas. *Rabelais ressuscité.* Texte présenté et annoté par Neil Goodley. Textes Littéraires, no. 20. Exeter: University of Exeter, 1976. xlix + 49 pp.

*Le disciple de Pantagruel (Navigations de Panurge).* Edited by G. Demerson and C. Lauvergnat-Gagnière.Société des Textes Français Modernes. Paris: Librairie Nizet.

Habert, François. *Le Songe de Pantagruel.* Introduction by John Lewis. Études Rabelaisiennes no. 18. Geneva: Librairie Droz, 1985. pp. 103–62.

*Les Chroniques gargantuines.* Édition critique publiée par Christiane Lauvergnat-Gagnière et Guy Demerson. Avec la collaboration de R. Antonioli, C. Bonilauri, M. Huchon, J. Lewis et B. Teyssot. Société des Textes Français Modernes. Paris: Librairie Nizet, 1988. 304 pp.

*Les Songes drôlatiques de Pantagruel.* Cent vingt gravures attribuées à François Rabelais. Introduction de Michel Jeanneret. La Chaux-de-Fonds: Éditions [vwa], 1989. xl + 120 pp.

# Reprints of Some Important Works on Rabelais First Published before 1950

BROWN, HUNTINGTON. *Rabelais in English Literature.* New York: Octagon Books, 1967. 254 pp.

BUSSON, HENRI. *Les sources et le développement du rationalisme dans la littérature française de la Renaissance (1533-1600).* Seconde édition, revue et augmentée. Paris: Librairie philosophique Vrin, 1957. 655 pp.

CLEMENT, NEMOURS H. *The Influence of the Arthurian Romances on the Five Books of Rabelais.* New York: Phaeton Press, 1970. 257 pp.

COLLETET, GUILLAUME. *François Rabelais.* Geneva: Slatkine Reprints, 1969. 73 pp.

COUTAUD, ALBERT. *La Pédagogie de Rabelais.* Edited by Gabriel Compayre. Geneva: Slatkine Reprints, 1970. 278 pp.

FEBVRE, LUCIEN. *Le Problème de l'incroyance au XVIe siècle: La religion de Rabelais.* Paris: Albin Michel, 1968. 512 pp. Translated by Beatrice Gottlieb under the title *The Problem of Unbelief in the Sixteenth Century: The Religion of Rabelais.* Cambridge: Harvard University Press, 1982. xxxiii + 516 pp.

GILSON, ÉTIENNE. "Rabelais Franciscain." In *Les Idées et les Lettres*, 197–241 Paris: Librairie philosophique Vrin, 1955. Also reprinted in *De la Bible à François Villon*, 35-79. Paris: Librairie philosophique Vrin, Vrin Reprise 1981.

HUGUET, EDMOND. *Étude sur la syntaxe de Rabelais comparée à celle des autres prosateurs de 1450 à 1550.* Geneva: Slatkine Reprints, 1967. 458 pp.

LEFRANC, ABEL. *Rabelais: Études sur Gargantua, Pantagruel, le Tiers Livre* Avant-Propos de Robert Marichal. Paris: Albin Michel, 1953. 377 pp.

———. *Les Navigations de Pantagruel.* Geneva: Slatkine Reprints, 1967. 333 pp.

LOTE, GEORGES. *La Vie et l'œuvre de François Rabelais*. Geneva: Slatkine Reprints, 1972, 574 pp.

PLAN, PIERRE PAUL. *Bibliographie rabelaisienne. Les éditions de Rabelais de 1532 à 1711*. 1904. Reprint. Nieukoop: B. de Graff, 1965. xiii + 277 pp.

PLATTARD, JEAN. *François Rabelais*. Geneva: Slatkine Reprints, 1972. 342 pp.

―――. *L'Œuvre de Rabelais: Sources, Invention et Composition*. Paris: Honoré Champion, 1967. 374 pp.

SAINÉAN, LAZARE. *L'Histoire naturelle et les branches connexes dans l'œuvre de Rabelais*. Geneva: Slatkine Reprints, 1972. 449 pp.

SCHWOB, MARCEL. *Rabelais*. Paris: Éditions Alia, 1990. 64 pp.

THUASNE, LOUIS. *Etudes sur Rabelais*. Paris: Librairie Honoré Champion, 1969. 450 pp.

―――. *Rabelais et Villon*. Paris: Librairie Honoré Champion, 1969. 54 pp.

―――. *Villon et Rabelais*. Geneva: Slatkine Reprints, 1969. 472 pp.

# Collections of Articles Devoted Exclusively to Rabelais

*Études Rabelaisiennes.* Published by Librairie Droz at irregular intervals in the Travaux d'Humanisme et Renaissance series.

*Europe* 95–96 (November–December 1953).

*François Rabelais: Ouvrage publié pour le quatrième centenaire de sa mort, 1553-1953.* Travaux d'Humanisme et Renaissance, no. 7. Geneva: Librairie Droz, 1953.

*Rabelais écrivain-médecin, par vingt-deux médecins français et italiens.* Paris: Éditions Garance, 1959.

*Esprit Créateur* 3, no.2 (Summer 1963).

*Rabelais.* Edited by August Buck. Wege der Forschung, no. 284. Darmstadt: Wissenschaftliche Buchgesellshaft, 1973.

*Cahiers de l'Association Internationale des Études Françaises* 30 (1978).

*Berenice* 1, no. 1 (November 1980).

*A Rabelais Symposium. Esprit Créateur* 21, no. 1 (Spring 1981).

*François Rabelais, 1483(?)–1983.* Études Rabelaisiennes, no. 17. Geneva: Librairie Droz, 1983.

*Études de Lettres. Revue de la Faculté des Lettres, Université de Lausanne,* no. 2 (April–June 1984).

*Rabelais in Glasgow: Proceedings of the Colloquium held at the University of Glasgow in December 1983.* Preface by Christine Scollen-Jimack. Edited and published by James A. Coleman and Christine M. Scollen-Jimack. Glasgow: Glasgow University Printing Unit, 1984. 150 pp.

*Rabelais's Incomparable Book: Essays on His Art.* Edited by Raymond C. La Charité. French Forum Monographs, no. 62. Lexington, Ky.: French Forum, 1986. 247 pp.

*Rabelais en son demi-millénaire. Actes du Colloque International de Tours (24–29 septembre 1984)*. Publiés par Jean Céard et Jean-Claude Margolin. Études Rabelaisiennes no. 21. Geneva: Librairie Droz, 1988.

# Abbreviations

BAARD     Bulletin de l'Association des Amis de Rabelais ct de la Devinière

BHR       Bibliothèque d'Humanisme et Renaissance

CAIEF     Cahiers de l'Association Internationale des Études Françaises

PMLA     Publications of the Modern Language Association

THR       Travaux d'Humanisme et Renaissance

# Writings about Rabelais

**1950**

1   AUERBACH, ERICH. "The World in Pantagruel's Mouth." *Partisan Review* 17, no.2:672–94.

First appearance in English of a text previously published in the original German in 1946. Notes the popular origins of the episode (the *Gargantuan Chronicles*), its sources in the literature of antiquity (Lucian's *True History* and his *Menippus seu Nekyomantia*), and underscores the originality of Rabelais' treatment of the theme. Discusses the shifting of locales and the interplay of the various stylistic levels, and shows this same freedom at play in episodes drawn from Rabelais' other books: "The revolutionary thing about his way of thinking is not his opposition to Christianity, but the freedom of vision, feeling, and thought which is produced by his perpetual playing with things, and which invites the reader to deal directly with the world and its wealth of phenomena" (p. 684). Finds Rabelais to be basically anti-Christian in his valorization of nature and natural life as intrinsically good and his affirmation of the "vitalistic-dynamic triumph of the physical body and its functions" (p. 685). Questions, on the other hand, whether individualism plays as large a part in his thinking as it does among other writers of the Renaissance. Believes in the existence of a core of seriousness in his work, but thinks it a mistake to attempt to seek it elsewhere than in his Pantagruelism. "To describe it more in detail is not a wise undertaking...for one would immediately find oneself forced to compete with Rabelais" (p. 690). Acknowledges that Rabelais' style is limited in that it excludes deep feeling and high tragedy, but admires him as a poet of everyday life. Reprinted, with slight modifications, in 1953.2.

2   BART, B.F. "Aspects of the Comic in Pulci and Rabelais." *Modern Language Quarterly* 11:156–63.

Accepts Plattard's conclusion that certain episodes in Rabelais are probably drawn from Pulci, but claims that such borrowings are put to a very different use. Rabelais' book is essentially comic; Pulci's is only incidentally so. In Rabelais, the comic is inherent in the very fabric of the work; in Pulci, it is external, manifest only in the interventions of the author in his fiction. "Each man, conditioned by his approach, has viewed his comic material from his own vantage point and has handled it, within those confines, in terms suggested by his own temperament" (p.160). With the exception of the character of Panurge, deems Rabelais' debt to Pulci to be unimportant or irrelevant.

3   CARPENTER, NAN COOKE. "Rabelais and Musical Ideas." *Romanic Review* 41:14–25.

Gathers evidence of Rabelais' knowledge of musical theory and practice in his work: metaphorical allusions, references to singing, to Boethius' division of music into *musica mundana, musica humana*, and *musica instrumentalis*, to Plato's idea of the soul as harmony, to medieval discussions on the relation between music and health. Notes Rabelais' "use of identical or similar metaphors in the same book or in the one next chronologically" (pp. 24–25), and points out that "all references to *musica mundana* and *musica humana* appear only in the last three books" (p. 25), in line with Rabelais' increasing interest in Platonism generally. The author's attempt to bring the use of musical imagery to bear on the question of the authenticity of Book V is left inconclusive.

4   ———. "Rabelais and the Chanson." *PMLA* 65, no. 2:1212–32.

Points to general references to "chansons," quotations from specific songs (either contemporary or more ancient, but in either case often of a ribald nature), the list of 175 chansons sung at the Court of Lantern Land in Book V. Believes that Attaingnant's publications are the chief source for Rabelais' catalogue. Claims that the two lists of musicians in the "nouveau Prologue" to Book IV are set in an order which suggests an insight into the relative merit of the composers as well as an awareness of stylistic distinctions. Observes that Panurge and Friar John are "the two men most consistently characterized by lines from chansons and given to quoting such lines in their own speech" (p. 1231). On the basis of chanson references, believes that Book V was either largely compiled from Rabelais' notes, or was the work of a very careful imitator.

5   CONNANT, M., et COUTON, G. "Rabelais, curé de Meudon." *BHR* 12:29–30.

Reprints document whereby Rabelais, "curé de Meudon" from January 1551 to January 1553, gives "à son vicaire, et au frère de son vicaire," an order to pay in his name an annual contribution to the convent of Saint-Germain-des-Près.

6   CORDIÉ, CARLO. "Recenti studi sulla vita e sulle opere di François Rabelais, 1939–50." *Letterature Moderne* 1:107–20.
    Supplements Saulnier's overview of Rabelais scholarship in his "Dix années d'études sur Rabelais (1939–1948)." *BHR* 11 (1949):105–28.

7   FRANÇON, MARCEL. "Note sur Rabelais et les nombres." *Isis* 41, parts 2–3, no. 125–126 (December):298–300.
    Notes the importance of the number 6—the first "perfect number"—its multiples (12 and 312) and its divider (3), in the architecture of Thélème and in the *Cinquiesme Livre*. Finds also a reference to the "nombre d'or" in the *Pantagrueline Prognostication...pour l'an perpétuel*. Concludes that Rabelais shared his contemporaries' interest in the practical as well as the mystical aspects of numbers, and that his choice of numbers reveals a preoccupation with Pythagorean and gnostic numerology.

8   MASSANT, RAYMOND. "Balzac disciple de Rabelais et maître du conte drôlatique." In *Balzac et la Touraine*. Congrès d'histoire littéraire, Tours, 28–31 mai 1949. Tours: Gilbert-Claray, pp. 69–76.
    Recalls the high esteem in which Rabelais was held by the Romantics, but argues that Balzac's admiration was more than merely a matter of fashion. Believes that there was a Rabelaisian constant in Balzac's character, and quotes F. Baldensperger to the effect that there was in Balzac "une façon qu'on pourrait dire *panurgienne* d'envisager l'existence" (p. 71). Notes traces of Rabelais' influence in Balzac's earliest novels, and points out that admiration for Rabelais turns to worship in the *Cent contes drôlatiques* (which Balzac considered to be his masterpiece).

9   NERI, FERDINANDO. *Rabelais e il suo tempo*. Turin: A. Viretto, 149 pp.
    Provides a short overview of Rabelais' life and work. Stresses Italian influences, particularly Colonna's *Hyperotomachia Poliphili* and Folengo's *Maccheronee*. Follows the development of Rabelais' "fantasia creatrice" through a series of key episodes. Compares the False Diamond episode in *Pantagruel* with its source in one of Masuccio Salernitano's stories in his *Novellino* (pp. 59ff.). Suggests that "Messere Francesco di Nianto, le Thuscan," mentioned by Rabelais as the author of a book on the art of reading "lettres non apparentes" is Francesco de Nanto, "artista di un certo pregio" (p. 67), and not an imaginary character invented by Rabelais, as Plattard and Boulenger believed him to be. The second half of the book is devoted to a discussion of Panurge ("un angelo cattivo," p. 84) in some of the main episodes in which he plays a major role: the encounter with Pantagruel, the victory over the Dipsodes, the praise of debts, Dindenault's sheep, and the storm at sea.

1951

10  O'KANE, ELEANOR. "The Proverb: Rabelais and Cervantes." *Comparative Literature* 2, no. 1 (Winter):360–69.

Takes exception to Sainéan's assertion that Rabelais uses proverbs in a much more interesting way than Cervantes. Claims that for Rabelais (and Erasmus) the proverb is merely a stylistic adornment, whereas for Cervantes, and for the Spanish paroemiological tradition as a whole, it has an intrinsic value. Finds the "psychological exploitation of the inner content of proverbs" to be "almost entirely lacking in Rabelais" (p. 364). Concedes that Rabelais is something of a master in the medieval use of proverbs, but believes that "we really leave Rabelais and his countrymen behind" when it comes to the Renaissance use of proverbs as "a psychological resource" (p. 368).

11  PITOU, SPIRE. "Rabelais, La Fontaine, Richelet, and *la touselle*." *Modern Language Notes* 65, no. 6 (June):399–403.

The diet of the unicorns sent by Pantagruel to his father in the *Quart Livre*, chapt. 4, consists of "pommes, poyres, orge, touzelle, brief toutes especes de fruitctz et legumaiges." La Fontaine borrowed the word in *Le Diable de Papefiguière*. Pierre Richelet, in his *Dictionnaire*, wrote that La Fontaine first admitted using the word without knowing its meaning, then claimed in a later edition to have learned what it signified: "une sorte de froment, qui a une tige assez haute, un épi qui n'a point de barbe," from "un habile Tourangeau." Suspects that Richelet's conversation with La Fontaine is fictitious.

## 1951

1  FLOWERS, RUTH CAVE. *Voltaire's Stylistic Transformation of Rabelaisian Satirical Devices: A Study in Epoch Styles, Renaissance Transformed into Rococo.* Washington, D.C.: The Catholic University of America Press, 138 pp.

Compares Rabelais and Voltaire in terms of their satirical techniques, and seeks in this comparison a key to the change in style and taste from the grotesque realism of the Renaissance to the Rococo style of the eighteenth century. Distinguishes the various types of satire upon which each writer drew, gives numerous examples of the forms which satire assumes in their work, and discusses Voltaire's changing attitude towards Rabelais from his initial dislike in 1734 to the much more positive reaction as expressed in his letters to Madame Du Deffand in 1759–60. Compares the use of satire by the two writers in their treatment of thematically similar passages, and concludes that the fundamental grotesqueness of Rabelaisian satire is toned down in Voltaire with wit, logic, and detachment, and made to conform to the restraint and sense of propriety of his own age.

2   FRANÇON, MARCEL. "Note pour le commentaire du *Quart Livre.*" *Modern Language Notes* 66, no. 3 (March):184.

   In Dindenault's praise of his sheep (chapt. 7), *vere* may be a play on "verrat" meaning "verres," and it is possible that *pourreaux* is a misreading of *pourceaux.*

3   ———. "Nouvelle note sur l'été 1532." *BHR* 13:334–35.

   Completes a previous note (*Modern Language Notes*, November 1947) with a document (*Cronique du roy Françoys premier de ce nom*) contradicting the assertion made by Pierre Jourda that in France the summer of 1532 was particularly dry. The assertion had been made to explain Rabelais' statement that Pantagruel was born during a period of severe drought.

4   ———. "Rabelais et Folengo." *Italica* 28:251–53.

   "Pantagruel prit Loup Garou par les deux pieds..." (*Pantagruel*, chapt. 29). Believes that the idea of thus using a character as if he were a bludgeon represents yet another borrowing from Folengo's *Maccheronee* (Book XIX).

5   ———. "Sur une source possible de Rabelais." *Modern Language Notes* 66, no. 7 (November):466–69.

   Makes the same point as 1951.4: The image of Pantagruel taking Loup Garou by his foot and lifting his body "comme une picque en l'air" (*Pantagruel*, chapt. 29) may have as its source a passage in Folengo's *Le Maccheronee.*

6   KELLER, ABRAHAM. "The Idea of Progress in Rabelais." *PMLA* 66:235–43.

   In matters relating to progress, "the conservative, traditional humanist of the first two books has become in the last three a forerunner of Bacon and a herald of the values of the seventeenth and eighteenth centuries" (p. 236). Offers a "suggestive rather than definitive" explanation for the development of the idea of progress in Rabelais from its embryonic stage, as manifested in his interest in trades as part of Gargantua's educational program, to its fully mature statement in the episode of the Pantagruélion. Detects three factors in this evolution: the passing of the old generation of such venerated scholars as Erasmus and Budé, the emergence of the notion of progress in the works of such contemporary writers as Louis Leroy, Vesalius, and Ambroise Paré, and "accomplishments which might have fortified Rabelais' progressive hypothesis" (p. 240).

7   KRAILSHEIMER, A[LBAN] J. "Rabelais et Postel." *BHR* 13:187–90.

   Expands on the suggestion, first made by Lucien Febvre, that it is in Postel (chapt. 7 of his *De Orbis Concordia*, 1543) that Rabelais found the idea of identifying the great Pan with Christ. Notes that Postel used the word

1952

"Deus" when referring to Pan in his *De Etruriae regionis...originibus* of 1551. Does not hesitate to see in Rabelais' "Maniacles Pistolets" (chapt. 32 of the *Quart Livre*) a reference to his old enemy: "Pistolet, c'est Postel. Le jeu de mots est assez précis pour être évident, l'adjectif convient spécialement bien au malheureux érudit dont la folie visionnaire était notoire partout en Europe" (p. 190).

8   SCREECH, M[ICHAEL] A[NDREW]. "Rabelais, de Billon and Erasmus." *BHR* 13:241–65.

Reexamines Lefranc's belief that Rabelais is the leader of the anti-feminist camp in the "Querelle des Femmes." Notes that the thesis is based on de Billon's testimony, and suggests that the latter's authority to judge the matter is not beyond question. Moreover, points out that the Rabelaisian texts alleged to support the idea of Rabelais' misogyny do not necessarily support it. Believes that the place given to women in the Abbaye de Thélème suggests the very opposite, although admits that the romantic, idealistic view characteristic of the episode was soon to be abandoned. Argues that Rabelais' "maturer attitude to women" (p. 253) should be sought in the *Tiers Livre*, and more specifically in the views expounded by Pantagruel rather than Panurge or Rondibilis. Claims that the *Tiers Livre* is less concerned with the "Querelle des Femmes" than with "the projected reform of the Cannon Law by the Council of Trent of 1545.... Rabelais' objections to love-matches derive from the great importance he attaches to the institution of marriage, which for him is the corner-stone of society, and from his great faith in the value of good birth and education" (p. 256). Here as in so many areas, Rabelais' thought is very close to that of Erasmus in his *Christiani matrimonii institutio*, and not, as is generally believed, to Tiraqueau and his *De Legibus connubialibus*.

9   THIOLLIER, ANTONIN. "Rabelais et les beaux-arts." *Romanic Review* 42:3–17.

Rabelais' silence before the masterpieces of contemporary Italian art, his laconic allusions to painting and sculpture, the very secondary role assigned to the visual arts in his concept of an ideal education suggest that— with the notable exception of music—he was curiously lacking in aesthetic sense and appreciation of the fine arts. Essentially an intellectual and a sensualist, "il se détourne de l'art pour aller au livre" (p. 17).

**1952**

1   CARPENTER, NAN COOKE. "The Authenticity of Rabelais' Fifth Book: Musical Criteria." *Modern Language Quarterly* 13:299–304.

The association of bells with ecclesiastical satire reaches its climax in the "Isle Sonante." The harmoniousness of the organ finds its most vivid dramatization at the court of Entelechie, in an episode which also provides "Rabelais' loftiest and at the same time most practical expression of the therapeutic value of music" (p.300). Rabelais' use of the chanson and the dance is at its most effective at the court of Lanternois. Such observations lead the author to conclude that on all points of musical rhetoric Book V represents the logical and artistic culmination of the preceding four, and that the persistence of these musical patterns strengthtens the argument that this final book is largely Rabelais' own work.

2   KELLER, ABRAHAM C. "Anti-War Writing in France, 1500–60." *PMLA* 67, no. 2 (March):240–50.

Notes a turnabout in Rabelais' outlook on war in the prologue to the *Tiers Livre*. Accounts for the abandonment of his earlier pacifistic stand by Rabelais' lack of understanding of aggression, and a desire to court royal favor as a protection against the hostility of the Sorbonne. Finds a similar lack of "an actual foundation on which to build a pacifistic program" (p. 244) and a similar desire for royal patronage in other humanists, such as Budé, and in such poets "in the erudite tradition" as Ronsard and Du Bellay.

3   LEBÈGUE, RAYMOND. "Rabelais et la parodie." *BHR* 14:193–204.

Defines parody as a conscious (though not absolutely faithful) imitation of a literary work or of the language characteristic of a genre, presupposing "un clin d'œil complice" (p. 195) between the author and the reader who is meant to recognize the original. Notes that during the Renaissance, the word does not imply—as it will later—a satirical or derisory intention. Lists twelve types of parody to be found in Rabelais' work, and concludes that its aim is most often the amusement of the reader. "Mais, le plus souvent, Rabelais ne cherche pas à ridiculiser et attaquer le texte, le genre, ou les disciplines qu'il parodie" (p. 203).

4   MARICHAL, ROBERT. "Rabelais et la réforme de la justice." *BHR* 14:176–92.

The Bridoye episode in Book III contained a violent diatribe against the "Parlement myrelinguois en Myrelingues." In the 1548 version of Book IV, only three years after the famous trial of Chancellor Poyet, Rabelais' satire of legal practices aims essentially at the Chicanous: "les sergents, les huissiers, les procureurs et d'une façon générale tous les auxiliaires subalternes de la justice" (p. 176). Referring to the trial of Poyet, the author shows the relevance of Rabelais' satire to contemporary events and the extent to which it is in line with official attempts at legal reform: "Ces chapitres en apparence si révolutionnaires ne sont que la paraphrase et la mise en 'gestes' de la politique du chancelier et du roi" (p. 190). In 1552, however, the diatribe against the Parlement ends, surprisingly, with a bitter denunciation of culprits of a different ilk: "ces juges pedanées soubs l'orme" whom the author identifies as "les juges seigneuriaux," independent of the king and of royal justice. This deflected criticism becomes less surprising when one realizes that it merely echoes one of the main objectives of Chancellor Olivier's *Edit d'érection des sièges présidiaux dans toute l'étendue du royaume* summarizing the efforts of both Francis I and Henry II in favor of judicial reform. Concludes tentatively that once again Rabelais may be enlarging upon a minor incident and using it as a weapon of royalist propaganda.

5 MAYER, C.A. "The Genesis of a Rabelaisian Character: Menippus and Frère Jean." *French Studies* 6:219–29.

Argues that in *Gargantua*, if not in the *Tiers Livre*, Frère Jean is much more than the embodiment of courage he is often taken to be. Finds him to be the mouthpiece of Rabelais' anti-monasticism, while being at the same time the typical monk of Renaissance satiric literature. Notes that he is likened by Philibert de Vienne, in his *Le Philosophe de Court* (1547), to Menippus, as the sixteenth century knew him: that is as the "jeering, caustic scoffer" of Lucian's *Dialogues*. Compares the two characters, and finds them similar in that each is an "inside witness" of what his author attacks. Just as Menippus is a Cynic used by Lucian to ridicule other Cynics, so Frère Jean is a monk mocking other monks. Argues that the vices with which Rabelais unexpectedly saddles his character—his slovenliness, his ignorance—are in reality the vices of monks in general. Dismisses Morçay's interpretation of the Abbaye de Thélème as a joke, on the grounds that it is built to reward an ignorant monk. Believes the Abbey deserves to be taken seriously, as an anti-monastic monastery built, in all logic, for a champion of anti-monasticism.

6 PITOU, SPIRE. "The MS. Commentary on Rabelais at Chateau-Thierry." *Modern Language Review* 47, no. 2 (April):209.

Draws attention to an eighteenth-century manuscript in the municipal library of Chateau-Thierry containing 188 explanations of obscure terms found in Rabelais' works, but warns that these are merely copied *verbatim* or abbreviated from the *Alphabet de l'Auteur François* contained in the 1663 and 1711 Amsterdam edition of Rabelais.

7 TELLE, ÉMILE V. "L'île des Alliances (*Quart Livre*, Chap.IX) ou l'anti-Thélème." *BHR* 14:159–75.

Notes that the meaning of the episode has hitherto eluded all critics. Since the Ennasins inhabiting the island are characterized by their flattened, misshapen noses, believes they are meant to stand for the mass of the *mal nez*, in contrast to the *bien nez* who alone are welcome in Thélème. Argues that the social organization on the island is intended to be an exact antithesis of the harmonious life led by the Thelemites in Frère Jean's Abbey.

8 ———. "La situation géographique (?) de la Dive Bouteille." *BHR* 14:329–30.

Mentions the belief in the existence of a Bottle worshipped by some tribes in Peru, to which Thévet alludes in his *Les Singularitez de la France Antarcticque*. Since the book appeared in 1558, what Thévet says cannot be considered to be a source of the Dive Bouteille (assuming the authenticity of Book V), but suggests that Rabelais may have found an allusion to the legend elsewhere.

## 1953

1 ASTRUC, PIERRE. "Rabelais médecin." *L'Éducation nationale* (16 June):15–16.

Follows Rabelais to Lyons, where Sébastien Gryphe publishes his scholarly editions of Manardi, Galien and Hippocrates, where he practices medicine at the Hôtel-Dieu, and meets Jean du Bellay who will take him as his private physician on his journeys to Rome. Quotes a series of anecdotes related to Rabelais' reputation for indulging in food and drink, and quotes Rabelais himself on the duties of the physician towards his patients.

2 AUERBACH, ERICH *Mimesis: The Representation of Reality in Western Literature*. Translated from the German by Willard R. Trask. Princeton, N.J.: Princeton University Press, 563 pp.

Chapt. 11, "The World in Pantagruel's Mouth," is a reprint of a text which first appeared in English translation in 1950.1. Reprinted: 1957.1.

3 BENOT, YVES. "Rabelais et le sentiment national au XVIe siècle." *Europe* 95–96 (November–December):134–52.

Claims that Rabelais' political thought is not that of a royal spokesman, as is sometimes believed, but that it was fashioned independently, from his experience of political realities in Lyons and from his collaboration with the Du Bellays. In the Picrochole episode, for instance, "Rabelais s'adresse bien à la nation française, et rien n'autorise à le rabaisser au rang d'un propagandiste officiel" (p. 14).

4 BERTHOUD, GABRIELLE. "*Le Livre des Marchans* d'Antoine Marcourt et Rabelais." In *François Rabelais: Ouvrage publié pour le quatrième centenaire de sa mort, 1553–1953*. THR VII. Geneva: Librairie Droz, pp. 86–92.

Notes that this work by the pastor of Neuchatel contains not only the first reference to Rabelais' Pantagruel, but also the first allusion to the lawsuit between Baisecul and Humevesne, as well as to Panurge. Having first appeared in August of 1553, it testifies to the immediate success of Rabelais' book, and to the fact that *Pantagruel* appealed to the general public as well as

1953

to the most pious of Reformed readers. Points out that all allusions to Rabelais were suppressed in the second edition (December 1534), for a variety of possible reasons.

5   BROCHON, PIERRE. "Rabelais et la littérature de colportage." *Europe* 95–96 (November–December):73–82.

Believes that the influence of Folengo's *L'Histoire macaronique de Merlin Coccaïe* on Rabelais has been grossly exaggerated, at the expense of what he owes to the popular literature of his day. Emphasizes Rabelais' debt to the *Grandes et inestimables cronicques*. "Il faut, pour le moins, reconnaître que l'œuvre de Rabelais est tellement liée à la littérature populaire qu'elle peut s'en inspirer, l'inspirer à son tour, et s'inspirer des œuvres populaires influencées par elle, et que ces influences réciproques forment un écheveau inextricable d'emprunts et d'imitations" (p. 82).

6   CARPENTER, NAN COOKE. "Rabelais and the Androgyne." *Modern Language Notes* 68:452–57.

Believes Rabelais to have been the first to make use of Plato's Androgyne in Renaissance literature, before Héroet (1542) and des Périers (1550). Notes that Rabelais goes back to Plato rather than to the "attenuated version given by Ficino" (p. 454). Sees in Rabelais' Androgyne a characteristic materialisation of Plato's figure. Notes the use of Greek for the motto around the figure, and underscores the irony and the ambiguity of that motto. Sees in the recourse to Saint Paul a characteristically humanistic reconciliation of Christianity and Platonism. Also believes that in his treatment of the figure, Rabelais reveals in miniature some of the most characteristic facets of his rhetorical style, with its juxtaposition of the physical and the spiritual, of erudition and humor.

7   COHEN, MARCEL. "Comment Rabelais a écrit." *Europe* 95–96 (November–December):45–72.

Begins with bibliographical details concerning the circumstances of publication of Rabelais' books, and an overview of the major critical studies on Rabelais from Brunet's *Notice* of 1843 through Lebègue's articles of 1952 and 1953. Offers a generally negative assessment: "ouvrages de grammairiens sans perspectives à historiens de la littérature négligeant la langue ou la traitant avec un manque déplorable de précision" (p. 51). Own contribution focuses on Rabelais' sentence: on the dramatic, theatrical aspects of those texts which are meant to be read aloud; on the rhetorical devices used in the passages which are presented as having been written; on rhythm; on the cinematographic in Rabelais; on his so-called "mannerism." Offers stylistic comparisons with du Fail and Béroalde de Verville. Does not provide a full-scale analysis, but indicates what such a stylistic analysis would entail.

8   DE GRÈVE, MARCEL. "Le Rabelais de légende." *Le Flambeau* 36th year, no. 6:585–604.

Quotes in its entirety Ronsard's "Epitaphe" to prove that for some of Rabelais' contemporaries his work seemed devoid of any significance: "Nulle trace, parmi les témoignages des années qui entourent la mort de Rabelais, d'une portée profonde attribuée à cette œuvre de génie" (p. 592). In the second half of the century, sees a tendency to view Rabelais only as an inconsequential buffoon, whereas earlier he had been taken seriously. Upon the publication of *Gargantua*, had been welcomed as a spokesman by an entire generation clamoring for intellectual and religious reform. Around 1540–45, began to be viewed as heretical both by those who saw in him a disciple of Calvin and by Calvin himself, who denounced him in *De Scandalis* as a drunken blasphemer. At the time of his death, both Catholics and Huguenots were unanimous in ignoring the work's "substantifique moelle" and condemning the author, assimilated to his fictional characters, for his immorality. "A partir du moment où ses romans sont réduits à d'impies et graveleuses railleries, à d'extravagantes ripailles, Rabelais ne tardera pas à prendre lui-même l'aspect d'un bouffon mécréant, d'un goinfre effréné, d'un ivrogne insatiable" (p. 600). Thus Ronsard's "Epitaphe" is not a personal attack: it echoes the feelings of an entire generation of readers and merely lends the prestige of the poet's name to the already accredited legend of a Rabelais in every way as debauched, as cynical and as devoid of serious intellectual stature as the most disreputable of his heroes. Only in the following century will the "Libertins spirituels" discover in him a kindred spirit and rediscover in his work its ideological significance.

9   ———. "Les contemporains de Rabelais découvrirent-ils la 'substantificque mouelle'?" In *François Rabelais: Ouvrage publié pour le quatrième centenaire de sa mort, 1553–1953*. THR VII. Geneva: Librairie Droz, pp. 74–85.

The earliest allusion to the serious message behind the frivolous exterior of Rabelais' work is to be found in Hugues Salel's "Dizain," in François Juste's 1534 edition of *Pantagruel*. Salel was the first to discover the book's "substantificque mouelle." The ensuing silence on the part of Rabelais' friends was to last until his death. Argues that the contemporary humanists were not insensitive to the message in Rabelais' work, but that they were even more sensitive to the danger of drawing attention to it after the "Affaire des Placards." Sees in their silence the very proof that, as of 1534 and the publication of *Gargantua*, they were conscious of the real importance of Rabelais' political and religious thought.

10  DELAUNAY, PAUL. "Rabelais physicien." In *François Rabelais: Ouvrage publié pour le quatrième centenaire de sa mort, 1553–1953*. THR VII. Geneva: Librairie Droz, pp.36–44.

"On ne saurait demander à une oeuvre, ou la science s'éparpille et se dissimule sous l'allégorie et le burlesque, les précisions et inventaires d'un traité didactique" (p. 43). Within these limitations, examines Rabelais' scientific knowledge. Finds him to be abreast of the past and curious of the present, but not an innovator, not even in the field of medicine: "il a laissé à Vesale le mérite de renover la connaissance du corps humain" (p. 36). His cosmology is essentially that of the Cabbalists. His philosophy of nature is essentially pagan. His notions of physiology go back to Aristotle and Galien. His scientific nomenclature is incoherent and unsystematic, as is his classification. In sum, he is an old-fashioned "physicien" whose knowledge of nature is primarily derived from books, rather than a naturalist, even in the relative sense in which this term can be applied to such contemporaries as Belon and Thévet.

11   DENOIX, L. "Les Connaissances nautiques de Rabelais." In *François Rabelais: Ouvrage publié pour le quatrième centenaire de sa mort, 1553–1953. THR* VII. Geneva: Librairie Droz, pp. 171–80.

Challenges Jal's excessively harsh opinion of Rabelais' knowledge of nautical maneuvers and vocabulary in his 1840 article in *Archéologie Navale*. Concedes that the information pertaining to naval matters in the first chapter of Book IV and the "storm-at-sea" episode is somewhat scant, but points out that everything Rabelais says is perfectly comprehensible and suggests that, in writing these chapters, Rabelais may have benefited from the help of a professional sailor.

12   DESONAY, FERNAND. "En relisant l'*Abbaye de Thélème*..." In *François Rabelais: Ouvrage publié pour le quatrième centenaire de sa mort, 1553–1953. THR* VII. Geneva: Librairie Droz, pp. 93–103.

Wary of critical commentaries, reads the episode itself and fails to see in the chapters on Thélème the key to Rabelais' thought, or the paean to the Renaissance that Raoul Morçay, among others, had read into them. Finds Rabelais to be insensitive to Renaissance architecture, notes that he devotes only two lines to the "librairies," that he says nothing about the paintings, and that he gives us a lackluster, monotonous description of the clothes worn by the Thelemites, in a style that has lost momentarily its musical and rhythmic qualities. Only the reference to the Evangelicals and Rabelais' words in defense of human freedom can be said to usher in the Renaissance. For the rest, the whole episode—including the celebrated "Fay ce que vouldras"—springs from the initial idea of creating a world in every way antithetical to the monastic life he had known and despised. "Thélème n'est qu'une farce" (p. 102), rather than an expression of the Renaissance ideal.

13   DONTENVILLE, H[ENRI]. "François Rabelais en ses 'mythologies galliques'." *Bulletin de la Société de Mythologie Française* 14:43–53; 15:57–61.

1953

Notes Rabelais' allusion, in his *Pantagruéline prognostication* for 1533, to the "mythologies galliques" of Jean de Gravot (the author himself). Calls attention to Rabelais' interest in France's pre-Roman past, evokes the traces of Gargantuan folklore in the region surrounding Chinon, and follows—"page à page"—the numerous references to Gallic mythology in the first four books of Rabelais' novel. Points out that these references are most frequent in *Pantagruel*, and that they grow progressively fewer as the novel unfolds.

14   DUMONT, FRANÇOIS. "La donation du Salmigondin." In *François Rabelais: Ouvrage publié pour le quatrième centenaire de sa mort, 1553–1953. THR* VII. Geneva: Librairie Droz, pp. 156–63.

Equates the episode in which Pantagruel offers Panurge the "Chatellenie de Salmigondin" after the conquest of Dipsodia with the conquest of the Piémont and its thoughtful administration at the hands of the wise Guillaume du Bellay. Sees the episode as an occasion for Rabelais to criticize the excessive liberality with which Francis I dealt with the estates of the Crown.

15   FEBVRE, LUCIEN. "Comment lire Rabelais." *L'Éducation nationale* (16 April):3–5.

Suspects that at the time of the fourth centenary of Rabelais' death his work is more often explicated by specialists than read by the wider public for whom it had been written. Seeks to prevent Rabelais' work from falling "dans la fosse commune de l'érudition morte." Warns against the danger of using his book as a subject of scholarly investigation rather than a source of inspiration and entertainment. Believes that his own historical approach is not incompatible with the kind of ahistorical reading he now advocates. "C'est que l'histoire n'est pas la mémoire du passé mort....Elle travaille sur le passé pour le rendre assimilable aux hommes du présent" (p. 5).

16   FRANÇON, MARCEL. "Influence des *Chroniques Gargantuines* sur Ronsard et sur J. du Bellay." *Studies in Philology* 50:144–48.

Believes that the allusions to Gargantuan meals in Ronsard's *Baccanales* (1552) and in Sonnet 104 of *Les Regrets* point to an influence of the *Chroniques* via Rabelais. Claims that other Pléiade poets were also influenced by the *Chroniques*, by way of folklore as well as literature.

17   ———. "Rabelais et les *Chroniques Gargantuines*." In *François Rabelais: Ouvrage publié pour le quatrième centenaire de sa mort, 1553–1953. THR* VII. Geneva: Librairie Droz, pp. 53–59.

In his edition of the *Vroy Gargantua*, author had suggested (without convincing most critics) that it was Rabelais who had quoted from three chapters of the *Chroniques admirables* in the episode of Pantagruel's birth, and not vice versa, as is commonly held. Restates what he admits are conjec-

1953

tures, but maintains that they are more plausible than the conjectures of the other critics. Adds one further argument: the allusion to the drought "en tout le pays de Africque," while difficult to explain in the context of *Pantagruel*, makes perfect sense in *Les Chroniques admirables*: "J'en conclus que cette mention de l'Afrique par Rabelais est un reste d'un récit d'une chronique gargantuine" (p. 58).

18  FRÉVILLE, JEAN. "Initiation à Rabelais." *Europe* 95–96 (November–December):3–6.

Introductory, general, panegyric. Emphasizes what is most forward-looking in Rabelais: "Hardiment, résolument, Rabelais se range du côté des novateurs" (p. 3).

19  GAREL, RENÉ. "Rabelais et la justice." *Europe* 95–96 (November–December):99–109.

During the Renaissance, the administration of justice is in the hands of the newly risen bourgeoisie, but the legal system is built on feudal foundations. The bourgeoisie "doit s'appuyer sur un droit d'origine féodale pour essayer de forger un droit plus conforme à ses intérêts de classe, et qui plus est elle exerce ce droit en contradiction avec ces intérêts" (p. 102). Rabelais, of bourgeois origin, contests this feudal legal system insofar as it has not kept up with economic and social evolution, but is moving on the contrary towards "un renforcement du pouvoir judiciaire, non pas dans le sens désiré par la bourgeoisie, mais sous forme d'un renforcement de l'absolutisme" (p. 105).

20  GIRALDI, GIOVANNI. *Rabelais e l'educazione del Principe*. Milan: Edizioni Viola, Biblioteca di Pedagogia, 81 pp.

"Rabelais è filio della cultura italiana, egli viene dal nostro Rinascimento più di quanto non si voglia ammettere" (p. 69). In particular, is convinced that Rabelais found in Italian humanistic literature the central motif of his work. Believes that Rabelais the thinker is less concerned with philosophy or religion than with education. Studies the theme in the text itself, without recourse to the potentially obfuscating context of Rabelais criticism. Reminds us that Rabelais' novel is the story of kings, and that the education Rabelais has in mind is that of the ideal Renaissance prince as embodied for example by Francesco Sforza. Discusses at length the place of religion in the prince's education, and describes Rabelais' religious position, or rather his *religiosity*, as being in "una categoria a sè" (p. 34), neither Evangelism nor Protestantism, but Christian deism. As independent of the jurisdiction of any specific church, finds such a form of religion to be particularly consonant with the prince's position of absolute authority, since it is he, and no one else, who teaches his subjects how to serve God. Questions whether belief in the immortality of the soul is an element of this religious teaching. Discusses the other duties of the prince, as prescribed by Italian humanists and embodied in

Rabelais' giants: to encourage the search for truth, to be firm but not insensitive, to decide matters of peace and war with the help of divine guidance, to resist the temptations of territorial expansion. Returns to the question of Rabelais' "deismo christiano," acknowledges it to be to a certain extent an inconsistent notion, but argues that Rabelais is not a philosopher but an educator, that he does not build abstract systems but men, and that he adopted the position of Christian deism, with its belief in God and in the truth of the Gospels, for very much the same reasons that will determine two centuries later the religion of Rousseau: namely because it provides the most solid foundation for their educational goals. Concludes that Rabelais' emphasis on the education of the aristocracy and not of the people makes of him, in matters of pedagogy, an author of the past.

21 GRANDGEORGES, PIERRE. "La pédagogie 'nouvelle' effrayante et allègre de Rabelais." *Europe* 95–96 (November–December):83–99.

The satirical aspect of Rabelais' texts on education belongs to Rabelais only by virtue of its comic verve. Nor is Rabelais original in the positive aspects of his pedagogy. The development of true science and of modern humanism owes him very little. The value of the pages devoted by him to pedagogical ideas is essentially literary: "Il reste de lui un chef-d'œuvre littéraire incomparable, une satire purgative, un élan, un espoir, et, peut-être, finalement, plus de bonne humeur que de bon sens" (p. 99).

22 GYERGYAI, ALBERT. "Rabelais en Hongrie." *Europe* 95–96 (November–December):155–58.

Rabelais was on the shelves of Hungarian libraries as early as the seventeenth century. The first Hungarian monograph devoted to Rabelais—A. Neményi's *Rabelais et son époque*—dates from 1877. But only the first three books have so far been translated; the earliest of these dates from 1936.

23 HAFFEN, LOUIS. "Johann Fischart, humaniste alsacien, 'Rabelais de l'Allemagne.'" *Europe* 95–96 (November–December):159–66.

Both Rabelais and his German translator were humanists, both fought for religious toleration and freedom of thought, both hid their serious ideas under a cloak of irony. But whereas Rabelais addressed himself solely to a cultivated public of aristocrats and members of the haute bourgeoisie, Fischart wrote for the common people. His translation of *Gargantua* is an adaptation of Rabelais' book to the taste of the working masses.

24 HUON, ANTOINETTE. "Le roy sainct Panigon dans l'imagerie populaire du XVIe siècle." In *François Rabelais: Ouvrage publié pour le quatrième centenaire de sa mort, 1553–1953*. THR VII. Geneva: Librairie Droz, pp. 210–25.

The discovery of an engraving (picture and text) published in Lyons by Pierre de Maison Neuve around 1560, representing "sainct Panigon" and pro-

1953

viding a versified description of the "royaume panigonnais" as a "pays de Cocagne," leads author to trace the theme of the "pays de Cocagne" in various European literatures, and to note some similarities between the versified description and chapt. 10 of the *Quart Livre* on the island of Chéli, in the hope of shedding light on Rabelais' mysterious Panigon. But concludes that it is unlikely that the versifier identified the island with the "pays de Cocagne" or that he borrowed from Rabelais the name "Panigon."

25 JANEAU, HUBERT. "La pensée politique de Rabelais." In *François Rabelais: Ouvrage publié pour le quatrième centenaire de sa mort, 1553–1953. THR VII.* Geneva: Librairie Droz, pp. 15–35.

Studies Rabelais' conception of royalty and royal power by examining the "trinity" of good kings (Grandgousier, Gargantua and Pantagruel), and contrasting them with the tyrannical Picrochole. Rabelais does not express himself unequivocally about the basis of royal power (Do kings reign by natural or by divine right?). He is clearer on the question of what makes a good prince: "la *piété*, la *sagesse*, la *bonté*" (p. 20). He seeks counsel, is a wise legislator, carefully manages the finances of the state. Finds that Rabelais' liberalism is stronger in religious than in political matters: the freedom he proclaims is the freedom of conscience. Politically, as in many other areas, finds him to be a disciple of Erasmus and an adherent of political evangelism.

26 JOURDA, PIERRE. "A Montpellier." *L'Éducation nationale* (16 April):13–14.

Reminds us that Rabelais was already around forty when he enrolled in September 1530 as a medical student at Montpellier. With the help of documents preserved at the Medical School Library and allusions gleaned from Rabelais' work, reconstructs in some detail Rabelais' academic and professional activity in Montpellier during his two sojourns in that city (in 1530–31 and again in 1537–38, when he received his doctorate). Believes that the Montpellier experience marks, with the discovery of human suffering, an essential stage in Rabelais' intellectual development: "C'est à Montpellier qu'il a compris que tout le savoir humain n'est pas dans les livres" (p. 14).

27 KRAILSHEIMER, ALBAN [J]. "The Andouilles of the *Quart Livre*." In *François Rabelais: Ouvrage publié pour le quatrième centenaire de sa mort, 1553–1953. THR VII.* Geneva: Librairie Droz, pp. 226–32.

Puts to the test Abel Lefranc's remark to the effect that everywhere in Rabelais "l'élément réel apparaît sous le mythe," by applying it to a passage most often considered as mere fantasy. On the basis of geographic, historic, and linguistic considerations, identifies Quaresmeprenant with Charles V, Mardigras (tentatively) with Martin Luther, the Andouilles with the German Lutherans, the Council of Chesil with that of Trent, and suggests that the whole episode was inspired by the Schmalkaldic War of 1546.

28 LAHY-HOLLEBECQUE, MARIE. "Rabelais et la Querelle des Femmes."
*Europe* 95–96 (November–December):116–34.
　　Believes that Rabelais places woman at the very center of his conception of the world. Notes the numerous instances in which women are treated
mercilessly and derisively, but underscores those passages in which the balance is redressed, most specifically the Thélème episode: "La grande nouveauté de Thélème, c'est l'admission sans réserve de l'égalité entre l'homme
et la femme à qui l'on reconnaît même intelligence, mêmes goûts artistiques et
aspirations morales" (p. 132).

29 LEBÈGUE, RAYMOND. "Le personnage de Pantagruel dans les *Tiers* et
*Quart Livres.*" In *François Rabelais: Ouvrage publié pour le quatrième centenaire de sa mort, 1553–1953. THR* VII. Geneva: Librairie Droz, pp. 164–70.
　　Are Rabelais' characters coherent individuals? Believes that a valid
answer to this question must take into account the distinction between the
giants and the other characters in the novels. Whereas Panurge and Frère Jean
are coherent characters from the very start, the giants of Book I and II keep
surprising the reader by appearing in turn as comic creations and as idealized
embodiments of humanist and Christian principles. In Books III and IV,
Panurge and Frère Jean continue to be true to themselves; they are types (as
are the characters in the comic theater of the time), whereas the giants, and
Pantagruel in particular, lose whatever human reality they possessed and
become personifications of Rabelais' human ideal.

30 ———. "Rabelais et le théâtre." *L'Education nationale* (16 April):11–12.
　　Briefly notes Rabelais' indebtedness to the various forms of medieval
theater. Underscores Rabelais' knowledge of the mysteries, his interest in their
staging, in the role of the devils, as well as his indifference to their more serious, moralizing side. Comments on Rabelais' familiarity with the farces and
*soties*, from which he borrowed a significant number of stylistic devices, and
which had an influence on the nature of Rabelaisian dialogue and characterization without compromising Rabelais' fundamental originality.

31 LEFEBVRE, HENRI. "Panurge ou la naissance de l'individu." *Europe* 95–96
(November–December):15–30.
　　A two-part article, presented as an excerpt of 1955.7. The first part, "Le
thème des géants," emphasizes the giants' origin in popular mythology. The
second, bearing the title of the article as a whole, underscores in Panurge
"l'homme de l'époque nouvelle" (p. 23). In Book III, the hero becomes more
individualized, and the work becomes more of a novel and less of an epic.

1953

32  LE PORRIER, HERBERT. "Le docteur François Rabelais." *Europe* 95–96
(November–December):30–40.
"Rabelais, qui êtes-vous?" (p. 31). Answers, for the most part, in terms
of traits which Rabelais lends to Panurge.

33  MARICHAL, ROBERT. "L'attitude de Rabelais devant le néoplatonisme et
l'italianisme (*Quart Livre*, ch.IX à XI)." In *François Rabelais: Ouvrage publié pour le quatrième centenaire de sa mort, 1553–1953. THR* VII. Geneva:
Librairie Droz, pp. 181–210.
Does Rabelais owe as much to Plato as Lefranc and, more recently,
Lucien Febvre have thought, or has this debt been exaggerated, as suggested
by Plattard? Believes Rabelais' attitude towards Plato and Platonism to have
been ambiguous. By 1525, some twenty years before Platonism became fashionable in the literary world, Rabelais had read Plato, and he quotes him more
often than any other author (although mostly through Erasmus). But in the
episode on debtors and borrowers in Book III, he seems to parody Plato's
conception of love as the soul of the world, at least indirectly, through
Ficino's commentary on the *Symposium*. In Book IV, the chapter on the
"Ennasés" (a near-anagram of "Esséniens," a Jewish sect sworn to celibacy
but which manages nevertheless to renew itself perpetually) can be taken as
deriding the notion of Platonic love, and the "île des Alliances" derives most
probably from the "amours d'alliance," or spiritual marriages fashionable at
the court of Marguerite de Navarre as well as in some monastic circles.
Rabelais continued to admire Plato's style, his concept of dialogue and his use
of myth. But he grew impatient with the neoplatonism of his day. Concludes
that "Rabelais, après avoir été en France l'un des premiers adeptes du
Platonisme, a éprouvé, après 1540, un certain agacement devant la vogue
qu'il connaissait dans les milieux mondains, y a vu, peut-être, l'un des aspects
de l'influence, à son gré excessive, que les idées et les moeurs italiennes
exerçaient à la Cour, et que contre ce snobisme il a réagi avec une certaine
vivacité" (p. 209).

34  MAYER, C.A. "Rabelais' Satirical Eulogy: the Praise of Borrowing." In
*François Rabelais: Ouvrage publié pour le quatrième centenaire de sa mort,
1553–1953. THR* VII. Geneva: Librairie Droz, pp. 147–55.
The study of Rabelais' sources for the episode leads the author to conclude that it is a satirical eulogy modeled on Lucian's *De parasito* and that as
such it is not to be taken as a serious exposition of Rabelais' economic theories (E. V. Telle) or as an example of his "irrealism" (L. Spitzer).

35  ———. "Réalisme et fantaisie dans l'œuvre de Rabelais." *L'Information
Littéraire* 4 (September–October):127–31.
Reacts against Spitzer's contention that Rabelais is fundamentally a
poetic, anti-realistic writer. Points out that reality and fantasy often coexist in

Rabelais' text. Acknowledges that Rabelais frequently transforms reality through his creative imagination into fantastic allegory. But argues that he also works in the opposite direction: "au lieu d'aller du réel vers l'irréel, Rabelais transforme des données fantastiques en quelque chose de plus réel" (p. 128). Claims this to be almost always the case with Rabelais' borrowings. Denies him the gift of invention, but concedes that he has a talent for artistic transformation by endowing what he borrows—episodes, characters—with an added degree of reality. Thus *Pantagruel* and *Gargantua* are more realistic than the *Grandes Chroniques*. Similarly, the *Tiers Livre* is more realistic than François Habert's *Songe de Pantagruel*, or Jean du Pontalais' *Les Contredicts de Songecreux*, from which Rabelais supposedly borrowed the framework of his novel. Studies from that point of view the character of Panurge in comparison with Folengo's Cingar, and that of Frère Jean in relation to Lucian's Menippus. Argues that Rabelais is similarly successful when he transforms a traditonal genre to suit his purpose. Gives as an example the praise of debtors in Book III, an adaptation of a satirical encomium borrowed from Lucian. Spitzer had singled out the chapter as an example of Rabelais' irrealism. Argues that here again Rabelais borrows an essentially fantastic genre and endows it with an astonishing degree of reality, to the point of leading many a critic to believe that the episode contains Rabelais' thought on as realistic a subject as that of political economy.

36    MONOD, GUSTAVE. "Rabelais et l'éducation." *L'Éducation nationale* (16 April):7–8.
    Insofar as Rabelais is at all concerned with pedagogical principles, believes that his ideas on the matter should be sought in the Abbaye de Thélème episode, where education is pursued in an atmosphere of freedom and trust in human nature, rather than in the chapters on the education of Gargantua, whose gruelling schedule and strict discipline are incompatible with the spirit of freedom and independence of mind evident throughout the rest of Rabelais' work.

37    NIKOULINE, L. "François Rabelais." *Europe* 95–96 (November–December):152–55.
    Is convinced that bourgeois conspiracy has sought to expurgate from Rabelais' masterpiece its revolutionary social and political significance. But his fight against the forces of political tyranny, religious fanaticism, and ignorance cannot be ignored. "Et c'est pourquoi Rabelais est tant aimé au pays des Soviets où on en a fini une fois pour toutes avec l'obscurantisme" (p. 154).

38    PERRAT, CHARLES. "Sur 'un tas de Prognostications de Lovain.'" In *François Rabelais: Ouvrage publié pour le quatrième centenaire de sa mort, 1553–1953. THR* VII. Geneva: Librairie Droz, pp. 60–71.
    Rabelais makes deprecatory allusions to "ces folz astrologues de

1953

Lovain" at the beginning of his own *Pantagrueline Prognostication*. Author traces the origin of the astrological school of Louvain. Lists twenty-nine prognostications dating from 1476 through 1560, and describes some of these at length. Rabelais' own contribution to the genre "nous apporte un nouvel écho du grand débat sur le déterminisme astrologique qui, avec Bonaventure des Périers, a passionné la plupart des écrivains de son temps" (p.61).

39   RABERIN, MARGUERITE. "Rabelais et la guerre." *Europe* 95–96 (November–December):109–16.
      Of the three military episodes in Rabelais' work, limits herself to the only truly significant one—the Picrocholine War. Views the latter as a confrontation between two regimes: Picrochole, representing the feudal system, and Grandgousier the modern state, "plus idéal que réel, qui, dans l'esprit des penseurs bourgeois, devait correspondre à la nouvelle organisation économique et sociale en voie de formation" (p. 110). Rabelais' ideas about war are those of a number of bourgeois thinkers of his day. They are now the ideas of the proletariat. "C'est pourquoi les idées de Rabelais ont pour nous une telle actualité et qu'aux yeux de la classe ouvrière ce penseur bourgeois fait figure de précurseur" (p. 116).

40   RENAUDET, AUGUSTIN. "Rabelais et l'Italie." *L'Éducation nationale* (16 April):9–10.
      Does not believe that Rabelais' three journeys to Italy had a profound influence upon him. Notes his interest in the architecture of Florence, but also his apparent indifference to the works of such artists as Donatello and Michelangelo. Notes also Rabelais' curious silence about painting: not a word about the frescoes of the Sistine Chapel. Suggests that in Rome Rabelais seems to have been mostly struck by the contrast between general licentiousness and the rigid dogmatism of the Roman church, which he proceeded to denounce as early as 1532 in *Pantagruel*, joyously at first, then with increasing audacity in the Isle des Papimanes episode of Book IV. Notes traces of literary influence of such works as *Orlando Furioso*, Pulci's *Morgante Maggiore*, and Folengo's *Macaronea*. Acknowledges also the influence of Italian humanism of the Quattrocento, but believes that Rabelais remained essentially rooted in the "gothic" past of his native country. "En réalité, l'Italie n'est, dans l'œuvre de Rabelais, qu'un décor éclatant et fugitif" (p. 10).

41   ROMAINS, JULES. "Rabelais et le Pantagruélisme." *La Revue de Paris* (May):8–14.
      Better than Cervantes, better than Dante, Rabelais represents the Renaissance at its most profound, its most daring: "Personne de ce temps-là ne l'égale tout à fait, que ce soit par la nouveauté, la hardiesse, le caractère adulte de la pensée, ou par la puissance de la figuration" (p. 8). Finds in his work an audacity of thought that went well beyond the Reformation and

explains Rabelais' refusal to join it. Believes that Rabelais' thought was too complex to be expressed in a single register: "Le comique de Rabelais est consubstantiel à sa vision du monde" (p. 13). Attempts a definition of Pantagruelism. Finds Pantagruelism particularly important in times of crisis, and gives it preference over stoicism which it in some ways resembles, but which lacks the therapeutic effects of laughter.

42   ROQUES, MARIO. "Aspects de Panurge." In *François Rabelais: Ouvrage publié pour le quatrième centenaire de sa mort, 1553–1953. THR* VII. Geneva: Librairie Droz, pp. 120–30.

Raises the question of the character's coherence. Draws his psychological portrait in Book I. Finds him essentially true to himself in the *Tiers Livre*; if he is not entirely the same, it is only because he has grown older. "Il n'en reste pas moins l'ancien Panurge, l'égoïste jouisseur, qui fanfaronne encore, mais s'inquiète: c'est Panurge à l'âge d'Arnolphe" (p. 124). Remains inventive and vindictive in the *Quart Livre*. Has not grown pious, nor more cowardly; what he exhibits is neither fear nor cowardice, but terror in the face of real danger. Sees in Panurge "une création originale, une dans sa variété et naturelle dans sa fantaisie, et dotée d'une vie morale cohérente sous des aspects divers, mais nécessairement liés dans leur succession" (p. 128).

43   SAULNIER, V[ERDUN]-L[OUIS]. "Le Silence de Rabelais et le mythe des paroles gelées." In *François Rabelais: Ouvrage publié pour le quatrième centenaire de sa mort, 1553 1953. THR* VII. Geneva: Librairie Droz, pp.233–247.

Aims to reveal, behind the poetic beauty of the episode, its "contenu de pensée" (p. 233). On the mythological level, sees in the battle between the Arismaspians and the Nephelibates an allusion to the perpetual struggle opposing the Arimaspians and the Griffons of classical mythology, as mentioned in Herodotus and Pliny the Elder. The reference to a war that has been momentarily suspended but risks flaring up again suggests, on the level of political intentions, that in evoking this mythical struggle Rabelais is in fact thinking of the hostilities between the German Protestant princes and the subjects of Charles V. Lastly, on the "philosophical" plane, the myth of words which do not immediately reveal their message shows that Rabelais is fully aware of the fundamental problems raised by language ("celui de sa légitimité, celui de ses privilèges et de ses pouvoirs," p. 241) and marks a return to the problem of intepretation raised in the prologue to *Gargantua*. But most importantly, the episode is an expression of Rabelais' "hésuchisme": his religious thought remains basically unchanged, but his evangelism is now based on the conviction that to preach the doctrine is both useless and dangerous, since the message risks at best to fall upon deaf ears, and at worst to lead the preacher directly to the stake.

1953

44 ———. "Notes sur le thème 'lex exlex' pour le commentaire de Rabelais (*Pantagruel*, V, 12)." *BHR* 15:306–14.

Does not believe that the comparison between laws and cobwebs, insofar as only the small and the weak are caught therein, was borrowed from Erasmus. Claims that the idea belongs to the "domaine public," and traces its evolution from antiquity through the Renaissance.

45 ———. "Rabelais défini par Jean-Jacques Ampère." *Revue Universitaire* 62, no. 3:160–63.

Notes the pertinence of Ampère's critical evaluation of Rabelais the artist and the thinker, as expressed by this minor Romantic in his "Portraits de Rome à différents âges" published by the *Revue des Deux Mondes* in 1855, and in his *Mélanges d'histoire littéraire et de littérature* (1867).

46 ———. "Rabelais et Mellin de Saint-Gelais, pronostiqueurs. Une édition inconnue de l'*Énigme en prophétie*." *Bulletin du Bibliophile*, no. 6:277–82.

Attracts attention to a hitherto unknown edition of the poem, published in †583 in Lyons by Jacques Pons under the title *Pronostication merveilleuse, sur le temps présent & advenir*, and attributed to "M. De S.G." Finds the separate edition of the *Énigme* to be important insofar as it suggests that the text was somehow used, at least occasionally, as a weapon during the Wars of Religion. "Ainsi peut-on surprendre, dès avant la fin du XVIe siècle, un peu de ce qu'on pourrait appeler la circulation souterraine du *Gargantua*" (p. 281). Believes that scholars are perhaps too hasty in their willingness to ascribe to Saint-Gelais the authorship of the poem.

47 SAUREL, LOUIS. "Quelques repères biographiques." *Europe* 95–96 (November–December):7–14.

Summarizes what is known of Rabelais' life: "sur certains points nous ne pouvons encore faire que des hypothèses" (p. 7).

48 SCHELER, LUCIEN. "Un quatrième exemplaire des *Grandes et inestimables croniques*: Lyon 1532." In *François Rabelais: Ouvrage publié pour le quatrième centenaire de sa mort, 1553–1953*. THR VII. Geneva: Librairie Droz, pp. 45–52.

Attracts attention to a fourth copy of the chronicles, typographically different from the three copies previously known. Describes other works which had been bound with the *Cronicques*. One of these confirms that *Les Grandes Cronicques* had been printed "à l'atelier de la veuve Chaussard" (p. 49).

49 ———. "Rabelais et l'anagramme." *Europe* 95–96 (November–December):40–44.

Contends that Rabelais' two anagrams—Alcofrybas Nasier, which he used to sign his work, and Séraphin Calobarsy, which he gave to the physician chosen by Ponocrates to correct "la manière vicieuse de vivre de Gargantua" in the first edition of Book II—are not merely haphasard transpositions of the letters in Rabelais' name, but that, as was often the case with sixteenth-century anagrams, they provide a key to his temperament and his character.

50  SCREECH, M[ICHAEL] A[NDREW]. "A Further Study of Rabelais's Position in the Querelle des Femmes: (Rabelais-Vives-Bouchard-Tiraqueau)." In *François Rabelais: Ouvrage publié pour le quatrième centenaire de sa mort, 1553–1953. THR* VII. Geneva: Librairie Droz, pp. 131–46.

Denies that Rabelais' *Tiers Livre* owes anything to Vives, either in the original or in Changy's translation. Concedes that there is between their views a certain degree of agreement, but finds the influence of Erasmus to be much more telling. Similarly, questions the influence of Tiraqueau and claims that Rabelais had much more in common with Bouchard. Even stylistic similarities between Tiraqueau and Rabelais are deceptive, for similar stylistic devices are used for very different effects (serious in Tiraqueau, comic in Rabelais). On the question of women, believes that the antifeminist streak in Tiraqueau is much stronger than in Rabelais. An examination of Tiraqueau's and Rabelais' approach to the problems raised by the Querelle des femmes leads him to conclude that the influence of *de Legibus connubialibus* is not as significant as has been claimed.

51  SPITZER, LEO. "The Works of Rabelais." In *Literary Masterpieces of the Western World*. Edited by Francis H. Horn. Baltimore: The Johns Hopkins Press, pp. 126–47.

Presents Rabelais' work as "the acme of disorderliness and improvisation" (p. 127), the Abbaye de Thélème as "a bold sixteenth-century anticipation of the American coeducational college" (p. 129), the invitation to extract from Rabelais' book a *substantifique moelle* as "a humanistic taunt directed against the medieval habit of allegorical explanation of literature" (p. 133). Argues that the spirit of the farce present in the passages where Rabelais is expounding his most serious ideas is not a precaution against censure but "a primary element of his creative mind" (p. 134). Restates his thesis of an essentially anti-realistic Rabelais: "The Rabelaisian in Rabelais is his capacity for comic visualization of what has never been seen" (p. 135). Sees in the Panurge of the episode in praise of debtors an embodiment of Rabelais himself, part clown and part mystic. Stresses in Rabelais the discoverer of the World of Words, "with its own laws over which Rabelais ruled as a king" (p. 140). Compares Rabelais with Dante: for Dante the simile is functional, for Rabelais it is autonomous. Comments on the "grotesque art" of the inscription over the gate of Thélème, and sees in it a "transition from a medieval to a humanistic treatment of language" (p. 144).

1954

52   TELLE, ÉMILE V. "Thélème et le paulinisme matrimonial érasmien: le sens
     de l'énigme en prophétie (*Gargantua*, chap. LVIII)." In *François Rabelais:*
     *Ouvrage publié pour le quatrième centenaire de sa mort, 1553–1953. THR*
     VII. Geneva: Librairie Droz, pp. 104–19.
         Sees in the episode of the Abbaye de Thélème the expression of an anti-
     monastic bias which Erasmus had voiced earlier throughout his work, and the evo-
     cation of the kind of ideal retreat that Erasmus describes in his *Vita S. Hieronymi*.
     Considers the Enigme as an integral part of the Thélème episode, to be interpreted
     as a warning against the dangers of religious persecution which the Evangelicals had
     faced in the past and were likely to face again in a not-too-distant future.


## 1954

1   ANON. "Epiphanies rabelaisiennes." In *Rabelais Pataphysicien. Cahiers du*
    *Collège de Pataphysique* 13–14:113–16.
        A *sottisier* of Rabelais criticism, mostly drawn from Marxist texts pub-
    lished in the special issue devoted to Rabelais in *Europe* (November–December
    1953).

2   AULARD, MARIE-LOUISE. "Rabelais et l'Immaculée Conception." In
    *Rabelais 'Pataphysicien. Cahiers du Collège de Pataphysique* 13–14:55–64.
        Behind the general facetiousness of the article, one serious argument:
    challenges Gilson's thesis of a "Rabelais scotiste" in spite of the abuse poured
    on Duns Scotus in Rabelais' work. Points out that the presence of scholastic
    vocabulary, upon which Gilson based his thesis, proves nothing.

3   BOLGAR, R.R. *The Classical Heritage and its Beneficiaries*. Cambridge:
    Cambridge University Press, 591 pp.
        Scattered references to Rabelais, mainly to his corrected version of
    Hippocrates' *Aphorisms* (pp. 290–91), his criticism of medieval law (pp.
    293–94), and his classical borrowings (pp. 320–23).

4   CARPENTER, NAN COOKE. *Rabelais and Music*. University of North
    Carolina Studies in Comparative Literature, no. 8. Chapel Hill: Univ. of North
    Carolina Press, 149 pp.
        Attempts a comprehensive study of Rabelais' use of musical terms and
    ideas, and finds an astonishing understanding of musical theory and practice
    on the part of a non-professional. Notes that Rabelais draws more upon music
    than any other discipline, and that he does so mainly for rhetorical purposes.
    Discusses Book V for its abundance of musical references and for the light
    they might shed on the question of the book's authenticity. Sees Rabelais'
    musical allusions as falling into five categories: musical instruments (princi-
    pally the bagpipe and the drum), secular music (proving his acquaintance with

the works of leading composers of his day), liturgical music (as a satirical device used most often to characterize evil situations), the dance (both courtly and folkloric, with an emphasis on ancient dances in Book V), and musical ideas ( their role in Rabelais' educational program and their importance in the context of humanist thought). In the last chapter brings out the general patterns emerging from the preceding detailed investigation, and sees in their evolution an argument for believing that Rabelais played at least a significant part in the authorship of Book V.

5  DE BOUILLANE DE LACOSTE, H[ENRI]. "La première navigation de Pantagruel." *Mercure de France* (1 April):604–29.
　　Exposes the weaknesses of Lefranc's interpretation of the voyage to Utopia as retracing the steps of Vasco de Gama's voyage to India, Cathay, and Manchuria. Points out that More's Utopia, which is where Lefranc believed Pantagruel to be heading, is in the Northern, and not the Southern Hemisphere. Stresses the adventurous nature of Lefranc's "jeux de mots géographiques" upon which he bases his identification of the various cities mentioned by Rabelais. Believes that the episode shows no signs of interest in Vasco de Gama's voyage of discovery, and that Rabelais did not make any effort to make Pantagruel's journey geographically believable. Argues that Rabelais meant to underscore the imaginary nature of the journey by providing pseudo-realistic details of patent absurdity; for instance the North-Northwest wind which is supposed to have helped the voyagers out of Honfleur would have had no such effect, given the location of the ship. Notes how more than one  generation of critics blindly followed Lefranc in his misguided interpretation, presumably because they too had read More's *Utopia*, if at all, in Stouvenel's incomplete translation. Concludes that Pantagruel's voyage to Utopia is "un voyage au pays des chimères," of no significance as to nautical geography, but of utmost literary importance as an element of transition between two very different series of narrative.

6  DONTENVILLE, HENRI. "Traductions de Rabelais." *BAARD* 1, no. 3:25–28.
　　Questions the validity of adaptations into modern French, but comments favorably on the adaptation of Rabelais' work into German by Fischart, and on the English translations by Urquhart and Le Motteux. Notes the Rabelaisian character of Fischart's interpolations, and points out that when Urquhart went wrong, it was often because he had been misled by Cotgrave's Dictionary.

7  ETIENNE, LUC. "Rabelais contrepétiste." In *Rabelais Pataphysicien. Cahiers du Collège de Pataphysique* 13–14:36-38.
　　Offers a list of examples drawn from the first four books.

1954

8    FEBVRE, LUCIEN. [Untitled]. In *Congrès de Tours et Poitiers: Actes du Congrès de l'Association Guillaume Budé, 3–9 Septembre 1953.* Paris: Société d'Édition "Les Belles Lettres," pp. 74–82.

Reiterates his thesis, expounded in *Le Problème de l'incroyance au XVIe siècle* (1946), that in matters of religious and scientific truth, Rabelais' ideas were limited to the common beliefs of his day. "Capable de devancer ses contemporains et souvent de les dépasser par l'imagination, il ne l'est pas, il ne saurait l'être de s'élever, seul, au-dessus de ce qu'ils savent, connaissent et croient" (p. 75).

9    FRANÇOIS, ALEXIS. "Rabelais et les Suisses." *BHR* 16:119–23.

"Dans l'allégorie des Andouilles, Rabelais, une fois de plus bon serviteur du roi de France et de ses hommes d'Etat, les Du Bellay, attaque les Suisses comme à Marignan et renouvelle allégoriquement l'exploit de François Ier pour le compte de Henri II" (p. 119). Sketches the political background of relations between France and Switzerland which he believes must be kept in mind as one reads chapt. 35 through 42 of the *Quart Livre*.

10   FRANÇON, MARCEL. "Francesco Colonna's *Poliphili Hypnerotomachia* and *Pantagruel*." *Italica* 31, no. 1 (March):136–37.

Argues that Colonna's text is the source for Rabelais' description of the heptagonal fountain and the round chapel mentioned in the Book V of *Pantagruel*. Reinterprets Colonna's passage on the heptagon in such a way as to suggest that his knowledge of geometry is more sound than critics have taken it to be.

11   ———. "La géographie de *Pantagruel* et les chroniques gargantuines." *Modern Language Notes* 69, no. 4 (April):260–64.

Notes how closely the story of Pantagruel follows that of Gargantua as told in the chronicles. Argues that the text of *Pantagruel* can only be understood in the light of these chronicles. Thus when Rabelais announces at the end of *Pantagruel* that the giant will marry, he merely echoes what the chronicles tell us about Gargantua. Suggests that Pantagruel was born in Utopia, where Gargantua had gone to marry, and that Rabelais' Utopia is probably where it is located according to the chronicles, "vers les côtes orientales de l'Afrique, près de la Turquie."

12   HUON, ANTOINETTE. "Les hiéroglyphes dans les derniers livres de Rabelais." In *Congrès de Tours et Poitiers: Actes du Congrès de l'Association Guillaume Budé, 3–9 Septembre 1953.* Paris: Société d'Édition "Les Belles Lettres," pp. 137–40.

Summary of a paper documenting Rabelais' serious interest in hieroglyphic literature in Books IV and V. Proves that Rabelais had read Horapollonius and Colonna's *Poliphile*, that he was introduced to the allegor-

ical art of Fontainebleau by Philibert Delorme, and suggests that his new interest in archeology and allegorism is reflected in the Medamothi and the
Macréons episodes of the *Quart Livre*, as well as in the heavily allegorical
character of the *Cinquiesme Livre* as a whole.

13 IMBS, PAUL. "Le diable dans l'œuvre de Rabelais: Étude de vocabulaire." In
*Mélanges de linguistique française offerts à M. Charles Bruneau*. Geneva:
Librairie Droz, pp.241–61.

Seeks to further our knowledge of Rabelais' imagination by studying his
representation of the world of devils. Regroups the elements of demonological vocabulary in Sainéan's study of Rabelais' language in order to show the
existence of a clearly characterized semantic field, organized around a unifying principle: namely, the representation of a third realm, coexisting with the
world of men and with Heaven. Analyzes the semantic associations within the
field in question, and seeks to show how Rabelais offers a concrete representation of essentially spiritual, "transhuman" beings. Studies their physical
description, their habitat, their number, their names, their principle of social
organization. Seeks to determine in each case what Rabelais owes to the
medieval tradition, and the nature and extent of his contribution to the traditional picture. Finds that on the conceptual level Rabelais does not innovate:
his devils are beings both spiritual and carnal, monstrously repulsive, grouped
into a crowded and rationally organized kingdom, potentially dangerous but
easily duped. Attempts to bring out also the medieval origins of Rabelais'
demonological vocabulary. With the relative exception of Book V, finds that
Rabelais' personal contribution, in both concept and form, is minimal: "un
peu d'humanisme grec et hébreu, venant grossir la tradition de l'humanisme
latin; un peu plus de réalisme aussi, dans le sens d'un anthropomorphisme
plus accusé, mais à peine; tel semble être l'apport personnel de Rabelais.
C'est peu de chose en face du poids de la tradition médiévale" (p. 260).
Differs only in his comic use of traditional materials. Wonders why Rabelais
leaves intact the universe of devils, while drastically transforming Pantagruel
("qu'il avait cueilli parmi les petits diables des mystères," p.261) into a symbol of his philosophy of life.

14 JOURDA, PIERRE. "Rabelais, peintre de la France de son temps." In
*Congrès de Tours et Poitiers: Actes du Congrès de l'Association Guillaume
Budé, 3–9 Septembre 1953*. Paris: Société d'Édition "Les Belles Lettres," pp.
132–36.

Reinforces Lefranc's thesis of Rabelais' fundamental realism by stressing Rabelais' novels as subjective documents of geographical and social
importance. "Rabelais peintre de la société de son temps n'est à aucun degré
un adepte de l'art pour l'art, qui décrit pour décrire; c'est un moraliste qui
décrit pour instruire" (p. 136).

1954

15   JUMEAU, GUY. "La grande jument et Anne de Pisseleu, ou les Belles
     Dames du temps jadis." *Rabelais Pataphysicien. Cahiers du Collège de
     Pataphysique* 13–14:89–92.
          Reviews, tongue-in-cheek, the various attempts to identify the beast.

16   LEBÈGUE, RAYMOND. "La Pensée de Rabelais dans le *Gargantua*."
     *Mercure de France* (1 April):630–48.
          Reminds us that *Gargantua* was thought for a long time to have been
     written before *Pantagruel*, briefly compares the two novels, notes the greater
     seriousness of the former, and feels justified in seeking in that novel "la pen-
     sée profonde de Rabelais" around 1534. Evokes the intellectual climate of the
     time, comments on Rabelais' readings, emphasizes what he believes to have
     been Erasmus' decisive influence, and notes Rabelais' awareness of the polit-
     ical and religious debates around him. Summarizes the pedagogical ideas con-
     tained in *Gargantua*, shows them to have been shared by many contemporary
     humanists, underscores the idea of temperance in the novel, the condemnation
     of religious formalism, Rabelais' silence about the sacraments and the mass,
     his sympathy towards "les bons docteurs évangéliques." Sees in the Abbaye
     de Thélème a valuable social document on the life of the court, and on
     Rabelais' thought concerning individual freedom, the monastic life, and mar-
     riage. In the Picrocholine War sees the influence of Erasmus' pacifism, but
     warns that Rabelais' thought does not always coincide with that of Erasmus.
     Sees *Gargantua* as richer in intellectual content than any other sixteenth-cen-
     tury novel. "Rabelais n'est pas seulement un inégalable artiste, il est un des
     penseurs les plus représentatifs de la première Renaissance française; en choi-
     sissant la langue 'vulgaire,' il a, plus que quiconque, répandu en France
     l'humanisme 'évangélique' et érasmien"(p. 648).

17   ———. "Ronsard lecteur de Rabelais." *BHR* 16:82–85.
          Seeks to determine the extent of Ronsard's knowledge of Rabelais from
     the versified epitaph of 1554 and the sixth book of Ronsard's *Poèmes* (1569).
     Notes that the first poem in that book contains "une imitation certaine et
     textuelle" of the passage in which Socrates is compared to the famous Silènes.
     Concludes from the numerous errors contained in the epitaph and from the
     allusion to one of the most widely known passages in Rabelais, that Ronsard's
     knowledge of Rabelais was superficial and far removed from the lucid admi-
     ration shown towards the writer by Joachim Du Bellay.

18   LECUYER, MAURICE A. "Balzac et Rabelais." Ph.D. dissertation, Yale
     University.
          See *Doctoral Dissertations Accepted by American Universities*, No. 21,
     1953-54, p. 271. Published in expanded and revised form: 1956.6.

19   LENOIR, PAULETTE. *Quelques aspects de la pensée de Rabelais*. Paris: Éditions Sociales, 93 pp.

Rapid overview of Rabelais' thought from a Marxist-Leninist perspective. Sides with Abel Lefranc and Henri Busson against Lucien Febvre, and sees in Rabelais a precursor of rationalism and materialistic thought. Is convinced that Rabelais wrote primarily for the people, for whom he does not show any of the contempt expressed by other humanists, and whose weaknesses he views with smiling indulgence. Ascribes to this concern for the "vulgaire" Rabelais' decision to write in French and to draw from contemporary reality. Concedes that he is perhaps less daring in his thought than such contemporaries as Erasmus and Thomas More, but finds him to be more important than these humanists, since by writing for the bourgeoisie and the people in a language they can understand, he was able to have a more direct influence on an increasingly important segment of society. Underscores Rabelais' relatively cautious—but thereby all the more effective—participation in the ideological struggle against the Catholic church, his criticism of the monastic life, his denial of miracles, his ambiguous position toward astrology. Believes that the Abbaye de Thélème episode offers "une ébauche de morale laïque" (p. 62), and denies that evangelism plays any role in the life of the Thelemites. But concedes that the first four books are marked by a religious fervor of unmistakable sincerity. Argues, however, that at the end of Book IV and in all of Book V this fervor is tempered with growing doubt. Believes that chapt. 28 of Book IV (the death of Pan episode) may cast doubt on the divinity of Christ. "Pendant que ses héros invoquent Dieu, tout-puissant, omniscient, garant de la morale et de la justice, Rabelais met en doute la providence, la justice, la prescience et la puissance divines" (p. 75). Notes a similar hesitation on the subject of the immortality of the soul. But sees as a constant throughout the work, at its very core, the triumphant presence of man, in the full complexity of his nature, forever striving for mastery over the world around him and for victory over the gods.

20   LIE. "Les solutions imaginaires de Rabelais et celles d'Abel Lefranc." *Rabelais Pataphysicien. Cahiers du Collège de Pataphysique* 13–14:71–88.

Claims to pay homage to Lefranc, and judges him to be almost worthy of belonging to the Collège de Pataphysique. Believes his hypothesis as to Rabelais' date of birth to be totally groundless. Discusses Lefranc's thesis of a thoroughgoing geographical realism in Rabelais, pointing out the limits of this realism: "La réalité n'est...pas le *fond* (ni le fondement) du récit. Elle y joue ...un rôle *nominal*" (p. 83). Believes Rabelais is consciously playing with this pseudo-realism. Reminds us that most of Rabelais' readers were unaware of the geography of the Chinonais, so that for them the names of the various villages were, as they were meant to be, mere names.

1954

21  LUTEMBI. "Le Problème de la Croyance au XXe siècle et la religion de M. Lucien Febvre, professeur au Collège de France." *Rabelais Pataphysicien. Cahiers du Collège de Pataphysique* 13–14:49–53; 15:49–57.

Conceals, behind an obvious anagram, the name of its author (Etiemble), and behind the facetiousness of its pataphysical style, an indictment of the various historical methods used to define Rabelais' thought. Takes to task Lucien Febvre and a group of studies which appeared on the occasion of the fourth centenary of Rabelais' death, and which are claimed to bear traces of Febvre's influence. Finds Febvre's critical approach in *Le Problème de l'incroyance au XVIe siècle* to work well in the case of *Cymbalum mundi*, but believes that no historical method could be fruitfully applied to Rabelais. Neither the texts, especially when "destructurés, mis en fiches" as they are by Febvre, nor their context could ever reveal what Rabelais really thought. Does not believe that Rabelais was either an atheist (as Lefranc would have it) or its opposite (as Febvre contends): "Il ne prenait pas ces choses assez au tragique, ni même assez au sérieux, pour se donner la peine d'être athée" (*Cahier* 15, p. 52). In matters of ideas, such as religion, why not believe that Rabelais is as descriptive, as realistic, as historical as in everything else? Here as elsewhere, he reflects contemporary reality, rather than providing a profession of faith. Reminds us that whatever ideas we come upon in Rabelais have been put in the mouth of specific characters. What reason is there to suppose that when they speak seriously, they speak for Rabelais himself? In his text, Rabelais is neither an Erasmian nor an Evangelical. When he makes room for humanistic ideas, it is not for ideological but for aesthetic reasons: "Ni pédantisme, ni satire. Mais ornement" (p. 57).

22  MARGAROT, JEAN. "Rabelais médecin: La médecine dans son œuvre." *BHR* 16:25–40.

Notes in Rabelais a harmonious fusion of somewhat contradictory tendencies: "la découverte des connaissances anciennes perdues ou déformées et la primauté accordée à la recherche destinée à les étendre, fût-ce au détriment de notions que l'on avait crues définitives" (p. 28). As an anatomist, Rabelais bears comparison with Vésale. As a surgeon, he deserves to be considered among the precursors of Ambroise Paré. In the area of experimental medicine, his ideas are often those of Fernel: "La science de Rabelais le situe en bonne place parmi les médecins de son siècle" (p. 30). As a practitioner he is generous towards the poor, tolerant towards his colleagues. Resists the temptation to see in Rabelais a forerunner of psychosomatic medicine in the modern sense of the term. Suggests that his medical practice may explain why his novels were written at irregular and long intervals; it may also explain the crudity of his language. Agrees with Mario Roques in seeing in Panurge signs of knowledge of both pathological and normal psychophysiology derived from medical observation. Comments on the frequency and accuracy of anatomical and physiological descriptions, but underscores their literary function.

23   MARICHAL, ROBERT. "Le dernier séjour de Rabelais à Rome." In *Congrès de Tours et Poitiers: Actes du Congrès de l'Association Guillaume Budé, 3–9 Septembre 1953*. Paris: Société d'Édition "Les Belles Lettres," pp. 104–32.

Notes how little is known of Rabelais' third and last trip to Rome in the company of Jean du Bellay. Questions whether Rabelais was there chiefly as the Cardinal's physician. Points out that the only certain document concerning Rabelais' activities is his *Sciomachie*. Underscores the political importance of the festivities organized by Jean du Bellay upon the birth of Henry II's son; points out that the Diane mentioned in the festivities is not Diane de Poitiers but Diane de France, whose marriage to Horace Farnese the cardinal wanted to bring about in the interest of the French court in order to improve his compromised position. Rejects as gratuitously damaging to Rabelais' reputation the idea that he may have sought the protection of the Cardinal de Guise while remaining in the service of Jean du Bellay (primarily as his secretary), and gives reasons for believing that the Medamothi episode of the *Quart Livre* was written in Rome and contains allusions to Rabelais' Roman experience.

24   MAUVOISIN, J. "Agathê tukhê." *Rabelais Pataphysicien. Cahiers du Collège de Pataphysique* 13–14:1–2.

Introduces the studies in the special issue of the *Cahiers* devoted to Rabelais. Warns of the deliberately limited scope of the articles. Suggests that perhaps one should take seriously the absence of seriousness in Rabelais, and that Rabelais' "fantaisie" is nothing less than the "substantifique mouelle" he would have us seek.

25   MAYER, C. A. "A propos du réalisme de Rabelais." In *Congrès de Tours et Poitiers: Actes du Congrès de l'Association Guillaume Budé, 3–9 Septembre 1953*. Paris: Société d'Édition "Les Belles Lettres," pp. 143.

Summary of a paper in which the author argues that Rabelais does, on occasion, and as Spitzer would have it, poetically transform the real into the unreal, but that he also does the opposite, treating with realism what in his sources is totally devoid of reality. See 1953.35.

26   NAUDON, PIERRE. *Rabelais franc-maçon*. Paris: Éditions La Balance, 171 pp.

Is convinced that Rabelais and his contemporaries did not think the way we do: "leur logique n'était pas la nôtre et ne peut même y être comparée" (p. 9). Theirs was an essentially symbolic, esoteric mode of thought, appealing both to intuition and to reason, and grounded in a strong belief in the occult. Feels entitled to conclude that Rabelais was a member of an esoteric sect such as that of the Freemasons, and that he sought to transmit, under the veil of his amusing fiction, "un profond message initiatique" to light men's way to knowledge. Believes that Rabelais fulfilled all the conditions for being thought worthy of initiation: "à la seule exception de Scaliger, tous les témoignages concordent pour souligner les bonnes moeurs de Rabelais" (p. 32). Sees Rabelais' philosophy as a synthesis of Christianity and the hermetic theory of Unity. In chapt. 5 studies Rabelais' symbolism; believes that Rabelais himself underscored in the first two prologues the esoteric character of his work. Argues that the many symbols borrowed from arithmosophy, the symbolism of salt and wine, of the letter *g*, all have an esoteric—masonic, rosecrucian—meaning. Claims that Rabelais believed in astrology and the prophetic arts; if he denounced them as "abus et vanités" in Gargantua's letter to Pantagruel, it was merely to avoid persecution. Believes that the two enigmatic poems in *Gargantua* (attributed without sufficient proof to Mellin de Saint-Gelais) are of a prophetic nature. Stops short of claiming that *Pantagruel* and *Gargantua* contain a systematic cryptographic message, but sees in the exchange of signs between Thaumaste and Panurge, in the choice of Thaumaste's name, in Panurge's interrogation at the court of Queen Quintessence, among other instances, solid proof of an intimate knowledge of esoteric rites. Concludes that the basic tenets of Rabelais' thought are those of Freemasonry, in their common effort to reconcile reason with faith, and materialism with spirituality.

27 PERRAT, CHARLES. "Autour du juge Bridoye: Rabelais et le *De Nobilitate* de Tiraqueau." *BHR* 16:41–57.

Sees in *De Nobilitate* one of the main sources of the *Tiers Livre*, even though Tiraqueau's book appeared fully three years after that of Rabelais. More specifically, question 15 of the second part of the book, entitled *De iure primigeniorum*, seems to him to be the source of the episode in which Bridoye settles problems of justice by recourse to dice, and that in which Panurge seeks to decide whether he should marry by recourse to Homeric or Virgilian "sorts." Believes the *De Nobilitate* also inspired the passages in the *Quart Livre* on the praise of good physicians. Suggests that far from having quarrelled with his friend at the time of the publication of Tiraqueau's book, as is often thought, Rabelais may even have collaborated in its writing.

28 PLOMB, V., and BRUNET, J. "Le lecteur de Rabelais au seuil de l'occulte." *Rabelais Pataphysicien. Cahiers du Collège de Pataphysique* 13–14:97–106.

Reviews studies dealing with the esoteric aspects of Rabelais' thought; finds them excessively timid. Traces throughout the novel the theme of the "chasse au trésor." Concludes with a series of methodological considerations.

29 QUATREZONEILLES. "Rabelais dans la Vie Imaginaire." *Rabelais Pataphysicien. Cahiers du Collège de Pataphysique* 13–14:21–24.

Draws attention to the legends surrounding Rabelais in seventeenth- and eighteenth-century texts. Although they have been discredited by serious critics, finds them significant because "le mythe fait partie de l'homme" and because the myth of Rabelais is in some respects as interesting as his reality.

30 ———. "L'Hebreu de Rabelais." *Rabelais Pataphysicien. Cahiers du Collège de Pataphysique* 13–14:25–35.

With a typically pataphysical mixture of fantasy and erudition, comments upon a series of Hebrew words used by Rabelais. Believes that his knowledge of Hebrew was probably greater than it was thought to be by such critics as Sainéan and Plattard, who impute to Rabelais errors for which his transcribers are most probably responsible.

31 ROE, FREDERICK C. "Urquhart traducteur de Rabelais." In *Congrès de Tours et Poitiers: Actes du Congrès de l'Association Guillaume Budé, 3–9 Septembre 1953.* Paris: Société d'Édition "Les Belles Lettres," pp. 143–45.

Summary of a paper stressing the affinities between Rabelais and his Scottish translator, and bringing out the main features of his masterful translation.

32 ROQUES, MARIO. "Aspects de Panurge." In *Congrès de Tours et Poitiers: Actes du Congrès de l'Association Guillaume Budé, 3–9 Septembre 1953.* Paris: Société d'Édition "Les Belles Lettres," pp. 61–73.

Slightly modified version of 1953.42.

33 SAMARAN, CHARLES. "Le Paris de Rabelais." *Mercure de France* (1 April):667–89.

Notes that we know very little about Rabelais' sojourns in the capital. Conjures up the *ambience* of Paris in the 1530's, often with the help of Lefranc's remarks. Provides information about the Hôtel Saint-Denis where Rabelais found lodgings for Pantagruel, and the Benedictine abbey of Saint-Maur-les-Fossés, in the suburbs of Paris, where Rabelais himself resided. Finds in Rabelais a keen observer of city life, especially in the case of artisans and students; notes with some surprise that Rabelais says nothing of the many Parisian printers and booksellers. Seeks to clarify the question of Rabelais' probable death in Paris. Deplores the lack of documents on the circumstances of this event.

34 SAULNIER, V[ERDUN]-L[OUIS]. "François Rabelais, patron des pronostiqueurs. (Une pronostication retrouvée)." *BHR* 16:124–38.

Describes the *Pronostication perpetuelle* published by Antoine Houic; dates it approximately between 1566 and 1586; summarizes its contents and discusses its importance; gives reasons for believing that it may have been written by Rabelais. Reprints part of the text in appendix 1. A second appendix contains a table of contents and a partial reprint of *Pronostication fort utile,* the other prognostication known to have been published by Houic.

1954

35 ———. "Le festin devant Chaneph, ou La Confiance dernière de Rabelais."
*Mercure de France* (1 April):649–66.

Argues that Rabelais' evangelism undergoes an evolution under the
pressure of external circumstances; studies its modalities, from the initial exuberance and generosity of its expression in *Pantagruel* and *Gargantua*, to the
final form it acquires in the *Quart Livre*, and especially in the feasting episode
off the coast of Chaneph (chapt. 63–65). Reads Chaneph, allegorically, as the
island of religious hypocrites, "une citadelle de l'intolérance" (p. 652), the
very antithesis of Thélème. Refuses to see the episode as an invitation to seek
in food and drink the solution to life's problems. Sees in the feast an allusion
to the Last Supper and to the Eucharist, and in the Pantagruelists' ensuing
happiness the joy of those who have placed their faith in God. Detects in the
episode the influence of Erasmus' *Colloquia*, and believes that Rabelais is
expressing an essentially Erasmian conception of religion, but adapted to the
contemporary climate of persecution and torture. Argues that behind the
image of the feast and its "interpretation jambonnique" lies a new evangelical
message of confident, intransigent, but patient and non-militant faith.

36 ———. "Pantagruel au large de Ganabin." *BHR* 16:58–81.

Is Ganabin, in chapt. 66 of the *Quart Livre*, merely the Isle of Thieves,
as the *Briefve Declaration* and Sainéan would have it? Or is it England, as
suggested by Abel Lefranc, who claimed to see in the name something like
the anagram of *Anglais*? Notes that it is the only island both Panurge and
Pantagruel refuse to visit. Based on significant details concerning the topography, the character of the inhabitants, and of the Pantagruelists' reaction to the
island, suggests that the island is a symbol of religious repression. Sees in the
double mount that dominates the island not only an anti-Parnassus but also an
allusion to the Châtelet and the Conciergerie, the two Parisian prisons *par
excellence*, and the double seat of the *Chambre ardente*. Similarly, the most
beautiful fountain in the world which is said to be located nearby is Jean
Gougeon's *Fontaine des Innocents*, and the adjoining forest consists of the
scaffolds and *piloris* erected everywhere in Paris for the punishment of
heretics. Evokes in passing Rabelais' friendship with Marot and Dolet; sees a
connection between the island and Marot's *Enfer*. Argues that in the concluding episode (chapt. 67), Panurge's cowardice is meant to underscore the difference between an undignified fear of repression and the prudent silence of
Pantagruel's *hésuchisme*. Stresses some analogies with the Isle du Guichet in
Book V, and draws from his proposed interpretation a double conclusion: that
the *Quart Livre* owes less than had been claimed to the contemporary voyages
of discovery and more to polemical symbolism; and that the book is less
open-ended than it is often said to be. For in political and religious circumstances that did not make it possible to lead his heroes to the Oracle of the
Divine Bottle, Rabelais may well have meant to give, in the evangelical mes-

sage of the final Ganabin episode, his provisional solution to the problem of the Pantagruelists' quest.

37 ———. "Position actuelle des problèmes rabelaisiens." In *Congrès de Tours et Poitiers: Actes du Congrès de l'Association Guillaume Budé, 3–9 Septembre 1953.* Paris: Société d'Édition "Les Belles Lettres," pp. 83–104.

Notes the absence of any definitive study of any of the problems raised by Rabelais' work. Lists the existing bibliographies, the various available editions, general studies that have retained some relevance, biographies, studies of a particular aspect of Rabelais' work. Defines the contribution of Abel Lefranc and his disciples, notes recent signs of interest in the aesthetic and psychological aspects of the Rabelaisian text; sees no urgent need for yet another series of studies of the man and his work; notes that certain problems, such as those touching upon Rabelais' pedagogical ideas, have fallen out of fashion, and welcomes further studies on Rabelais' political role, his medical humanism, his scholastic background, the traces of popular culture and folklore in his books; summarizes present positions on the question of Rabelaisian realism and Rabelais' religious orientation, and welcomes signs of international interest in Rabelais' work.

38 SMARAGDIS, JEAN. "Recherche de la Sibylle de Panzoust." *Rabelais Pataphysicien. Cahiers du Collège de Pataphysique* 13 14:65 66.

Reviews the various attempts to identify the character: St. Theresa, Postel's Virgo Veneta, Diane de Poitiers. Purports to regret the absence of modern attempts at such identification.

39 ———. "Le plus ancien portrait de Rabelais." *Rabelais Pataphysicien. Cahiers du Collège de Pataphysique* 13–14:2.

Refers to the painting reproduced in Jean Martin's Lyons edition of 1569. Sees no reason to believe that it is not a true portrait.

40 VALSENESTRE, JEANNE DE. "Le Quartier Latin de Pantagruel et de Panurge." *Rabelais Pataphysicien. Cahiers du Collège de Pataphysique* 13–14:68–69.

Reproduces a map of the Latin Quarter from the Bibliothèque de Bâle, published only about twenty years after *Pantagruel*. Locates on the map the various places mentioned by Rabelais.

41 VAUBERGLIN, PHILIPPE. "Panomphée." *Rabelais Pataphysicien. Cahiers du Collège de Pataphysique* 13–14:107–11.

Devoted to the paradoxical proposition that there are works—and those of Rabelais are among them—which should be interpreted in the light of what followed, and not in the light of what preceded their publication.

1955

42    VOTKA, O. "Grabuge à Thélème." *Rabelais Pataphysicien. Cahiers du Collège de Pataphysique* 13–14:3–7.

Argues against Erasmian interpretations of the Abbaye de Thélème episode and its concluding *Énigme*, as well as the progressive interpretations of the team of contributors to the Rabelais issue of *Europe* published in November–December 1953. Admits that Gargantua's interpretation of the *Énigme* is indeed along Erasmian lines, but claims that it is far from certain that Gargantua represents Rabelais' thought. Finds excessively simplistic the view that characters whom Rabelais does not ridicule can automatically be assumed to be speaking for him. As for the motto "Fay ce que voudras," it means only that the sole ethical ideal of Thélème is that of freedom.

43    WILL, SAMUEL F. "Rabelais en Amérique." In *Congrès de Tours et Poitiers: Actes du Congrès de l'Association Guillaume Budé, 3–9 Septembre 1953.* Paris: Société d'Édition "Les Belles Lettres," pp. 145–47.

Summary of a paper on the state of Rabelaisian studies in the United States. Points to Protestant dogmatism as an obstacle to the understanding of Rabelais' work in the past, but sees optimistic signs of recent critical activity, even if the work on Rabelais is not as extensive as it is on Montaigne.

44    ———. "The Rabelais Quadricentennial, 1953." *French Review* 28, no. 2 (December):233–40.

Reports on the scholarly activities prompted in 1953 by the anniversary of Rabelais' death. Believes the highlight to have been the fifth colloquium of the Association Guillaume Budé, held in Tours. Notes the emphasis on Platonism in many of the papers read on that occasion (many of which subsequently appeared in the selected proceedings published by Société d'Édition "Les Belles Lettres.") Points out that the occasion marked for Rabelais his first recognition by "his old enemy the Sorbonne" (p. 235). Among other tributes, singles out for comment the articles published in the special issue of *Europe*, whose contributors tend to see in Rabelais "the founding father of Communism." Finds them worthy of attention insofar as they illustrate "how even the classic authors can be misread and misinterpreted to serve the purposes of propaganda" (p. 235).

**1955**

1    BRUGMANS, H. "De Lach in de Franse Literatuur: Rabelais, Molière, Voltaire." In *De Lach in de Literatuur*. Lezingen gepubliceerd die worden gehouden voor de School voor Taal- en Letterkunde te 's- Graventage. The Hague: Servire, pp. 45–65.

Claims that Rabelais is not above all a realist or a satirist, but what Voltaire called "le premier des bons bouffons." Stresses the optimistic, liberating, gratuitous nature of Rabelaisian laughter.

2   DE GRÈVE, MARCEL. "Une exposition 'Rabelais et les Pays-Bas' à Bruxelles." *BHR* 17:88–89.
    Alludes to the wealth of information in the catalogue of the exhibition held in June 1954 at the Bibliothèque Royale de Belgique, in Brussels. Suggests that much work remains to be done on Rabelais in the Netherlands.

3   ———. "Rabelais au pays de Breugel: Réflexions sur la popularité de Rabelais dans les Pays-Bas au XVIe siècle." *BHR* 17:154–87.
    Documents Rabelais' early influence in the Netherlands, in spite of the fact that no translation of his work existed before 1682. Shows that French was understood not only by the aristocracy but by the bourgeoisie as well, and even to some extent by the common people. Determines that Rabelais not only *could* have been read but that his work was actually known, a full century before his books were available in translation. Argues that his influence was not as insignificant as has been thought, especially in the south, and that it can be more clearly felt on serious, rather than on vulgarly comic works.

4   D[ROZ], É[MILIE]. "A propos du *Tiers Livre* de 1546." *BHR* 17:296–97.
    Draws attention to the existence of a third Parisian edition of the *Tiers Livre* of 1546; only two such editions are described by Lefranc.

5   FRANÇON, MARCEL. "A quelle époque se rapporte la *Pantagruéline Prognostication?*" *Modern Language Notes* 70, no. 7 (November):510–12.
    Believes that the pamphlet refers to a specific year, rather than to the "an perpetuel" mentioned in the title of certain editions. Speculates that Rabelais' refusal to come up with the "nombre d'or" for that year may be due to the fact that, for 1532, that number is 13. Believes the *Prognostication* may well have been written and published before *Pantagruel*, in which case it can tell us nothing about the date of publication of Rabelais' first book; nor can it bear witness, as some critics would have it, to that book's success.

6   JODOGNE, O[MER]. "Rabelais et *Pathelin*." *Les Lettres Romanes* 9, no. 1 (February):3–14.
    Notes, after Plattard and Cohen, the direct allusions to the farce; lists linguistic borrowings, but hesitates to include among them the expression "revenir à ses moutons," since one cannot be sure it did not pre-exist *Pathelin*; rejects other expressions, considered to be "de pures rencontres d'expression, de simples coincidences" (p. 7). Discusses the use of such derivatives as *patelin, patelinage, patelineux, patelinois*, and concludes that they did not all originate with the play.

1955

7  LEFEBVRE, HENRI. *Rabelais*. Paris: Les Éditeurs français réunis, 286 pp.
   In conscious opposition to Lucien Febvre's psycho-sociological interpretation of the Renaissance and of Rabelais as essentially pre-logical and mystical, presents Rabelais from a Marxist-Leninist perspective. Adopts a deliberately non-historical approach: "Il ne saurait être question de nous demander de faire abstraction de nous-mêmes, de notre culture, pas plus que des époques intermédiaires" (p. 21). Rejects all attempts at reductive interpretations, and offers an early example of a polyvalent reading, emphasizing the work's plurality of meanings. Studies Rabelais as both poet and novelist, and labels him "un visionnaire réaliste" (p. 33). Adopts for his study a Marxist structure, beginning with an analysis of economic and social aspects of the sixteenth century before proceeding to an account of the man and his work. This structure is related to the fundamental thesis underlying the study, namely that as a great work of art, Rabelais' book is a successful attempt to reflect, on the thematic level, every aspect of contemporary reality. Generically, the author finds it to have a transitional form between the epic of antiquity and the modern novel: "Encore épopée, c'est une Odyssée burlesque. Déjà romanesque, c'est le roman du premier individu moderne: Panurge" (p. 49).

8  LIVINGSTON, C[HARLES] H. "Masuccio Salernitano en France en 1515." *BHR* 17:350–64.
   Believes that Philippe de Vigneulles knew Salernitano's *Novellino* and made use of it in two of his *Cent nouvelles nouvelles* (written between 1505 and 1515). But claims that Salernitano's collection of stories remained otherwise nearly unknown in the first half of the century, "et si Rabelais en a eu connaissance, il n'aurait imité qu'un épisode secondaire d'un seul conte" (p. 351). Neglects to say what that episode might be.

9  SAULNIER, V[ERDUN]-L[OUIS]. "Le départ de l'Escadre, ou Pantagruel à la recherche du grand Passage." *BAARD* 1, no. 4:13–15.
   "Le voyage doit beaucoup moins au réalisme géographique qu'à l'intention symbolique" (p. 15). Stresses the allegorical dimension of the journey described in the *Quart Livre*, and provides an allegorical reading of the departure episode. Notes that before setting out to sea on the *Thalamège*— "une sorte de Thélème flottante"—the fleet sings Marot's French version of Psalm 114: "Quand Israël hors d'Egypte sortit." Sees the departure as an exodus from a land become inimical to Evangelists under Henri II ("quelque peu Pharaon"). Believes that if the voyagers, in their quest for the Dive Bouteille located in India, eschew the customary route through the Cape of Good Hope and head northwest instead, it is because Rabelais wishes to express his refusal to join the Reformation, and his determination to seek a new, albeit more difficult, solution to the religious dilemma facing the true Evangelicals.

10 ———. "Rabelais maître de volonté." *Rivages* (June).
Argues that the author of *Pantagruel*, although not a philosopher, aimed at more than amusing the reader. Stresses the double moral message underlying the work: that "science sans conscience n'est que ruine de l'âme," and that lucid deliberation must be followed by action.

11 ———. "Sur un personnage de Rabelais: Frère Bernard Lardon." *Bulletin de l'Association Guillaume Budé*, 4e série, no. 1 (March):122–25.
In an anecdote recounted by Épistémon in chapt. 9 of the *Quart Livre*, a monk named Bernard Lardon fails to share the enthusiasm of a group of tourists for the city of Florence, and deplores the absence therein of the kind of "roustisseries antiques et aromatizantes" that can be found everywhere in his city of Amiens. On the strength of a manuscript found in the Bibliothèque Nationale, suggests that in spite of the seemingly made-up name, a Frère Bernard Lardon appears to have existed, lived in Amiens, and shared with the Rabelaisian character a predilection for the rotisseries of his city and the wines of the neighbouring town of Laon.

12 SCREECH, M[ICHAEL] A[NDREW]. "The Death of Pan and the Death of Heroes in the Fourth Book of Rabelais. A Study in Syncretism." *BHR* 17:36–55.
Finds the episode most significant in that it reveals in Rabelais' religion a blend of various aspects of Christian thought and of pagan elements, used to "enrich and to some extent to modify, but certainly not to replace, essentially Christian beliefs" (p. 36). Agrees with Krailsheimer (see 1951.7) that Rabelais may have been inspired by Postel in identifying Pan with Christ, but believes that Postel's influence was only one factor among many others, and that their interpretation of the death of Pan varies greatly. Among other influences, finds that of Bigotius' *Christianae Philosophiae Praeludium* (1549) to be minimal, Paul Marsus' commentary on Ovid's *Fasti* to have been more important; cites the linking of Pan the god of shepherds with Christ the Good Shepherd as a current theme in the allegorical pastoral, such as Marot's *Complaincte d'un pastoureau chrestien*, and most importantly in François Habert's *Songe de Pantagruel*. Finds the context of the episode to be strongly influenced by Stoic thought, mainly in Rabelais' eulogy of Guillaume de Langey, whose death is presented as that of a *hero*, but believes that in Rabelais' syncretic conception there is no intention to paganize the Christian sage; nor is there any intention, in the episode of the death of Pan/Christ, to make of Christ a *hero* in the classical sense. Finds in Rabelais' syncretism a note of Pauline serenity and mysticism absent from other contemporary attempts to fuse Christian and classical thought.

1956

13   SCHUTZ, A. H. "Why did Rabelais satirize the Library of Saint-Victor?"
*Modern Language Notes* 70:39–41.
The humanists' high hopes for a reform of the order by its Dutch lead-
ership had been crushed by the recalcitrance of the order's Parisian members.
Argues that Rabelais' choice of the Library of Saint-Victor as a target of his
satire despite the library's considerable humanistic holdings was motivated by
his disillusionment when the attempt at reform proved fruitless.

## 1956

1   BAMBECK, MANFRED. "Epistemons Unterweltbericht im 30. Kap. des
*Pantagruel.*" *Etudes Rabelaisiennes* 1:29–47.
Rejects Lefranc's contention that the episode of Epistemon's visit to the
underworld reveals Rabelais' "pensée secrète" in matters of religion. Refuses
to read it as an attack on papacy or a parody of the resurrection of Lazarus.
Compares the episode with Lucian's *Menippus seu Necyomantia* (which
Lefranc had indicated as a source), and notes that the two texts have in common only the theme of reversal of fortune. Draws some detailed parallels with
Lucian's *Catalpus*. Points to similarities with an episode in *Aucassin et
Nicolette*, as well as with passages in a short story and a farce dating back to
the fifteenth century, to show that Rabelais' episode takes its place in a
medieval tradition. Concludes by suggesting that chapt. 30 of *Pantagruel*
shows us "le savant en vacances" rather than a Rabelais seeking to express his
opposition to the Church. Reprinted: 1973.2, pp.184–212.

2   DE GRÈVE, MARCEL. "François Rabelais et les libertins du XVIIe siècle."
*Études Rabelaisiennes* 1:120–50.
Notes that for the "libertins" as well as as for such Catholic apologists
as the famous Jesuit Father Garasse, Rabelais represented, even more so than
Montaigne, the very embodiment of the "libertinage intellectuel et moral" (p.
126). Shows that the "libertins" appreciated his "pantagruélisme" and his
attacks on religion, although they did not consider him to be an atheist but
merely a heretical, irreverent critic of Christian dogma.

3   FRANÇON, MARCEL. "Note sur l'épitaphe de Rabelais par Ronsard."
*Modern Language Notes* 71, no. 2 (February):101–103.
Suggests that when Ronsard, in his epitaph, makes Panurge the son of
Gargantua, he merely repeats the mistake made in the title of the first edition
of Rabelais' complete works (1553), which the author had presumably been
unable to oversee.

4   HUON, ANTOINETTE. "Alexandrie et l'Alexandrinisme dans le *Quart
Livre*: l'escale à Medamothi." *Études Rabelaisiennes* 1:98–111.

From a close reading of chapt. 2 of the *Quart Livre*, argues that the Medamothi episode cannot be explained merely, as had been done previously, by reference to Cartier's discovery of Newfoundland, or as a satirical allusion to the ambitions of the Guise family. Compares the episode with a fragment of Tatius's *Les Amours de Leucippe et de Clitophon*, with its description of Alexandria, and suggests that it is this Egyptian city that Rabelais had in mind, at least in part, when describing Medamothi. Shows that this hypothesis helps to explain a number of details otherwise difficult to account for. Extends her remarks to traces of "alexandrinisme" in other aspects of Rabelais' work: his references to the art of Fontainebleau with which he became familiar through Philibert Delorme around 1550–51, his interest in architecture and allegorism dating from his stay in Rome. Suggests that the allegorical character of much of Book V, used by some critics to question the authenticity of the work, might very well prove the opposite, since with Book IV Rabelais was already moving in that direction. In that light, Book V can be seen not as an aberration but as a logical *aboutissement.*

5   JEFFELS, RONALD R. "The 'Conte' as a Genre in Renaissance France." *Revue de l'Université d'Ottawa* (October–December):435–50.

Takes exception to what he believes to be an indiscriminate use of the term "conteur" as applied by critics to a number of Renaissance writers. Argues that in the modern sense of *conte* as a brief narrative centered upon a single episode or situation, the term applies only to the works of Bonaventure des Périers and Béroalde de Verville. As for Rabelais, contends that he is not primarily a *conteur*, either in the sense in which the word is used today, or in its sixteenth-century meaning of writer of tales "in which Philosophy is married with Humour for the entertainment of the general reading public" (p. 436).

6   LECUYER, MAURICE. *Balzac et Rabelais*. Paris: Société d'Édition "Les Belles Lettres," 222 pp.

Finds traces of a similarity of thought, feeling, and style between Rabelais and Balzac, not only in the *Contes drôlatiques* but throughout the *Comédie humaine*, in such early works as *Jean-Louis*, in Balzac's articles, in his theater—even in his unpublished manuscripts. Refers to previous studies by Pietro Toldo (1905), Spitzer (1910), and Fernand Baldensperger (1927). Begins by noting that all the romantics (with the exception of Lamartine) admired Rabelais. In part 2, studies the affinities between Balzac and Rabelais, the extent of Balzac's knowledge of Rabelais' life and work, his conception of the author of *Pantagruel*. In part 3 notes echoes of Rabelais' "philosophy" in Balzac's works from *La philosophie du mariage* through *La Peau de chagrin*, and of his verbal realism in the *Contes drôlatiques*. Corroborates Baldensperger's thesis: "il y a chez Balzac une façon panurgienne d'envisager l'existence" (p. 195), but notes that the *Comédie humaine* is

1956

entirely free from what Balzac believed to be Rabelais' fundamental skepticism. Plots the curve of Rabelaisian fever in Balzac: shows its earliest manifestation in 1822, notes a sharp rise between 1829 and 1831, then sees it losing ground in the novels following *La Peau de chagrin*, before another bout in 1837. But believes that in spite of the waxing and waning of Rabelais' direct influence, Balzac's admiration for "le grand Chinonais" remained intact throughout.

7   MALLAM, DUNCAN. "Joyce and Rabelais." *University of Kansas City Review* 23, no. 2 (December):99–110.
      Among the affinities between Rabelais and Joyce, notes the enormous scope of their work, its universality, its "comic profundity." Stresses similarities of purpose, attitude toward the reader, tone, and outlook on life. Draws parallels between the education of Rabelais' giants and the chapter on the education of children in *Finnegans Wake*. Points to differences in attitude toward religion and morality, and to a similarly satirical treatment of law. "But what is crucial is their technical complexity, resulting in a comparable obscurity" (p. 102). Finds that both make use of familiar geographical and physical reality as a stepping stone for their whimsy, and stresses a similar diversity of rhetorical forms: letters, speeches, anecdotes, riddles. Notes a similar use of purposeful, functional digressions, a similar use of a variety of languages, and a similar preoccupation with language *per se*. Suggests that for both words are physical entities; notes their fondness for "polysyllabic monsters" and the impression both create of "prodigal abundance" rather than prolixity. Also comments on their fondness for epic catalogues and lists which aim at all-inclusiveness. Finds Joyce to be "more continually and consistently funny than Rabelais," although both "run the gamut of the comic from the extremes of slapstick to the ultimate refinements of intellectual delicacy and subtlety" (p. 109).

8   MARICHAL, ROBERT. "Le nom des vents chez Rabelais." *Études Rabelaisiennes* 1:7–28.
      Whereas in his first book Rabelais' nomenclature belonged to the nautical vocabulary related to the Atlantic ("la langue du Ponant"), in Book IV it is related for the most part to the Mediterranean ("la langue du Levant"). Finds that in *Pantagruel* Rabelais uses oceanic terms seemingly without any knowledge of their meaning. But notes that in the *Quart Livre* he shows himself to be perfectly informed in all matters related to the sea. Had Rabelais ever sailed? Had he met Jacques Cartier, the "Jamet Brahier" mentioned in the 1552 edition of the *Quart Livre*? Finds no evidence that Rabelais had personal knowledge of nautical matters, but is convinced that he used the professional competence of real sailors as well as his own imagination to create, before the nineteenth century, the only literary storm which gives the impression of having been based on personal experience.

9   ———. "*Quart Livre*: Commentaires." *Études Rabelaisiennes* 1:151–202.
    Offers a linguistic commentary on Rabelais' text as published in volume
6 of the Lefranc edition of 1955. Comments primarily on the confrontation
between Panurge and Dindenault (chapt. 5–8), and the pages concerning
Messere Gaster (chapt. 57–62). In connection with the latter, questions previous interpretations of the episode as an expression of historical materialism or
as a socialist platform. Underscoring the negative aspects of Gaster's portrayal, concludes that the whole episode is nothing more than an ironic encomium.
Is thus able to integrate the series of chapters on Gaster among the surrounding episodes as yet another obstacle in the Pantagruelists' quest for a Promised
Land.

10  ROE, F[REDERICK] C. "Urquhart traducteur de Rabelais." *Études
    Rabelaisiennes* 1:112–19.
    Offers a brief account of the life and works of Thomas Urquhart, whose
translation of Rabelais' first three books was published in 1653. Underscores
parallels in personality and ideas between Rabelais and his translator. Notes
that Urquhart's was still the most popular translation in English at the time
the article was written. See also 1954.31.

11  SAULNIER, V[ERDUN]-L[OUIS]. "L'Énigme du pantagruélion, ou: du
    *Tiers* au *Quart Livre*." *Études Rabelaisiennes* 1:48–72.
    Reviews the various interpretations hitherto proposed of the chapters
related to the "pantagruélion," seen in turn as hemp, a rope with which to hang
the Protestants, a learned enigma, the glorification of human genius, a display
of botanical erudition. Rejects them all as either manifestly untenable or at
best insufficient, just as he rejects the idea that the episode is entirely devoid
of meaning. Notes the length of the episode, its consciously pedantic tone, its
insistence upon the contrast between the visible and the hidden. Sees in these
aspects of the text an invitation to decipher, to interpret the episode "à plus
haut sens." Reads the "pantagruélion" as a symbolic expression of Rabelais'
"hésuchisme," a non-militant, prudent form of evangelism adopted by
Rabelais in the face of growing religious intolerance and oppression.

12  ———. "Rabelais et les provinces du Nord." In *La Renaissance dans les
    provinces du Nord*. Edited by François Lesure. Paris: Éditions du Centre
National de la Recherche Scientifique, pp. 127–52.
    Among a number of points of contact between Rabelais and the
Northern provinces, mentions the possibly Northern origins of the Gargantuan
legends, Rabelais' personal relations (with Pierre de Vingle and Jean Second,
with such friends as Erasmus and such enemies as Calvin), and brief allusions
to the North (more frequent than to any other provinces he does not know
from experience). Discusses the expression "Martin de Cambrai" in the new
prologue to Book IV as an example of a popular motif related to the Northern

provinces. Most importantly, raises the question of a possible affinity with the art and thought of the Northern Renaissance. In connection with the realistic trends of Northern art, mentions Rabelais' affinity with Bosch and Breugel the Elder, and the narrative art of the *Quinze joies de mariage* and the *Cent nouvelles nouvelles*. Stresses the difficulties involved in attempting to connect the art of Rabelais with Franco-Flemish realism, but ventures to suggest a number of common traits: vitality, concreteness, avoidance of the morbid and the unhealthy, earthiness, comic expression of seriousness, absence of tragic overtones, tendency toward caricature. Historically, sees Rabelais as an intermediary between Northern realism and the baroque.

13 SCHELER, L. "François Rabelais pronostiqueur et son succès jusqu'en 1769." *BHR* 18:384–91.

Notes, in connection with an article by Saulnier (see 1954.34) that the name Seraphino Calbarsi, which Rabelais had used to sign one of his *Pronostications*, was discovered to be his pseudonym only in 1852, by J. Ch. Brunet. Shows that Rabelais' *Pronostication perpetuelle* and his *Pronostication fort utile*, or *des Laboureurs*, kept being reprinted, by such publishers as Jean Bessault, Jean Oursel, Pierre Seyer, and the so-called Anthoine Maginus, throughout the sixteenth and seventeenth centuries, and at least until 1769.

14 SCREECH, M[ICHAEL A[NDREW]. "Some Stoic Elements in Rabelais' Religious Thought: (The Will -Destiny -Active Virtue)." *Études Rabelaisiennes* 1:73–97.

While recognizing that they form only one of "many strands" in Rabelais' syncretic thought, studies—after many other critics—the Stoic influences that can be detected in *Gargantua* as well as in Books III and IV. Considers them insofar as they raise, within the framework of Evangelical Christianity, "the question of the human will and its relation to the divine; the question of divine intervention into human affairs; [and] the search for standards of judgment in face of the complexity of human problems" (p. 74). In the episode of Thélème, where the rule of doing what one wills leads paradoxically to a free conformity to the will of others rather than to chaos, finds "a vision of the perfect state as seen through stoic eyes" (p. 84) and not a careless contradiction on Rabelais' part. Rejects the view that Rabelais is fundamentally hostile to divination; finds him hostile only to its "popular forms" (p. 87), which he views as a typically Stoic attitude. Argues that Rabelais believes, as do the Stoics, in fate and destiny, but understood here as Providence and the will of God. Insists on the continuity of thought between the three books, and on the compatibility between Stoic and Christian thought in the area of ethics (if not of metaphysics). Sees a fusion of Stoic and Evangelical ethics in such episodes as the Abbaye de Thélème, the Bridoye episode, the chapters on the storm at sea, as well as in the character of

Pantagruel himself. Concludes that the "primary contribution of stoicism to Rabelais' Evangelical Christianity" lies in "the insistence on an *active* acquiescence in the will of God, and a stressing of the concept of virtue" (p. 96).

15 ————. "The sense of Rabelais' *Énigme en prophétie* (*Gargantua*, 58): A Clue to Rabelais's Evangelical reactions to the persecutions of 1534." *BHR* 18:392–404.

Sides with E. V. Telle in thinking that it is Gargantua's interpretation of the enigma that is to be taken seriously, but believes that the critic overstates the influence of Erasmus on Rabelais' religious thought, here and elsewhere in his writings. Argues on the contrary that the main sources of the enigma are to be sought in Matthew, Mark, and Luke, "with a little of Peter thrown in" (p. 394). Indicates some of these biblical sources, and concludes that in Rabelais' version of Mellin de Saint-Gelais' enigma, with its added last stanza, the text "is above all a call to steadfastness in the face of persecution" (p. 399). Underscores the similarities between Rabelais' attitude to persecution and that of Lefèvre d'Étaples.

16 SILVER, ISIDORE. "La prima fortuna di Omero nel Rinascimento francese." *Convivium* 29:30–49, 560–78.

Contains a list of allusions to Homer in Rabelais' works.

17 VALLET, EUGENE-CHARLES. "Panurge et l'obscénité dans le roman rabelaisien." *BAARD* 1, no. 5:136–40.

Does not share the conviction, prevalent among some Marxist critics, that Rabelais is a social visionary, and that Panurge represents the emergence of a new type of man: "l'individu bourgeois." Prefers to see him as a character whose curiosity and perplexity provides the motivation for the series of dialogues in the *Tiers Livre*, and the journey to the Oracle of the Divine Bottle in Book IV. As for the obscenity prevalent in Rabelais' novel, points out that it is present also everywhere in the sixteenth century ("dans l'air de l'époque"). Sees it as a sign of a healthy sexuality and of Rabelais' refusal to deal hypocritically with this or any other topic.

18 WADSWORTH, JAMES. "*Les Alibantes* of Rabelais." *Modern Language Notes* 71, no. 8 (December):584–87.

When Rabelais speaks, in chapt. 2 of *Pantagruel*, of those who try to escape the effects of the drought afflicting Africa at the time of the giant's birth by seeking refuge in the belly of a cow ("d'aultres se mettoient au ventre d'une vache pour estre à l'umbre: et les appelle Homere *Alibantes*"), he is satirizing a remedy proposed by the old-fashioned writer on medical matters, Pietro d'Abano, in his *Tractatus de Venenis*, later recommended by Ambroise Paré.

**1957**

1 AUERBACH, ERICH. *Mimesis: The Representation of Reality in Western Literature.* Translated from the German by Willard R. Trask. Garden City, N.Y.: Doubleday, Anchor, 498 pp.

Chapt. 11, "The World in Pantagruel's Mouth," contains an analysis of *Gargantua*, chapt. 32. Reprint of 1953.2. See also 1950.1.

2 BOUCHER, A. "Les caves peintes et l'authenticité du Ve Livre." *BAARD*, no. 6:157–60.

Notes the numerous allusions to Chinon in Book V, stresses the passage concerning the painted cave (chapt. 30), recalls the existence of a painted cave corresponding to Panurge's description, and concludes that only Rabelais, or a contemporary inhabitant of Chinon, could have introduced so many exact references to the town.

3 FRANÇON, MARCEL. *Autour de la lettre de Gargantua à son fils (*Pantagruel, 8). Rochecorbon: Éditions Charles Gay, 173 pp.

Reproduces the text of the earliest edition of the letter, with footnotes of an essentially linguistic nature. The text is preceded by an introduction providing the historical and intellectual context, an account of Rabelais' life up to the publication of his first book, as well as an analysis of the letter, whose seriousness is never questioned: "En résumé, Rabelais présente un programme d'études pour la formation totale d'un homme....C'est, en outre, un idéal plutôt qu'un programme" (pp. 49–50). Appendices comprise a set of twenty-two scholarly notes on a variety of topics (history, politics, geography), most of them unrelated to the letter, or indeed to *Pantagruel* as a whole.

4 FRANÇON, MARCEL, et FRAUTSCHI, RICHARD. "Sur des variantes de *Pantagruel*." *Bulletin Folklorique de l'Isle de France* 20:1052–53.

Draw attention to a passage in chapt. 27 of *Pantagruel* in which each of three characters—Pantagruel himself, Epistemon, and Panurge—are made to utter a sentence built on a common pattern: three nouns, each of them followed by an appropriate "complément déterminatif." The first sentence refers to an army, the second to food, and the third to matters sexual; each thus reflects the character of the person making the statement. A similar series of three sentences can be found in the twenty-ninth tale of Nicolas de Troyes' *Parangon des Nouvelles Nouvelles*. This had led such critics as Pietro Toldo and Henri Clouzot after him to conclude that Nicolas de Troyes had imitated Rabelais. But the authors point out that the series of three in Rabelais occurs for the first time in the François Juste edition of 1542. In the earlier editions there were only two characters, and two series of expressions. Thus Nicolas de Troyes series of three statements predates Rabelais' original text, and it is

Rabelais, as Gaston Paris had already pointed out, who in the 1542 edition borrows from Nicolas de Troyes and not the other way round.

5   LEWIS, D. B. WYNDAM. *Doctor Rabelais*. London: Sheed and Ward, 273 pp.

Offers an account of Rabelais' life and work from the perspective of a non-specialist, and thus perhaps free from the "Olympian aplomb" which tends to disfigure the studies of the man and the author by Rabelais scholars. Among the aspects presented as being possibly new, singles out the attempt to connect Panurge with the old Italian comedy, the hypothetical explanation of how Rabelais may have acquired his command of the language of the sea, and the discussion concerning the attribution to Rabelais of Béroalde de Verville's *Moyen de parvenir*. Suggests that his acquaintance with men who have embraced the monastic life gives him a small advantage over scholars totally unfamiliar with this important target of Rabelais' satire, be it only in helping him to avoid the mistake—which he claims to have found in the work of a Rabelaisian scholar "operating from a famous British University"—of believing that "frère mineur" refers to a friar under the age of twenty-one.

6   MEYER, HERMAN. "Das Zitat als Strukturelement in Rabelais Erzählwerk." In *Gestaltprobleme der Dichtung. G. Müller zu seinem 65. Geburtstag*. Bonn, pp. 49–66.

Argues that Rabelais' vast erudition, his wide knowledge of the past as well as of humanistic science and thought, is never used for its own sake or as background, but is thoroughly integrated as an important (most often comic) element of his narrative. Notes Rabelais' tendency to juxtapose the learned and the trivial for comic effect, but points out that Rabelais is less playful in his allusions to antiquity than to Christianity. Shows that his general references are sometimes made in pure seriousness (as in Grandgousier's prayer), but that with literal quotations this is almost never the case. Notes that they represent an irresistible challenge for the verbal humorist, who does not hesitate to use them as objects of a parody occasionally bordering on the blasphemous (as for instance in the Propos des Bien-Yvres, where Christ's last words are made to echo in a broadly comic context). Sees in the tensions thus created between text and context an important structural function of quotations in Rabelais' narrative. Reprinted in *Das Zitat in der Erzahlkunst. Zur Geschichte und Poetik des europäischen Romans*. Stuttgart: J. B. Metzlersche Verlag, 1967, pp. 28–53, and in 1973.2, pp. 229–56.

7   ROE, F[REDERICK] C. *Sir Thomas Urquhart and Rabelais*. Oxford: Clarendon Press, 23 pp.

Points out that the first translations of Rabelais appeared in Northern Protestant countries. Urquhart's was "the first, the most popular, the richest and raciest English version" (p. 4) and Urquhart's surest claim to fame.

1957

Sketches his life and works, stressing affinities with Rabelais which allow him sometimes, in spite of a total lack of humour in his own writings, to outdo his model in the matter of "unsavory epithets" (p. 16) with the help of Cotgrave's dictionary. "Cotgrave not only eased the labours of the erudite translator but has more than once supplied French Rabelais scholars with decisive clues in their attempt at elucidating some of the more abstruse passages" (p. 17). The Taylorian Lecture for 1957. See also 1954.31 and 1956.10.

8    SAULNIER, V[ERDUN] L[OUIS]. "Médecins de Montpellier au temps de Rabelais." *BHR* 19:425–79.

Elaborates on Marcel Gouron's *Matricule de l'Université de médecine de Montpellier* (Geneva: Librairie Droz, 1957). Seeks to bring out what such a study can tell us about the life of a medical student in the sixteenth century. Devotes pages 440–45 to "Rabelais à Montpellier"; shows to what extent Gouron's study supplements what was already known of Rabelais' life as a medical student and practitioner in that city. Notes in particular that the record time in which Rabelais received his degree was not in itself exceptional, and that earlier studies, perhaps in Paris during 1528–30, may have been taken into account by the authorities.

9    TELLE, ÉMILE V. "A propos de la lettre de Gargantua à son fils (*Pantagruel*, chap. VIII)." *BHR* 19:208–33.

Notes the contrast between this example of *epistola hortatoria* and the rest of the book. Sees in the first part of the letter, written in praise of legitimate marriage as a means of reaching seminal immortality, an integral part of the whole text. Brings out the similarities between this chapter of *Pantagruel* and Erasmus' *Encomium Matrimonii*, thrice condemned by the religious authorities of the day, and concludes that Rabelais' rehabilitation of the sexual act within the framework of legitimate marriage could have been signed by Erasmus.

10    ———. "Notes pour servir au commentaire du *Quart Livre*." *Romanic Review* 48:81–89.

Had previously suggested that the first edition of the *Quart Livre* could pass for an anti-monastic pamphlet. The epistle to the Cardinal Odet de Châtillon (1552), the nature of the islands visited by Pantagruel on his seafaring journey, the acknowledged borrowings from the Jewish historian Flavius Josephus, and the prologue to the 1552 edition lead author to believe that what was true of the first edition of 1548 is equally valid for the definitve edition published by Rabelais a year before his death. See 1952.7.

**1958**

1 CHAUVELOT, R. "Le vocabulaire médical de Rabelais." *La Presse médicale* 66, no.19, (8 March):427–28.

Surveys the scientific terminology in the years 1480–1540, and shows that many of the medical terms which Rabelais is held to have invented were already in use at the time. Provides a list of twenty-five terms whose earliest use was wrongly attributed to Rabelais by such dictionaries as Dauzat and Wartburg. Notes that at first these neologisms merely find their place alongside medieval terminology, and are used widely in medical circles, if not by physicians of humanistic inclination, at least by what were called at the time "les médecins de la petite manière": French-speaking possessors of an abnormally accelerated medical degree often given out by universities on condition that their recipients were not to exercise their profession in the town where such a degree was obtained. Points to the great number of French translations of Latin medical texts as proof of the vast number of these "médecins de la petite manière."

2 HARTLEY, K.H. "Rabelais and Pulci." *AUMLA:Journal of the Australian Universities Language and Literature Association* 9 (November):71–78.

Sees in Pulci's *Il Morgante* one of Rabelais' sources. Bases his opinion on Pulci's reputation at the time when Rabelais was in Italy, and above all on internal evidence of "similarities in expression, incident and character" (p. 71). Stresses how much Panurge owes to Margutte, and notes common elements in the authors' treatment of their giants, although finds Rabelais to be less detailed in his physical descriptions, and less coherent. "Pulci sometimes forgets he is dealing with different orders of magnitude: Rabelais sometimes remembers it" (p. 74). Notes that Pulci's Morgante carries off church bells as do the Rabelaisian giants; notes in particular the similarities in the episode of the storm at sea (where in both cases the dead whales are made to rise to the surface belly up, whereas in reality they would sink straight down). Points out the existence in both works of references to the Turks' custom of roasting their enemies. Finds similarities in Pulci's and Rabelais' humor, though "Rabelais is beyond comparison the coarser" (p. 77).

3 LEBÈGUE, RAYMOND. "Rabelais et les Grands Rhétoriqueurs." *Lettres Romanes* 12, no.1:5–18.

Sketches a history of the personal relations between Rabelais and the Grands Rhétoriqueurs, principally Jean Bouchet, whom Rabelais knew in Poitou; stresses their common interest in the theater, and Rabelais' imitation of Bouchet's stylistic devices. Notes Rabelais' acquaintance with Clément Marot and Mellin de Saint-Gelais, "deux fils de rhétoriqueurs" (p. 9). Reminds us that Rabelais borrowed a *rondeau* by Cretin and put it in the mouth of

1958

Raminagrobis in the *Tiers Livre*. Discusses Lefranc's identification of Raminagrobis with Lemaire de Belges, point out the similarities between the inscription on the portal of Thélème and Genius' speech in the *Concorde des deux langages*, and notes common stylistic features as well as a common conception of life: "Thélème est une synthèse du Temple de Vénus et du Temple de Minerve" (p. 13). Sees in Molinet a precursor of Rabelais in matters of verbal virtuosity. Underscores in Rabelais the humanist interested, as many of his colleagues were not, in all facets of contemporary life, including contemporary artistic forms which he occasionally borrowed and raised to new heights.

4   RENAUDET, AUGUSTIN. *Humanisme et Renaissance: Dante, Pétrarque, Standonck, Érasme, Lefèvre d'Étaples, Marguerite de Navarre, Rabelais, Guichardin, Giordano Bruno.* Geneva: Librairie Droz, 279 pp.
    Chapt. 15, "Rabelais et l'Italie" (pp. 236–39) is a reprint, in slightly modified form, of 1953.40.

5   SAULNIER, V[ERDUN]-L[OUIS]. "Une dissection de Rabelais célébrée par Étienne Dolet." *Revue Lyonnaise de Médecine*, pp. 84–86.
    Provides the text of a poem first published in Dolet's *Carminum libri quatuor* (1538), celebrating a human dissection performed by Rabelais (or, more precisely, under his direction) in Lyons a short time earlier. The Latin text is accompanied by a metric translation into French.

6   SCHRADER, LUDWIG. *Panurge und Hermes. Zum Ursprung eines Characters bei Rabelais.* Romanistische Versuche und Vorarbeiten, no. 3. Bonn: Romanisches Seminar an der Universität, 213 pp.
    Reviews previous interpretations of Panurge's character, provides his own definition, compares Rabelais' character with Hermes, and concludes that Panurge represents mercurial man.

7   SCREECH, M[ICHAEL] A[NDREW]. *The Rabelaisian Marriage: Aspects of Rabelais's Religion, Ethics and Comic Philosophy.* London: Edward Arnold, 144 pp.
    Rejects the view of the *Tiers Livre* as an extremely antifeminist expression of Rabelais' position in the Querelle des Femmes. Finds it to bear upon that quarrel only insofar as it relates to the wider debate on the relative merits of marriage and celibacy. Claims that Rabelais scorns the rhetoric of *pro et contra* leading his contempraries to extreme antifeminism or its extreme opposite, and adopts a compromise in keeping with his general ethics of moderation. Sees in the passage of Gargantua's letter to his son on the notion of immortality through children an antimonastic manifesto in favor of marriage, and in Gargantua's lament for Badebec a proof of at least "hesitant feminism" (p. 26). Stresses the antimonasticism of the chapters on the Abbey of

Thelema, and sees in its mathematical mysticism clear evidence of Rabelais' philogamy. Believes that the entire episode "breathes an air of feminism": with its enthusiasm for the civilizing qualities of women's company, "Thelema is poles apart from anything approaching contempt for women" (p. 34). In the *Tiers Livre*, underscores the allusions to Old Testament attitudes towards matrimony, the uncharacteristically violent denunciation of clandestine marriages, and Pantagruel's exemplary submission to his father (resurrected expressly for the occasion) in matters of matrimonial choice; sees these elements as reinforcing a positive view of marriage grounded in the values of Evangelical humanism. From the chapters on the consultation of various oracles, concludes that Rabelais is not hostile to divination, so long as it is used in a spirit of humility and acceptance of the inevitable. Accepts the identification of the theologian Hippothadée with Lefèvre d'Etaples, although believes Rabelais may also have been thinking of Melanchthon. Detects in Hippothadée's sermon the influence of Saint Paul's *Epistles* (used somewhat freely) and Plutarch's *Conjugal Precepts*. In the discourse of Rondibilis, sees Rabelais' "progressive" support of Plato against Galen on the question of the animal nature of the uterus. But stresses that Rabelais does not use his (and what he takes to be Plato's) negative opinion of female physiology to score misogynous points in the Querelle des Femmes; on the contrary, he takes the opportunity to praise those chaste women who manage to bring their wild and unreasonable uterus under control. Argues that the physiological wisdom of Rondibilis is perfectly compatible with the theological wisdom of Hippothadée, when one is considered against the background of the other. Believes that for Rabelais, marriage is in itself neither good nor bad; like other fortuitous matters, it is fundamentally *indifferent*, but eminently "promotable" if contracted responsibly, after careful deliberation, and in a spirit of submission to the will of God. Panurge's inability to make up his mind, his insistence upon a guarantee of a favorable outcome, define him as arrogant, stupid, ignorant, and ultimately evil (since Pantagruel detects behind Panurge's *philautia* a Satanic influence). In the concluding chapter, suggests that Rabelais' unfounded reputation as the leader of antifeminists in the Querelle des Femmes, derived from Billon's judgment in his *Fort inexpugnable de l'honneur du sexe fémenin* (1555), may have been based on Billon's reading of parts of Rondibilis' unflattering remarks about women in the anonymous *Louenge des Femmes*, "which carefully leaves out all modifications and all the learning to be found in Rabelais' original" (p. 132).

8   STEVENS, LINTON C. "Rabelais and Aristophanes." *Studies in Philology* 55, no. 1 (January):24–30.
        Given Rabelais' stature as a satirist and his general indebtedness to Latin and Greek sources, critics have found it puzzling that neither Juvenal nor Aristophanes appear to have had a significant influence on his work. In the case of Aristophanes, seeks to demonstrate, by pointing to "borrowings

of themes, illustrations, and words" (p. 24), that Rabelais' knowledge of the Greek satirical writer was both extensive and direct. Believes Aristophanes' political and economic ideas were too democratic and thus too dangerous to have found an echo in Rabelais. But claims that in such relatively safe areas as satire of tax collectors, philosophers, and lawyers, he does follow in Aristophanes' footsteps. Notes borrowings from *The Clouds, The Knights, The Wasps*, and *The Birds*, but believes that Rabelais owes most to *Plutus*. Also finds traces of Aristophanes' influence in Rabelais' linguistic experiments.

## 1959

1  ALBERTI, G. "Rabelais médecin humaniste à Rome." In *Rabelais écrivain-médecin, par vingt-deux médecins français et italiens*. Paris: Éditions Garance, pp. 65–70.

Briefly evokes Rabelais' three visits to Rome. "Il aimera passionnément l'Ancienne dont il recherchera avec respect les vestiges, mais il condamnera la Moderne et ses institutions qu'il jugera indignes de sa pureté primitive et qu'il fustigera de ses sarcasmes audacieux et parfois peu orthodoxes" (p. 70).

2  AURY, GABRIEL. "Rabelais navigateur." In *Rabelais écrivain-médecin, par vingt-deux médecins français et italiens*. Paris: Éditions Garance, pp. 147–59.

One of the few non-medical papers read at the second Congrès International des Sociétés d'Ecrivains-Médecins held at Evian in 1957. Comments on Rabelais' technical and linguistic knowledge of nautical matters in Book IV. Admits his debt to L. Denoix's "Connaissances nautiques de Rabelais" (1953.11).

3  BAILBÉ, J[ACQUES]. "Rabelais et Aubigné." *BHR* 21:380–419.

Recalls Rabelais' intellectual influence on many of his contemporaries, and shows that Aubigné was one of his fervent admirers. Finds traces of Rabelaisian gaiety in the *Confession de Sancy* and the *Aventures du Baron de Faeneste*. Notes the direct allusion to Rabelais in these two works, discusses features of style and narrative devices borrowed from Rabelais, and the presence of Rabelaisian satire touching upon religion, politics, justice, and magic. Concludes by pointing out that Rabelais' influence in matters of thought and art was considerable, but without altogether obliterating Aubigné's bitterness and the intolerance which he was prone to display in his defense of toleration. "La franchise téméraire, la verve bouffonne et cynique ne parviennent pas à dissimuler le tempérament de l'homme et de l'écrivain" (p. 418).

4    BONFANTINI, MARIO. "L'influence de sa qualité de médecin sur l'oeuvre de Rabelais." In *Rabelais écrivain-médecin, par vingt-deux médecins français et italiens*. Paris: Éditions Garance, pp. 111–14.

    Does not see any specific traces of such an influence: "De l'étude des faits et des thèmes de ses livres il résulte que rien, ou peu de choses, ne laisse présupposer nécessairement chez l'auteur la qualité spécifique de médecin" (p. 111). In a more general way, however, the study and practice of medicine may account for Rabelais' feeling for the physical and material aspects of existence, of his organic conception of life as manifested, for example, in the myth of Gaster.

5    CHAUMARTIN, HENRI. "Rabelais et Dame Vérole." In *Rabelais écrivain-médecin, par vingt-deux médecins français et italiens*. Paris: Éditions Garance, pp. 219–28.

    Describes the treatment undergone by the "vérolés" in Rabelais' day, sometimes referred to metaphorically as a journey to "Surye" and "Bavières." "Le feu Sainct-Antoine" of which Rabelais speaks repeatedly has often been identified as syphilis. Wrongly, claims the author: since Rabelais often localizes the disease in the legs, it is more likely to be a form of gangrene.

6    CHERUBINI, ARNALDO. "Médecin...non médecin." In *Rabelais écrivain-médecin, par vingt-deux médecins français et italiens*. Paris: Éditions Garance, pp.107–10.

    Suggests that Rabelais considered himself first and foremost a physician. Underscores Rabelais' importance in that regard. "Dans la médecine il ouvre la voie à Vésale et à Paré" (p. 110).

7    CLEMENTS, ROBERT J. *The Peregrine Muse: Studies in Comparative Renaissance Literature*. Studies in the Romance Languages and Literatures, no. 31. Chapel Hill: The University of North Carolina Press, pp. 53–75.

    References, mostly in chapt. 4, to J.-C. Scaliger's attacks upon Rabelais in the latter's lifetime as well as after his death.

8    CRUCHET, RENÉ. "Rabelais à Bordeaux." In *Rabelais écrivain-médecin, par vingt-deux médecins français et italiens*. Paris: Éditions Garance, pp.43–49.

    Believes that Rabelais used medicine for strictly literary ends. Suggests that he may have stopped in Bordeaux on his way to Montpellier in the Summer of 1530. Points out that he witnessed Jean du Bellay's "acte de soumission aux usages de l'archevêché de Bordeaux" in 1545 (p. 45). Notes that in that document Rabelais is said to belong to the parish of Saint Christophe de Jambet: "il n'est pas question de la cure de Meudon" (p. 45n).

1959

9   DENIER, ANDRÉ. "Rabelais à Grenoble, 1535–1536." In *Rabelais écrivain-médecin, par vingt-deux médecins français et italiens*. Paris: Éditions Garance, pp.61–63.
    Seeks to account for Rabelais' absence from Lyons by a hypothetical sojourn in Grenoble, where Rabelais' hypothetically pregnant girlfriend may have given birth.

10  DESSE, GEORGES. "Rabelais rhumatologue." In *Rabelais écrivain-médecin, par vingt-deux médecins français et italiens*. Paris: Éditions Garance, pp. 115–26.
    Believes that the variety of Rabelais' medical knowledge notwithstanding, his concern for the gouty, the rheumatic, shows that he was most particularly interested in rheumatology, which is now (in 1959) considered to be one of the new medical specializations.

11  DIAMANT-BERGER, LUCIEN. "Rabelais chirurgien." In *Rabelais écrivain-médecin, par vingt-deux médecins français et italiens*. Paris: Éditions Garance, pp. 127–46.
    Points out that in Rabelais' day the practice of surgery was considered a degrading activity, left by physicians to barbers, a prejudice shared by Rabelais himself. Claims that Rabelais' theoretical knowledge of the subject is documented by his invention of a technique for the treatment of fractures of the femur, and of a surgical instrument for the cure of strangulated hernia, as illustrated in a 1537 translation of Galien's *Fourth Book* (reproduced in the article). Also reproduces passages from Dr. Ledouble's work on the anatomy of Carême-Prenant, tending to prove that "l'extravagant Carême-Prenant,...n'était, à tout prendre, qu'un homme normal" (p. 146).

12  ESKIN, STANLEY G. "Hedonism and the Concept of Nature: The Work of Rabelais and Montaigne in the Context of Western Literature." Ph.D. dissertation, Columbia University, 296 pp.
    Studies the hedonistic aspects of Rabelais' thought in "his concept of joy, his ideas on education, the principles underlying the Abbaye de Thélème, the philosophy of "Pantaguelism," his concern with the physical appetites, his realistic attitude toward sex, his concept of nature and antinature (Physis and Antiphysie), and the symbolic implications of wine and drinking." Relates this emphasis on pleasure and sensuality to trends in intellectual history. See *Dissertation Abstracts* 20 (1960):4109–10A.

13  EYLAUD, J. M. "Rabelais et le vin." In *Rabelais écrivain-médecin, par vingt-deux médecins français et italiens*. Paris: Éditions Garance, pp. 199–211.

Notes that Rabelais speaks of wine as a vintner, a physician, and a humanist. His temperament, as well as his legendary predilection for wine, suggest that he may have been "un véritable diabétique" (p. 200).

14    FRANCIS, K. H. "The Mechanism of Magnetic Doors in Rabelais, Bk V, Chapter 37." *French Studies* 13, no. 4 (October):293–303.
       Seeks to explain the significance of the *diamant Indique* suspended in front of the closed doors to the Temple. Is it a diamond, or a magnet? Compares the episode of the magnetic doors in Rabelais with its source in Colonna's *Hypnerotomachia,* and finds that the comparison testifies to Rabelais' "impressive interest in the scientific why and wherefore" (p. 300). Sees in the substitution of *aimant* for *diamant* at the end of the chapter an indication that we are in the presence of a rough draft that the author had not had the opportunity to work over before publication. Compares chapt. 37 with the scientific chapt. 42 on the fountain (see 1959.15), finds it "dull, colourless and lacking in detail," and suggests that chapt. 42 "proceeded from the pen of Rabelais himself," whereas chapt. 37 betrays the work of a lesser hand.

15    ———. "Rabelais and Mathematics." *BHR* 21:85–97.
       Seeks to determine the extent of Rabelais' knowledge of mathematics. Finds evidence of "a mind interested in the world of mathematics, and notably in that part of it which is related to mysticism and numerology" (p. 88). Finds him also to have a grasp of geometrical problems, especially in his description of the *fontaine fantastique* in Book V, chapt. 42, with its problem of constructing a regular heptagon in a circle. Notes that Rabelais uses numbers for exactitude, for comic effect, and for their significance "or because of their superstitious overtones" (p. 94). Selects numbers in each category, and notes the frequency of certain numbers which seem to have for him a particular meaning.

16    FROHOCK, W[ILBUR] M. "Panurge as Comic Character." *Yale French Studies* 33 (Summer):71–76.
       Challenges the prevalent notion of Panurge as "an inconsistent character." Admits that he may leave an impression of inconsistency, but only because we judge him by the canon of consistency "forced upon us by the dynamics of the modern novel" (p. 71). Underscores within Panurge the mixture of the gentleman, the scholar, the charmer. Notes the disquieting nature of his tricks, which are invariably acts of aggression of potential interest to the police, were it not for "the immunity from the civil arm with which Rabelais regularly invests his characters" (p. 73). Contrasts him with Frère Jean and compares him at some length with Falstaff. Sees in the concept of both characters the influence of "the old stage comedy." Argues that in both characters what we take to be inconsistencies are mutations with which the sixteenth-century reader would be familiar through his experience of the stage. In the

case of Panurge, "[t]he various mutations, from Villonesque trickster to quailing coward, would represent nothing that had not been represented on the comic stage. They would be recognized by the reader as latent in the type, and would not surprise" (p. 76).

17 GAUTHIER, GEORGES. "Rabelais à Lyon." In *Rabelais écrivain-médecin, par vingt-deux médecins français et italiens*. Paris: Éditions Garance, pp. 51–57.

Notes that only two documents attest to Rabelais' medical presence in Lyons. In the face of this lack of reliable information, critics have given their imagination free run. Admits that he does likewise: "Comme eux, nous ne pouvons nous faire qu'une idée très approximative de la carrière hospitalière de Rabelais, en nous replongeant dans l'ambiance de l'époque" (p. 52).

18 GERMANI, GIUSEPPE MARIO. "François Rabelais à Ferrare." In *Rabelais écrivain-médecin, par vingt-deux médecins français et italiens*. Paris: Éditions Garance, pp. 71–74.

Underscores affinities between Rabelais and Giovanni Manardi, whose *Epîtres Médicales* he published in Lyons with a preface in 1532. Evokes Rabelais' two visits to Ferrara, where he may have met Manardi (but no document to that effect exists).

19 GODLEWSKI, GUY. "Rabelais à Montpellier." In *Rabelais écrivain-médecin, par vingt-deux médecins français et italiens*. Paris: Éditions Garance, pp. 29–41.

Seeks to reconstruct Rabelais' life at Montpellier in 1531, his surprising career at the Grand Hôtel-Dieu in Lyons, and his brief return to Montpellier in 1537, where he received his *licence*, followed by a doctorate in medicine after an appropriate period of time since his baccalaureate, but without, it seems, any medical preparation. Holds his scientific and therapeutic contributions to have been negligible. Believes that it is through his novels that Rabelais came closest to have had any influence on medicine.

20 HOSIASSON, STÉPHANE. "Rabelais et la musique." In *Rabelais écrivain-médecin, par vingt-deux médecins français et italiens*. Paris: Éditions Garance, pp. 189–97.

Quotes passages bearing witness to Rabelais' interest in music, and discusses the phonetic aspect of his work: "c'est au point de vue sonore et musical que l'oeuvre de Rabelais constitue une réussite" (p. 190). Sees in Rabelais a precursor in the field of music therapy.

21 KOHLER, ERICH. "Die Abtei Thélème und die Einheit des Rabelais'schen Werks." *Germanisch-Romanische Monatsschrift* 40:105–18.

Reprinted: 1973.2, pp. 296–314; 1966.11, pp. 142–57. Reminds us that Rabelais' literary production spans a period of over twenty years, and notes that his first two books were written at a time when it could not be foreseen that the link between humanism and Reformation would soon be broken. Offers a close reading of the Abbaye de Thélème episode, and argues that on fundamental issues—religion, human nature, women and marriage, human will—what Rabelais writes in the last chapter of *Gargantua* echoes what he had said before in *Pantagruel* and foreshadows what he will say in the books that were yet to come.

22 KOHN, RICHARD. "Rabelais et le théâtre." In *Rabelais écrivain-médecin, par vingt-deux médecins français et italiens*. Paris: Éditions Garance, pp. 167–87.

Stresses the theatrical aspects of Rabelais' fiction, and surveys the dramatic literature inspired by Rabelais' characters and the author himself. Claims that Rabelais' work bears witness to his knowledge of the theater as well as his talent for such dramatic techniques as the soliloquy and the dialogue. Points out Rabelaisian reminiscences in Molière.

23 LORAS, OLIVIER. "Vers une psychanalyse de Rabelais." In *Rabelais écrivain-médecin, par vingt-deux médecins français et italiens*. Paris: Éditions Garance, pp. 237–50.

Offers a psychoanalytic interpretation, by a professional psychiatrist, of Rabelaisian laughter (both destructive and constructive), and the Rabelaisian smile (symbolic of a trusting optimism).

24 MÉRY, FERNAND. "François Rabelais, animalier." In *Rabelais écrivain-médecin, par vingt-deux médecins français et italiens*. Paris: Éditions Garance, pp. 161–66.

Rabelais' work testifies to his knowledge of animal anatomy and psychology, but shows no sign of "fraternité animale" (p. 166).

25 NOEL, PAUL. "Rabelais, curé de Meudon." In *Rabelais écrivain-médecin, par vingt-deux médecins français et italiens*. Paris: Éditions Garance, pp. 87–105.

Recalls the scarcity of documents relating to the "cure de Meudon," to which Rabelais was named on January 1540, and which he resigned on January 9, 1552, a few days before the publication of Book IV. "Tout son passé semble s'inscrire contre cette fin de vie ecclésiastique et en constitue une opposition flagrante" (p. 88). Adds to the meager dossier an "acte notarié" (quoted on p. 95), whereby Rabelais gives to a certain Me Pierre Richard and his brother the power to act on his behalf in a lawsuit with the abbots of Saint-Germain-des-Près.

1959

26 O'FOLLOWELL, LUDOVIC. "L'Humour dans Rabelais." In *Rabelais écrivain-médecin, par vingt-deux médecins français et italiens*. Paris: Éditions Garance, pp. 213–18.

Contrasts the frank and spontaneous gaiety of Rabelais' humor with the modern variety, "si plein d'amertume et de férocité" (p. 218).

27 POISSONNET, HENRI. "Rabelais à Fontenay-le-Comte." In *Rabelais écrivain-médecin, par vingt-deux médecins français et italiens*. Paris: Éditions Garance, pp. 13–28.

Traces Rabelais' intellectual awakening at Fontenay-le-Comte and later at Maillezais ("à moins de trois lieues de là," p. 19) among the Franciscans, evokes his friendship with Pierre Amy and Tiraqueau. Seeks to evaluate, in Rabelais' work, "l'apport de la culture acquise en Poitou" (p. 21).

28 SCHMITT, BERNARD. "Rabelais à Metz." In *Rabelais écrivain-médecin, par vingt-deux médecins français et italiens*. Paris: Éditions Garance, pp. 75–85.

In the absence of any archives for the period, attempts to give some idea of Rabelais' life—as a physician, a priest, a philosopher and a writer—in Metz, to which he fled after the publication of the *Tiers Livre*, and which he left in June 1548 after writing the first version of Book IV.

29 SCREECH, M[ICHAEL] A[NDREW]. *L'Evangélisme de Rabelais: Aspects de la satire religieuse au XVIe siècle*. Études Rabelaisiennes, no. 2. Geneva: Librairie E. Droz, 101 pp.

Leaving aside the question of Rabelais' syncretism, studied by the author elsewhere (see 1955.12 and 1956.14), seeks to underscore the Evangelical aspects of Rabelais' religious thought in the passages on the birth of Gargantua, Pantagruel's prayer before the battle with Loup Garou, the two versions of the storm at sea, and Rabelais' Almanachs. Aims to trace the biblical passages to which Rabelais alludes, and to place them in their theological and historical context. By drawing parallels with other religious authors of the time, hopes to bring out the true significance of these biblical allusions for Rabelais himself. Claims that in his novels Rabelais' primary concern is to expound and defend his religious views: "La propagande religieuse n'est pas pour lui une affaire secondaire; elle commande le choix de ses sujets et la forme qu'ils prennent dans ses romans; elle est la principale raison d'être de quelques-uns des épisodes les plus connus et les plus géniaux" (p. 10). Following Gilson and Febvre rather than Lefranc, does not see in Gargantua's birth any element of parody, but rather a deep knowledge of theology and the Scriptures. Believes that the parallel between the miraculous nativity of Gargantua and the equally miraculous birth of Isaac and Jesus is meant to underscore the fundamental difference in attitude between the true Christian believer and a simple-minded believer in superstition:

"Pourquoi le chrétien ajoute-t-il foi aux unes et non pas à l'autre? Parce que foi n'est pas crédulité" (p. 15). Believes Rabelais' conception of faith to be close to that of Erasmus and Luther, but notes also a fundamental opposition to Luther's ideas, evident for example in some details of the Loup Garou episode. Notes the emphasis in Rabelais on the ethical aspect of Christian life, on *active* virtue, as seen in the character of Frère Jean, or the 1548 version of the storm at sea episode in Book IV. Also notes the synergism of the second version, where the notion of helping God is replaced by that of cooperating with him. Finally, makes a case for giving Rabelais' Almanachs and prognostication a privileged place among his works. Notes the solidity of their theological erudition and the clarity of their religious message. Finds that they are informed by a theology very similar to that of the novels, in its attempt to preserve both predestination and free will with an intention similar to that of Erasmus and Lefèvre d'Etaples: "décharger Dieu de la responsabilité des mauvaises actions de l'homme, tout en les retenant dans l'orbite de la Providence" (p. 70). Believes that the radical evangelism of the Papimanes episode in the *Quart Livre* owes as much to Rabelais' "gallicanisme" as to his sympathies for the Reformation, and that his religious attitude also informs his political ideology, as when he charges the ideal prince with the mission to defend Evangelical faith and to put an end to religious abuses. Concludes by summarizing Rabelais' religious position as equally hostile to both Calvin and the Sorbonne, close in some respects to that of Luther, tolerant of certain Catholic dogmas but rejecting others—a position that was never able to take hold on French soil. "Il y a lieu de soupçonner que la réforme que Rabelais envisage est une réforme à l'anglaise" (p. 94).

30 ———. "Rabelais and the Sarabaites: Peter Crinitus and St. Augustine, sources of an addition to *Pantagruel*." *BHR* 21:451–52.
    Believes that the strong attack against the hypocrisy of monks added to the end of *Pantagruel* after the first edition is derived from Peter Crinitus' *De honesta disciplina*.

31 TRIBOUILLET DES ESSARDS, PAUL HENRI. "Rabelais ou la bonne conscience." In *Rabelais écrivain-médecin, par vingt-deux médecins français et italiens*. Paris: Éditions Garance, pp. 229–36.
    Reviews Rabelais' attitude towards religion, women, and paternity. Seeks to capture Rabelais "en sa pensée quotidienne, ses goûts et ses dégoûts, bien autant qu'en l'épopée de ses livres" (p. 229).

32 VOIVENEL, PAUL. "Sur Rabelais par campagnou." In *Rabelais écrivain-médecin, par vingt-deux médecins français et italiens*. Paris: Éditions Garance, pp. 251–58.
    A witty *mise-en-garde* against the simplistic tendency to seek the author in his work. Militates in favor of a common-sense, non-specialist view

of Rabelais. Suggests that there may be nothing "Rabelaisian" in Rabelais the man.

33    WHITAKER, THOMAS R. "The Drinkers and History: Rabelais, Balzac, and Joyce." *Comparative Literature* 9, no. 2 (Spring):157–64.

Recalls that Leopold Bloom brought home for Molly a copy of *Gargantua and Pantagruel* in the translation by Urquhart and Le Motteux. Points out a number of Rabelaisian echoes, and compares "Les propos des bien yvres" (*Gargantua*, chapt. 5) with the party at the hospital in *Ulysses*. Notes similarities in the use of language to suggest a speaker's identity, and in the treatment of the theme of wine.


## 1960

1    DE DIÉGUEZ, MANUEL. *Rabelais par lui-même.* Écrivains de Toujours. Paris: Éditions du Seuil, 184 pp.

Begins by sketching a "biographie parallèle de Rabelais et des géants"; insists on how little is known of Rabelais' life; accepts Lefranc's hypothesis of 1494 as being the date of Rabelais' birth. In the rest of the work, offers a *lecture commentée* of the most important episodes. Sees in the lawsuit between Baisecul and Humevesne the first attempt at "écriture automatique" (p. 64). Questions whether Rabelais meant to write *Pantagruel* for the general public ("un public populaire"); sees in Rabelais' very first novel all the essential qualities of the work to come. Finds that in *Gargantua* Rabelais' ability to transfigure reality has become so powerful that recourse to fantasy is no longer required: the real has acquired a thoroughly Rabelaisian stamp. In the prologue to the *Tiers Livre* reads an intention to create an essentially verbal universe: "remplacer les choses par les mots,...substituer à l'épaisseur et à la durée du monde une épaisseur et une durée verbales équivalentes" (p. 84). Does not believe that Rabelais takes sides in the Querelle des Femmes; finds him indifferent to the problems of women, but fascinated by the prophetic arts. Sees in the Pantagruélion episode a successful attempt to blend science with poetry, and to prove that poetry is a matter of tone and style rather than subject matter. Finds Book IV to be the strangest and most innovative of all, at once the most mysterious and the most committed. "Racine, Molière, La Fontaine,...pilleront littéralement le *Quart Livre*." Believes Book V to have been written by Rabelais. Sees in Rabelais' style the most unmistakable sign of his greatness and modernity: "Rabelais est le premier écrivain français pour lequel les mots sont une matière, qui donne une réalité aux mots en tant que *choses*—non seulement en tant que *sens*" (p. 125). Insists on Rabelais' work as a meditation on the problems of language. Underscores the essentially interrogative character of his quest. Provides a selection of excerpts.

Concludes with a few critical appraisals, including those of a number of contemporaries interviewed by the author.

2   DE GRÈVE, MARCEL. "La légende de Gargantua en Angleterre au XVIe
    siècle." *Revue Belge de Philologie et d'Histoire* 38:765–94.
        Reminds us that the most famous allusion to Gargantua in English liter-
    ature is to be found in Shakespeare's *As You Like It* (Act III, scene 2). On the
    basis of somewhat mystifying entries in the *Stationer's Register*, concludes
    that at least one book on Gargantua was published in England at the end of the
    sixteenth century. Excludes the possibility that it was a translation from
    Rabelais, since none appeared in English before 1653. Notes the connection of
    the Gargantuan chronicles with the Arthurian legends, the taste of the English
    public for popular romances, and the contemporary listings of *Gargantua*
    among popular works, and concludes that the entries in the  *Stationer's
    Register* refer to an English version of one or another of the Gargantuan
    chronicles. Points out that the first allusion to Gargantua in English occurs in
    1547, but given the contemptuous reference by Edward Fenton in 1569 to a
    *History of Gargantua* in which only the "unlearned sorte" take pleasure, con-
    cludes here again that the reference could only have been to an English ver-
    sion of the chronicles and not to Rabelais' work. Notes echoes of the
    legendary Gargantua in a variety of texts in the second half of the century.
    Believes that even Thomas Nashe, who alludes to Gargantua and is claimed to
    have been influenced by Rabelais, was referring to the Gargantua of legend
    and was unfamiliar with Rabelais.

3   FRANÇON, MARCEL. "A Note on the Word 'Symbolisation' in the *Tiers
    Livre*." *Modern Language Review* 55, no. 1 (January):84–85.
        When Rabelais says that in a world devoid of debtors and borrowers
    "entre les élémens ne sera symbolisation, alternation ne transmutation aul-
    cune," he uses *symbolisation* in the Greek sense of exchange. Hence, the three
    terms are "practically synonymous with one another."

4   GRUBER, VIVIAN MERCER. "François Rabelais and Miguel de Cervantes:
    Novelists of Transition." Ph.D. dissertation, Florida State University, 154 pp.
        Studies Rabelais' novels as transitional works between the Middle Ages
    and the Renaissance, and the *Quijote* as typifying the changes in cultural his-
    tory between the Renaissance and the modern period. Finds the works to be
    comparable in their choice of subject, "personal development," and variety of
    stylistic techniques. On the other hand, contrasts the excesses of Rabelais with
    the restraint of Cervantes, and "the near-pagan pessimism and skepticism of
    the French writer as opposed to the essential Christian optimism of the
    Spanish novelist." See *Dissertation Abstracts* 21 (1961):2294.

1960

5    GUITER, HENRI. "De Rabelais à Cervantes, ou Les héros de la démesure."
     *Bulletin de l'Association Guillaume Budé* 19, no. 4:579–622.
         Compares the two writers, seen as the two greatest representatives of
     their time. Stresses analogies between their life and their work. Limits his
     comparison to the *Quijote* and to *Gargantua*. Notes that their heroes are both
     "démesurés," one in body, the other in his dreams. Believes that both works
     have their origin in a traumatic memory ("un mauvais souvenir"), in Rabelais'
     case the feud between his father and Gaucher de Sainte-Marthe, and explains
     the moral *démesure* of Picrochole by Rabelais' alleged desire for revenge.

6    KAISER, WALTER JACOB. "Praisers of Folly: Erasmus, Rabelais, and
     Shakespeare." Ph.D. dissertation, Harvard University.
         See *American Doctoral Dissertations*, 1959–60, p. 115. Published in
     book form: 1963.13.

7    PONS, ROGER. "Rabelais: Hymne de la Paternité." *L'Information Littéraire*
     2 (March–April):82–89.
         Provides an *explication de texte* of the first five paragraphs of
     Gargantua's letter to his son, "ce début  méconnu" of an otherwise celebrated
     chapter. Brings out the emotional dimension of the relation between father
     and son, and finds the passage particularly moving in that it combines with
     unaccustomed simplicity the feeling of deep attachment to the world and of
     serene detachment from it.

8    REICHENBERGER, KURT. "Studien zu Rabelais' Rechtsdenken." *BHR*
     22:185–91.
         Studies the Bridoye episode in the *Tiers Livre* by bringing out the impli-
     cations of the image of the bear licking her cub into shape, used by Bridoye to
     justify his tendency to temporize before rendering his verdicts. Traces the
     myth to Pliny the Elder, notes its persistence in Virgil and Ovid, and during
     the early Renaissance in the *Hieroglyphica* of Horapollo Niliacus (1505).
     Points out that it acquires an exemplary value in Saint Ambrose's *Hexameron*,
     and is used in Du Bartas as a metaphor of divine creation. Notes the recur-
     rence of the bear motif (and the expression "Comme vous, Messieurs")
     throughout the chapter, and sees both as structural elements underscoring
     Rabelais' skepticism as to the foundations of the legal system. Sees
     Pantagrel's obvious approval of Bridoye's recourse to the *sort des dez* as a
     sign of Bidoye's superiority over his colleagues, in that he alone recognizes
     the fallibility of human judgment in the legal sphere, as well as elsewhere.
     Argues that this idea had already been prefigured in *Pantagruel* in the episode
     of the lawsuit between Baisecul and Humevesne.

9    SAULNIER, V[ERDUN]-L[OUIS]. "Hommes pétrifiés et pierres vives: (Autour d'une formule de Panurge)." *BHR* 22:393–402.

"Je ne bastis que pierres vives, ce sont hommes" (*Tiers Livre*, chapt. 6). Stresses the beauty of the expression, its humanistic tone despite its farcical context, its pedagogical importance. Traces the idea of stones endowed with life to such chemists as Cardano, such poets as Du Bellay. Reminds us that the Collège des lecteurs royaux was known as an institution built of men rather than stones (since it had no fixed location). Believes that the origin of the expression should be sought in the myth of Deucalion and Pyrrha, repopulating the world after the Flood by throwing stones over their shoulders. Or in Agesilas' remark, quoted by Rabelais himself, to the effect that a city needs no walls if it has heroic inhabitants ready to protect it. But that Rabelais found its exact wording in the Bible, namely in the *lapides vivi* mentioned by Saint Peter. "Il a très évidemment repris une formule religieuse...pour en faire beaucoup plus généralement une formule d'humanisme" (p. 401). Notes echoes of the concept elsewhere in Rabelais' work.

10   ——. "Pantagruel et sa famille de mots." *L'Information Littéraire* 2 (March–April):47–57.

Studies the derivatives of "Pantagruel" in Rabelais' text: *pantagruélin, pantagruéliste, pantagruélique*, and so on. Finds them used mostly in a liminary position, or at the end of the books. Notes that derivatives of "Gargantua" are much fewer, and speculates that Rabelais chose Pantagruel to represent his philosophy because, much more than Gargantua, who is a product of the Middle Ages to which he remains attached by his upbringing, Pantagruel belongs to the enlightened climate of the Renaissance. Notes the near absence of pantagruelistic vocabulary in Book V, but stops short of finding it significant in the context of the problem of that book's authenticity. Argues that the evolution of the pantagruelistic vocabulary reveals a progression in Rabelais' thought. Detects three stages in that progression, corresponding to three different meanings given to the word *pantagruélisme*: at first the meaning is prephilosophical and is merely synonymous with good cheer; then, in 1534–35, it suggests a philosophy of quiet tolerance, before acquiring in the years 1546–52 a stoical resonance with its emphasis on steadfastness and courage. Closes with brief remarks on the posthumous use of pantagrueulistic vocabulary, and points out that it signals almost from the very start a marked trivialization of Rabelais' thought. Reprinted in 1983.33.

11   ——. "La Philosophie de Rabelais." *BAARD* 1, no. 9:249–51.

Excerpts of a paper read in Tours in March 1960. Argues that Rabelais' method is essentially that of a physician, that his laughter means above all to be therapeutic, and that pantagruelism—a constant throughout his work—is an attitude rather than a philosophy.

1960

12 SCHRADER, LUDWIG. "Die Rabelais-Forschung der Jahre 1950–60: Tendenzen und Ergebnisse." *Romanistische Jahrbuch* 11:161–201.

For the period in question, lists and comments upon new editions of Rabelais' work, general studies, biographies, studies of sources, works on language, attempts to bring out the work's *substantifique moelle*, studies dealing with literary history, as well as specific characters and episodes. Deplores the prevailing emphasis on Rabelais' thought, and calls for an approach grounded in literary aesthetics. Ends with a review of works on Rabelais' fortune in France and abroad.

13 SCREECH, M[ICHAEL] A[NDREW]. "Further Precision on the Stoico-Evangelical Crux: *chascun abonde en son sens (Tiers Livre,* VII)." *BHR* 22:549–51.

Insists on the boldness of Rabelais' position when he invokes Saint Paul's injunction: *Unusquisque in suo sensu abundet* (Rom. 14:5) and makes it apply ostensibly to matters external and indifferent, but in fact to "everything outside the mind and below the heavens, including much of what many of his contemporaries would have regarded as basic moral issues for Roman Catholics" (p. 550), such as celibacy and matrimony.

14 ———. "The Meaning of Thaumaste: (A double-edged satire of the Sorbonne and of the *prisca theologia* of cabbalistic Humanists)." *BHR* 22:62–72.

Argues that the Thaumaste episode is more than the satire of Scholasticism it is often considered to be. Believes it to be a satire of those who do not seek after the truth, as well as those who seek it where it is not to be found. Likens Thaumaste's journey to sit at the feet of the Sages to the Queen of Sheba's visit to Solomon as narrated in both the Old and New Testaments. Sees also a parallel with Pico della Mirandola's journey in search of truth as related by his son in Pico's biography. Notes that both Pico and Thaumaste seek truth in magic, alchemy, and the Cabbala, as well as in philosophy. Points out that the signs with which Thaumaste wishes to argue, as well as the first syllable of his name, underscore his sympathy for the Cabbalists and their search for *signs* revelatory of truth. Contends that if Thaumaste is in the end a figure of fun naively taken in by Panurge's antics, it is because his belief in *prisca theologia* makes him an easy prey to superstition and diabolical persuasion. Believes that Rabelais admires him for his humility (in contrast to the arrogance of the Sorbonne theologians), but that he also condemns him for seeking truth in esoteric knowledge. Compares this to the similarly ambiguous attitude of the Scriptures towards the Queen of Sheba, admired by Saint Matthew and Saint Luke as a seeker of truth (in contrast to the arrogance of the Jews), but condemned by Christ for her misguided belief in the revelatory power of signs.

15  SPITZER, L[EO]. "Rabelais et les 'rabelaisants.'" *Studi Francesi* 4, no. 12 (September–December):401–23.

In strong reaction to the volume of articles published by Droz in the Travaux d'Humanisme et Renaissance series on the occasion of the four-hundredth anniversary of Rabelais' death, rejects any exclusively historicist approach to Rabelais insofar as it sacrifices the work's artistic merit to its documentary value. Attacks in particular Saulnier's article on the Frozen Words (1953.43), in which the critic seeks to explain the episode as an allusion to a particular event in the war between the German Protestant princes and Charles V. Generally accuses the French critics of stifling Rabelais' poetry under what they believe to be history; deplores historical ignorance in some, and an impeccable but misplaced erudition in others. Believes Rabelais' work to be realistic only to the extent that it gives to myth the appearance of reality: "Chez Rabelais le réel ne transparaît pas autant dans le mythe que le mythe ne transforme le réel dont il a besoin pour s'incarner" (p. 422). Calls for studies on Rabelais' cosmic and mythical laughter, on the poetry of his ideas and of his language, rather than studies of the pseudo-problems of an outmoded historical realism.

16  WEINBERG, BERNARD. "Rabelais as an Artist." *Texas Quarterly* 3, no. 3 (Autumn):175–88.

Precisely because the *Great and Inestimable Chronicles of the Great Giant Gargantua* and Rabelais' *Pantagruel* follow the same pattern, the same over-all organization of materials, a comparison of the two works brings out with particular force the artistic superiority of Rabelais' novel, and the way it enriches the canvas of an essentially dull story. Sees this superiority in the novel's "contemporancity" and its "localism" (the fact that the times as well as the basic intellectual attitudes and the geographical location are those with which the reader is most familiar); in the creation of numerous and clearly diversified secondary characters; in the handling of individual episodes; and in the quality of its humor. Believes that all these virtues are brought to an even higher level of artistic perfection in *Gargantua*, which moreover is no longer a mere entertainment, but art put to the service of philosophy. "What is important to recognize from the artistic point of view is that Rabelais' art grows and improves as a result of this philosophical orientation" (p. 186). Claims that the improvement can be seen in both narrative and dramatic technique, and that it is even more evident as the novel progresses.

17  WILLIAMS, EDWARD BAKER. "Rabelais and the *Cinquiesme Livre*." Ph.D. dissertation, Brown University, 129 pp.

Reviews the positions of Birch-Hirshfeld, Tilley, and Sainéan on the problem of the work's authenticity. Finds all three approaches to use subjective or "surface" criteria. Suggests as a more valid criterion the degree to which the central theme of moderation pervading the first four books is also present in the fifth. Finds Book V to be "inconsistent with the concept of the mean and with what the characters represent in the earlier books," and thus to show no understanding "of an essential element in Rabelais' humanism." See *Dissertation Abstracts* 28 (1967):1453A.

## 1961

1   BÉNÉ, CHARLES A. "Erasme et le Chapitre VIII du premier *Pantagruel* (Novembre 1532)." *Pædagogica Historica: International Journal of the History of Education* 1:39–66.

That *Pantagruel* contained two chapters numbered 9 was believed to be due to the fact that 9 bis, "the First Encounter with Panurge," had been written at the last minute and inserted in the wrong place by the printer. Claims that it is chapt. 8, namely Gargantua's letter to Pantagruel, that was the last-minute change responsible for the error. Further suggests that chapt. 8 was inserted after the book had been set, which would explain not only the presence of two chapters bearing the same number 8, but also the fact that chapt. 7 and 9 (which presumably had to be shortened to accommodate chapt. 8) were suddenly lengthened, in the subsequent edition (1534), by exactly as many pages as make up chapt. 8. The hypothesis would also account for the difference in tone between Gargantua's letter and the rest of the book. Reviews the literature concerned with the sources of the letter. Believes the closest models are to be found in Erasmus' *Methodus* and *Ratio verae Theologiae*, especially in the version in which they figure in his *Ecclesiastes*. The latter was published only in 1535, but Rabelais may have known it in manuscript form as early as 1532 through Erasmus' secretary, who was in Lyons at the time.

2   DAY, HEM. *Erasme Hérétique et Libre Penseur. Rabelais et la Pensée Libre. Du Pantagruélisme au Subjectivisme.* Brussels and Paris: Editions Pensée & Action, 71 pp.

In "Rabelais et la Pensée Libre" (pp. 33–56), claims that from the very first words of the prologue to *Pantagruel*, Rabelais' work is imbued with an irreligious spirit. Shares Lefranc's belief in Rabelais' "foi rationaliste." Is convinced that Thélème, Gargantua's letter to his son, as well as countless other episodes reveal "ce Rabelais mécréant, ce Rabelais sacrilège, ce Rabelais hérétique, apostat, athée, impie, blasphémateur, cet apôtre de la liberté de conscience" (p. 49). In the last section (pp. 59–71), seeks to draw parallels between Rabelais' "pantagruélisme" and the subjectivism of Han Ryner, the author's spiritual father.

3   DE GRÈVE, MARCEL. *L'Interprétation de Rabelais au XVIe siècle.* Études Rabelaisiennes, no. 3. Geneva: Librairie Droz, 310 pp.

Intended as the first of a number of works studying the posthumous fate of Rabelais' work in the four centuries since its publication. Presents his study as different from that of such predecessors as Boulenger or Sainéan in that the latter had neglected the most essential point, namely "Rabelais lui-même et son œuvre tels qu'ils réapparaissent et se renouvellent à travers ses lecteurs, imitateurs et interprètes" (p. 9). Notes that the first attempts at interpreting Rabelais date from 1534, the very year in which *Gargantua* was published. Traces these attempts to discover the hidden meaning of the work, from Hugues Salel's *dizain* placed at the head of the 1534 edition of *Pantagruel* onwards. Interprets the silence immediately following the publication of *Gargantua* as proof that Rabelais' friends were aware of the dangerous nature of his ideas at the time of the king's hostile reaction to the Affaire des Placards: "En un temps où parler mène au bûcher, le silence est un aveu" (p. 33). Notes that Postel praises Rabelais' erudition in the dedicatory epistle of *De Originibus* in 1538 (when Rabelais is still considered as a physician and a scholar rather than a novelist), before attacking him in the most virulent terms in the *Alcorani Concordia* of 1543 as one of the "Cénévangélistes" who threaten his ideal of unity. Shows how after being considered a heretic by both sides in the religious quarrels of the day, Rabelais comes to be viewed at the time of his death as the inconsequential, drunken author of a work both Catholics and Calvinists find it convenient to dismiss as devoid of any ideo-logical significance. Considers the role of Ronsard's famous epitaph in the birth of that legend. But also notes that among the "new Erasmians" (Le Caron, Etienne Pasquier), Rabelais remains a humanist whose work is impor-tant above all for the "substantifique moelle" it contains. Shows that Rabelais also remains an important thinker among such precursors of the *libertins* as Pierre de l'Estoile and Marc de Papillon, as well as in Protestant countries. In the concluding chapter, insists that linguistic and other difficulties were an obstacle to the understanding of Rabelais' work even for his contemporaries. Notes the earliest attempts to "interpret," often allegorically, a difficult text. Appendices contain excerpts of contemporary texts referring to Rabelais.

4      ———. "Les variantes de *Pantagruel* et de *Gargantua* et l'évolution de la pensée rabelaisienne." In *Fin du Moyen Age et Renaissance: Mélanges de philologie française offerts à Robert Guiette*. Antwerp: De Nederlandsche Boekhandel, pp. 249–69.
Challenges the common belief that the changes made by Rabelais to his first two books in the 1542 edition—namely the suppression of irreverent allu-sions to the Church, the Sorbonne, and the Bible—were made in reaction to the Sorbonne's decision to condemn the books. Compares the variants in the different editions which Rabelais had had a chance to correct. Notes that many of the most daring allusions remain through the various editions right up to 1542. Admits that Rabelais had good reasons to fear the Sorbonne, and that he did fear it, as strongly suggested by his decision soon after the original publi-

1961

cation of *Gargantua* to leave Paris, and eventually France itself. But believes that the changes made in 1542 were due primarily to an evolution in Rabelais' own thought, more specifically to his loss of faith in the ability of the Church to reform itself without falling into the intolerant ways of a Calvin. So that if he tempers his criticism and his satire, it is because he has come to believe that the struggle no longer justifies the risks he had been willing to run when he still believed in the cause of evangelistic reform.

5   FRAUTSCHI, R[ICHARD] L. "Nicolas de Troyes and the Presumed Borrowings from *Pantagruel*." *Modern Language Quarterly* 22:345–50.
   Reexamines the question of the presumed debt of Nicolas de Troyes towards Rabelais, first suggested by Henri Clouzot and reiterated more recently by Marcel de Grève. Claims that the resemblances between *Le Grand Parangon des nouvelles nouvelles* and *Pantagruel* are either tenuous, or could be accounted for by a common tradition. Concludes that there is insufficient evidence to affirm that Nicolas de Troyes is directly obligated to Rabelais.

6   KRAILSHEIMER, A[LBAN] J. "The Significance of the Pan Legend in Rabelais' Thought." *Modern Language Review* 66, no. 1 (January):13–23.
   Stresses the importance of the Macreons episode in Book IV for a study of Rabelais' religious thought. Points out passages in Book III which bear a striking resemblance to this episode, most notably chapt. 31, with its reference to the Platonic idea that men nearing death are endowed with the gift of prophecy, and the allusion to the death of Guillaume du Bellay and to the exemplary death of Raminagrobis. Analyzes Rabelais' account of the death of Pan, studies its antecedents, notes that Rabelais must have known—from Postel, Marsus, or Bigot—that Pan had been identified with Christ, emphasizes the importance of Scholastic as well as classical and humanistic sources, and concludes that Rabelais' "treatment of the theme of immortality and of portents differs in no material respect from the teachings of his masters at Fontenay" (p. 23). See also 1963.17.

7   SAULNIER, V[ERDUN]-L[OUIS]. "Le formulaire rabelaisien." *Revue de la France-Ancienne*, no. spécial, pp. 73–79.
   Notes in Rabelais, alongside a tendency toward expansive development, an equally strong need to encapsulate his thought in a striking, aphoristic form. Finds in his work a significant number of *formules*, and comments on their diversity, their origins, and their possible intention: to amuse, but also to serve as an effective instrument of humanistic propaganda. Reprinted in 1983.33.

8   ———. "Les idées pédagogiques de Rabelais." *BAARD* 1, no. 10:279–81.
   Notes the negative, destructive aspect of much that Rabelais has to say about traditional pedagogy, as well as his constructive concept of education as

1962

an instrument in the humanistic struggle for enlightenment. Emphasizes the notions of freedom, experience, encyclopedic knowledge, and harmonious development of the whole individual. Underplays the traditional distinction made between Rabelais and Montaigne with respect to their conception of education, and shows that Rabelais' tutor does not merely fill his student's mind but sharpens it as well. Reprinted in 1983.33.

9  ZILLI, FREDERICK J. "A Critical Analysis of the Pedagogy of Rabelais and Montaigne with its Reflections on Curriculum Today." Ph.D. dissertation, University of Connecticut, 206 pp.
   Studies Rabelais as one of the two great theorists of education in the sixteenth century. Finds in the pedagogical ideas of Rabelais and Montaigne the same importance given to nature and freedom, and to the training of the body as well as the mind; also the same assumption that "life is fundamentally good and worth living." But notes that whereas Montaigne defines the goal of education as the formation of judgment and the teaching of ethics, Rabelais stresses the acquisition of knowledge, the development of the speculative rather than the practical faculties, and the importance of science. Believes that both thinkers have influenced modern education in matters of methodology as well as curriculum. See *Dissertation Abstracts International* 22 (1962):2672A.

## 1962

1  CAMPROUX, CHARLES. "Du Pantagruélisme: A propos de la *Coupe Testée.*" *Studi Francesi* 6, no. 16 (January–April):19–30.
   Seeks to show that the tenets of Pantagruelism—rejection of constraint, quest of joy, duty towards the state and towards others—are not in contradiction to the tenets of Christian ethics. Argues that the tone and style in chapt. 30 of *Pantagruel* are not those of an atheist but of a "bon pantagruéliste." Rejects the idea that the episode is a sacrilegious parody of the resurrection of Lazarus. "Et ce chapitre XXX du *Pantagruel*, loin de nier quoi que ce soit, est une affirmation de plus, enthousiaste, simple, franche du Pantagruélisme qui est école de civilisation parce qu'il se refuse à penser que la confiance en Dieu doive nier la confiance en l'homme" (p. 30).

2  DONTENVILLE, HENRI. "Le site de Thélème." *BAARD* 2, no. 1:19–20.
   Attempts to localize Thélème in the landscape of the Touraine. Believes the idea of calling the Abbey by the name Rabelais chose for it may have been triggered by the existence of the "île de Thelot," near the forest of Chinon.

85

1962

3   ESKIN, STANLEY G. "Physis and Antiphysie: The Idea of Nature in Rabelais and Calcagnini." *Comparative Literature* 14, no. 2 (Spring):167–73.

Examines a fable by the Italian humanist Celio Calcagnini, from which Rabelais borrowed the myth of Physis and Antiphysie as retold by Pantagruel upon seeing Quaresmeprenant (*Quart Livre*, chapt. 33). Mentions two other fables portraying Nature as a benevolent force and a standard of behavior justifying a hedonistic point of view and warning against the perverse tendency in man to distort natural life. Concludes by recalling the various forms of Antiphysie denounced by Rabelais elsewhere in his work, notably in the episodes dealing with the Ecolier Limousin, Maistre Janotus, and the inhabitants of the island of Ennasin.

4   FRANÇON, MARCEL. "Rabelais a-t-il participé à la rédaction des *Grandes et Inestimables Chroniques?*" *BAARD* 2, no. 1:24–26.

Nicolas Bourbon, in his *Nugae*, had seen in Rabelais the author of the chronicles (1532), and reproached him for having wasted his time in a manner unbecoming to a humanist. Believes this hypothesis to be quite plausible.

5   KELLER, ABRAHAM C. "The Books and Stories of Rabelais." *Romanic Review* 53:241–59.

Suggests a development, in Rabelais' narrative art, from that of a novelist to that of a story-teller. Noting that Rabelais "produces almost exactly four times as many stories and anecdotes in Books III and IV as he did in Books I and II" (p. 242), points out further that only one of the "stories" in the first two books was unrelated to the main plot, whereas the situation in the later books is precisely reversed. On the basis of the increasing number of stories, the increasingly painstaking manner of introducing the stories, and an examination of the anecdotes contained in the various books, concludes that "in his late period Rabelais had come to regard himself, more than before, as a teller of short tales" (p. 248), and that "in Books III and IV it is the stories and anecdotes, and not the long narrative, which are to be the principal source of our pleasure and the special object of his story-telling gifts" (pp. 258–59). Appears, in slightly different form, as chapt. 2 of 1963.15. See also 1963.14.

6   LANDER, JOHN LAMBERT. "The New Life and its Educational Correlates in France from Rabelais to Rousseau." Ph.D. dissertation, University of Pennsylvania, 269 pp.

Chapt. 1 studies, in part, Rabelais' role in the reaction against the medieval concept of education (as narrowly synonymous with instruction). See *Dissertation Abstracts International* 23 (1963):1265A.

7   MAYER, C. A., and DOUGLAS, C. M. "Rabelais poète." *BHR* 23: 42–46.

Among his contemporaries, Rabelais had the reputation of being a poet, which the versified parts of *Pantagruel* and *Gargantua* alone hardly seem to justify. Argue that a "Chant Royal de la fortune des biens mondains," an "Epitaphe de Marie fille aisnée de monsieur d'Estissac," and a "Dixain de l'ômage de Vénus armée," published together with Marot's *Adolescence Clémentine*, signed FR (or RF in the case of the third poem), and hitherto attributed without discussion to François Robertet, were in fact composed by Rabelais. Base their attribution on Rabelais' friendship with François Juste, who published the first Lyons edition of *Adolescence Clémentine*, and on his presence in the Estissac family, where he was preceptor to Louis d'Estissac, little Marie's father.

8    NARDI, ENZO. *Rabelais e il diritto romano.* Seminario giuridico della Università di Bologna, no. 34. Milan: Dott. A. Giuffré, 250 pp.
       Chapt. 7 offers a legal specialist's account of the *Tiers Livre* in the light of Rabelais' knowledge of Roman law. Reviews the external as well as the internal evidence of Rabelais' interest in Roman law: his correspondance with Budé, his dedication of the second volume of Manardi's *Epistolae Medicinales* to Tiraqueau, his edition of the *Testament of Cuspidius*, Pantagruel's studies of law at Bourges and other allusions to Roman law in Book I, as well as the circumstances of Gargantua's birth and the few references to the subject in Book V. Concludes that these "elementi romanistichi" can be found throughout Rabelais' work, with the exception of Book IV, and that they bear witness to a passion and semi professional competence in the matter, which constitute an important component of Rabelais' culture and personality. Includes a most useful "repertorio analitico e delle fonti."

9    SAULNIER, V[ERDUN]-[LOUIS]. "Ce que Rabelais dénonce." *BAARD* 2, no. 1:21–23.
       Excerpt from an unpublished paper read at Cambridge University in 1960. Underscores Rabelais' attacks on hypocrisy, especially in religious matters.

10   ———. "Histoire d'un conte rabelaisien: La nonne surprise et le devoir de silence (*Tiers Livre*, XIX)." *BHR* 24:545–58.
       Discusses the anecdote of "sœur Fessue," who failed to call for help when sexually assaulted, for fear of breaking the rule of silence in her dormitory, and who confessed herself there and then to her aggressor, so as to remain as short a time as possible in the state of sin. Questions whether the source of the anecdote is to be found in Erasmus' *Ichthyophagia*, as has been advanced. Notes that the anecdote can already be found in Georges d'Esclavonie's *Le Chasteau de Virginité* (1505), and can be traced in several farces, notably in *L'abbesse et ses sœurs* (in the La Vallière manuscript, which may predate the *Tiers Livre* and be the true source of Rabelais' passage). Finds it also in a group of Latin and French epigrams. "Parce que Rabelais a beaucoup lu Erasme, on n'a pas tout dit, pour avoir inscrit un texte d'Erasme

1962

dans la colonne de gauche, et un texte parallèle de Rabelais dans la colonne de droite" (p. 555). Suggests that in many cases both Erasmus and Rabelais may have found their source in the public domain. Finds that Rabelais' decision to end his anecdote with the reference to the confession shows his ability to adapt the narrative to a specific ideological end: in this case, the desire to ridicule religious formalism and its blind respect for religious rules at the expense of true morality.

11  SCHELER, LOUIS. "Une édition inconnue du *Quart Livre* (1552)." *BHR* 24:47–49.
    Notes the discovery of a hitherto unknown edition of Rabelais' Book IV, published by Jehan Chabin in Lyons and faithfully reproducing the Fézandat edition, but with a different layout.

12  SPITZER, LEO. *Linguistics and Literary History: Essays in Stylistics.* New York: Russell & Russell, 236 pp.
    In the introductory chapter on the unity of linguistics and literary history, briefly discusses Rabelais' word-formation as evidence of a tendency toward the creation of a world of irreality. Sees Rabelais' neologisms, his menacing "word-monsters," as creating an intermediate zone midway between reality and irreality, "between the nowhere that frightens and the 'here' that reassures" (p. 17). Points out that Rabelais' word-families have reality only in the world of language.

13  TETEL, MARCEL. "La Valeur comique des accumulations verbales chez Rabelais." *Romanic Review* 53:96–104.
    "Lorsque Rabelais nous a invités à extraire la 'substantifique mouelle' de son ouvrage, il a certainement dû vouloir faire allusion à ses édifices verbaux" (p. 104). Invites the reader to examine Rabelais' verbal accumulations (enumerations, litanies, lists, catalogues) as manifestations of the author's verve, consciously organized into intricate structural patterns of sound and, to a lesser degree, of meaning.

14  ———. "Le comique de Rabelais." Ph.D. dissertation, University of Wisconsin, Madison, 306 pp.
    Argues that Rabelais' works are "essentially comic in spirit and in tone," characterizes each novel in terms of the different forms of the comic to be found therein, suggests that the choice of imagery and language—rather than satire and parody—are "the essential components of his mastery of the comic," and proceeds to study these two components of the Rabelaisian text. See *Dissertation Abstracts* 22 (1962):4020A. Revised for publication: 1964.19.

**1963**

1 BOSSUAT, ROBERT. "Un précurseur de l'écolier limousin au XVe siècle."
*Le Moyen Age* 69:883–92.

Notes that Rabelais' chapter on the *écolier limousin* reproduces almost
to the letter a passage from Geoffroy Tory's *Champ fleury*. Traces the infiltration of Latin vocabulary with French endings to the twelfth century. Attracts
attention to a certain *Littera Philippi*, preserved in a manuscript of the
Bibliothèque Nationale, dating perhaps from the middle of the fifteenth century, and similar to the speech of Rabelais' *écolier* in that it implicitly condemns
the excessive use of latinisms by underscoring their absurdity.

2 CIORANESCU, ALEXANDRE. "Rabelais et les îles Canaries." *BHR*
25:88–96.

Notes the various instances when Rabelais refers to the Canary Islands
and their inhabitants, indicates the context and meaning of these references,
and examines them more thoroughly than has been done before. Points out
that Rabelais, unlike many a humanist, had a clear knowledge of the islands'
geographic location ("entre Madère et le Cap Blanc"). Rejects as futile and
unfounded the numerous attempts to identify "Marotus du Lac," the imaginary author of a history of the Kings of Canarre. Argues that the intention
behind Rabelais' longest reference to the inhabitants of the islands as worthy
of the magnanimity of Grandgousier toward them (*Gargantua*, chapt. 50), the
*primum movens* of the episode, is to express his belief in the fundamental
nobility of these "savages": "la satire l'ayant porté naturellement vers l'éloge
de l'âge d'or de l'humanité, n'était-il pas aussi naturel de voir dans les
sauvages récemment découverts, les derniers représentants de ce même âge
d'or?" (p. 96).

3 DERRETT, J. DUNCAN M. "Rabelais's Legal Learning and the Trial of
Bridoye." *BHR* 25:111–171.

Assumes that Rabelais meant his more diligent readers to look up every
reference in his text, lest they be content with the surface meaning of the
work. Believes that no one has done the job adequately in the case of chapt. 39
to 42 of the *Tiers Livre*. Attempts the task of "reconstructing all that was in
Rabelais' mind, all that he intended the more industrious of his readers to
think about" when reading these chapters. Proposes to show that Plattard was
wrong in his notes to the Bridoye episode, and proceeds to verify each of the
119 references to civil and canon law in Bridoye's self-defense, indicating
their meaning, their relevance to Bridoye's situation, and the category of
humor to which they belong. Believes that the references reveal, behind the
surface humor of the text, "a very sad man, a worried man, whose satire of the
complacent and soon-to-be-overthrown elements of contemporary Europe
does not hide his fear that nothing better will take their place" (p. 116). Notes

that on the Bartoli-Alciati issue, Rabelais was squarely on the side of Alciati and all those who wished to return to the original texts of Roman law as the basis of a new legal system. But argues that Rabelais did not realize that by attacking the methods of the Bartolists "he might help to undermine the authority of the universal Western legal system itself" (p. 125).

4   DONTENVILLE, HENRI. "Rabelais au quartier Saint-Paul." *BAARD* 2, no. 2:21–24.

Evokes the district where Rabelais is supposed to have spent the last days of his life. Suggests that the *épitaphier* of the Church of Saint Paul is on shaky ground when it states that Rabelais died at the age of seventy, since the date of Rabelais' birth is not known.

5   EHRMANN, JACQUES. "La Temporalité dans l'œuvre de Rabelais." *French Review* 36, no. 2:188–99.

Although exceptional by their size and supernatural by their origin, the Rabelaisian giants live in a time and space which they share with characters on the human scale. Their extraordinary exploits are achieved by essentially human, and thus limited, means. Their immortality is merely "seminal." They do not transcend time and its debilitating effects upon man, but Rabelais dwells on the positive aspects of this subjection: on the fact that it is only through time that man develops his potential and becomes master of the future. Time is viewed by Rabelais as an agent of becoming rather than an agent of death; the consciousness of one's temporality is thus a source of joy rather than anguish. But neither past nor future are as important as the present: "les personnages de Rabelais sont principalement marqués par l'action présente" (p. 193). Not being shaped by a personal past, the characters—with the exception of Gargantua—are not individualized: their adventure is that of the Renaissance itself, and that of their author. Their fragmentation is emphasized by the structure of the novel, made up of a series of chapters each of which tells a new experience, a new adventure. This discontinuity—both vertical and horizontal, experienced on the level of the individual's relation to his past as well on the level of his relationship with others—accounts for the lack of continuity of individual experience, and for the lack of simultaneity of action. Notes an opposition between time as an idea (conceived by the author), and time as reality (experienced by the characters). As a theoretical element of Rabelais' philosophy, time is a marvellous continuum which enables the individual to evolve and progress; as a practical element of Rabelais' narrative technique, it is time experienced in everyday life: "un temps où l'action se confond avec la vie et est égale à elle" (p. 198).

6   FOULET, ALFRED. "Les Adventures des gens curieux." *Romanic Review* 54:3–5.

1963

Upon meeting Panurge for the first time, in chapt. 9 of Book I, Pantagruel accounts for Panurge's sorry appearance by the misadventures which inevitably befall "les gens curieux." For historical, as well as logical and contextual reasons, suggests that *curieux* is a misprint for *curiaux*, meaning courtiers, and that what Pantagruel had in mind were the proverbial misfortunes of courtiers and not of the *curieux* in the modern sense of "désireux de voir et de savoir," a meaning the word had not yet acquired in Rabelais' day.

7   FRANÇON, MARCEL. "Pour le commentaire du *Cinquiesme Livre*." *Romance Notes* 5, no. 1 (Autumn):187–91.
    Comments on various allusions in chapt. 20, and on the rhinoceros mentioned in chapt. 29.

8   ———. "Le 'Prestre Jehan.'" *BAARD* 2, no. 2:27–28.
    At the end of *Pantagruel*, Rabelais promises to recount in a subsequent volume how his hero married the daughter of the "roy de Inde, dit Prestre Jehan." Attracts attention to recent scholarly work on this twelfth-century personage.

9   ———. "Note sur le prologue du *Tiers Livre*." *BAARD* 2, no. 2:29–30.
    Believes that the prologue alludes to the invasion of the province of Champagne by Charles V in 1544.

10  GRAY, FLOYD. "Structure and Meaning in the Prologue to the *Tiers Livre*." *Esprit Créateur* 3, no. 2 (Summer):57–62.
    Argues that the scope and significance of the prologue are best revealed when it is considered "as an artistic creation rather than the transposition of reality for propaganda purposes" (p. 57). The significance of the anecdote concerning Diogenes is neither military (Lefranc) nor religious (Saulnier) but literary (as it already is in Lucian and Budé). The prologue is above all a defense of Rabelais' own style and inspiration, "a defense of creative writing at a time when it was considered frivolous, fit only for popular or court circles" (p. 60). It is also a defense of the peculiarly circular structure of the *Tiers Livre*, without equivalent in the reader's experience, as well as a "défense et illustration" of literature as an ambiguous verbal creation.

11  GRIFFIN, ROBERT. "Rabelais' *humanisme dévot*." *Esprit Créateur* 3, no. 2 (Summer):75–79.
    Argues that Rabelais' belief in man's free will and his ability to perfect his faculties is not irreconcilable with his equally strong belief in an "overriding moral order which is God's will" (p. 75), and to which human freedom is implicitly subordinated. Whereas other humanists tended to see "an apparent contradiction in the opposition of faith and reason" (p. 77), Rabelais sees here

1963

again "a naturally proportioned cooperation rather than an antagonism" (p. 77). If Rabelais grew increasingly hostile, after 1535, towards Catholics and Protestants alike, it was not from an intolerant attitude towards religion itself, but because both forms of organized religion had become less tolerant of man. His attacks on dogma are carried out not in the name of atheism but in that of a "purified and enlightened Christianity" (p. 77), and if he is wary of metaphysical speculation, it is because he has come to see it as useless and arrogant, and because for him, as later for Pascal, "faith is not a truth but a state of mind" (p. 77). Unlike many of his contemporaries, Rabelais strikes a comfortable balance between his humanism and his religious faith.

12  GRUBER, VIVIAN M[ERCER]. "Rabelais: The Didactics of Moderation." *Esprit Créateur* 3, no. 2 (Summer):80–86.

Rabelais' work is a denunciation of all forms of human excess. But he cannot be dismissed as a mere rebel or caricaturist: "These roles enabled him to achieve his deeper purpose of destroying the blindness of his time in order to construct a new order in a renascent society based on the universal truths of the ages" (p. 86).

13  KAISER, WALTER [JACOB]. *Praisers of Folly: Erasmus, Rabelais, Shakespeare.* Cambridge: Harvard University Press, pp. 101–92.

Contains an eight-part discussion of the *Tiers Livre* centered on the character of Panurge. Considers it a perfect Erasmian blend of the playful and the serious, allowing Rabelais to express his subversive ideas without risking the accusation of sedition and heresy. Argues that the message contained in the prologue is so successfully concealed "that no one has yet seen it for what it is" (p. 109). Reads the story of Diogenes as Rabelais' autobiography, and sees in the portrait of the Cynic philosopher a portrait of the artist himself. Reads Rabelais' prologue as "an eloquent and moving defense of his role as author" (p. 112), which is to observe and to tell the truth. Reads it also, in the ironic mode, as a definition of Rabelais' political role: not that of a royal propagandist, as Lefranc had claimed, but of an out and out pacifist. Believes that the prologue also hints at Rabelais' religious position of freedom of choice in the Utraquist controversy concerning the Eucharist. Takes the subject of the book to be truth rather than marriage: "Panurge the fool is not taking a wife; he is seeking an answer" (p. 125). In the episode of Panurge in Salmiguondin, stresses the contrast between Panurge's folly (his uncertainties and worry) and Pantagruel's wisdom (his calm optimism, his acceptance of the inevitable, his Pantagruelism). In the series of consultations, dwells on the encounter with Her Trippa; accepts Lefranc's identification of the character with Cornelius Agrippa, but finds his *De nobilitate et praecellentia foeminei sexus* less relevant than the famous *De incertitudine et vanitate scientiarum et artium*; in fact sees Rabelais' work, from the symposium onward, as a fictional adaptation of that philosophical text. Reads the symposium at the heart of the book as bringing out the opposition between reason (the physician Rondibilis) and faith (the theologian Hippothadée), an opposition which human wisdom (the philosopher Trouillogan) cannot reconcile. Notes that it ends in Pyrrhonism, transcended by Bridoye who represents the knowledge of one's folly: "In that knowledge there is wisdom; in that wisdom there is salvation" (p. 174). Sees Bridoye as the fool in Christ that Panurge, in the stubborn pride of his learning, his rhetoric and sophistry, his *philautia*, is incapable of becoming. Alludes to Le Caron's dialogue entitled "Valton, de la tranquillité d'esprit, Ou du souverain bien," in which Rabelais is a participant. Argues that what Rabelais is made to say is an accurate representation of his thought. Finds his apology of pleasure (*volupté*) to be essentially Epicurean (despite Rabelais' disclaimer), and concludes that what Rabelais says in the dialogue, especially his concluding remarks on the vanity of learning rejected in favor of the order of nature, represents the message of the *Tiers Livre* as embodied in the Pantagruélion. In connection with the indestructibility of the plant, avoids the traditional comparison with Pliny in favor of Erasmus' *Epicureus*, and reads in it a daring warning that the fire of intolerance, if unchecked, will destroy even the salamander, that is the king himself and the kingdom of France. Attracts attention in a footnote (pp. 169–70) to a "serious textual confusion" concerning the story of Dolabella and its commentary in the 1552 edition, and suggests a return to the original text of 1546, where the anecdote belongs in the mouth of Epistémon and not Pantagruel, and where it is Pantagruel, and not Epistémon, who explains Bridoye as a Christian fool.

14  KELLER, ABRAHAM C. "Pace and Timing in Rabelais' Stories." *Studies in the Renaissance* 10:108–25.

Conjectures that Rabelais "might well have preferred to be regarded above all as a teller of tales" (p. 109). Sees in their "studied spontaneity" their chief characteristic. Studies the structure of the story of Couillatris in the prologue to the *Quart Livre* and the tale of Dindenault, notes the "interludes" that break the story line, and suggests that Rabelais' handling of pace is primarily that of a teller of oral tales. Argues that Rabelais stages the Dindenault episode as a show for a live audience. Notes that "time-killing," through interruption or prolongation, is a device used by Rabelais in both episodes to make of what is basically a very short tale a substantial story, but that he is equally capable of bringing his tale to a swift conclusion, or to tell a whole story rapidly and directly. Concedes nevertheless that not all tales are equally successful, and detects in some of the best known episodes in *Pantagruel*, for example, marks of strain. Believes that Rabelais reached mastery of the art of storytelling only in Book IV. Reprinted in 1973.2. See also 1963.15.

1963

15 ———. *The Telling of Tales in Rabelais: Aspects of His Narrative Art.*
Analecta Romanica: Beihefte zu den Romanischen Forschungen, no. 12.
Frankfurt: Vittorio Klosterman, 81 pp.

Explores, in four chapters, Rabelais' skill as a narrative artist. Believes
it to be the aspect of his art which most clearly shows an evolution, as
Rabelais becomes more and more a story-teller and less and less a novelist, a
moralist, a philosopher. Chapt. 1 ("Pace and Timing in the Stories") studies
the pace of narrative and the structure of two episodes—those of Couillatris
and of Dindenault—as the most successful examples of Rabelais' "oral manner." Chapt. 2 ("Of Books and Stories") analyzes the relationship between the
stories and the whole narrative of which they are a part. Notes that the stories
and anecdotes are almost four times as numerous in Books III and IV as in the
first two books, that they grow more and more independent of the over-all
plot, and that they tend more and more to be staged. Chapt. 3 ("The Imaginary
World of Alcofrybas Nasier") discusses Rabelais' world, identified largely
with that of Panurge, as a unifying element in the novels. Chapt. 4 ("Art and
Exhortation") shows that in the stories which are not merely entertaining, the
narrative artist and the humanist are often at odds. But concludes that this
imperfect integration of art and exhortation grows less pronounced as
Rabelais allows himself more and more "the freedom of telling stories primarily for his and his readers' pleasure" (p. 81). Chapt. 1 first appeared, in
slightly different form, in 1963.14; chapt. 2 in 1962.5.

16 KLINE, MICHAEL B. *Rabelais and the Age of Printing*. THR, no. 60. Études
Rabelaisiennes, no. 4. Geneva: Librairie Droz, 59 pp.

Views Rabelais' career and his works in the light of the changes in the
intellectual climate brought about by the advent of printing. Notes the new
importance of such problems as censorship and plagiarism. Discusses
Rabelais' relationship with his printers. In the case of Gryphius, Juste, and
Wechel, notes his efforts to associate himself with men who could best further
his literary reputation and who shared his humanistic values. Finds Rabelais'
choice of Michel Fezandat and Balthazar Aleman somewhat more puzzling;
nor can he quite explain Robert Estienne's violent attack on Rabelais, since
both were defending essentially the same cause. Sees Étienne Dolet's publication of *Pantagruel* and *Gargantua* in 1542 as motivated by ideological
rather than monetary considerations, and explains Rabelais' reaction to his
friend's betrayal by a desire to protect his literary reputation and try to discourage the publication of pirated editions of his work. Stylistically, comments on the changes in tone brought about by the existence of a reading
public, and argues that the possibility of numerous rereadings of the printed
page allowed Rabelais to endow his language with a greater capacity to conceal meaning and disguise more effectively the satirical dimension of his text.

1963

17 KRAILSHEIMER, A[LBAN] J. *Rabelais and the Franciscans*. Oxford: The Clarendon Press, 334 pp.

In the wake of Gilson's famous essay on "Rabelais Franciscain," offers a full-scale study of Rabelais' *années de moinage* as an Observant friar in the Franciscan order. In part 1, seeks to characterize the kind of training Rabelais must have received at Fontenay-le-Comte as a Franciscan novice and friar. By comparing Rabelais' linguistic audacities in religious matters with the clerical norms prevailing among Franciscan preachers of his day, argues that what may strike us as irreverent or even sacrilegious need not lead us to doubt the sincerity of his vocation. Making extensive use of printed Franciscan sermons, shows how their imagery, narrative technique, vocabulary, satire of clergy and laity alike, and their power of invective prepared Rabelais for his literary career as a popular writer. In part 2, studies the intellectual infrastructure of Rabelais' world-picture, his epistemology and the main tenets of his philosophy, his ethics and his political thought, as expressed in theoretical terms and embodied in his characters. Assesses Rabelais' debt to his classical and biblical sources in part 3, and argues in part 4 for a strong influence of Franciscan doctrines, most particularly the Platonism of Bonaventura, the voluntarism of Duns Scotus, and "the peculiarly Franciscan tradition of *caritas*" (p. 312). Finds this influence on Rabelais' habits of mind and speech even in the later books, long after the "bedrock of Scholasticism" had been repudiated.

18 POMEAU, RENÉ. "Rabelais et le folklore." *Studi Francesi* 7, no. 20 (May–August):218–25.

Lefranc, relying on information provided by Sébillot, believed that the legendary charactersistics of Gargantua were limited to the vastness of his size and his appctitc. Henri Dontenville, in his *Mythologie française* (1948), showed that the Gargantua of legend and folklore was a far richer and more complex character, assimilated to solar divinities, waterways, stones, and mountains. Rabelais may have borrowed many of the legendary characteristics with which he endows Pantagruel (and to a lesser extent Gargantua himself) from the anonymous authors of the *Grandes Chronicques* or the *Gargantua translaté*. But in the case of such folkloric reminiscences— unknown to these authors—as the giants' association with a number of megaliths and the numerous urinal downpours unleashed by Rabelais' giants upon their hapless victims, Rabelais' information must have come from local legends. Concludes by suggesting that Rabelais' choice of a pagan hero as his spokesman (albeit "transmué en évangéliste") may have been dictated, at least in part, by the opposition of ecclesiastical authorities to the legendary giants from the very time of their birth.

19 ROSS, D. J. A. "'Je lui livre chanse...'" *BHR* 25:172–73.

Notes that the actual method used by Bridoye in throwing his dice when deciding for the plaintiff or the defendant has gone without comment, presumably because the meaning of the expression "Je lui livre chanse" was never understood. Believes that it should be sought in the medieval rules of the game of hazard, briefly summarized on page 173.

20  SAULNIER, V[ERDUN]-L[OUIS]. "Aspects et motifs de la pensée rabelaisienne." In *Studi in onore di Carlo Pellegrini*. Biblioteca di Studi Francesi, no. 2. Turin: Società Editrice Internazionale, pp. 119–31.

Distinguishes three stages in the cycle formed by Rabelais' five books: the humanistico-evangelical phase of the first two books, embodied in Gargantua's wisdom; a second phase, represented by the *Tiers Livre*, in which Rabelais questions the belief that in deciding upon the course of our lives we can be guided by others; and a third phase in which that belief is rejected in favor of a personal quest undertaken in Books IV and V. Yet argues that throughout the three stages one can see the recurrence of certain principles dictating behavior: charity towards those who need it, courage in the defense of truth against hypocrisy, formalism and sophistry; also, from the very start, the consciousness that fortune is fickle, and consequently that wisdom dictates detachment from all that is fortuitous and thus beyond our control. Argues that in its principles, if not in matters of strategy, Rabelais' thought remains essentially true to itself. When, between 1534 and 1546, it becomes dangerous for him and for the other Evangelicals to express themselves overtly, Rabelais merely becomes more prudent, less militant in the expression of his beliefs, perhaps under the influence of Guillaume du Bellay. "De là le passage de Rabelais, d'un évangélisme, d'un érasmisme prédicant des jours d'espoir à un hésuchisme, à un érasmisme prudent ou secret" (p. 30). Reprinted in 1973.2.

21  ———. "Mythologies pantagrueliques. L'utopie en France: Morus et Rabelais." In *Les Utopies à la Renaissance: Colloque International (avril 1961), Université libre de Bruxelles*. Travaux de l'Institut pour l'étude de la Renaissance et de l'Humanisme, no. 1. Brussels: Presses Universitaires; Paris: Presses Universitaires de France, pp. 135–62.

Seeks to define *utopia*, lists some of its variants, notes its positive as well as its negative aspects, points out its connection with the humanistic tendencies of the Renaissance, and with myth. Argues that Rabelais' is a fundamentally *mythic* form of thought, with its characteristic superpositions of meaning. Notes that More's influence on Rabelais is rather minimal. Does not believe that Rabelais had him in mind when he created the character of Thaumaste. Finds Rabelais to be closer to Erasmus on the subject of war and tolerance. Concludes with remarks on the utopian dimension of Thélème.

22  SCREECH, M[ICHAEL] A[NDREW]. "Girolamo Cardano's *De Sapientia* and the *Tiers Livre de Pantagruel*." *BHR* 25:97–110.

Suggests that the ideas for the chapters on Her Trippa and the Virgilian Lots, as well as for the first part of the chapter on dice, were derived from the fourth book of Cardano's *De Sapientia*. Quotes at length, side by side, from Cardano's text and from the *Tiers Livre*, and notes that nearly all methods of divination mentioned by Her Trippa in the first version of the episode are to be found in Cardano. Rejects as totally without foundation Plattard's claim that they can also be found in Agrippa's *De Occulta Philosophia*. As for Pictorius, another traditionally accepted source, points out that his text had not yet been written at the time Rabelais published his *Tiers Livre*. Although some problems remain unclear, and Rabelais' attitude towards decisions made by dice is very different from Cardano's scepticism towards prophecy, believes that Cardano's *Sapientia* must be considered as the main—if not the sole—source of Rabelais' erudition in these matters. Concludes by indicating briefly how the "dry, pedantic and uninspiring" material in both Agrippa and Cardano was transformed by Rabelais into a successful comic text.

23  STAROBINSKI, JEAN. "Note sur Rabelais et le langage." *Tel Quel* 15 (Fall):79–81.

Comments on Rabelais' need to mobilize all the resources of existing language, and to create a synthetic language of his own. Sees in him an epic poet who uses language not only as a narrative tool but also as an ambiguous object of investigation. Notes how often an absurd episode in the novels is "rectified" in the one that follows. Sees in this "mouvement obstiné de la rectification" (p. 80) the secret structure of the work, as well as a sign of Rabelais' fundamental optimism.

24  TETEL, MARCEL. "Aspects du comique dans les images de Rabelais." *Esprit Créateur* 3, no. 2 (Summer):51–56.

Rather than grouping Rabelais' images into categories, prefers to study them in relation to the various aspects of reality from which they are derived. Generalizes about the nature and comic effects of Rabelais' metaphors and comparisons: their vigor, their concreteness, their conscious inappropriateness. "La forme plutôt que le fond représente le processus créateur de l'auteur et la valeur de l'image" (p. 51).

25  ———. "Rabelais and Folengo." *Comparative Literature* 15, no. 4 (Fall):357–64.

Notes that previous critics had identified similarities between Rabelais and Folengo in the episodes of the sheep and the storm at sea in Book IV, and commented on the resemblance between Panurge and Cingar, one of the characters in Folengo's *Baldus*. Stresses the literary transformation which the borrowings undergo in Rabelais' works, and argues that the most significant similarity between the two authors is their verbal exuberance. "Future Folengo-Rabelaisian studies should follow the path of stylistic analogies" (p. 361).

1964

26 WILLIAMS, EDWARD B. "The Observations of Épistémon and Condign Punishment." *Esprit Créateur* 3, no. 2 (Summer):63–67.

Viewed as a whole, Épistémon's report on his experience in the Other World is not an expression of religious skepticism (Lefranc) or Erasmian thought (Febvre). Like the Lazarus story told in the Gospel of St. Luke, it expresses a conception of divine judgement as "a system of retributive justice," a compensation for the injustices suffered in life on earth.

27 ZELDIN, JESSE. "The Abbey and the Bottle." *Esprit Créateur* 3, no. 2 (Summer):68–74.

In search of unity in Rabelais' group of novels, argues that the Oracle episode in Book V is Rabelaisian in spirit, and consonant with Rabelais' thought in the earlier parts of his work, "although much of Book V may not in fact have been written by Rabelais himself" (p. 74). In its emphasis on the responsible exercise of the will, finds the episode to be consistent with the characters of Pantagruel and of his father, as well as with the principle upon which the Abbey of Thélème was founded.

## 1964

1 ARVEILLER, R. "La *Briefve declaration*: Est-elle de Rabelais?" *Études Rabelaisiennes* 5:9–10.

Short note comparing the definitions of two terms in the *Briefve Declaration* with the usage of the same terms in Rabelais' work. Finds grounds to question Rabelais' authorship: "il est fort douteux que la *Briefve Declaration* soit de Rabelais, ou du seul Rabelais" (p. 10).

2 AUERBACH, ERIC. "Die Welt in Pantagruels Mund." In *Mimesis: Dargestellte Wirklichkeit in der abendländischen Literatur.* 3. Aufl. Bern and Munich: A. Francke, pp. 250–70.

Reprint of original German version of article, first published in 1946. See 1950.1.

3 BÉNÉ, CHARLES. "Contribution à l'histoire du texte du *Pantagruel*: L'édition lyonnaise de 1533." *Études Rabelaisiennes* 5:11–18.

Attracts attention to the second edition of *Pantagruel*, published by Juste in 1533, of which the only surviving copy is to be found in Dresden. Points out that the edition had been disregarded because of the numerous textual errors it contained. But argues that it is nevertheless of great interest for its numerous variants, many of which were maintained by Rabelais in the subsequent editions, either because they represented stylistic improvements, were less archaic and pedantic, or because of their stronger aggressiveness against the pope, the monks, and the Sorbonne theologians. Finds it to be valuable also for its surer handling of comic devices.

4  BERTALOT, ENRICO U. "Rabelais et la Bible d'après les quatre premiers livres." *Études Rabelaisiennes* 5:19–40.

Rapid study of biblical allusions in Rabelais. Notes Rabelais' attraction to Saint Paul, but also his deliberate effort to ignore the side of the apostle that is incompatible with his own "pantagruélisme." Touches briefly on "Rabelais et la Réforme," to conclude that "Rabelais se tient à un carrefour où se rencontrent les avenues du catholicisme, du protestantisme et de l'incrédulité" (p. 25). The last fifteen pages contain remarks on J. Boulenger's Pléiade edition of 1955, and several "tableaux synoptiques et chronologiques" of biblical quotations and allusions.

5  BUTOR, MICHEL. *Répertoire II*. Paris: Editions de Minuit, 301 pp.

In a short chapter on Rabelais (pp. 135–38), and incidentally throughout "Le livre comme objet" (pp. 104–23), comments on the structural aspects of Rabelais' enumerations and the linguistic difficulties of what is paradoxically at one and the same time a popular and a learned work. "Le contraire de la littérature populaire, ce n'est pas la littérature savante, mais la littérature de salon" (p. 135).

6  DE GRÈVE, MARCEL. "Les Érudits du XVIIe siècle en quête de la clef de Rabelais." *Études Rabelaisiennes* 5:41–63.

Acknowledges Rabelais' vogue among the *libertins* and the *précieux* early in the century, and notes that as time goes by, the interest in Rabelais diminishes in the "milieux mondains," whereas it actually increases among the disciples of such *libertins* as Théophile de Viau and Gassendi. Insists in particular upon the historical commentary appended by Le Motteux to Thomas Urquhart's translation of Rabelais' work, in which Rabelais is seen as a Protestant witness of the religious and political events of his day, and his novel is presented as a *roman à clef*, with an historical figure behind every literary character. Also mentions the attempts made by Le Duchat, Jean Bernier, the abbé de Marcy, and Johanneau to extract the "substantifique mouelle" from Rabelais' work by seeking historical allusions behind every allegory, character, or event. Underscores the socio-political bent of Bernier's commentary, and notes that it represents "la dernière tentative de faire accepter le joyeux moine par les âmes bien-pensantes" (p. 58). After that, Rabelais becomes the banner of the "esprits forts," the intellectual ancestors of Voltaire and of the *Encyclopédistes*: of all those who will have paved the way for the advent of the French Revolution.

1964

7 ———. "Limites de l'influence linguistique de Rabelais en Angleterre au XVIe siècle." *Comparative Literature Studies* 1:15–30.

Reiterates his conviction that Rabelais' literary influence in sixteenth-century England has been vastly exaggerated, and suggests that his linguistic influence was equally negligible. Questions the so-called Rabelaisian origin of a number of expressions in Claude de Sainliens' *Dictionarie French and English*, and similarly disputes the contention that certain terms found in the works of Thomas Nashe are of a "typically Rabelaisian" character. Acknowledges that Ben Jonson had indeed read Rabelais and been influenced by him, but doubts that the expression "lick figs," used in *The Alchemist* and thought to be at the source of "to give (a person) the fig," is an allusion to the anecdote concerning Emperor Barbarossa and the citizens of Milan, as recounted by Rabelais in the *Quart Livre* (chapt. 45). Notes that Jonson could have found the anecdote in Albert Krantz's *Saxonia* (1520), or in Guillaume Paradin's *De Antiquo Burgundiae Statu* (1542). "Aucune raison valable ne permet d'attribuer à Maître François cet enrichissement du lexique anglais" (p. 27). Nor is there any reason to believe that Rabelais had any linguistic influence whatsoever in England during the second half of the sixteenth century.

8 DONTENVILLE, HENRI. "Le mot 'farfelu' de François Rabelais à André Malraux." *BAARD* 2, no. 3:83–86.

Points out that the word first occurs in Rabelais, that it is used on four occasions, and that its recent vogue has been launched by André Malraux, who admits to having found it in Rabelais.

9 ESKIN, STANLEY G. "Mythic Unity in Rabelais." *PMLA* 79:548–53.

Finds the essential seriousness of Rabelais' work in its mythic dimension. Concedes that the "chivalric myth" which structures the narrative of the first two books is treated mostly in the burlesque mode, but contends that it leads to the discovery of values in which the author strongly believes. The myth reappears in the equally chivalric quest for truth in the last three books, this time as a "comic modulation on the Holy Grail pattern" (p. 549). Other myths are related to characterization, description, and theme, rather than to plot. The myth of giganticism is an expression of Rabelais' belief in the innocence of childhood. The myth of Thélème is seen as an attempt to preserve that innocence in maturity, by listening to the voice of instinct. The double myth of Physis and Antiphysia reiterates Rabelais' belief in the goodness of nature "at a farther remove," in a story within a story. In the Dive Bouteille episode, myth is reintegrated into the quest, as yet another expression of man's harmony with nature. All these myths are thus intimately related to each other as variants of Rabelais' philosophy of nature, and as such they endow the work with its most significant principle of unity.

1964

10  FRANÇON, MARCEL. "Mentions du rhinocéros par Rabelais." *Le Lingue Straniere* 13 no. 2:222–27.

Lists all the references to the rhinoceros in Rabelais, recalls the arrival of such an animal in Lisbon in 1515, and the subsequent staging of a fight between it and an elephant (recounted by Damiao de Goìs). Reminds us that Dürer had made a drawing of a rhinoceros in that very year, with an inscription that Rabelais seems to have read, since he reproduced part of it in his allusion to a rhinoceros in Book V.

11  ———. "Rabelais et la langue 'chaldaïque.'" *BAARD* 2, no. 3:88–90.

Claims that by "chaldaïque" Rabelais means Aramaic and not Syriac. In the immediately following note (p. 92), believes that at the end of *Pantagruel*, where Rabelais promises to give an account of his hero's journey by "mer Athlanticque," he means in fact the Red Sea, and that Pantagruel's is a journey to the Near East. In "Rabelais et Anatole France" (p. 93), notes with some surprise Anatole France's predilection for the *Tiers Livre*, and in "Verlaine, Rabelais et le XVIe siècle"(p. 94–95), remarks on Verlaine's interest in Rabelais.

12  ———. "Rabelais et le folklore." *Bulletin folklorique d'Ile-de-France* 24 (Winter 1963–64):744–45.

In connection with an article by René Pomeau (see 1963.18), comments on the relationship between "Monte Gargano" and "le mont des Pouilles," believed by Pomeau to have been the first abode of Gargantua and his parents.

13  ———. "Two notes on *Gargantua* and *Pantagruel*." *Modern Language Review* 59, no. 3 (July):371–74.

Reflects on the meaning of *Chaldaicque* in Gargantua's letter to Pantagruel ("it corresponds to Aramaic and/or Syriac"), and suggests that in his description of a rhinoceros in the *Cinquiesme Livre* Rabelais may have been influenced by the caption on Dürer's famous woodcut. Both can be traced to Pliny. See also 1964.10.

14  LONIGAN, PAUL R. "Cicero *De oratore*—Rabelais *De homine*." *Studi Francesi* 8, no. 23 (May–August):272–80.

Seeks to show "just how Maître François has taken the skeleton of Ciceronian stress upon knowledge and excellence for their own sake and built upon it the flesh and blood of Man searching for self and for truth" (p. 274). Believes that attaining the perfection of an ideal orator was for Cicero an end in itself, whereas in Rabelais education prepares the giants to assume their place as responsible leaders of men and obedient servants of God.

1964

15 MARICHAL, ROBERT. *"Quart Livre*: Commentaires." *Études Rabelaisiennes* 5:65–162.

An addition to the notes published in 1956.9. Offers linguistic and historical commentaries—some very brief, others much more elaborate—on Rabelais' vocabulary in Book IV. Occasionally draws out the ideological implications of his lexicological study. The expression "Dieu en terre" in the Papimanes episode, for example, gives rise to what amounts to a long article (pages 100–133) on Rabelais' religion and the relationship between the episode and contemporary reality. Comments, among other things, on the lack of zeal on the part of the Sorbonne and the Parlement to attack the *Quart Livre*. Explains the decision to censor the book but not to condemn it outright by the fact that despite its religous satire it did militate in favor of royal authority.

16 SAULNIER, V[ERDUN]-L[OUIS]. "Rabelais entre Bigot et Baduel: Sur la correspondance d'Antoine Arlier." *Études Rabelaisiennes* 5:163–73.

Of minimal relevance to Rabelais scholarship. Seeks to attract attention to Arlier's as yet unpublished correspondance, on the grounds that Arlier "valut surtout par ses relations," Rabelais among them.

17 SCREECH, M[ICHAEL] A[NDREW]. "The Legal Comedy of Rabelais in the Trial of Bridoye in the *Tiers Livre de Pantagruel*." *Études Rabelaisiennes* 5:175–95.

A chapter by chapter commentary, explaining the legal jokes by reference to a variety of legal texts, from an elementary compilation of legal commonplaces called *Brocardia Juris* to Tiraqueau's *Commentarii de nobilitate et de jure primogeniorum*. Concludes that "the primary source of the comedy lies in Bridoye's misuse of commonplaces" (p. 177) rather than the use of his legal erudition, as claimed by J. D. M. Derrett (1963.3).

18 SOZZI, LIONELLO. "Rabelais, Philelphe et le 'fumet du rôti.'" *Études Rabelaisiennes* 5:197–205.

Reviews all the texts hitherto proposed as a source for the anecdote in chapt. 37 of the *Tiers Livre*, wherein "Seigny Joan le fol" invites the *rôtisseur* to content himself with the sound of money in exchange for the smell of the roast. Adds yet another possible source: the fable entitled "De paupere advena et divite caupone," by the Italian humanist Phililpho, whose fables were known in France throughout the sixteenth century; one of them may have been a source for Des Périers's Nouvelle 87: "De la pie et de ses piauz."

19 TETEL, MARCEL. *Étude sur le comique de Rabelais*. Biblioteca dell'Archivum Romanicum, no. 61. Florence: Leo S. Olschki, 148 pp.

Reviews the various definitions of the comic from Cicero to Bergson, and notes that it can be didactic (that is, satirical) or pure, expressing the author's "joie de vivre." Emphasizes, as Plattard and Boulenger had done before him, the therapeutic aspect of Rabelais' laughter rather than "le comique significatif." Believes that Rabelais himself meant to stress the gratuitous nature of his comedy by framing *Gargantua* and the *Tiers Livre* with enigmatic or insignificant episodes, and by ending *Pantagruel* and the *Quart Livre* on a burlesque note. Sees the "logical" ending of Book V as an indication of its inauthenticity (except for the first sixteen chapters). Believes that each book is characterized by its own brand of comedy, and by the use of contemporary themes as a springboard for Rabelais' comic verve. Devotes separate chapters to satire ("grotesque" in the first four books, "biting" in the fifth), parody (generally more refined), and "le comique populaire," which tends to disappear in the later novels. In chapt. 5 studies "le comique des détails," and the various forms of verbal exuberance. Discusses Rabelais' imagery in chapt. 7, deplores that the existing studies are content with classifying the images into categories without drawing any meaningful conclusions. Studies the nature and effect of Rabelais' comparisons; discusses "les images proprement dites" (i.e., metaphors) and periphrasis. Devotes chapt. 8 to "le comique du mouvement," based on effects of surprise and amplification, and reflected in the movement of the sentence. Concludes by stressing that the target of the satire or parody is less important than the comic quality of any given episode. "En définitive ce qui reste éternel dans l'œuvre de Rabelais c'est le comique" (p 143), especially in its purest, most gratuitous, most exclusively verbal form.

20 ———. "Rabelais: A Precursor of the Baroque Style." *Rivista di Letterature Moderne e Comparate* 17 (March):5–16.

"Viewed as a whole, Rabelais' books fit the definition of a baroque novel" (p. 7). After Spitzer, Saulnier, and Rousset, finds in Rabelais' text an illustration of the various criteria of the literary baroque as defined by such theoreticians as Hatzfeld and Buffum: absence of a linear structure, lack of unity and logic, theatricality, tension between being and becoming, a predilection for the pictorial and the magnificent, for the gory and the macabre, indulgence in movement, hyperbole and verbal energy, accumulation and antithesis, and a syntax reflecting in its "style coupé" the meandering process of thought. But acknowledges that these characteristics of style and imagination do not reflect in Rabelais, as they do in the writers of the last years of the sixteenth century and the beginning of the seventeenth, the "metaphysical irrationalism" of the true baroque, and thus rejects the label as not entirely appropriate. "Because he died in 1553 and because his style and philosophical thought do not blend harmoniously, one has to refer to him as a pre-baroque or mannerist" (p. 16).

1965

21  WENDELL, CHARLES WARNER. "Narrative Style in Rabelais and Sterne." Ph.D. dissertation, Yale University, 193 pp.

Studies the narrative forms and devices in the works of each writer. Finds that Rabelais transforms concrete reality "into a gigantic superrealism" within "a loose and chaotic, dynamically creative" structure, whereas Sterne, with greater subtlety, "projects more fully developed characters." Finds similarities in their technique (most of all in their use of comic devices), and in their conception of laughter "as an antidote to all that man opposes, an optimistic belief in the goodness of human nature, and a diffidence toward life's ambivalences." See *Dissertation Abstracts* 25 (1965):4711–12.

## 1965

1  BAKHTIN, MIKHAIL. *Tvorchestvo Fransua Rable i narodnaia kultura Srednevekovia i Renessansa.* Moscow: Khudozhestvennia literatura.

Russian original of *Rabelais and His World*. See 1968.1.

2  BUSSON, HENRI. "Les dioscures de Fontenay-le-Comte. Pierre Amy. François Rabelais." *Études Rabelaisiennes* 6: 1–50.

Two-part study. The first, "Les mystères de Pierre Amy," deals with Rabelais' friend during his Franciscan years. Claims that of the two, it was Amy who was more inclined toward religion, and that he had warmer relations with Budé. Notes that both had condemned Aristotle for his religious thought, and that Amy had been attracted to Pythagorism. In the second part, "La morale de Thélème: Essai sur la morale chrétienne de 1515 à 1535," seeks the key to the meaning of the Thélème episode in an analysis of Rabelais' position on the question of free will. Argues against Lucien Febvre and Raoul Morçay, who refuse to take the Thelemites' motto seriously. "La critique et la satire toujours répétées des abus de l'Eglise masque souvent pour le public le sens profond de la Réforme" (p. 23). They also explain why Rabelais is so often seen as an Erasmian Evangelical in religious matters. Comments on Budé's Dantesque vision of man, forever tarnished by original sin and unable to achieve salvation without God's help. Claims that without denying the existence of free will, Budé denies that man can, by the exercise of free will alone, avoid sin and attain virtue. Points out that Erasmus too, at the end of his life, will adopt an essentially Lutheran stance in his insistance that man recognize his weakness and glorify God's mercy. Argues that the evolution of Rabelais' religious thought took an exactly opposite course, and led him to proclaim in *Gargantua* "l'entière liberté humaine" (p. 35). Claims that in the famous "Fay ce que vouldras" and the commentary that follows Rabelais' position is neither Christian nor even Erasmian, in spite of occasional pious allusions borrowed from Saint Paul and invariably ascribed to the noble representatives of an outdated Christianity. "Tout autre est l'esprit nouveau: 'Autant vaut l'homme comme il s'estime,' proclame Panurge"(p. 36). Claims that Rabelais' contention that man is naturally drawn to the Good represents an essentially non-religious position. Does not see in the ethical thought of the episode any religious foundation or component: "proposer l'honneur pour idéal de vie est une prétention qui aurait fait bondir Erasme comme elle a déchaîné l'indignation de Bossuet"(p. 37). Believes this position to be directly borrowed from Cicero's *De finibus* and Cato's defense of the ethics of stoicism, a position adopted before Rabelais by such other Franciscans as Duns Scotus and William of Ockham, and taught in Rabelais' own day by such theologians of "Pelagist" persuasion as Gabriel Biel and Jérôme de Hangest. Referring back to his original thesis in *Le Rationalisme en France*, argues that even in his *Hyperperaspistes*, often compared with the Thelemites' rule, Erasmus speaks like a Catholic theologian: "Rabelais pense en stoïcien" (p. 40).

3   CÉLINE, LOUIS-FERDINAND. "Rabelais, il a raté son coup." *Cahiers de l'Herne*, no. 5:19–21.
    "Rabelais avait voulu faire passer la langue parlée dans la langue écrite": in an interview, claims to admire Rabelais mainly as an artist who sought to attract the readers' attention by addressing them in their own language. Deplores that he should have failed to exert any influence upon the subsequent development of accepted literary style.

4   DONTENVILLE, HENRI. "Les cloches de Notre-Dame." *BAARD* 2, no. 4:115–20.
    Is convinced that François Poncher, bishop of Paris between 1519 and 1532, had written a Gargantuan chronicle predating any of the existing versions.

5   FRANÇON, MARCEL. "Note sur l'emploi du mot 'chaldaïque' par Rabelais." *Études Rabelaisiennes* 6:51–52.
    When Rabelais uses, in the *Almanach pour l'an 1533*, the term "chaldaïque," he means Aramaic and not Syriac, as implied by M. A. Screech in a note to a passage in *L'Evangélisme de Rabelais* (p. 59). See 1964.11, 13.

6   ———. "Notes rabelaisiennes." *BAARD* 2, no. 4:121–25.
    Rewrites part of the "itinéraire" provided by Saulnier in his edition of *Pantagruel*, assuming that Rabelais was born in 1494 and not in 1483. Notes the list of languages both Rabelais and Erasmus recommend for the study of the Bible. Believes that the text of the seventh speech in chapt. 9 of *Pantagruel* is in Flemish and not in Dutch, and that it may have been provided by Hilarius Berthulfus.

1965

7 ———. "Pantagruel et le Prestre Jehan." *Studi Francesi* 9, no. 25 (January–April):86–88.

Believes that the Prestre Jehan, "roy de Inde" mentioned by Rabelais in the last chapter of *Pantagruel*, was an historical character best known as the author of a letter he was said to have written around 1165 to various Christian leaders, containing miscellaneous texts about Alexander the Great as well as about certain monsters and marvels of the Orient. Notes that the first French translation appeared in 1488, and gave rise to a legend which eventually made of him the emperor of Ethiopia. "Nous pouvons conclure qu'en mentionnant 'Prestre Jean,'...Rabelais ne faisait pas seulement allusion au personnage légendaire, mais qu'il désignait le personnage historique—encore mal connu—qu'était l'empereur d'Éthiopie" (p. 88). Argues that by marrying off Pantagruel to the daughter of Prestre Jehan, Rabelais follows the pattern of many another Gargantuan chronicle by returning his hero to the Orient, where he was born. See 1963.8.

8 GRAY, FLOYD. "Ambiguity and Point of View in the Prologue to *Gargantua*." *Romanic Review* 56:12–21.

Comparisons with such essentially programmatic texts as Lucian's introduction to his *Verae Historiae* and Erasmus' dedicatory epistle to the *Moriae encomium* underscore the extent to which Rabelais' prologue is, on the contrary, dramatic, and functions "as an integral part of the fictional world" (p. 21). Studies the prologue not as "the transparent expression of an authorial injunction" which it is not, but as the "simultaneous presentation of conflicting claims" that it is. Argues that the ambiguity underlying the prologue is a means of expression whose main function is to establish an "aesthetic distance" between author and narrator, and to force the reader "into an immediate state of reaction and receptivity" (p. 12).

9 LIVINGSTON, CHARLES H. "A propos de *Pantagruel* II, ch. XXVII: Un conte de Philippe de Vigneulles." *BHR* 27:30–36.

Henri Clouzot had remarked on the resemblance between chapt. 27 of *Pantagruel* and the twenty-ninth story in Nicolas de Troyes's *Le Grand parangon des nouvelles nouvelles* (1535), and had concluded that Nicolas de Troyes had known Rabelais' first book and had borrowed from it. Points out that the fifty-ninth of Philippe de Vigneulles' *Cent nouvelles nouvelles* (1505–15) contains a similar episode, and that all three may be independent versions of a common traditional tale, probably of oriental origin.

10 MARICHAL, ROBERT. "Notes pour le commentaire des œuvres de Rabelais." *Études Rabelaisiennes* 6:89–112.

Comments upon three notes in Lefranc's edition of *Gargantua*; offers lexicographical remarks upon the expression "autant pour le brodeur" (in *Gargantua*, chapt. 13, and *Quart Livre*, chapt. 32), the terms *border/broder*, and syntactical observations on the place of the subject in Rabelais' sentences: "Nous n'avons pas d'étude vraiment valable sur l'ordre des mots dans la phrase de Rabelais" (p. 107). The author's own study of "postposition du sujet...dans les propositions dites 'introduites'" (p. 108) suggests that this archaic feature is much more frequent in Rabelais than in any of his contemporaries.

11  MICHEL, PIERRE. "Réminiscences rabelaisiennes dans les *Essais.*" *Bulletin de la Société des Amis de Montaigne* 4, no. 1 (January–March):3–5.

Stresses the affinities between the two writers. Finds echoes of the Baisecul and Humevesne episode (*Pantagruel*, chapt. 10–13) in "Du pédantisme" (*Essais* I, chapt. 25), and of the debate in sign-language between Panurge and Thaumaste (*Pantagruel*, chapt. 19) in what Montaigne says on body language in the "exemplaire de Bordeaux" edition of the "Apologie de Raymond Sebonde": "On dirait que Montaigne, relisant le texte primitif de l'Apologie, a voulu non seulement étoffer l'argument, mais aussi l'égayer en recourant aux procédés qui avaient assuré le succès du 'plaisant' Rabelais auprès du public" (p. 5).

12  MUIR, EDWIN. "Panurge and Falstaff." In *Essays on Literature and Society*. London: The Hogarth Press, pp. 166–81.

Brings out the similarities in their characters: their love of drink and of words, their fondness for company, their tendency to flout the law. Argues that Falstaff is a "greater" character  than Panurge (or any other character in Rabelais' work), but notes that he is much more repulsive. Underscores the acceptance of Panurge into Pantagruel's circle and the spirit of friendship and tenderness that surrounds him, and sees in this aspect of Rabelais' work the author's willingness to accept all that exists and that is human.

13  NARDI, ENZO. "Seigny le Fol e il fumo dell'arrosto." In *Studi in onore di Biondo Biondi, II*. Milan: Dott. A. Giuffrè, pp. 243–67.

Investigates the possible sources of the anecdote of the man who pays for the smell of a roast with the sound of his money (*Tiers Livre*, chapt. 37). Concludes that the direct source of Rabelais' anecdote is still unknown. As for the list of Rabelais' judicial references in connection with the anecdote, Plattard had thought it had originated in Tiraqueau's *De legibus connubialibus*. Sees no reason to believe that this was indeed the case, and suggests that Rabelais and Tiraqueau may well have consulted the same judicial source.

14  NYKROG, PER. "Thélème, Panurge et la Dive Bouteille." *Revue d'Histoire Littéraire de la France* 3 (July–September):385–97.

Without significantly modifying the meaning of the episode, a philological study of the name given by Rabelais to his abbey nevertheless enriches that meaning in important ways, and throws light on Panurge's quest in Book

III, as well as on the result of that quest in Book V. Claims that the usual translation of Thélème as "volonté" is somewhat misleading in that it suggests a link with the Latin *voluntas* and its homologues in the modern languages. In fact, Rabelais found the Greek form of the word in the New Testament, where it designates the will of God, a spontaneous, instinctive force clearly contrasted with the act of reflective reason. An awareness of the Greek origin of the word underscores the perfect adequacy of the term to designate the kind of life that is led in the abbey. If the consultations in Book III are fruitless, it is because Panurge does not realize that will is the only guide through the perplexities of human judgment, and that the solution to his existential problems should thus be sought on the level of will and not of reason. In the last episodes of Book V, under the influence of wine, Panurge is able to hear at last the voice of his *thelema*: his will is now free, as is the will of the inhabitants of Thélème.

15  RAWSON, C. J. "Rabelais and Horace, A Contact in *Tiers Livre*, ch. III." *French Studies* 19 (October):373–78.

Examines the relationship between Rabelais' reference to "la cohorte de tous maulx" in a world without lenders or borrowers, and Horace's "febrium...cohors" in the list of ills befalling mankind after Prometheus stole the fire from Heaven (*Odes* I, iii, 29–31). Discusses the extended usage of the term in Horace to refer to things as well as people. Sees an "incidental parodic note" in Rabelais' use of the term. Suggests that the allusion to fishes in the air and stags in the sea may also come from Horace's account of the age of Pyrrha, in a contiguous ode, and not from Erasmus, as Screech's critical edition of the *Tiers Livre* has it.

16  ROBERTS, JOHN WINDSOR. "Les Images dans l'œuvre de Rabelais." Ph.D. dissertation, University of Michigan, 165 pp.

Classifies the images into categories, studies their various functions, considers them as part of Rabelais' general exploration of language and its limitations, and deems the nature and function of the images in Book V to be so consistent with their nature and function in the previous books that finds himself compelled to conclude that it too is an authentic Rabelaisian text. See *Dissertation Abstracts* 26 (1965):3349.

17  SAREIL, JEAN. "Voltaire juge de Rabelais." *Romanic Review* 56:171–80.

At the time when he mentions Rabelais in his letters to Madame du Deffand (1759–60), Voltaire has just launched his campaign against "l'Infâme." If he now tempers his originally harsh opinion, it is for "philosophical" and propaganda reasons, rather than from any evolution of his literary aesthetics. Having just reread Rabelais, "il y découvre les éléments d'une lutte identique à celle qui constitue alors le centre de ses préoccupations" (p. 175).

18  SAULNIER, V[ERDUN]-L[OUIS]. "Divers échos de Rabelais au XXe siècle." *Études Rabelaisiennes* 6:73–88.

    Attracts attention to a series of generally brief references to Rabelais in
such twentieth-century authors as Francis Jammes (a moving letter to Arthur
Fontaine), Anatole France (who wrote a whole book about Rabelais), Paul
Claudel, André-François Poncet (notes made during his imprisonment from
1943 to 1945 and published in *Carnets d'un captif*). Also mentions a poem by
Charles Vildrac, one of the founders of the "phalanstère de l'Abbaye," "l'un
des plus beaux avatars de l'Abbaye de Thélème" (p. 88).

19  SCHEURER, RÉMY. "François Rabelais et la cure de Meudon." *Études
Rabelaisiennes* 6:53–55.

    Attracts attention to a deed found in the National Archives whereby
Rabelais, after having leased his "cure de Meudon" to a certain Pierre
Richard, leases it again, on February 20, 1552, to two priests of the region. In
the lease, Rabelais is referred to as a "noble et discrette personne," which may
or may not signal a change in Rabelais' social status. In the preface to the
sixth *Études Rabelaisiennes*, in which this note appears, Robert Marichal sees
the date of the deed as of possible importance, in connection with the purported "condemnation" of the *Quart Livre*: "l'affermage de sa cure de Meudon a
donc toute l'apparence d'une mesure de précaution; s'apprête-t-il a fuir? à se
cacher?" (pp. vii–viii).

20  SCREECH, M[ICHAEL] A[NDREW]. "Some Recent Rabelais Studies."
*Études Rabelaisiennes* 6:61–71.

    Reviews a number of books and articles published in 1962 through
1964, of purportedly varying quality ("from first-rate works of scholarship to
works of very doubtful merit," p. 61), but testifying to the seriousness with
which Rabelais' work is being studied.

21  SKARUP, POVL. "Le Physétère et l'île farouche de Rabelais." *Études
Rabelaisiennes* 6:57 59.

    Points to the *Carta marina* of the Swedish geographer Olaus Magnus,
published in Venice in 1539, as a possible source of the "île Farouche"
episode of the *Quart Livre* (chapt. 33ff.). Believes it to be more likely than the
current explanation whereby the île Farouche is a transformation of the "mer
des Farouches" found in *Le Disciple de Pantagruel ou les Navigations de
Panurge* (1538) to which Rabelais merely added a *physétère* he had found in
Pliny.

22  SPITZER, L[EO]. "Ancora sul prologo al primo libro del Gargantua di
Rabelais." *Studi Francesi* 9, no. 27 (September–December):423–34.

    Posthumous article reiterating the charge that Rabelais specialists have
been treating a literary text for its documentary value instead of viewing it as

the supreme work of art that it is. Considers Rabelais criticism to be at a standstill. Disputes once again Lefranc's contention that Rabelais' work represents the most wonderful example of pure, powerful, triumphant realism. Challenges Lefranc's interpretation of the prologue, and his belief that atheism and materialism make up the secret message, the *substantificque moelle* of the novel. Argues that the reference to a *substantificque moelle* does not signal the presence of any secret message at all; to the contrary, "alla fine, Rabelais ha rigettato esplicitamente questa interpretazione" (p. 429). In the Middle Ages the image of the *moelle* (in contrast to the *écorce*) is associated with a poetic that tolerates secular elements in the romances only when they can be interpreted in an allegorical, spiritual manner. Would a man like Rabelais, who welcomed all of life, its carnal as well as its spiritual side, refer to such a poetic with any other motive in mind than to hold it up to ridicule? Concludes that the reference to the *substantificque moelle* and to the poetics of allegorical interpretation does not invite the reader to seek a higher meaning behind the façade of the work, but that it merely introduces yet another *idée* into the immense "*jeu des idées*" which forms the essence of Rabelais' text.

23  TETEL, MARCEL. "Pulci and Rabelais: A Revaluation." *Studi Francesi* 9, no. 25 (January–April):89–93.
    Points out that Rabelais' debt toward Pulci, in terms of character and scenes, is by now well established and does not need to be reiterated. Claims that what does deserve further attention is "an affinity of mind" between the two writers, the influence of oral and popular tradition upon them, a similar attitude towards women, a common tendency to intersperse their narrative with anecdotes, and above all a similar linguistic verve, characterized by a penchant for amplification and verbal play.

24  WINTER, JOHN F. "Visual Variety and Spatial Grandeur in Rabelais." *Romanic Review* 56:81–91.
    Claims that "visual variety and grandeur are intrinsic and artistically well-conceived elements of the work of Rabelais, and that they develop naturally from the Renaissance outlook on the world" (p. 81).

## 1966

1  BOUCHER, A. "Rabelais était-il le fils ou le frère de l'avocat Chinonais?" *BAARD* 2, no. 5:155–57.
    Disputes Lefranc's presupposition that the Antoine Rabelais who died in 1534 without leaving any of his money to François, was his father. Believes him to have been one of François Rabelais' brothers.

1966

2   BRAULT, G[ERARD] J. "*Ung abysme de science*: On the interpretation of Gargantua's letter to Pantagruel." *BHR* 28:615–32.

Examines the letter as a whole in the context of the entire work, challenges the prevalent opinion that it represents a paean to the Renaissance, and claims that the text has been "vastly misunderstood" (p. 616).

3   COLIE, ROSALIE L. *Paradoxia Epidemica: The Renaissance Tradition of Paradox.* Princeton: Princeton University Press, 553 pp.

In chapt. 1, studies the rhetorical use of paradox in Rabelais. Considers his book a macaronic for its mingling of scale, its reliance on the "parodic pattern of the world upside down" (p. 45), as well as its use of a variety of languages. Discusses the paradoxical aspects of the Abbaye de Thélème; notes the pervading use of "rhypographical" paradox—which consists in praising "low" things in opposition to things conventionally considered "high"— throughout the *Tiers Livre*, with its paradoxical praise of debtors and borrowers, that of the codpiece, and the relation of both to the theme of marriage. Regards Pantagruel's attitude to women as signalling an important shift in the way literature traditionally views women: "regarded neither as a succubus necessarily intent upon destroying men nor as a chilly piece of property, women could be considered as fully human or, like men, as mixtures of good and bad traits, capable of development or degeneration, different in different relationships" (p. 58). Discusses Rabelais' work as "recreative" in both senses of the word: "a book of recreation, a book to amuse and divert its readers and to restore them to themselves by means of that recreation" (p. 62). Links eating and drinking with inspiration; scatology and copulation with intellectual conception and creation. Notes Rabelais' interest, which he shares with his contemporaries, not only in words, but also in alternate systems of communication.

4   DONTENVILLE, HENRI. *La France mythologique: Travaux de la Société de mythologie française sous la direction de Henri Dontenville.* Nancy: Tchou, 379 pp.

The two parts of chapt. 6, "Le Gargantua médiéval populaire" (pp. 277–339) and "Derrière Gargantua, le Panthéon Gaulois" (pp. 340–74), discuss the folkloric origins of the giant. Finds the name of Gargantua mentioned in over 400 locations. Believes that the legend of Gargantua was partly spread by the *Chroniques gargantuines*, but that it also preexisted these works. Notes that sometimes the anecdotes have no equivalent in either the chronicles or in Rabelais. Argues that Rabelais cleansed the giant of his diabolical connotations.

1966

5 DROZ, ÉMILIE. "Frère Gabriel DuPuyherbault, l'agresseur de François Rabelais." *Studi Francesi* 10, no. 30 (September–December):401–27.

Provides a biographical study of the author of *Theotimus*, in which Rabelais found himself denounced as an atheist. Both Abel Lefranc and Lucien Febvre had explained DuPuyherbault's attack as instigated by the Sainte-Marthe family. Finds this to be an unnecessary assumption: "Pour DuPuyherbault, son attaque est une œuvre de salubrité publique: que les membres des parlements et des commissions de censure sachent que les écrits de Rabelais sont néfastes; par conséquent, brûlons ses livres" (p. 407).

6 FRANÇON, MARCEL. "Rabelais et le système musical de Guido d'Arezzo." *BAARD* 2, no. 5:151–52.

Comments on Rabelais' allusions to d'Arezzo's terminology. In the following "Note rabelaisienne" (p. 153), believes that Rabelais' reference to *alibantes* in the early pages of *Pantagruel* may allude to the episode of the massacre of the pretenders in the *Odyssey*.

7 ———. "Sur l'Abbaye de Thélème." *BAARD* 2, no. 5:149–50.

Disagrees with Per Nykrog's interpretation of the meaning of Thélêma, which he takes to refer to the rational will and not, as does Nykrog, to "impulsions spontanées et irréfléchies" (see 1965.14). Prefers to see Rabelais as following the medieval tradition rather than anticipating Diderot and Rousseau.

8 ———. "Thélème." *Annali del'Istituto Universario Orientale* 8:57–59.

Restates the argument made in 1966.7.

9 GLAUSER, ALFRED. *Rabelais créateur*. Paris: Editions A.-G. Nizet, 284 pp.

Approaches Rabelais' four authenticated books as the creation of a poet and novelist rather than that of a thinker. In chapt. 1 studies the presence of Rabelais in his novels in a variety of disguises. In chapt. 2 discusses Rabelais' text as the creation of a poetic universe characterized above all by its fecundity and its exaltation of the forces of life. Devotes chapt. 3 to the work's various forms; stresses its "lopinisme," that is, its fragmented structure, within an admittedly global conception; notes Rabelais' awareness of the book as an object, to be held and seen as well as read; comments on its "calligrammatic" dimension, as groups of words creating patterns on the page as well as referring to a metalinguistic reality. Studies the Rabelaisian characters, mostly Panurge (pp. 126–69): "Il est ce que Rabelais a conçu de plus profond" (p. 132). Sees him as "un personnage en formation," an actor, a spectator, and a poet. In a much shorter section on Frère Jean (pp. 169–79), sees the latter as an embodiment of energy and freedom, superior to Panurge in vitality and efficacy of action, but in the main rather similar, until the presence of both characters in Book IV forces Rabelais to differentiate between them. In chapt.

5, discusses the themes of education and of war as "mouvements de l'œuvre." In chapt. 6, studies the journey of Book IV as an essentially verbal quest of the world and of the self: "ce voyage d'humaniste nie en somme le voyage" (p. 232). Sees the book as a mental journey, with the islands as so many obstacles to self-knowledge. Studies the episodes dealing with Quaresmeprenant and the Andouilles as expressions of Rabelais' somewhat unexpected anti-materialism, reads the storm episode as "une fête de style" (p. 264), and concludes with a discussion of the Unfrozen Words, in which Rabelais is taken to reflect on the power and limits of language. "Ce qui pouvait n'être qu'un récit est devenu le lieu d'un débat essentiel sur les secrets de la création littéraire, où tous les sens ont participé" (p. 282).

10  GOEBEL, GERHARD. "Zwei Versuche zur Architekturbeschreibung in der Dichtung der Renaissance." *Romanische Forschungen* 78:280–311.

In the first pages of the article, notes that in connection with hieroglyphics the *Briefve Declaration* refers to Francesco Colonna's *Hypnerotomachia Polyphili* (although gratifying him with an erroneous first name). Points out that the architectural descriptions of the island of the Macraeons owe much to that work, as does the description of the Temple of Venus in the Dive Bouteille episode of the *Cinquiesme Livre*, and Rabelais' architectural terminology in general from Book IV onwards.

11  KÖHLER, ERICH. "Die Abtei Thélème und die Einheit des Rabelais'schen Werks." In *Esprit und arkadische Freiheit*. Frankfurt and Bonn: Athenäum Verlag, pp. 142–57.

Reprint of 1959.21.

12  LARMAT, JEAN. "La vigne et le vin chez Rabelais." *Revue des Sciences Humaines* 122–123:179–92.

Shows that in *Gargantua* (notably in chapt. 5 and 27), wine is most often a "realistic" theme, reflecting the economic importance of wine in Rabelais' day. Notes its association with laughter, except in Book III. Points out that it can have a structural function, accelerating the rhythm of the narrative. Acknowledges that it may also have on occasion a symbolic value. "Dans son roman, le vin est sans doute un des mots les plus chargés de sens" (p. 192).

13  LEONARDUZZI, ALESSANDRO. *F. Rabelais e la sua prospettiva pedagogia*. Trieste: Tipographia Moderna, Istituto di filosofia, Facoltà di Lettere e Filosofie, Università degli Studi di Trieste, 163 pp.

Provides a brief overview of the general tendencies of Rabelais criticism (chapt. 1), gives a brief account of the man and his work (chapt. 2), studies the work from a scientific and cultural perspective, summarizing Rabelais' ideas on law, medicine, philosophy, and above all religion (chapt. 3), and deals in

chapt. 4 with the theme of education, said to receive deep and sincere attention even though it is not a prevalent aspect of Rabelais' thought. Against the
background of scholarly studies of Rabelais' pedagogy and of medieval education as the target of Rabelais' satire, reconstructs the pedagogical ideas of
Alcofribas as expressed not only in the chapters dealing with the education of
the giants, but also in the episode of Thélème. Admires Rabelais' intuition
into the psychology of the child, and his emphasis on hygiene and physical
education as a necessary complement of intellectual training. Notes the differences in matters of curriculum between Gargantua's letter to Pantagruel and
later, in Gargantua's own education, the new importance given to the arts of
the quadrivium and to close contact with life in Book II. But finds weaknesses
in Rabelais' rather stereotyped (though essentially accurate) account of traditional education, in the traces of that very education in Rabelais' own pedagogy, in an inadequate treatment of the concept of educational development,
and in Rabelais' insufficient awareness of the difficulties inherent in the task
of education, resulting from an excessive faith in the resources of human
nature. Compares Rabelais' pedagogy with that of Montaigne, Comenius,
Locke, and Rousseau (on whom Rabelais' influence is claimed to be at best
indirect, and not nearly as important as that of Montaigne and Locke). Warns
in conclusion against the mistake of underestimating the seriousness underlying the whimsical surface of Rabelais' novel, but also against the temptation
to overvalue the pedagogical dimension of his work and to view as a system
what are after all mere glimpses into matters which will receive full and systematic treatment only much later.

14 LEVI DELLA VIDA, G. "Un'aporia rabelaisiana." In *Studi in onore di Italo
Siciliano, II.* Florence: Leo S. Olschki, Biblioteca dell'Archivum Romanicum,
pp. 651–56.

In a mystifying note on the Cataracts of the Nile, the author of the
*Briefve Declaration* at the end of Book IV claims to have come by his knowledge of Arabic from the bishop of Caraminth when they were both in Rome.
Suggests that Caraminth is a transcription of Qarâ Amid, capital of a province
in Mesopotamia, and notes that a high Church official by the name of Simon
Sullâqâ did indeed visit Rome, but at a time when the *Briefve Declaration* had
already appeared in print. Argues that in the middle of the century in France
only Guillaume Postel could boast "una discreta conoscenza dell'arabo" (p.
655), and that Rabelais' claim to a knowledge of the language was pure
invention. Finds it uncanny, however, that Rabelais should have foreseen that
in a few months the patriarch of Caraminth, if not exactly the bishop, would
visit Rome to be received by the pope.

15 MASTERS, GEORGE MALLARY. "The Platonic and Hermetic Tradition
and the *Cinquiesme Livre* of François Rabelais." Ph.D. dissertation, The Johns
Hopkins University.

See *American Doctoral Dissertations*, 1965–66, p. 137. Revised for publication: 1969.15.

16 ———. "The Hermetic and Platonic Traditions in Rabelais' *Dive Bouteille.*" *Studi Francesi* 10, no. 28 (January–April):15–29.

Argues that the "silènes" and the "os médullaire" of the prologue to *Gargantua*, the Pantagruélion of Book III, the "parolles gelées" of Book IV, and the "febves en gousses" of the prologue to the *Cinquiesme Livre* are all part of a network of imagery having an essentially Platonic basis. As such, believes that they unify the earlier books and prepare the ground for the Platonic symbolism of the episode of the *Dive Bouteille* as the crowning literary expression of man's search for truth. Sees the various images in the first four books as refering to the Platonic opposition between physical appearance and transcendent reality. As for the experience of Pantagruel in the temple of the Divine Bottle, claims that it is fundamentally similar to the experience of the Platonic sage attaining a vision of the Real World of Ideas at the center of the World Soul before going back to interpret the vision for the rest of mankind.

17 RAIBLE, M. W. "Der Prolog zu *Gargantua* und der Pantagruelismus." *Romanische Forschungen* 78:253–79.

Sees the structure of the prologue as ternary, with a thesis, an antithesis, and a synthesis in which the apparent contradiction between the first two stages of Rabelais' argument is satisfactorily resolved. Insists on the symbolism of wine and its curative powers. Seeks to prove that, Rabelais' assertions in the prologue notwithstanding, there is no real dichotomy between the exterior form and the inner content of Rabelais' work, since its *substantifique moelle* is a philosophy of laughter.

## 1967

1 BAILLOT, A.-F. "Rabelais et Schopenhauer." *BAARD* 2, no. 6:174.

Notes Schopenhauer's interest in Rabelais and hints at the pessimistic undertone of Rabelais' so-called optimistic laughter. "Sous des dehors burlesques, il constate amèrement les injustices sociales, les hypocrisies perfides et l'absurdité de la condition humaine."

2 BICHON, JEAN. "Rabelais et *la vie œconomicque.*" *Études Rabelaisiennes* 7:107–17.

In the prologue to *Gargantua*, Rabelais promised to reveal "de tres haultz sacremens et mysteres horrificques, tant en ce qui concerne nostre religion que aussi l'estat politicq et vie œconomicque." Analyzes the meaning of "estat politicq" and "vie œconomicque," which the reader is likely to interpret anachronistically, as they were used before Rabelais and in his day. Points out that "œconomicque" pertains to the science of managing one's household, an area in which human relations are at least as important as financial management, whereas "politicq," in the Aristotelian sense (which is also the sense in which the term continues to be used during the Renaissance), pertains to the govermnent of the city, often in opposition to "religieux" and thus synonymous with "civil." "Vie" is to be taken as "manière de vivre" and "estat" as a near-synonym of it. What is "political" in Rabelais is not, as we might have thought, the Picrocholine War, but rather the chapters on education, or on life at the Abbaye de Thélème. Similarly, what is "economical" is not the praise of borrowers and debtors in the *Tiers Livre* but rather Grandgousier's management of his "maison" (synonymous with "royaume"): "son attachement à la paix, sa joie paisible et patriarchale au milieu des siens, ainsi que le joyeux empressement de ses amis, de ses domestiques, de ses alliés, nous avertissent que c'est là le but même du gouvernement" (p. 116). Thus when Rabelais promises to deal with politics and economics, his are not empty promises, so long as they are understood for what they were meant to be. As for the economic realities of Rabelais' day, and to a lesser extent the political ones, in the modern sense of these words, they find surprisingly few echoes in the book.

3   BOUCHER, A. "Rabelais et le voyage de François Ier à Bourgueil au mois de septembre 1532." *BAARD* 2, no. 6:179–81.
    Believes it may have been on this occasion that Rabelais came back for a brief visit to his "Pays de vache."

4   BUSSON, HENRI. "Les Eglises contre Rabelais." *Études Rabelaisiennes* 7:1–81.
    The diatribe that DuPuyherbault (a sometime monk of Fontevrault) had inserted in his *Theotimus* against Rabelais was seen by Abel Lefranc as a vengeful epilogue to the quarrel that had set Rabelais against the Sainte-Marthe family during the protracted lawsuit between the Communauté des Marchands de Loire and Gaucher de Sainte-Marthe, the physician of the Abbess of Fontevrault and the real-life model of Rabelais' Picrochole. Brings out the full significance of the diatribe, and suggests a new hypothesis as to its authorship. Parts 1 through 4 provide background on the two theologians involved in the diatribe: DuPuyherbault himself, and Le Picart, whom Busson finds likely, given his tempestuous temper on the one hand, and DuPuyherbault's meekness on the other, to have been the author of the part of the *Theotimus* attacking Rabelais. Points out that the seventy-eight lines of the diatribe against Rabelais are the only part of the text to be set between quotation marks, leading the reader to believe that DuPuyherbault is quoting someone other than himself. Further suggests that Le Picart, as a determined enemy of religious heresy, took advantage of the publication of the *Theotimus* to

insert the violent attack because Rabelais's book was lewd, because it manifested certain Lutheran tendencies, and because in denouncing the book as
progressive and thus morally dangerous, he was able to get even with Rabelais
for having attacked his friend Pierre Descornes, portrayed as Maistre de
Cornibus in chapt. 14 of the *Tiers Livre* and as Frater de Cornibus in chapt. 15
of *Pantagruel*. Attacked the man, rather than the priest or the writer, in what
constitutes, with Calvin's *Traité des Scandales*, the most violent pages written
against Rabelais. Through Rabelais, was also aiming at Jean du Bellay, sus-
pected of Lutheran sympathies but too powerful to be attacked directly.
Suggests that the gift of "la cure de Meudon" may have been, on the part of
Rabelais' protector, "un adieu à un personnage compromettant" (p. 70). In
conclusion, presents Rabelais as a victim of attacks from two opposite sides.
"Les deux malédictions des deux églises ennemies se rejoignent sur la tête de
Rabelais " (p. 78), judged by both the orthodox Church and by Calvin to be a
man without religion.

5   CHARPENTIER, FRANÇOISE. "Une page rabelaisienne de Des Périers: La
Première Nouvelle en forme de *Préambule*." *Revue d'Histoire Littéraire de la
France* 3:601–05.
        The reading of Des Périers's *Nouvelles  Récréations* often suggests a
Rabelaisian model. Sees Rabelais as an influence (if not necessarily as a
source) in a number of instances: turns of phrase, imagery, manners of expression, and even moral attitudes, and reads the "préambule" in the light of these
*rapprochements*: "La lecture de ce Préambule laisse apparaître des habitudes,
une problématique, communes à Des Périers et à Rabelais; on est assez tenté
de croire que ce dernier fut pour l'autre un maître. Mais de toute façon cette
influence n'est que partielle."

6   CHOLAKIAN, R[OUBEN C.]. "A Re-Examination of the Tempest Scene in
the *Quart Livre*." *French Studies* 21, no. 2 (April):104–10.
        Examines Rabelais' use of his sources (Erasmus and Folengo), and
studies the way in which "he alters the theme in order to integrate it with his
philosophical objectives" (p. 104). Attributes the changes brought to the
episode between 1548 and 1552 to circumstances in Rabelais' life, namely
Gabriel Du Puy-Herbault's accusations of impiety and Calvinism, and to
Calvin's denunciation of Rabelais' Erasmian tendencies. Reads the episode as
an allegory in which the participants are reduced to their essential characteristics: Panurge to religious superstition, Frère Jean to excessive pride in human
resourcefulness, with Epistemon and Pantagruel providing a lesson in religious moderation by their insistence on the necessity for man to cooperate
with God in achieving salvation. Argues that the episode is used by Rabelais
to express his position on the question of free will and the efficacy of prayer,
and to propose a conception of religion that reconciles faith in God with faith
in man.

1967

7   COLEMAN, DOROTHY [GABE]. "The Prologues of Rabelais." *Modern Language Review* 62:407–19.

In the wake of Spitzer's plea for an aesthetic approach to Rabelais' work, studies such features of Rabelais' literary technique as mockery, parody, irony, and creation of the author's *persona*. Looks at each prologue in turn, studies its character and structure, as well as the way in which they "suggest in miniature the technique of the books" (p. 419). Believes Rabelais' art to have reached its fullest perfection in the prologue to Book III, in which he seems to be "indicating his unwillingness to be committed at the political and religious level and declaring instead his unique commitment to his writing" (p. 417). In the prologue to Book IV, believes the artist disappears behind the self-effacing narrator, and that this "foreshadows the narrative technique of the *Quart Livre* itself" (p. 419).

8   DERRET, J. DUNCAN M. "Rabelaisian Kyrielles and their Source." *Études Rabelaisiennes* 7:85–89.

Looks at some possible sources and rejects them all. But along the way is led to conclude, from Rabelais' slight misuse of terms such as "Massorets" and because he does not seem to know that "cherubim" is a plural, that Rabelais knew no Hebrew and that he had not interested himself in Jewish studies.

9   DONTENVILLE, HENRI. "Mythologies gallicques." *BAARD* 2, no. 6:171–72.

Believes that the allusion to Jean de Gravot and his *Mythologies gallicques*, in the *Pantagrueline Prognostication* of 1533, refers to nothing other than to Rabelais himself and his *Pantagruel*.

10  FRANÇON, MARCEL. "Notes." *BAARD* 2, no. 6:185–92.

Points out that Pantagruel's itinerary upon leaving Honfleur at the end of *Pantagruel* resembles the itinerary described by Münster in his *Novus Orbis* of 1532. Makes further remarks on d'Arezzo's terminology, on Gargantua's itineraries in the *Gargantuan Chronicles*, and on "Prestre Jean": "he is not a mythical character but the Emperor of Ethiopia."

11  FRASER, THEODORE PAUL. "Jacob Le Duchat, First Editor of Rabelais." Ph.D. dissertation, Brown University, 338 pp.

Studies Le Duchat's 1711 edition of Rabelais' works, and assesses his contribution to Rabelais criticism. Finds Le Duchat's notes very helpful in elucidating proverbial expressions and old provincial terms, and sensitive to Rabelais' use of language. Observes that in the historical notes Le Duchat sought to moderate somewhat the prevailing interpretation of the work as primarily a *roman à clef*, and that he reacted strongly against the tendency to read the episodes in the *Gargantua-Pantagruel* as merely "figurative recountings of religious and political issues of Renaissance history." In Le Duchat's own interpretation of Rabelais, sees an emphasis on the obscene writer and the committed Protestant. Concludes by pointing out that much of Le Duchat's commentary survives in such modern critical editions as those of Screech and Marichal. Revised for publication: 1971.12.

12  GOODRICH, N.L. "The Dream of Panurge." *Études Rabelaisiennes* 7:93–103.

Examines the dream of Panurge (chapt. 13 through 15 of the *Tiers Livre*) in the light of Freud's *Introduction to Psychoanalysis*, as well as a more recent study, Edwin Diamond's *The Science of Dreams* (1952). Finds that Panurge's dream exhibits signs of infantilism, "the wish to be a normal adult...and a repudiation of sexual maturity attended by the usual retrogression into childhood" (p. 102). Takes this to be convincing proof of Rabelais' stature as a scientist. Interesting comments on the subject by Robert Marichal in his preface to the issue of *Études Rabelaisiennes* in which this article was published.

13  HENRY, BERNARD-M. "Maitre François Rabelais en Olonne." *BAARD* 2, no. 6:182–84.

Alludes to Rabelais' visit to the ocean when still a monk at Fontenay-le-Comte, and comments on Rabelais' six references to "Olone."

14  KRAILSHEIMER, A[LBAN] J. *Rabelais*. Les écrivains devant Dieu. Paris: Desclée de Brouwer, 140 pp.

Concentrates almost exclusively on Rabelais' religious thought. Believes that Rabelais' early religious vocation had been as sincere as his later contempt for monks, and that he left the Franciscans for the Benedictines because Franciscan rules did not allow medical studies and did not encourage the pursuit of higher education in general. Argues that neither Alcofribas nor Rabelais are ever indifferent in religious matters. Traces to Bonaventure Rabelais' conception of God as an *active* agent, both physically and meta-physically. Defines Rabelais' theology as a synthesis of Platonic and biblical doctrines. Underscores the importance of the 1552 version of the storm at sea episode, and of the death of Pan (*Quart Livre*, chapt. 28). Sees them as incontrovertible proof of Rabelais' belief in the immortality of the soul. Claims Rabelais believed not only in God but also in Providence, and in the Devil. Defines Rabelais' faith as requiring man's cooperation, and submission to the will of God. Believes that his anticlericalism was expressed in the name of an Evangelical conception of Christianity, based on the notion of love as tolerance, compassion, and responsibility. Explains Pantagruel's friendship towards Panurge as an act of pure Christian charity rather than admiration for any qualities Panurge may have possessed. "Comme la plupart des humanistes Rabelais ne croyait pas à une religion séparée de la morale" (p. 71). In the last

1967

chapter, discusses "pantagruélisme" as a Christian philosophy. Does not take Book V into account: concentrates on the quest for oracular wisdom rather than the solution proposed in the last book. Does not believe that the Thélème episode, however atypical and boring, stands in contradiction with the rest of Rabelais' religious and ethical thought.

15  KRISTEVA, JULIA. "Bakhtine, le mot, le dialogue et le roman." *Critique* 23 (April):438–65.
    Brief references to Rabelais' work as an example of "roman ménippéen" and "discours carnavalesque," considered as essentially modern and subversive, and thus maintained, in the past as well as the present, "en marge de la culture officielle" (p. 461).

16  MAUNY, RAYMOND. "Les Caves peintes à Chinon, modèle de la Cave de la Dive Bouteille?" *BAARD* 2, no. 6:175–78.
    Draws attention to the similarity between the "Cave de la Dive Bouteille" and one of the "Caves Peintes" that can still be seen in Chinon. Believes Rabelais used the latter for his description of the entrance to the Temple of the Divine Bottle in Book V.

17  MÖLK, ULRICH. "Das Rätsel auf der Bronzetafel (Zu Rabelais, *Gargantua*, Kap. 58)." *Zeitschrift für romanische Philologie* 83:1–13.
    Does not question the attribution of the *Énigme en prophétie* to Mellin de Saint-Gelais, but reminds us that lines 99 through 108 are by Rabelais himself, and comments on their stylistic interest. Relates the *Énigme* to the *Fanfreluches antidotées* at the beginning of the novel; finds it reminiscent of another *énigme* by Saint-Gelais and notes that both poems framing the novel seem to refer to the persecution of true believers. Questions the validity of trying to determine who, of Gargantua or Frère Jean, interprets the riddle correctly. Believes that the chapter cannot be understood without reference to the *énigme* as a poetic genre. Of the three types practiced in the sixteenth century, argues that the *Énigme en prophétie* belongs to the second, that is the *allégorie obscure*, which demands both a literal and an allegorical interpretation. Notes that Leonardo da Vinci's *indovinelli* could have served as examples of prophetic riddles of this nature. Argues that the solutions of Gargantua and Frère Jean are meant to be viewed as correct, and relates the prophetic riddle to the prologue to *Gargantua*, the golden rule of the Thelemites and the consultations in the *Tiers Livre* as illustrations of Rabelais' belief that the reader should be free to exercise his or her own judgment in matters of literary interpretation. Reprinted in 1973.2, pp. 473–88.

18  PAULSON, RONALD. "The Satirist as Knave and as Hero. Panurge and Pantagruel." In *The Fictions of Satire*. Baltimore: Johns Hopkins University Press, pp. 80–88.

Discusses Panurge as an example of double-edged Lucianic satire: a knavish character used as a satirical device. Sees Panurge not only as a rogue, but also as an embodiment of Pantagruelian values carried "to their utmost extreme"—of a type of knavery that exposes other people's folly (p. 83).

19  SAULNIER, V[ERDUN]-L[OUIS]. "François Rabelais veillant aux portes?" *Études Rabelaisiennes* 7:121–26.
Notes that the list of names in a manuscript in the Archives Communales of Lyons entitled "Etablies de la ville de Lyon [faictes au mois de mars MVc trente cinq. Devers le Rosne]" includes that of "Me Françoys Rabellaiz" among the local urban militia at a time when Lyons is at war. Conjectures that Rabelais, together with the other men mentioned in the list, may have been given the task of defending the "Grande Porte du Rhône," one of the four gates leading out of the city. Believes the list dates from Rabelais' return to the city between two sojourns at Montpellier, between June and September 1537; more specifically, before August, for by then Rabelais was already regarded with suspicion by the cardinal François de Tournon, governor of Lyons, for having committed a political indiscretion, and as such would not have been trusted with the defense of the city. Suggests that the evocation of the siege of Corinth in the prologue to the *Quart Livre* may owe something to this episode in Rabelais' life.

20  ———. "Michel d'Amboise, l'âne de Rabelais et quelques autres." *BHR* 29:545–56.
Brings out the various themes which link the fable of the horse and donkey in the Isle Sonnante episode of Book V (chapt. 7) to the rest of Rabelais' work. Believes Rabelais' source to be Aesop's fable 268, in the Chambry edition, and perhaps a versified apologue on the same subject published by a certain Michel d'Amboise in 1542.

21  TETEL, MARCEL. *Rabelais.* Twayne's World Authors Series, no. 11. New York: Twayne Publishers, 153 pp.
Surveys Rabelais' first four books, with emphasis on their aesthetic rather than ideological dimension. Omits any discussion of Book V, since its authenticity is in doubt. Presents *Pantagruel* as "an attempt at the grotesque," a disconnected series of essentially crude and vulgar episodes, a novel in which Rabelais has not yet learned the art of story telling. Sees in *Gargantua* a broader scope, a better structure, and a fuller mastery of the grotesque, a novel in which vulgarity is "surpassed," the grotesque is "achieved and exceeded," and satire comes "to full fruition." Notes in Book III a "sharp thematic break" with the two earler works, a preponderance of verve over satire, a greater display of "self-taught erudition," a greater number of tales only tenuously related to the action. Sees it as a quest for truth, wisdom, and happiness, rather than a statement of Rabelais' position in the Quarrel of Women or

his views on marriage. Finds in Book IV evidence of further maturity; notes that satire and parody recede into the background in favor of verbal inventiveness and playful imagery. In chapt. 5 seeks to "rehabilitate" the prologues, and views them as "microcosms of the books they precede." In chapt. 6 comments on Rabelais' views on education and his ethics. In chapt. 7 examines Rabelais' religion, the definitions of Pantagruelism, and considers Rabelais' work as an "artistic exercise."

## 1968

1   BAKHTIN, MIKHAIL. *Rabelais and His World.* Translated by Helene Iswolsky. Cambridge: MIT Press, 484 pp.
  Believes that Rabelais can only be understood in the context of popular culture, and more specifically in the tradition of folk humor. Sees popular culture as manifesting itself in the Middle Ages and the Renaissance in three distinct forms: the ritual spectacle, the comic verbal composition, and such various genres of billingsgate as curses, oaths, and popular blazons. Underscores the importance of carnival festivities in the life of medieval and Renaissance Europe, and emphasizes what he believes to be their "nonofficial, extraecclesiastical and extrapolitical" view of the world (p. 6), characterized by the suspension of hierarchical distinctions and of the norms and prohibitions of everyday, official life. Traces the origins of these festivities in the folklore of primitive peoples, but believes that in the Middle Ages the carnival rituals have lost their original ties to magic and religiosity, and that they now emphasize a universal sense of the world's revival and renewal. Finds them to be grounded in "carnival laughter," defined as festive (and thus not individual but communal), universal in scope, and ambivalent in that they both assert and deny, bury and revive. Traces the "carnival spirit" in the comic literature of the Middle Ages, especially in the medieval theater, and in the colloquial speech of the marketplace. Sees it as characterized by the representation of the body in its physiological and sexual functions, and as a gay, constructive transfer (or degradation) of the abstract and spiritual to the plane of material bodily images as a condition of renewal and regeneration. Applies the term "grotesque realism" to the aesthetics underlying these manifestations of folk culture. Sketches the history of the grotesque as an aesthetic phenomenon, and of the term used to designate it. In "Rabelais in the History of Laughter," traces the ancient sources of the Renaissance philosophy of laughter as a positive, regenerative, creative activity. Sees laughter in the Middle Ages as confined to popular culture, then breaking into literature during the Renaissance with its images of "bodily lower stratum," its universality, its relation to freedom and to "unofficial culture" (p. 90). Sees the tradition of grotesque laughter as reaching its highest artistic level with Rabelais, then

plots its "degradation" as laughter becomes used solely for satirical purposes and loses its "essential link with a universal outlook" (p. 101). Traces the historical and allegorical method of interpreting Rabelais (as critics lose sight of the popular origins of his work), from Jacques de Thou through Le Motteux and the *Variorum* edition of 1823–26. Believes Rabelais to be most misunderstood in the eighteenth century, when carnival forms subsist but are made to serve exclusively aesthetic aims, or when—as in rococo literature—the carnivalesque spirit becomes private, erotic, and skeptical. Believes him also to have been misunderstood (although appreciated) during the French Revolution, when his grotesque exaggeration is seen merely as negative satire. Notes the romantics' appreciation of Rabelais' genius, comments at some length on Hugo's "series of free Romantic variations on the theme of the absolute material bodily stratum and bodily topography" (p. 125) in Rabelais, and commends him for his understanding of the role of the lower stratum as the organizing principle of the network of Rabelaisian imagery. But rejects Hugo's narrow ethical and philosophical interpretation, his conception of laughter as merely destructive and degrading. Follows the development of Rabelais scholarship from the foundation in 1903 of the Société des Etudes Rabelaisiennes, with emphasis on Lucien Febvre and on Russian studies devoted to Rabelais (pp. 137–44). In "The Language of the Marketplace in Rabelais," justifies its place in the artistic texture of the novel as an organic part of the whole system of images and style: "the terms were then universal and far removed from pornography" (p. 146). Stresses the ambivalence of the scatological vocabulary, both debasing and regenerating. Reviews elements of Rabelais' biography which point to his familiarity with the world of the marketplace, underscores his interest in the popular aspects of the festivities of his time, and traces the manifestations of this experience in the work, particularly in the language and imagery of the prologues to Books I through IV. Sees the banquet and kitchen imagery, the echoes of the "cris de Paris" resounding throughout, the language of advertising and abuse as all contributing to the atmosphere of "freedom, frankness, and familiarity" (p. 195) which permeates Rabelais' work. In "Popular-Festive Forms and Images in Rabelais," sees the same ambivalence in the scenes of massacre or thrashing, in which the punishment of the victims (representing the old, repressive world) is transformed into festive laughter and paves the way for the birth of a new freedom. Underscores the same festive spirit in the scenes of feasting, recreational amusements, and games. Views the recourse to the carnivalesque as Rabelais' solution to the Renaissance problem of finding forms that would allow freedom of thought and speech in the struggle against the official culture of the Middle Ages. Studies banquet imagery in chapt. 4; examines the role of banquets as popular rather than private, individual feasts; notes that they are omnipresent, in themselves or as metaphors, organically combined with all other popular-festive forms and interwoven with images of the grotesque body, and intimately connected with man's work, as representing its last, joyously triumphant stage. Traces the source of this banquet imagery to medieval grotesque realism rather than the ancient symposium, and underscores how fundamentally different it is from the images of private gluttony and drunkenness in bourgeois literature. In "The Grotesque Image of the Body and Its Sources," reviews various attempts to define the grotesque, and rejects the prevalent idea that it is primarily satirical. Believes the grotesque to be a fundamentally ambivalent mode of representation, anti-classical and anti-naturalist, and based upon a whimsical conception of the body as represented in colloquial forms of speech, in the tradition of comic giants, in the various compilations of legends dealing with the "Indian Wonders," the medieval mysteries and the Renaissance conception of man as microcosm. In "Images of the Material Bodily Lower Stratum," notes a characteristically downward movement throughout Rabelais' work: "Rabelais' world in its entirety, as in every detail, is directed toward the underworld, both earthly and bodily" (p. 370). Uses the episode of Gargantua's discovery of the "torchecul" and Epistémon's descent into hell to illustrate the meaning of this downward movement; behind the parodic nature of such episodes sees the valorization of the lower stratum as the productive center of transformation and renewal. Argues that Panurge's journey in Book IV is also in essence a journey to the underworld. Sees the philosophical meaning of this downward movement as related to the transformation of the medieval picture of the universe during the Renaissance, as its hierarchical, vertical, extratemporal character gives way to a horizontal movement in time and space, making at last possible the idea of progress. Concludes the chapter by studying Rabelaisian ambivalence in the author's use of negation and destruction as reconstruction rather than annihilation, and in the Rabelaisian fusion of praise and denigration throughout the novel. In the last chapter, uncovers behind the popular-festive universalism of Rabelais' images their realistic dimension, acknowledging what they owe to Rabelais' personal experience and to his observation of the political, social, and even linguistic problems of his day. Is thus able to show how in Rabelais' work "the cosmic breath of myth is combined with the directness of a modern survey and the concrete precision of a realist novel" (p. 438).

With a foreword by Krystyna Pomorska, relating Bakhtin's methodology in his book on Dostoyevsky's poetics to the structuralist phase of the Russian formalist school and the linguistics of F. de Saussure. Notes at that time Bakhtin's interest in the nature of poetic language and in literature as product rather than process, and underscores in *Rabelais and His World* a new semiotic orientation, which allows Bakhtin to investigate pictorial and gestural sign systems as well as verbal language. Reminds us that *Rabelais and His World* was probably begun in the early 1930s, and that it was completed by 1940.

2 ———. "The Role of Games in Rabelais." *Yale French Studies* 41:124–32.
   Reprint of an excerpt from chapt. 3 of 1968.1. Examines the *Énigme en prophétie* and the dice-casting episode of Bridoye in the *Tiers Livre* in terms of images built on games.

3 BARRAULT, JEAN-LOUIS. "Approches et distances, notes relevées dans Michelet pouvant servir à *Rabelais*." In *Rabelais. Cahiers de la Compagnie Madeleine Renaud–Jean-Louis Barrault* 67 (September):3–81.
   Excerpts from Michelet's *Histoire de France au XVIe siècle* on the Renaissance and on Rabelais, with brief comments and illustrations from Dalibon's edition of *Les Songes drôlatiques de Pantagruel*.

4 ———. *Rabelais: "Jeu dramatique" en deux parties tiré des cinq livres de François Rabelais.* Paris: Gallimard, Nouvelle Revue Française, Le manteau d'Arlequin, 195 pp.
   Draws on all five books as well as Rabelais' letters and prognostication, in an enterprise aiming to bring out the theatricality of Rabelais' text.

5 BASTIAENSEN, MICHEL. "L'hébreu chez Rabelais." *Revue Belge de Philologie et d'Histoire* 46, no. 3:725–48.
   Does not seek to document or evaluate Rabelais' knowledge of Hebrew but to define its function in Rabelais' work. Surveys the various references to Hebrew and the use of Hebrew words. Notes that the Hebrew inscription on the Parisian lady's ring (*Pantagruel*, chapt. 24) is independent of the narrative, so that Hebrew is here merely part of a verbal game illustrating Rabelais' materialistic conception of language and underscoring its autonomy. Notes the great number of words of Hebrew origin in Book V, where they are used less grammatically than elsewhere. Explains the use of such words as Bacbuc, Thohu, and Bohu by Rabelais' interest in their phonic, onomatopoeic character. Believes that the most important function of Hebrew words is to add by their strangeness to the fantastic nature of Rabelais' world, while lending it at the same time an element of credibility, since their meaning can be verified.

6 BOWEN, BARBARA. "Rabelais and the Comedy of the Spoken Word." *Modern Language Review* 63, no. 3 (July):575–80.
   Sees in the emphasis on the spoken word in the four authenticated books an underlying basis for Rabelais' comic art hitherto neglected by critics. Stresses the importance of the theme of hearing, and Rabelais' awareness of the problems involved in oral communication. Notes that words—both written and spoken, but mainly the latter—become the very subject of Rabelais' work from the *Tiers Livre* on: in Book III Rabelais examines and questions their use; in Book IV he illustrates their creative possibilities. Suggests that "the

spoken word can be considered as providing a basic unity for Rabelais' work" (p. 580), and sees in Book V a logical continuation of Rabelais' increasing emphasis on the positive and creative aspects of verbal communication.

7   BRAULT, GERARD J. "The Comic Design of Rabelais' *Pantagruel*." *Studies in Philology* 65, no. 1 (January):140–46.

Raises the question of *Pantagruel*'s unity, and the related question of "the order in which the various parts of the book were written" (p. 141). Challenges the then-prevailing view that *Pantagruel* is a mere "hodgepodge of unrelated stories" (p. 140). Develops Saulnier's idea that the novel is a work in the baroque style by following through "certain recurring motifs and literary devices" which for the author define that style (equated here with mannerism). Finds previous attempts to discover a degree of unity unconvincing, and contends that this unity is to be found in a pattern of recurring themes (such as that of thirst), and in a number of "episodic parallels resulting in an amusing series of contrasts" (p. 143), for example between Panurge and the Eschollier Lymousin, or between the visit of Epistémon to the Other World and Alcofrybas' descent into Pantagruel's mouth. Draws attention to the links provided at the beginning of chapters between seemingly unrelated episodes. Above all, points to the all-pervasive comic tone as the book's most effective unifying device: "Irony and parody inform this work throughout and assure its essential unity" (p. 145).

8   BUTOR, MICHEL. "La faim et la soif." *Critique* 257:827–54.

Remarks on Rabelais' *Quart Livre* and Francesco Colonna's *Le Songe de Poliphile*, whose first edition in French appeared in 1546. Rabelais identifies his protectors (Geoffroy d'Estissac, Jean du Bellay) with his giants, which explains why they are presented as good Christians. Self-preservation forces him to say what he does not always mean. His conception of Christianity is as different from that of the Sorbonne as from that of Calvin. Is convinced that Rabelais' work does contain a meditation on ethics and religion, but that it is so dangerously removed from orthodoxy that he is unwilling to bear full responsibility for it. Believes that Rabelais wants to share this responsibility with his reader. Interprets in this vein the "Epître en prophétie," in which he sees a three-way dialogue. Rabelais' Evangelical interpretation is voiced by Gargantua, the simple-minded one by Frère Jean, while Mellin de Saint-Gelais' text is consciously, deliberately ambivalent: it is left to the reader to choose an interpretation, and to bear the responsibility for the choice. Underscores a group of "allégories" or "hiéroglyphes" in the text: thirst, hunger, sexuality, viewed as symbols of restoration and as "métaphores de la lecture" (p. 850). Notes that the temple reached by the lovers at the end of the first part of the *Songe de Poliphile* is of a very similar nature. Sees in the final episode an expression of Rabelais' essential optimism, of his belief that all is possible: "l'utopie aura lieu, la faim, la soif auront raison de tout obstacle" (p. 853) in spite of the horrors of contemporary oppression.

9 ———. "Le parler populaire et les langues anciennes." In *Rabelais. Cahiers de la Compagnie Madeleine Renaud–Jean-Louis Barrault* 67 (September):83–98.

Discusses Rabelais' use of language in the encounters with the Écolier Limousin, Panurge, and Nazdecabre, as well as in the chapter on Gargantua's childhood made up entirely of proverbs. "Le langage populaire découvre la nature avec modestie; il ne cherche jamais à s'imposer, il reconnaît l'existence et la vertu du langage distingué...; au contraire, le langage savant, lorsqu'il s'opacifie, terrorise; il peut être une technique d'intimidation, d'asservissement et d'exploitation" (p. 85).

10 ———. "Rabelais et les hiéroglyphes." In *Saggi e Ricerche di Letteratura francese.* Vol. 9. Pisa: Libreria Goliardica, pp. 9–75.

An extended version of 1968.8. Offers remarks of a linguistic nature on the student from Limoges, Panurge's multi-lingual self-introduction, the rebirth of Latin through French, sign language, and Rabelais' use of proverbs. Insists on the chapter in which, according to the author, Rabelais "dénonce une fausse lecture des couleurs" (p. 43) and expresses his attraction for hieroglyphics viewed as an ideal language. "Tout son effort va donc tendre à constituer dans son récit, à partir de l'étude, du passage au crible de tous les langages qu'il connait, de gigantesques idéogrammes" (p. 47).

11 CATACH, NINA. *L'orthographe française à l'époque de la Renaissance.* Geneva: Librairie Droz, 495 pp.

Pages 153 through 160 are devoted to Rabelais. Briefly studies his spelling (of his name, of his manuscripts—of which only copies are known—of his printed texts). It had been previously noted that his style and grammar are simple at first, more complicated later. Points out that the same is true of his spelling. The typography of his works becomes progressively more archaic. In 1542, Dolet imposes his own spelling, corrects mistakes, imposes punctuation, cuts down on abbreviations. Compares three stages of spelling and punctuation in a sample of eighty-five words from *Gargantua* (François Juste, 1535; Dolet, 1542; Pierre de Tours, 1542). Notes that the changes are mainly in spelling, which becomes more modernized as the characters become roman. Deplores that Abel Lefranc had not chosen Pierre de Tours' 1548 text as the basis for his own critical edition. Concludes that if Rabelais' works look more archaic in spelling, syntax, and typography than those of lesser writers of the day, it is because Rabelais found these archaisms more in keeping with the nature of his texts.

1968

12    CHARPENTIER, FRANÇOISE. "Variations sur des litanies: A propos du *Tiers Livre de Pantagruel.*" *Revue des Sciences Humaines* 33, no. 131 (July–September):335–53.

    Acknowledges the poetic dimension of Rabelais' art, but believes that there is also in his work a resistance against the temptation of poetry; detects a movement from poetry to prose, through laughter as well as through the attitude of the characters. Studies the litanies of Book III (chapt. 26, 28, and 38) as yet another example of such a reduction of poetry to prose. Evokes their religious origin ("c'est une des plus anciennes et vénérables formes de la liturgie chrétienne," p. 340). Shows how Rabelais adopts the form, but to a very different purpose. Analyzes the complex structure of the litanies, and notes that they revolve somewhat unexpectedly around two of Rabelais' most important themes: procreation and folly. Sees in them an example of Rabelais' attempt to raise prose, by entirely prosaic means, to the dignity of a privileged mode of expression.

13    COLEMAN, DOROTHY [GABE]. "Rabelais: Menippean Satirist or Comic Novelist?" In *The French Renaissance and its Heritage: Essays Presented to Alan Boase.* London: Methuen, pp. 29–42.

    Studies the persona created by Rabelais to present his fiction, in its effect on characterization and narrative technique. Notes that it "splits into a host of narrative voices" (p. 31)—Alcofrybas, the "pseudo-chronicler" who first appears in chapt. 1 of *Pantagruel*, the third person omniscient author—enabling us to watch the story from a variety of points of view. Argues that Rabelais is a Manippean satirist, but only to a point, insofar as his characters do have some personality of their own and do not always, as should be the case in pure Manippean satire, speak unmistakably for the author. But finds that this personality, especially in the case of the giants, becomes more and more "abstract" as the work progresses. Concludes that unlike Cervantes, who makes us believe in the reality and truth of his characters, Rabelais "does not make truth and reality around his characters, but around the whole world" (p. 42).

14    DONTENVILLE, H[ENRI]. "La dent creuse et le cure-dents de Gargantua." *BAARD* 2, no. 7:205–08.

    Argues that the allusions to the tooth and the toothpick, left unexplained in Lefranc's critical edition as well as elsewhere, have their source in the folkloric tradition, and become clear in the light of a number of episodes in *Le Vroy Gargantua* and *Les Admirables Chronicques*.

15    ENGSTROM, ALFRED G. "A Few Comparisons and Contrasts in the Word-Craft of Rabelais and James Joyce." In *Renaissance and Other Studies in Honor of William Leon Wiley.* Edited by George B. Daniel. University of North Carolina Studies in the Romance Languages and Literatures, no. 72. Chapel Hill: University of North Carolina Press, pp. 65–82.

Without raising the question of a possible influence of Rabelais on Joyce, compares these "two gigantic representatives of the comic spirit in the Western world" (p. 65) in terms of their attitudes towards language. Finds an equivalent of Rabelais' *parolles gelées* in Joyce's tangible words, compares the comic effects each achieves through the use of pedantic, artificial language, comments on the "vital rhythm" of their prose, the creative power with which they endow their vocabulary, their delight in meaningless sounds and in word-play. Notes elements in Joyce which suggest a kinship with the romantic and symbolist poets, an undercurrent of guilt and anxiety absent from Rabelais' healthier, more optimistic work.

16  FOURNIER, PIERRE-FR. "Gargantua: Essai d'étymologie." *Revue Internationale d'Onomastique* 20:25–47.
    Traces the history of the name before and after Rabelais. Believes it to be of Auvergnat origin, and to date from the end of the twelfth century.

17  FRAME, DONALD M. "The Impact of Frere Jean on Panurge in Rabelais's *Tiers Livre*." In *Renaissance and Other Studies in Honor of William Leon Wiley*. Edited by George B. Daniel. University of North Carolina Studies in the Romance Languages and Literatures, no. 72. Chapel Hill: University of North Carolina Press, pp. 83–91.
    Notes that Frère Jean's sudden appearance at the end of chapt. 13 in Book III recalls the similarly sudden appearance of Panurge in chapt. 9 of *Pantagruel*. Ascribes them to the same need for new characters who could take on a comic function borne hitherto, with increasing unease, by the giants. Points out that Panurge and Frère Jean do not know each other, and that they are potential rivals competing for the king's and the reader's attention. Finds inconsistencies in the character of Panurge which suggest that Rabelais uses him as he will, whereas Frère Jean is a more three-dimensional, flesh-and-blood character. Studies the way they affect each other in the last three-quarters of the *Tiers Livre*. Shows that Panurge becomes more concerned with heresy, that he becomes an unmitigated coward, "in striking, direct contrast with the courageous Frère Jean." Ascribes to a similar desire to contrast the two characters Rabelais' insistence on Panurge's old age, although in this case the contrast is achieved against all chronological plausibility, since "the greatest ado over Panurge's old age is made by Frère Jean, who is theoretically a generation older" (p. 91).

18  FRANCIS, K. H. "Some Popular Scientific Myths in Rabelais: A Possible Source." In *Studies in French Literature Presented to H. W. Lawton*. Manchester: Manchester University Press; New York: Barnes and Noble, pp. 121–34.
    Attracts attention to the works of Joachim Sterck van Ringelberg, whose *Experimenta* may have been the source of some scientific lore used by

1968

Rabelais. Recalls that Ringelberg, born in Antwerp, had lectured on scientific subjects in Paris in 1529–30 and that he had been celebrated in a public session of the Parlement de Paris. Jourda had mentioned his *De ratione studii* in connection with references to astrology in *Pantagruel*. Suggests other passages that may have been inspired by Rabelais' readings of *Experimenta* and other works by Ringelberg: the magnetic doors in Book V, chapt. 36; the deciphering of "lettres non apparentes" in *Pantagruel*, chapt. 24; the myth of the ivy funnel allowing one to separate wine from water in *Gargantua*, chapt. 24 and in *Tiers Livre*, chapt. 52; as well as the trick played by Panurge with glasses of water and a javelin in *Pantagruel*, chapt. 27.

19  FRANÇON, MARCEL. "Notes Rabelaisiennes." *BAARD* 2, no. 7:220–24.
On numbers, the chess ballet in Colonna's *Hypneromachia*, Calvin in Orléans, the rhinoceros mentioned in Book V, the notion of state in Rabelais, the *Cymbalum Mundi*, some variants in *Pantagruel*, and Damiââo de Gois.

20  JOSIPOVICI, GABRIEL. "Rabelais." In *French Literature and Its Background.* Edited by John Cruickshank. London: Oxford University Press, pp. 17–31.
Sees in literary interpretation, and in the relationship between literature and reality, the central theme of Rabelais' work. Reads Rabelais' invitation to seek a higher, hidden meaning behind the comic surface of his book as a parody of allegorical approaches to literature, and as an attempt to ridicule the belief that literature is capable of offering a glimpse into the mysteries of reality. Argues that the world of Rabelais' book is the world of words and not the world of nature. Stresses Rabelais' insistence upon the subjective, and exclusively linguistic character of his work. Argues that Rabelais' descriptions, by their focus on minute details, draw attention to themselves rather than to an external reality they might have been thought to reflect; that they destroy the illusion of reality, and affirm the self-referential nature of literature. Reprinted: 1971.17.

21  KELLER, ABRAHAM C. "The Geophysics of Rabelais' Frozen Words." In *Renaissance and Other Studies in Honor of William Leon Wiley*. Edited by George B. Daniel. University of North Carolina Studies in the Romance Languages and Literatures, no. 72. Chapel Hill: University of North Carolina Press, pp. 151–65.
Studies the episode not so much for its literary sources (Plutarch, Aristotle, the Vulgate Bible, Caelius Calcagninus, and Castiglione, as well as possible contemporary reports of "unidentified sounds in the air"), or any possible hidden meaning (a controversial matter left unresolved), as for its connection with natural phenomena. Notes that reports of unidentified sounds in the air, often similar to Rabelais' version, are being taken seriously by atmospheric scientists today, and includes some of these reports in an appendix.

Points out that these sounds are sometimes explained in terms of noise made by distant thunder, transmitted by the process of "anomalous sound propagation." Believes this to be the most plausible explanation of the noises heard by the passengers of the Talamège as it navigated, in all likelihood, in the waters of the North Atlantic.

22    LA CHARITÉ, RAYMOND [C]. "An Aspect of Obscenity in Rabelais." In *Renaissance and Other Studies in Honor of William Leon Wiley*. Edited by George B. Daniel. University of North Carolina Studies in the Romance Languages and Literatures, no. 72. Chapel Hill: University of North Carolina Press, pp. 167–89.

Offers a linguistic commentary, in alphabetical order, on each of the thirty-six synonyms used by Rabelais to designate the sexual act; touches upon their etymology, their possible sources, their occurrence in other authors. Notes that approximately fifteen of these terms are of his own invention, and that in twenty-two cases, Rabelais extends the existing metaphorical connotations of the act of copulation. Points out that Rabelais finds his images primarily in the animal world and in human anatomy, but that he also derives them from the vocabulary of trades, the army, agriculture, and navigation. In Rabelais' own inventions, notes the effort to blend sound, motion, and rhythm with meaning. "In a word, there is in Rabelais a poetry of obscenity" (p. 189).

23    LONIGAN, PAUL R. "Rabelais' Pantagruélion." *Studi Francesi* 12, no. 34 (January–April):73–79.

Stresses the "centrality" of the Pantagruélion episode, and reminds us that the plant was named for its "inventor" and at least one of his virtues, namely the "joyeuse perfection" which forms the essence of Pantagruelism. It is that quality that will allow man to find his place in the universe: "It is a type of perseverence and acceptance, an aspect of self that seeks an equilibrium of contemplation and usefulness, of physical place and spiritual experience" (p. 78).

24    MURPHY, RUTH. "Rabelais, Thaumaste and the King's Great Matter." In *Studies in French Literature Presented to H. W. Lawton*. Manchester: Manchester University Press; New York: Barnes and Noble, pp. 261–85.

Offers a political interpretation of the Thaumaste episode. Rejects, after others, the identification of Thaumaste with Thomas More, and sees the episode as related to the two visits made by a group of learned Englishmen to Paris in 1529 and 1530, with the purpose of persuading the Faculty of Theology to give an opinion on the divorce of Henry VIII and Catherine of Aragon. Provides a detailed account of the ensuing consultations on what became known at the time as the "King's Great Matter." Believes that Rabelais must have been aware of these events, and that when he wrote in *Pantagruel* of the visit of a learned Englishman to Paris to dispute of difficult

1968

matters, it is to the King's Great Matter that he meant to allude. Among the details which strengthen this hypothesis, notes Rabelais' mention of a treatise published by Thaumaste in London on the subject (a treatise on the King's Great Matter had indeed appeared in the English capital in 1530), and the numerous allusions in the episode to the English royal house. Concludes that the Thaumaste chapters "are not a pointless though entertaining sketch, but a deliberate and sustained allusion to the Great Matter of the King of England" (p. 281).

25 PARKER, DOUGLAS VERNON. "François Rabelais, Playwright." Ph.D. dissertation, University of Washington, 196 pp.

Studies the traces of theatrical forms in Rabelais' work. Stresses Rabelais' ability to "block out" specific scenes (especially in the prologue to the *Tiers Livre* and the final episode of Book V), notes the congruence of dialogue with situation and character in selected scenes. Sees a development away from the theatrical presentation prevalent in the earlier books, as Rabelais makes increasingly frequent use of indirect discourse. Suggests "that the weaker sections of the controversial fifth book should be considered as a series of preliminary sketches" for scenes eventually perfected and inserted in Books III and IV. Credits the Benedictine order and "its established reputation in the production of religious drama" with offering Rabelais the opportunity to become acquainted with the theatrical tradition he was to exploit in his novels. See *Dissertation Abstracts International* 30 (1969):1176A.

26 REBHORN, WAYNE ALEXANDER. "Renaissance Optimism and the Limits of Freedom: Educational Theory in the Quattrocento. Erasmus, Castiglione, and Rabelais." Ph.D. dissertation, Yale University, 300 pp.

Finds Rabelais' fundamental optimism to be "darkened" by his realization that man's freedom of choice must of necessity be exercised in the context of essentially arbitrary systems of thought. See *Dissertation Abstracts International* 30 (1969):735A.

27 SCREECH, M[ICHAEL] A[NDREW]. "Aspects du rôle de la médecine dans la philosophie comique de Rabelais." In *Invention et imitation: Etudes sur la littérature du seizième siècle publiées sous la direction de J. A. G. Tans*. The Hague and Brussels: Van Goor Zonen, pp. 39–48.

Reminds us that satirical or philosophical laughter presupposes a norm in relation to which a particular situation can be seen as justifying the reaction of laughter, and that lacking such a norm, what was meant to be funny can be taken as serious and vice versa. In the case of Rabelais' Christian comedy, warns that it is particularly important to realize that the norm is Rabelais' Evangelical conception of religion, a syncretic belief founded on his knowledge of the Bible (especially of the New Testament), and enriched with elements borrowed from antiquity, in particular from the philosophy of

Plato. In order to appreciate the medical aspects of Rabelais' comic philosophy, notes that it is also important to realize that in the medical quarrels of his time, Rabelais sided with the Platonists against the disciples of Galen, partly because of his admiration for Plato, but also because Plato's medical theories, such as his ideas about the relative role of the brain and the testicles in the secretion of sperm, were more easily reconcilable with Christian thought. Argues that knowledge of Rabelais' bias in favor of Plato is all the more essential since the ideas of Galen, though mocked by Rabelais, are in fact closer to the concepts of modern medicine. Thus when Panurge, in the *Tiers Livre*, expounds his Platonico-medical theories and launches into his praise of testicles as the source of seminal immortality, the modern reader risks siding with him and against Rondibilis, who upholds the "cerebral" theory of sperm production, without realizing that for Rabelais, Panurge's "error" in this matter contributes to make of him a figure of fun. Concludes by remarking that these questions transcend the sphere of comedy by their moral implications; thus Plato's and Galen's theories relating to the production of sperm or the nature of the uterus can be shown to imply two distinctly opposite conclusions as to the function of procreation and the nature of woman, which in turn can shed significant light on such important moral questions as Rabelais' misogyny.

28 ———. *Aspects of Rabelais's Christian Comedy.* London: H. K. Lewis & Co., 19 pp.

Centered mainly on the *Tiers Livre* ("by far his most intellectual book," p. 10), and concerned with the norms of Rabelais' work as comic propaganda. "Rabelais's norm, both implicit and explicit, is over and over again, a Renaissance Christian one, a markedly Classical-Christian syncretism, in which Platonism, Stoicism, Skepticism all play a role, and which is enriched by medical and legal learning, not to mention a tough and sinewy theology" (pp. 8–9). Summarizes for an academic audience of non-specialists a set of ideas developed at greater length and in more scholarly fashion in 1968.27, and 1958.7. Text of an inaugural lecture given at University College, London, in 1967.

29 SHAFFER, WILLIAM GAYLORD. "Rabelais and Language: Studies in Communication." Ph.D. dissertation, Case Western Reserve University, 98 pp.

Studies the episodes dealing with language as a means of communication. Stresses ambiguity as a "protective measure" in the context of religious persecutions. Notes a similar use of language in other writers of the time, and relates it to the silence adopted by the Evangelists when "all hopes of peaceful reform between factions had been destroyed." See *Dissertation Abstracts International* 30 (1970):4464A.

1968

30  SMITH, BROTHER ROBERT. "Rabelais and the Nature of Comedy." *Revue de l'Université Laurentienne/Laurentian University Review* 1, no. 2:80–93.

Offers "a long walk" through the episode of the bells of Notre Dame (*Gargantua*, chapt. 17–20). Purports to see in it an allusion to some hypothetical earlier version of the *Affaire des Placards*. Notes the "Scotist ring" of Janotus' speech, identifies him with a certain John Major, "an electic [*sic*] Scotist" (p. 88) and a theologian at the Sorbonne. Argues that he is viewed with "cold hatred" (p. 92) as a representative of the repressive Faculty of Theology, that he is presented as "detestable" and dangerous, and that he is comic only to the extent that he does not realize (as does Rabelais and his ideal reader), that he and his likes are mere entertainers, at the mercy of the prince's will.

31  TETEL, MARCEL. "Thème et structure du *Quart Livre*." *BAARD* 2, no. 7:217–19.

Believes that even as episodic a work as the *Quart Livre* possesses its own order and equilibrium. Sees a principle of unity in the theme of moderation, introduced in the prologue and developed in the main episodes. Thinks the three episodes of Enassins, Ruach, and the Frozen Words amount to a kind of "art poétique," and that the last five chapters form a thematic conclusion and present the work as a possible "moyen d'évasion à la peur de la mort et pour l'auteur et pour le lecteur" (p. 219).

32  VESCOVI, GERHARD. *François Rabelais: Arzt und Schriftstelle der französischen Renaissance.* Stuttgart: Verlag A. W. Gentner, 40 pp.

An illustrated account of Rabelais' life, with brief references to his work.

33  WEINBERG, FLORENCE MAY. "Rabelais and Christian Hermetism: The Wine and the Will." Ph.D. dissertation, University of Rochester, 225 pp.

Treats two of the aspects which relate Rabelais' novels to the tradition of Christian Hermetism: wine, "as symbol and allegory of divinity...and divine possession"; and the will, "as expression of the innate nobility of the soul, by which man may choose to attune himself with the divine will." Studies the protagonists as archetypes on Rabelais' "anthropomorphic ladder of being," from the "magnanimous giant" to Panurge the fool, "to whom alone the divine revelation of the *Dive Bouteille* is granted." See *Dissertation Abstracts International* 29 (1968):279A. Revised for publication: 1972.34.

34  WORTLEY, W. VICTOR. "From *Pantagruel* to *Gargantua*: The Development of an Action Scene." *Romance Notes* 10, no. 1 (Autumn): 129–38.

Examines Pantagruel's duel with Loup Garou (*Pantagruel*, chapt. 29) as a prefiguration of the scene in which Frère Jean defends the abbey vineyard against Picrochole's army (*Gargantua*, chapt. 27). Notes elements of autoplagiarism, and finds "an enormous improvement of technique" (p. 138).


## 1969

1  BEAUJOUR, MICHEL. *Le Jeu de Rabelais: Essai sur Rabelais*. Paris: Editions de l'Herne, 179 pp.

First major Western study in the wake of Bakhtin's *Rabelais and His World* (1968.1, see also 1965.1). Claims merely to supplement Bakhtin's book. Uses the same methodological approach borrowed from the Russian formalists, but widened to include such Western points of reference as Joyce and the surrealists. In opposition to academic criticism and its emphasis on the humanistic content of Rabelais' novel, follows Bakhtin in underscoring its popular, carnivalesque spirit: "Le roman ne postule pas tant un nouveau monde ouvert par l'humanisme, que la permanence d'un contre-univers populaire, collectif, anonyme, anti-individualiste, qui intègre vie et mort dans une chaîne sans fin de destruction et de renouveaux" (p. 9). Minimizes the importance of Rabelais' message ("Rabelais *ne veut rien dire*," p. 26), just as it reduces the significance of French humanism itself, defined in terms of essentially trivial pursuits: "recopier, commenter, traduire, bêtifier" (p. 14). Rabelais does not *mean*; he merely *plays*, with language as well as images and ideas. Argues against any attempt at interpretation; the whole history of Rabelais criticism seen as a "tissu de contradictions et de sottises" (p. 26). The chief ideological interest of Rabelais lies in the fact that it turns its back upon the conventional notions of knowledge and culture propounded by humanism. Concedes that Rabelais' work does have a subversive dimension, but claims that the subversion is less ideological than artistic: it lies less in the attacks upon accepted values than in the negation of any hierarchy between the various stylistic registers which Rabelais allows to coexist in the texture of his prose.


2  BERK, PHILIP ROBERT. "Evangelical Irony: Allegory and Design in Rabelais." Ph.D. dissertation, University of Pittsburgh, 437 pp.

"Is there an Evangelical esthetic which consciously informs his work?" Seeks to relate Rabelais' style to his religious conviction, and finds such a connection in Rabelais' ironic, theological perspective, and in the Hermetic symbolism of a work deemed to be modelled in both style and structure upon the Bible. See *Dissertation Abstracts International* 30 (1970):3448A.


3  BICHON, J[EAN]. "Sagesse humaine ou sagesse canine?" *Études Rabelaisiennes* 8:87–90.

"A l'exemple d'icelluy vous convient estre *saiges*": in this exhortation to seek out the "substantificque moelle" of *Gargantua* by following the example of the dog worrying his bone, suggests that Rabelais is using *saiges* in the technical sense the term had acquired in the Middle Ages and will retain to the end of the seventeenth century, namely in reference to a dog considered remarkable for its sense of smell and its ability to follow the scent of its prey without allowing itself to be distracted. Notes the relatively few examples in Rabelais of the use of "sage" in the sense of "wise," and sees in the cynegetic use of the term in the prologue to *Gargantua* an example of Rabelais' penchant for archaic and technical vocabulary.

4   CHATELUX, JEAN. "Le bois de gaïac au XVIe siècle ou de Hutten au Pantagruélion." *Études Rabelaisiennes* 8:29–50.
    Evokes the discovery of "gaïac" by the Spaniards on the island of Hispaniola (today Santo Domingo), designated as "lignum sanctum" or "lignum indicum"; notes its introduction into Europe, where it was prized as a remedy against syphilis and other venereal diseases. Points to the propaganda in its favor by Ulrich de Hutten in 1519, after a cure during which he was able to experience its medicinal virtues in the treatment of syphilis. Notes its subsequent praise by medical authorities and its widespread use, despite the fact that the ancients had not spoken of it. Shows that Rabelais was aware of it as early as 1532. Without disputing the various symbolic interpretations of the Pantagruélion episode in the *Tiers Livre*, and its debt to Pliny's praise of flax, suggests that Rabelais may also have been influenced by the discovery of a new plant which, at the time when he was writing, "avait déjà fait couler beaucoup d'encre" (p. 46).

5   COLEMAN, DOROTHY [GABE]. "Rabelais: Two Versions of the 'Storm at Sea' episode." *French Studies* 23, no. 2 (April):113–30.
    Compares the 1552 version with that of 1548, and discusses their artistic and religious significance. Notes variants and additions, finds the Erasmian source of the episode to be much more bitingly satirical than either of Rabelais' versions, to insist on the importance of praying directly to God (as against confessing to a priest), and to have generally a much greater religious significance (in spite of Eudémon's contribution). Argues that the focus of the episode is not on the religious attitude of the characters but on the grotesque interplay between them, and on the life, energy, and humanity with which Rabelais endows Frère Jean and Panurge. Concludes that the chapters on the storm at sea should not be read as a philosophical or religious allegory, but rather as an artistically satisfying episode in a comic romance. See 1967.6.

6   DONTENVILLE, HENRI. "Rabelais et Dolet." *BAARD* 2, no. 8:245–52.
    Points out intellectual affinities between Rabelais and Dolet, and stresses the difference in their attitudes in specific circumstances. Thus while both work for Gryphe, during strikes Rabelais is on the side of the "patrons dont il tire profit" (p. 248), whereas Dolet sides with the strikers.

7   DUMONT, F. "Territoires et tenures chez Rabelais." In *Mémoires de la Société pour l'Histoire du Droit et des Institutions des anciens pays bourguignons, comtois et romands*. Faculté de Droit et de Science Politique de Dijon, no. 29. Dijon: Siège de la Société, pp. 215–30.

Examines the juridical status of the giants' possessions, and that of the various regions mentioned by Rabelais. Reminds us that Utopia, although its exact location is not specified, is clearly independent of the king of France, and that the giants are not French. Reviews the history of the giants' kingdom, discusses their various annexations, defines and distinguishes the various forms of "tenures" mentioned in the texts. Concludes that on these matters as on many others, Rabelais "a conservé le souvenir de ses conversations avec Tiraqueau à Fontenay-le-Comte" (p. 230).

8   FRANÇON, MARCEL. "Note sur *Le Tiers Livre* de Rabelais." *Études Rabelaisiennes* 8:81–83.

Suggests that the reference to the siege of Corinth in the prologue is not, as Lefranc believed in his critical edition, a historical allusion to the defense of Paris under Jean du Bellay in 1536, but rather to the second expedition of Charles V into France in September of 1544. Concedes that the suggestion had previously been made by Gaston Zeller in 1936, and by the author himself in the "Note sur le prologue du *Tiers Livre*" (1963.9).

9   ———. "Notes Rabelaisiennes." *BAARD* 2, no. 8:256–62.

Brief notes on the geographic itinerary of Pantagruel's voyage to Utopia, the picaresque tradition, remarks on Rabelais by Jacques-Auguste de Thou (to the effect that by the end of his life Rabelais had totally abandoned the scholarly life and sank into debauchery), on the term "Cannibals" (which for Rabelais denotes a monstrous African tribe), and on the structuralist and folkloric dimension of Bakhtin's study on Rabelais.

10  HENRY, BERNARD-M. "Sur la jument de Gargantua." *BAARD* 2, no. 8:244.

Suggests that the name of certain rocks along the coast near Sables-d'Olonne may have given Rabelais the idea of having Gargantua's mare be brought to him by sea at that particular point.

11  HORNIK, HENRY. "Rabelais and Idealism." *Studi Francesi* 13, no. 37 (January–April):16–25.

Seeks signs of a spiritual itinerary that would provide a unifying thread in an otherwise fragmented work. Proposes to see in *Pantagruel* and *Gargantua* an initial, intuitive stage, followed in Books III and IV by a rational phase, and culminating, in the transcendent level reached in Book V, in the Platonic symbolism of the Dive Bouteille sequence, as "merely recapitulating a theme and its variations of man's quest for illumination about the ultimate answers" (p. 76).

1969

12    ———. "Time and Periodization in French Renaissance Literature: Rabelais
and Montaigne." *Studi Francesi* 15, no. 39:477–81.
      Questions the validity of traditional periodization by pointing out that
Rabelais' and Montaigne's works, although written at significantly different
times, both show a similar evolution through three phases corresponding to
the beginning, the peak, and the decline of the Renaissance.


13    LARMAT, JEAN. "Picrochole est-il Noël Beda?" *Études Rabelaisiennes*
8:13–25.
      Believes that *Gargantua* as a whole symbolizes the predicaments of the
Evangelicals at the time of its publication, and the Picrocholine War symbol-
izes more specifically the accusations and persecutions launched by the
Faculty of Theology. Does not question Lefranc's interpretation of the
episode as a transposition of a legal quarrel between Gaucher de Sainte-
Marthe and the "marchands et bateliers de la Loire" (p. 13), in which
Rabelais' father may have had an interest. But beyond this local quarrel sees
a war of much greater importance: "celle qui opposa la Sorbonne aux
Réformés" (p. 14). Documents the key role played by Noël Beda as theolo-
gian, principal of the Collège de Montaigne and "syndic" of the Faculty of
Theology in the religious persecutions against the humanists and the
Evangelicals in the fifteen years before *Gargantua* was written. "Dans
l'épisode de la guerre picrocholine, [Rabelais] se venge de l'homme qui, à lui
seul, représente à ses yeux l'adversaire sans scrupules, l'ennemi buté" (p. 21).
Draws parallels between Beda and the leader of the "fouaciers de Lerné."
Finds the "higher meaning" of the Picrocholine War in the fact that it symbol-
izes the conflict between Beda and the theologians of the Sorbonne on the one
hand, and the humanists and Evangelicals on the other. "A notre avis,
Picrochole est Noël Beda" (p. 13).


14    MASTERS, G[EORGE] MALLARY. "Rabelais and Renaissance Figure
Poems." *Études Rabelaisiennes* 8:53–68.
      Discusses the poem in the form of a bottle in the Dive Bouteille episode
of Book V, considered authentic. Traces the tradition of the genre from its origins in the sixth-century Alexandrian *Technopægnia*, through the "carmina
figurata" of the Christian era, and the revival of the genre during the
Renaissance. Believes Rabelais may have known of both traditions through
the works of Rabanus Maurus, and may have had knowledge of such contemporary examples of the form as Mélin de Saint-Gelais's *Aelles* and Alciati's
emblems. Argues that the Dive Bouteille episode is "replete with Platonic and
Dionysian symbolism," that the visit to the temple is "an initiation to the mysteries of ancient Greece," and that the poem itself is part of a ritual initiation
(p. 63) summarizing the symbolism of Panurge's quest. Sees in the "tem-
perie" mentioned in the poem an ideal of conduct closely related to the

Socratic ideal of moderation echoed elsewhere in the novels, and in the poem itself a sign of Panurge's conversion to the tenets of *pantagruélisme*.

15 ———. *Rabelaisian Dialectic and the Platonic-Hermetic Tradition*. Albany: State University of New York Press, 152 pp.

Offers an allegorical reading of the five books as a synthesis of Platonic idealism and Hermetic naturalism into a philosophy of the divine as both imminent and transcendent, and of man as a dynamic combination of body and soul. In chapt. 1, "Rabelais Platonicus," studies Platonic imagery (the *Silènes*, the *os médulaire*, the androgyne) as a play on appearance and reality, and an expression of the dialectical coincidence of opposites. In chapt. 2, "Homo bibens," focuses on the images of wine and the symposium as reflecting the spirit of conviviality at the heart of Rabelais' *pantagruélisme* and, in the last two books, the symbolism of the Dionysian mysteries. In chapt. 3, "Rabelais hermeticus," investigates the function of the Hermetic sciences in the novels, shows Rabelais' naturalism to be inseparable from such notions as harmony, reason, and moderation, and interprets Panurge's quest in terms of the Cabalistic search for completion through erotic union. In an appendix, brings the discussion to bear on the problem of the authorship of Book V. Notes the continuity of Platonic and Hermetic themes throughout the five books, argues that they all converge in the episode of the Divine Bottle, and suggests that this convergence demonstrates the unity of Rabelais' work and "points to the authenticity of the *Cinquiesme Livre*" (p. 107).

16 MAUNY, RAYMOND. "Rabelais et les Saints." *BAARD* 2, no. 8:239–43.

Comments on Rabelais' attitude towards the various categories of saints, and notes that being a good Christian does not prevent him from putting the saints "à leur place."

17 PAISSE, JEAN-MARIE. "Une page d'ironie Rabelaisienne." *BAARD* 2, no. 8:253–55.

Attracts attention to examples of irony in the chapter on Gargantua's education under the tutelage of his earlier masters (*Gargantua*, chapt. 21). Stresses the "caractère discrètement narquois" of a work whose broad satire has perhaps been studied at the expense of this aspect of Rabelais' comic style.

18 PARIS, JEAN. "Rabelais et le langage antinomique." *Modern Language Notes* 84, no. 4 (May):505–31.

Argues that the most revolutionary aspect of Rabelais' work consists not so much in the audacity of its thought as in Rabelais' emphasis on the contingent, arbitrary nature of language, and in his refusal to reduce the function of language to mere communication. Studies the "destructive intention" behind Rabelais' use of language. Suggests that his linguistic profusion does not aim at naming the innumerable facets of reality; notes the tendency of his lists and inventories to dissolve into irreality. Finds a similar tendency in Rabelais' recourse to neologisms and onomatopoeia ("Si les mots inventés irréalisent le signifié, les onomatopées irréalisent le signifiant," p. 522) as well as in his use of *isotopies*, whereby words coexist on various semantic levels between which the reader finds himself incapable of choosing. Notes that this linguistic ambiguity extends to the reader, in passages where Rabelais dissociates the characters from their verbal utterances (as in the *Propos des bien yvres* in chapt. 5 of *Gargantua*), or in his incoherent inner monologues. Nor is silence free from ambiguity, in passages where gestural language takes over from verbal expression: "Ces gestes mystérieux, si nettement décrits, se veulent autant d'equivalents physiques de nos messages, et comme eux ne parviennent qu'à porter à l'extrême l'ambiguité, l'absurde qui les sous-tend" (p. 531).

19  RIGOLOT, FRANÇOIS PAUL. "Problématique et poétique du langage chez Rabelais." Ph.D. dissertation, University of Wisconsin, Madison, 339 pp.

Notes in Rabelais the simultaneous presence of a desire to express what he believes to be truth, and to use words for an exclusively ludic purpose, resulting in a conflict between thought and expression. Suggests that this *agonistic* dimension of Rabelais' text is counterbalanced by the *encomiastic* episodes, which thus bring a poetic resolution to the problematics of language. See *Dissertation Abstracts International* 31 (1970):766A. Revised for publication: 1972.29.

20  SCREECH, M[ICHAEL] A[NDREW]. "Eleven-Month Pregnancies: a Legal and Medical Quarrel a propos of *Gargantua*, Chapter Three: Rabelais, Alciati and Tiraqueau." *Études Rabelaisiennes* 8:93–106.

Claims that in order to understand Rabelais' comic treatment of serious subjects it is not necessary—it is in fact often wrongheaded—to go back to primary sources. "He makes his points over and over again by exploiting commonplaces which were available to his readers (and to himself) through secondary sources" (p. 94). To find the immediate sources of Rabelais' ideas on the subject of long pregnancies, one need only to look at texts which dealt with the subject at the time Rabelais was writing about it. Points out that the controversy had been made fashionable by Alciati in his *Problemata* of 1531, and taken up by his follower Tiraqueau in his commentary on *L. Si unquam, c. de revoc. donat* published probably after *Gargantua*, but which Rabelais could have consulted in manuscript. Claims that paragraph 171 of Tiraqueau's work was the source of Rabelais' erudition on long pregnancies, a subject which attracts him mostly by its satirical aspect. Acknowledges that Rabelais is careless with the text, and that his conclusion is perhaps different from Tiraqueau's, but reminds us that Rabelais does not set out to be fair to all parties in the controversy. He merely intends "to get the maximum of fun out of this problem" (p. 105).

21 ———. "Rabelais: Le *Tiers Livre* de Pantagruel." In *The Art of Criticism: Essays in French Literary Analysis.* Edited by Peter H. Nurse. Edinburgh: The University Press, pp. 27–39.

"To appreciate Rabelais we must first understand him" (p. 29). Explicates an excerpt from chapt. 25 of Book III, on the consultation with Her Trippa. Argues that both literary sensibility and "patient erudition" are required to arrive at Rabelais' meaning in this example of "intellectual comedy at its best." "What we have here is a farce raised almost miraculously to the heights of moral laughter" (p. 38). Confronts the text with its sources and stresses Rabelais' "ability to select and reject," and to use the materials for his own comic purpose.

22 ———. "Some Reflexions on the Abbey of Thelema." *Études Rabelaisiennes* 8:109–14.

Suggests that both the Picrocholine War and the Abbey of Thelema episodes were conceived independently of the rest of *Gargantua*. Sees the idea of rewarding Frère Jean with the abbey of Thelema as an afterthought, clumsily grafted onto the rest of the book. Notes that whereas the abbey was to be founded "à son devis," it is Gargantua who is credited with establishing the rules. Notes also that the supposedly ignorant Friar declines the offer of his own abbey with a quotation from Plato which would have been more fitting in Gargantua's mouth. Finds at the heart of the episode the rejection of subservient obedience, and the paradox of freedom leading to moral conformity. Underscores the fundamental optimism of the episode, but finds it surprisingly at odds with the inscription over the gate and the concluding enigma. "Both these chapters introduce into the book a new tragic dimension,...both are last minute interpolations" (p. 112) making Thelema unexpectedly a refuge from religious persecution or a preparation for martyrdom. "The parts simply do not fit together" (p. 113). To explain these inconsistencies, suggests that the interpolations were written after the Affaire des Placards, which had put an end to a period of Evangelical optimism. Believes that the book itself was published later than is generally thought, "after the onset of persecution in October, 1534" (p. 113).

23 TELLE, É[MILE] V. "Une allusion (?) de Charles Estienne à Rabelais en 1553." *Études Rabelaisiennes* 8:75–78.

Notes that in his translation of Landi's *Paradossi* in 1553, Charles Estienne adds to Landi's list of illustrious scholars who died victims of their own erudition, the names of Jean Tissier, Erasmus, and that of "le poete Françoys." Suggests, by a process of elimination but also for more positive reasons, that the latter may well refer to Rabelais, noting that the term "poète," besides its modern meaning, could also designate what we would now call a "romancier." Sees in this first allusion to Rabelais after his death a touching

1970

testimonial, especially in the light of Rabelais' bad reputation with Charles Estienne's brother Robert.

24 TETEL, MARCEL. *Rabelais et l'Italie*. Florence: Leo Olschki Editore, Biblioteca dell'Archivum Romanicum, 314 pp.

Not concerned with Rabelais' sojourns in Italy or with possible Italian sources of Rabelais' work. Shows that even in as Catholic a country as Italy, and despite the absence of any Italian translation of Rabelais until that of *Gargantua* in 1886, Rabelais' influence was not as insignificant as has been asserted. Studies the various points of contact, stylistic as well as thematic, between Rabelais and Italian writers of the second half of the sixteenth century and beyond. Notes that the first reference to Panurge occurs as early as 1540, and that Rabelais himself is mentioned for the first time in 1568–69 by Corbinellei, who admires his erudition; Gargantua will not be mentioned until 1595, in a tale by Poncino della Torre. Notes similarities between Lando's *Paradossi* (1547) and Rabelais, especially in matters of verbal exuberance and a search for serenity in paradox. In chapt. 2 finds points of contact with sixteenth-century Italian comedy: Aretino, Della Porta (for "la thématique du Ventre"), Giordano Bruno (same nonconformism, same verbal energy, same disregard for linear structure of narrative). Admits that during the baroque period traces of Rabelais are more difficult to find, but insists that they are present nonetheless, for instance in the dithyrambic poetry of Francesco Redi. Shows that Rabelais' presence can also be felt in the works of Giulio Cesare Croce, Gianbattista Basile, and Francesco Fulvio Frugoni, before surfacing in the eighteenth century when, despite a general predilection for the aesthetics of classicism, he is mentioned favorably by Bettinelli and Baretti, imitated by Gozzi in his *Marfisa*, and relives in the personality and the works of the abbé Galiani. Brought to the attention of the early romantics, Rabelais earns the admiration of Ugo Foscolo and the scorn of the Church and Cesare Cantù, before being raised to the ranks of the great humorists of world literature by De Sanctis and Dossi. In chapt. 7, insists on the relationship between Rabelais and Belli, the author of hundreds of sonnets in Roman dialect: finds identical targets of satire, the same interest in poetic fragmentation, the same use of imagery and verbal play. In the last two chapters, notes the contribution of Italian scholars to Rabelais criticism. The appendix contains a translation of Lodovico Arrivabene's *Sylvius ocreatus*, Frugoni's catalogue of the Gastrimargiti Library (compared with that of Saint Victor in Rabelais), and critical reviews of the first performances of Marinetti's *Le Roi Bonbance*.

## 1970

1 ARONSON, NICOLE HABATJOU. "Les idées politiques de Rabelais." Ph.D. dissertation, City University of New York, 214 pp.

Rejects Lefranc's view of Rabelais as spokesman for royal policies. Finds Rabelais' conception of royalty to be essentially an idealized amalgam of Plato's philosopher-king and the father-king of Erasmus. Believes Rabelais to be equally idealistic in his pleas for a system of stable alliances and in his position on peace. Notes that the tone of Rabelais' satire grows more bitter and violent in Book V, and that his caricature of the excesses of the Valois court contrasts dramatically with the idealistic view of royalty in the earlier books. Even in these, however, Rabelais cannot be considered to have acted as a tool of the monarchy, whose autocratic regime was "so obviously in direct contradiction to his beliefs." See *Dissertation Abstracts International* 31 (1970):2866A.

2    BAKHTIN, MIKHAIL. *L'œuvre de François Rabelais et la culture populaire au moyen âge et sous la Renaissance.* Traduit par Andrée Robel. Paris: Gallimard. 471 pp.

French translation of 1965.1. English translation: 1968.1.

3    BECK, WILLIAM JOHN. "Le Cas de Gymnaste: (*Gargantua*, chap. XXXV)." *BAARD* 2, no. 9:290–91.

When Gymnaste states that his "cas va au rebours," he does not use *cas* in its legal meaning, as commentators have it, but in the sense of "membre viril." Points out that given the position in which Gymnaste finds himself ("le cul tourné vers la teste du cheval"), he is merely making a statement of fact.

4    CHESNEAU, ALBERT. "Un point de sémiotique pantagruélique: Problèmes et valeur du langage par signes selon Rabelais." *Bulletin des Jeunes Romanistes* 17 (December):35–43.

In the three chapters of *Pantagruel* dealing with the debate in sign language with Thaumaste, highlights certain aspects of the relationship between signal and message in the act of communication that anticipate important principles of the new science of semiology. Through the character of Thaumaste, Rabelais calls into question the value of language and claims the superiority of signs over words, presumably because they are more natural, more spontaneous, more true. In the course of the gestural "dialogue," he shows himself to be conscious of certain necessities of semiotic discourse: proper conditions of emission and reception, the use of one coherent code understood by both the "émetteur" and the "récepteur." Sees the comic aspect of the scene as lying in a "substitution de code": in the fact that Panurge has substituted for a set of neutral signals a set of insolent ones. "La drôlerie du texte provient précisément de ce que le lecteur s'aperçoit de la substitution d'un code grossier à un code noble, alors que les personnages du récit n'en sont pas conscients et qu'à leur niveau l'ambiguïté des signes subsiste" (p. 42), thanks to the presence of the ever serious Pantagruel. Sees in Rabelais' attempt at such a complex experiment a sure sign of his interest in the problems of language.

1970

5   DE GRÈVE, MARCEL. "L'évolution de la pensée de Rabelais." *BAARD* 2, no. 9:281–84.

Reiterates his opinion that the elimination of irreverent allusions to the Church and the Sorbonne in the 1542 edition had nothing to do with the fact that Rabelais' first two books had been condemned by the Sorbonne, and everything to do with his growing disillusionment with the evolution of evangelism toward Calvinistic reformation. Argues that Rabelais had come to believe that the cause of evangelism was no longer worth fighting for: "La position de Rabelais sera dorénavant une attitude de non-engagement" (p. 283). See 1961.4.

6   DIXON, JACK EDMUND GARRARD. "Une concordance du *Gargantua* de Rabelais: (Volumes I and II)." Ph.D. dissertation, Stanford University, 2387 pp.

Provides a concordance of the "pre-edited text," and discusses the problems related to the use of a computer-generated concordance of a prose work. Published by Droz in 1992.

7   DONTENVILLE, HENRI. "Rabelais édulcoré par le révérend père Niceron." *BAARD* 2, no. 9:285–89.

Reminds us that in his biography of Rabelais, Niceron insists—rather surprisingly—on the latter's exemplary piety, on his orthodoxy in his works as well as in his life. Notes that Niceron could not have been blind to Rabelais' obscenity and irreverence, but argues that for him the essential consideration is that Rabelais should have remained officially in the bosom of the Roman Catholic church.

8   FONVIEILLE-ALQUIER, FRANÇOIS. *Rabelais.* Collection "Les Géants de la littérature mondiale," Périodique Paris-Match. Verona: Arnoldo Mondadori, 134 pp.

A synthesis, for the general public, of what is known of the man ("Rabelais vu de plus près") and his work. Summarizes the five books, offers a series of excerpts, studies the characters, takes note of the work's reception ("Rabelais de siècle en siècle") and discusses the main contemporary approaches. Abundant iconography.

9   FRANÇON, MARCEL. "Notes Rabelaisiennes." *BAARD* 2, no. 9:301–06.

On the prologue to the *Tiers Livre* (less optimistic than is sometimes thought); on Rabelais and Samuel Beckett; on the *Sciomachie*.

10  GAIGNEBET, CLAUDE. "Une coutume de folklore juridique dans l'œuvre de Rabelais (La redevance du pet)." In *Approches de nos traditions orales*. Arts et Traditions Populaires, no. 18. Paris: G. P. Maisonneuve et Larose, pp. 183–94.

Notes that Rabelais' references to everyday reality, proverbial expressions, or popular customs are often more difficult to understand than erudite allusions that scholarly investigation can hope to clarify. Explains a passage in the *Tiers Livre*, chapt. 5 ("Tous les peteurs du monde petans disent 'Voyla pour les quittes'") in the light of three early texts which allude to the custom of farting as partial settlement of one's debt ("les quittes" being related in Rabelais' expression to "être quitte," "être acquitté"). Shows that two other passages referring to breaking wind (in *Pantagruel*, chapt. 25, and the *Quart Livre*, chapt. 9) are related to a folkloric theme.

11    GREENE, T[HOMAS] M. *Rabelais, A Study in Comic Courage.* Englewood Cliffs, N.J.: Prentice Hall, 119 pp.
      "We are only beginning to have a body of criticism commensurate in quality with the body of Rabelais scholarship" (p. v). Seeks to help right the balance by presenting Rabelais' work as both courageously committed to a number of humanist causes, and as distinguished by the fecund invention of a comic artist of the highest rank. Notes that Rabelais' treatment of character and his conception of narrative structure defy conventional expectations. Stresses his experimental use of language and the interplay between the comic and the angelic voices throughout the work. Judges *Pantagruel* to be "the crudest and the least coherent" (p. 20) of the five books, but argues that it also contains some of the most memorable pages of the entire work, and displays a richness of ironic effect "without precedent in French literature" (p. 21). Beyond surface similarities, finds *Gargantua* to be genuinely original and structurally superior to its predecessor, with "a core of serious intellectual content neither to be ignored nor easily isolated" (p. 38). Underscores the polemical rather than the utopian dimension of the Thélème episode, and finds Rabelais' religious orientation in Book II to be particularly controversial in its sympathy for the Evangelical movement and its incompatibility with it. Presents the *Tiers Livre* as darker in tone, and less concerned with women and marriage than with the nature of truth and the nature of action. Sees it as a long meditation on the notion of courage, culminating with the expression of an ideal of "lofty indifference to the contingencies of Fortune" (p. 71), embodied in the symbol of the Pantagruelion, and derived from the Stoic ideal of *ataraxia*. In the *Quart Livre*, notes "a partial shift of emphasis from individual to social experience" (p. 82), remarks on the difficulty for the modern reader to give its full value to the relatively discredited notion of *médiocrité* at the heart of the book, and finds the latter to be less exuberant in its imagination, less open in its spirit, less generous in its laughter than the earlier novels. On the other hand, suggests that much of Book V is much finer than is generally admitted, and finds in "the glories of the *Cinquiesme Livre*" an argument in favor of the book's at least partial authenticity.

1970

12  GRIFFIN, R[OBERT]. "The French Renaissance Commonplace and Literary Context: An Example." *Neophilologus* 54, no. 3 (July):258–61.

Claims that when Pantagruel compares Panurge to a mouse trapped in pitch ("la souriz empeigée") in *Tiers Livre*, chapt. 37, he is not so much using "un terme provincial" (Lefranc) as alluding to a proverb in Erasmus' *Adagia*; that Rabelais is taking into account the Erasmian context of the proverb; and that in so doing he is following a tradition that defines for the Renaissance writer the rhetorical use of such commonplaces as *sententiae, exempla*, proverbs, and apophthegms.

13  KIRSTEIN, BONI H.-J. "Could the Lion-Fox Episode in Chapter XV of *Pantagruel* Be a Fable?" *Romance Notes* 12, no. 1 (Fall):180–85.

Argues that the episode could (and should) be read in isolation from the rest of the chapter, that it is inspired by Aesop like the other episode contained in the same chapter, and that it corresponds to the definition of a fable since it presents animals (the lion) acting like human beings (a monk), and implies a moral thesis: that monks are blindly pious and ignorant of female anatomy.

14  KLEIS, CHARLOTTE COSTA. "Structural Parallels and Thematic Unity in Rabelais." *Modern Language Quarterly* 31, no. 4 (December):403–23.

Provides a rapid overview of recent criticism dealing with the question of unity in Rabelais' fictional work. Argues that the first four books are bound together "by one intellectual attitude and one way of experiencing it" (p. 405). More specifically, finds them to be linked by a common preoccupation with the nature of knowledge and truth, and by the same structural device: an "antithesis between those who understand this problem and those who do not." Sees Book IV, with its message of moderation and tolerance, as the practical resolution of "the philosophical problem intuitively explored in the first, consciously elaborated in the second, and systematically demonstrated in the third" (p. 406). Finds this unity to be maintained by a group of recurring ideas, and by scenes which "lend a pictorial quality to the dramatic presentation of the moral" (p. 422).

15  MAUNY, R[AYMOND]. "Rabelais et l'amour." *BAARD* 2, no. 9:292–96.

Stresses the ambiguity of the text as it relates to women. Admits that most of the time women are badly treated, but points out the presence of a "Rabelais respectueux des femmes, ami du mariage" (p. 293), even though finds himself forced to conclude that Rabelais' general attitude is that of an antifeminist.

16  PARIS, JEAN. *Rabelais au futur*. Paris: Éditions du Seuil, 252 pp.

Argues for an analogy between Rabelais' discovery of the arbitrariness of language and current linguistic preoccupations with what he terms "la problématique du langage." "Une chose semble acquise: c'est que le signifiant cesse ici de participer du signifé, qu'entre eux le lien est désormais tranché, qui jusqu'alors les unissait en Dieu" (p. 126). Finds Rabelais to be most revolutionary in his "contestation du langage," insofar as this denunciation of the arbitrariness of language—centuries before Saussure—undermines the foundations which had justified the totalitarian orientation of the various modes of medieval thought. Casts doubt on the ideological importance of Gargantua's letter to Pantagruel in Book I, and of Rabelais' encyclopedic program in Book II, by suggesting that the texts are subverted by their immediate context. Underscores the importance of economics in the *Tiers Livre*, and sees in the journey of Book IV above all "une métaphore de la critique" (p. 218). In general, ascribes to Rabelais' discovery of the contingency of language the ambiguities, paradoxes, and discontinuities of his text.

17  PHILLIPS, MARGARET MANN. "Quelques pensées sur Rabelais lecteur des *Adages*." In *Hommages à M. Delcourt*. Revue d'Études Latines, no. 14. Brussels: Collection Latomus, pp. 332–41.

  Discusses the classical allusions which Rabelais can be said with certainty to have borrowed from Erasmus' *Adagia*. Finds that the borrowings grow more frequent with time, and that by Books III and IV they have become systematic. Confines the discussion to the quotations to be found in *Pantagruel* and *Gargantua*. Points out that in *Pantagruel* the borrowings are primarily decorative. In *Gargantua*, provides brief notes on the quotations drawn from the longer and more celebrated commentaries, such as *Sileni Alcibiadis* (in the prologue) and *Festina lente* (in a passage on hieroglyphics). Concludes that Rabelais used the *Adagia* in any number of ways: "de Rabelais à Érasme, c'est une association à la fois libre et filiale" (p. 341).

18  RIGOLOT, FRANÇOIS [PAUL]. "Rabelais et l'éloge paradoxal." *Kentucky Romance Quarterly* 17, no. 3:191–98.

  Credits the Renaissance predilection for the paradoxical encomium to Lucian's satirical dialogues and Erasmus' *Praise of Folly*. Notes its presence throughout Rabelais' work, even in seemingly serious passages, before Rabelais gives it pride of place in the opening and closing episodes of the *Tiers Livre*. Reads the description of the world without debts as a prefiguration of the central theme of lack of meaningful communication pervading the rest of Book III and taken up again in Book IV. Sees in the section on the praise of debts an original mixture of metaphysical poetry tinged with burlesque. Notes in the chapters on the Pantagruélion a similar duality ("la voix qui décrit et la voix qui chante," p. 195), and the same movement from descriptive prose to lyric poetry. In Book IV, focuses on the six chapters devoted to Gaster. Accounts for the divergent interpretations of the episode by the duality of its semantic structure ("le thème du Ventre" and "le thème de l'Art," p. 197). Concludes by suggesting that the significance of the paradoxical encomium for Rabelais lies in the opportunity it offers to express his ambiguous stance

1970

towards lyricism and verbal extravagance: "En adoptant le genre de l'éloge paradoxal, le poète a su à la fin stigmatiser toutes les outrances du lyrisme et s'abandonner naturellement à l'enthousiasme spirituel et sanguin qui le caractérise" (p. 198).

19  RUSSELL, DANIEL. "Some Observations on Rabelais's Choice of Names: Nazdecabre." *Romance Notes* 12, no. 1 (Fall):186–88.

Sees possible associations, in the consultation with Nazdecabre (*Tiers Livre*, chapt. 20) between the deaf-mute's name, the bearded Apollo of the Assyrians (whose prophecies were made manifest through gestures), and the proverb used by Bartélémy Aneau in his portrait of the goat: "Sage n'est, pour barbe estre portant." These associations would underscore the ambiguity of Rabelais' attitude towards the various means of predicting the future.

20  SCREECH, MICHAEL ANDREW. "Emblems and Colours: The Controversy over Gargantua's Colours and Devices (*Gargantua* 8, 9, 10.)." In *Mélanges d'histoire du XVIe siècle offerts à Henri Meylan.* Geneva: Librairie Droz, pp. 65–80.

Seeks to "elucidate the sense and background" of the chapters in *Gargantua* dealing with colors in heraldry and with emblems. Underscores the satirical aspects of the episodes, and their comtemporary relevance. Accounts for Gargantua's androgynous "image" in terms of the vogue of emblems in the wake of Alciati's *Emblemata*, around 1535. Points out that the "Admiral" mentioned by Rabelais in connection with good emblems is not Bonnivet, as the critical edition has it, but Philippe Chabot, an intimate and powerful friend of Francis I. Gargantua's "image" and Rabelais' satirical attack on false emblems is part of his design to champion Alciati's new emblems favored by Chabot. For Rabelais, the sense of the emblems is not arbitrary, nor is the meaning of colors. As with emblems, the true meaning of colors is reserved for the initiated few. The "Blason des Couleurs" used to mock false "armoirie" is probably that of Sicile, herald to King Alphonso V of Aragon. Rabelais' statement that it is anonymous strongly suggests that he had not read the "Blason" he attacks. Underscores the legal aspects of the quarrel over the meaning of the heraldic colors, of which Rabelais was aware. Relates Rabelais' satire to Tiraqueau's attack on Chassanaeus and his *Catalogus gloriae mundi*. Concedes that the seriousness with which Rabelais treats the subject may be puzzling to the modern reader, but suggests that it becomes understandable when one realizes how fascinating and important it was to the Renaissance gentleman for whom Rabelais was writing. Concludes by pointing out that Rabelais' justification for his non-arbitrary interpretation, although ostensibly based on faultless Aristotelian logic, is in fact seriously flawed. Does not believe Rabelais to have been aware of this flaw.

21  SCREECH, M[ICHAEL] A[NDREW], and RUTH CALDER. "Some Renaissance Attitudes to Laughter." In *Humanism in France at the End of the Middle Ages and in the Early Renaissance*. Edited by A. H. T. Levi. Manchester: Manchester University Press; New York: Barnes and Noble, pp. 216–28.

Presents itself as part of a wider projected study, an "interim report" on the evolution of theories of laughter and comedy from Plato to Descartes. Notes that Joubert's *Traité du ris* never mentions Rabelais. Points out that Rabelais' claim in the liminary poem to *Gargantua* that laughter is the property of man had not gone unchallenged by Rabelais' contemporaries, and that what Rabelais says of the physiology of laughter is also expounded by Nicolas Nancel in his *De risu*. Sketches the connection between Rabelais' comic practice and the attitude of some of his contemporaries to laughter: Joubert's idea that laughter is not compatible with compassion, or Fracastorio's contention, shared by Erasmus, that the sage and the old laugh less often than the young and foolish. Notes Rabelais' "disquiet about laughter from the third book onwards" (p. 224). Closes with references to the Calvinists' attempts to argue that laughter can be a dignified and effective vehicle of religious propaganda. Notes with particular emphasis Viret's apology of laughter in the "Avertissement" to his *Disputations chrestiennes*, a justification based on the precepts of Horace and on examples of what he takes to be biblical humour.

## 1971

1  BENSON, EDWARD GEORGE, Jr. "'Engin mieulx vault que force': Rabelais's Treatment of Warfare in Its Literary and Historical Context." Ph.D. dissertation, Brown University, 264 pp.

Seeks to throw light upon every military incident in Rabelais' first four books by studying the sources of his war imagery. Believes that Rabelais grew increasingly critical of rationalistic pacifism as exemplified by Erasmus, and that he became almost defiantly nationalistic in the *Quart Livre*. Suggests that Rabelais' progressive disinterest in war parallels "a general shift in his perspective from the social to the individual and from the terrestrial to the theological." See *Dissertation Abstracts International* 32 (1972):5219A.

2  BRAULT, GERARD J. "The Significance of Eudémon's Praise of Gargantua (Rabelais, I, 15)." *Kentucky Romance Quarterly* 18, no. 3:307–18.

Argues that Eudémon's oration in praise of Gargantua, seemingly proposed by the narrator as an exemplary product of humanistic education, but "embarrasingly flattering and artificial...to modern readers" (p. 309), follows in almost every respect the rules prescribed by the Greek rhetoretician Aphtonius for the composition of encomia, an exercise recommended by Erasmus as part of his humanistic educational program.

1971

3    BRENT, STEVEN T. "Concerning the Resurrection of Epistémon." *Romance Notes* 12, no. 2 (Spring):392–96.

Finds previous readings by Lefranc and Febvre to be inconsistent with the facts of the narrative. Stresses Epistémon's "humanistic thought," and proposes to read the episode as a symbol of the Renaissance. "The death and subsequent resurrection of Epistémon symbolically suggest the decline and rebirth of the arts in Europe" (p. 394).

4    BUTOR, MICHEL. "6/7 ou les dés de Rabelais." *Littérature* 2 (May):3–18.

Random reflections on the significance of numbers in Rabelais' work, especially in relation to the dice-throwing episodes, the Fountain of the Three Graces, the languages represented in the library of Thélème. "Au seizième siècle les numérologies abondent et toutes celles qu'il rencontrait devaient intéresser Rabelais, mais il les récuse dans la mesure où elles se présentent comme de simples tables d'équivalences sans apporter leurs justifications, sans nous éclairer la vie sémantique des nombres" (p. 9). Finds that Rabelais' own interpretations are predominantly erotic.

5    CHARLES, MICHEL. "Rabelais coryphée." *Nouvelle Revue Française*, no. 222 (June):91–96.

Discusses Bakhtin's *Rabelais and His World* (1968.1, 1970.2). Stresses, over and above the question of Bakhtin's theory, the quality of his reading of specific texts. Notes certain weaknesses, such as his inability to account for an episode such as that of Thélème. Believes that his analyses lead one to question to what extent Rabelais, rather than language, is in control of his text, and suggests that in the last resort "l'objet de l'étude de Bakhtine est plus le livre que le carnaval" (p. 96).

6    COLEMAN, DOROTHY G[ABE]. *Rabelais: A Critical Study in Prose Fiction*. Cambridge: Cambridge University Press, 241 pp.

Begins with an analysis of a passage from chapt. 4 and 5 of *Gargantua* as an example of the literary approach to Rabelais adopted throughout the book. Briefly sketches Rabelais' "general intellectual, metaphysical and moral assumptions" (p. 22) before considering Rabelais in the following chapters primarily as a comic artist rather than a moralist or a religious thinker. Studies the prologues, the relationship they establish between author and reader, the *persona* of the author as narrator, the tone of parody and irony which will color the work as a whole and which prevents us from taking literally Rabelais' promise of a "substantifique moelle" in his text. Argues that the narrative point of view is that of the omniscient, Olympian author. Brings out the structure of the four books whose authenticity is not in doubt; rejects the term "novel" as adequately describing the books: prefers to see then as examples of Manippean satire. Uses the *Tiers Livre* as a "test case" of her hypothesis, and concludes that the book cannot be regarded as a moral treatise expressing

Rabelais' position in the Querelle des Femmes or on any other subject treated in the text. Suggests that Rabelais manages to give life to essentially "flat," "cardboard" figures through mere linguistic inventiveness. Argues that in a Manippean satire such as Rabelais' narrative, the reader is not called upon to assess such comic characters as Panurge or Frère Jean "as moral, immoral, or amoral people" (p. 150). In the creation of giants, on the other hand, "Rabelais the real man and Rabelais the creative author" (p. 168) come together. The gigantic figures of Grandgousier, Gargantua, and Pantagruel are both fictional characters and on occasion, but by no means always, representatives of Rabelais' intellectual attitudes, spokesmen for his religious convictions and his general view of the world. Closes with a chapter on Rabelais' "poetic prose" and the shifting meaning of Pantagruelism. Reissued in paperback in 1978.

7 ———. "Rabelais and *The Water-Babies*." *Modern Language Review* 66, no. 3 (July):511–21.

Finds that "the form in which Rabelais couched his work is particularly relevant to the form that Kingsley chose" for his fairy-tale (p. 512). Seeks to clarify the sense in which *The Water-Babies* and Rabelais' books are, as Northrop Frye had stated in his *Anatomy of Criticism*, examples of Menippean satire. Finds echoes of Rabelais, particularly from chapt. 4 onwards.

8 DEFAUX, GÉRARD. "Rabelais et les cloches de Notre-Dame." *Études Rabelaisiennes* 9:1–28.

According to two letters in the *Correspondance des Réformateurs dans les pays de langue française* edited by Herminjard, Gérard Roussel delivered a number of Evangelical sermons in March of 1533 and aroused thereby the opposition of a group of preachers, stirred up by the Sorbonne in an effort to set the people of Paris against him. Three of the preachers, together with Noël Béda, were subsequently sent into exile by the king, whereupon several delegations from the Sorbonne petitioned the king for the return of the exiles. Attracts attention to the resemblance between this historical event and the episode in *Gargantua* dealing with the bells of Notre-Dame. Concedes that the episode is thematically related to the preceding and following chapters on sophistic and humanistic education, but believes it to be more than a satire of the medieval concept (and reality) of education. Argues that the bells of Notre-Dame, while remaining mere bells on the literal level of interpretation, are also, on the allegorical level, the theologians exiled by the king in the aftermath of the hostilities generated by Roussel's sermons. Believes that this evidence of strife between the Evangelicals and their enemies in 1533 renders unnecessary Screech's hypothesis that *Gargantua* was written later than is generally thought, namely *after* the Affaire des Placards. Develops his thesis within the framework of a discussion on the various methodological approaches to Rabelais, with emphasis on the opposition between the histori-

1971

cal and the aesthetic perspectives on his work. Warns of the limitations of both approaches when considered as mutually exclusive: "il s'agit de reconnaître que les qualités esthétiques d'une œuvre n'ont jamais empêché cette œuvre de posséder en même temps une signification historique" (p. 7). Ascribes the multiplicity of levels of meaning in Rabelais to the influence of Scholastic philosophy and medieval humanism.

9 DE FÉLICE DE NEUFVILLE, ARIANE. *Rabelais, le théâtre et la tradition.* Paris: Imprimerie Robert, 35 pp.

Recalls and supplements the studies by Émmanuel Philippot and Gustave Cohen on Rabelais' debt to the medieval French theater and to the French oral tradition. Reminds us that Grandgousier owes his name to a character in a French farce of the fifteenth century, that there was a devilish Pantagruel not only in the *Mystère des Actes des Apôtres* but also in the *Mystère de saint Louis*, and that Triboulet had been a member of the Sottie. Notes also that Gargantua, as a prodigious ingestor of food, figures in *La Farce du Gouteux* (mid-sixteenth century), although he does not share any specific traits with Rabelais' giant. Draws comparisons between Rabelais' work and the tradition of the "conte mensonger."

10 ELDRIDGE, PAUL. *François Rabelais: The Great Story Teller.* South Brunswick, N.J. and New York: A. S. Barnes & Co.; London: Thomas Yoseloff, 215 pp.

A retelling, in resolutely non-academic style, of Rabelais' life, with an account of the contents of his fictional works.

11 FRANÇON, MARCEL. "Notes Rabelaisiennes." *BAARD* 2, no. 10:341–47.

On Erasmus and Rabelais, on Rabelais and Michelet, on numbers, and on the term *encyclopédie.*

12 FRASER, THEODORE P[AUL]. *Le Duchat, First Editor of Rabelais.* Études de philologie et d'histoire, no. 21. Geneva: Librairie Droz, 204 pp.

Studies Le Duchat's 1711 edition of Rabelais. Sketches Le Duchat's life and work, notably his relations with Pierre Bayle and the latter's role in persuading Le Duchat to edit Rabelais. Describes the 1711 edition, analyzes its "Préface," Le Duchat's defense of Rabelais against the charges of obscenity and of the profane use of Scripture, of heresy and atheism; examines Le Duchat's revisions of the text, notes the faulty editing of the *Tiers Livre* (where Le Duchat does not follow the Fézandat text of 1552); evaluates the originality of Le Duchat's notes, his debt to Urquhart and Motteux; studies Le Duchat's notes on language and style; agrees with Sainéan that Le Duchat's linguistic commentary remains of great value. Studies Le Duchat's remarks on the "sens historique" of Rabelais' five books, and his attempts to identify fictional characters and events. Notes his professed unwillingness to read a "sens mystérieux" into the work, but also his actual forays into hidden meaning; comments on the social and cultural aspects of Le Duchat's commentary and notes "a virtually complete silence on the intellectual currents that flow through the text" (p. 129). Notes that such contemporary editors as Screech continue to pay close attention to Le Duchat's commentary. Draws out the religious implications of the commentary, underscores the extent to which the Protestant perspective of the annotations contributed to the reputation of Rabelais as a partisan of the early Reformation. Takes note of the mixed reactions to the commentary, from 1711 through the publication of the *Edition Variorum* in 1823. Assesses Le Duchat's work as pointing the way to modern scholarship by providing "the indispensable framework for our more comprehensive understanding and appreciation of Rabelais" (p. 191). Bibliography lists French and English editions of Rabelais from the seventeenth century on; works written or edited by Le Duchat as well as articles and books related to Rabelais and Le Duchat.

13  GABAY, SIMONE. "Rabelais: Des années 30 à 1970." *Littérature* 1 (February):116–19.

The title notwithstanding, attempts a brief assessment of Bakhtin's strengths (his break with the historico-allegorical interpretative tradition, his awareness of the autonomy of artistic production, of an artistic logic, a "système d'images" which structures the work and reveals an original conception of the world), and of his weaknesses: awkward style, repetitive structure, shaky methodological underpinnings, cumbersome and often outdated documentation, and an unjustifiably optimistic trust in the liberating power of carnival. Shows how Bakhtin has paved the way for the work of such young Rabelais critics as Paris and Beaujour, more brilliant and elegant than that of their master, but "d'une richesse moins inépuisable" (p. 119).

14  GAUNA, S. M. "De genio Pantagruelis: An Examination of Rabelaisian Demonology." *BHR* 33 (September):557–70.

After Screech and Krailsheimer, studies Rabelais' adaptation of certain tenets of Neoplatonic demonology. When Rabelais refers to "les bons daemons" in Book III, when he provides Pantagruel with his own tutelary demon in Book IV, he places himself squarely within the Neoplatonic tradition exemplified by such works as Apuleius' *De Deo Socratis* and Plutarch's *De Genio Socratis*. "While Rabelais always rejected vulgar and obvious superstition, his attitude, especially in the later books, is anything but incredulous. He appears to have been progressively more interested in the Platonic tradition, finally incorporating many of its ideas into his syncretistic picture of the universe" (p. 570).

1971

15  HOLBAN, MARIE. "Autour de Jean Thenaud et de Frère Jean des Entonneurs." *Études Rabelaisiennes* 9:49–69.

Draws a parallel between Frère Jean and Jean Thenaud, author of the *Voyage et Itinéraire de Outre Mer*, traveler and Cabbalist who lived in the entourage of the Angoulême family. Attracts attention to the similarity between their two names. Sees a certain number of allusions to Thenaud's work in various remarks by Rabelais' characters, especially in the *Quart Livre*. Notes that Rabelais was familiar with the *Voyage et Itinéraire*.

16  INGLIS, ANNE EDWARDS. "Parody in Rabelais' Treatment of Aggression and a Heroic Ideal." Ph.D. dissertation, Case Western Reserve University, 262 pp.

Treats Rabelais' political references not as propaganda but as comic criticism of war and traditional heroism on Christian, popular, or humanistic grounds. Believes that in his subversive attitude in these matters, Rabelais went as far as to question the possibility of a "just war." In such episodes as the Death of Heroes and the Frozen Words, sees the transformation of parody into myth. See *Dissertation Abstracts International* 32 (1972):4568A.

17  JOSIPOVICI, GABRIEL. "Rabelais: Language and Laughter." In *The World and the Book: A Study of Modern Fiction*. Stanford: Stanford University Press, pp. 100–21.

Reprint of 1968.20.

18  KOPENFELS, WERNER VON. "Thomas Nashe und Rabelais." *Archiv für das Studium der Neueren Sprachen und Literaturen* 207, no. 4:277–91.

Attracts attention to a number of textual parallels between the works of Nashe and those of Rabelais, and argues that Rabelais' influence on the author of *Pierce Penilesse* and *The Unfortunate Traveller* was much greater than can be gathered from such otherwise authoritative studies as Huntington Brown's *Rabelais in English Literature* or from the critical edition of Nashe's works published in 1958 by McKerrow and Wilson.

19  LAURENT, MARCEL. *Rabelais: Le Monde paysan et le langage auvergnat.* Saint Laure, Clermont-Ferrand: Chez l'Auteur, 107 pp.

Proposes "une modeste lecture paysane" (p. 5) of Rabelais' work. Underscores the popular, folkloric origins of the legend of Gargantua. Comments on a series of excerpts of strongly peasant character. Discusses a number of peasant themes in a section on "Images de la vieille France rurale," and comments on a list of words offering similarities with the dialect of the Auvergne, with which Rabelais may have become familiar during his sojourn in the South.

20 MAILLET, ANTONINE. *Rabelais et les traditions populaires en Acadie.* Les Archives de Folklore, no. 13. Quebec: Les Presses de l'Université Laval, 201 pp.

"Les Acadiens n'ont pas lu le *Gargantua-Pantagruel,* ils l'ont vécu." (p. 27). Comparing two parallel traditions stemming from what the author believes to have been a common source, studies the persistence of the folkloric background of Rabelais' novels in the oral traditions of the French-speaking population of New Brunswick, Nova Scotia, and Prince Edward Island. Brings out Rabelaisian reminiscences in Acadian folklore by stressing thematic similarities (legends, customs, beliefs, psychological types), as well as the recurrence of similar formal and linguistic elements: proverbs, expressions, vocabulary, imagery, and comic devices. Published version of a Ph.D. dissertation for Laval University, 1971. See *American Doctoral Dissertations* (1970–71):236.

21 MARICHAL, ROBERT. "Le *Quart Livre* de 1548." *Études Rabelaisiennes* 9:131–74.

Reproduces a facsimile of the eleven chapters of the 1548 edition, from the Rothschild collection, on the grounds that any serious research into the authenticity of the *Cinquiesme Livre* should be based upon a comparison with the 1548 edition of the *Quart Livre* and not that of 1552. Studies the conditions surrounding the publication of the text, clarifying—to the small extent that documents permit—Rabelais' relationship with the Sorbonne censors, the circumstances of Rabelais' move to Metz in March 1547, his second stay in Rome at the summons of an increasingly ailing Jean du Bellay. Narrows down the composition of Book IV to a period stretching from the completion of Book III to June 20, 1547, and suggests that Rabelais brought out the hasty and incomplete 1548 version at a time when hostility towards evangelism had reached a new high from sheer "bravade" (p. 150), and not, as Plattard had thought, in order to impress the censors with the innocuous nature of his work. Although not as violently satirical as the 1552 text, the *Quart Livre* of 1548 had much in it to fan the anger of the censors. Suggests that if Rabelais published it nevertheless, it was because of his confidence in the power and willingness of his protectors to shield him from wrath.

22 MASTERS, BRIAN. *A Student's Guide to Rabelais.* London: Heinemann Educational Books, Student Guides to European Literature, 108 pp.

An introduction for undergraduates, with emphasis on the main recurring themes.

1971

23 MORGAN, DAVID RUSSELL. "The Pantagruelion Enigma and the Structure of François Rabelais's *Tiers Livre.*" Ph.D. dissertation, Columbia University, 187 pp.

Suggests that the final episode of the *Tiers Livre* may hold the key to the meaning of the work. Believes that the episode requires an allegorical reading, in which the plant "comes to stand for Man himself," and that its praise is a hymn to mankind's immortality through procreation. Sees this theme as being foreshadowed in key episodes of the previous books (such as Pantagruel's birth, Gargantua's letter to his son and the "philogamic aspects of Thélème"), and as unifying the book through its obvious relation to the theme of marriage. Considers the enigma as more important than the consultations for an understanding of the *Tiers Livre.* See *Dissertation Abstracts International* 35 (1975):4441–2A.

24 NAUDEAU, OLIVIER. "Autour de l'anagramme 'Nature Quite.'" *Études Rabelaisiennes* 9:91–92.

The 1564 edition of the *Cinquiesme Livre* and the two editions of the following year end with an epigram signed "Nature Quite." Provides phonetic reasons for suggesting we return to the idea of seeing in that enigmatic expression the anagram of André Tiraqueau.

25 PACKER, DOROTHY S. "François Rabelais, vaudevilliste." *Musical Quarterly* 57, no. 1 (January):107–28.

Studies parallelisms between the works of Rabelais and the French vaudevilles of the late-seventeenth and early-eighteenth centuries. Notes the same exhortation to drink, the same philosophy of free will, the same ribald approach to love, the same contempt for women and marriage, the same anti-clerical streak. Puts down these similarities to a "mutual association with the Old Italian Comedy" (p. 107). Argues that the vaudevillistes "absorbed the Rabelaisian stock of words and phrases," and suggests that Rabelais may be seen as the father of the vaudeville, the ancestor of a long line of satirical song writers extending down to Georges Brassens.

26 PARIS, JEAN. "Hamlet et Panurge." In *Hamlet et Panurge, suivi de Entretiens du cercle Polivanov.* Paris: Editions du Seuil, pp. 9–103.

Discusses the notion of *comparative* literature, concludes that the comparison in question is justified only when it delves below the surface of the works down to the level of their "problématique," and sets out to compare "deux créations apparemment incomparables: le Panurge de Rabelais/le Hamlet de Shakespeare" (p. 12). Notes a series of resemblances, rejects this "analogie de surface," but finds *Hamlet* and the *Tiers Livre* to be identical "dans leur projet" (p. 27) since both raise the same problem, namely the relationship between language and reality, between the signifier and its referent. Studies Panurge and Hamlet as representations of self-doubt; views their story as a quest for a solution to the dilemmas of uncertainty. Sees them both as aware of the arbitrariness of the linguistic sign, and puts down their passivity, their procrastination, the paralysis of the will which afflicts them both, to this awareness of the contingency of language and of its inadequacy to express the truth.

27   PLAISANT, FRANÇOIS-MARCEL. "Rabelais, maître ou disciple de Guillaume du Bellay." *Bulletin de l'Association Guillaume Budé* (March):95–102.

Notes similarities, in both style and theme, between the Picrocholine War episode in *Gargantua*, and Guillaume du Bellay's *Mémoires* for the years 1536–40 touching upon diplomatic language and procedure. Shows that the points of contact are often so close that the reality of the *Mémoires* seems to be modelled on the fiction of *Gargantua*. Argues that Rabelais was familiar with the diplomatic usage of his time, that once again he does not invent from scratch but lets his imagination embroider upon the canvas of contemporary events, and that what is often taken as an expression of his political ideas (for instance his purported royalism) is perhaps nothing more than a parody of current political ideas. Given Rabelais' familiarity with the language of diplomacy, wonders whether *Gargantua* may not have been written *after* the author's first trip to Italy rather than before—in other words, "près d'un an après la date couramment admise" (p. 101).

28   POUILLOUX, JEAN-YVES. Introduction to *Le Quart Livre des faicts et dicts héroïques du bon Pantagruel*. Paris: Garnier-Flammarion, pp. 7–20.

Attempts to counter traditional criticism leveled against Book IV by underscoring certain "facteurs de cohésion" which provide a link with the other parts of Rabelais' novel: recurrence of characters, thematic and structural connections, intermingling of reality and fiction, parody of humanistic values, reassertion of the vanity of all knowledge. In relation to Book III, the *Quart Livre* represents a further step towards scepticism. It is the narration of a voyage, but without any true progression: "Tout se passe comme si, pour l'esprit aussi bien que pour le roman, l'existence consistait dans ce mouvement dilatoire, ajournement d'une réponse définitive à la fois souhaitée et redoutée, procrastination vitale" (p. 8).

29   ———. "Notes sur l'Abbaye de Thélème." *Romantisme*, no. 1–2:200–04.

Offers a set of preliminary remarks on the way the Thélème episode is inserted into the narrative, and on the ideological presuppositions underlying the sequence. Points out that the sentence referring to the circumstances in which the abbey was conceived is grammatically ambiguous, so that both Gargantua and Frère Jean can be taken to be the abbey's founders. Argues that the conditions of inclusion and exclusion, as well as the picture of life at Thélème, clearly imply that the utopian Thelemites are not a group of individ-

1971

uals but a collection of essences, wherein difference—and thus alterity—has no place: "Les Thélémites ne sont que le *même*, répété au nombre d'exemplaires voulus" (p. 204).

30  REGOSIN, RICHARD L. "The Artist and the *Abbaye.*" *Studies in Philology* 68, no. 2 (April):121–29.

Agrees with Spitzer and others that a number of "unreal and grotesque" elements relate Thélème to the rest of *Gargantua*, but recognizes also those characteristics that do distinguish it stylistically from the rest of the first two books. Notes a preponderance of elements that mimic reality and a shift to a descriptive prose style, which give Thélème a "tangible" quality, but sees in the overabundance of details and their frequently grotesque nature a sign of the simultaneous presence of the fantastic, which provides an "ironic counterpoint" to the dominant seriousness of the episode. Despite the general impression of reality it conveys, "Thélème does not exist outside of the context of the poetic world created by the artist" (p. 125). Concludes that in thus juxtaposing the serious and the comic, the realistic and the fantastic, Rabelais illustrates the Renaissance concept of the poet as *facteur*, whose function is "to rearrange matter already created in new and original ways" (p. 129).

31  REBHORN, WAYNE A. "The Burdens and Joys of Freedom: An Interpretation of the Five Books of Rabelais." *Études Rabelaisiennes* 9:71–90.

Notes a change between the author of Books III, IV, and V on the one hand, and the author of *Pantagruel* and *Gargantua* on the other. Ascribes this change to a growing religious intolerance which puts into question the optimism of Rabelais' first two books and leads to the Evangelical Stoicism which marks Rabelais' ideological position in the *Quart Livre*. Thus believes that if Thélème on dry land has been replaced by what Saulnier had called "une Thélème flottante," it is not merely for reasons of relative security, but because it symbolizes a new "detachment and non-involvement Rabelais must have wished for individual and community alike" (p. 80). Also sees in the substitution of the Thalamège for Thélème Rabelais' newly adopted "conviction of man's need for externally imposed social order" (p. 81), since the ship has a captain at the head of a hierarchic order, whereas at Thélème all were equal. Concludes with a discussion of the biblical exodus of the Jews from Egypt to the Promised Land as an analogue for the Rabelaisian quest.

32  SAFFREY, H.-D. "'Cy n'entrez pas, hypocrites...': Thélème, une nouvelle académie? [Rabelais, *Gargantua*, Chap. LII (LIV)]." *Revue des Sciences Philosophiques et Théologiques* 55, no. 4 (October):593–614.

Sees in the inscription over the portal of Thélème an allusion to the inscription over Plato's Academy in Athens. Argues that Thélème was meant to be a new Platonic Academy, open only to those who are in a state of grace, and thus will only what God himself wills. Believes that the natural instinct which spurs the Thelemites toward virtue is the *syndérèse* of Thomistic theology, and that of Saint Bonaventure. "Thélème est une utopie qui combine ensemble le rêve de la Renaissance des Humanistes de restaurer l'Académie de Platon et l'effort des Évangélistes français pour réformer la vie monastique" (p. 613).

33   SCHRADER, LUDWIG. "Die Rabelais-Forschung der Jahre 1950–1960: Tendenzen und Ergebnisse." In *The Present State of French Studies: A Collection of Research Reviews*, edited by Charles B. Osborn. Metuchen, N.J.: Scarecrow Press, pp. 107–60.
     Reprint of 1960.12.

34   SPANOS, MARGARET. "The Function of the Prologues in the Works of Rabelais." *Études Rabelaisiennes* 9:29–48.
     Sees the various prologues—especially those which introduce *Gargantua*, and Books III and IV—as "keys to some structural and thematic elements of these books" (p. 29). Finds the *narrés*, the anecdotes contained in the prologues, in opposition to the more discursive *devis*, to be particularly significant: "in the exploration of the demonstrably close structural and thematic relationship between each of these *narrés* and the following book lies a clarification of the essential unity behind the seemingly episodic structure of Rabelais' major works" (p. 29). Argues that the comparison between Socrates and the *silènes*, by introducing the concept of a double level of reality, makes it possible to integrate the Abbaye de Thélème episode into the totality of *Gargantua*: "The society of Thélème is related to its enclosing society precisely as Socrates' virtues are related to his appearance: it exists simultaneously with it and completes its nature" (p. 32). Believes the relationship between prologue and book to be even clearer in the *Tiers Livre*. Argues that the siege of Corinth and Diogenes' resolve to leave that city for Cranie, where he will indulge in tub-tumbling as a substitute for waging war, prefigures the various controversies making up the book that follows, and Pantagruel's attitude towards them. Believes that the Pantagruélion episode, whose dramatic link with the rest is tenuous, emerges as the logical conclusion of the action when considered in the light of the thematic and structural patterns of the prologue. In the *narré* involving Couillatris and his axe, believes that Rabelais manages even better than elsewhere "to achieve a complex but unified narrative that expands the significance of the prayer for health introduced in the *devis* into the quest for ultimate truth" which structures the voyage of Book IV (p. 40). The parallel between the *narré* and the novel it introduces leads the author to reinterpret the meaning of the islands and to view them not as elements of evil or error, but as partial perspectives rendered dangerous or absurd by their isolation from "the total body of Truth" (p. 44).

1972

35  THOMAS, DAVID H. "Rabelais in England: John Eliot's *Ortho-epia Gallica* (1593)." *Études Rabelaisiennes* 9:97–126.

Eliot's bilingual dialogues offered to the English reader the first contact with Rabelais' prose (not identified as such). Finds Eliot's borrowings to be infinitely more numerous than the "few pleasant conceits" to which Eliot admits.

36  WEINBERG, FLORENCE M[AY]. "Frère Jean, Evangélique: His Function in the Rabelaisian World." *Modern Language Review* 66:298–305.

Given his bawdiness, violence, and lack of polish and elegance, the presence of Frère Jean "in the Evangelical circle around the giants" (p. 298) and in the Abbey of Thélème may seem puzzling but is in fact appropriate. During the invasion of the Abbey of Seuillé he guards and defends the vineyard, "which represents the *true* Church established by Christ" (p. 301). At Thélème he aptly acts as guardian, representing, like the watchdogs of Plato's *Republic*, "the irascible soul." "Despite his obvious faults, Jean incarnates the Rabelaisian ideal of Christianity in the guise of a knight of the *roman chevaleresque* or of a Bishop Turpin of the *Chanson de Roland*" (p. 303).

## 1972

1  ALCOFRY, ETIENNE. "Récompenses distribuées aux capitaines victorieux." *BAARD* 3, no. 1:20–22.

Claims to read a hidden meaning in the name of every participant in the Picrocholine War.

2  ARONSON, NICOLE. "Les reines et le *Cinquième Livre* de Rabelais." *Studi Francesi* 16, no. 46 (January–April):324–29.

Attracts attention to a change in the treatment of royalty: whereas it had hitherto been treated with respect, the queens in Book V are an object of satire, and are denounced for their sumptuousness and love of etiquette. Since nothing in the historical context during Rabelais' lifetime would explain such a change in attitude, suggests that the courts of Quinte Essence and of the queen of Lanterns were inspired by the regency of Catherine de Medicis, whose court was criticized in many quarters precisely for its excessive luxury and the rigidity of its etiquette. "Les chapitres de la Quinte Essence et de la reine des Lanternes représentent, peut-être, le premier d'une longue série d'ouvrages qui vont attaquer la régente, sa politique et sa vie privée" (p. 327). Since the regency began in 1559, suggests that these considerations may strengthen the argument according to which Book V was written by someone other than Rabelais.

3  BADY, RENÉ. *Humanisme chrétien dans les lettres françaises: XVIe -XVIIe siècles*. Je sais–Je crois: Encyclopédie du catholique au XXe siècle. Paris: Librairie Arthème Fayard, pp. 31–45.

In the chapter on Rabelais, points out that Rabelais attacks stupidity and wickedness in the name of a high humanist ideal and in a spirit of faith in the possibility of human regeneration. Notes also that despite Rabelais' criticism of religious abuse, his characters, with the exception of Panurge, are endowed with the essential elements of Christian faith. Denies that Rabelais has no conception of sin or of divine grace as a prerequisite for salvation, but admits that in his boundless faith in nature he fails to take into account the necessity of constraints to minimize the corrosive effect of sin. Thus concludes that Rabelais is in the final analysis more of a humanist than a Christian for having failed, like many another humanist of his day, to meditate with sufficient fervor on the mystery of the cross.

4  BARAZ, MICHAEL. "Le Sentiment de l'unité dans l'œuvre de Rabelais." *Études Françaises* 8, no .1:3–53.

Studies the imagery and mythology through which Rabelais expresses his feeling of unity. The Silenes and Socrates embody the unity of the sublime and the grotesque, the corporeal and the spiritual. Utopia embraces the ideal and the everyday reality. The notion of human microcosm emphasizes the interdependence of the various organs of the body. The notion of "panta gruélisme" is ultimately based on a feeling of cosmic unity. The kingdoms of Gaster and Quaresmeprenant represent the interdependence of nature and anti-nature. Rabelaisian laughter and Rabelaisian imagination free us from the distinctions and separations inherent in our practical consciousness and promote a feeling of unity with nature. "C'est surtout dans ce sentiment qu'il faut chercher le secret de l'immense joie d'être qui anime son œuvre et celui, non moins étonnant, d'une grande élévation spirituelle naissant de représentations basses au possible" (p. 53).

5  BOUCHER, A. "Rabelais était-il le père ou le frère de l'avocat Chinonais?" *BAARD* 3, no. 1:18–19.

Cites a document strengthening his thesis that the Antoine Rabelais who died in 1535 was not the author's father but a brother. See also 1966.1.

6  BOWEN, BARBARA C. *The Age of Bluff: Paradox and Ambiguity in Rabelais and Montaigne*. Urbana: University of Illinois Press, 168 pp.

Seeks to supply a general framework for the study of individual writers of the French Renaissance. Believes that French literature of the Renaissance possesses a unity of outlook and technique comparable in kind, although antithetical in detail, to the aesthetics that underlie the works of the major classical writers. Detects in the writers of the sixteenth century a preference for "paradox, enigma, argument, antithesis, and ambiguity" (p. 6), a tendency to ask questions rather than provide answers, to stimulate rather than to satisfy. Believes that these characteristics apply not only to the baroque period but to the century as a whole, and that they betray "a general intention, which is to disconcert the reader" (p. 6). Suggests the term "bluff" to designate the result of this effort to disconcert and mystify, and applies the notion to Rabelais in chapt. 2 of the study. Without denying the serious purpose of much of Rabelais' work, emphasizes Rabelais' "delight in ambiguity and paradox" (p. 39) in reaction to the tendency of the previous generation of critics to over-stress the ideological content of Rabelais' text at the expense of its humor. Comments on each of the first four books in the order in which they were written, and notes an evolution in the degree of importance that the notion of bluff acquires in Rabelais' work: "What began as an intellectual game became a profound interest in the very nature of ambiguity and our reactions to it" (p. 39). Insists on the contradictory aspects of a book that presents itself as "un roman d'aventures" but in which less than half of the number of chapters are concerned with action, the others dealing with intellectual and linguistic matters when they are not downright enigmatic or incomprehensible. In *Pantagruel*, finds "plenty of shock tactics but little ambiguity" (p. 49). In *Gargantua*, notes the first appearance of such "ambiguous themes" as wine, reproduction, madness, an "interest and delight in double bluff" (pp. 52–53), notably in the prologue, and an increased subtlety in the use of ambiguity as well as in shifts in atmosphere and the production of shock effects. Whereas the first two books were merely ambiguous, finds the *Tiers Livre* to be about ambiguity itself, and to treat paradox and ambiguity in a totally new way. "There is less emphasis on the verbal forms of bluff,...less emphasis on individual bluff techniques, but paradox has expanded until it has become the pre-text and basic theme, as well as the main comic device, of the book" (p. 83). As for Book IV, purporting to tell an adventure story but containing only two episodes of action—the storm at sea and the encounter with the Physetere—it is "just as fundamentally paradoxical and disconcerting as the *Tiers Livre*, a doubly false epic in which the impression of action is entirely illusory, and "incident is created, literally, out of words" (p. 99).

7   BRAULT, GERARD J. "A Neglected Aspect of Rabelaisian Pedagogy: Associating with Men of Letters." *Romance Notes* 14, no. 1 (Autumn): 151–54.

In the chapters on Gargantua's education, finds that Rabelais is more interested in satirizing contemporary pedagogical practices than in proposing a serious program of his own. Notes Rabelais' insistence on the educational advantages of associating with men of letters, and explains it by Rabelais' awareness that the enthusiasm for the kind of humanistic learning he had in mind was not likely to be aroused by schools but by contact with other humanists.

8   BROWN, JACK DAVIS. "Hans Carvel's Ring: Elements, Literary Tradition, Rabelais's Source." *Romance Notes* 13, no. 3 (Spring):515–22.

Breaks down the story into its elements, notes their presence or absence in Rabelais as well as in Ariosto, *Les Cent Nouvelles Nouvelles*, and in Poggio's *Facetiae*, and concludes that the last of these is in all probability "not only the original source of the entire literary development of the story, but also Rabelais's unique source" (p. 522).

9   BUCKLEY, CHARLES ROBERT, Jr. "Narrative Techniques in Rabelais' Later Books and in the *Cinquième Livre*." Ph.D. dissertation, University of Chicago.

See *American Doctoral Dissertations*, 1971–72:229.

10   BUTOR, MICHEL, et HOLLIER, DENIS. *Rabelais, ou c'était pour rire*. Larousse Université, Collection "Thèmes et Textes." Paris: Librairie Larousse, 143 pp.

Contains fragments of articles published by Michel Butor elsewhere. Interspersed with notes by Denis Hollier on the political and religious context of the *Gargantua-Pantagruel*, as well as on the scholarly activity generated by Rabelais' work.

11   CLAUDE, CATHERINE. *Rabelais*. Collection "Précurseurs." Paris: Éditeurs Français Réunis, le Livre Club Diderot, 292 pp.

Presents the man and his work for the general public, in a "materialistic" perspective (p. 137). Stresses Rabelais' "rapport au peuple" (p. 19), his medical knowledge and its influence on his work, the nature of the work as that of a *romancier*: "Il l'est comme on l'est de nouveau depuis Joyce, Proust, le Nouveau Roman" (p. 81). Reads the Picrocholine War in terms of class struggle ("dans un moment où l'idée de lutte de classes n'existe même pas" (p. 141). Sees Thélème as fundamentally antichristian. Believes that in the *Tiers Livre* Rabelais identifies with Panurge: "Pantagruel, c'est l'autre" (p. 191). Discusses the Querelle des Femmes and Rabelais' participation in terms borrowed from Engels and Marx. Finds Rabelais' misogyny, and that of the Gallic tradition in general, less objectionable than the idealization of woman in the tradition of courtly love: "Les femmes sont menteuses, elles sont ceci, elles sont cela.... Ce n'est pas grave: elles existent" (p. 209). Sees in the *Tiers Livre* an open system of contradictions requiring an interpretation in Marxist terms. Sees in the prologue a lesson in civic duty worthy of Saint-Just (p. 251). Deals more rapidly with Books IV and V as a moving quest *forward* rather than *upward*, as is the case with medieval peregrinations.

1972

12   DE ROCHER, GREGORY DAVID. "A Renaissance Conception of Laughter: Rabelais's Laughters and Joubert's *Traité du Ris*." Ph.D. dissertation, University of Michigan, 229 pp.

   Studies Rabelais' comic practice in the light of the theory of laughter in Laurent Joubert's *Traité du Ris* (1579). Finds Joubert's system to be a mixture of Aristotle's comic theory and sixteenth-century medical doctrine. Claims that it "furnishes a means of understanding [Rabelais'] achievement as a literary organism." See *Dissertation Abstracts International* 33 (1973):6305–6A.

13   DEFAUX, GÉRARD. "Le Prince, Rabelais, les Cloches et l'Énigme: Les dates de composition et de publication du *Gargantua*." *Revue de l'Université d'Ottawa* (July–September):408–38.

   "Le but de cette étude est de montrer, d'une façon je crois conclusive, que le *Gargantua* a été composé dans sa presque totalité au cours de l'année 1533, et publié de toute nécessité avant l'Affaire des Placards" (p. 412). Examines and rejects Screech's contention that the book had appeared *after* the persecutions triggered by the affair—that is after October 17, 1534— rather than in the summer of that year, as had been argued by Lefranc and accepted by most scholars, most recently by Saulnier. Bases his conclusions on an attempt to date, directly and decisively, three of the book's episodes. Claims that the chapters on the color symbolism of Gargantua's livery (*Gargantua*, chapt. 8–9) date from the end of 1532 or the beginning of 1533 since Le Prince, mentioned by Alcorfybas in the episode as being still alive (and mistakenly identified by Screech with Francis I), is in fact the publisher Claude Nourry, who died in early 1533. Sees in the episode of the bells of Notre-Dame an allusion to the efforts on the part of the Sorbonne to intercede on behalf of Noël Béda and three other Sorbonne theologians—the "grosses cloches" in question—exiled by the king as a result of Gérard Roussel's pro-Evangelical sermons of March 1533. Argues that the "beaulx placars de merde" mentioned in *Gargantua* do not refer to the Affaire des Placards but to documents relating to Béda's exile, and that the *Enigme en prophétie* can be understood without reference to the persecutions following the affair, since the Evangelicals had been a target of religious and political persecution well before then. Concludes with a number of syntactical and stylistic considerations tending to strengthen the hypothesis that *Gargantua* was indeed both written and published before the *Pantagruel* brought out by François Juste in 1534.

14   DRESDEN, S. "Érasme, Rabelais et la *festivitas*." In *Colloquia Erasmiana Turonensia: Douzième stage international d'études humanistes, Tours 1969*, vol. 1. Toronto: University of Toronto Press, pp. 463–78.

   As a figure of ancient rhetoric, *festivitas* implies grace and brevity. Notes that in Renaissance texts *festivus* is often associated with *doctus*, so that *festivitas* and *gravitas* are no longer incompatible in practice as they are in rhetorical treatises, and *festivitas* refers to a serious game in which life is viewed as an amusing, and yet also a serious spectacle—as in Erasmus' *Encomium moriae* or in Rabelais' work. Points to the rapid passage from the serious to the playful in the prologue to *Gargantua*, a process that will become a feature of nearly every page of Rabelais' text. As another example of the fusion of the serious and the comic, refers to the world in Pantagruel's mouth, comic in itself but leaving the reader with the serious—not to say disquieting—impression that the world in which he lives is no more real than that which the narrator discovers within Pantagruel. As for *festivitas* in the psychological sense of the term, identifies it with Rabelais' definition of Pantagruelism, and notes that the "gayeté d'esprit" that makes up its main component is not pure, exuberant, pagan vitality associated with the period in most Renaissance manuals, but a state of mind akin to Erasmus' "gravité souriante" (p. 472), a deeply religious and Christian joy, behind which the author senses a parallel undercurrent of sadness and melancholy.

15  FLECNIAKOSKA, J.-L., et RECOULES, H. "*Les Têtes coupées* en Espagne et Rabelais." *Revue des Langues Romanes* 80:129–38.
     Attracts attention to similarities between Epistémon's descent into the underworld (*Pantagruel*, chapt. 30) and the adventures of the pilgrims in the giant's mouth (*Gargantua*, chapt. 38) on the one hand, and on the other to *Entremés de la burla del ropero* and *Las noches de invierno y perdone el enfermo*, the picaresque novel entitled *Vida y hechos de Estrebanillo González*, and chapt. 10 of the *Quijote*. But acknowledges that the motif of the severed heads may in fact go back to the *Legenda aurea* of Jacobus da Voragine.

16  FRANÇON, MARCEL. "Humanisme, *Bonae Literae*, Encyclopédie." *Romance Notes* 13, no.3 (Spring):523–28.
     Rabelais was not the first to use the word *encyclopédie*. But whereas it had been used until then as nearly synonymous with *humanisme*, Rabelais was the first to use it in its modern sense of "ensemble de connaissances diverses" (p. 528).

17  ———. "Notes Rabelaisiennes." *BAARD* 3, no. 1:27–34.
     Notes on Rabelais and history, the prologue to the *Tiers Livre*, "le prestre Jean," and the "Alibantes."

18  GRIFFIN, ROBERT. "The Devil and Panurge." *Studi Francesi* 16, no. 46 (January–April):329–36.
     Argues in favor of Panurge's demonic ancestry. Notes his knowledge of the demons, and draws parallels between Panurge and Satan: their nobility and beauty, their curiosity, their predilection for fire and aversion to water. Insists on Panurge's mastery of the diabolic arts, such as "his expertise in language

and eloquence in logic" (p. 334), and on his deceitfulness, although stops short of seeing in him an incarnation of the devil, which would provide him with a coherence that the character does not possess. Suggests that the demonic aspect of Panurge may account for the otherwise puzzling attachment of Pantagruel to his lifelong friend, given the giant's own demonic antecedents.

19  KALWIES, HOWARD H. "Hugues Salel et François Rabelais." *Romance Notes* 14, no. 2 (Winter):341–46.

Points out that Salel's *dizain* first appeared in the François Juste edition of 1534 and not in 1542, as was thought by Vaganay and Boulenger. Notes other editions in which the *dizain* appears before 1543, with or without its *devise* ("Vivent tous bons pantagruelistes"). Reminds us that Salel is mentioned in the prologue to Book V as a defender of women, and thus a target of the narrator's contempt. "The only thing we know for certain that these two humanists had in common was their deaths in 1553" (p. 346).

20  KELLER, ABRAHAM C. "Absurd and Absurdity in Rabelais." *Kentucky Romance Quarterly* 19, no. 1:149–57.

Studies one aspect of Rabelais' comic vision: "the taking seriously of phenomena which are manifestly absurd" (p. 149). As a preliminary step towards a full-scale study of the absurd in Rabelais, analyzes the structural handling of absurd material in a series of particular episodes—the roast-shop story involving Seigny Jean (*Tiers Livre*, chapt. 37), Perrin Dandin and his son (*Tiers Livre*, chapt. 41), the Devil-Farmer story (*Quart Livre*, chapt. 45–47)—and shows how carefully Rabelais arranges the elements of the narrative to achieve the intended effect.

21  LA CHARITÉ, RAYMOND C. "The Unity of Rabelais's *Pantagruel*." *French Studies* 26, no. 3 (July):257–65.

Seeks to absolve "the resonantly raucous and rollicking *Pantagruel*" of the accusation of lacking "structural and thematic integrity" (p. 257). Argues for the presence of at least two unifying patterns which provide what is often viewed as a series of unrelated episodes with a significant degree of inner cohesion: "repeated use of trickery and theatre" (p. 258) as a means of deflating the pomposity of a group of assorted impostors, and "the structural and thematic design of opposition" (p. 262) at play in the relationship between Panurge and Pantagruel and in a number of key episodes. Adds to these "the motif of temporality," which imbues the work with its characteristic spirit of generation and rebirth. See also 1980.30.

22  MARTINEAU-GÉNIEYS, CHRISTINE. "Un apport au réalisme de Rabelais: l'Affaire Baisecul-Humevesne et son règlement par Pantagruel ou Meschinot source de Rabelais." *Réseaux: Revue Interdisciplinaire de Philosophie Morale et Politique*, no. 18–19:59–76.

Rejects the interpretations of such "modern" critics as Manuel de Diéguez, Jean Paris, and Michel Beaujour, who tend to see in the episode (*Pantagruel*, chapt. 10–13) an example of language operating in a vacuum, without reference to any other reality than that of the linguistic signs. Argues that the debate between Baisecul and Humevesne, as well as Pantagruel's verdict, is modeled on a real event, documented in a letter written by the poet Meschinot to the duke of Brittany, requesting the latter's intervention in a quarrel between the poet's son and a certain Jean de Boisbrassu. Suggests that Rabelais must have known of the existence of the document, since it was published throughout the first half of the sixteenth century together with Meschinot's *Lunettes des Princes* (to which Rabelais refers in a chapter almost immediately preceding the episode). Provides the text of Meschinot's *Supplication* as well as the duke's response, underscores their similarity to the Baisecul-Humevesne episode, and interprets the latter as an "inside joke" meant to amuse those of Rabelais' friends who, like Tiraqueau and Rabelais himself, were eager to reform the existing judicial system, but were also aware of the obstacles that human folly, in the shape of the Baiseculs and the Humevesnes of this world, continually erects in the path of progress.

23 MESSERT, MARTINE. "Rabelais and Mythology." Ph.D. dissertation, University of Wisconsin, Madison, 244 pp.

Studies Rabelais' use and interpretation of classical mythology by examining "his most significant references to the best known and most widely acknowledged sources of mythological erudition": Homer, Hesiod, Virgil, and Ovid. Challenges the view that Rabelais' mythological references are drawn at random and that they are used only to display the extent of his learning. Argues that Rabelais possessed "a complete familiarity with the ancient texts," and that he used mythology almost exclusively for a humorous purpose. See *Dissertation Abstracts International* 33 (1973):6368A.

24 NASH, JERRY CARROLL. "The Stoic Nature of Rabelaisian Thought." Ph.D. dissertation, University of Kansas, 200 pp.

Studies the influence of Stoicism on Rabelais' moral philosophy, with emphasis on the Stoic themes of reason, justice, fortitude, and moderation. Sees Pantagruel as an illustration of the "optimistic view of the human condition governed by the Stoic ethic," reflecting the optimism of the early Renaissance. See *Dissertation Abstracts International* 33 (1973):6369A.

25 NEW, MELVYN. "Sterne's Rabelaisian Fragment: A Text from the Holograph Manuscript." *PMLA* 87:1083–92.

Offers an annotated edition of the "true text" (p. 1083) of Sterne's "A Fragment in the Manner of Rabelais," presenting the main characters Longinus Rabelaicus and Homenas, surrounded by such "Rabelaic fellows" as Panurge, Gymnaste, Triboulet, and Epistemon. Sterne may have hoped to include it somewhere in *Tristram Shandy*, but ultimately abandoned it as unusable.


26  POUILLOUX, JEAN-YVES. "Notes sur deux chapitres du *Quart Livre*." *Littérature* 5 (February):88–94.

Structural study of chapt. 55 and 56 (the myth of the Frozen Words). The "organisation cyclique" (p. 89) of this parenthetical episode and the structural parallelism of its two chapters lead the author to suggest a new reading of the text as "une *réduction progressive* des possibilités de sens" (p. 92); whereas in relation to the whole novel the episode has a particular meaning, within the episode itself the second chapter neutralizes the meaning of the first, and the novel can resume its forward thrust.


27  RAGLAND, MARY ELOISE. "A Modern Perspective on Rabelais's Panurge in *Pantagruel, Le Tiers Livre*, and *Le Quart Livre*." Ph.D. dissertation, University of Michigan, 265 pp.

"This study considers how a sixteenth century character can interest a twentieth century reader and thereby purports to explain both Panurge's magnetism and his importance in Rabelais' work." From the perspective of twentieth-century psychology, views Panurge's evolution as paralleling a child's quest for maturity, identity, and understanding. Triumphantly egotistical in *Pantagruel*, Panurge loses his security and identity in the *Tiers Livre*, seeks to adapt to the demands of society by wishing to marry, but is unable to accept the restraints of responsibility and is reduced, in the *Quart Livre*, "to a state of cowardice and infantile fear." Believes that the reader is fascinated with the character because he can re-create him from his own effort at socialization, and recognize in him the universal "life impulse to seek, to grow and to survive" which all people share "without regard to time and place." See *Dissertation Abstracts International* 33 (1972):2391A. Revised for publication: 1976.27.


28  QUINONES, RICARDO J. *The Renaissance Discovery of Time*. Cambridge: Harvard University Press, pp. 187–203.

In chapt. 5, notes that in Rabelais procreation, more than fame itself, is viewed as a means of triumphing over time. Contrasts the disregard of time in the portrayal of education under Gargantua's first pedagogues, and the emphasis on the most effective use of time in Gargantua's education under his new mentors. Notes a new temporal persective in the *Tiers Livre*, particularly in connection with Bridoye and his habit to delay rendering his verdicts because time is the father of truth.

1972

29  RIGOLOT, FRANÇOIS [PAUL]. *Les Langages de Rabelais*. Études
Rabelaisiennes, no. 10. Geneva: Librairie Droz, 186 pp.

Studies the ambiguity of the Rabelaisian text as it manifests itself in the
author's playful use of language. Sees in the "problématique du langage" the
most important aspect of Rabelais' novel, "la grande aventure intérieure du
roman" (p. 12). Studies the various voices heard in the work, beginning with
that of the crier, "le langage du présentateur." Underscores the semantic
duplicity of the prologues to the first two books, each of them introduced by a
dedicatory *dizain* whose function is to alert the reader to the prologue's fundamental ambiguity. In chapt. 2, points to the paradox of a written text aiming
to create the impression of orality, and of giants whose greatest prowess lies
in the verbal expression of their awesome exploits. Notes also, in an analysis
of the lawsuit between Baisecul and Humevesne, the dichotomy between a
logical syntax and an absurd vocabulary, and in the episodes dealing with gestural communication, the paradox involved in the necessity to evoke in words
the language of gesture. In chapt. 3 studies the language of the humanist, as
heard for instance in Gargantua's letter to his son. Argues that, as a fictional
text, the letter "n'échappe pas à la problématique du langage" (p. 60), and
should not be read as a direct expression of Rabelais' ideas. In the chapters on
Gargantua's education, sees an opposition of styles rather than pedagogical
systems. Attributes the relative failure of the pages on the Abbey of Thélème
to a momentary victory of Rabelais the humanist over Rabelais the artist, and
to a resulting lack of congruence between theme and style. Notes that the
notion of freedom is expressed in terms of coercive, albeit negative rules, and
that the beauty of the architectural aspects is rendered in a cold, weighty, prosaic style: "L'exposition défait en toute subtilité ce que promettait l'invention"
(p. 97), which again leads to question the importance of Rabelais' humanistic
passages as expressions of the author's philosophical stance. In the case of the
concluding *Énigme en prophétie*, argues for the validity of both Frère Jean's
and Gargantua's interpretation, as underscoring the ambivalence of the entire
book. In the analysis of the language of the storyteller (chapt. 4), shows that
whatever the register chosen by the narrator, the choice of language tends to
betray the author's original intention, by raising the obscene to lyrical heights,
lowering the gigantic to the level of the everyday, or raising the everyday to
the level of the mythic. Finally, in "Langage du topiqueur" (chapt. 5), studies
the passages belonging to the genre of the paradoxical encomium (including
the "folie verbale" of the chapters dealing with the visit to Triboullet in the
*Tiers Livre*), and finds that only here is the "problématique du langage" at
last—triumphantly—transcended: "Sous la poussée du lyrisme, le *jongleur* se
fera *vates*; il franchira en un instant le seuil des catégories sémantiques en
empruntant un parcours rayonnant où les mots et les choses ont même sympathie" (p. 12).

1972

30 ———. "Rabelais présentateur de ses œuvres." *Revue des Sciences Humaines* 35, no. 147 (July–September):325–37.

Follows the various phases of the author's dialogue with his readers by studying the language of the *présentateur* in the liminary texts ("ces textes-avant-le-texte"). Notes the difference in the public's reception of the first two books: the readers found the first to be merely amusing, the second to be full of daring ideas. Suggests that if they had paid more attention to what the *présentateur* of *Pantagruel* was saying, they would have realized that the book was meant to express "une certaine sagesse, non précisée, mais qui dépassait les apparences bouffonnes" (p. 327). Claims the readers equally misunderstood the ambiguity stressed by the *présentateur* of *Gargantua*. In both cases, "à la duplicité sémantique posée par le texte le lecteur avait substitué la linéarité d'une lecture univoque" (p. 329). Sees the *dizain* by Hugues Salel in the 1534 edition of *Pantagruel* as an effort to correct the reader's misreading of the text's intention. Notes the same motive behind Rabelais' own *dizain* introducing the second edition of *Gargantua*. Argues that both were meant to reorient the public toward a reading that takes into account the text's essential ambiguity, reemphasized in the liminary texts of Books III and IV. Developed more fully in 1972.29.

31 SCHWARTZ, JEROME. "Gargantua's Device and the Abbey of Thélème: A Study in Rabelais' Iconography." *Yale French Studies* 47:232–42.

Distinguishes between an emblem, where a visual element is followed by its verbal equivalent, and a device (or *impresa*), made up of a visual sign and a motto which reciprocally interpret each other. Argues that Gargantua's *image* is a device and not an emblem; accordingly, rejects Screech's interpretation of Rabelais' androgyne as an emblem of Christian love. Argues that "Rabelais' version of the androgyne is a parody of the Platonic (or Aristophanic) original " (p. 237), and that the visual component of the *image* represents "the egocentric conception of eros" (p. 238), so that it undercuts ironically the Pauline motto inscribed around the picture. Relates the picture to Picrochole's self-love, and the motto to Gargantua's charitable treatment of his prisoners and to the love of God and neighbor in the life of the Thelemites. Thus sees in Gargantua's *image* an example of Rabelaisian irony and a structural element in the architecture of the novel.

32 SCREECH, M[ICHAEL] A[NDREW]. "Comment Rabelais a exploité les travaux d'Erasme: Quelques détails." In *Colloquia Erasmiana Turonensia: Douzième stage international d'études humanistes, Tours, 1969*, vol.1. Toronto: University of Toronto Press, pp. 453–61.

Discusses a few examples of direct borrowings from Erasmus. Notes that Rabelais never mentions the writer, but that one can speak of direct Erasmian influence from *Gargantua* onward, on the grounds of the obvious allusion to the *Sileni Alcibiadis* in the prologue, the chapter on eleven-month pregnancies which owes much to the *Annotationes in Novum Testamentum*, and in the pages on color symbolism. Cites as one last example the direct influence of the *Colloquia* on certain passages in the *Tiers Livre*.

33 ————. "Folie erasmienne et folie rabelaisienne." In *Colloquia Erasmiana Turonensia: Deuxième stage international d'études humanistes, Tours, 1969*, vol. 1. Toronto: University of Toronto Press, pp. 441–52.

Believes that Erasmus had a profound influence on Rabelais' life and thought, but doubts that this influence was strictly speaking literary. "Il n'est pas seulement la voix française de son maître" (p. 442). Points to the danger of misreading his work by imposing upon it an Erasmian perspective. Argues for instance that the pages on war in the prologue to the *Tiers Livre* are at odds with Erasmian pacifism, and that the closest Rabelais comes to Erasmus on the subject is in his notion of appeasement as consonant with honor. Also warns against the risks of misinterpreting Book III as a whole by viewing it in the light of the *Encomium moriae*, and of misunderstanding Rabelais' attitude toward Panurge by identifying him with Stultitia. Argues that Rabelais' notion of Christian folly derives from the New Testament and not from the *Moria* (so that Erasmus' *Annotationes in Novum Testamentum* are more relevant in this context). Nor does he believe that Rabelais' views on prophecy, or on the place of the love of one's country and one's family in the life of a true Christian are exactly those of Erasmus (on that last score they can be said to be poles apart). "La folie rabelaisienne est paulinienne, mais moins authentiquement biblique que celle d'Érasme" (p. 449).

34 STONE, DONALD, [Jr]. "A Word About the Prologue to *Gargantua*." *Romance Notes* 13, no. 3 (Spring):511–14.

Notes recent instances of careless reading of the prologue by critics intent on exploring its meaning. Points out in particular that at the pivotal point where Rabelais seems to retract his suggestion that his work possesses an underlying seriousness, the conjunction *combien que*, often taken to mean "since," is in fact equivalent to "although," and that consequently what follows does not really contradict his earlier suggestion. "Thus the complexity of the Prologue cannot be defined in terms of an invitation to study the book and an abandonment of that invitation. The complexity arises because at a given moment Rabelais moves away from the idea of "mouelle" and "haultes matieres" to talk about certain approaches to Homer and to discourage his reader from applying such techniques to his own work" (pp. 512–13). Warns against the temptation to see in what Rabelais says of allegorical interpretations of Homer a rejection of all attempts to find a "doctrine plus absconce" behind the literal sense of a given text. Argues that Rabelais only condemns interpretations that introduce into the discussion elements which are totally foreign to the text at hand.

1973

34  WEINBERG, FLORENCE M[AY]. *The Wine and the Will: Rabelais' Bachic Christianity.* Detroit: Wayne State University Press, 188 pp.

Examines the metaphor of wine and the theme of the will as leading to "the heart of Rabelais's Christian message" (p. 10). Relies heavily on the *Cinquiesme Livre* in the absence of arguments proving "the total inauthenticity of the work" (p. 11). Recalls Rabelais' Christian heritage, and argues for the presence of a hidden truth behind Rabelaisian laughter: "The cumulative evidence tends to indicate that Rabelais meant literally what he promised in the thesis of the prologue to *Gargantua*, and that his disclaimer in the antithesis proposed to throw his enemies off the track" (p. 44). Discusses the numerous references to Bacchus, and claims that Rabelais uses him as a symbol of Christ, as do such other Renaissance humanists as Nicholas of Cusa, Pico della Mirandola, and Cornelius Agrippa. Sees in the temple of the Divine Bottle "the most striking version of the Eucharist" (p. 90), in Gargantua an allegory of divine love, and views Pantagruel as "a compendium of all the wisdom accessible to man" as well as "a Christ figure" (p. 106). Argues that Frère Jean is also an embodiment of the Rabelaisian ideal of Christianity, and that his will is naturally attuned to the divine, which justifies his presence in the Evangelical circle and at the head of the Abbaye de Thélème, whereas Panurge is a representation of "misguided will" and folly, and is entitled as such to receive the divine revelation at the end of Book V. Concludes that Rabelais' message, as embodied in the symbol of wine, is "a combination of Christian and humanistic Neoplatonism" (p. 149), based on the conviction that man can achieve wisdom through free acceptance of divine grace. Published version of 1968.33.

**1973**

1  BERRY, ALICE [FIOLA]. "Rabelais: Homo Logos." *Journal of Medieval and Renaissance Studies* 3, no.1 (Spring):51–67.

Investigates the philosophical background of Rabelais' ambivalent attitude towards language—questioning its legitimacy, drawing the limits of its power—as it manifests itself in Books III and IV, where the problem of language acquires its fullest significance in the context of Panurge's and Pantagruel's quest for truth. Stresses the Platonic background of Rabelais' reflection on language, especially in the episode of the Frozen Words. Argues that Rabelais' position concerning the nature of words is similar to that of Plato in *Cratylus*, as reinterpreted by Plotinus: "the word, derived from the world of the senses, can attain, at the highest, the expression of rational concepts, but it can never attain the expression of that which is suprasensible and suprarational" (p. 64). In Rabelais as in the Neoplatonic tradition, notes the same attempt to solve the dilemma by recourse to paradox and symbolic language. But notes also that, coexisting with this consciousness of the limitations of language, there is within Rabelais "a voice which persistently ridicules these Platonic concerns" (p. 66), believes in the limitless creative power of words, and explores this power to the fullest extent.

2   BUCK, AUGUST. *Rabelais*. Wege der Forschung, no. 284. Darmstadt: Wissenschaftliche Buchgesellshaft, 488 pp.

Collection of twenty-two articles written between 1931 and 1967. The introduction ("Rabelais und die Renaissance: Eine Eintleitung") stresses the opposition between the historical and the aesthetic orientation of the articles. Contains the following studies published since 1950: Manfred Bambeck, "Epistemons Unterweltbericht" (1956.1); Herman Meyer, "Das Zitat als Strukturelement in Rabelais Erzählwerk" (1957.6); Émile Telle, "A propos de la lettre de Gargantua à son fils (*Pantagruel*, chap. VIII)" (1957.9); Erich Köhler, "Die Abtei Thélème und die Einheit des Rabelais'schen Werks" (1959.21); Charles A. Béné, "Érasme et le chapitre VIII du premier *Pantagruel* (Novembre 1532)" (1961.1; takes into account critical reactions to the original version of the article); Marcel Tetel, "La valeur comique des accumulations verbales chez Rabelais" (1962.13); Abraham C. Keller, "Pace and Timing in Rabelais's Stories" (1963.14); V.-L. Saulnier, "Aspects et motifs de la pensée rabelaisienne" (1963.20); Floyd Gray, "Ambiguity and Point of View in the Prologue to *Gargantua*" (1965.8); Per Nykrog, "Thélème, Panurge et la Dive Bouteille" (1965.14), Leo Spitzer, "Ancora sul prologo al primo libro del *Gargantua* di Rabelais" (1965.22); George Mallary Masters, "The Hermetic and Platonic Tradition in Rabelais's *Dive Bouteille*" (1966.15); Ulrich Mölk, "Das Rätsel auf der Bronzetafel (Zu Rabelais, *Gargantua*, Kap. 58)" (1967.17).

3   DEFAUX, GÉRARD. *Pantagruel et les Sophistes: Contribution à l'histoire de l'humanisme chrétien au XVIème siècle.* Archives Internationales d'Histoire des Idées. The Hague: Martinus Hijhoff, 233 pp.

Adopts an intermediate critical approach between the extremes of pure historicism and an exclusively aesthetic interpretation. Sees contextual criticism as necessary, since Rabelais is a committed writer ("un écrivain politiquement, religieusement, et culturellement engagé"), but also potentially detrimental to the understanding of the text itself, especially of its satirical dimension. Confronts key passages from *Pantagruel* with hitherto untranslated texts by such neo-Latin writers as John of Salisbury, Peter of Spain, Agrippa, and Vivès, quoted abundantly in the original. Proposes as a hermeneutic model the Augustinian concept of allegorical exegesis as practiced throughout the Middle Ages and the Renaissance on sacred as well as non-religious texts. Detects in *Pantagruel* (and indeed in the whole of Rabelais' fictional work) an echo of the polemic between Socrates and Gorgias, a manichean opposition between good and evil. "Pantagruel, par la nature même de son savoir, achève...de s'identifier avec le sophiste type tel

1973

qu'on le définit depuis Aristote, non seulement chez les humanistes du XVIe siècle, mais aussi chez les logiciens et les penseurs médiévaux" (pp. 136–37). The giant first appears as a personification of merely apparent knowledge, in contrast to the true knowledge of him who knows that he does not know. But as Panurge finds his way into the book and takes his master's place as an embodiment of sophistry, Pantagruel emerges as the champion of truth, a Christian Socrates, a spokesman for humanism. From Grandgousier through Gargantua to Pantagruel, the author notes an ideological shift: "Evolution exemplaire, à la fois historique et symbolique, d'une sagesse divine primitive à la tentation de la sagesse humaine, jugée et refusée, à une sagesse divine élargie et librement choisie" (p. 199). The whole work is thus studied as a meditation on the role of knowledge and culture in the perspective of Christian humanism.

4    DEMERSON, GUY. "*Extraits de haulte mythologie*: La mythologie clas-
sique dans les *mythologies pantagruélicques* de Rabelais." *CAIEF* 25
(May):227–45.
     Points to the limitations of studying mythology in Rabelais from an exclusively epic or folkloric perspective. Underscores the importance of classical mythology both for Rabelais and for a clear understanding of his work. Argues that *myth* is not used by Rabelais in a Platonic sense but in the humanistic sense of *fabula* ("la véritable mythologie est récit et non construction intellectuelle," p. 231). Contests the validity of explaining Rabelaisian characters by reference to archetypal mythological models. Argues that mythology is used in Rabelais mainly as *allusion*, in the playful sense the etymology of the word suggests. Shows how recourse to classical mythology affects the temporal structure of the Rabelaisian narrative and the stature of the Rabelaisian characters. Defines Panurge in terms of his misunderstanding of the nature of myth as representation of the ultimate mystery of reality ("pour lui le temps du mythe est le temps du désir," p. 242). Argues that for Rabelais, on the other hand, classical myth represents "une occasion d'exercer l'esprit critique contre les fantasmes qui ont tendance à faire déborder l'imaginaire dans le réel" (p. 242). As such, classical myth has both a didactic and a narrative function. "C'est en cela qu'il demeure véritablement *mythe*, vivant et sérieux, au lieu de se scléroser en une métonymie décorative" (p. 244).

5    ———. "Rabelais et le Calendrier." *BAARD* 3, no. 2:68–73.
     "Rabelais s'acharne à réduire l'importance de ses almanachs à celle d'un calendrier" (p. 68). Finds Rabelais to be attracted to the calendar as a tool that provides an essentially reassuring conception of temporality.

6    DONTENVILLE, HENRI. *Histoire et géographie mythiques de la France.*
Paris: G. P. Maisonneuve et Larose, pp. 229–332.

In chapt. 8, "Géographie de Gargantua," discusses the folkloric sources of the Gargantuan legend.

7 FRANÇON, MARCEL. "Notes Rabelaisiennes." *BAARD* 3, no. 2:76–78.
On Rabelais' religious vocation, on the theme of the three wishes (*Pantagruel*, chapt. 27) and its possible connection with the fifty-ninth of Philippe de Vigneulles' *Cent Nouvelles Nouvelles*.

8 HALL, ELLEN WOOD. "A Study of Rabelais' Thought in the Context of Jean de Meung's *Roman de la Rose*." Ph.D. dissertation, Bryn Mawr College, 256 pp.
Underscores the medieval origins of Rabelais' ideas in matters of education, religion, and philosophy, as influenced by his education at a university "which had changed little since the Middle Ages." Uses Jean de Meung's *Roman de la Rose* as a basis of comparison in an attempt to show that *Pantagruel* and *Gargantua* owe more to the twelfth-century Renaissance than to that of the sixteenth. Emphasizes thematic similarities (often of Aristotelian origin), but concludes that the two authors were essentially dissimilar in their intellectual and spiritual attitude toward such fundamental matters as knowledge and wisdom. "Pantagruel, the Rabelaisian hero, learns that human wisdom, as exemplified by Panurge, is folly; man must look to God for true wisdom. Ultimately, Jean de Meung champions the intellectual prowess of the Middle Ages, Rabelais, the humanistically oriented faith of the Renaissance." See *Dissertation Abstracts International* 35 (1975):5344–5A.

9 HAYMAN, DAVID. "Au-delà de Bakhtine: Pour une mécanique des modes." *Poétique* 13:76–94.
Believes that Bakhtin is right in seeing the carnivalesque as an appropriate frame of reference for the study of comic effects, but claims that he has not convincingly argued his case, oversimplifying the popular modes of which he speaks by not taking into account their dialectical aspect. Seeks to complete Bakhtin's analysis of the mechanism underlying the conventions of the carnival in a discussion of the character of Panurge, seen as both an emblem of fear and evil, and as a popular hero endowed with boundless culture and energy. Studies chapt. 7–9 of *Pantagruel* with emphasis on "rhythms," "attitudes," and "other modal variants," notes the interpenetration of the farcical and the "romanesque," the ordered and the chaotic. Underscores in these chapters as elsewhere in the novel the coexistence of seemingly incompatible elements, held in a precarious yet never totally disrupted equilibrium, and in which allusions to existing locations and to contemporary events, far from anchoring the fiction in reality, reinforce the discordance between the real and the imaginary and lead to a rejection of formal coherence.

1973

10 KAPLAN, ELIZABETH W. "Sources and Functions of Visual Humor in Rabelais' First Four Books." Ph.D. dissertation, Indiana University, 234 pp.

Studies the humorous mental pictures evoked by Rabelais' text in the light of a distinction between joyous and aggressive laughter. Finds that scenes dealing with the overcoming of natural or social limitations give rise to joyous laughter, whereas those dealing with the desire to kill physically or socially the inferior members of the species provoke laughter of an aggressive type. Also finds that when humor is used—as it is in the prologues—to describe Rabelais' books, "joyous laughter aids in presenting what they are not to be." When used to present major characters, any traces of aggressive humor are absorbed by joyous humor, whose function is to make the characters acceptable to the reader. In the case of satire, the predominantly aggressive humor is frequently mitigated. See *Dissertation Abstracts International* 34 (1974):4266–7A.

11 LANIUS, EDWARD W. "Sense of Group and Accomodation in Rabelais's Comic Universe." *Zeitschrift für Romanische Philologie* 89:167–81.

Taking as a point of departure Saulnier's claim that from the end of Book III the characters abandon any attempt to change the world around them and merely seek accomodation with it, argues (with reference to the Bergsonian theory of laughter) that in all instances Rabelaisian laughter stems from the way in which the personages seek to maintain a sense of group participation through word or action.

12 LARMAT, JEAN. *Le Moyen Age dans le "Gargantua" de Rabelais.* Publications de la Faculté des Lettres et Sciences Humaines de Nice, no. 12. Nice: Les Belles Lettres, 583 pp.

Not a study of influences and sources, but of the mentality of Rabelais, seen essentially as a man of the Middle Ages. *Gargantua* chosen in preference to the last three books because the latter admittedly bear traces of a belated conversion to the Renaissance, and in preference to *Pantagruel* insofar as it is viewed as a mere "ébauche" of Rabelais' second book. The preliminary pages offer a summary of *Gargantua*, as well as a study of Rabelais' notion of time. Chapt. 1 studies the work's major themes. The freedom with which Rabelais speaks of food and of body functions, including sexuality, is considered to be essentially medieval. His conception of women, far from being exclusively misogynous, reflects the many guises under which women appear in the various currents of medieval literature: the lascivious cause of man's perdition, the idealized object of courtly love, as well as the serious, loyal partner, and man's equal companion. Suggests that Rabelais' ideal in this respect would be "Gargamelle élevée à Thélème" (p. 576). Claims that Rabelais' themes in themselves, their convergence, and the frankness with which they are expressed bring to mind the Middle Ages rather than the Renaissance. In chapt. 2, argues that the work is also fundamentally medieval in its indebtedness to folklore, to scholastic modes of thought, and to the symbolic modes of literary interpretation; even Rabelais' humanism, as expressed in *Gargantua*, is seen as a legacy of the Middle Ages. Contends, in chapt. 3, that in his pedagogy Rabelais is as close to such fourteenth and fifteenth century theoreticians as Aegidius Romanus and Vittorino da Feltre as he is to Erasmus and Vives, and that his political ideas owe more to St Thomas Aquinas, Jean de Meung, or Ockham than to the political thinkers of his time. Even the religious ideas which Rabelais holds in common with the Evangelical movement and Luther's Reformation are already those of the second part of the *Roman de la Rose*. In chapt. 4, offers a number of stylistic analyses and suggests that Rabelais' style, whether colloquial, technical, or humanistic, is that of an essentially medieval author. Concludes by presenting Rabelais as a transitional figure: "Au confluent de deux époques, en une période de crise, il choisit les temps modernes, et c'est avec les armes du Moyen Age qu'il combat pour la Renaissance." Extensive bibliography.

13 ———. *Rabelais*. Connaissance des Lettres. Paris: Hatier, 255 pp.
General survey of Rabelais' life and work, with emphasis on Rabelais' ideas, and on his debt to the Middle Ages: "Il doit beaucoup à Erasme et à Luther. Mais, en dépit des générations qui les séparent, il est de la famille intellectuelle et spirituelle de Jean de Meun" (p. 104). Finds him equally indebted to medieval literature in his choice of themes and their treatment: "A Rabelais, le Moyen Age a donné plus que l'Antiquité, peut-être plus que la Renaissance" (p. 77). Studies *Pantagruel* in terms of liberating laughter, and *Gargantua* as offering a new vision of the world. Provides episode-by-episode summaries, followed by a literary analysis of their content. Agrees with many that the question of marriage in the *Tiers Livre* is merely a *mise-en-scène* of a more fundamental, philosophical problem of knowledge and prophecy. Finds Screech's emphasis on Panurge's *philautia* somewhat excessive. Insists on the variety of possible readings of the work's meaning. Compares the two versions of Book IV: "rien ne laisse prévoir, en 1547, ce que sera le *Quart Livre* de 1552, la place capitale qu'y auront les problèmes religieux et surtout la satire antivaticane, ni le caractère fantastique qu'y prendra l'imagination de Rabelais" (p. 152). Sees the book as Rabelais' contribution to an ideological struggle: "une œuvre de combat" (p. 170). Argues that the comparison also underscores a stylistic evolution towards a consciously more archaic syntax and vocabulary. In connection with Book V, notes the significant number of arithmological interpretations to which it has given rise, and the necessity of allegorical readings of a number of episodes. Believes that all told the message of the last chapters is similar to that of Rabelais' previous books, with its insistence on the the notions of grace, charity, and action. Studies in the last chapter the art of Rabelais, the various aspects of his work's comic dimension, his characteristic juxtaposition of a variety of styles: "Merveilleux conteur, incomparable dramaturge, il est, par-dessus tout, poète" (p. 234). Ends with a

1973

brief section on Rabelais' influence and reputation, and a long "note bibliographique."

14 LORIAN, ALEXANDRE. *Tendances stylistiques dans la prose narrative française au XVIe siècle*. Bibliothèque Française et Romane. Paris: Éditions Klincksieck, 343 pp.

Scattered references to Rabelais as the most prestigious of the "auteurs-témoins" used to illustrate the stylistic tendencies under investigation. Remarks on Rabelais' use of numbers, reduplication of synonyms, enumeration, and a variety of stylistic devices.

15 LOSSE, DEBORAH NICHOLS. "Thematic and Structural Unity in Rabelais's *Tiers Livre*." Ph.D. dissertation, University of North Carolina, Chapel Hill, 113 pp.

Studies the *éloge* and the consultation as structural patterns in the *Tiers Livre*. The function of the *éloge* is to express the author's opinion, to praise certain ideas or significant aspects of his characters' personality, or to satirize, in the case of the ironic *éloge*. The common pattern discernible in the series of consultations "lends continuity to the individual episodes and to the behaviour of Panurge and his companions." On the other hand, the contrasts in tone which also characterize the consultations underscore the temperamental differences between Panurge and Pantagruel. "Comparison and contrast are thus essential elements of unity within the *Tiers Livre*." Concludes by suggesting that the unifying elements of the book lie hidden "beneath the deceptive guise of diverse episodes." See *Dissertation Abstracts International* 34 (1974): 5979A.

16 MASTERS, G[EORGE] MALLARY. "Panurge at the Crossroads: A Mythopoetic Study of the Pythagorean Y in Rabelais's Satirical Romance (QL/33-34)." *Romance Notes* 15, no. 1 (Autumn):134–54.

Sees in the Physétère episode of the *Quart Livre*, with its central image of the Pythagorean Y, "a microstructure of Panurge's allegorical quest" (p. 134). Relates the quest to the moral dilemma of Hercules at the crossroads to Vice and Virtue, the moral choice between wisdom and folly as illustrated in the woodcuts of Brant's *Narrenschiff*, and the crossroads in hell leading to the sufferings of Tartarus or the happiness of the Elysian fields. Sees in the numbers associated with the killing of the whale (assimilated to Leviathan) a symbol of wholeness and perfection. Notes the recurrence of the Pythagorean Y at the foot of the stairway leading down to the Temple of the Dive Bouteille in Book V. Reads the various steps of Panurge's voyage toward the oracle as a descent into hell before initiation. "Having taken the inverted route of Vice and Folly, Panurge has descended into hell. Conquering the dragon of the deep, he ascends to the right path of Wisdom and Virtue symbolized by the image of marriage, a figure of wholeness and completion" (p. 153). Sees in

Panurge's spiritual voyage a symbolic expression of modern psychological theories.

17  METTRA, CLAUDE. *Rabelais secret*. Collection Histoire des personnages mystérieux et des Sociétés secrètes. Paris: Culture, Arts, Loisirs, 286 pp.

Argues that Rabelais' work contains a hidden truth, "un savoir initiatique" (p. 13). Believes the kitchen to have been the "lieu privilégié" of Rabelais' childhood, and underscores the close relationship between the kitchen and the art of alchemy. Dwells on the period when, having left his convent, Rabelais lives among the poor and the vagrants, in search of a truth that cannot be found in books alone. Believes Thélème to have been designed as a refuge from the horrors of wars and the incertitudes of history, as a capitalistic attempt to recreate in materialistic terms the happiness of man in the Garden of Eden. Also underscores the theatrical side of Thélème, as a restitution of the *Theatrum mundi* which haunted men's imagination throughout the fifteenth century and had its roots in the alchemic tradition. But believes that it is only in the *Tiers Livre* that Rabelais begins in earnest, through the character of Panurge, his initiatory quest. Sees Panurge as an orphan, "un homme de nulle part," an outsider in search of his own truth. Believes that Panurge's perplexity on the problem of marriage reflects one of the fundamental teachings of the alchemist tradition: "nul ne peut avancer dans la possession du monde sans avoir pénétré d'abord dans la connaissance de ce monde" (p. 178). Finds in Rabelais' attempt to destroy language as a means of communication, and in his emphasis on the functions of the body, yet another link with the occult tradition: "C'est...à travers les fonctions corporelles que les hommes parviennent à la conscience et à l'intelligence du monde" (p. 208). Sees in the itinerary of Book IV the very prototype of the initiatory quest, and interprets Book V as open-ended quest in need of perpetual renewal. "Et c'est là le sens véritablement alchimique de son entreprise, si l'on veut bien voir dans l'alchimie la tentative de chaque individu pour découvrir sa propre vérité, son propre secret, pour trouver la connaissance suprême, c'est-à-dire la connaissance réservée à chaque itinéraire humain" (p. 249). In an appendix, gives an excerpt from Béroalde de Verville's *Moyen de parvenir* and quotations from Hugo and Michelet which underscore the nocturnal and magical character of Rabelais' work.

18  MULHAUSER, RUTH. "Rabelais and the Fictional World of Alcofribas Nasier." *Romanic Review* 64:175–83.

Studies Rabelais' narrative technique in the first two books, in an effort to discover "the relationship between the author, the book and the public" (p. 175), and the effect of this narrative technique on the totality of the work. Notes that the dialogue between Alcofribas and his readers is not confined to the prologues. Of the thirty-four chapters making up *Pantagruel*, "fourteen carry some direct dialogue between narrator and audience" (p. 177). Notes also that in chapt. 17 and especially chapt. 32 (on the world in Pantagruel's mouth), the narrator becomes a protagonist. Sees this as part of a progressive evolution in the relationship between the author-narrator and his readers as one passes from *Pantagruel* to *Gargantua*. Alcofribas progressively fades away into the absent writer, while the principal characters themselves now "carry the burden of Rabelais's view of life" (pp. 182–83).

19  PUISSEGUR, M. "Rabelais géomètre, ou A propos de la fontaine fantastique (*L[ivre] V*, XLII)." *BAARD* 3, no. 2:74–75.
     Suggests a hermetic, esoteric interpretation of the fountain episode in Book V.

20  THOMPSON, PAUL L. "Thematic consistency in *Tiers Livre*, chapter 28." *Romance Notes* 14, no. 3 (Spring):577–82.
     Argues that the chapter "hangs together" in spite of the meanderings of Rabelais' thought, as a set of variations on the link between age and sexual potency.

21  VALETTE, FRANCIS C. "Notes pour le commentaire de Rabelais." *Romance Notes* 15, no. 2 (Winter):323–27.
     Philological remarks on the meaning of *coulouoir* (*Pantagruel*, chapt. 29) and *ennicrochez* (*Gargantua*, chapt. 16).

## 1974

1  BABCOCK-ABRAHAMS, BARBARA. "The Novel and the Carnival World: An Essay in Memory of Joe Doherty." *Modern Language Notes* 89, no. 6 (December):911–37.
    In the second section of the article, discusses Rabelais as "[t]he oft challenged but still unseated literary master of polyphonic revel" (p. 921), and his work as intentionally defying classification. Believes that the revolutionary dimension of Rabelais' work lies in his joyous breaking down of the boundaries within which medieval thought confines itself, rather than in his opposition to medieval systems of thought and its feudal and ecclesiastical hierarchies. Studies the complexity of Rabelais' polyphonic novel from a semiotic perspective, in which the grotesque world of the carnival is superimposed upon the traditional patterns of epic and romance.

2  BAKHTIN, MIKHAIL. *La Cultura popular en la Edad Media y Renacimiento.* Translated by Julio Forcat and Cesar Conroy. Barcelona: Berral.
    Spanish translation of 1965.1.

3  BASTIAENSEN, MICHEL. "La rencontre de Panurge." *Revue Belge de Philologie et d'Histoire* 52, no. 3:544–65.

In opposition to prevailing critical opinion, believes that chapt. 9 of *Pantagruel*, in which the reader first meets Panurge, is of utmost importance to the understanding of the work, and that its place after chapt. 8 (the letter from Gargantua to his son) is due neither to error nor to chance, but corresponds to a very conscious design. Notes that Panurge's answers to Pantagruel's inquiry as to his identity fall into two groups: those which are made in languages that Pantagruel and his followers do not understand, and the last four replies before the final answer in French. Believes that the aim of the nine answers forming the first group is to delay communication by deliberately using codes unknown to the person addressed. Although the answers in the second group are meant to be understood, Panurge does not give his auditors the time to reply before he moves to the next linguistic register. Applying Jakobson's theory of communication and his terminology to this example of "interlingual code switching," notes that the referential and injunctive functions of the message are underplayed in favor of functions pertaining to the conditions and modes of reception rather than to the message itself, and are designed mainly to elicit astonishment and admiration. Nor is the poetic function forgotten, whereby attention is called to the message through such means as imagery and a variety of literary allusions. Finds in this emphasis on form the proof of Panurge's paradoxical yet real tendency to give a privileged status to language *per se*. In attempting to bring out the significance of Panurge's plurilingualism, suggests that besides being related, as had previously been noted, to his tendency to play and to mystify, Panurge's recourse to such intellectual intermediaries as linguistic signs, even if they delay the alleviation of his physical suffering, is a vigorous affirmation of his humanity: "il refuse de céder à la déshumanisation qui guette l'affamé et l'humilié...; il se raccroche à la dignité humaine par le seul moyen dont il dispose à ce moment-là: le langage, même si cela doit prolonger ses souffrances" (p. 556). Believes that Panurge reconciles within himself, in this scene as well as elsewhere, the humanistic and folkloric currents inextricably mingled in Rabelais' work. Underscores what Panurge has in common with primeval man ("Urmensch"), the "trickster" of Winnebago Indian mythology, and with its Greco-Roman equivalent, Hermes. Insofar as he represents an antithetical (yet equally valid) ideal to that proclaimed by Gargantua in his letter, Panurge contributes to Pantagruel's emergence as "un homme complet." Argues that in the light of this interpretation, chapt. 9 is placed exactly where it ought to be, since Gargantua's letter and the meeting with Panurge follow each other naturally and logically as the two components of an ideal, complete education.

4  BURRELL, PAUL. "*Aubeliere*: A Note on Rabelais' Vocabulary." *Études Rabelaisiennes* 11:145–46.

Notes that the word *aubeliere*, which appears in chapt. 12 of *Gargantua*,

1974

is glossed in Pierre Jourda's edition as being of unknown origin and meaning. Suggests that *museliere* (in immediate proximity to our word) is to *museau* what *aubeliere* is to *aube*, in the sense of "derrière, anus" in Godefroy's *Dictionnaire de langue française*.

5  COOPER, RICHARD. "Rabelais et l'occupation française du Piedmont." In *Culture et politique en France à l'époque de l'Humanisme et de la Renaissance*. Études réunies et présentées par Franco Simone. Turin: Accademia delle Scienze, pp. 325–39.

Suggests that Rabelais may have come to Turin in order to help Langey's four doctors to deal with the great number of Frenchmen who had fallen ill because of the climate and the unsanitary conditions in the city. Evokes the large group of Frenchmen whom Langey had gathered around him. Believes Rabelais to have been one of Langey's secretaries in charge of cultural matters. Speculates on Rabelais' role in the writing of Langey's *Ogdoades*. Ascribes the disparity between Rabelais' description of Dipsodia in *Pantagruel* and in the *Tiers Livre* and Rabelais' return to the subject, after a period of twelve years, to his desire to make use of his intervening political experience in the Piedmont, and to stress the virtues of colonization as carried out by Langey. Finds further echoes of Rabelais' Piedmontese experience in the Diogenes episode in the prologue to Book III, and most of all in the *Sciomachie* with its passages on artillery and fortifications.

6  DEFAUX, GÉRARD. "Au cœur du *Pantagruel*: Les deux chapitres IX de l'édition Nourry." *Kentucky Romance Quarterly* 21, no. 1:56–96.

Notes the generally dismissive attitude of French scholars towards the earliest of Rabelais's books. Thus the presence of two chapters numbered 9 in Claude Nourry's *editio princeps* has been taken as an example of the supposed haste with which *Pantagruel* had been put together. Recalls that Charles Béné had sought to explain the anomaly by suggesting that chapt. 8 had been inserted belatedly in an attempt to ennoble with a humanistic manifesto an otherwise popular and comic work (see 1961.1). Challenges this explanation and seeks to challenge by the same token *Pantagruel*'s reputation as hastily written, loosely organized, incoherent, and largely insignificant. "Rabelais y a inscrit, à travers l'opposition complice du divin Pantagruel et du sophiste Panurge, les dilemmes et les grandeurs, les espoirs et les échecs, la parabole entière de l'humanisme évangélique érasmien" (p. 61). Stresses the medieval aspects of chapt. 8 (Gargantua's letter to his son): "Ce qui s'y découvre est moins le 'chant triomphal de la Renaissance' que l'étendue et la nature *franciscaine, patristique et scholastique* de la culture de Rabelais" (p. 66). Reads this chapter as part of a linear sequence of episodes imbued with the same comic tonality, and written in the same popular vein as the Gargantuan chronicles. Believes that the decisive turning point of the novel occurs with the appearance of Panurge in the following chapter, when the sophistry of Pantagruel is transferred to Panurge, thus allowing the giant to begin to assume in the second of the chapters numbered 9 (the legal dispute between Baisecul and Humevesne) a genuinely heroic stature as a representative of enlightened humanism. From that point on the work as a whole acquires its structural originality as a *locus* of dialogue and tension between contadictory, yet friendly forces, and assumes the ideological significance it is customarily denied.

7 ———. "Les Dates de composition et de publication du *Gargantua*: Essai de mise au point." *Études Rabelaisiennes* 11:137–42.

Notes that the problem of dating *Gargantua* is intimately related to the question of its meaning, and of the historical circumstances in which the work was composed. Supports Lefranc's solution ("composition en 1533, publication en août 1534," p. 137) with factual information enabling to date with precision three of the episodes: the passage about the meaning of the colors white and blue (late 1532 or early 1533), the episode of the bells of Notre-Dame (June–July 1533), and the *Enigme en prophétie* (December 1533 or January 1534). On the basis of stylistic considerations, believes that *Gargantua* was published before the 1534 edition of *Pantagruel*.

8 ———. "Rabelais et son masque comique: *sophista loquitur*." *Études Rabelaisiennes* 11:89–135.

Submits that the art of the storyteller or the novelist is essentially akin to that of the sophist as defined by Socrates in the *Gorgias*, namely an art of persuasion whose effects are achieved primarily through words. "Le conteur est naturellement et nécessairement sophiste, et d'autant plus sophiste qu'il est meilleur conteur" (p. 89). Reminds us that the master of the verbal game is Alcofrybas Nasier and not Rabelais himself. ("Anagramme ne signifie pas identité," p. 91). Sees Alcofrybas as the comic mask behind which Rabelais can hide in his attempts to unmask evil and expose it to ridicule. Notes Alcofrybas' omnipresence throughout *Gargantua*, where he is made to take on the sophistic function ascribed earlier to Panurge. Warns of the danger of confusing author and narrator, and consequently of taking *Gargantua* for an essentially serious work. Notes that by being placed in Alcofrybas' mouth, even the most serious ideas lose their seriousness: "L'imposante science humaine se résout en une sorte de fête du langage dont l'intelligence sort désarmée et conquise, l'esprit critique anéanti" (p. 107). Argues that Alcofrybas' dissertations on lengthy pregnancies, miraculous births, heraldic symbolism are all to be read as parody. Offers a detailed study of the chapters on heraldic symbolism in this light. Believes that the reference to "le Prince" at the end of the episode is not to Francis I but to Rabelais' publisher, Claude Nourry, who died in 1533. Sees in this one reason to conclude that *Gargantua* dates from that year. Contests the generally held view that *Gargantua* is the most transparent, least mysterious of Rabelais' books, since it is entirely nar-

1974

rated by Alcofrybas. Argues that the book's interest does not lie in its ideas ("Car la 'pensée' du *Gargantua* est dénuée de toute originalité, elle relève du lieu commun," p. 130) but rather in their "mise en œuvre," that is in the verbal, sophistic game which begins as early as the first sentence of the prologue. In that game, which is primarily a game of contrasts, ideas exist and find their justification in their relation to their opposites, rather than in themselves, as expressions of Rabelais' thought. To think otherwise is to forget that *Gargantua* is first and foremost a work of art: "C'est oublier en Rabelais l'artiste, le joueur, le maître du langage, et proposer du *Gargantua* une image appauvrie" (p. 135).

9    DEMERSON, GENEVIEVE. "Rabelais auteur latin." *BAARD* 3, no. 3:110–13.

Notes a certain clumsiness in Rabelais' use of Latin and Greek in his letters and his poetry. Finds that he improved as time went by, due perhaps to the influence of Jean du Bellay, who spoke and wrote Latin admirably. Notes that at all times Rabelais' vocabulary is much less rich, and his syntax much less free, in Latin than it is in French.

10   DEMERSON, GUY. "Rabelais et les météores." *BAARD* 3, no. 3:114–17.

Defines meteorology as it was understood in Rabelais' day, notes that among meteors were included such atmospheric phenomena as rain, snow, and hail, as well as such luminous phenomena as the rainbow, comets, and lightning. Points out that if meteorology was not included in Pantagruel's program of studies, it was because the latter comprised only *descriptive* sciences, whereas meteorology depended not on observation but on *ratio philosophica*. Comments on the allusions to meteors in Rabelais' novels, and notes that they are treated derisively when denoting a tendency towards superstition, but also with curiosity and seriousness when viewed as constitutive elements of man and of the world around him. Part 2 of article: 1975.2.

11   DISTELBARTH, WERNER. *François Rabelais: Aspecte seiner Erzählkuntzt*. Tübingen: Fotodruck Präzis, 336 pp.

Systematic analysis of narrative techniques, with emphasis on the relationship between the writer and his audience, narrative point of view, and the process of integration of ideas into what remains essentially a work of fiction.

12   DOWNES, MICHAEL. "Arbre=Mat: Why Pantagruel Does Not Hold the Rudder (*Quart Livre*, XIX)." *Études Rabelaisiennes* 11:73–80.

Pantagruel is seen, throughout the storm at sea episode, as holding on to the ship's "arbre." What in fact is he holding? Georges Lote had preferred to see in "arbre" a stern rather than a mast, mainly because this interpretation avoids having to tax Pantagruel with cowardice. But "arbre" is most often defined in dictionaries as "mat," and there is no rudder to hold on to since it was removed at the beginning and put back at the end of the storm, whereas Pantagruel holds on to the "arbre" throughout. Rises from this lexicographical discussion to an ideological commentary, and views Pantagruel as abandoning "the rudder of human control, powerless and even dangerous as it is in a crisis," and "preparing himself for the supreme moment of submission" to the will of God (p. 78).

13  FRANÇON, MARCEL. "Note sur la datation de *Gargantua*." *Études Rabelaisiennes* 11:81–82.
     Supports Screech's thesis that *Gargantua* was published *after* the Affaire des Placards, by pointing out that there was nothing in the political climate that would make it impossible for Rabelais to bring out his book at that particular time.

14  ———. "Notes Rabelaisiennes." *BAARD* 3, no. 3:118–19.
     On Thélème and its motto; on Sextus Empiricus; and on the date of publication of *Gargantua* (agrees on 1535, with Screech).

15  GAIGNEBET, CLAUDE, and FLORENTIN, MARIE CLAUDE. *Le Carnaval: Essais de mythologie populaire*. Collection Le Regard de l'Histoire. Paris: Payot, 170 pp.
     A folklorist's account of popular carnivalesque culture in France, with occasional references to Rabelais.

16  GENDRE, ANDRÉ. "Le Prologue de *Pantagruel*, le prologue de *Gargantua*: Examen comparatif." *Revue d'Histoire Littéraire de la France* 74:3–19.
     Compares the prologues in an effort to bring out the evolution of Rabelais' art in manner and intention ("une évolution du dessein et du faire," p. 3) between 1532 and 1534. Underscores the improvisational character of the structure, syntax, and argumentation in the first prologue, and notes the fluctuations in tone characterizing the interpolations to the reader and the latter's responses. Finds that in the second prologue Rabelais is more clearly conscious of what he aims to do, and a greater master of his means of expression. Whereas his purpose in the prologue to *Pantagruel* was merely to convince the reader that he had before him a genuine work of literature, in the prologue to *Gargantua* he raises for the first time the more important question of interpretation. The systematic use of comparisons underscores the relativistic nature of interpretation as Rabelais understands it. As for the structure of the prologue, argues (against such critics as Spitzer) that the second part merely corrects the first without really contradicting it. Thus when Rabelais claims that Homer had not consciously used in his work the allegories that later commentators claim to have discovered in it, he does not contradict his earlier suggestion that the reader search for a "plus hault sens": he merely underscores the reader's responsibility in the act of interpretation.

1974

17    GIERCZYNSKI, ZBIGNIEW. "Rabelais ou l'humanisme des Lumières."
      *Roczniki Humanistyczne* 22, no. 4:7–99.
         Believes that the recent tendency to view the work exclusively in terms
      of comedy and paradox reduces it to its most superficial dimension. Argues
      that humor and fiction merely allow Rabelais to express a set of daring,
      strongly held convictions representing the most radical form of humanistic
      rationalism. Finds him to be contemptuous of the occult sciences and of the
      Neoplatonism in vogue among his contemporaries. Explains his sympathy
      towards the Evangelical movement as a tactical adherence to a sect whose
      victory might bring about greater tolerance and a more humane form of
      religion.

18    GRAY, FLOYD. *Rabelais et l'écriture*. Paris: Librairie A.-G. Nizet, 215 pp.
         Proposes to read Rabelais' text "dans l'optique du langage" (p. 12),
      studying the interplay of the various languages heard as well as seen in the
      course of the narrative, and showing to what extent language is the very sub-
      ject of Rabelais' book. Sees the prologues as *loci* of linguistic experimenta-
      tion. Shows that they are not an apology of the work they introduce, but that
      each becomes "scène et mouvement" in a preliminary effort to substitute the
      perspective of the author's work for the everyday perspective of the reader.
      Discusses their linguistic texture, and the relationship they establish between
      narrator and reader, between *parole* and *écriture*, and follows the changing
      modalities of this relationship throughout the four books whose authenticity is
      not in question. Notes how the text is generated by other texts, pre-existing or
      sometimes imaginary; sees the multiplicity of languages brought into play as
      a way to achieve stylistic diversity, but above all as a sign of a reflection on
      the nature of language and the relationship between words and things. Sees as
      early as in *Pantagruel* a preoccupation with the arbitrary nature of language;
      notes instances where words are treated as objects, signifying nothing beyond
      their linguistic form: "L'univers du *Pantagruel* est essentiellement verbal" (p.
      62). Believes this to be even more true of *Gargantua*; Rabelais does not
      recount the giant's childhood: "il la refait par l'écriture" (p. 89). In the chap-
      ters on education, on the war with Picrochole, at the abbey of Seuillé, at
      Thélème, believes Rabelais to be less interested in what he is saying than in
      the relationship between language and the reality it is meant to express. In the
      *Tiers Livre*, sees words as a substitute for both psychology and action, in an
      attempt to free the writer from narrative and characterological constraints. In
      the *Quart Livre*, argues that the dynamics of the book depend, once again,
      directly on the confrontation of a diversity of languages, as the exploration of
      language (through enumeration, anecdotes, literary allusions to the past)
      stands in the way of narrative progression: "Rabelais entreprend un voyage
      de lecteur, emportant sa bibliothèque avec lui" (p. 168). Insists on the gener-
      ating power of proper nouns (chapt. 27), and proposes for many of the islands
      on the travellers' itinerary a linguistic interpretation: thus reads the Ruach

episode as underscoring the autonomy of language, its independence from any theme it may be used to express, and sees in the chapter on Papimanie "un essai de langage interrogatif et surtout exclamatif" (p. 189). Insists on the importance in Rabelais of the *written* word (related to the invention of printing), meant to be seen as well as heard. Sees throughout his work an oscillation between "une écriture nourrie de lectures" and writing as pure invention, and notes that the ambiguity of the Rabelaisian text—more ludic than semantic—stems directly from Rabelais' innovative use of *écriture* as self-referential, rather than implying, as it did in the Middle Ages, a reference to a transcending reality from which it derived its unequivocal meaning.

19  GUERLAC, RITA. "Vives and the Education of Gargantua." *Études Rabelaisiennes* 11:63–72.

Argues that Rabelais' ideas on education are much closer to those of Vives than to any other humanist of his day: "Both shared an Erasmian piety, a belief in the value of physical as well as moral and intellectual training and, most significantly, a lively interest in the life of the world around them, which manifested itself in nature study, observation, curiosity about crafts and trades, and the application of learning to daily life" (p. 63). Shows that the pedagogical part of the letter from Gargantua to Pantagruel derives very closely from the first part of Vives' *De disciplinis*: "De causis corruptarum artium," and not, as Michaud had thought, from the second part, entitled "De tradendis disciplinis"; the latter bears much closer relation to the chapters on the giant's education in *Gargantua*, which represent a ten-page compression of Vives' twelve books.

20  GURNEY, GEORGIE AUGHERTON. "Rabelais and Renaissance Color Symbolism." Ph.D. dissertation, University of North Carolina, Chapel Hill, 330 pp.

Believes that the chapters on Gargantua's livery mock the excesses of medieval color symbolism as superstitious and arbitrary, in the name of the "purer" symbolism of antiquity. On the basis of a study of color-systems in literary works with which Rabelais could have been familiar, argues that color, while prevalent in "passages of an emotive nature" is rare in those that narrate actions or depict psychological states, and that white is the dominant color discussed. See *Dissertation Abstracts International* 35 (1975):5344A.

21  LA CHARITÉ, RAYMOND C. "Interpenetration in Rabelais's *Pantagruel*: A Study of the Lion-Fox Episode." In *Renaissance Studies in Honor of Isidore Silver: Essays on French Renaissance Literature*, edited by Frieda S. Brown. *Kentucky Romance Quarterly* 21, supplement no. 2:239–64.

Sets out to dispel the mistaken belief on the part of many critics that *Pantagruel* lacks structural coherence. Argues for the presence of a "necessary and coherent interrelationship between the various constituent elements" of the novel. Finds two unifying patterns: the recurrence of "deflationary episodes" in which Pantagruel and Panurge poke fun at a series of pompous secondary characters, and "a thematic structure of opposition and corrective progression" (p. 240) between paired episodes and characters. Examines the generally neglected episode of the lion, the fox, and the hag (chapt. 11 of the original *Pantagruel*; chapt. 15 in later editions), rejects the prevalent opinion that it is totally unrelated to the rest of the novel. Notes the absence of any analogues for the coupling of the lion and the fox, and justifies it here by identifying the lion with Pantagruel and the fox with Panurge, and seeing the coupling as yet another example of the oppositions which account in part for the coherence of the novel. Relates the episode to the whole on the thematic level by pointing to the connection between the motif of the *playe* and the theme of healing pervading the novel, and shows by an analysis of the sequence of actions that "the oppositive and ameliorative mechanisms which unify the novel as a whole are operative" in this episode as well (p. 246). Concludes that beyond its immediate purpose of telling a racy story, the episode functions as part of a pattern of thematic opposites which contributes to *Pantagruel*'s inner cohesion if not to the linear progression of its narrative units.

22 ———. "The Drum and the Owl: Functional Symbolism in Panurge's Quest." *Symposium* 28, no. 2 (Summer):154–65.

Without questioning the possible validity of recent psychological interpretations, believes that Panurge's dream has primarily a poetic significance, and that it embodies in the two symbols of the drum and the owl the two main themes of the novel, namely procreation and cognition. Reads the metaphor of the drum as polyvalent, suggesting copulation but also passivity, a sign of emotional menopause; believes that in its ambivalence it "brings together the physical and emotional tensions prevalent in Panurge and in the book" (p. 161). As for the owl, which Panurge sees as beauty and Pantagruel as risk, claims that it is both, as it symbolizes at the same time the attraction and the dangers of Panurge's quest for truth. Notes that although the owl has been considered mainly as a sinister bird, it was also endowed by Greek legend with positive attributes and associated, through Pallas Athena, with wisdom and knowledge. In its ambivalence, considers it a particularly appropriate metaphor for "the ramifications of the cognitive pattern in the *Tiers Livre*" (p. 162), and sees the two symbols of the owl and the drum as drawing into a coherent whole the kaleidoscopic nature of the book's thematic structure.

23 LAUVERGNAT-GAGNIERE, CHRISTIANE. "Rabelais et le libertinage: Position du problème." In *Aspects du libertinisme au XVIe siècle: Actes du Colloque International de Sommières*. De Pétrarque à Descartes, no. 30. Paris: Vrin, pp. 50–58.

Bears within the volume itself (as against the table of contents) the title: "Le 'libertinage' de Rabelais dans la critique contemporaine." More specifically still, discusses the interpretations of Rabelais' religious position as they emerge from the works of Bakhtin, Beaujour, and Jean Paris. Doubts whether the concept of *libertinage* applies to the "popular" Rabelais as viewed by Bakhtin, since it is heavily charged with intellectual and polemical connotations; argues it may apply in the context of Beaujour's analysis, but in a much more radical sense than usual, since Beaujour's Rabelais rejects all recourse to reason as a guide in man's search for truth; considers the term to be even more problematic for Paris, and concludes that in the context of contemporary criticism the question of Rabelais' *libertinage* may very well be a "faux problème" (p. 57).

24 LEMELAND, CHARLES A. "La Bouche et l'estomac des géants." *Romance Notes* 16, no. 1 (Fall):183–89.

Comments on the three trips inside the body of the giants. Notes their "autobiographical" framework, since the trip into Pantagruel's mouth is undertaken by Alcofrybas the narrator; the crew that cleanses Pantagruel's stomach immediately afterwards is a crew of physicians; the hapless fellows eaten "en salade" by Gargantua are pilgrims driven by monks on their religious quest; and since monks, physicians, and the narrator form "le triple visage de l'écrivain" (p. 189). Compares the three inner worlds, notes the "atrophied" itinerary taken under the sign of medicine and religion, and contrasts it with the richness, the fullness of the world in Pantagruel's world—a literary, verbal world both fuller and richer than the world of reality it is taken to mirror.

25 LISTON, SUSAN. "Rabelais and Medieval Epic Parody: *Gargantua* and *Pantagruel*." Ph.D. dissertation, Michigan State University, 155 pp.

Accepts the notion that *Gargantua* and *Pantagruel* parody the structure of the *chanson de geste*, and analyzes the means by which Rabelais "burlesques" the medieval epic. Finds the same parodic devices in both cases, although believes that they appear in *Gargantua* in a more refined state, and that the portrayal of war in the latter work follows more closely the medieval models in its emphasis on physical prowess rather than ruse. An appendix summarizes the plot of the "gest romances" and the "romances of adventure" known to Rabelais and parodied by him in his first two books. See *Dissertation Abstracts International* 35 (1975):6100A.

26 NASH, JERRY C. "Rabelais and Stoic Portrayal." *Studies in the Renaissance* 21:63–82.

In line with his view that Rabelais' main interest lies in the field of ethics, studies the moral and literary influence of Stoicism on Rabelais' five books through character analysis. Charts Pantagruel's moral progression toward Stoic perfection, notes his "detachment from external things" (p. 68), the *ataraxia* that allows him to achieve knowledge and wisdom. Sees in this Stoic attitude of detachment the main tenet of Pantagruelism. Views Panurge's "moral deterioration" as paralleling Pantagruel's progression and underscoring by contrast the absence of that "active virtue" that would have enabled him to will the proper moral choice and help him enforce his decision through appropriate action. Argues that it is this absence of active virtue that accounts for Panurge's hesitation and self-deception in the *Tiers Livre*, and his reaction to fear in Books IV and V. Presents Pantagruel as a positive foil throughout these episodes: "Through the active virtue of Pantagruel, Rabelais is pointing out the infinite possibilities of human potential" (p. 81). Sees in the persistence of Stoic themes in Book V a possible argument in favor of its authenticity.

27 OLIVER, RAYMOND. "Urquhart's *Rabelais*." *Southern Humanities Review* 8:317–28.

Despite its inaccuracies, Urquhart's translation of Rabelais' first two books in 1653 is widely acknowledged to be a masterpiece of English style. Notes that Urquhart often exaggerates Rabelais' stylistic features, doubling for instance, and even tripling to achieve isocolon and parallel construction. Accounts for the distinctiveness of Urquhart's prose, "its greater sense of violent movement and contrast, its often grotesque extravagance" (p. 326) by the influence of the euphuistic prose of the Elizabethan period, Randle Cosgrove's dictionary, the verbal extravagance peculiar to the Scotch tradition, and above all the nature of the English language. Thus the irony which stems in Rabelais from the "clash between high and low diction" (p. 323) is heightened in Urquhart by juxtaposing English words of Romance and Germanic origin, and the more "emphatic" quality of the English language results in a more expressive account of physical action.

28 REUTINGER, MARTIN. "Swift's Authorial Voice in *A Tale of a Tub* Compared with Montaigne, Rabelais, Erasmus, La Rochefoucauld and Robert Burton." Ph.D. dissertation, University of California, Berkeley.

See *American Doctoral Dissertations* (1974–1975):295.

29 ROLOFF, VOLKER. "Zeichensprache und Schweigen." *Zeitschrift für Romanische Philologie* 90:99–140.

Studies the debate in sign language between Panurge and Thaumaste (*Pantagruel*, chapt. 18–20) and the consultation with Nazdecabre (*Tiers Livre*, chapt. 19–20). Notes the relationship of Rabelais' text in these matters with Plato's *Cratylus* and the position of Heraclitus as stated in Plutarch's *De garrulitate*. But stresses at the same time Rabelais' ironic treatment of the subject in the anecdote concerning soeur Fessue and the theme of monastic silence. Sketches the history of the motif, through Juan Ruiz's *Libro del buen amor* and the tradition of medieval farces, and concludes that the comedy of sign language serves a double purpose in that it allows Rabelais to raise the question of ambiguity and misunderstanding inherent in spoken communication as well.

30  RUSSELL, DANIEL. "A Note on Panurge's 'Pusse en l'aureille.'" *Études Rabelaisiennes* 11:83–87.

Interprets Panurge's piercing of his ear "à la Judaïque" as a willingness to submit to the servitude of marriage. Whereas Screech, in his edition of the *Tiers Livre*, sees in Panurge's "pusse en l'aureille" a sign that he will be forever a slave of his desires, argues that in one of its meanings the proverb has an sexual connotation, so that Panurge's "pusse en l'aureille" could be seen as "a sign both of his sexual desire and of an accompanying uneasiness or anxiety" (p. 87).

31  SCREECH, M[ICHAEL] A[NDREW]. "Some Aspects of Rabelais's *Almanach* and of the *Pantagrueline Prognostication*: (Astrology and Politics)." *Études Rabelaisiennes* 11:1–7.

Ascertains the correctness of Rabelais' astrological data in the *Pantagrueline Prognostication* by comparisons with Johannes Stoeffler's astrological tables. Suggests, on the basis of a reference to the comet of 1532, that the work was composed and published early in 1533. Shows that the almanacs of 1533 and 1535 also conform to astrological reality; Le Roy, who transcribed them, probably did not have sufficient knowledge of astrology to have falsified the data. Confirms Rabelais' reputation as a scientific astrologer. Concludes that all these astrological works "may be seen as forming (together with *Gargantua*) part of the propaganda Rabelais wrote on behalf of the Du Bellays" (p. 6).

32  ———. "Some Reflexions on the Problem of dating *Gargantua*, A and B." *Études Rabelaisiennes* 11:9–56.

Discusses in great detail the problems related to the dating of these two texts. On the basis of a reference to Barbarossa and Tunis and of Rabelais' relationship with his printers, argues that *Gargantua*, usually taken as dating from 1534, was in fact published in 1535, and thus *after* the Affaire des Placards. Notes that errors in *Gargantua* A are often corrected in B. Believes that this suggests that Rabelais had left with the printer a defective manuscript and that he did not see the manuscript through the press; this in turn suggests that Rabelais was at the time absent from Lyons and that he had left in haste. Points out that the only documented absence that presupposes a hasty departure occurred in July 1535 and lasted probably through April 1536. On that occasion, Rabelais had left Lyons and the Hôtel-Dieu, "abandoning post and patients with precipitous and mysterious haste" (p. 45). This lends further weight to the thesis that *Gargantua* was in fact published in 1535 and not ear-

1974

lier. Finds unconvincing the attempts to link the *Enigme en prophetie* with "milder earlier persecutions" (p. 50) rather than with the Affaire des Placards. Dates *Gargantua* B from "late in 1535 (o.s.) or early 1536 (n.s.), at any rate before Easter."

33   SIMON, ROLAND HENRI. "Les Prologues du *Quart Livre*." *French Review* 47, no. 6 (Spring):5–17.
          Comparative study of the two prologues to Book IV, with emphasis on the relatively neglected prologue of 1548. Argues that the anecdotes in both prologues are more significant than they have been taken to be. Believes that whereas earlier Rabelais had left the reader free to interpret his work, in the 1548 prologue he acts as "le seul lecteur accrédité de son œuvre" (p. 5), and imposes upon the reader his own "lecture seconde." Finds the message contained in the episode of the jays and the magpies to be essentially optimistic ("les choses doivent éventuellement rentrer dans l'ordre," p. 11). But interprets the central anecdote in the second prologue as subverting its explicit appeal to moderation, and to invite an "anti-lecture" by emphasizing the intensity of man's cry of distress, and contrasting it with the disdainful magnanimity with which the gods come to grant Couillatris's wish, "afin que cesse ce bruit insupportable à leurs augustes oreilles" (p. 16). Although seemingly less ideologically committed and less aggressive in its tone, "ce prologue propose une révolte" (p. 16).

34   STABLER, A.P. "Rabelais, Thevet, L'île des Démons, et les Paroles Gelées." *Études Rabelaisiennes* 11:57–62.
          Argues that Rabelais' mention of the story of Marguerite de Roberval and the episode of the frozen words, in Book IV, owe nothing to Thevet's *Cosmographie*. Shows Thevet's accusation of plagiarism to be unfounded, since Rabelais was dead by the time Thevet's *Cosmographie* appeared in print. On the other hand, believes that both Rabelais' frozen words and certain features of Thevet's account of the Ile des Démons are drawn from a passage in Postel's *De Orbis Concordia*.

35   TELLE, ÉMILE V. "Notule sur '...leur robidilardicque loy...' (*G*, iii)." *Études Rabelaisiennes* 11:143–44.
          Suggests that the adjective is formed on the name of Martin Robillard, a lawyer and contemporary of Rabelais.

36   WEINBERG, FLORENCE [MAY]. "Francesco Colonna and Rabelais's Tribute to Guillaume du Bellay." *Romance Notes* 16, no. 1:178–82.
          Notes, after Gœbel (see 1966.10), that the architectural landscape of the Isle des Macreons resembles the ruins which Colonna's Poliphilus encounters on two occasions in the *Hypnerotomachia*; argues that the two sets of ruins "presage a shift from one plane of existence to a higher one through the aid of

the wisdom of classical antiquity" (p. 181). Suggests that this reference to Colonna underscores the seriousness of the immediately following chapters dealing with the death of Guillaume du Bellay, and that it helps to heighten Guillaume du Bellay's stature as a "man of great wisdom like the sages of old" (p. 182).

## 1975

1   BERRY, ALICE [FIOLA]. "Apollo versus Bacchus: The Dynamics of Inspiration (Rabelais' Prologues to *Gargantua* and the *Tiers Livre*)." *PMLA* 90:88–95.

Examines the prologues as expressing Rabelais' ideas about the art of literary creation. Before the poets of the Pléiade, Rabelais equates literary inspiration with two of the forms of divine madness mentioned in the *Phaedrus*, and views it in terms of a pre-Nietzschean "creative tension" between Apollonian and Bacchic frenzy. Claims that both principles coexist in Socrates and Diogenes, alternating in the first prologue, simultaneously present in the second. In the last paragraph of the latter, "inspiration is perceived as agony rather than joy" (p. 93).

2   DEMERSON, GUY. "Rabelais et les météores." *BAARD* 3, no. 4:169–72.

Second installment of a two-part article. First part: 1974.10.

3   GIERCZYŃSKI, ZBIGNIEW. "Rabelais et la religion: Le Problème du libertinage au XVIe siècle." *Roczniki Humanistyczne* 23, no. 4:5–77.

Brackets Rabelais with Montaigne and stresses their common belief in human reason and in science, which will channel the forces of nature to the benefit of mankind. Finds Rabelais' work to be fundamentally critical and sceptical, but also liberating. "Il est vrai que le fond de sa philosophie est sceptique, mais son scepticisme a une fonction positive, car il y voit le meilleur moyen de la lutte contre l'erreur, la superstition et l'abus" (p. 40). Underscores the daring nature of Rabelais' attempt to impose a new conception of man and of life by calling for a return to paganism. Sees in wine one of Rabelais' key symbols; interprets it along pagan lines as the symbol of a new Revelation, and sees in the work as a whole a new Bible, a libertine manifesto. Refuses to see Rabelais as an Evangelical. Sees in his apparent Evangelicalism a strategy rather than a religious conviction, a platform from which he can criticize established (and even reformed) religion. "Le plus grand des lucianistes français, Rabelais est aussi le plus radical des libertins de son siècle" (p. 51).

1975

4   GLAUSER, ALFRED. *Le Faux Rabelais, ou, De l'inauthenticité du Cinquième Livre*. Paris: Librairie Nizet, 191 pp.

Believes Book V to be among the most flagrant cases of literary forgery. Reviews the various arguments previously brought to bear on the problem; whether based on the presence or absence of any particular themes, or any particular syntactic patterns, finds them all equally inconclusive. Believes the book should not be judged chapter by chapter but as a whole. From that perspective sees no evidence of artistic control, by Rabelais or anyone else. Argues that the circumstances of its publication all point to its being an inauthentic work; even the *Isle sonante* is no exception. Believes that an analysis of its structure leads to similar conclusions: notes too many fragments lifted from previous works (whereas Rabelais never repeats himself), too much order, too little narrative thrust: "ce voyage est un piétinement" (p. 61). Takes the uncharacteristic bitterness of the satire to be the result of mediocre writing rather than any change in historical circumstances: "Car ce qui est proféré sans la force qui est inhérente au style prend un aspect de dureté exceptionnelle" (p. 95). Finds the harshness of the satirical passages to be due to the absence of Rabelais' characteristic ambiguity. Similarly, suggests that the scatological aspects of the text seem here more offensive for being deprived of the poetic resonance and the ludic dimension they possess in the other books. Notes an impoverishment in characterization; the characters lack presence: "Ces personnages ne sont pas eux-mêmes car ils ne *sont pas*" (p. 114). Often mere spectators, they show none of the communal links that Rabelais had created between them. What they say does not spring from any inner necessity: "un monologue fait, semble-t-il, de paroles apprises" (p. 118). Finds Panurge to be particularly betrayed by the plagiarist author(s). Argues that women occupy more narrative space, but to infinitely less effect. Similarly, the first person narrator is more frequently present, but he seems much more anonymous than before. Finds none of Rabelais' ambiguity in the treatment of the various themes; notes that the theme of sickness is developed with a literalness not present elsewhere: "Les malades de l'œuvre ne sont pas de ceux que l'on soigne" (p. 159). On the subject of music, finds it inconclusive that what is said here does not contradict what Rabelais has said elsewhere; is struck by the fact that music is treated in itself, divorced from the comic context in which one finds it in the earlier books. Notes also that the list of 179 songs sung at the court of Lanternois is lifted entirely from the *Navigations de Pantagruel*. Even finds grounds for suspicion in the frequent references to Chinon. Admits in his conclusion that the question of the authenticity of the *Cinquiesme Livre* is likely to remain problematic, and calls for a moratorium in the search for the possible author(s) of a book undeserving, by its artistic weaknesses, of our critical attention.

5   GOUMARRE, PIERRE. "Rabelais: Les possibilités de l'écriture, et celles de la nature." *Rivista di letterature moderne e comparate* (December):245–51.

Sees in the distinction between the possible and the impossible one of the major themes of Rabelais' chronicles. Shows that Rabelais is keenly aware of the limits imposed upon men and giants alike by the human condition (disease, suffering, old age, death) and by the "fatales destinées"—Christian predestination? pagan fatality?—but that he manages to preserve for his characters, through the notion of cooperation with God, a certain degree of freedom in the face of God's omnipotence. And argues that Rabelais himself finds as a writer, in the act of literary creation, the total freedom which he is denied in life as a mere human being.

6   GROOS, ROBERT STOW. "Foregrounding and Defamiliarization in the Rabelaisian Narrative." Ph.D. dissertation, University of Wisconsin, Madison, 256 pp.

Understands by foregrounding the throwing into relief of particular episodes, and by defamiliarization the process whereby "objects and acts are torn away from their normal context through creative deformation." In the light of these two concepts borrowed from Russian formalism, studies how Rabelais "de-automatizes" the reader's reaction to his text through his original use of language and paradox. See also 1978.16.

7   IANZITI, GARY. "Rabelais and Machiavelli." *Romance Notes* 16, no. 2 (Winter):160–73.

Rejects Plattard's and Lefranc's contention that in the first chapter of the *Tiers Livre* the "espritz tyrannicques," whose views on colonization are diametrically opposed to those held by Pantagruel, are Machiavelli and his followers. Argues that the chapter cannot be seen as an attack upon Machiavelli since the latter advocates humane treatment of the conquered as most likely to win their loyalty, and that he does so expressly in *Dell'Arte della guerra* which Guillaume du Bellay follows very closely in his *Instructions sur le faict de la guerre*. Notes an evolution in Rabelais' views on colonization: finds them to be aggressive in *Pantagruel*, Erasmian in *Gargantua*, and believes that in the *Tiers Livre* "the emphasis shifts to political realism and the procedure adopted is very similar to that practiced by Du Bellay in the Piedmont and outlined by Machiavelli in *Il Principe* and other works" (p. 470). Argues that if Plattard believed Rabelais to have been hostile to Machiavelli, it was because he took into account "events and ideas which developed long after Rabelais had composed his *Tiers Livre*" (p. 463).

8   JEANNERET, MICHEL. "Les Paroles dégelées (Rabelais, *Quart Livre*, 48–65)." *Littérature* 17 (February):14–30.

At the core of these episodes, sees Rabelais' dynamic and polyvalent conception of language and its ability to lend itself to a multiplicity of interpretations. Reads the satire against the Papimanes as a denunciation of literalism and its tendency to immobilize words in a straight-jacket of fixed

1975

meaning, and the episode of the "paroles gelées" as underscoring the dangers of the written word. In the opposition between Pantagruel's and his companions' attitude before the phenomenon of the frozen words, sees the opposition between two conceptions of language: the one according to which words are an inert, petrified commodity of fixed value, and the one that sees language as essentially dynamic, creative, polyvalent. In his equivocal nature, Gaster illustrates the ambivalence of signs and the necessity of a dialectical vision, and chapt. 63 through 65, in which Pantagruel's ship is immobilized off the island of Caneph, reiterate Rabelais' belief in the resources of symbolic language and the necessity of the quest for a higher meaning. Here as elsewhere, Rabelais' concerns are broadly philosophical. "Mais d'un bout à l'autre de la séquence, il est question de littérature autant que de morale et des implications de l'une sur l'autre. Le problème que traite Rabelais est celui du comportement du récepteur face aux messages extérieurs ou aux signes" (p. 30).

9  KITTAY, JEFFREY SAMUEL. "From Telling to Talking: The Description of a Stylistic Sequence in Rabelais." Ph.D. dissertation, New York University. 206 pp.

"In the Prologue to *Gargantua*, the narrator claims that his book contains a secret meaning, and then denies that claim." Sees in this contradiction a "fundamental shift of discourse, a shift from a discourse which presumes to encompass the world and to define its properties to a discourse which makes no such presumption, but simply names what is manifest." Argues that this shift from telling to talking can be perceived throughout Rabelais' text, on the level of paragraphs as well as sentences, calls the phenomenon a *stylistic sequence*, defines its three moments (the first discourse, the fulcrum where the shift occurs, the second discourse), describes the stylistic criteria of each moment in a number of passages, and uses the notion to suggest new interpretations of Rabelais' work. See *Dissertation Abstracts International* 6 (1976):3691A. Revised for publication: 1977.20.

10  LA CHARITÉ, RAYMOND C. "Devildom and Rabelais's *Pantagruel*." *French Review* 49, no.1 (October):42–50.

Finds it significant that Rabelais should have endowed Pantagruel, his "crusading hero," with devilish origins. Stresses the demonic nature of Panurge, and the demonic motifs with which Rabelais surrounds him (eating, fire, linguistic agility, association with dogs). Sees in the devilish Pantagruel an "organizing myth" (p. 50) providing a particularly appropriate basic structure for the novel's thematics of revolt and regeneration. See 1980.30.

11  LOSSE, DEBORAH [NICHOLS]. "Thematic and Structural Unity in the Symposium of Rabelais' *Tiers Livre*." *Romance Notes* 16, no. 2 (Winter): 390–405.

Studies the structural and thematic continuity of the symposium, and argues that Trouillogan's "terse responses," puzzlingly dismissed by Gargantua "as a futile exercise in Pyrrhonism," in fact "expand and confirm the conclusions of the speakers who precede him" (p. 390). Notes that the structure of the episode follows closely that of Plato's *Symposium* and Ficino's *Commentaries* upon it, and believes that the recurrent images, ideas, and phrases create links with the rest of the *Tiers Livre*. "The continuity of the banquet dialogues is evident to all but the interrogator" (p. 401). Attracts attention to those elements in Panurge's nature and behavior that show him unable to profit from the discussions.

12  LYDGATE, BARRY. "*Ars artificialiter scribendi*: Rabelais and the Printed Book." Ph.D. dissertation, Yale University, 304 pp.
    Examines Rabelais' first four chronicles for evidence that he was aware of "the artistic potential and cultural consequences of the medium of print." Argues that his narrative strategies, in the prologues as well as in the novels themselves, were dictated by this awareness of the new status of the book as an object of active interpretation by the reader. See *Dissertation Abstracts International* 5 (1976):2880A. See 1980.32.

13  MAUNY, RAYMOND. "Rabelais et l'Afrique." *BAARD* 3, no. 4:165–68.
    Studies the numerous references to Africa (its geography, its history, its flora and fauna). Finds Rabelais' information to be borrowed most often from antiquity: "Il n'existait pas de son temps d'ouvrage de vulgarisation sur l'Afrique" (p. 168).

14  SCANLAN, TIMOTHY M. "An Echo of Marot, Rabelais and Scarron in Rousseau's *Les Confessions*." *Romance Notes* 16, no. 2 (Winter):335–37.
    Refers to Rousseau's use of "au demeurant le meilleur fils du monde" in connection with Wintzenried. Takes the "original occurrence of this phrase" to be in Marot's *Epitre au roy pour avoir été desrobé* ("dated 1551," p. 333), and believes that Rabelais borrowed it to characterize Panurge in 1552. Since Rousseau does not acknowledge his source, thinks it likely "that in this case he is not aware, on a conscious level, of the fact that he is echoing Marot, Rabelais and Scarron" (p. 336).

15  SIMONEAU, JOSEPH ROBERT. "Literary Affinities Between François Rabelais and Denis Diderot." Ph.D. dissertation, Pennsylvania State University, 139 pp.
    Studies a number of Rabelaisian references in Diderot's work, analyzes Rabelaisian antecedents in *Jacques le Fataliste* (principally the master-slave relationship between Pantagruel and Panurge, the theme of masks, role-playing, and dialogue), and concludes that there is an affinity between the two

1975

authors, rather than an influence of Rabelais on Diderot. See *Dissertation Abstracts International* 37 (1976):1012A.

16  SPILLEBOUT, GABRIEL. "Ronsard et Rabelais." *BAARD* 3, no. 4:157–59.
    Does not find Ronsard's *Epitafe* to be as hostile as some commentators would have it.

17  TETEL, MARCEL. "The Function and Meaning of the Mock Epic in Rabelais." *Neophilologus* 59, no. 2:157–64.
    Believes that Rabelais chose the mock epic because it provided him with a loose framework in which his satire and imagination could unfold in total freedom. Sees the mock epic background of *Gargantua* as derived mainly from medieval models. Speaks of Panurge's quest as an "Ulyssian voyage" (p. 160). Detects in the background of Book IV echoes of the quest for the Holy Grail, as well as of the Homeric epic. Argues that Book IV brings to the fore the question of imitation and literary creation in general. Focuses on the "Chitterlings" episode as a prime *locus* of verbal invention. Believes that Rabelais' Italian models, the mock epics of Pulci and Folengo, reflect the same preoccupation with irony and verbal exploration. Finds also a similarity of spirit in *Orlando Furioso*. Argues that the mock epic served as a perfect vehicle for Renaissance writers in allowing them to express both their admiration of the past and their desire to destroy it, and in encouraging them "to free themselves from the linguistic limitations of their national past" (p. 163).

18  WASSERMAN, JERRY. "The Word as Object: The Rabelaisian Novel." *Novel* 8, no. 2 (Winter):123–37.
    In *Language and Science* (New York: Atheneum, 1967), George Steiner had dated from the middle of the seventeenth century the decline of humanistic confidence in the ability of verbal language to apprehend reality and experience. Argues that this phenomenon had already begun in the sixteenth century with Rabelais in the field of the novel. "His book is in large part an exploration of the relationship between signifier and signified and the silences that lie between them, an examination of the ability of words to "mean" anything other than themselves" (p. 125). Discusses Rabelais' determination to question the ability of words to carry meaning in such episodes as Panurge's self-introduction in a variety of languages, the lawsuit between Baisecul and Humevesne in *Pantagruel*, the harangue of Janotus de Bragmardo in *Gargantua*, the paradoxical encomia and the consultations in the *Tiers Livre*. Also notes Rabelais' interest in visual and corporeal attempts at communication in Book IV. Attracts attention to Rabelais' "objective, corporeal" rather than referential use of language, his attempt to create a linguistic world analogous to the visual world of objects with which the reader is familiar. Discusses the "pure phenomenality" of Rabelais' world of words as manifested, notably, in his numerous lists and catalogues, in which he under-

mines the nominative properties of words. Argues, however, that this world is not an end in itself, but is meant to lead us to the world outside the novel, and allow us to experience it "as though for the first time" (p. 137).

## 1976

1  ANTONIOLI, ROLAND. *Rabelais et la médecine*. Études Rabelaisiennes, no. 12. Geneva: Librairie Droz, 394 pp.

Devotes the first part of his study to Rabelais' medical career and the medical ideas of Rabelais' contemporaries up to the publication of *Gargantua*. Notes the influence of Tiraqueau at Fontenay-le-Comte, and Rabelais' first encounter with medical quackery in Poitou. Follows him to Montpellier, where Rabelais begins his studies at the time when the works of Galien and Hippocrates have just been published in their Greek original. Notes Rabelais' interest in botany and surgery. At Lyons, notes his double activity as editor of Galien and Hippocrates on the one hand, and as physician at the Hôtel-Dieu at a time of hospital reforms, on the other. Discusses Rabelais' involvement in "la querelle des simples," and his dual interest in medecine and astrology. In part 2, studies the main medical themes in the context of the evolution of Rabelais' thought and the medical controversies of the day. Limits the investigation to the first three books, since the authenticity of Book V is still in doubt, and since in Book IV medical themes appear only as symbols and myths. Draws attention to the ambiguous relationship of Rabelais' medical thought and the text in which it is expressed: "L'humour rabelaisien se joue en effet parfois de la science médicale ou joue librement avec elle" (p. 125). In *Pantagruel*, sees some evidence of medical preoccupations in the themes of fire and thirst, as well as in the parody of occult sciences; notes a more realistic expression of Rabelais' medical knowledge in his account of the war against the Dipsodes. In *Gargantua*, notes it in the passages on gestation, childbirth in the early chapters, and on hygiene and dietetics in the chapters on education. Returns in chapt. 7 to Rabelais' medical career before the publication of the *Tiers Livre*, during his second sojourn at Montpellier, and his stay in the Piedmont with Guillaume du Bellay: "Les routes du voyage deviennent...les routes de la pensée, et transforment la médecine polémique des deux premiers livres, dirigée contre les Arabes et les 'Barbares' en une plus sereine méditation sur l'homme" (p. 201). Detects an ever-growing irony towards medicine in the *Quart Livre*: "Ce n'est plus seulement la médecine arabe, ignorante et routinière, qui sert de cible au comique, mais l'art médical tout entier, inefficace et intéressé, dont la satire reprend les thèmes traditionnels de la farce" (p. 210). As for the *Tiers Livre*, whose medical themes are studied in detail in chapt. 8 (with strong emphasis on Rondibilis' theory of generation), notes that it marks an evolution in Rabelais' medical doctrine towards "antigalénisme," and underscores the questions of female sexuality behind the

1976

"Querelle des femmes" theme. In part 3 ("La science médicale et la thérapeu-
tique"), assesses Rabelais' debt towards Hippocrates and Galen, as well as his
less evident debt towards Arab medicine. Assesses also Rabelais's medical
knowledge of anatomy, physiology, and botany, noting his love of experi-
mentation: "Il a autant le goût de l'expérimentation que de dégoût pour la
spéculation vaine" (p. 303). Discusses the various conceptions of medicine in
the sixteenth century: that of popular tradition, that of humanism, and their
convergence in Rabelais' work. Concludes that in the field of medicine
Rabelais was not an innovator, as had been claimed, but that his role has nevertheless been of major importance: "Il a ouvert sur la place publique les
dossiers de la médecine, méditant sur le présent, rêvant sur le futur, et il les a
éparpillés au vent de sa fantaisie, pour instruire, pour éveiller, pour libérer les
esprits et les hommes" (p. 367). Extensive bibliography.

2   BALDINGER, KURT. "A propos du mot *aubeliere*, néologisme de
    Rabelais." *Études Rabelaisiennes* 13:181.
        The scatological meaning of *aube* in Godefroy had suggested to Paul
    Burrell (1974.4) an ingenious interpretation of the word *aubeliere*. Finds it
    unacceptable, however, since *aube* is, he claims, "un mot fantôme, une simple
    erreur de copiste." Takes up the matter again: 1978.3.

3   ———. "Beiträge zum Glossar der *Pantagrueline Prognostication*." *Études
    Rabelaisiennes* 13:183–90.
        Supplements the glossary in M. A. Screech's edition of the
    *Pantagrueline Prognostication* with lexicological and dialectological infor-
    mation drawn from von Wartburg's *Französisches Etymologisches
    Wörterbuch*.

4   BENSON, ED[WARD]. "Rabelais's Developing Historical Consciousness in
    his Portrayal of the Dipsodean and Picrocholine Wars." *Études
    Rabelaisiennes* 13:147–61.
        Proposes to study Rabelais' use of sources for the military details in
    *Pantagruel* and *Gargantua*, because it "reveals his attitude not only towards
    the sources themselves, but also towards the civilizations which produced
    them" (p. 147). Believes that Rabelais uses "his characters' attitude towards
    military sources to suggest their natures" (p. 152), as well as their develop-
    ment in the context of military episodes. Notes that in *Gargantua* political
    questions acquire as much importance as religious matters had in *Pantagruel*.
    Argues for Jean du Bellay's influence on *Gargantua*, and Langey's on the
    *Tiers Livre* and the *Quart Livre*.

5   BOUCHER, A. "Rabelais et le prieur de Saint-Louant." *BAARD* 3, no.
    5:197–99.

Notes that in the 1552 edition of the *Quart Livre* the diatribe against the Chicanous becomes much more violent and more personalized. Seeks to account for Rabelais' animosity towards the prior of Saint-Louant.

6   BOWEN, BARBARA C. "Rabelais and P.G.Wodehouse: Two Comic Worlds." In *The French Renaissance Mind: Studies Presented to W.G. Moore. Esprit Créateur* 16, no. 4 (Winter):63–77.

By comparing some of their comic techniques in the matter of plot, characterization and "intellectual parlor-games," and their use of certain rhetorical devices, brings out "an astonishing, and instructive, similarity of literary method between a Renaissance Evangelical humanist and a twentieth-century English gentleman." Argues that Wodehouse's comic technique "repays detailed analysis," and that by their constant debunking—"pricking the balloons of tyranny, hypocrisy and pretension which threaten civilisation"—both Rabelais and Wodehouse have a therapeutic effect upon the reader.

7   CAMERON, KEITH. "Panurge and the Screech-Owl: An Interpretation of Rabelais, *Le Tiers Livre*, Ch. XIV." *Neuphilologische Mitteilungen* 77:161–65.

Points out that in wanting to know about his future conjugal life, Panurge uses his dream in a way expressly condemned by St. Thomas Aquinas, and that he shows himself in that instance to be possessed by Satan in the traditional shape of a beautiful woman.

8   CHARPENTIER, FRANÇOISE. "Notes pour le *Tiers Livre de Rabelais*, ch. 32: Le discours de Rondibilis." *Revue Belge de Philologie et d'Histoire* 53, no. 3:780–96.

Notes that the anatomy of the male sexual organs is described in Rabelais with a wealth of verbal invention curiously lacking in the case of female organs. Relates this to the near-absence of women from Rabelais' novels ("si total que soit son projet," p. 781). Reviews the female figures in all five books, shows them to be most often grotesque, or over-generalized and lacking any but verbal reality. Notes that the giants' is a family without wives or mothers; points out how sketchily they are drawn, and how quickly disposed of. In Rabelais' most aggressively vulgar references to women, detects an infantile conception of sexuality. Compares the pseudo-scientific discourse of Rondibilis with its Platonic source in the *Timaeus*, and finds Rabelais' version to be marked by an emotional vocabulary which betrays a veritable terror of female sexuality. In the childhood episode of Gargantua and his *gouvernantes* (*Gargantua*, chapt. 13), takes note of Rabelais' pre-Freudian intuition of infantile sexuality and fear of castration. Suggests that the reasons for Rabelais' negative portrayal of women should be sought in these deeper, darker zones of the subconscious rather than in any conscious, ideological antifeminism. Concludes with a number of caveats limiting the significance of such a psychoanalytic interpretation.

9   CHESNEY, ELIZABETH ANNE. "The Counter-Voyage of Rabelais and Ariosto: Myth, Madness, and Multiplicity." Ph.D. dissertation, Duke University, 242 pp.

Despite their many differences, detects thematic and structural similarities in Rabelais' novel and *Orlando Furioso*. Focuses on structure, whose chief characteristic is "fragmented thematic development," and shows how it contrasts with and conforms to other literary expressions of High Renaissance humanism. The study of the theme of voyage brings out the "subversive undercurrents" which neutralize the theme's positive thrust. Finds that in their treatment of myths both authors use classical comparisons to satirical ends, provoking a critical attitude towards "commonly accepted truths." By intervening in their work, they both color the value of their narrative with their own "definitional uncertainty." In the fourth chapter, finds an "intratextual tension between creative and destructive time," and sees in the treatment of the theme of madness the most perfect expression of the authors' "antipodal world view." Concludes that the tensions inherent in all these structures reveal a "critical attitude towards humanistic aspirations," but shows that this critical attitude is itself characteristic of Renaissance humanism and its tendency towards self-appraisal. See *Dissertation Abstracts International* 37 (1976):3668–A. Revised for publication: 1982.8.

10   DEFAUX, GÉRARD."De *Pantagruel* au *Tiers Livre*: Panurge et le Pouvoir." *Études Rabelaisiennes* 13:163–80.

Believes Panurge to be one of Rabelais' most attractive characters, as well as the most complex and disconcerting, and thus also the most modern. Acknowledges that he changes significantly from one book to the other, but does not think he loses his coherence in the process. Seeks to show the close connection between *Pantagruel* and the *Tiers Livre*; reads both as a continuous meditation on the nature of power, wisdom, and folly, with Panurge acting in each novel as a "silène renversé" (p. 167). Sees the *Tiers Livre* as a reworking and amplification of *Pantagruel*. Claims that Panurge's ascendency over Pantagruel and his subversive tendencies reveal his political dimension, his fundamental if unconscious obsession with power. "Le besoin de dominer constitue le principe unificateur de Panurge" (p. 171). Notes the behavioral sequence *dominé–agissant–dominateur* in both books, and sees Panurge's need of others as defining both his power and its limitations: "Pour être, Panurge a besoin du regard d'autrui. Car c'est à travers lui qu'il établit son empire" (p. 173). In *Pantagruel*, the diabolical Panurge represented for the wise Pantagruel the temptation of the world and of power. But in the *Tiers Livre* Pantagruel acquires an ever greater moral stature and self-assurance as

Panurge, on the contrary, sinks into fear and superstition. By freeing Panurge from his past (that is by paying his debts), Pantagruel deprives him of all power over himself and over others. But claims that Panurge was already powerless, incapable of self-domination, even in *Pantagruel*. "Il y a moins ici rupture, contradiction, ou même métamorphose véritable que description, face et pile, d'une même réalité" (p. 180).

11   DE GRÈVE, MARCEL. "Le Discours rabelaisien ou la raison en folie." In *Folie et déraison à la Renaissance*. Brussels: Éditions de l'Université de Bruxelles, pp. 149–57.

Notes the preponderance of paradox and ambiguity in the literary discourse of the Renaissance. Sees them as tools allowing the writer to question reality and introduce an element of madness ("déraison") into a medium that is rational and reasonable by its very definition. Explicates three fragments from *Pantagruel* to illustrate the self-destructive use of paradox. Finds the excerpt from the section on Pantagruel's birth remarkable above all for having nothing to do with the subject at hand. In the passage from the chapter on Gargantua's contradictory feelings at the death of his wife, notes how sorrow is undercut ("contesté") by the use of colloquial expressions. And in an excerpt from the chapter on the library of Saint-Victor, finds it most remarkable that writing ("l'écriture") should be self-generating. Argues that in all three passages language is no longer conceptual: "la vérité du discours n'est pas, n'est plus dans la signification exacte des mots, dans l'adéquation du signifié au signifiant, mais dans les structures rythmiques, visuelles, phoniques et surtout symboliques que l'écriture entretient avec le contexte" (p. 157).

12   DELAVEAU, FRANÇOISE. "Rabelais et la magic." *BAARD* 3, no. 5:200–204.

Sees in the Sibylle de Panzoult episode of Book III a strong indictment of sorcery, and studies the way in which Rabelais' treatment of the character ("ni tout à fait sibylle, ni tout à fait sorcière") allows him to reach his goal. Comments on the structural and the comic aspects of the episode.

13   DOWNES, MICHAEL. "Panurge, Ulysse et les 'Gens Curieux.'" *Études Rabelaisiennes* 13:139–45.

Presents Panurge in the light of a "courtisan," and claims that Philibert de Vienne had also seen him as such. On the basis of Ulysses' reputation among some authors of the sixteenth century as the very prototype of the courtier, argues that there is a relationship between the two literary characters. Admits that Panurge never speaks of himself as having any links with the life of the court. "Mais c'est son silence qui est éloquent" (p. 144).

1976

14   FARRELL, MARY MACLENNAN, II. "Mentors and Magi in Ariosto and Rabelais." Ph.D. dissertation, Yale University, 306 pp.

Seeks to establish a similarity of aesthetic preoccupations in the *Orlando Furioso* and Rabelais' five books by exploring the role, powers, and functions of magicians, doctors, teachers, prophets, and men of God. Notes that while Ariosto's magicians are among his most powerful characters, "Rabelais rejects magic in favor of education, medicine, and prophecy." Finds that in many instances the mentors and magi are figures of the artist himself. Also studies the images of the work of art. As magic and prophetic creation, they are related to some extent in Ariosto to the central image of the tapistry; in Rabelais, to the image of wine as language. The study of magic, medicine, prophecy, and pedagogy as metaphors for art enable the author to proclaim Ariosto's and Rabelais' faith in the powers of art, especially its ability "to bring about a positive, even therapeutic or visionary reconciliation of the conflicts and tensions inherent in the text." See *Dissertation Abstracts International* 37 (1977):4395–A.

15   GENDRE, ANDRÉ. "La 'geste' de Frère Jean dans le *Gargantua*." In *Mélanges de langues et de littératures romanes offerts à Carl Theodor Gosse*, edited by Germán Colón and Robert Kopp. Bern: Francke Verlag; Liège: Marche Romane, pp. 239–74.

Begins with a close reading of the chapter introducing the character (*Gargantua*, chapt. 27). Studies the chapter's narrative structure through an analysis of its syntax. Notes the arbitrary nature of the punctuation as we have it, and suggests certain modifications. Analyzes the relationship between narrative and description, brings out the author's interventions, and notes a "duality" between Rabelais and his character. In the central episode of the battle, studies the dynamics of style and meaning, and the way in which the imagery structures the sentence. Seeks to account for the reader's sympathetic reaction to an inherently horrifying carnage, and finds the answer beyond the chapter's parodic and satirical dimension. "Frère Jean va plus loin. Nous l'aimons parce qu'il pratique gaiement la transgression et que son entreprise équivaut à une libération" (p. 259). Takes him seriously when he proclaims his ambition to be a true monk in the midst of all the false monks around him. Sees in his antimonastic stance something more significant than Franciscan prankishness; views it as a call for a new monastic ideal mobilizing man's instinct and energy in the spiritual struggle against the forces of evil. In an "asyndetic" reading of *Gargantua*, contrasts Frère Jean's antimonasticism (in the name of instinct) with the humanistic antimonasticism of Grandgousier, Gargantua, and Ponocrates (in the name of mastery of instinct). Argues that Rabelais had sacrificed Frère Jean's ideal at Thélème ("paradigme parfait du siècle de François Ier," p. 272), but that he reintroduced it at the "asyndetic" end of the book, in the *Enigme en prophétie*, which the reader is left free to interpret at will, but where the voice of transgression is heard once again, proclaiming the rights of instinct alongside the anti-instinctive tendencies of Renaissance humanism.

16  GIRAUD, YVES. "Deux notes rabelaisiennes." *Études Rabelaisiennes* 13:191–95.

In the first note, confirms M. A. Screech's interpretation of "avoir la pusse en l'aureille" (*Tiers Livre*, chapt. 7) as meaning "to be pray to sexual desire"; provides further textual evidence for considering that in the sixteenth century the expression has strictly sexual connotations. In the second note, cites various examples of the use of the expression "Adieu, paniers: vendanges sont faites," in the sense of "il n'y a plus rien à faire."

17  JEANNERET, MICHEL. "Rabelais et Montaigne: L'écriture comme parole." In *The French Renaissance Mind: Studies Presented to W. G. Moore. Esprit Créateur* 16, no.4 (Winter):78–94.

Studies what he calls "l'infiltration de l'écriture par la parole" (p. 80) as one aspect of the general tendency to "naturalize" art during the Renaissance. Although the antithesis between the oral and the written is not quite as strict as it is in the *Essais*, argues that *Gargantua* reveals for the most part a similar preference for the oral over the written word, for essentially similar reasons. The written word, exemplified in the *Fanfreluches antidotées* and the *Enigme en prophetie*, is denounced by Rabelais for being self-referential, complacent, and arbitrary, for obstructing rather than revealing the object of its discourse, whereas oral use of language is seen as a genuine mode of communication: between man and the material world on the one hand, between the individual and the collectivity on the other. The association between the spoken word and sensory satisfactions of all kinds (as in the theme of the banquet) further underscores this bond between the individual and the world of nature and the world of other men. Unlike its written form, spoken language is not viewed by Rabelais as a substitution for action: "le langage des Pantagruélistes est un foyer d'énergie et se prolonge en gestes" (p. 90). The efficacy of Ponocrates' pedagogy is due in large measure to his constant recourse to oral modes of discourse: "faire parler les livres, c'est les rapprocher du physiologique et les engager dans une connaissance pragmatique du monde; dans la parole fusionnent l'esprit et le corps, la notion et l'acte" (p. 91). The privileged status of the spoken word can also be seen on the narrative level, in the dialogue between the narrator and his reader, "traité plutôt comme auditeur ou interlocuteur" (p. 92). Behind this promotion of the spoken word, sees an awareness of the criticism leveled since Plato against the written sign, considered as merely mediating (and at worst perverting) the reality it represents. Whereas the spoken word, insofar as it arises spontaneously from the speaker's inner being, minimizes by its immediacy the gap between the sign and the object of its representation: "dans son immédiateté, la parole ne serait même plus un signe,

1976

c'est-à-dire instituée, substitutive; elle ne représenterait plus, elle *serait*, au même titre qu'une chose, une matière, un vivant, non pas seconde quant au réel, mais identique ou contiguë" (p. 93). Concludes by stressing a double paradox: the denunciation of the written word is carried out, as it is the *Essais*, within the confines of what remains after all a literary, written text; the clear consciousness of its shortcomings does not prevent Rabelais from (somewhat perversely) exploiting the written linguistic sign, albeit for an essentially ludic purpose.

18  LANHAM, RICHARD A. "The War Between Play and Purpose: *Gargantua and Pantagruel*." In *The Motives of Eloquence: Literary Rhetoric in the Renaissance*. New Haven: Yale University Press, pp. 165–89.
    Attracts attention to the text's refusal to commit itself to any one genre. Notes the extent to which it makes room within its fictional framework for speech and "a reality overwhelmingly literary"; argues that Rabelais treats style and words "as objects, as things" (p. 165); and suggests that these features make of Rabelais' chronicles, among other things, an important rhetorical treatise, comparable in breadth and range to Quintilian (p. 167). Touches upon every prologue in turn; notes that in each the reader is first invited to allegorize Rabelais' text, then mocked for so doing. Suggests that the reader's tendency to allegorize at the level of "mythic reality" (between the plane of physical reality where things merely *are*, and the plane of obvious allegory where Eusthenes, for example, represents strength and Carpalim swiftness) is perfectly natural, and that Rabelais condones it, although interpretation is doomed to remain subjective since fables do not have intrinsic meaning and people "see in them what it suits them to see" (p. 175). Believes that in such episodes as the gestural debate between Thaumaste and Panurge Rabelais acknowledges our urge to find significance, and that by having this search for a serious purpose constantly dissolve in play, he merely reminds us how subjective, how relative the search for meaning necessarily is. Sees *Gargantua and Pantagruel* as neither wholly serious nor wholly rhetorical, but as trying to build "a dynamic model for our perpetual movement between the two," and argues that by continually defending play against the encroachments of purpose, Rabelais—that "purposeful champion of purposeless play"—does so "in the name of right purpose, to defend the balance of human nature" (pp. 188–89).

19  LERNER, JULIANNA KITTY. "Rabelais and Woman." Ph.D dissertation, City University of New York, 235 pp.
    Studying him against a "historically accurate" background, shows Rabelais to have been much less misogynous than the Church: for the burden of original sin was not carried by women alone. Rabelais was in favor of marriage and legitimate procreation; he found infidelity equally unacceptable in either sex; he mocked those who taxed women with sexual insatiability,

acknowledged that they were as intelligent as men and ought to be educated accordingly. Concludes that, "contrary to prevailing critical opinion which considers him to have been at best a moderate, Rabelais was truly a feminist." See *Dissertation Abstracts International* 37 (1976):1595–A.

20   MARIN, LOUIS. "Les corps utopiques rabelaisiens." *Littérature* 21 (February):35–51.
    Presents itself as an extension of the author's previous studies of utopia. Underscores the playfulness of the Thélème episode ("la ludicité du texte," p. 36). Sees on every discursive level of the text a principle of duality, of contradiction (between law and desire). Remarks on the word Thélème ("ce n'est ni la volonté divine ni le désir humain et c'est l'un et l'autre." p. 37), on the function of the *calembour* ("mur/murmur"), on the architectural features ("Où sont les cuisines? Les salles à manger?") which favor play and culture at the expense of food and work. Sees the architecture and the text as reflections of the human body. With reference to the *Enigme en prophetie*, suggests that for Rabelais utopia does not imply the rejection of reality but is *"l'autre de la réalité et de l'histoire"* (p. 46). Concludes by suggesting a thematic comparison between the Thélème episode and chapt. 32 of *Pantagruel*, between the *ailleurs* of the New World and the *nulle part* of the utopian voyage into Pantagruel's mouth.

21   MILLET, E. "La sibylle de Panzoult et la réalité." *BAARD* 3, no. 5:207–09.
    Insists on the local origins of the episode, and the existence of a healer who may have served as a model: "La Sibylle de Panzoult était tout simplement une guérisseuse, peut-être diseuse de bonne aventure."

22   MORRISON, IAN R. "Ambiguity, Detachment, and Joy in *Gargantua*." *Modern Language Review* 71:513–22.
    The fictional nature of the work allows Rabelais to set up a network of ambiguities (in the sense of contradictions or divergencies without any unequivocal indication as to which  should be taken more seriously) closely related to the "theme of fundamental detachment from worldly things and the theme of joyous living" (p. 513). The ambiguous allusions to the importance of his book in the prologue, the divergent attitudes towards war as expressed by Gargantua and Frère Jean, point to a conception of life essentially summarized in the notion of Socratic detachment and *joie de vivre*, which takes on a "distinctly Christian connotation" (p. 520) in the *Enigme en prophetie*.

23   MUSTACCHI, MARIANNE. "The Harangue in Rabelais' *Gargantua* and *Pantagruel*." *Kentucky Romance Quarterly* 23, no. 2:225–30.
    Looks for common elements in the various orations, debates, and harangues throughout Rabelais' first two books. Finds that they all stress form

1976

at the expense of content, and suggests that this similarity contributes to the structural unity of the works.

24  PALLISTER, JANIS L. "Three Renaissance Sojourns in 'Hell': *Faifeu, Pantagruel, Le Moyen de parvenir.*" *Romance Notes* 17, no. 2 (Winter):199–203.

Draws attention to analogies between Epistémon's account of his visit to the underworld and that of the narrator in Bourdigné's *Légende joyeuse de Maistre Pierre Faifeu* (1526 or 1531–32). Shows that, shortly before Rabelais, Bourdigné had made room in his "post-classical" hell for countless ecclesiastical figures evoked in general terms, and to such specific characters as Pathelin and François Villon.

25  PETROSSIAN, GEORGE A. "The Problem of the Authenticity of the *Cinquiesme Livre de Pantagruel*: A Quantitative Study." *Études Rabelaisiennes* 13:1–64.

Seeks to provide an objective solution to the problem of authenticity of Book V. Offers a highly technical analysis, illustrated with thirty-three statistical tables, using chiefly the principles of stylo-statistics based on frequency counts. Discusses the attempts to solve the problems by qualitative analysis. Defines his own method and procedure. Among his findings, notes a quantitative stylistic difference between *Pantagruel* and *Gargantua* on the one hand, and the *Tiers* and *Quart Livre* on the other. Finds similar stylistic differences between the *Isle Sonante* and the last thirty-two chapters of the *Cinquiesme Livre*. Notes that the *Navigations de Panurge*, used as a control text, does not contain any of the stylistic characteristics associated with Rabelais' novels. Concludes that there is no reason to doubt the authenticity of Book V: "the suggestions of many past critics that the *Cinquiesme Livre* was the work of a very skilled *pasticheur* seem most unlikely" (p. 43).

26  RAGLAND, MARY ELOISE. "A New Look at Panurge." *University of Hartford Studies in Literature* 8:61–81.

Instead of seeing in Panurge, as many critics tend to do, a mere symbol of Rabelais' quest for certainty and truth, studies him "as a character in his own right," whose main characteristics—immaturity, irresponsibility—assimilate him to "a child seeking to create an identity in and rapport with his society" (p. 61). Argues that Rabelais, a "pre-Freudian visionary" (p. 75), meant to create in Pantagruel and Panurge, each an incomplete individual in himself, a couple standing in a relation of complementarity and integrating the multiple and antithetical aspects of man.

27  RAGLAND, MARY E[LOISE]. *Rabelais and Panurge*. Amsterdam: Editions Rodopi N.V., 165 pp.

Psychological study of Panurge and attempt at an existential interpretation of Rabelais' work as a whole. Published version of a doctoral dissertation: 1972.27.

28  RIGOLOT, FRANÇOIS. "Cratylisme et Pantagruélisme: Rabelais et le statut du signe." *Études Rabelaisiennes* 13:115–32.

Given Rabelais' obvious interest in the question of language, what exactly is his position concerning the status of linguistic signs? Does he, as some new critics would have it, consider them as totally arbitrary, and language, consequently, as mere usage and convention? Or does he, along with other Renaissance humanists, attempt to narrow the gap between words and things, and assert the existence of clear links between them? Admits the difficulty of arriving at a firm conclusion, since on these matters as on all others Rabelais does not express himself directly but through his characters, even in the so-called "humanistic" passages. Studies the chapters on color symbolism in *Gargantua* (chapt. 9 and 10), which deal with the relationship between words and things on the one hand, and between the *symbolisant* and the *symbolisé* on the other. Argues that Rabelais (here through Alcofrybas) rejects symbolism when the relationship it posits is grounded in private authority and unconfirmed by anything in our experience of reality, but that he finds it valid and valuable when it is founded on *jus gentium* and on rational interpretation. Similarly word-play is scorned, at least in theory, when based on arbitrary sound associations, but valued when sound and meaning converge to attract our attention to a profound truth, although in practice both arbitrary symbolism and gratuitous word-play find their place in the comic context of the work. Finds a parallel with the double attitude of Socrates on these points in Plato's *Cratylus*, and underscores the relevance of Pantagruelism to the subject at hand. For insofar as it is defined both as "certaine gayeté d'esprit" and "mespris des choses fortuites," Pantagruelism allows for a coexistence, in a kind of schizophrenic utopia, of the two Socrates and the two Rabelais: "mespris des choses fortuites" justifies the theoretical position, whereas "certaine gayeté d'esprit" allows the practitioner to coexist alongside the theoretician.

29  SCHWARTZ, JEROME. "Panurge's Impact on Pantagruel (*Pantagruel*, chapter IX)." *Romanic Review* 67:1–8.

Studies the encounter between Panurge and Pantagruel in relation to the immediately preceding letter from Gargantua to his son. As a figure of *indignitas hominis*, as an embodiment of that *curiositas* in which Christian tradition sees an enemy of *sapientia*, Panurge—*homo ironicus*—ironically undercuts the values inherent in Gargantua's letter. In clear contradiction to his father's injunction to avoid the company of undesirable characters, Pantagruel is attracted to Panurge by "that appetite for adventure and that curiosity which are his own unarticulated, unavowed desires for freedom" (p. 6). The

1976

encounter with Panurge thus marks a crucial stage in Pantagruel's "progress towards self-consciousness and freedom" (p. 8). Views the scene of the encounter as a *mise en question* of the concepts of *dignitas hominis* and Christian charity inherent in Gargantua's system of values.

30    SCREECH, M[ICHAEL] A[NDREW]. "Commonplaces of law, proverbial wisdom and philosophy: their importance in Renaissance scholarship (Rabelais, Joachim du Bellay, Montaigne)." In *Classical influences on European Culture, A.D. 1500–1700: Proceedings of an International Conference held at King's College, Cambridge, April 1974*. Cambridge: Cambridge University Press, pp. 127–34.

       Insists upon the necessity, for a proper understanding of a Renaissance text, of recognizing an "authoritative commonplace" for what it is, and not mistaking it for a sign of erudition. In the case of Rabelais, draws examples from the prologue to *Gargantua* and the *Tiers Livre*.

31    ———. "The Earliest Reference to a *Gargantua* and *Pantagruel* (*Gargantua Rex*, Pantagruel Filius ejus): Petrus Baptista Cremonensis's *Epistolae Tres* (Medical controversy at Nantes in 1534)." *Études Rabelaisiennes* 13:69–78.

       Notes that the allusion to Gargantua and Pantagruel in Baptista's work is dated 9 September 1534. Had hoped that this might provide a "terminus ante quem" for the publication of *Gargantua*, which the author considers to have been published later than is commonly thought. But concedes that the reference to Gargantua as "King" suggests that Baptista had in mind the *Grandes Croniques* rather than Rabelais' work. In an appendix provides the text of the prologue to Baptista's very rare *Letters*. Notes that the letters themselves contain interesting allusions to life in the medical circles of Montpellier in Rabelais' day.

32    ———. "Lorenzo Spiritu's *Du passetemps des dez* and the *Tiers Livre de Pantagruel*." *Études Rabelaisiennes* 13:65–68.

       Suggests various reasons for Pantagruel's vehement attack on the French version of Spiritu's *Libro delle sorti* in chapt. 9 of the *Tiers Livre*.

33    ———. "Medicine and Literature: Aspects of Rabelais and Montaigne (with a Glance at the Law)." In *French Renaissance Studies, 1540–70: Humanism and the Encyclopedia*, edited by Peter Sharratt. Edinburgh: Edinburgh University Press, pp. 156–69.

       Observes that by the nature of their work, both Rabelais and Montaigne were led to draw their scientific material from the same "public domain of shared and accessible knowledge" (p. 156). Argues that Rabelais, although a doctor and not a lawyer by profession, writes more as a student of law than of medicine. Stresses Rabelais' debt to Budé's *Annotationes in Pendectas*. In matters of medicine, finds Rabelais and Montaigne to be at their most reveal-ing when dealing with the theories of generation and birth. On the question of prolonged pregnancies, neither turns to the authority of doctors (most of whom believed in eleven-, and even thirteen-month gestations): Rabelais turns to legal authorities, Montaigne to his own experience (he had been himself an eleven-month child). Denies that Rabelais' own medicine was truly experi-mental. Observes that on the question of seminal production Rabelais sides through Pantagruel with Hippocrates, for whom it occurs in the brain, and who was considered to have acquired his knowledge of nature's secrets through divine revelation. Similarly, notes that Rabelais sides with the alleged authority of Plato and concludes to a basic difference between man and woman in terms of the woman's allegedly greater subordination to her sexual-ity. (Whereas Montaigne goes back directly to the *Timaeus*, reads therein that both men and women are subjected to the whims of "un membre inobedient et tyrranique," and concludes that men and women are "jettez en mesme moule; sauf l'instruction et usage, la difference n'est pas grande," quoted p. 165). Both Rabelais and Montaigne are Christian sceptics; both believe in revela-tion. But whereas Montaigne gives ultimate authority to the Roman Catholic church, for Rabelais it lies in the Holy Scriptures, by which the Church itself must be judged.

34 ———. "Some Further Reflexions on the Dating of *Gargantua* (A) and (B) and on the Possible Meanings of Some of the Episodes." *Études Rabelaisiennes* 13:79–111.

Clarifies his position in the controversy surrounding the dating of *Gargantua* and responds to objections raised against it by Marichal and Defaux. Considers it probable that *Gargantua* A was *published* (but not writ-ten) after the Affaire des Placards, most likely in 1535. To bolster his thesis, adds a series of observations to his earlier argument (see 1974.32). Notes that the *Enigme en prophétie* which concludes *Gargantua* is indeed a call to resist persecution, and concedes that persecution refers to events which predate the Affaire des Placards. Sees the satire of Janotus in the episode of the bells of Notre-Dame as centered "probably round the Shrovetide revels of 1533" (p. 111), but referring also to events which took place in 1532 and 1534. Believes it to be aiming at Noël Béda and recalling "the long drawn-out battle between Rabelais's patrons, the du Bellays, and Béda's faction in the Sorbonne" (p. 103). But thinks that the allusions to Barbarossa and Tunis refer most likely to events associated with the armada against Tunis by Charles V in July 1535, and not to the Tunis of Mully Hassan, before its conquest by Barbarossa; they are thus part of what the author believes to be a satire against Charles V, rep-resented by Picrochole. Argues that subsequent revisions strengthen the con-nection between Picrochole and Charles V. Rejects the suggestion that *Gargantua*'s satire of events in 1533 or earlier must have appeared early in

1976

1534 for fear of becoming outdated; notes that it was equally topical in 1534. Concludes that *Gargantua* was written over a period of time, and probably—but not certainly—published in 1535.

35    SIMONE, FRANCO. "La notion d'Encyclopédie." In *French Renaissance Studies, 1540–70: Humanism and the Encyclopedia*, edited by Peter Sharratt. Edinburgh: Edinburgh University Press, pp. 234–62.
        Comments on Rabelais' secularization of Erasmus' encyclopedic ideal in the famous letter of Gargantua to his son (*Pantagruel*, chapt. 8). Béné (see 1961.1) had noted that Rabelais seems to forget that the encyclopedic curriculum discussed in the *Enchiridion militis christiani* and elsewhere is defined for the benefit of the future Christian orator and not of the future knight. Suggests that this secularization may have been quite conscious, and that the step towards secularizing the notion of *encyclopédie* was imposed by the turn of contemporary events, more specifically "par l'évolution d'une civilisation qui s'apprêtait à entreprendre des guerres fratricides à cause de la liberalisation des esprits et des consciences" (pp. 249–50).

36    SPILLEBOUT, GABRIEL. "Note conjointe sur la sibylle de Panzoust." *BAARD* 3, no. 5:205–06.
        Finds in the episode a poetic, mysterious coloration, owing to its relationship with the Sibylle de Cumes, emphasized by the presence of Epistémon.

37    ———. "La Fantaisie de Rabelais." *BAARD* 3, no. 5:210–17.
        Defines "fantaisie" as a personal vision of the world, coexisting with reality, but setting itself in opposition to it in an act of total artistic freedom. Argues that this world possesses its own coherence, its own equilibrium, its own harmony; that it is neither anti-real nor anti-logical, but para-real and para-logical, the product of an imposition of logic "sur des faits qui n'ont pas de réalité" (p. 215).

38    STEEVES, MARGARET ANN. "Joyce and Rabelais: Processes of verbal creativity." Ph.D. dissertation, Johns Hopkins University, 230 pp.
        Seeks to analyze "the deep structures that account for the similarities of surface structure" between the texts of Rabelais and Joyce. Acknowledges thematic reminiscences of Rabelais in Joyce as well as biographical evidence of familiarity with Rabelais' work, but detects a more profound evidence, linguistic in nature, between the literary projects of the two writers. Both aim at the creation of human caricatures through verbal structures. Each situates his preoccupations on the level of *écriture*, each uses multi-lingual lexical elements, each distorts the linguistic resources at his disposal. But also underscores dissimilarities, for example in their use of syntax. Notes in this regard that whereas in Rabelais the signifier tends to "obscure, confuse and subvert"

the signified, in Joyce there is equivalence, "or at least homology," between the two. Studies the "multi-dimensional significance" of both texts as epitomized in the *mot-valise*, through which meaning is achieved by the process of association. The *mot-valise* is also studied as an agent of ambiguity and equivocation, "a fundamental feature common to both writers." Concludes by showing how they both transcend antithesis and equivocation in "a final synthesizing perspective." See *Dissertation Abstracts International* 41 (1980):694A.

39  STEGMAN, ANDRÉ. "Sur quelques aspects des fous en titre d'office dans la France du XVIe siècle." In *Folie et déraison à la Renaissance*. Brussels: Éditions de l'Université de Bruxelles, pp. 53–73.

In the context of a discussion of court jesters, refers to Panurge's Triboulet in the *Tiers Livre* as vaguely suggesting the superiority of madness over rational wisdom and the inspired state of the insane, but does not believe that Rabelais treats the subject with any degree of seriousness: "Rabelais s'amuse et n'a mis en scène le fou royal que pour mieux allécher le lecteur, avide d'actualité" (p. 62).

40  TOURNON, ANDRÉ. "La *Briefve Declaration* n'est pas de Rabelais." *Études Rabelaisiennes* 13:133–38.

To arguments previously advanced for doubting the authenticity of the glossary to the *Quart Livre*, adds a list of nine terms whose definition, although sometimes correct in itself, is contradicted by the context in which the term is to be found in Rabelais' book. Notes that six other definitions are gratuitous displays of erudition that do nothing to explain Rabelais' texts. Moreover, believes that the absence from the glossary of a certain number of obscure Hellenisms as well as of every nautical term mentioned in chapt. 18 through 22, inexplicable if we hold Rabelais to be the author, becomes clear when we postulate that it was compiled by Rabelais' first "exégète": it could be alleged that he merely abstained from glossing words he did not understand.

41  TUTTLE, LAURENCE HEATH. "Clues to Vocabularic Structure: Comparative Suffixal Productivity in the Five Books of Rabelais, Using a Computer-Generated, Reverse Dictionary." Ph.D. dissertation, University of North Carolina, Chapel Hill, 203 pp.

Groups Rabelais' vocabulary by suffix, eliminates all words that were attested before 1500, chooses some seventy suffixes, and studies the sixteenth-century derivatives with these suffixes in each of Rabelais' five books. The second of the author's three conclusions bears directly on Rabelais: "For the ten suffixes in Rabelais' five books with the greatest sixteenth-century productivity, rising or falling productivity between his first two works was an accurate predictor of rising or falling productivity for the same suffix between his third and fourth books." See *Dissertation Abstracts International* 38 (1978):3451A.

**1977**

1 BAKER, PAUL V. "Loup Garou and the Green Knight: A Reassessment of the Deaths of Loup Garou and Epistémon (*Pantagruel* XXX)." *Études Rabelaisiennes* 14:47–57.

The indication that Gargantua "avoit esté translaté au pays des Phées par Morgue" (*Pantagruel*, chapt. 23) leads author to link the episode of the war against Anarche with the Arthurian legends, more specifically with Gawain and the Green Knight and its Irish and French antecedents. Sees in these a source for the battle between Pantagruel and Loup Garou. The resuscitation of Epistémon has a medieval rather than a biblical character, and is thus not, as Lefranc had argued, "a parody of Christ's raising of Lazarus and of Jairus's daughter" (p. 47).

2 BALDINGER, KURT. "Rabelais' Späße und die Humorlosigkeit der Lexikographen." In *Imago Linguae: Beiträge zu Sprache, Deutung und Übersetzen, Festschrift zum 60. Geburtstag von Fritz Paepcke*, edited by K.-H. Bender, K. Berger, and M. Wandruszka. Munich: Wilhelm Fink, pp. 25–27.

Remarks on *aller le camelin et l'onagrier* in the episode of Gargantua's horses (*Gargantua*, chapt. 12).

3 BERRONG, RICHARD MICHAEL. "Genealogies and the Search for an Origin in the *Oeuvres* of Rabelais." *South Atlantic Bulletin* 42, no. 4 (November):75–83.

Notes the fascination of the sixteenth century with genealogies, as a strategy for arguing in favor of the preeminence of the French race (in Jean Lemaire de Belges), of the French language (in Henri Estienne), of Calvinism (in Calvin). Studies the preoccupation with lineage and origins in Rabelais. Notes a progression from the first chapter of *Pantagruel*, which establishes the hero's descent from Adam, through *Gargantua*, where the validity of genealogies is thrown into question, to the *Tiers Livre*, where "the genealogy strategy, for want of a generally recognized point of departure, is rendered altogether useless" (p. 80). Relates the recurrence of the theme in the Andouilles and the Quaresmeprenant episodes of Book IV to the disintegration of world order, and of narrative itself, in Rabelais' last authenticated work.

4 ———. "The Triumph of Madness: Rabelais' Tragic Vision." Ph.D. dissertation, Cornell University, 197 pp.

In the light of Michel Foucault's definition of the Renaissance concept of madness, seeks to demonstrate that Rabelais' novels are structured by a conflict between the forces of madness and reason. Unrestrained in *Pantagruel*, the forces of madness are "systematically restricted" in *Gargantua*, then further limited in the *Tiers Livre* (in which they are "enclosed within the character of Panurge alone"), before regaining ascendency in the *Quart Livre*, where they shatter the foundations of society and of language. Sees Book V as abandoning the conflict and developing strategies for the obfuscation of madness. Believes that most critics have sought to negate or minimize the disquieting forces at work in the novels. See *Dissertation Abstracts International* 39 (1978):1613A.

5   BERRY, ALICE FIOLA. "'Les Mithologies Pantagruelicques': Introduction to a Study of Rabelais' *Quart Livre*." *PMLA* 92, no. 3 (May):471–80.
      Believes that Rabelais' apocalyptic vision in the *Quart Livre* owes most to the Old Testament, more specifically to the myth of Jonah in the mouth of the whale and to the story of the Exodus. Like "The World in Pantagruel's Mouth" at the end of Book I, Book IV too is "a dream voyage into the body" (p. 475). And just as Moses had brought down from the mountain the healing Word of God, so Rabelais "the logotherapist" (p. 476) sends his characters in search of the Word that will heal the world.

6   CÉARD, JEAN. *La Nature et les prodiges: L'Insolite au XVIe siècle, en France*. Geneva: Librairie Droz, 512 pp.
      In chapt. 6, "Le *Tiers Livre* et les problèmes de la divination" (pp. 132–58), studies Rabelais' interest in prophecy, and argues that the central problem of Book III is not, as is often believed, that of marriage but that of the knowledge of the future, of which the question of marriage is but an illustration: "Le mariage a valeur d'exemple" (p. 132). Notes among other arguments that if this were not so, it would be difficult to justify the presence of the Bridoye episode, in which the problem of marriage is never mentioned. Finds Rabelais to be very familiar with the debates that the subject occasions among his contemporaries. Believes it is impossible to assign any one specific source to his statements on the subject. Contests Perrat's thesis that the passage on the "sorts homeriques et virgilianes" has its origin in Tiraqueau (see 1954.27). Finds it equally impossible to name one single source for what Rabelais says about dreams (suggests Scaliger's commentary on Hippocrates' *De Somniis*, but also Vives' *Somnium*). Notes Rabelais' particular hostility to the subject of prophecy in the Sybille de Panzout episode, where divination takes on satanic overtones. For the consultation with Her Trippa, doubts that the main source is Cardano's *De Sapientia*, as suggested by Screech (see 1963.22). Underscores the numerous divergences between the two texts and proposes to consider Agrippa's *De Occulta Philosophia*, where certain aspects of divination meet with the author's approval, as a second important source. Finds new grounds to justify the identification of Her Trippa with Cornelius Agrippa and Jean Trithème, both suspected of sorcery, and whose combined names may well have inspired the name given by Rabelais to his character. Concerning the series of consultations in general, suggests that Rabelais meant to distinguish between the first five, which propose self-effacement and humility as a

possible way to receive God's message about the future, and the consultation with Her Trippa, "dont la divination toute artificielle confine à la sorcellerie" (p. 148). Notes Rabelais' unmistakable hatred of this type of divination, as well as of astrology, against which Gargantua had already warned Pantagruel in his famous letter to his son. But reminds us that Rabelais had also written a number of almanacs and prognostications, some of which treat of astrology with utmost seriousness. Has Rabelais now changed his mind? Appearances to the contrary, argues that Rabelais' attitude towards astrology remains unchanged throughout his work: what he abhors here as before is "l'astrologie divinatrice," which leaves no room for human freedom, whereas that astrology which merely proclaims a general influence of the heavenly bodies on earthly matter he finds both acceptable and useful. Proposes a reading of the Bridoye episode as an apologue in which the throw of dice is not an arrogant and cynical substitute for a genuine search for truth and justice, but a humble surrender, in all simplicity, to the will of God. Concludes by remarking that in the entire series of consultations there is not one recourse to the miraculous or the unnatural: "personne n'a proposé de tenir compte de quelque comète, de quelque prodige, de quelque monstre" (p. 155). Tentatively suggests that Rabelais thought too highly of "les prodiges" (as can be seen in the episode on the death of heroes in Book IV) to associate them with the prophetic arts which he wholeheartedly condemns, without thereby condemning prophecy itself.

7   CHARLES, MICHEL. *Rhétorique de la lecture.* Paris: Éditions du Seuil, 297 pp.
In "Une rhapsodie herméneutique" (pp. 33–58), shows by structural analysis that the prologue to *Gargantua* is built on a complex series of oppositions. Argues that when Alcofrybas rejects the kind of allegorical reading of Ovid provided by Frère Lubin near the end of the text, he does not—as is commonly believed—contradict his previous injunction to seek a "substantifique moelle," and that the apparent contradiction is in fact a logical consequence of what precedes: the narrator merely completes the series by stressing the opposition between author and reader, between what the writer intended to write and what the reader claims to be reading. Suggests that the references to Plato and to the tradition of poetic and theological exegesis throughout the prologue underscore Rabelais' new conception of the act of reading a literary text, in which the reader is responsible for the interpretation he chooses to impose on a text whose meaning (as intended by the author) will never be known. Sees the prologue as encouraging any number of possible interpretations, but within certain limits: "Avec Rabelais, le lecteur est libre, *mais* il y a, sinon une bonne, du moins une mauvaise lecture" (p. 33). In "Le prévu et l'imprévu" and his subsequent "Remarques (V)" (p. 263–88), seeks to define the conditions of this "mauvaise lecture" by sketching a typology of possible

readings of the novels on the basis of a structural analysis of the frozen words episode in Book IV. By contrasting this episode with that in which Thamous is charged with announcing the death of Pan (*Quart Livre*, chapt. 28), distinguishes between the "hieroglyphic" and the "symbolic" levels of meaning. Pantagruel, unlike Thamous, understands the meaning of Pan's death because the Christian allegorization of pagan myths provides him with a deciphering code. On the other hand, the frozen words—or Rabelais' novel, or indeed *any* fictional text—demand to be interpreted but fail to provide the code that alone would guarantee the validity of the interpretation. Concludes that of the three approaches to reading envisaged by Rabelais: reading as a free, joyous, playful *passetemps*; reading as a (utopian, ever-deferred) search for a higher, allegorical meaning; and *lecture-calomnie*, reading as imposition of a univocal, arbitrary signification to be used as a weapon against the author), only the last is unwarranted, because it violates the one cardinal rule of the fictional game. By claiming to possess the key to the work's intended meaning, when no such key is provided, it sets itself apart as the only *impossible* reading in Rabelais' otherwise generous hermeneutics.

8  CHESNEY, ELIZABETH [ANNE]. "The Theme of Folly in Rabelais and Ariosto." *Journal of Medieval and Renaissance Studies* 7, no. 1 (Spring): 67 93.
    Studies the "dialectic of folly and reason" (p. 83) in the two authors, on the thematic, psychological, and linguistic levels. Argues that in *Orlando Furioso*, as in Rabelais' novel, the embodiments of folly pervert both intellectual and esthetic order and give rise to "a sense of metaphysical vertigo" on the one hand, and an "esthetic of the grotesque" on the other (p. 67). Sees the dialogue between folly and reason in these works as an essential element in their authors' quest for knowledge, enriching with ambiguity what would otherwise have been an impoverished, one-dimensional point of view: "Whereas the medieval idiot was an outsider, the Renaissance's voyage-fool is at the same time Everyman, different from readers only in the intensity of his experience and the paradoxical clarity of his perspective" (p. 75). His presence in the work allows the author to test the pretensions of socially acceptable behavior: "When manifested in characters, folly is not absolute but polemic in value, used largely to question the sanity of society's comfortable institutions" (p. 85). Sees this dialectic as also informing Rabelais' and Ariosto's conception of art and truth. But argues that due to the relativity of wisdom and folly, the universality of madness proclaimed by both authors does not lead to the morbidity of the medieval view as expressed for instance in the *Dance de Macabré*. It informs, instead, the authors' "thoroughly modern brand of humanism" (p. 93), expressed in works that are "a hymn to life rather than death" (p. 92).

9  COOPER, RICHARD. "Rabelais' Edition of the *Will of Cuspidius* and the *Roman Contract of Sale* (1532)." *Études Rabelaisiennes* 14:59–70.

Did Rabelais know that these documents were forgeries? They were taken seriously by other scholars; Rabelais had previously been clearly taken in by a forgery when he published his edition of Marliani's *Topographia* containing another purported Roman will. Argues that the discovery of two editions of the *Contract of Sale* predating that of Rabelais, and of two editions of the *Will* which may also have predated it, adds further reasons to suggest that Rabelais believed the documents to have been genuine.

10  ———. "Rabelais and the *Topographia Antiquae Romae* of Marliani." *Études Rabelaisiennes* 14:71–87.

Notes that there is disagreement over the circumstances of publication of Rabelais' edition of Marliani's work. Adds a few observations to what is known from Rabelais' prefatory letter to his edition. Suggests that "Du Bellay and his circle were at least aware of Maliani's research and its imminent publication" (p. 74), and that Rabelais had probably planned to publish a book of his own on Roman antiquities upon his return from his first Roman sojourn. As it was, he only published Marliani's work, with a dedication to Du Bellay (whereas Marliani's own edition was dedicated to de Cupis). But the author shows that Rabelais' edition was not a "mere reprint" (p. 76) by calling attention to numerous revisions, due either to Rabelais or to the printer Gryphius.

11  COTTRELL, ROBERT D. "The Poetic Function of *io* in Rabelais's *Quart Livre*." *Revue du Pacifique* 3, no. 2 (Fall):93–101.

When Frère Jean asks the inhabitants of *Procuration* which of them would be willing to be beaten in exchange for a sum of twenty *escuz* (*Quart Livre*, chapt. 16), every Chiquanou answers "Io!" Why have them break into Italian when hitherto they had all been made to speak French? Suggests that it is because of the poetic, connotative function of the Italian pronoun, with its resonance evoking the commedia dell'arte, the Feast of the Ass, and above all the Dionysian cult, of which the passage is a transposition.

12  DEFAUX, GÉRARD. "Un *extraict de haulte mythologie* humaniste: Pantagruel, *Picus Redivivus*." *Études Rabelaisiennes* 14:219–64.

Proposes that we modify the traditional view of *Pantagruel*'s structure as reflecting the tripartite division of the romances of chivalry and their parodic versions, since the latter offer no precedent for the episode of Pantagruel's education. Sees such a precedent in the biography of Pico della Mirandola by his nephew, especially the pages dealing with Pico's projected *disputatio* of 900 theses at Rome in 1486. Is aware of the "mythic" character of the biography, but views the theses episode as all the more significant since it draws the biographer's disapproval in an otherwise eulogistic text. Notes that many modern critics have been struck by the parallelism between Pantagruel defending his theses at the Sorbonne and Pico's intention to do so in Rome, and adds many other significant parallels: "leur existence tout entière, la crise spirituelle qu'en des circonstances identiques ils traversent à tour de rôle, l'itinéraire exemplaire que, sur le plan des valeurs et de la conscience, ils décrivent tous deux, l'évolution intérieure qu'ils subissent...à quelque quarante-cinq ans d'intervalle" (p. 223). Calls for a reassessment of chapt. 8, which he considers to be essentially a parody, rejects the view of Pantagruel as a "partisan d'un idéal de culture rationnel et encyclopédique analogue à celui de l'Antiquité" (p. 260), and pleads for the recognition of Rabelais as a foremost representative of Christian scepticism.

13 ———. "Plaidoyer pour l'histoire: Rabelais, les *Brocardia juris*, Démosthène et l'Antiquaille." *Revue d'Histoire Littéraire de la France* 77, no. 5 (September–October):723–48.

Noting a hardening of positions between practitioners of historical and esthetic criticism in the wake of Spitzer's overemphasis on Rabelais the poet at the expense of the thinker, pleads for a return to historical erudition as an indispensible prerequisite for a sound understanding of a text grounded in social and intellectual history: "Pour comprendre ce que Rabelais a voulu dire, pour restituer à l'œuvre sa richesse originelle de signification, pour éviter les contresens, les anachronismes, les interprétations aventureuses ou injustifiées, la documentation historique, si elle n'est pas un but en soi, reste cependant...la condition *sine qua non* de toute autre spéculation" (p. 726). Proves his point by showing how a knowledge of the legal texts in use at the time throws light on the literal meaning of an obscure passage in the original prologue to *Pantagruel*. Also argues for the importance of historical erudition for a sound interpretation of Rabelais' text. Points out that only when we are aware of the unflattering reputation of Demosthenes among the humanists do we realize that when Rabelais compares Pantagruel to Demosthenes in the chapter in which the giant posts his 9,764 "conclusions" throughout the city, his intention is ironic and not laudatory. At that point in the novel, Pantagruel is the embodiment of medieval sophistry and not yet, as most critics would have it, the champion of the new humanism.

14 DEMERSON, GUY. "Le *Cinquiesme Livre*: Le Problème de l'authenticité est-il résolu?" *Réforme Humanisme Renaissance*:12–15.

In the search for an answer to the question of the authorship of Book V, rejects the criterion of inner coherence as too subjective and that of stylistic coherence as excessively impressionistic. Welcomes the recent quantitative analyses based upon computer-generated statistical data. Summarizes the conclusions drawn by Petrossian (see 1976.25). Contrasts them with the diametrically opposed conclusions of Glauser (see 1975.4) and seeks to reconcile them by pointing out that the former are based upon considerations of language whereas the latter are grounded in considerations of style: "Le livre V peut être du langage de Rabelais sans être du style de Rabelais" (p. 15).

15 ———. "Rabelais et l'analogie." *Études Rabelaisiennes* 14:23–41.
 For Bakhtin, Rabelais' world is firmly rooted in medieval culture, based as it is on a system of analogies between microcosm and macrocosm; and Rabelais' philosophy is "un matérialisme conséquent" (p. 24). For Jean Paris, on the contrary, Rabelais rejects medieval symbolism, destroying not only the analogical bond between one thing and another, but also the bond between the thing and the word that signifies it. Both agree, however, in refusing to see in Rabelais the principle of analogy as it applies to temporal succession in the history of humanity: both see a Rabelais projected into the future, "un Rabelais progressiste, étranger à la vision humaniste d'un monde où le présent a même structure que l'antiquité, ce qui rend possible la *restitutio* des lettres humaines et de la civilisation après une époque de barbarie" (p. 30). Argues that Rabelais conceives of beings, and of God, through the principle of analogy, and that he thus does believe in analogy as a *modus cognoscendi*. But what of analogy as a *modus significandi*? Does he reject, as both Bakhtin and Paris would have it, the belief in an analogy between the sign and what it signifies? Argues that Rabelais rejects only false analogies, namely the arbitrary analogies between *voces*, but not the analogy between *vox* and *verbum*, between sounds and concepts. Contends that Rabelais remains squarely on the side of the humanists in that for him verbal allusion is *al-lusion*, "c'est-à-dire jeu à *l'intention* des connaisseurs"(p. 40). Concludes that Rabelais remains influenced by medieval modes of knowing and thinking, but that he represents at the same time a new spirit, insofar as he, together with his contemporaries, was proposing a new concept of language, not only as a means of knowing, but also as a forming agent of intuitive thought.

16 FRAME, DONALD. M. *François Rabelais: A Study*. New York: Harcourt Brace Jovanovich, 238 pp.
 Written in the hope of earning both the confidence of the scholar and the interest of a wider public. Sees Rabelais' greatness in the masterful interplay of voices and attitudes, rather that in any specific aspect of his art or thought. Finds *Pantagruel* filled with the spirit of the carnival, but chooses to take at face value the seemingly serious tone in Gargantua's letter and in Pantagruel's prayer before battle, in opposition to recent critics (Brault, Paris, Defaux) whose parodic readings he finds unconvincing. On the question of *Gargantua*'s date of publication, opts for the traditional view (late summer, early fall 1534), and believes the book was written in reaction to accusations of frivolity leveled at *Pantagreul*. Interprets the prologue as offering the reader a choice between two possible readings, inviting us to choose the second ("à plus hault sens"), but not at the expense of the first (as pure *divertissement*). Finds the traditional contrast between Rabelais' ideas on education and

those of Montaigne to be overstated. Enumerates the various problems raised by the Thélème episode without seeking to resolve them (other than by putting them down to Rabelais' seeming decision to daydream the episode rather than think it through). On the general meaning of the *Tiers Livre*, sides with Screech's interpretation as expounded in *The Rabelaisian Marriage* (see 1958.7) and the introduction to his critical edition. Of the thirteen interpretations hitherto offered of the Pantagruélion, finds the view that it represents human industry and progress to be the most solid, and Saulnier's theory of *hésuchisme* (or "crypto-Evangelism," p. 64) to be also quite plausible. Attracts attention to the changes in the chapters of the *Quart Livre* that appeared in both 1548 and 1552, and notes that they all stress Pantagruel's piety. Finds the 1548 material to be generally unpolemical, the rest Evangelical, and more outspokenly Gallican. As for the problem of authorship of Book V, notes that several episodes appear in only one of the three texts we possess, that the book makes one reference to a work published four years after Rabelais' death, that it abounds in repetitions from earlier books (whereas in those earlier books Rabelais hardly ever repeats himself), that it is hardly Evangelical at all; finds some of it uninspired and even boring, and much more heavily imitative than anything in the first four books; and all of it too long to have been written in the year and a half between the *Quart Livre* and Rabelais' death. Opts for partial authenticity. Finds the prologue unworthy of attention, the chapters on the Frères Fredons particularly Rabelaisian. Notes the near-absence of satire. Wants to believe that the conclusion—"superb and appropriate"—was mainly, if not entirely, written by Rabelais. Finds the message of the oracle of the Dive Bouteille to be consistent with Rabelais' earlier invitation to drink in philosophy, knowledge, and truth. Agrees with Bakhtin that Rabelais' comedy is mainly carnivalesque and grotesque (rather than witty), finds it obscene though not pornographic. Claims that satire is scarce in *Pantagruel*, hardly more frequent in *Gargantua* and the *Tiers Livre*, more prevalent in Book IV and the first third of Book V. "Unnecessary in the first two, scanted probably for reasons of caution in the third, it emerges in the last two as the best way for an admitted but unresigned underdog to get back at powerful and oppressive enemies" (p. 121). Does not believe that storytelling is Rabelais' greatest achievement, or that Alcofribas, as critics would have it, possesses one, coherent *persona* ("Now that we have several good studies of Rabelais' *persona*, I hope to see more of his *personae*," p. 127); emphasizes the oral aspect of his exuberant style, notes its variety (grotesque, erudite, "quintessential," and lofty), stresses the mixture of the lofty and the grotesque. Thinks that the importance of gigantism in Rabelais has been exaggerated. Finds his humanism to be less dominant in the last two books, his evangelism to be most prominent in *Gargantua*, and "evident, but mainly covert" (p. 156) thereafter. Discusses Rabelais' creation of characters (not his greatest gift) and their interaction (dependent mainly on their creator's needs and purposes). Follows Rabelais' documented fortunes in France and abroad from the time of the first

1977

publication of his work, glances at a few "high spots" of Rabelais criticism, and ventures into the "uncharted" territory of Rabelais' reception from the late nineteenth century to the present. Concludes by noting traces of Thélème in such twentieth-century educational experiments as Summerhill, in the thought of such post-Freudian psychotherapists as Fromm, May, and Maslov, and in the optimistically permissive attitude towards child rearing of Benjamin Spock.

17  GOUMARRE, PIERRE. "Entre le signal et l'indice." *Renaissance and Reformation/Renaissance et Réforme*, 2d ser., vol. 1, no. 1:16–23.

Adopts a semiological approach to Rabelais, "un grand créateur et un grand explorateur de signes" (p. 16). Notes his interest in signs as predicting the future, but also as revealing present realities. Wonders to what extent the signs in Rabelais' work can be said to be related to contemporary semiological concerns. Choosing an example in each of Rabelais' authenticated four books, shows that signs often are, indeed, used in a semiological sense of the term, as means of communication (*signals*), even if they coexist with *indices*, to which no communicative intention can be attached, and even though Rabelais refuses to establish a clear distinction between the two.

18  ——. "La Forêt Rabelaisienne des signes." *Romanische Forschungen* 89, no. 4:462–66.

In the wake of a number of semiological studies presenting Rabelais as a precursor of Saussure and Jakobson, seeks to define the nature and function of the vast forest of signs in Rabelais' work. Suggests they can be classified as physiological, sociological, and cosmic, as well as gestural and linguistic. Argues that their function is equally diverse, since they are used to foretell the future, to categorize characters, to express feelings and to communicate ideas.

19  ——. "Le toucher dans l'œuvre de Rabelais." *Les Lettres Romanes* 31, no. 2 (May):178–86.

Attracts attention to the number and importance of references to the sense of touch. "C'est par le toucher, surtout, que les personnages de Rabelais entrent en contact avec le monde qui les entoure" (p. 178). Traces the emphasis on touch to the author's personality: "le toucher est par excellence le sens du plaisir" (p. 183). Relates it also to Rabelais' profession ("Le docteur est fondamentalement un toucheur"), and to Rabelais' conception of experience: "peut-on avoir l'expérience réelle d'une chose sans la toucher? " (p. 186).

20  KITTAY, JEFFREY S. "From Telling to Talking: A Study of Style and Sequence in Rabelais." *Études Rabelaisiennes* 14:109–218.

Near book-length stylistic analysis of "*one* stylistic sequence" in Rabelais. The sequence is said to be characterized by a shift in direction on various stylistic levels, and "can span varying portions of the text" (p. 114), from a sentence to a paragraph and beyond; it is susceptible of a variety of interpretations, only some of which are suggested in the study. The first chapter proposes the prologue to *Gargantua* as a key example of the sequence. It is seen as being organized around a series of axes: outside/inside; you/me; oil/wine; best/worst. But "the fundamental stylistic action in the Prologue as a whole" is not thematic, but is located in a "shift of discourse," from language as medium to language as activity (p. 122), with a concomitant "increase in illocutionary force" (p. 123). This movement from telling to talking, from the "constative" to the "performative," is seen as representative of the general movement of the last three books. Subsequent chapters study the sequence on the level of episodes and sentences; chapt. 6 studies the "break of closure" by the addition of gratuitous clauses. The last chapter uses the sequence "as a prism through which to view smaller and larger portions of the text" (p. 182), and discover new characteristics of the sequence, such as shifts form high to low, from meaning to soundplay, away from redundancy towards animation. Revised version of 1975.9.

21  KOTIN, ARMINE. "*Pantagruel*: Language vs Communication." *Modern Language Notes* 92, no. 4 (May):691–709.

Studies the four episodes of *Pantagruel* illustrating the failure of communication through language: the Limousin scholar (chapt. 6), the first encounter with Panurge (chapt. 9), the lawsuit between Baisecul and Humevesne (chapt. 10–13), and the debate with Thaumaste (chapt. 18–20). Sees in all four a conscious obstruction of meaning, an "intentionally destructive" use of language. In a terminology borrowed from Jakobson and Barthes, analyzes the cause of linguistic failure: "It is the disappearance of the intelligible in the four episodes under consideration that determines the failure of language to communicate" (p. 693). Yet language is shown to be essential, a compulsive act like eating or drinking, with communication being only one of its many possible functions.

22  KRITZMAN, LAWRENCE D. "La quête de la parole dans le *Quart Livre* de Rabelais." *French Forum* 2, no. 3 (September):195–204.

Reads Book IV as a linguistic fable on the generative power of words, "un tourbillon au centre duquel se dessine une disponibilité verbale qui crée le voyage fictif en même temps qu'elle le nie" (p. 195). Studies this power of words on four levels: words as they become characters, characters as they are reduced to words, words as generating action, and linguistic expressions which serve as commentary upon the narrative. Focuses the discussion on the Isle des Alliances, the Andouilles episode, the storm at sea, and Quaresmeprenant. Concludes that the quest is that of Rabelais the writer, seeking a new freedom through an essentially poetic adventure.

1977

23 KUSHNER, EVA. "Was King Picrochole Free? Rabelais between Luther and Erasmus." *Comparative Literature Studies* 14, no. 4 (December):306–20.

In a close reading of the chapters on the Picrocholine War, underscores the ambiguity of Rabelais' position on the question of free will; sees in the episode an oscillation between the stands taken by Luther and Erasmus ten years previously, at a time when it was still unnecessary to choose between Evangelical optimism and Luther's belief that man was condemned to will and to do evil. Sees in the opposition between Grandgousier and Picrochole the dramatization in narrative form of the theological and ethical problem of man's will. Argues that by choosing to give in to his choleric temperament rather than to obey God's commandments, Picrochole—like the Pharaoh of the hardened heart in Erasmus' *De libero arbitrio*—succumbs momentarily to the influence of Satan and temporarily abdicates his spiritual freedom. Recalls that Rabelais sides with Luther in permitting the kind of wars that are waged to correct sinful princes and peoples. Thus correction is admitted as a possibility, and on the question of free will "a relative optimism prevails" (p. 317), along the lines of Erasmian compromise between God's omnipotence and man's freedom.

24 LA CHARITÉ, RAYMOND C. "*Mundus Inversus*: The Fictional World of Rabelais' *Pantagruel*." *Stanford French Review* 1, no. 1 (Spring):95–105.

Argues that "*Pantagruel* is a far more coherent and esthetically rewarding work than it is normally perceived to be" (p. 95), and that its unity and coherence should be sought on the thematic level rather than in its narrative line. Finds the unifying element of Rabelais' first book in its "thematics of upheaval."

25 MAUNY, RAYMOND. "Rabelais et la Sorbonne." *BAARD* 3, no. 6:252–61.

Argues that the Sorbonne, as the official guardian of Catholic orthodoxy, could hardly have reacted towards Rabelais and his work in any other way than it did. Reminds the reader that the allusions to the Sorbonne cease in 1542. Takes this to mean that Rabelais decided to remain in the bosom of the Church, and that he must have paid heed to his friends' advice to attenuate his criticism at a time when the danger of being led to the stake for heresy was all too real. Lists all the references to the Sorbonne, defines the situation of the Church at the beginning of the Reformation, and concludes that the Sorbonne could not have remained indifferent to Rabelais' contestatory stance, although it was forced to limit its actions to mere warnings, since Rabelais had distanced himself from Calvin just in time.

26 MILITZ, HELGA. "François Rabelais: Vom Volksbuch zum Weltbuch." In *Realismus in der Renaissance: Aneignung der Welt in der ezählenden Prosa*, edited by Robert Weimann. Berlin and Weimar: Aufban-Verlag, pp. 437–521.

Argues that Rabelais' work is characterized above all by the representation of a new reality, and stresses its preconditions: a new relationship between truth and fiction; a new proportion between description and narration on the one hand, and reflection on the other; emphasis on the physical description of the body; the use of language as a means of social intercourse; a new way of playing with forms and meanings in an attempt to master the world through the power of art and of words.

27  MUIR, LYNETTE R. "The Abbey and the City: Two Aspects of the Christian Community." *Australian Journal of French Studies* 14:32–38.

Can Thélème be considered a genuine Christian community? Notes certain inconsistencies, such as the differences in requirements for admission listed in chapt. 50, and those that figure in the inscription over the door to the abbey in chapt. 52: "there are really two abbeys, that suggested by Frère Jean and that carried out by Gargantua" (p. 34). Acknowledges the absence of communal worship, the self-centered nature of the Thelemites' existence, and the exclusion from their midst of the ugly and the stupid, but stresses on the other hand the extent to which Thélème resembles the New Jerusalem described in the book of Revelation and St. Augustine's City of God. Concludes that in describing the abbey Rabelais did not have in mind an exemplary religious community as it could exist in practice: "It is not the earthly monastic ideal of a hard-working, ministering, worshipping community within a temporal and mundane dimension, but a redeemed, elect, glorified, eschatological vision" (p. 38).

28  MURPHY, PATRICIA. "Rabelais and Jarry." *French Review* 51, no. 1 (October):29–36.

Notes the influence of Rabelais as revealed in direct quotations throughout Jarry's work; detects it also in various aspects of his *Gestes et Opinions du Docteur Faustroll*, and most notably in the opéra-bouffe *Pantagruel*, where Jarry surprisingly underplays the misogyny and cruelty of Panurge. Finds similarities in the authors' use parody, and in "the interplay of rigidity and fluidity in their use of the grotesque" (p. 29). Argues that "Jarry's admiration and emulation of Rabelais was much more enduring and much more extensive" than is commonly recognized (p. 36).

29  POLINER, SHARLENE MAY. "Versions of Death and Renewal in Rabelais' Five Books." Ph.D. dissertation, Yale University, 281 pp.

Studies the patterns of death and renewal in a group of "thematically significant" episodes. In *Pantagruel*, discovers "positive horizontal imagery of (re)generation and formation" as well as "vertical revelation distorted by fiction's prophetic, self-perpetuating lie" in Alcofrybas' "medlar myth" and Epistemon's resurrection, respectively. Detects essentially similar, albeit more

1977

complex, patterns in *Gargantua*. In Panurge's praise of debts at the beginning of Book III, and in his "ensuing plunge into existential crisis," finds that the earlier optimistic patterns have been replaced by "images of negative horizontality," a new metaphysical dimension, and "pronounced moral overtones." Views Book IV as a "journey into negativity," in which the storm episode, the Isle Sonante, Gaster, and the visit to Grippeminault "invert themes previously used to express joyful renewal." Traces the recapitulation of major themes in Book V, and sees in the oracular pronouncement of the Dive Bouteille "a potential link which spans the abyss of negative experience and affirms [moral] recuperation" as well as artistic rebirth. See *Dissertation Abstracts International* 39 (1978):2321–A.

30   RIGOLOT, FRANÇOIS. *Poétique et onomastique*. Geneva: Librairie Droz, pp. 84–104.
      In "Livre III: Dichotomie épistémologique chez Rabelais," draws attention to the importance of proper nouns (of both people and places) in Rabelais' fictional world. Discusses the significance of "Alcofrybas Nasier" both as pseudonym and as anagram. Notes the dichotomy between the first and second part of the fictional name: "Par la physionomie de son nom composé, le narrateur allie Socrate et Bacchus, le *Banquet* et *Fessepeinte*, le rire et la moelle" (p. 84). As anagram, believes that the name signals the duality of a text in need of decoding, and that it acts as a symbol of the ideology of *inversion* at work in Rabelais' carnivalesque text. Within the work itself, studies the various descriptive and ideological functions of onomastics, particularly in the episode of Epistémon's visit to the underworld, and in the first stanza of the inscription over the portal of Thélème. Devotes a separate section to the treatment of proper nouns in Book V. Finds that it lacks the complexity, the dynamic force, the inventiveness that characterize the onomastics of the earlier volumes, and that onomastic analysis thus corroborates the observations which had led Alfred Glauser (see 1975.4) to question the authenticity of the *Cinquiesme Livre*. Comments on chapt. 37 of the *Quart Livre*, in which Rabelais provides a theoretical discussion of the problem of the relations between words and things with reference to Plato's *Cratylus*. Notes the ambiguity of Socrates' position on the matter. Suggests a similar ambiguity over the question in Rabelais the philosopher and the poet. Concludes by bringing onomastics to bear on the characters of Panurge and Pantagruel. Notes that Panurge is literally contained in Pantagruel, and that Pantagruel contains within himself the negative characteristics associated with Panurgism right up to his encounter with Panurge, a pivotal point in Pantagruel's characterization: "La lecture onomastique rend bien compte à la fois du dédoublement des deux personnages et du rapport profond qui les unit; leur dialogue est aussi celui de leurs noms anagrammatisés" (p. 104).

31  ———. "Sémiotique de la sentence et du proverbe chez Rabelais." *Études Rabelaisiennes* 14:277–86.

Proposes a framework for further study of the way in which proverbs function as language and as knowledge in Rabelais. Defines the proverb, distinguishes it from the *sentence*, but notes that from the point of view of their rôle in the text, both function as "l'expérience formalisée en locution" (p. 279). Studies, as one particular example, the proverb "l'habit ne faict point le moyne" in the prologue to *Gargantua*. Points out that in the context of the opposition between a worthless exterior hiding an interior of great price (the "Silènes," the marrow bone, the bottle of wine), the reversal of values in the proverb (since here it is the exterior that is valorized at the expense of the interior) seems to subvert the meaning of the text it is meant to illustrate. In fact, however, the proverb acts as an *avertisseur* (since it warns us to distinguish appearance from reality) and a *rectificateur* (for it suggests that the marrow is not necessarily where we may think it is). As such, it is part of the ironic discourse of the text. Shows that the proverb plays a similar rôle in relation to elements of the text that it foreshadows, such as Frère Jean's cassock, the monks of Seuilly, and the inhabitants of Thélème. Contrasts the proverbs in the chapter on Gargantua's activities as a child (*Gargantua*, chapt. 11) with those associated with Panurge just before the series of consultations (*Tiers Livre*, chapt. 2). In both cases, notes that language is "démétaphorisé," so that the proverbs are taken literally. As in the example of the "paroles gelées," however, "le proverbe et la sentence entrent dans le texte pour 'rendre son en dégelant,' pour s'actualiser et donc reprendre vie" (p. 286).

32  ROMER, JAMES WILLIAM. "François Rabelais and the New World: A Study of Geography and Navigation in Rabelais' Romance." Ph.D. dissertation, University of North Carolina, 259 pp.

Argues that Rabelais was "an intelligent and informed observer of the Renaissance voyages of discovery," and that he understood the economic and religious implications of the discovery of the New World, but that his knowledge of this New World was limited not only by his ignorance of the specific "geographical entities" concerned, but also by an "archaic vision of the world" inherited from antiquity and the Middle Ages. Believes that Rabelais' information in *Pantagruel* and *Gargantua* was derived in the main from generally available texts and maps, whereas the last three books show knowledge of recent French voyages to Canada. But finds it unlikely that "the real navigations had a significant influence on the romance beyond the early chapters of the fourth book." See *Dissertation Abstracts International* 39 (1978):311A.

33  RUSSELL, DAVID. "Panurge and His New Clothes." *Études Rabelaisiennes* 14:89–104.

Panurge's change of costume in the *Tiers Livre* signals his attempt "to change with the help of the talismanic potency of his allegorical costume's symbolic associations" (p. 91). He hopes to reflect his new desire for the bourgeois values of marriage, thriftiness, tranquility, and family life, but ends up projecting an altogether different image. Three images, in fact: that of the burgher, the lay Franciscan brother, and the cuckold, none of which comes into clear focus. Suggests that Panurge's attempt was doomed to failure because of what is permanent in his character, namely hesitancy, and intellectual bad faith.

34 ———. "Réponse à M. Giraud." *Études Rabelaisiennes* 14:105–07.
   Replies to his critic that Gargantua's *image* is indeed a *devise*, and that nothing makes it impossible to associate the expression "avoir la puce en l'aureille" with both sexual desire (as Giraud would have it) and the worry that he may be a cuckold. See 1976.16.

35 SACRÉ, JAMES. "Les métamorphoses d'une braguette." *Littérature* 26 (May):72–93.
   Lists every mention of the word *braguette*, and provides a linguistic commentary—semantic as well as phonic, grammatical as well as rhetorical. Notes the word's figurative associations (with the head, the feminine sex organ, the book), the process by which it is made to acquire a positive or an ironic value. Suggests that such a study only begins to indicate the complexity and the importance of the erotic and the obscene in Rabelais' work.

36 SAULNIER, V[ERDUN]-L[OUIS]. "Le doute chez Rabelais. Un programme circonstancié: Le premier *Pantagruel*." *Études Rabelaisiennes* 14:1–21.
   Offers a close reading of the letter from Gargantua to his son in *Pantagruel*. Believes it to be, in essence, neither a utopian dream nor a comic episode, but a text the author calls "circonstancié," that is adapted to a particular fictional, intellectual, and historical context: a letter from a father to his son, in a particular place and at a particular moment in history. Argues that it defines the aspirations of a whole generation, and that it proposes, when read attentively, an attainable goal in accordance with sound pedagogical principles. Admits that the text reaches sometimes beyond realism, but only to the extent that it bears the mark of the humanist's mental set, his taste for rhetoric, ornamentation, a pedagogically justified enlargement of the truth. No doubt about it: "Rabelais croit bien à ce qu'il dit, tel qu'il le dit" (p. 19). Concludes with three brief "notes annexes," on the conception of God in *Pantagruel*, the meaning of *philautia*, and the desire to know as a *natural* impulse in Aristotle's *Metaphysics*.

37 SCHWARTZ, JEROME. "Scatology and Eschatology in Gargantua's Androgyne Device." *Études Rabelaisiennes* 14:265–75.
   Distinguishes between emblem and device, and studies Gargatua's device in an iconographical and verbal context. Reminds us that the two faces

of Rabelais' Androgyne look at each other, whereas Plato's, before separation, has a head with two faces pointing in opposite directions. Rabelais' version was seen by Sainéan as an illustration of the expression "faire la beste à deux dos." But rather than being a parody of the vogue of Neoplatonism, suggests it may be, as in Ficino, a symbol of the return to the original state of wholeness "through conversion and mutual *amor* or *caritas*" (p. 272). Or it could be related to Ebreo's interpretation of the Androgyne—when its heads are turned towards one another—as a symbol of postlapsarian carnality. "Gargantua's *image* remains equivocal" (p. 274).

38 SCREECH, MICHAEL-ANDREW. "Erasmus, Gilbertus Cognatus and Boniface Amerbach: A Link through the *Lucii Cuspidii Testamentum.*" *Etudes Rabelaisiennes* 14:43–46.
    The discovery of a copy of the *Testament* sent by Gilbert Cousin to Boniface Amerbach, Erasmus' secretary, allows the author to "tie Rabelais a little more tightly to the *entourage* of Erasmus" (p. 44), to confirm Rabelais' reputation as a legal scholar, and to suggest that the publication of the *Testament* was not, as is sometimes thought, a deliberate act of deception.

39 SIDER, SANDRA C. "Emblematic Imagery in Rabelais." Ph.D. dissertation, University of North Carolina, Chapel Hill, 107 pp.
    Believes that all the emblematic images in Rabelais, defined as "visual images with allegorical meanings," are related to the revelation and application of the Platonic principles of harmony, and that they are meant "to function hieroglyphically in their mystical hinting toward higher realities." Notes the Renaissance tendency to embody metaphysical truths in hieroglyphic emblems, points to such emblems in Rabelais' text, and discusses "the epistemological basis for their efficacy." See *Dissertation Abstracts International* 39 (1978):273A.

40 SPILLEBOUT, GABRIEL. "Des chevaux factices de Gargantua, ou Comment Rabelais 'brave l'honnêteté' (*Gargantua*, chapitre XIII)." *BAARD* 3, no. 7:246–49.
    Discusses Rabelais' use of scatological language in the episode, and its pertinence to the subject-matter.

41 VACHON, G.-ANDRÉ. *Rabelais tel quel*. Montreal: Les Presses de l'Université de Montréal, 144 pp.
    Begins by referring to the ambiguities of the "Énigme" discovered in the foundations of Thélème and in *Les Fanfreluches antidotées*, in which the author sees allusions to the most important episodes in Rabelais' novel. Extends his remarks to the work as a whole, and insists on the enigmatic character of Rabelais' text. Questions the possibilty of any valid interpretation: "C'est le texte entier d'Alcofribas qui est énigme. Il est tout entier: question.

1978

Une énigme, ou bien n'a pas de sens, ou bien a des sens contradictoires. C'est un texte sur lequel l'explication, l'interprétation n'ont aucune prise. Je puis tout au plus décrire" (p. 16). Provides a lengthy discussion of Book V, whose authenticity is not put in doubt. Stresses the ambiguities of Rabelais' novel. Questions the specificity of the characters and of the episodes in which they take part: "L'histoire de Pantagruel, c'est en fin de compte celle de Panurge.... Pantagruel, c'est aussi son père, Gargantua, puisque la deuxième tranche du roman est le livre premier *des aventures de Pantagruel* [author's emphasis]. Or, Gargantua, c'est Frère Jan" (p. 103).

42    VASSAL, PIERRE. "Le stoïcisme chez Rabelais." *BAARD* 3, no. 7:250–51.
      Claims that the language used by Panurge between the passages in classical Greek and Latin in his encounter with Pantagruel is not an imaginary dialect but the language of Greek poetry, "avec force fleurs de rhétorique," and that it is used to express the main tenets of Stoicism.


**1978**

1    ANTONIOLI, ROLAND. "Rabelais et les songes." *CAIEF* 30:7–21.
      On three occasions Rabelais' characters are seen to stop in their tracks and seek in dreams the solution to their problems: before his sign dispute with Thaumaste (*Pantagruel*, chapt. 18), an anxious Pantagruel spends the night thinking (Rabelais uses the word "revasser") of a list of books—most of them never written—that might ensure his victory over the English philosopher. In the *Tiers Livre* (chapt. 13 and 14) the same Pantagruel suggests to Panurge that he seek in dreams a solution to his matrimonial dilemma, on the authority of such ancient sages as Hippocrates, Aristotle, and Plato, as well as such Neoplatonists as Plotinus and Synesius. In Book IV, Pantagruel and Ponocrates fall to dreaming off the coast of Chaneph as they wait for the wind to fill their sails. Suggests that Rabelais' very different tone in each of the three episodes is related to the three categories of dreams—vain, natural, and prophetic—into which they fall as well as to the kind of solution the characters are seeking. If Pantagruel, for all his physical, social, and intellectual stature is made into a figure of fun as he frets in preparation for his dispute with Thaumaste, it is because at the time *Pantagruel* is written, the humanists, and Rabelais among them, view with deep suspicion if not with downright hostility the use of dreams for Cabbalistic purposes now that the Cabbala dabbles in magic and thaumaturgy. The seriousness with which the dream episode is treated in the *Tiers Livre*, on the other hand, reflects the increased interest of physicians and philosophers alike in psychic activity as manifested in dreams, an interest fueled perhaps by Cornarius' edition of Artemidorus' *Interpretation of Dreams*, and later by the growing preoccupation with prophetic dreams under the influence of poets and of Catherine de Médicis'

court. In the interpretation of Panurge's dream Rabelais seems to echo these preoccupations, without failing to distinguish—as some around him do not—between dreams that are false and those that are true. Concludes by relating the treatment of dreams to the rest of Rabelais' work, and argues that the search for meaning in the interpretation of dreams is a model for the interpretation of history and myth as practiced by Rabelais' characters in the last two books. Sees it also as a model for literary interpretation as developed by Rabelais in the prologue to *Gargantua*.

2 ———. "Rabelais: Médecine et politique dans le chapitre premier du *Tiers Livre*." In *Culture et pouvoir au temps de l'Humanisme et de la Renaissance*, edited by L. Terreaux. Paris and Geneva: Slatkine and Champion, pp. 285–98.
    Studies the relationship between medicine and politics in the introductory chapter of Book III on the theme of colonization. Suggests that the source of the ideas on governing newly conquered territories should be sought less in the benevolent policies of Langey in the Piedmont than in More's *Utopia* and in the French king's plans for colonization of Newfoundland by Cartier, since 1533, and in his policy of *entente* with the German Protestants. Believes that the political ideas expressed in the chapter are grounded less in politics than in medicine, and that the functions of the king are essentially similar to those of the physician. "Nourrir, protéger, instruire: ces trois fonctions du roi sont aussi celles du médecin" (p. 290).

3 BALDINGER, KURT. "M fr *aubelière*, mot créé par Rabelais." In *Mélanges de philologie romane offerts à Charles Camproux*, vol. 2. Montpellier: Université Paul Valéry, pp. 835–39.
    Contests Paul Burrell's interpretation. See 1974.4 and 1976.2.

4 ———. "Premier, terme de jeu de paume méconnu dans Rabelais." In *Mélanges d'études romanes du Moyen âge et de la Renaissance offerts à Monsieur Jean Rychner*. Travaux de Linguistique et de Littérature publiés par le Centre de Philologie et de Littératures Romanes de l'Université de Strasbourg, no. 16. Paris: Éditions Klincksieck, pp. 45–48.
    Identifies the word *premier*, used in the *Enigme en prophetie* (*Gargantua*, chapt. 58), as a technical term referring to the gallery closest to the net.

5 BERRONG, RICHARD M[ICHAEL]. "Note for the commentary on the *Cinquième Livre*: 'un pot aux roses' (ch. 4)." *Romance Notes* 19, no.1 (Fall):78–82.
    Notes the silence on the part of modern commentators—or an admission of ignorance—in connection with the possible meaning of the expression "un pot aux roses" in the last line of the chapter. Points out that Le Duchat, in his 1741 edition, had suggested it referred to the author's attempt to find in the

1978

Hebraic and Greek sources of the Scriptures "les raisons qui portoient tant d'honnêtes gens à renoncer à la Communion du Pape" (quoted p. 79). Le Duchat had also alluded to Marot's *Epitre du Coq à l'Asne*, where the expression is used in a similarly humanistic context. Points out that Henri Estienne's *Apologie pour Hérodote* had already contained a similar allusion, and that the expression occurs twice, each time in reference to maneuvers by the Church to prevent its impostures from being discovered. Notes one last sixteenth-century appearance of the phrase in the *Satyre Menippée*.

6   BRAULT, GERARD J. "For what audience did Rabelais write *Pantagruel* and *Gargantua*?" In *Mélanges de littérature du Moyen Age au XXe siècle offerts à Mademoiselle Jeanne Lods*, vol. 2. Paris: École Normale Supérieure de Jeunes Filles, pp. 611–16.
      Without denying that the books may have been written for the general public and for humanist readers, argues that they were also aimed at an audience of students. Believes that in their obscenity, their irreverence towards authority, their antifeminism, and their erotic bent, the books reflect male student attitudes and fantasies. Notes the attraction of "that rascal Panurge" for such an audience. Insofar as they represented the nation's future, argues that it is this public that Rabelais the humanist must have wished to reach above any other audience.

7   CÉARD, JEAN. "La querelle des géants et la jeunesse du monde." *Journal of Medieval and Renaissance Studies* 8, no. 1 (Spring):37–67.
      Suggests that the sixteenth-century debate on the role of the giants in the creation of the world sheds significant light on Rabelais' choice of giants as heroes of his novel. Believes that through his genealogy of the giants Rabelais means to add his own—admittedly facetious—commentary to the dispute, and side with the Talmudists against Viterbo and Lemaire de Belges by discrediting the prevalent theory of the progressive *vieillissement* of the world. Sees Rabelais' genealogy as inspired less by the Gospel of St. Matthew than by the fourth chapter of Genesis, especially as glossed by Viterbo. "Il faut lire les trois premiers chapitres du *Pantagruel* comme un commentaire irrespectueux des commentaires de la Genèse" (p. 52), rather than as an irreverent satire of a biblical text.

8   COLEMAN, ANTONY. "Sterne's Use of the Motteux-Ozell *Rabelais*." *Notes and Queries* 223 (February):55–58.
      A certain Edmund Ferrers, rector of Cheriton, Hants, noted in the margins of a copy of *Tristram Shandy* now in the British Museum, a number of passages he believed to have a Rabelaisian source, and had claimed that Sterne's debt was to Odell's translation of Rabelais rather than to Rabelais himself. Records eighteen of these purported borrowings, giving in each case the reference in *Tristram Shandy* and its supposed source in Ozell. Observes

that in some cases the rector is more assiduous than accurate, "but [that] he does establish convincingly Sterne's use of [Ozell's] translation" (p. 58).

9    COOPER, RICHARD. "Rabelais et l'Italie: Les lettres écrites de Rome." *CAIEF* 30:22–40.
        Discusses the three letters sent by Rabelais to Geoffroy d'Estissac from Rome during his second trip to Italy. Notes the textual problems they raise, and sees no reason to doubt that the second letter (the contrary opinions of Lefranc, Boulenger, and Plattard notwithstanding) is not from Rabelais' own hand. As for their content, argues that they are for the most part historical and political documents rather than accounts of Rabelais' personal preoccupations. Notes Rabelais' reliance on Roman *bolletini* and *avvisi*: if Rabelais' account of the defeat of Soliman II, for instance, is confusing and inaccurate, it is not due to personal incompetence but because of the inaccurate reporting by the Roman "press." Shows that as historical documents the letters are not particularly valuable, since what Rabelais reports is already widely known. Believes their political interest to be greater, since they often reflect his own opinions, particularly his nationalism. Stylistically, believes the letters have been dealt with too harshly: does not find them as boring, or as devoid of Rabelaisian verve as their reputation suggests. Concludes by underscoring their biographical interest. Notes in particular that nothing in the letters suggests that Rabelais was in Rome as du Bellay's physician, or indeed that they lived under the same roof. "Tout porte à croire que, jusqu'au mois de février 1535, quand du Bellay lui obtint un canonicat à Saint Maur, Rabelais n'était pas au service du Cardinal, mais qu'il s'était rendu à Rome en partie pour les affaires de d'Estissac, et aussi pour résoudre le problème de son apostasie" (p. 39).

10   DEFAUX, GÉRARD. "Deux paraboles de l'humanisme chrétien: Pantagruel et Pic de la Mirandole." *CAIEF* 30:41–56.
        Notes that none of the romances of chivalry which are taken as having furnished Rabelais with a framework for *Pantagruel* contain the *topos* of education, which plays such an important part in Rabelais' first novel. Rather than a knight, Pantagruel traveling from one university to another in search of knowledge brings to mind the vagrant scholars of the Middle Ages and the Renaissance, and in particular the young Pico della Mirandola, as described by his nephew in a biography published in 1498 and translated in 1510 by Thomas More. Acknowledges that the parallel between Pantagruel advertizing his 9,764 theses throughout Paris and the 900 theses argued by Pico in Rome has not escaped the attention of modern commentators, but notes that they fail to take into account how strongly Pico's thirst for glory is condemned by his nephew for its arrogant ambition, how close it is to sophistry, and how antithetical to the spirit of true humanism. In the light of this parallelism, suggests that the traditional interpretation of Gargantua's letter to his son as a Renaissanace manifesto deserves to be reevaluated: "Comment en effet quali-

1978

fier de 'chant triomphal de la Renaissance' ou d' 'Hymne aux temps nou-veaux' une lettre qui contient une exhortation à la *disputatio* scolastique?" (p. 52). Notes that Pico himself came to think of public disputations as unworthy of a true philosopher and rejected worldly glory in favor of humble submission to the word of Christ. Argues that Pico's entire spiritual itinerary from sophistry to Christian humanism parallels exactly the spiritual evolution of Pantagruel, as well as that of such Christian humanists as Erasmus, Lefèvre d'Etaples, Budé, and More. See also 1977.12.

11 DEMERSON, GUY. "Les facéties chez Rabelais." *Studi Francesi*, no. 64 (January–April):1–12.
     Points to chapt. 39 of Book IV as proof that Rabelais was aware of the technical meaning of the *facétie*, and claims that in this episode as well as in many others, Rabelais makes use of such characteristics of the genre as *comitas* (a sense of lively dialogue), and *dicacitas* ("art des effets aigus et brefs," p. 3), an essential element of the genre, since in contrast to the *narrés* (which are given ever more importance from the *Tiers Livre* onward), "la facétie n'est pas une esthétique du développement mais de l'explosion" (p. 4). Argues that such episodes are organically related to the whole: "les facéties ne font pas grumeau dans la pâte de l'œuvre " (p. 5), and that it is from the *facéties* that Rabelais' humor derives many of its most characteristic features and its capacity to laugh at the human condition.

12 FRANÇON, MARCEL. "Erasme, Rabelais, Maurice Scève, Hobbes et Spinoza." *Romance Notes* 19, no. 1 (Fall):72–73.
     "Homo homini lupus": notes Rabelais' use of the French equivalent of Hobbes' phrase in chapt. 3 of the *Tiers Livre*.

13 ———. "Sur les Cannibales." *BAARD* 3, no. 7:320.
     Argues in favor of his belief that for Rabelais the Cannibals are an African tribe (and not Brazilian, as for Montaigne).

14 GENDRE, ANDRÉ. *Humanisme et folie chez Sébastien Brant, Erasme et Rabelais*. Vortäge der Aeneas-Silvius-Stiftung an der Universität Basel, no. 14. Basel and Stuttgart: Verlag Helbibg & Lichtenhahn, 41 pp.
     Focuses primarily on Rabelais. Traces the disquieting presence of "folie" (which the author prefers not to define) in Rabelais' language, where-as Erasmus speaks of it in rational discourse ("sagement"). Notes the historical antecedents of such verbal experimentation in the *sotties* and in popular language, but underscores its fundamental originality: "seul de son espèce, en France du moins, Alcofribas confronte tous les langages, pousse à bout tous les non-sens, mène à leur point de rupture toutes les folies" (p. 20). Notes also the presence of folly in Rabelais' characters, especially in Panurge, who is

said to suffer from "philautie," in Erasmian terminology, or "narcissism," in that of the author. But notes that Rabelais seems to side with Panurge (as does Pantagruel). Ascribes this to Panurge's basic function in the novel, which is to raise embarrassing questions and to remind us of certain fundamental values (freedom, sexuality) as well as of the limits of humanistic knowledge. Concludes by arguing that in Book IV folly loses its positive, redeeming value at the same time as Panurge loses his prestige: "Il n'est plus le valeureux contradicteur, mais le farceur cynique dans l'épisode des moutons ou le couard impénitent dans les épisodes de la tempête ou de Ganabin" (p. 29). As the enemies of humanism emerge victorious in the struggle for enlightenment, folly becomes, in Rabelais' novel, the unredeeming flaw of the enemies of truth.

15  GLAUSER, ALFRED. "Le Gouffre chez Rabelais considéré comme espace scriptural." In *Renaissance et Nouvelle Critique: Quatrième Symposium sur la Renaissance, Modern Language Association of America, State University of New York at Albany, 16–19 octobre 1975, Directeur: Raymond Ortali.* Valencia: Artes Gráficas Soler, pp. 39–54.

"Rabelais se réfère souvent au gouffre comme à un lieu vaguement structuré, qui a dû représenter pour lui un espace scriptural à explorer, à remplir, figurant par son ombre les hasards et les dangers de l'écriture" (p. 39). Claims that writing, *l'écriture,* is the central theme, the true adventure narrated in Rabelais' novels. The birth of the giants is thus, above all, the birth of the text: "Avant la naissance du géant, s'impose la véritable naissance, celle du livre" (p. 40). Studies the *gouffre*, the shadowy enclave, as scriptural space in the episode of the pilgrims swallowed by Gargantua with his salad, and in Alcofrybas' exploration of the world in Pantagruel's mouth.

16  GROOS, ROBERT S[TOW]. "The Enigmas of Quaresmeprenant: Rabelais and Defamiliarization." *Romanic Review* 69:22–33.

Studies the chapter entitled "Continuation des contenenses de Quaresmeprenant" as an example of linguistic defamiliarization, defined as "the use of language in such a way that we are compelled to reassess the significations we commonly attach to words" (p. 22). Instead of considering the propositions making up the chapter as a series of non sequiturs, proposes that we view them as "enigmas which Rabelais expected his audiences to decipher" (p. 23). See also 1975.6.

17  HAUSMANN, FRANK-RUTGER. "Rabelais und...kein Ende, ein Forschungsbericht." *Romanistische Zeitschrift für Literaturgeschichte* 2:326–49.

Reviews Rabelais scholarship of the previous twenty years, with emphasis on recent critical trends.

1978

18 HUCHON, MIREILLE. "Rabelais grammairien: De l'histoire du texte aux problèmes d'authenticité." *Réforme, Humanisme, Renaissance* 8 (December):46–49.

Summary of doctoral dissertation. See 1981.17.

19 HYDAK, MICHAEL G. "Rabelais, Erasmus and Sixteenth-Century Woman." *Degré Second* (June):1–20.

Contests Saulnier's view that Erasmus is an antifeminist precursor of Rabelais, by arguing that Erasmus is not an antifeminist, either in his *Praise of Folly* or elsewhere. Contests with equal vigor Screech's opposite contention that Rabelais was influenced by Erasmus' feminism: sees no trace of such feminism anywhere in Rabelais. Concludes that "however large the debt Rabelais may owe to Erasmus, it is certainly not in the domain of woman and marriage" (p. 18).

20 KENNEDY, WILLIAM J. *Rhetorical Norms in Renaissance Literature*. New Haven: Yale University Press, 229 pp.

In the section devoted to Rabelais (pp. 105–27), studies Rabelais' rhetorical strategies, and more specifically the way in which the characterization, style, and world-view of the "speaker" mediates the characterizations, styles, and world-views of the other characters. Notes the stylistic and rhetorical contrasts developed by the narrator to differentiate the major characters in the first two books, whole professional classes in Book III, and whole societies in Book IV. Points out how changes in Pantagruel's style signal his ever increasing importance as the "moral center of the book" (p. 108). Emphasizes the complexity of the relationship between the speaker and his audience, and the effect that the role ascribed to the reader has on the reception of the text. Studies the strategies whereby the narrator ensures the complicity of the reader. Believes that the purpose of this strategy, somewhat limited in *Pantagruel*, assumes greater importance in *Gargantua* where the strategy allows the author to draw his audience, through "comic intimidation," "into an ever expanding conspiracy against the customs, conventions, and accepted mores of the day " (p. 113). Notes that in the *Tiers Livre* the speaker's role loses importance since the book is for the most part a dialogue which the audience is invited to interpret without the controlling intervention of the narrator. Sees this as problematic in the context of humanistic philosophy underlying the narrative, since the audience is likely to give a subjective interpretation to words which have, in a humanistic perspective, an absolute meaning grounded in philology. Speculates that this may be why Rabelais returns to conventional narrative in the *Quart Livre*. Notes the conciliatory attitude of the narrator in that book, a new mastery of narrative art, and a new subtlety in the speaker's manipulation of an audience invited to accept the fictional validity of increasingly improbable episodes. Sees the episode of the frozen words as illustrating the essential autonomy of the text, containing within itself its fictive audience. Concludes that Rabelais' attitude toward style, embodied in the shifting relations between speaker and audience throughout the book, questions the claims of philological humanism by challenging "language's potential to reveal absolute truth or to communicate straightforward objective content" (p. 123).

21 KOPPEL, PETER. *La cohérence du Tiers Livre de François Rabelais.* Zurich: Juris Druck, 72 pp.

Seeks to establish the structural as well as the thematic coherence of Book III, seen as representing a critical moment in the evolution of Rabelais' narrative, a crisis that puts into question the narrative act itself. "Il n'y a, au *Tiers Livre*, que des commencements, des départs et des actes qui n'aboutissent pas" (p. 2). In the first three chapters, offers a reading of chapt. 1–8 of the novel. Sees them as preparing "le récit de l'arrêt du récit" (p. 5), in which fiction becomes theory (chapt. 1), and action becomes disarticulated (chapt. 2–5), before coming to an end altogether in chapt. 6–8. In chapt. 4, studies the series of consultations, insists on their endless and obsessive repetition, but argues that they achieve a kind of coherence in the episode of the Pantagruélion, seen as embodying the energy of experience and "l'humanité naturelle de l'homme" (p. 71).

22 LA CHARITÉ, RAYMOND C. "Chapter Division and Narrative Structure in Rabelais's *Pantagruel*." *French Forum* 3, no. 3 (September):263–70.

Argues against the then-prevalent view of *Pantagruel* as structurally weak and full of careless inconsistencies. Studies the problem of chapter divisions in the original edition of 1532, stresses the episodic nature of the book, suggests that this episodic structure does not denote "a compositional flaw," but that it expresses a particular view of the world, acting as a comic device and reinforcing the book's "thematics of *dis*-integration, upheaval, and openness" (p. 268). See also 1980.30.

23 LARMAT, JEAN. "Formes et fonctions des récits chez Rabelais." *CAIEF* 30:57–70.

With a terminology borrowed in turn from Gérard Genette, Roland Barthes, Greimas, Propp and Todorov, studies the forms and functions of Rabelaisian narrative, including dialogue as an integral part of the process. Distinguishes three types of narrator: the voice of the prologues, the king's historiographer who is also an occasional actor in the story, and in Book IV one of Pantagruel's companions, whose identity dissolves into a common "we." Argues that with the possible exception of Panurge and Frère Jean, the other protagonists should be thought of as "actants": characters who do or say things, or to whom things are done and said, rather than as genuine characters with a clearly discernible psychological identity. Finds that Rabelais uses most of the literary forms of his day while managing to preserve a fundamen-

1978

tal sense of unity, and that these forms are made to fulfill their dual function of entertaining and enlightening the reader. Throughout, stresses the freedom with which Rabelais uses the literary structures at his disposal.

24  LAUVERGNAT-GAGNIERE, C[HRISTIANE]. "Rabelais lecteur de Lucien de Samosate." *CAIEF* 30:71–86.

Seeks to assess and explain the extent of Lucian's influence on Rabelais' work. Notes Rabelais' thorough knowledge of Lucian, whom he may even have translated. But points out that references to the Greek writer are surprisingly few, and that an author such as Virgil, to whom he owes much less, is more frequently mentioned. Locates Lucian's influence in three areas: "la contamination des genres et sa conséquence la plus immédiate, le mélange du sérieux et du comique, la fantaisie dans l'invention et l'utilisation ludique d'un héritage culturel" (p. 75). Notes that the playful references to their cultural past—in Rabelais' case to both antiquity and the Bible—does not imply any fundamental skepticism as to its inherent value. Notes also that similar devices found in both writers are often put to a different purpose: for instance, fantasy, a mere ornament in Lucian, becomes an inherent element of Rabelaisian reality. Concludes by stressing the difference in quality between the two writers: the relative timidity of Lucian's linguistic innovations, the narrow confines of his cultural world, his inability or unwillingness to bring his satire to bear on the realities of his day.

25  MARTIN-LEFF, ANN. "Aspects of Gigantism in Rabelais: Characters, Style, Vision." Ph.D. dissertation, Yale University, 233 pp.

Views gigantism as "an essential and vital component of Rabelais' imagination." Studies the functions and characteristics of the giant-figure as they change in each of the five books, and relates them to the "style and vision" of Rabelais' text. Underscores the ambiguous nature of gigantism, its powers and limitations. Compares Rabelais' giants to other giants of literature and folklore, and sees them as protean symbols of transition and transformation. Stresses the "interconnectedness of characters, style, and vision" in an effort to bring out "patterns and greater coherence" in a work most often perceived as disjointed. See *Dissertation Abstracts International* 40 (1979):251A.

26  MASTERS, G[EORGE] MALLARY. "On *Learned Ignorance*, or How to Read Rabelais: Part I, Theory." *Romance Notes* 19, no. 1 (Fall):127–32.

"The much-debated Prologue [to *Gargantua*] is really a clear statement when read in the light of Erasmian reform of Biblical exegesis; for Rabelais reflects in a secular context Erasmus' method of scriptural interpretation" (p. 128). Draws attention to Filippo Beroaldo's *Symbola Pythagorae moraliter explanata*, which asserts the polysemy of Pythagorean symbols and uses the image of the marrow bone. Sees the prologue as authorizing an allegorical interpretation, provided it avoids excess.

27 ―――. "On *Learned Ignorance*, or How to Read Rabelais: Part II, Application." *Romance Notes* 19, no. 2 (Winter):254–60.

In the light of the prologue to *Gargantua*, viewed as authorizing an allegorical interpretation of the work in matters ethical, political, and economic, sees the giant as a silenus, incorporating the grotesque and the spiritual perfection of Socrates. Argues that Gargantua's education, as well as his behavior in war, offers a secular version of the ideas promoted by Erasmus in his *Christian Prince*. Sees Thélème as a symbol of the prince's accomplishments. Suggests that a similarly allegorical interpretation could be given of Pantagruel, at least from Book III onward.

28 MÉNAGER, DANIEL. *Pantagruel et Gargantua: Rabelais*. Profil d'une œuvre, no. 62. Paris: Hatier, 79 pp.

Like the other guides in the same series, provides the student with a general critical analysis of Rabelais' first two chronicles. Discusses the diversity of the public for whom Rabelais was writing, the plot, the particular nature of the characters, the choice of narrative techniques, Rabelaisian laughter, and Rabelais' conception of man as embodied in the figure of the giant-king. Concedes that *Gargantua* may legitimately be seen as a work of greater maturity and artistic mastery, but warns against underestimating the striking originality of Rabelais' first book, or reducing the second to a *roman à thèse*.

29 ―――. "La politique du don dans les derniers chapitres du *Gargantua*." *Journal of Medieval and Renaissance Studies* 8, no. 2 (Fall):179–91.

Proposes an "economic" reading of the chapters on the Abbaye de Thélème, in the modern sense of the term. Views the episode as a reflection of the new economic order, of a new relationship between power and money. Underscores the ambiguity of the act of giving, as manifested in the liberality of the giants. Argues that the gifts with which Gargantua rewards friends and foes alike make of him the very model of the humanist prince, whose calculated prodigality ensures the eternal gratitude of the receiver, and strengthens his power through the display of his wealth. Argues that only Panurge and Frère Jean remain free from the constraint imposed by the acceptance of gifts: by immediately squandering their reward or by refusing to be rewarded, they manifest their individuality and love of freedom. "En acceptant les dons de Gargantua, les Thélémites perdent tout, jusqu'aux noms qu'ils avaient dans leur vie antérieure" (p. 187), whereas the prince, through his liberality and the charitable use of his money, acquires power over God himself and ensures not only his political survival but also his place in Heaven. Concludes by claiming that the prince's liberality does not only alienate his subjects' freedom but that it also stifles the productive activity extolled by the Renaissance humanists.

1978

Only in the last chapters of Book IV, in the myth of Gaster, does Rabelais give expression to this important Renaissance ideal: "L'homme de ce nouveau mythe n'aura plus besoin de rois ou de dieux protecteurs puisqu'il gagne, par son travail, une totale autonomie. Ses exploits annoncent, qu'on le veuille ou non, ceux qu'est en train d'accomplir, historiquement, la bourgeoisie" (pp. 190–91).

30   RIGOLOT, FRANÇOIS. "Rabelais rhétoriqueur?" *CAIEF* 30:87–103.
   Leaving aside stylistic similarities, questions of versification, and considerations of a biographical nature, seeks to uncover those characteristics of Rabelais' writing practice which he possesses in common with the so-called "école des Grands Rhétoriqueurs." Insists on certain formal analogies, but also on the "travail différentiel" whereby Rabelais puts his own stamp on what he borrows from the Rhétoriqueur tradition. Sets the episode of Epistémon's resurrection squarely within the literary tradition of the "songe" (already present in the *Roman de la Rose* before being systematically exploited by Molinet and Lemaire de Belges), and that of the resurrection of the speaker who can then share with his audience his experience of the beyond. Notes telling similarities between the episode in which Picrochole is encouraged by his counsellors to conquer the world (*Gargantua*, chapt. 33) and André de la Vigne's *Ressource de la Chrétienté* which mocks the grandiose political ambitions of Charles VIII. Points out that Rabelais often "corrects" the stylistic devices of the Rhétoriqueurs by an amplification designed to bring out their full comic potential. Argues that the circular structure of the *Tiers Livre* owes something to the formal model known as *la couronne littéraire*, used among others by Lemaire de Belges in his *Couronne Margaritique*. And that the episodic structure of the *Quart Livre* is similarly related to the structure of the *chapelet*, as practiced before Rabelais by Cretin and Molinet; whereas his ideological model, which it shares with Brant's *Narrenschiff* and Erasmus' *Moria*, had already been used (albeit without the moral ambiguity it possesses in Rabelais) by such Rhétoriqueurs as Pierre Gringore in his *Folles entreprises*. Notes that Rabelais' narrator in the first two books has much of a Rhétoriqueur about him, before discovering his own voice in Books III and IV and rejecting the rhetorical tradition as a narrative framework. "Le rhétoriqueur, évacué de l'instance narrative sinon des schémas littéraires, se réfugie au plan de la fiction: il devient personnage" (p. 101). The character in question is of course Raminagrobis, previously identified in turn with Cretin, Lemaire, and Gringore, but best seen as a composite figure, lying on his death bed at a time when all three Rhétoriqueurs he resembles have left this world. "Tout se passe donc comme si les chapitres sur Raminagrobis constituaient une sorte d'éloge funèbre paradoxal de la grande rhétorique" (p. 102).

31 SORRELL, GREGORY. "Panurge, the Protean Rogue: A Study in Rabelaisian Mutations." Ph.D. dissertation, University of Wisconsin, Madison, 206 pp.

Studies Panurge, "the most fully delineated *Urschelm* in literature," as a literary mutation of an archetypal human phenomenon. Underscores in particular the two most substantial mutations: Panurge as the wise fool, and as the Socratic-Diogenic seeker of wisdom. After reviewing Rabelais criticism, with emphasis on the polemic between the "Lefranc school" and Leo Spitzer, surveys the critical attitudes towards Panurge and discusses Rabelais' own treatment of his "beloved rogue." Claims to provide the first convincing evidence that Rabelais knew Brant's *Narrenschiff* and that he makes use of this knowledge in Books III and IV. Concludes with a review of the picaresque novel and its critical literature, and attempts to offer a justification for seeing in Panurge the embodiment of "a complete picaro," as well as a prefiguration of the modern existential hero. See *Dissertation Abstracts International* 40 (1979):1504A.

32 SPILLEBOUT, GABRIEL. "Rabelais et le désastre de Pavie." *BAARD* 3, no. 7:303–08.

Reads the Picrocholine War as a mock-heroic transposition of the famous battle, of which Rabelais may have had a very precise knowledge thanks to the brothers du Dellay.

33 SCHWARTZ, JEROME. "Aspects of Androgyny in the Renaissance." In *Human Sexuality in the Middle Ages and Renaissance*, edited by Douglas Radcliff-Umstead. University of Pittsburgh Publications on the Middle Ages and Renaissance, no. 4. Pittsburgh: Center for Medieval and Renaissance Studies, pp. 121–31.

In the context of a more general discussion, interprets Gargantua's medallion (*Gargantua*, chapt. 8) as a fusion of sexual love and Pauline charity. Contrasts this optimistic synthesis of contraries with the pessimistic Freudian notion of an irreconcilable conflict between the self-centered *eros* and the altruistic *agape*.

34 TAYLOR, EDWARD FRANK. "Rabelais' Inner Voyages: Psychoanalytic and Generational Aspects of His Narrative and Characterization." Ph.D. dissertation, Northwestern University, 174 pp.

Structural and psychoanalytic study of Rabelais' five books, principally in the light of Otto Rank's *Trauma of Birth*. Part 1 studies the episode of Thélème, the four instances of corporeal entry into the giants bodies, and the confrontation with the Dive Bouteille as forms of vertical and horizontal penetration. Part 2 is concerned with "The Hero's Struggle," chiefly as compensation for the trauma of birth. The conclusion relates the penetration and struggle of man to the phenomenon of death, "the antithesis of his birth-oriented anxiety." See *Dissertation Abstracts International* 37 (1979):4973A.

35  VALESIO, PAOLO. "Structures rhétoriques chez Rabelais, dans le texte et autour du texte." In *Renaissance et Nouvelle Critique: Quatrième Symposium sur la Renaissance, Modern Language Association of America, State University of New York at Albany, 16–19 octobre 1975, Directeur: Raymond Ortali*. Valencia: Artes Gráficas Soler, pp. 55–90.

Offers an outline and a methodological justification of the author's forthcoming (but to my knowledge hitherto unpublished) *Antitextual Linguistics: An Essay on Middle French through Rabelais*. Chooses Rabelais' text as particularly representative of the last phase in the development of Middle French, and focuses his study on chapt. 9 of the *Quart Livre* (the Isle des Alliances) for its importance as a rhetorical system, its density of rhetorical figures explicitly presented as such. Seeks to account for the semantic and syntactical details of the text through rhetorical analysis. Finds earlier positivistic studies helpful, more so than later, impressionistic ones. Argues that rhetorical and philological studies should have as solid, as scientific a foundation as linguistic analysis. Claims that rhetorical analysis distinguishes itself by the scientific rigor of its methodology from literary criticism as currently practiced. Rejects all critical interpretations to the extent that they claim to read some meaning or other in a text whose linguistic code has yet to be discovered. Insists that the empirical analysis which alone will decipher this code must be brought to bear on a text that has previously been rediscovered in its specificity, its physicality, as a textual *idiolect* (p. 66), a specific variant of the *dialectal* text on which critical analyses are presently practiced. Describes the various stages of the rhetorical analysis brought to bear on chapt. 9 of the *Quart Livre* in the book-length version of the author's study, undertaken with the intention of bringing out "la politique réelle du complexe textuel" (p. 83), and relating it to the work as a whole as well as to the French literature of the period and to the Italian tradition of macaronic poetry.

36  VASSAL, PIERRE. "A propos des baragouins du ch. IX du *Pantagruel*: Patelinois, Lanternois ou Suédois." *BAARD* 3, no. 7:313–14.

Suggests that the sixth language used by Panurge in the 1542 edition may be Swedish, and offers a translation.

37  WEBER, HENRI. "La méthode marxiste et les études sur la Renaissance: L'exemple de Rabelais." In *Renaissance et Nouvelle Critique: Quatrième Symposium sur la Renaissance, Modern Language Association of America, State University of New York at Albany, 16–19 octobre 1975, Directeur: Raymond Ortali*. Valencia: Artes Gráficas Soler, pp. 91–102.

Acknowledges that Marxist criticism has only recently abandoned its hitherto exclusive preoccupation with ideology and history of ideas, provides an overview of Lefebvre's and Bakhtin's work on Rabelais, and notes their shortcomings. In the case of Lefebvre, points out that the characteristics of modern man seen by the critic in Panurge are already those of such types as the cleric errant and the *goliard* of the Middle Ages. Admits that Bakhtin's concept of "popular culture" lacks precision and that the critic all too easily dismisses the role of erudition and humanistic values. Deplores that this should have led such post-Bakhtinian critics as Paris and Beaujour to offer a "purely negative"—and thus essentially anti-Marxist—interpretation of Rabelais' work as an intellectual game where conflicting ideologies neutralize each other and dissolve into problems of language. But claims that Marxist criticism has performed an important task in highlighting in Rabelais's text the manifestations of popular or national culture which elitist criticism has tended to ignore.

38 WOOD, HADLEY. "An Interpretation of Rabelais's 'Ancien Prologue.'" *French Studies* 32, no. 4 (October):398–407.

Notes that the battle of the jays and the magpies appears to be thematically inconsistent with the rest of the 1548 prologue to the *Quart Livre*, but argues that it is interesting nevertheless as an allegory in which the jay represents Rabelais, the magpie is Gabriel du Puy-Herbaut (who had attacked Rabelais a year earlier in his *Theotimus*), and that the allegory itself hints at the hostile reception given to Rabelais' books. Believes that this interpretation helps explain the angry tone of the *Ancien Prologue*, which later gave way to the tone of moderation characterizing the *Quart Livre* of 1552.

39 ZIMMER, RUDOLPH. "Die Rhetorik der Zahl bei Rabelais." *Germanish-Romanische Monatsschrift*, no. 2:155–67.

Comments on previous work done on the subject by Francis (1959.15), Tetel (1964.19), Butor and Hollier (1972.10), and Lorian (1973.14). Comments on Rabelais' system of numerical notation, notes his "Art der Überpräzision," and argues that Rabelais' use of numbers is above all rhetorical.

## 1979

1 BAKHTIN, MIKHAIL. *L'Opera di Rabelais e la cultura popular; riso, carnevale e festa nella tradizione medievale e rinascimentale.* Translated by Mili Romano. Turin: Einaudi.

Italian translation of 1965.1.

2 BÉNÉ, CHARLES. "'Folie' et 'Sagesse' dans la littérature du XVIe siècle." *Studi Francesi*, no. 67 (January–April):1–14.

Brief references to Rabelais' portrayal of folly, pernicious and evangelical in Book III, sinful in Book IV. Comparisons with Bosch's paintings (of the Ship of Fools, but also of the Deadly Sins and of the Garden of Earthly Delights.)

3.   BERLOIZ, MARC. *Rabelais restitué. I. Pantagruel.* Paris: Didier Erudition, 609 pp.

Deplores the absence of a truly faithful and complete text of Rabelais' works; notes that aside from Claude Gaignebet's facsimile edition of *Gargantua* (1542), all the other available editions, including that of Lefranc and his disciples, have taken unwarranted liberties, be it only by attempting to improve upon Rabelais' punctuation. Argues that in their notes the various authors of critical editions are merely content to repeat Lefranc's opinions. Finds particularly inadequate the editors' reluctance to face squarely the prob-. lems raised by the erotic nature of much of the text. Casts a fresh eye on Rabelais' first book, using for his "lecture commentée" the 1542 edition (and occasionally the edition of 1532), comments upon the difference between the two editions, and offers a running commentary which questions at every turn the accepted opinions of Rabelais scholars (that is, in essence, the opinions of Lefranc). Is led by his philological considerations to propose new interpretations, especially of passages given up as meaningless by other critics.

4   BERRONG, RICHARD M[ICHAEL]. "From *Pantagruel* to *Gargantua*: Developing a Definition of Narrative Prose Fiction." *Degré Second* (July):39–60.

Stresses the differences between Rabelais' first two novels, seen more often by critics as similar even if unequal in artistic merit and philosophical depth. Notes Rabelais' insistence upon the veracity of *Pantagruel*, and his indifference to the truth of the story in the second novel, where he repeatedly casts doubt on the narrator's credibility, not only in the famous prologue but also in such episodes as Gargantua's birth through his mother's left ear or the discussion on color symbolism. Rejects as invalid the recent attempts to see in this emphasis on the uncertainties of the narrative a warning against confusing reality and literature, on the grounds that in Rabelais' day, if not in ours, no such dangers were threatening the reader, since literature had not yet laid claim to being a faithful representation of reality. Admits the plausibility of the "biographical" explanation, according to which Rabelais insists on the doubtful veracity of the text in the hope of shielding *Gargantua* from the censure to which *Pantagruel* had fallen victim at the hands of the Faculty of Theology, by discouraging potentially hostile readers from taking the text seriously. But argues that if *Gargantua* ceases to lay claim to veracity, it is chiefly because Rabelais wishes to establish his second novel as belonging to the genre of serious prose fiction rather than historiography, and as offering the reader the inspiration to recognize and confront the issues of the present rather than an accurate representation of the past.

5 ———. "The Significance of Rabelaisian Echoes in the *Cinquième Livre*."
*Studi Francesi*, no. 68 (May–August):299–308.

Seeks to shed light on the question of the authenticity of Book V by
examining the sixty-one borrowings from the other four books. Divides them
into five categories: classical references, references to French medieval literature, popular sixteenth-century expressions, possible expressions, and geographical references. Lists in an appendix the fifteen echoes found in the
prologue and the fifty-one scattered throughout the narrative. Notes that in the
narrative only one borrowing is complex and faithful enough to presuppose
that its author had actually copied it out from one of the earlier books. In the
case of the prologue, finds the situation to be different: "Of the fifteen possible 'echos,' at least four...are, by their content and complexity, without question direct quotations from the *Tiers Livre* (1546) and partial *Quart Livre*
Prologues" (p. 302). (By contrast, the "echos" in the narrative suggest passages in all four of the previous novels.) Concludes, as others had before him,
that the prologue, or at least its second part, is not by Rabelais, but that this
cannot be extended to the book as a whole. "The 'echos' in the *Cinquième
Livre* of the four assuredly authentic novels are not, for the most part (except
in the prologue), necessarily quotations from the earlier works, and so cannot
(again, with the exception of the prologue), be used to refute the *Cinquième
Livre*'s authenticity" (p. 303).

6 BERRY, ALICE FIOLA. *Rabelais: Homo Logos*. North Carolina Studies in
the Romance Languages and Literatures, no. 208. Chapel Hill: University of
North Carolina Press, 130 pp.

Studies Rabelais' ambivalent attitude to language, both in itself and as
the tool of the writer of fiction. Sees Rabelaisian language as fundamentally
"freed from the burden of signification and communication" (p. 15) and used
"as verbal creation for its own sake" (p. 16). Views certain key episodes of the
first four books (the encounters with Panurge and the Écolier limousin, the
frozen words), as a meditation on the problems of language in a Platonic context. Revised version of a doctoral dissertation. See also 1973.1.

7 BUSHELL, SCOTT. "Rabelais and Christian Initiation: Allegorical and
Typological Motifs in the Works of Rabelais." Ph.D. dissertation, University
of North Carolina, Chapel Hill, 191 pp.

Analyzes Rabelais' biblical allusions in the light of the major traditions
of exegesis, with which supposes Rabelais to have been familiar. The number
of Rabelaisian images having a "mystagogic significance" and the initiatory
aspect of the final episode of Book V leads the author to claim that Christian
initiation was of fundamental importance "in the Rabelaisian process of composition." Common allegorical images (the ship, the sea, the whale, the vineyard), as well as specifically biblical images of deliverance (the Flood, the

1979

crossing of the Red Sea) are seen to represent "the encounter with evil and subsequent transcendence of it." The Dive Bouteille represents the themes of spiritual illumination and the acquisition of ultimate wisdom, "intricately interwoven around the symbolic enactment of the sacrament of baptism and the Eucharist." Concludes by proposing a new interpretation of the prologue to *Gargantua*. Believes that the apparent contradiction in Rabelais' remarks on allegory disappears if one keeps in mind the distinction between "the allegory and typology peculiar to biblical exegesis" and "secular or poetic" allegory. When Rabelais both proclaims and denies that his work has an allegorical significance, he means that it is allegorical in the exegetic, and not merely the poetic sense of the word. See *Dissertation Abstracts International* 40, (1980):4619–A.

8   CAVE, TERENCE. *The Cornucopian Text: Problems of Writing in the French Renaissance*. Oxford: Clarendon Press, 386 pp.

Stresses the essential ambiguity of the prologue to *Gargantua*: "Its plurality...is always in excess of any gloss, any analytical discourse which may be added to it" (p. 100). In the context of a discussion of *copia* as a fundamental rhetorical device used for expanding discourse in Renaissance writing, studies in part 2, chapt. 2 (pp. 183–222), a long series of parallel episodes involving the figure of cornucopia: Gargantua's *braguette*, the chapters treating the theme of generation in *Pantagruel*, the appearance of Panurge without a codpiece in the *Tiers Livre*, the story of Couillatris in Book IV. Discusses the "cornucopian movement" of the Rabelaisian text, its methods of lexical productivity, its "duplicity" (p. 192), its equivocations, fragmentations and ruptures, the ways in which this "self-consciously fallen and deviant text" (p. 222) measures its distance from an ideal text untouched by the "scandal of language." Shows how various episodes of Book IV reflect thematically the problems of language and narrative.

9   CAZAURAN, N[ICOLE]. "Comparaisons et sagesse dans *Le Tiers Livre*: Rabelais et Plutarque." *L'Information Littéraire*, no. 1 (January–February):7–10.

Shows that in Rabelais even simple, everyday images may have literary antecedents. In chapt. 13 of the *Tiers Livre*, concerning prophetic dreams, Rabelais compares the soul leaving the body during sleep to regain its original abode in Heaven to nurses free to seek their amusement where they will while the babies placed in their charge are sound asleep. Notes that a comparison which seems to have been drawn from daily experience is in fact drawn from Plutarch's *Moralia*. Notes later in the text a similar Plutarchian reminiscence in the comparison between the light of the sun as refracted by the moon, and the soul's somewhat dimmed vision of the future as experienced in dreams. Shows that the images do not have the same tone or significance in Rabelais, but are subtly transformed to suit his particular purpose. These comparisons, as well as allusions to the Protean legend are made to serve Pantagruel's conception of the soul, and illustrate the tension between the divine origin of the soul and its proximity to the body during life on earth.

10  CHOLAKIAN, ROUBEN C. "Narrative Structure in Rabelais and the Question of the Authenticity of the *Cinquième Livre.*" *French Studies* 33 (January):1–11.

Compares Marguerite de Navarre's use of the frame in the *Heptaméron* with Rabelais' use of the same device in the *Tiers* and *Quart Livres.* "Like Marguerite's, Rabelais's characters are commentators and storytellers" (p. 2), and both authors establish a clear relationship between the personality of the narrators and the kind of stories they are made to tell. Studies Rabelais' use of characters as *raconteurs* in connection with Frère Jean, Panurge, and Pantagruel, and finds that it "parallels the narrative structure of the frame as it appears in the novella collections" (p. 5) of his time, though with greater "imaginative energy" than elsewhere. Suggests that the device may also have suited Rabelais' didactic aims, providing "a smoke-screen for the author against his potential critics" (p. 9), at a time when it had become particularly dangerous to express one's sympathies with the reform movement. Notes that the number of episodes not told by Alcofribas Nasier or Rabelais himself but by some of his actors-narrators increases significantly in Books III and IV, whereas in the *Cinquième Livre* this device disappears almost completely. Sees in this disappearance a sign of "the inauthenticity of the final book" (p. 8).

11  CLARK, CAROLE. "'The Onely-Languag'd-Men of all the World': Rabelais and the Art of the Mountebank." *Modern Language Review* 74, no. 3 (July):538–52.

Examines the "possible connexion...between Rabelais' rhetoric and the oral art of the mountebank" (p. 538) previously noted by Plattard and Lebègue in the prologues, and expounded here to the works as a whole. From contemporary descriptions and imitations by literary artists, describes the typical format of the charlatan's speech, its *topoi* and structure, as well as "what makes up the *elocutio* of mountebank rhetoric" (p. 542). Both Rabelais and the mountebank probably blended seriousness and playfulness, truth and illusion, sincerity and deception into a similarly ambiguous whole.

12  DASSONVILLE, MICHEL. "Sortilèges de Rabelais." In *Textes et Intertextes: Études sur le XVIe siècle pour Alfred Glauser.* Edited by Floyd Gray and Marcel Tetel. Paris: A. G. Nizet, pp. 69–77.

Suggests that the spirit of childhood and a readiness for every eventuality prepares one better than erudition to meet the challenges of Rabelais' world. Cites a series of instances of incoherence in Rabelais' novels and argues that "dans cet espace figuratif, les objets comme les personnages changent d'usage, de dimensions, et les relations qu'ils entretiennent entre eux

1979

ou avec les personnages varient en fonction des besoins du récit" (p. 71). Notes that many fantastic episodes seem to refer to a religious context predating Christianity, "une religion néolithique attestée en bien des lieux de la Gaule où vit encore le souvenir de Gargan et de sa femme Gallemelle" (p. 76), and calls for their reinterpretation in the light of myth, folklore, and anthropology. Claims that Rabelaisian space is above all "un espace psychologique" (p. 72), that as such it is freed from the constraints of time and logic, and that it is perhaps this freedom which accounts for the elation felt by readers when they first come into contact with Rabelais' magical world.

13    DE ROCHER, GREGORY [DAVID]. "Rabelais, le *Tiers Livre*, Prologue: The Homomorphic u/v." *Romance Notes* 20, no. 1 (Fall):114–15.
     Recalls that in chapt. 22 of the *Tiers Livre*, "Son asne" in the 1546 edition became "Son ame" in subsequent ones. Attracts attention to another such possible "play on letters" in the prologue, in which *pour cheureter* may mean either "for having upset" or "for having acted as a busy-body," if *cheureter* stands for *chevreter*, from which it could not be distinguished in a printed sixteenth-century text.

14    DESLEX, MARCELLA GIACOMELLI. "Il suffisso [go] nell'opera di Rabelais." *Studi di Letteratura francese* 5:40–54.
     Does the phonic group [go] (as in "bigots," "cagots," and so on) have a special meaning? Notes its unusual accumulation in the inscription on the portal of Thélème and in the "Ile sonnante" episode of Book V. Points out that many of the words containing the phoneme are of Germanic origin. Believes that in Rabelais the phoneme loses its habitually arbitrary value and becomes a symbol. Sees in the syllable "una ricchissima simbologia connotativa e, quasi, una parola chiave" (p. 54). Has a negative connotation, since it is very often associated with hypocrisy, but a positive value as well: "Il [go] dissacrante e deridente diventa anche simbolo di buonumore" (p. 53) in the word *gaudir* and its derivatives.

15    GAIGNEBET, CLAUDE. "*Histoire des Gorgias*: Les mondes intérieurs renversés de Rabelais." In *L'Image du monde renversé et ses représentations littéraires et para-littéraires, de la fin du XVIe siècle au milieu du XVIIe: Colloque international, Tours, 17–19 Novembre 1977*, edited by Jean Lafond and Augustin Redondo. Paris: Librairie philosophique J. Vrin, pp. 49–53.
     Presents itself as a study of the "topologie mystique et initiatique" of three key episodes: chapt. 38 of *Gargantua* wherein six pilgrims are eaten "en salade" by the giant, Alcofribas' investigation of the world in Pantagruel's throat, and Epistémon's descent into Hell. In all three texts, the author sees veiled allusions to Jonah, and claims that only the framework of Freemasonry can account for the symbolic allusions in these texts. All three form chapters in the *Histoire des Gorgias* which Rabelais promises his reader at the end of

*Pantagruel*, and which is, for the author, the history of men's souls and their peregrinations.

16  HAUSMANN, FRANK-RUTGER. *François Rabelais*. Stuttgart: Metzler, 156 pp.

Notes the lack of general studies on Rabelais in German. Intends to provide a general introduction to Rabelais and his work, but also to stress the problems raised by Rabelais' novels, and to take into account the most important results of current research on the author. In the new "Querelle des anciens et des modernes" dividing Rabelais' critics, sides for the most part with those scholars who seek to explain his work in the historic context of the Renaissance, but combines this historicist perspective with close attention to the narrative and comic values inherent in Rabelais' text. Sees in Rabelais a conservative thinker, rather than the destroyer portrayed by such critics of Marxist persuasion as Lefebvre and Jean Paris. Situates Rabelais in his time, provides a rapid overview of Rabelais criticism, brings out the unity of Rabelais' "Pentalogie," comments on the prologues, on the question of the authenticity of Book V, and on the relationship between Rabelais' novels and the "Chroniques gargantuines." Raises the question of sources and influences, discusses Rabelais' attitude towards Christianity, his political ideas, and briefly analyzes such aspects of his art as satire, parody, the carnivalesque spirit, imagination, and word-play. Extensive bibliography.

17  LA CHARITÉ, RAYMOND C. "Reflexion-Divertissement et Intertextualité: Rabelais et l'écolier limousin." In *Textes et Intertextes: Études sur le XVIe siècle pour Alfred Glauser*. Edited by Floyd Gray and Marcel Tetel. Paris: A. G. Nizet, pp. 93–103.

Even as playful a work as *Pantagruel* invites the reader's reflection, but keeps him in the dark as to where that reflection ought to lead: "le texte invite et mystifie simultanément tout commentaire" (p. 95). What could be the meaning, for instance, of the rather savage punishment meted out on the Écolier Limousin, seemingly so out of proportion with his "crime"? Concedes that Rabelais may have thought it a fitting punishment for the ignorant and lazy student's misuse of the human mind and high treason against language. But argues that from an intertextual perspective the episode may have been meant to illustrate a very different, in fact an altogether opposite message. As had previously been pointed out, the discourse of the Écolier Limousin was most probably suggested to Rabelais by a few lines in Geoffroy Tory's *Champ fleuri*. In that passage, Tory condemns the "escumeurs de Latin" in the name of an ideal of blandly refined expression which Rabelais most obviously did not share. Argues that when Rabelais puts in the mouth of the Écolier Limousin the words of which Tory so censoriously disapproves, and when he further embroiders upon them in a lengthy speech, he may be mischievously satisfying his taste for verbal eccentricity. By thus giving to the text a very different meaning from the one Tory intended, he may well be playing here with the author as he plays with his reader, in the confines of a constantly mystifying narrative which invites an endless variety of divergent readings.

18  LAZARD, MADELEINE. *Rabelais et la Renaissance*. Collection "Que saisje?" Paris: Presses Universitaires de France, 127 pp.

Presents Rabelais' work as a faithful reflection of the conflicting tendencies which characterize the intellectual, scientific, and spiritual climate of the Renaissance. Believes that the diversity of his personal experience, the wide range of his intellectual curiosity, and his commitment to the cause of humanism make Rabelais the most representative writer of the first phase of the Renaissance in France. Underscores the Renaissance character of his main themes: the glorification of the present, the praise of learning, a keen sense of man's essential dignity, an abiding love of life in all its forms, and the quest for a new moral philosophy set within the framework of Christian thought. Sees this new moral philosophy as first expressed in the myth of Thélème as a somewhat unorthodox trust in human nature, then in a significantly different (though not necessarily contradictory) form, as a synthesis of ancient Stoicism and Christian faith in the last two books. Suggests a relationship between Rabelaisian thought and Rabelaisian laughter: "C'est dans le rire qu'il faut saisir la pensée de l'auteur" (p. 72). Summarizes Rabelais' views on education, insists on aspects of his treatment of women which suggest that Rabelais is the very opposite of a misogynist, finds in him "un défenseur sincère de l'union conjugale" and of marriage founded on love (p. 90). Notes that in political matters Rabelais has not sought, as have many humanists around him, to propose an ideal system in an imaginary state and that he accepts the *status quo*. Points out that the ideal monarch embodied in Grandgousier owes much to Erasmus, admits that Rabelais' political ideas may have sometimes been opportunistic, but claims that they conform in the main to the general orientation of his thought. In matters of religion, sees Rabelais as "un défenseur de la cause évangélique," and notes his attempt to reconcile his optimistic belief in the goodness of human nature and his undeniable belief in God within the framework of Christian humanism. Concludes by underscoring in Rabelais' art a happy mixture of novelty and tradition, a successful synthesis of popular culture and humanistic aspirations.

19  LOSSE, DEBORAH N. "Frivolous Charm and Serious Bagatelle: Lyrical and Burlesque Paradox in the Works of François Rabelais." *Sixteenth Century Journal* 10, no. 3 (Fall):61–68.

Discusses the various eulogies in Books III and IV (Debtors, Pantagruélion, Gaster, Decretals) in terms of Marcel Tetel's distinction between lyrical (or poetic) and burlesque (or satirical) paradox. Singles out for close analysis Homenaz's praise of the Decretals in Book IV.

20 MORRISON, IAN R. "Peace and War in *Gargantua*: A Question of Didacticism." *Romanic Review* 70, no. 3 (May):219–33.

Argues that the overtly didactic passages on peace and war in *Gargantua* are not as commonplace or as utopian as is sometimes thought, and that they coexist with a number of comic passages in a harmonious relationship which brings out their underlying seriousness. Defines the didactic beliefs of such "exemplary characters" as Grandgousier and Gargantua himself, and of such "near associates" as Ulrich Gallet; studies them in practice; and contrasts them with the attitudes and activities of Frère Jean. Although finds them to be at odds with the attitudes of the giants, argues that they should not be "dismissed as a joke," for they provide a welcome variety of tone, and help to underplay the didacticism of the views represented by the giants. By pointing out that the kind of belligerence embodied in Frère Jean is sometimes necessary to restore order, the passages dealing with the friar acknowledge certain limitations to what would have been an excessively optimistic ideology, and provide the work with an originality absent from the writings of Erasmus and like-minded humanists. Concludes by suggesting that the thematically related episodes, whether serious or comic, should be considered together, since "the dissociation of the serious and the comic distorts the work by masking the light-hearted and self-critical nature of the didacticism" (p. 233).

21 NORTON, GLYN P. "Rabelais and the Epic of Palpability: *Enargeia* and History (*Cinquiesme Livre*, 38–40)." *Symposium* 33, no. 2:171–85.

Offers a new interpretation of the episode of the temple mosaics in the light of the Erasmian notion of *enargeia* as applicable to both art and rhetoric, icon and word. Notes that the episode does not involve, as has been claimed, a suspension of narrative progression in favor of description, since the described mosaics themselves tell a story—"la bataille que Bacchus gagna contre les Indians"—although they tell it without text. Finds it "fundamental to the meaning of the temple mosaics that they represent pictured sounds" (p. 181), rendered "palpable," that is "visible" to the reader through verbal opulence. Reads the episode as an illustration of a fundamental rhetorical problem: "how narrative, constructed by the compounded sequence of word falling upon word, can bring history to light, transforming it into the synchronic medium of picture" (p. 184). See 1984.28.

22 REA, JOANNE EWING. "Rabelais and Joyce: A Study in Verbal Humor." Ph.D. dissertation, University of Kentucky, 418 pp.

In both authors, notes a similar urge to explore the full range of their respective languages, a similar tendency to "reconstruct language forms," a similar "inclination towards polyglottism." Studies their use of puns as unifying contextual and thematic elements, the inventiveness of their word games,

1979

the mixture of innocence and obscenity, the disjunction between sound and meaning, the preoccupation with etymology. Views the "accretion of the denotative and the connotative powers of language" as a primary function of their linguistic humor. See *Dissertation Abstracts International* 41, no.2 (August 1980):664–A.

23    SCREECH, M[ICHAEL] A[NDREW]. *Rabelais*. Ithaca, N.Y.: Cornell University Press; London: Duckworth, 494 pp.

A synthesis, for a wider public, of the author's extensive work on the writer. Leaving technicalities, footnotes, and scholarly controversy aside, offers a contextual study of the major episodes of Rabelais' four authenticated chronicles against a background of humanistic comedy and Christian thought. Studies the works in the order in which they were published, and the episodes, for the most part, in the order in which they appear in the particular chronicle under study. Argues that the work of a comic writer, more than any other, requires to be understood in its historical, intellectual, and aesthetic context. In the first two chapters, sketches the development of humanistic comedy (with emphasis on Lucian and Erasmus), and discusses Rabelais' life before *Pantagruel* (favors 1483 as Rabelais' date of birth). Studies *Pantagruel* primarily as a humanistic book, a comic Utopia characterized by a gamut of laughters ranging from scriptural to scatological. Discusses *Gargantua* in relation to *Pantagruel* as well as in itself; underscores in the prologue Rabelais' concern with Erasmian syncretism, and finds it to have "a striking unity of tone and style" (p. 127); discusses it in relation to the Affaire des Placards of October 1534, but also with the "far worse events of January 1535," considered as marking "the real climax" (p. 203) of the persecution against the Evangelicals. Underscores the learned construction of the *Tiers Livre* and views the book as a watershed in literature: "Nothing at once so complex, so learned and so comic had ever been written in the French language" (p. 291) or in any other. Studies separately the two versions of the *Quart Livre*; in the 1552 version emphasizes the prologue, the storm episode, the death of Pan, Quaresmeprenant, the "linguistic comedy and linguistic wisdom" of chapt. 37 on proper names of persons and places. Considers Rabelais' other writings in their chronological place, but deliberately omits any discussion of the *Cinquiesme Livre*, pending publication of an edition of the text.

24    SPILLEBOUT, GABRIEL. "Le *Tiers Livre* et le problème de la connaissance." *BAARD* 3, no. 8:347–51.

In connection with Panurge's "Dois-je me marier?" points out the absurdity—which he believes Rabelais must have had in mind—of raising the question in universal terms and seeking to answer it on the level of the individual: "une question mal posée n'admet aucune réponse" (p. 348). Believes that in Gargantua's attitude towards Trouillogan Rabelais expresses his disdain of any philosophy unwilling to face the problems of everyday life. Sees in the violence of Panurge's reaction against the skepticism of Her Trippa yet another sign of Rabelais' indignation at what he must have taken to be a crime against human intelligence. Reads the *Tiers Livre* as a plea in favor of man, against those who would seek to question his dignity.

25 TETEL, MARCEL. "Genèse d'une œuvre: Le premier chapitre de *Pantagruel.*" *Stanford French Review* 3, no. 1 (Spring):41–52.

Studies the extent to which the first chapter prefigures the themes, the intertextual approach, and the attitude towards writing and towards reality that will inform the entire narrative. Suggests that the *mesles* to which Rabelais refers may be an Italianism (formed on *mela*=apples, and thus reinforcing the Edenic associations of the text), proposes a new etymology for the giant Hurtaly, argues that the chapter owes more than has been acknowledged to Aesop, and believes that the allusion to Lucian's *Icaromemenippus* is meant to shed light not only on *Pantagruel* but on Rabelais' entire fictional *œuvre*.

26 TUTTLE, HEATH. "Clues to Vocabularic Structure: Comparative Suffixal Productivity in the Five Books of Rabelais." *Lingua e Stile* 14, no. 1 (March):151–63.

Summarizes 1976.41.

27 VASSAL, PIERRE, and TRIKKI, A. "Langage des antipodes ou hispano-moresque? Un poème andalou au chapitre IX du *Pantagruel.*" *BAARD* 3, no. 8:352–54.

Believe Panurge's second answer in a foreign language to be an example of a Hispano-Moresque poem known as *muwashshah*. Provide a translation.

28 WALLACE, NATHANIEL OWEN. "John Skelton, *Ein Kurtzweilig lesen von dyl Ulenspiegel*, the *Epistolae Obscurorum Virorum*, and François Rabelais: An Inquiry into the Literary History and Historical Context of Renaissance Satire." Ph.D. dissertation, Rutgers, The State University of New Jersey, New Brunswick, 285 pp.

Examines "broad and basic questions of Renaissance satire" through a comparative study of the four texts alluded to in the title. In the second chapter, presents Panurge as a continuation of the German prototype of the picaresque hero embodied in Eulenspiegel, and as an antecedent of the "Elizabethan satyr/satyrist." Finds in Rabelais an abundance of images of violence related to the genre. Views Rabelais as "summing up the satiric techniques and cultural developments of the period." See *Dissertation Abstracts International* 40 (April 1980):5435A.

1980

29 WEINBERG, FLORENCE [MAY]. "Chess as a Literary Idea in Colonna's *Hypnerotomachia* and in Rabelais' *Cinquiesme Livre.*" *Romanic Review* 70:321–35.

Compares the chess ballets in Colonna and Rabelais with previous literary treatments of the theme. Seeks to find the meaning of chess in the ballet witnessed by Poliphile in the realm of Queen Eleutherillida, and by the Pantagruelists during their visit to the kingdom of Entelechie, "by a close scrutiny of the context in which the incidents occur" (p. 325n). Claims that in Colonna and Rabelais the symbolism is the same: the realm of both queens symbolizes the material world, and chess represents the process of spiritualization whereby the material world is transcended.

## 1980

1 ANTONIOLI, ROLAND. "Le Motif de l'avalage dans les *Chronicques Gargantuines.*" In *Etudes seiziémistes offertes à M. le Pr V.-L. Saulnier.* Geneva: Librairie Droz, pp. 77–85.

Studies the motif of the giant's mouth in the *Gargantuan Chronicles* as a parody of the Celtic and Arthurian theme of the other world representing a form of Christian hell. Contrasts it with the world in the giant's mouth in chapt. 33 of *Pantagruel*, with its resemblance to our own world and its as yet uncharted regions.

2 BARAZ, MICHAEL. "Rabelais et l'Utopie." *Études Rabelaisiennes* 15:1–29.

Seeks to highlight Rabelais' originality by comparing his utopian thought with those of Plato and of Thomas More. Studies the conception of man at the basis of these three utopian visions as the best way to bring out the structure of each utopian universe. Finds Plato's view pessimistic (since the bestial far outweighs the divine, except in those whom Plato calls "philosophers"), but coherent and "unitaire" (p. 4). Not so with More, for whom man is in turn capable of the moral perfection expected of the inhabitants of communistic Utopia, and hopelessly corrupted by original sin; hence the essentially totalitarian aspect of his Utopia, which leaves no place for the free development of the individual. Takes into account the extent to which Rabelais' utopia resembles the egalitarian Utopia of More, and the ways (less numerous, but more significant) in which it resembles the aristocratic utopia of Plato. But claims that Rabelais remains essentially original, by the place of popular culture in his universe, the rehabilitation of manual labor, the importance of technical innovations. Sees his utopia as based on the intuition of the One, considered as a particularly daring form of Evangelism, where there is no place for any form of external cult. Finds it significant that the Fountain of the Three Graces, rather than a church, should occupy the center of Thélème.

Sees in it a polyvalent symbol: an ideal of sensual beauty, of joy, and a symbol of love viewed as a principle of fecundity in nature. Points out that Rabelais' utopia is not isolated from reality, and claims that Rabelais purposely blurs the distinction between the two, "pour exprimer sa méfiance à l'égard de la perfection en vase clos et pour suggérer que la vraie perfection ne saurait être conçue comme isolée à l'égard de la réalité imparfaite de l'humanité qui souffre" (p. 20). Nor is this utopia totally out of time; it is not a refuge from the imperfection of reality, but a starting point from which to face reality. Most importantly, it is a utopia that favors, as most do not, the spiritual development of the individual. In sum, "une utopie réaliste jusqu'à un certain point, pour paradoxal que cela paraisse; la plus réaliste peut-être que nous connaissions" (p. 28).

3 BECK, WILLIAM J. "Additional insight into Rabelais' King Picrochole." *Neophilologus* 64, no. 1 (January):42–47.

In Xenophon's account of his life, King Cyrus asks his soldiers to follow him into battle for the love of themselves. Picrochole asks them to do it for the love of him ("qui me ayme, si me suyve!"). Adds Xenophon's *Cyropaedia* to the list of possible sources of the Picrocholine War episode in *Gargantua*.

4 BELLENGER, YVONNE. "Lecture critique tardive de la traduction française de *L'Oeuvre de François Rabelais et la culture populaire au Moyen Age et sous la Renaissance* de Mikhaïl Bakhtine." *Berenice* 1, no. 1 (November):30–42.

On the whole, a negative assessment. Finds the text badly written and/or translated, and circular in its methodology: "pour lire correctement Rabelais, il faut être initié à la culture populaire, mais pour connaître cette culture, il faut d'abord lire Rabelais" (p. 33). Also criticizes the work for being dogmatic, contradictory, and devoid of humor. In a postscript, alludes to the author's political situation which may explain some of the book's shortcomings, most specifically the unduly exaggerated distinction between the official and the popular forms of Renaissance culture.

5 BENSON, EDWARD. "'Jamais vostre femme ne sera ribaulde, si la prenez issue de gens de bien': Love and War in the *Tiers Livre*." *Études Rabelaisiennes* 15:55–75.

Studies the question of marriage in the *Tiers Livre* from the point of view of social history, as a social problem examined from contemporary perspectives. On war as on marriage, "the variety of fundamental changes occurring in France at the end of the first 'long' sixteenth century accounts for the extraordinary richness of Rabelais' text" (p. 74).

1980

6 BERLIOZ, JEAN-PAUL. "Aspects populaires des *Chroniques Gargantuines*." *Réforme, Humanisme, Renaissance* 11 (June):63–74.

Insists upon the difficulty of giving an adequate definition of the term "popular" as applied to such texts as the *Chroniques Gargantuines*. Points out that the latter remained "popular," in the sense of being widely read long after the publication of Rabelais' novels. Suggests that if most popular chronicles are anonymous, it is not because their authors were ashamed of being associated with them, but because they did not wish to interpose their personality between the texts and their readers. Believes that their lack of "literary" qualities is to be explained by the fact that each was a mere canvas, meant to be read aloud and "fleshed out" in the process. Points out that Rabelais himself did not share the disdain that most Rabelaisian scholars pour upon the *Chroniques Gargantuines*, but does not believe—as does Mireille Huchon (see 1981.17)—that he had anything to do with their composition.

7 BERRONG, RICHARD [MICHAEL]. "The *Cinquième Livre* and 'La Querelle de la *Deffence*.'" *Études Rabelaisiennes* 15:145–59.

Comments upon the author's promise, in the prologue to the *Cinquième Livre*, to rise to the defense of the French language. Argues that in so doing, the narrator sides with the opponents of the Pléiade in the quarrel concerning the relative merits of French and Latin (to the extent that Du Bellay's position is in fact, as the Quintil Horatian would have it, an "offence et dénigration"). Since the quarrel is supposed to have come to an end in 1552, suggests that the prologue was not written later than in the first two months of 1553, and thus before Rabelais' death—but probably not by him. The passage also leads the author to suggest a new, satirical interpretation of the Dive Bouteille episode, by reading the pages on the "fureur poëtique" with which all are seized as "a parody of Ronsard, de Tyard, and their fellow members of the Pléiade" (p. 155).

8 BERRY, ALICE FIOLA. "The Mix, the Mask and the Medical Farce: A Study of the Prologues to Rabelais' *Quart Livre*." *Romanic Review* 71:10–27.

Studies the relationships between the three prefaces to the *Quart Livre*: the ultimately discarded prologue of 1548, the prologue of 1552, as well as the letter to Odet de Chastillon. By creating the fiction of an ambassador come to plead before the writer on behalf of his readers, and misquoting the "do, dico, addico" of the Roman magistrate into "Vous donnez, vous dictes, vous adjugez," Rabelais stands on its head the traditional relationship between the writer and his audience, and implicates the reader in the writing of the book. Ascribes this novelty to the new-found awareness of literature as a form of written rather than oral communication, and of the reader's newly-acquired control over the written text and, through his text, over the writer himself. "It is the reader's power over the text and his participation in the creation of its meaning, that Rabelais means to express when he calls him (us) 'writer' of the fable of the bluejays and the magpies" (p. 13). The three prefatory texts were written by Rabelais to defend himself from potentially malicious readers by weakening the writer's authority. But this reversal of traditional roles has the serious drawback of undermining the "medical argument" based on the Platonic and Aristotelian concept of logotherapy through catharsis, by which Rabelais seeks to justify his enterprise and disarm his critics. Hence, in the 1552 prefatory texts, his return to a more traditional position. The later texts attempt "to separate and clarify the relationships which he had...confounded in 1548" (p. 11), but these attempts remain unconvincing, since the relationships as drawn in 1548 expressed, in their very confusion, the real problems and paradoxes inherent in the acts of reading and writing.

9   BICHON, JEAN. "L'enracinement du *Pantagruel* dans les genres médié-vaux." In *Études seiziémistes offertes à M. le Pr V.-L. Saulnier*. Geneva: Librairie Droz, pp. 87–89.

    Detects in the prologue to *Pantagruel* the influence of three medieval genres: the mountebank's patter, the monk's sermon, and the merry mono-logue. Since the prologue is probably the earliest text written by Rabelais, suggests that it sets the tone for the entire series of novels.

10   BILLACOIS, FRANÇOIS. "Thélème dans l'espace et en son temps." *Études Rabelaisiennes* 15:97–115.

    For the medieval mind, time was the reassuring mirror of eternity, whereas space represented danger and temptation. From the seventeenth cen-tury onwards, the relationship is reversed: space can be dominated, whereas time is proof of man's ultimate powerlessness. Sees the Renaissance as the point at which this reversal occurred, and seeks to document this fundamental change by an analysis of the Thélème episode. In the description of the archi-tecture, sees evidence of sensibility to color, shape, temperature, insertion in a particular landscape: the abbey is not merely a theoretical blueprint; it is meant to house people. Sees the inside as compartmentalized in accordance with the needs of its inhabitants: providing privacy, and the possibility to sat-isfy one's intellectual and esthetic curiosity. Notes that the plan of the abbey is also conceived in relation to the world beyond its walls, so that the Thelemites (*homo sapiens*) are seen in relation to the immediately contiguous world of artisans (*homo faber*) as well as the remote world of the American Cannibals (*homo ferus*). "Thélème, l'abbaye sans cloître, est à la fois le centre du monde, le lieu d'où comprendre le monde, et la retraite qui protège du monde" (p. 112). Suggests an unexpected *rapprochement* with the "Jésuitières" founded by Ignatius of Loyola at that very time: "Même rejet de la récitation des Heures et des contraintes de l'office divin; même refus des postulants venus d'un ordre monastique; même recrutement élitaire, et si pos-sible noble et fortuné; même importance vouée à la sociabilité et à l'art de conférer" (p. 114). Sees in Rabelais' "Fay ce que voudras" and the Jesuitic

1980

"obéissance de conspiration et d'amitié fraternelle" two related early modern forms of the categorical imperative.

11    CÉARD, JEAN. "L'Histoire écoutée aux portes de la légende: Rabelais, les fables de Turpin et les exemples de saint Nicholas." In *Études seiziémistes offertes à M. le Pr V.-L. Saulnier*. Geneva: Librairie Droz, pp. 91–109.
        In the 1542 edition of *Pantagruel*, having just witnessed Loup Garou's defeat at the hands of Pantagruel before proceeding with the miraculous cure of Epistemon, Panurge regales his companions with "fables" from Turpin's *Chronicles* and examples of Saint Nicholas' ability to perform miracles. Believes that the reference to these kinds of narrative has a specific purpose, and that both are connected with the adventures narrated at that point in the novel. Notes the similarity between Loup Garou's defeat from a blow to the stomach, and Roland's victory over the giant Ferracutus who, according to Turpin's *Historia Karoli Magni et Rhotolandi*, later adapted by Boiardo in his *Orlando Innamorato*, was immune to all bodily harm "nisi per umbilicum." Also notes that among the miracles attributed to Saint Nicholas is the resurrection of two donkeys whose severed heads were sewn back to their body by the ministrations of the saint, just as Epistemon's head was rejoined to his body by the skillful ministrations of Panurge. Suggests that Rabelais was familiar with the debates surrounding Turpin's *Chronicles* and the hagiographical narratives of the *Légende dorée* as to their authenticity. Believes that by referring to the *Chronicles* and Saint Nicholas' miracles as "fables," Rabelais pokes fun at the outdated methods of a certain type of historiography, and that implicitly he equates such pseudo-historical texts with his own brand of fiction. "Ecrit en marge des *Chroniques*, dont il assure être la continuation, *Pantagruel* a notamment pour dessein de dénoncer la supercherie d'une historiographie encore trop répandue et dont les séductions dissimulent le danger" (pp. 108–09).

12    CHARPENTIER, FRANÇOISE. "La guerre des Andouilles, *Pantagruel IV*, 35–42." In *Études seiziémistes offertes à M. le Pr V.-L. Saulnier*. Geneva: Librairie Droz, pp. 119–39.
        Acknowledges that the Andouilles episode has received some attention as reflecting certain aspects of political reality, but notes that in spite of representing the longest narrative block in the *Quart Livre*, it has yet to be studied both in itself and in its relation to the rest of the book. Finds it to be intentionally inept as narrative, but of great interest as a reflection on the problems of language, and as a poetic fragment in which Rabelais has sought for once to establish a positive relation between words and things: "Dans notre épisode, Pantagruel veut accorder aux signes une vérité essentielle et une rationalité rassurante" (p. 125). Notes, on the other hand, that food and sexuality lose the positive value they have elsewhere in Rabelais, and now stand in disquieting relationship to sterility and death. The Andouilles' bisexuality, in

particular, is now seen as a menacing, diabolical shadow over Rabelais' earlier project to make of his work *un livre de vie*, a monument of *pierres vives*, rather than the ideal synthesis it represents elsewhere in humanistic thought.

13 CROQUETTE, BERNARD. "Panurge & Pacorus: Le nom qui va sans dire, le nom qui en dit trop." *34/44: Cahiers de recherche de S.T.D., Université Paris VII*, no. 7 (Fall):11–17.

Admits that joining Panurge and Pacorus—one of the characters in Corneille's *Suréna*—may seem odd since they have nothing in common, but finds it interesting to compare their treatment by reason of their very difference, in that the one is "motivé" and the other arbitrary. In the case of Panurge, focuses on chapt. 9, where the character introduces himself in a variety of languages. Notes that when Panurge finally speaks in a language that Pantagruel and his companions can understand, they recognize the code but are unable to bring their attention to bear on the message. The reader, on the other hand, does perceive the sense of the message even before Panurge turns to French, if only because he can look up the translation given in the footnotes. He knows that Panurge is reiterating the idea that linguistic communication is here both superfluous and out of place. Alongside the traditional readings of Panurge's name, proposes a number of other possibilities: Panurge, for instance, can be read as "I urgently need bread." Notes that Panurge and Pantagruel are as inextricably linked as the hunger and thirst inscribed in their names: "En somme, le roi des altérés rencontre ici le roi des affamés" (p. 13). When Panurge reveals his name, he also reveals his essential nature. Whereas "Panurge" both designates and signifies, "Pacorus" merely designates the character who happens to bear the name.

14 DELOFFRE, FRÉDÉRIC. "Rabelais et la Sorbonne en 1979." *Berenice* 1, no. 1 (November):43–52.

Attracts attention to two doctoral dissertations directed by Roger Lathuillère and defended "en Sorbonne" by Mireille Huchon and François Moreau (see 1981.17 and 1982.20–22). Finds their methodology all the more fruitful for being grounded in philology rather than in linguistics.

15 DEMERSON, GUY. "Les Calembours de Rabelais." *Berenice* 1, no. 1 (November):5–17.

Argues that puns in Rabelais, and word-play in general, are not marginal adornments that a fastidious reader can deplore and disregard as irrelevant to the meaning of the work. In the form of Freudian allusions, they function as mechanisms of release from sexual inhibition; in the form of proper nouns taken to have abusive connotations, they act as substitutes for personal revenge which would not be otherwise tolerated by society; when directed against social types rather than specific individuals, they can have the "revolutionary" function of destroying official values, a function Bakhtin ascribes exclusively to the grotesque realism of popular culture, but which here is also the task of the serious humanist deriding ignorance and superstition wherever he finds them. Rejects, however, Jean Paris' notion that puns are above all a weapon against oppressive social structures, by pointing out that Rabelais' use of word-play is rooted in the tradition of Aristotle (rediscovered by Erasmus in his *Apophtegmes*) and in that of the Grands Rhétoriqueurs, and most importantly that Rabelais' conception of language, as Foucault had noted, is grounded in the medieval belief that there is an essential connection between the word and the thing it represents. Thus when Rabelais plays with language, his aim is not to question its ability to signify, and thereby to shake the foundations of a bourgeois social order built on that very premise, but merely to deride our fumbling handling of an intrinsically noble tool, while at the same time revealing the mysterious poetic possibilities of word games. Covers much of the same ground as a paper read in Warsaw at a symposium on "Le comique verbal" and published in *Cahiers de Varsovie* (see 1981.13).

16   ———. "L'Utopie populaire de Cocagne et *Le Disciple de Pantagruel*." *Réforme, Humanisme, Renaissance* 11 (June):75–83.

Defines the myth, wonders about its utopian as well as its popular character, discusses it in connection with *Le Disciple de Pantagruel* (where it has purportedly lost its evocative power at the hands of a mediocre compiler). But notes that in an author of Rabelais' genius it is integrated into a complex thematic network and manages to suggest the inherent wisdom of popular mythology.

17   DE ROCHER, GREGORY. "The Fusion of Priapus and the Muses: Rabelaisian Metaphors in the Prologue to the *Quart Livre*." *Kentucky Romance Quarterly* 27, no. 4:413–20.

Reads the story of Couillatris in the prologue as intertwining the double theme of procreation and eloquence as represented in the mythic figure of Priapus and reinforced by the network of imagery developed throughout the episode. Sees in Priapus a metaphor of health and well-being as well as *facundia*, and thus considers him a symbol of Rabelaisian esthetics and philosophy, an embodiment of the Muses through his association with Mnemosyne, as well as a symbol of virility.

18   DONALDSON-EVANS, LANCE K. "Panurge *perplexus*: Ambiguity and Relativity in the *Tiers Livre*." *Études Rabelaisiennes* 15:77–96.

Notes recent efforts to reevaluate the character of Pantagruel in Book I, and to emphasize his mediocrity, his weakness, in contrast with the traditional view which held him to be a dignified spokesman of Evangelical humanism. This revisionist view has not significantly affected the Pantagruel of Book III, whom critics continue to see as a Stoic-Christian sage, and Panurge essentially as a fool. Systematic analysis of suggestions by Greene and Coleman to the effect that Panurge is less a fool and Pantagruel less wise than is commonly thought have lead the author to reevaluate both characters as they appear in Book III. Wishes to show "that the *Tiers Livre* is primarily a work of comedy, and to present *both* Panurge and Pantagruel as comic characters, whose attempts to seek knowledge are illuminated not by the superior wisdom of the latter, but by a sly and humorous relativity supplied by Rabelais" (p. 80). Points out that both have "demonic antecedents," and that Pantagruel's pedantry, his "faulty scholarship," his "glaring inconsistencies" and his "faith in the rightness of his own interpretations of highly ambiguous signs and utterances" (p. 84) make of him a comically fallible character.

19  DUPÈDE, JEAN. "La date de la mort de Rabelais?" *BHR* 42:657.
      Quotes a document dated August 1554, stating that "dominus Rabeles" died on January 9 of the previous year (old style), and thus confirming—"à trois mois près"—the eighteenth-century *épitaphier* to the effect that Rabelais died on April 9 of that year, at the age of seventy. "Dès lors Rabelais ne serait pas né en 1494, mais bien en 1484."

20  FRANÇON, MARCEL. "Rabelais et les Canibales." *Berenice* 1, no. 1 (November):55–57.
      Notes that Rabelais uses the term in *Pantagruel* to refer to the natives of Africa.

21  ———. "Sur les variantes des romans rabelaisiens." *Études Rabelaisiennes* 15:141–43.
      Notes the addition of references to "Brésil" (as a type of wood and as the country) in 1542 and afterwards. Finds in these references a further confirmation of his thesis that it was only in the 1540s that France began to be interested in America.

22  GAUNA, MAXWELL. "Fruitful Fields and Blessed Spirits, or Why the Thelemites Were Well Born." *Études Rabelaisiennes* 15:117–28.
      "The part played by Stoic ideas in the Rabelaisian conception of right living has, I feel, been understressed" (p. 124). In the wake of Screech's studies of the Stoic elements in Rabelais's thought, complements what Screech has written on the subject concerning the Thélème episode. Emphasizes the Stoic resonance of the Thelemites' motto, but notes that Rabelais is more pessimistic, since by restricting the population of Thélème to those who are "bien nez," he refers to "an innate condition not modifiable by human or by environmental agency" (p. 124). Discusses the meaning of "bien nez" and its Latin equivalent from Varro through Dante and Calvin to Montaigne. Defines it as "naturally virtuous" (p. 126), and thus "destined to gaze upon the face of their Maker" (p. 128).

1980

23 GIRAUD, YVES. "La Fortune dans l'œuvre de Rabelais." *Berenice* 1, no. 1 (November):17–25.

Lists all the references to the Goddess Fortuna (or Occasion) in the five books. Finds Rabelais to be relatively uninterested in the allegorical dimension of the topic. Comments on its relationship with predestination and nemesis. Underscores Rabelais' belief in the possibility for man to influence the course of his destiny, expressed most clearly in the storm-at-sea episode of Book IV. Acknowledges that Rabelais occasionally uses the image of Fortune, but not in its pagan meaning: "Presque rien ne demeure de l'antique divinité: le *fatum* auquel il croit est entièrement chrétien et catholique" (pp. 22–23).

24 GLAUSER, ALFRED. "La poétique du nombre chez Rabelais: L'exemple du *Quart Livre.*" *Michigan Romance Studies* 1:73–97.

Fragment of a general study of the function of numbers in the first four books of Rabelais (see 1982.16). Studies the "idea of number" as poetic ferment, as image, as propelling force ("force promotrice du texte") in the prologue, in the theme of the journey, in the storm episode—wherever the predominance of numbers acts as "déterminant de texte" (p. 79). Notes that the idea of "number" in the *Quart Livre* has negative, inauspicious connotations, but that stylistically numbers underscore the positive value of Rabelais' *démesure.*

25 GOUMARRE, PIERRE. "La sexualité infantile: Rabelais, Freud, et Jung." *Renaissance and Reformation /Renaissance et Réforme* 16, no. 1:33–44.

Compares Rabelais' ideas on the sexual life of the child with those of Freud. Argues that Rabelais was not only a precursor of Freud, but that he also anticipated the discoveries of such disciples or critics of Freud as Melanie Klein, Wilhelm Reich, and above all Jung.

26 JEANNEAU, G. "Rabelais et le mariage." In *Études seiziémistes offertes à M. le Pr V.-L. Saulnier.* Geneva: Librairie Droz, pp. 111–18.

Notes Rabelais' seemingly ambivalent attitude towards women in the *Tiers Livre.* Traces Rondibilis' misogynous discourse to the Gallic and Platonic traditions; believes Hippothadée's diametrically opposed idealism, with its Evangelical respect for women and marriage, to be derived from the First Epistle to the Corinthians; and attracts attention to another possible source, namely Plutarch's precepts on marriage, as translated in 1535 by Jehan Lodé. But does the ideal woman, as described by Hippothadée and prescribed as the kind of wife Panurge ought to seek, really exist? Suggests that Panurge's negative answer to the question expresses Rabelais' own scepticism on that point.

27  KRITZMAN, LAWRENCE D. "The Allegory of Repression." *Sub-Stance* 28:72–85.

Part of a projected psychoanalytical study of narrative in the *Quart Livre*. Reads the fable of Couillatris "as a psychosexual allegory of writing" (p. 76), seen as "an instrument of repression" of the author's fear of punishment for excessive self-expression, from which Rabelais seeks to liberate himself through his use of texts written by others. Notes the obsessional character of Rabelais' call for moderation; attracts attention to instances where the ideal of moderation is "undermined," and suggests that the text "may be saying something quite other from what it purports to say" (p. 83). Ascribes to the repression of anxiety the motif of indecision running through the text and "the numerous philosophical inconsistencies in the *Quart Livre*" (p. 82).

28  LA BRETÈQUE, FRANÇOIS DE. "Rabelais, le lion et le coq." *Études Rabelaisiennes* 15:43–54.

Rabelais alludes twice in his work (*Gargantua*, chapt. 9 and *Quart Livre*, chapt. 62) to the fable of the lion frightened by the song of the white rooster. Reviews the sources of the fable, classical as well as medieval: Pliny and the Bestiaries, for the most part. Finds that Rabelais follows the medieval sources since he speaks of the *white* rooster, then seeks to analyse the "myth" by studying the context in which it appears. Notes that it is based in "une situation d'inversion, dans laquelle le vainqueur obligé habituel se trouve, pour une fois, en situation d'infériorité à plus petit et plus faible que lui" (p. 49). The bipolarity of the myth is accompanied by an interpretation, most frequently in terms of Christian symbolism. The Bestiaries see in it an opposition between Good and Evil; Lucretius offers a scientific, positivistic explanation in terms of his atomic theory: the particles emanating from the rooster wound the eye of the lion. In Rabelais, finds an attempt at synthesizing both interpretations.

29  LA CHARITÉ, RAYMOND C. "Rabelais: The Book as Therapy." In *Medicine and Literature*, edited by Enid Rhodes Peschel. New York: Neale Watson Academic Publications, pp. 11–17.

Argues that in Rabelais "the interpenetration of literature and medicine is so pervasive that one would have to say that, for him, literature is indeed medicine, and medicine the stuff of literature" (p. 12). Notes in particular the range of medical discussions, the place of human anatomy and physiology, both in themselves and as metaphors for the whole of human life. To illustrate the "restorative properties of the book," briefly discusses "the interplay of sickness and health as a structural principle" in *Pantagruel*.

1980

30 ———. *Recreation, Reflection and Re-creation: Perspectives on Rabelais's Pantagruel.* French Forum Monographs, no. 19. Lexington, Ky.: French Forum, 137 pp.

Views *Pantagruel* as an underrated masterpiece, and brings together, in sometimes significantly modified form, a series of previously published essays presenting Rabelais' first book as "a far more coherent and esthetically rewarding work than it is normally perceived to be" (p. 7). In "The World Upside Down," argues that Rabelais' *coup d'essai* should not be judged in relation to *Gargantua* but on its own terms; acknowledges that it does not possess a clearcut narrative line, but argues that it is held together, thematically and structurally, by the recurrent motif of *mundus inversus* (see 1977.24). In "Repetitive Form," discusses the chapter division of the book (in the original 1532 edition), and notes behind its episodic structure the unifying process of "re-creation," whereby various thematic and structural elements are echoed with variations throughout the novel, forming a network of recurring patterns which defines the work's essentially cyclical structure. Among such repetitive devices cites the motif of procession and spectacle, sickness and cure, various forms of catastrophic occurrence, travel, and above all "the characterological and artistic contrasts and parody which inform the Pantagruel-Panurge relationship" (p. 52). The coexistence of the playful and the serious, especially as it manifests itself in "Rabelais's endlessly inventive flirtation with language" (p. 69), concludes in chapt. 3 with a discussion of the Ecolier Limousin episode, emphasizing through the intertextual use of a passage from Tory's *Champ fleury* the ambivalence of Rabelais' attitude towards language as a medium of communication as well as creativity. In chapt. 4, "Le meilleur fils du monde," studies the diabolical dimension of "the most demonic of Rabelais's texts" (p. 82), stresses the devilish side of Pantagruel, sees in Panurge "all the attributes of the medieval devil of carnival and play" (p. 84), accounts for Pantagruel's friendship with Panurge by their "devilish ancestry," but notes that Rabelais has also endowed Panurge with a dose of humanity, so that he emerges as "a Pantagruelian deceiver and not the devil incarnate" (p. 91). The last chapter, "Au temps que les bestes parloient," studies the "interior architecture" of the lion-fox episode (chapt. 11) as well as its links with the rest of the book, in yet another effort to demonstrate that "*Pantagruel* is not a haphazard collage, but a remarkable work of art" (p. 115). See 1974.21.

31 LOSSE, DEBORAH N. *Rhetoric at Play: Rabelais and the Satirical Eulogy.* Utah Studies in Literature and Linguistics, no. 17. Bern, Frankfurt, and Las Vegas: Peter Lang, 132 pp.

Traces the panegyric tradition from Aristotle through Fabbri, considers the paradoxical encomium as a branch of "demonstrative oratory," and seeks "to assess Rabelais' contribution to the development of epideictic form in its satirical application" (p. 26). Studies the paradoxical elements of the prologues to the first four books, and stresses the rhetorical underpinnings beneath their apparent spontaneity of tone. Applies Tetel's distinction between lyrical and burlesque eulogy to the main encomiastic passages in Books III and IV, and discusses Rabelais' participation in the Querelle des Amyes. Finds him to be "somewhat detached" from its philosophical concerns, but "fully committed to its principal arm, rhetorical paradox" (p. 99). Underscores the parodic treatment of the praise of love in Charles Fontaine's *La Contr'Amye de Court*. Finds Rabelais to be drawn to satirical eulogy for its ability to lend expression to farce, fantasy, rhetoric, and popular culture, and as an ideal vehicle for a view of the world as at once ambivalent and transcendent.

32   LYDGATE, BARRY. "Printing, Narrative and the Genesis of the Rabelaisian Novel." *Romanic Review* 71:345–73.

In *The Nature of Narrative*, Scholes and Kellogg had ascribed the skeptical attitude which had led Renaissance writers to differentiate between myth and history, to the emergence of empirical habits of mind. Argues that the phenomenon was mainly due to the advent of printing. Among the effects of printing on the development of narrative forms, notes the emergence of vernacular prose fiction as a popular genre, and the introduction of "new kinds of narrative dynamics and the possibility of novel communicative acts between writer and reader" (p. 354). Believes that printing encouraged individuation and independence from tradition both in the writer and in his public. Uses Rabelais as a "litmus-test" for the validity of his conclusions (p. 356). Sees in the *Grandes Chronicques* a transitional work, the transcription of an essentially oral text without the necessary "esthetic transposition" that *Pantagruel* provides. "Once we examine *Pantagruel* in this light, the heterogeneity of its styles and the discontinuity of its narrative line appear as conscious effects, not unavoidable consequences of an attempt to capitalize on the popular success of the *Grandes Chronicques* by patching together, pot-boiler style, whatever came to hand" (p. 364). Traces back to the development of printing a number of Rabelaisian themes. Reads the facsimile edition of the *Fanfreluches antidotées* (*Gargantua*, chapt. 2) as Rabelais' skeptical reaction to the humanists' belief that printed editions "would reveal the uncorrupted original meaning of the texts of the past" (p. 371). And sees the prologues of the first two books as defining for the fictive reader the nature of the act of reading, as it has become modified by the development from scribal to printed texts: "The reader's real reward is neither an initiation into 'sacremens et mystères,' nor a mindless 'passetemps,' but the middle ground of an inner life enriched by his complex skills as performer, skeptic, evaluator, expounder, accomplice" (p. 373).

1980

33 MOREAU, FRANÇOIS. "Les Orteils de Quaresmeprenant: Note sur une comparaison de Rabelais." *Berenice* 1, no. 1 (November):53–54.

   In the first of the many comparisons making up the chapters describing the monster (*Quart Livre*, chapt. 30–32), Rabelais assimilates the monster's toes to "une espinette orguanisée." Notes that "organisée" has here the specific meaning of "organized like an *organ*," and that Rabelais is thus alluding to a specific type of musical instrument, with organ pipes attached underneath.

34 MOTTE, WARREN F., Jr. "Procédés anthroponymiques chez Rabelais." *Neophilologus* 64, no. 4 (October):503–13.

   Notes that of all the names invented by Rabelais in the first four chronicles, only three merely identify. All the others describe (and satirize) as well: "tous sauf trois renvoient au personnage de manière significative et non pas seulement appellative" (p. 504). Studies the "Cratylic" way in which Rabelais establishes a link between a character's name and a trait of his personality. Sees in this process a manifestation of Rabelais' nostalgia for a pre-Babelian adequacy of names to the objects they designate.

35 PARKIN, JOHN. "Frère Jean in the *Cinquiesme Livre*." *Études Rabelaisiennes* 15:161–78.

   Questions the validity of all previous attempts to solve the problem of the authenticity of Book V, whether based on considerations of style, characterization, or ideology. Without taking sides in the controversy, studies Frère Jean in the *Cinquiesme Livre* and draws a few comparisons with the character as he appears in the other books. Follows Bakhtin in viewing Frère Jean in *Gargantua* as a parody of the lower clergy, and the Seuillé episode as a parody of the Mass with Frère Jean's role "deliberately inverted from that of a comforter and confessor to that of a savage killer" (p. 165). In the other books, although a much more marginal character, he remains "the convivial and physical antithesis of the monastic ideal of abstinence" (p. 168). In Book V, the character becomes more erudite, more sympathetic towards Panurge, more priestly in his ministrations. But argues that these new aspects were "anticipated in the attested works and integrated successfully with contrary patterns which highlight precisely the dominant functions (ignorance, hostility to Panurge, violence and murder)" in the earlier books (p. 177).

36 SCHRADER, LUDWIG. "Rabelais lecteur des anciens." In *Actes du Colloque Nantes-Düsseldorf, 29–30 mars 1979. Textes et Langages*, no. 4, pp. 113–27.

   Acknowledges that Rabelais sometimes reveals a positive attitude of optimism and confidence in his reception of classical and biblical texts. But points out that he is also often sceptical in his interpretation of these texts, and that he appears to be fully conscious of their ambiguity. Suggests that in the prologues he invites the reader to share his own scepticism, that his ambiguous reading of ancient texts is only one instance of his ambiguous reading of the world in general, and that this ambiguity reflects the unease and the contradictions at the heart of humanism itself.

37 ———. "Rabelais und die Rezeption der Antike. Deutungs-Probleme im Humanismus." *Romanische Forschungen* 92, no. 1–2:1–49.

Believes that the humanists' attempt to recover the original meanings of the texts inherited from antiquity necessarily presupposes interpretation, and thus gives rise to an ambivalent, relativistic hermeneutics. Argues that Rabelais' attitude toward classical texts is characterized by this same relativistic ambivalence.

38 SCREECH, M[ICHAEL] A[NDREW]. "The First Edition of *Pantagruel*: Bibliographical details and their help in dating Rabelais' first Chronicle and in appreciating aspects of its impact." *Études Rabelaisiennes* 15:31–42.

Provides a photocopy of the only existing copy of the first edition of *Pantagruel*, as well as that of a number of title pages using the same frame. The frame, used by Claude Nourry only once, had been used earlier by Jean David and Jacob Myt for learned books in Latin. Argues that "*Pantagruel A* was deliberately made to look like one of the legal volumes" provided by these editors: "The format is part of the joke" (p. 38). A hypothesis as to how Nourry got hold of the frame, as well as other bibliographical evidence, lead author to suggest that *Pantagruel A*, thought to have been published in autumn 1532, may in fact date from late autumn or winter 1531 (p. 39).

39 ———. "Seraphino Calbarsy ('Phrançoys Rabelais'), *La Grant Pronostication Nouvelle Pour L'An Mille Cinq Cens Quarante et Ung*." *Études Rabelaisiennes* 15:179–209.

Facsimile and transcription of a text found in the National Museum of Hungary in Budapest, and bearing the anagram of Rabelais. Introduction gives a physical description of the manuscript, and gauges its dubious scientific value ("bourrée d'erreurs," p. 192). Compares it with the *Pronostication pour l'an 1544* previously discovered by Lucien Schèrer, bearing the quite similar anagram Seraphino Calbasy and attributed to Rabelais. Shows the preface to have been copied almost word for word from the *Pronostication pour l'an 1544*. Only astrological data differ. Neither is comical or learned, and both are markedly inferior to the fragments of the prognostication for 1541 that bears Rabelais' name. Doubts that either Seraphino is really Rabelais. "S'il l'était, non seulement ces opuscules n'ajouteraient rien à sa réputation, ils ne pourraient pas ne pas porter atteinte à son intégrité" (p. 194).

1980

40 ———. "The Winged Bacchus (Pausanias, Rabelais and Later Emblematists)." *Journal of the Warburg and Courtauld Institutes* 43:259–62.

Suggests that "Rabelais' wine is mainly to be taken literally, as a means of spiritual enhancement" (p. 259n). Although wine-drinking is often mentioned in Rabelais, argues that it is only in the *Quart Livre* that it attains to the status of myth. Claims that during the Renaissance the powers of wine were seen "in a context of moderation." Notes that the winged Bacchus who appears in the *Quart Livre* is borrowed from Pausanias (*Laconia*, xix, 6). Rabelais thus seems to have been the first author who was aware of its source.

41 SPILLEBOUT, GABRIEL. "Feu M. Alcofribas, Abstracteur de Quinte Essence." *BAARD* 3, no. 9:383–85.

Explains the meaning of *quintessence* (i.e., ether) in the cosmogony of the Stoic philosophers, and argues that it was for Rabelais the symbol of the human soul, and of man's action in the world around him.

42 STABLER, ARTHUR [P]. "Variations sur un thème: 'Instinct' chez Rabelais et Montchrestien." *Romance Notes* 21, no. 1 (Fall):89–91.

Notes in four lines from Montchrestien's *Reine d'Escosse* a possible echo of what Rabelais says in the Abbaye de Thélème episode about an instinct in man that spurs him on to virtue. Rabelais claims that some men have it "par nature." Montchrestien holds it to be "ne sçay quoi de plus qu'humain, / Que le Ciel de grace nous donne." But suggests that both may be saying one and the same thing.

43 VIER, JACQUES. "Humanisme et hermétisme chez Rabelais." *Berenice* 1, no. 1 (November):25–29.

Notes in Rabelais' novels the theme of travel and discovery of the earth and of man, but also that of a thirst for a higher truth, represented by Pantagruel, and a concomitant belief in man's ability to recover a prelapsarian purity: "il crut que son verbe restaurerait l'état de nature avant la Chute et que le mal rebelle aux disciplines de l'église serait vaincu ou plutôt réintégré par la science" (p. 29).

44 WEINBERG, FLORENCE M[AY]. "Comic and Religious Elements in Rabelais' *tempête en mer*." *Etudes Rabelaisiennes* 15:129–40.

Seeks to "add a few touches that will bolster the idea that Rabelais was consciously striving *both* to create a comic effect *and* to convey a religious message to those of his readers equipped to receive it" (p. 129). Compares the "tempête en mer" episode to a similar one in Folengo. Finds in Rabelais "a greatly heightened exploitation of the grotesque and comic possibilities of the scene" (p. 130), as well as a religious context and a religious message thoroughly lacking in Folengo.

## 1981

1 BALDINGER, KURT. "*Stupide* bei Rabelais: *Faux-amis* in der Überset-zung." In *Europäische Mehrsprachigkeit: Festschrift zum 70. Geburstag von Mario Wandruszka*, edited by Wolfgang Pöckl. Tübingen: Max Niemeyer, pp. 349–57.

Argues that Rabelais uses the term *stupide* in its medical sense of para-lyzed (with astonishment). Reprinted in 1990.2.

2 BAR, FRANCIS. "Répétition et énumération chez les auteurs burlesques du XVIIe siècle." In *Le Comique verbal en France au XVIe siècle: Actes du Colloque organisé par l'Institut d'Etudes Romanes et le Centre de Civilisation Française de l'Université de Varsovie (avril 1975)*. Cahiers de Varsovie. Warsaw: Les Éditions de l'Université, pp. 163–82.

Occasionally compares seventeenth-century practice with the use of the rhetorical devices of repetition and enumeration in Rabelais.

3 BATANY, JEAN. "Les 'Quatre Estats' de l'Ile des Papimanes." *BAARD* 3, no. 10:425–29.

Argues that the four characters who ask Pantagruel and Panurge whether they had seen the pope (*Quart Livre*, chapt. 48) represent the four social orders: the three traditional ones, plus the members of the legal profes-sion, who had long refused to be mingled with merchants and peasants into a "Third Estate." Believes that Rabelais got the idea for the allegorical repre-sentation of the four social orders from the group of statues adorning the tri-umphal arch erected on the occasion of the entry of Henry II into Paris in 1549.

4 BÉNÉ, CHARLES. "Agrippa d'Aubigné, émule de Rabelais?" In *La Nouvelle française à la Renaissance*, études réunies par Lionello Sozzi et présentées par V. L. Saulnier. Bibliothèque Franco Simone, no. 2. Geneva and Paris: Édi-tions Slatkine, pp. 671–82.

Argues that Aubigné sought to *use* Rabelais rather than to *imitate* him. Studies Rabelais' "présence" in the *Confession du Sieur de Sancy* in order to bring out Aubigné's debt, but above all his "génie créateur" (p. 673). Discusses brief, direct allusions (mostly to the Papimanes' episode in the *Quart Livre*), but also the presence of Rabelaisian devices: play on words, par-ody of scholastic argumentation, the use of the absurd *encomium*. Finds Aubigné to be more daring, less gratuitous, more committed than his model.

5 BERNARD, CLAUDIE E. "Le Pantagruélion entre nature et culture (*Tiers Livre*, chapitres XLIX–LII)." *Degré Second* 5:1–20.

Offers a close reading of the four chapters forming the Pantagruélion episode, considered as a pivotal point between Rabelais' three preceding chronicles and the journey narrated in the *Quart Livre*. Explicates the text around the interrelated notions mentioned in the title, and sees the plant above all as a purveyor of a new, liberating form of culture: "culture technique opposée à une culture livresque, culture vivante et fructueuse opposée à une érudition stérile, culture qui s'édifie grâce à la collaboration du locuteur et de l'auditeur, elle sert pleinement les valeurs de la 'civilisation'"(p. 11). Explains the Pantagruélion's puzzling use in the manufacturing of hanging ropes—its sinister "vertu oppilative"—as a kind of exorcism against institutionalized culture and its official language. Comments on the etymological connection between the plant and its "inventor" as an aspect of Rabelais' reflection on the relationship between words and things, and sees as the plant's most precious quality its ability to inspire the type of rich, poetic, persuasive language used by Rabelais in the episode under discussion.

6   BERRONG, RICHARD [MICHAEL]. "Rabelais's *Quart Livre*: The Nature and Decline of Social Structure." *Kentucky Romance Quarterly* 28, no. 2:139–54.
    Sees in the dyadic relationship holding together the inhabitants of Ennasin a harmonious societal bond. Notes that the subsequent dyadic relationships are characterized by hostility, not only on the various islands but also, and most particularly, on board the Thalamège. Interprets this as evidence of Rabelais' growing concern for the disintegration of social structure. Sees telling signs of this concern in the appeal to moderation in the 1552 prologue, and in the proliferation of monsters, which were absent from the 1548 version of the *Quart Livre*. Attributes Rabelais' pessimism not only to an awareness of growing religious tensions, but more generally to a belief in an imminent return to original chaos as God's punishment for man's increasing self-worship.

7   BOWEN, BARBARA C. "L'épisode des Andouilles (Rabelais, *Quart Livre*, chapitres XXXV–XLII): esquisse d'une méthode de lecture." In *Le Comique verbal en France au XVIe siècle: Actes du Colloque organisé par l'Institut d'Etudes Romanes et le Centre de Civilisation Française de l'Université de Varsovie (avril 1975)*. Cahiers de Varsovie. Warsaw: Les Éditions de l'Université, pp. 111–21.
    Brings out the complexity of an essentially ambiguous episode by underscoring the diversity of its literary sources and of its intellectual and linguistic contexts. "J'en distingue dix, et est-ce tout?" (p. 115). Is convinced that a knowledge of all these contexts is necessary for a thorough understanding of the text.

8   ———. "Lenten Eels and Carnival Sausages." In *A Rabelaisian Symposium*. *Esprit Créateur* 21, no. 1 (Spring):12–25.

Explores the episode of the battle with the Andouilles (chapt. 35–42 of the *Quart Livre*) "in the context of the age-old confrontation between Carnival and Lent" (p. 12). Follows the theme in literature from *De Caresme et de Charnage* (a thirteenth-century *fabliau*) through the *Libro de Buen Amor*, to French Renaissance carnival plays and Italian examples. One of the French plays, *La Bataille de Sainct Pensard à l'encontre de Caresme*, is considered as a possible source. Notes that the first pictorial representation of the theme occurs surprisingly late, at the hands of Frans Hogenberg (1558) and Brueghel (1559). Studies the connection between *andouilles* and *anguilles* (especially as it relates to the proverbs "Rompre les andouilles/anguilles au genou"), and comments on the sexual associations of the two terms. Claims that Rabelais is deliberately conflating *andouilles* and *anguilles*, and suggests that this confla-tion is a comment on the current religious situation, more specifically upon the doctrinal confusion that accompanies religious discord at the time when Calvin and Luther side with Charles V against the pope.

9 COOPER, RICHARD. "Les *contes* de Rabelais et l'Italie: une mise au point." In *La Nouvelle française à la Renaissance*, études réunies par Lionello Sozzi et présentées par V. L. Saulnier. Bibliothèque Franco Simone, no. 2. Geneva and Paris: Éditions Slatkine, pp. 183–207.

Discusses the divergent critical opinions on the extent of Italian influ-ences on Rabelais, and on the possible Italian sources of his anecdotes. Agrees with those who see Poggio's *Facetiae* as a source of the tale of Hans Carvel, and believes with Le Duchat that Rabelais may owe to Poggio the story of the jays and the magpies, but not the phrase "Voy là pour les quittes" (chapt. 5 of the *Tiers Livre*), the debate about eleven-month pregnancies, or the dispute between Baisecul and Humevesne. For the ring with the false diamond episode, considers Masuccio Salernitano and his *Novellino* to be the most like-ly source. Sees no influence of the *Decameron* on Rabelais' work. Sides with Sozzi on the question of the Italian sources of the Seigny Joan story (see 1964.18), but finds Nardi's thesis (see 1965.13) also attractive. Concedes that the story of Physis and Antiphysie is borrowed from Calcagnini, but disagrees with those who believe that Rabelais followed his model reasonably closely (see 1962.3). Acknowledges Rabelais' debt to Coelius Rhodiginus and to Aretino's *Dialogo del Giuoco* for the story of the man from Gascony in the *Tiers Livre*, chapt. 42. Notes that Rabelais situates only three of his stories in Italy, and that at most twelve stories—a small proportion of the total—have Italian sources.

10 COSTA, DENNIS. *Irenic Apocalypse: Some Uses of Apocalyptic in Dante, Petrarch and Rabelais*. Stanford French and Italian Studies, no. 21. Saratoga, Calif.: Anma Libri, 143 pp.

In the chapter on "Irenic Apocalypse," argues that the horror and vio-lence which for most readers summarize the Apocalypse are in fact mitigated

1981

in the biblical text, for the term is equivalent to *revelation*, "and discloses a mystery which claims to create a people who are free and at peace." Chooses to call "irenic" the peaceful images "which serve to qualify the violent, seemingly closed-ended, horrific content of the biblical book" (p. 3), and in chapt. 5, "Daily Bread: The 'Horrible Mysteries' of Rabelais," applies the notion of "Irenic Apocalypse" to Rabelais' "seemingly contradictory attitude towards language" (p. 136n), and to the concept of Pantagruelism as it emerges from Rabelais' text.

11 DEFAUX, GÉRARD. "Une rencontre homérique: Panurge noble, peregrin, et curieux." *French Forum* 6, no. 2 (May):109–22.

Although it may appear inconsequential from the point of view of literary history, the influence of Homer upon Rabelais proves to be of utmost importance from textual analysis, in this case a close reading of the chapter on Pantagruel's encounter with Panurge (*Pantagruel*, chapt. 9). Argues against a psychological interpretation of the episode, and in favor of an intertextual reading suggested by a multiplicity of allusions to the *Odyssey*. "C'est tout Homère qui est là, présent en lui, qui non seulement l'enrichit de sa substance, mais qui encore lui donne ses structures et, finalement, son sens" (p. 120). Notes the light shed on the chapter by the First Epistle to the Corinthians, and the Babel episode in Genesis. Adds to these texts the parallel drawn by Rabelais between Panurge and Ulysses: their nobility, their peregrinations, their intellectual curiosity. Defends the reading of "gens curieux,"that Foulet had challenged in 1963.6.

12 DEMERSON, GUY. "Le Plurilinguisme chez Rabelais." *Réforme Humanisme Renaissance* 14:3–19.

Briefly summarizes the state of research on Rabelais' knowledge of foreign languages, and seeks to discover Rabelais' intentions in using them, as he does, throughout his work. Does not believe they contribute to characterization. Argues that they are used as a springboard for reflection on the origin of language and on the process of its degeneration; that they serve to suggest that languages can separate as well as unite; that the occasional use of artificial languages serves to underscore the irreality of the narrative. Notes that the existence of a variety of languages endows the narrative with an exotic as well as an enigmatic dimension. Points to the use of multilingualism as a source of laughter, and sees in the verve with which plurilingualism is introduced a satirical function: that of underscoring the chaos of a disorganized world. But believes that it offers at the same time a glimpse into the potential harmony of society when it at last frees itself from the curse that the erection of the Tower of Babel had brought down upon it.

13 ———. "Les calembours de Rabelais." In *Le Comique verbal en France au XVIe siècle: Actes du Colloque organisé par l'Institut d'Etudes Romanes et le*

*Centre de Civilisation Française de l'Université de Varsovie (avril 1975).*
Cahiers de Varsovie. Warsaw: Les Éditions de l'Université, pp. 73–93.

Studies the functions of the pun in general, with specific reference to
Rabelais. Discusses its apparent absence of all meaning; its relation to the
unconscious according to Freud ("C'est surtout dans le domaine du langage
qu'on pourrait être tenté d'appliquer les analyses de Freud à l'univers essentiellement masculin de Rabelais," p. 74); its relationship to popular culture and
its revolutionary function according to Bakhtin and Jean Paris (whom the
author challenges on that score); its function as a weapon in Rabelais' humanistic struggle. Locates its origin in the medieval *équivoque*, which does not
promote cultural terrorism but offers an opportunity to escape from the banal-
ity and insignificance of everyday reality. "Rabelais se rattache à des traditions esthétiques pour qui le langage peut être matière à expériences, mais non
matière explosive" (p. 88). Believes with Foucault that for the Renaissance
and for Rabelais, as was the case for the Middle Ages, there is still a relationship between the word and the thing, so that a play on words can reveal inherent similarities between the things of which the word is the sign. Concludes
that Rabelais' is an essentially poetic use of the *calembour*, similar to that of
such modern poets as Apollinaire and Aragon.

14 GIERCZYÑSKI, ZBIGNIEW. "La fonction du non-sense chez Rabelais, et
les parties 'vides' de son œuvre." In *Le Comique verbal en France au XVIe
siècle: Actes du Colloque organisé par l'Institut d'Etudes Romanes et le
Centre de Civilisation Française de l'Université de Varsovie (avril 1975).*
Cahiers de Varsovie. Warsaw: Les Éditions de l'Université, pp. 122–40.

Studies the comic passages seemingly devoid of all meaning—such as
the episodes dealing with Baisecul and Humevesne, Panurge and Thomaste,
Nazdecabre, Triboulet—in their relationship to the serious content of the
work. Believes that their individual functions are as diverse as the contexts in
which they are inserted, but thinks that a careful consideration of the work in
its totality suggests that in general the use of the nonsense device has a satirical function and reinforces the positive aspect of Rabelais' message.

15 HAUSMANN, F. R. "Rabelais und das Aufkommen des Absolutismus:
Religion, Staat und Hauswesen in den fünf Büchern *Gargantua et
Pantagruel.*" In *Französische Literatur in Einzeldarstellungen.* Vol. 1, *Von
Rabelais bis Diderot,* edited by P. Brockmeier and H. H. Wetzel. Stuttgart:
J.B. Metzler, pp. 13–75.

Sketches the rise of capitalism and absolute monarchy during the second
half of the sixteenth century. Argues that the general intellectual climate of the
early Renaissance, and in particular the religious, political, and economic
developments characterizing the period are reflected in Rabelais' work, most
specifically in the chapters on Thélème (*G,* chap. 49–56), the bells of Notre
Dame (*G,* chap. 16–19), the Picrocholine war (*G,* chap. 23–48), the praise of

debtors and borrowers (*TL,* chap. 2–5), the sausage war (*QL,* 35–42) and the Frozen Words (*QL,* chap. 55–56). Provides close, contextual, multi-leveled readings of these episodes. Suggests that the prologues, taken as a whole, offer evidence of an evolution in Rabelais' position on matters of faith, politics, and economics. Finds Rabelais to be essentially conservative in his views on religion and politics, but modern in his rejection of all *a priori* forms of thought and in his empirical approach to intellectual inquiry.

16  HERRMANN, LÉON. *L'Utopien et le lanternois: Les pseudonymes et les cryptogrammes français de Thomas More et François Rabelais.* Paris: Editions A.-G. Nizet, 136 pp.
    Believes that it is from More's *Utopia* that Rabelais borrowed the idea of using cryptograms. Notes that Badebec, Pantagruel's mother, is a Utopian. Agrees with Lefranc in identifying the theologian Hippothadée (*Tiers Livre,* chapt. 29) with Erasmus. Does not see any reason not to identify Thaumaste (*Pantagruel,* chapt. 18–20) with Thomas More. Attempts to decode ("décrypter") Panurge's four cryptograms. Of the first three (*Pantagruel,* chapt. 9), the one written in "antipodien" is a warning against Calvin, the one in "lanternois" renews the urging that Francis I pursue Calvin in Geneva, and the one in "utopien" refers to Rabelais' intention to join Erasmus in Basel. All three warn against Reformation, urge the unity of true faith, and predict the triumph of the "Lanterne," an ecumenical organization transcending any particular sect. From the fourth cryptogram (*Tiers Livre,* chapt. 47), concludes that Rabelais may have contemplated seeking refuge in England in 1546. As for the pseudonyms, reiterates his belief that the Ecolier Limousin is Jean Dorat, suggests that Hans Carvel (*Tiers Livre,* chapt. 28) is none other than Jean Calvin, proposes to see in Pantagruel a cryptographic pseudonym decodable as "anti-Calvin," believes that Raminagrobis is neither Guillaume Crétin (as Etienne Pasquier had stated), nor Jean Lemaire de Belges (as suggested by Lefranc), but Clément Marot. Further suggests that Trouillogan refers to the philosopher Guillaume Bigot (1502–55), that Bridoye is Tiraqueau, that among the "domesticques" of Pantagruel Epistémon, Ponocrates, Gymnaste, and Rhizotome cannot as yet be identified, but that Carpalim, together with being "the swift one," according to the Greek etymology of the name, is also Jean Lascaris, from whom Guillaume Budé had acquired his knowledge of Greek. As for Bringuenarilles (*Quart Livre,* chapt. 17), of whom the *Briefve declaration* states that it is one of several names "faicts à plaisir," believes that it can be decoded as "François maranne," and that it could allude to Antoine Rabelais' first wife, a Spanish Jew converted to Christianity. "Je n'ai aucune *preuve* décisive et ce n'est point là *matière de bréviaire,* mais je crois avoir relevé un certain nombre d'indices qui doivent attirer notre attention sur les origines de Rabelais et la possibilité qu'il ait été, avant Michel de Montaigne, le fils d'une juive christianisée, donc un 'marrabais' ou 'marranne'" (p. 131).

17   HUCHON, MIREILLE. *Rabelais grammairien: De l'histoire du texte aux problèmes d'authenticité.* Etudes Rabelaisiennes, no. 16. Geneva: Librairie Droz, 534 pp.

Linguistic study of Rabelais' work in relation to sixteenth-century theories and applied research in matters of grammar and syntax (including spelling and punctuation) in an attempt to assess Rabelais' originality on this score. Based on an examination of different copies of the same edition (to separate what should be put down to the printer's habits from what reflects the author's intentions), as well as an exhaustive comparison of the various editions. Chooses as a touchstone Fezandat's 1552 edition of the *Tiers Livre*, since it had received Rabelais' particularly careful attention, and had been published at a time when printing habits had at last become stabilized. Part 1 ("Les enseignements des éditions") defines the main points of Rabelais' grammatical system, shows that his punctuation is not as whimsical as is generally thought, and dates the *editio princeps* of *Gargantua* as having appeared in the first quarter of 1535, and hence after the Affaire des Placards. Part 2 ("Censure antique et grammaire") bears on Rabelais' use of negation (especially the various reinforcements of *pas* or *point* in negative expressions) and on his spelling (shown to conform more frequently than that of contemporary usage to the Latin and Greek origin of words). Part 3 ("Une systématique des formes") correlates certain peculiarities of spelling (for example the use of both *ant* and *ent* in present participles, whereas only *ant* is in common usage) with Rabelais' wish to underscore the Latin etymology of certain verbs, and his insistence on the integrity of the radical part of a word (by adopting, for instance, *œillz* as the plural form against the common use of *yeulx*), by analogy with Hebrew. Part 4 compares Rabelais' spelling with that of a number of contemporaries, and concludes that for the most part Rabelais' usage is thoroughly original, and that it was not imitated by authors writing subsequently. In the last part, grammatical and linguistic analysis is brought to bear upon the problem of authenticity raised by certain texts, most notably by the *Cinquiesme Livre*. The letter to Geoffroy d'Estissac written in Rome on January 28, 1536, is thought to be from Rabelais' hand; the letter to Antoine Hullot (of March 1, 1542) is not. The *Grandes et inestimables cronicques* included a table of contents which the author ascribes to Rabelais as his "premier écrit en langue vulgaire" (p. 491). Rabelais is also thought to have modified the text of the first two subsequent versions of the chronicles. The *Briefve declaration* at the end of Book IV is authenticated on the basis of two points: "L'existence de toutes les caractéristiques du système grammatical de l'auteur et la concordance des gloses avec les conceptions linguistiques de l'auteur" (p. 409). As for Book V, a parallel reading of the manuscripts and a linguistic study of the book lead to the following conclusions: the prologue of Book V is the first version of the prologue to the *Tiers Livre*; the "Isle Sonante" episodes are a discarded alternate ending for Book IV; and the last thirty-two chapters are made up of drafts for a discarded ending to the *Tiers Livre*. The

1981

text is thus thought to be authentic (with the exception of the chapter on the Apedeftes), although it was not meant by Rabelais to form a sequel to Book IV: "ce n'est qu'un montage et l'une des plus extraordinaires supercheries de l'histoire littéraire" (p. 489).

18  JEANNERET, MICHEL. "Du mystère à la mystification: Le sens caché à la Renaissance et dans Rabelais." *Versants. Revue Suisse des Littératures Romanes*, no. 2 (Winter):31–52.

Notes the frequency with which the "topos des Silènes" recurs in the literature of the Renaissance, from Pico della Mirandola to Tasso and Giordano Bruno, and studies it specifically in Erasmus and Rabelais. Erasmus invokes it as a paradigm for recognizing the true nature of phenomena, since value and truth are always hidden. For Erasmus it forms the basis of a system of reading, and of an ethical system as well, since truth can only be reached through a spiritual interpretation of signs freed from their literal meaning. In the prologue to *Gargantua*, Rabelais uses a similar argument when he prompts the reader to interpret his text "à plus hault sens." But here the latonic fable does not illustrate the thesis of a hidden meaning: it problematizes it. When Rabelais disavows his thesis in the second phase of his argument, he and Erasmus seem to be poles apart. But claims that the two positions are not contradictory, when replaced within the context of humanism. For the humanist, allegorical interpretation is eminently valid—indeed necessary—in the case of the oracular literature (classical as well as biblical) of the past, when poets were mediators of supernatural truths that became progressively lost and must be rediscovered. But for modern texts, devoid as they are of any oracular message, allegorical interpretation is no longer justifiable. In rejecting this type of interpretation in the second phase of his argument, Rabelais is merely reacting against the medieval tendency to allegorize indiscriminately the works of the present as well as those of the past. Argues that the most advanced among humanist interpreters of religious texts, such as Erasmus, reject the mechanical formalism of scholastic exegesis in favor of a more supple, more personal, more intuitive approach to the discovery of the spirit behind the letter. In Rabelais' Books III and IV, Pantagruel keeps up his belief in a higher meaning and knows how to reach it. The other characters, however, are less and less sure. In much of the work, the promise of a message is constantly disappointed: mystery becomes mystification. In Book III, "Les sophismes de Panurge parodient la méthode allégorique et renvoient aux abus de la glose scolastique qui, au lieu d'éclaircir le texte qu'elle commente, y projette sa propre confusion et recule à l'infini la saisie de la vérité" (pp. 43–44). In Book IV, each step of the journey is an enigma which seems to require decoding, but mystery is again degraded. The work remains enigmatic, but there is no longer any guarantee that phenomena conceal a hidden meaning that can be apprehended. As a strategy for interpreting such a modern work of literature allegory is useless, for the work does not contain any hidden truth that the mechanical application of the principles of allegorical exegesis can uncover. Its secrets are those of life itself, and of language: "l'étrangeté des choses et l'opacité des mots" (p. 49). As such, they can only be experienced through the mediation of the work of fiction, and tentatively pondered in the light of one's own experience. This is what Rabelais means when, after inciting the reader to seek a higher meaning through allegorical interpretation, he ostensibly contradicts himself and enjoins us to savor the work for the pleasure it can afford.

19   JOUKOVSKY, FRANÇOISE. "Les narrés du *Tiers Livre* et du *Quart Livre*." In *La Nouvelle française à la Renaissance*, études réunies par Lionello Sozzi et présentées par V. L. Saulnier. Bibliothèque Franco Simone, no. 2. Geneva and Paris: Éditions Slatkine, pp. 209–21.

Studies the stories in Books III and IV from the point of view of their relation to the main plot line. Classifies the *apophtègmes* into groups: dry, concise apologues drawn from antiquity, and stories drawn from contemporary, popular sources, more diffuse and stylistically more closely related to the rest of the novel. But notes the shortcomings of such a classification. Some tales belong to both categories; amplification may also on occasion be a feature of both; and both have in common their exemplary function, bolstering the debate in Book III, and commenting on the voyage in Book IV. "Dans les deux livres, c'est en partie grâce au récit secondaire, notamment à l'apologue, que la vision du monde contemporain s'élève au mythe et dépasse la simple description" (p. 213). Stresses the parodic nature of the commentaries provided by the *apophtègmes*. Admits that they often appear as mere diversions whose only functions is to satisfy Rabelais' taste for storytelling. But argues for a deeper relationship between the stories and the episodes of the novel, in that they share the same vision of universal folly, while attenuating by their oral character and their humor the anguished tonality of the main narrative.

20   KRITZMAN L[AWRENCE] D. "Rabelais's Splintered Voyage." In *Fragments: Incompletion and Discontinuity*, edited by Lawrence D. Kritzman. *New York Literary Forum* 8–9, pp. 53–70.

Discusses the voyage in Rabelais' *Quart Livre* as "a series of delays in which the absence of a final destination disrupts the conventions of logical sequence and closure" (p. 53). Sees the characters as grotesque victims of an *idée fixe* that determines their behavior, and the structure of the book as the result of "literary bricolage" whereby groups of episodes are arranged haphazardly and could thus be moved about without interrupting the text's "narrative syntax" (p. 59). Finds the structure of each episode to be "both disjointed and digressive" (p. 60), and comments on Rabelais' frequent use of enumerations whose effect is to replace "sustained narrative sequence" and further splinter an already heterogeneous, ruptured text.

1981

21  LA CHARITÉ, RAYMOND C. "Gargantua's Letter and *Pantagruel* as Novel." *A Rabelaisian Symposium. Esprit Créateur* 21, no.1 (Spring):26–39.

Siding with those who see in the letter an essentially serious text, but refusing to read it merely as a document in the history of ideas, studies its meaning and function and seeks to show both its thematic importance and its fictional relevance to the novel as a whole. Argues that the letter is thematically related to the rest of the novel through "the theme of displacement and replacement, renewal and revitalization" (p. 33). Sees the text as "inextricably intertwined on all levels with the two basic generating principles of the book": intercourse and discourse, biological and verbal creativity (p. 31). Closes with an analysis of the structural function of the letter. Believes that by interpolating into the novel an epistolary text, Rabelais draws attention to the fact that the reader, who is elsewhere a participant, a spectator, an auditor, is also a reader, and that for all its spontaneity and oral character, the novel which surrounds it is also a written text.

22  LARMAT, JEAN. "Le comique verbal chez Rabelais et les personnages de Panurge et de Frère Jean des Entommeures." In *Le Comique verbal en France au XVIe siècle: Actes du Colloque organisé par l'Institut d'Etudes Romanes et le Centre de Civilisation Française de l'Université de Varsovie (avril 1975)*. Cahiers de Varsovie. Warsaw: Les Éditions de l'Université, pp. 97–106.

Notes that the two characters appear precisely at the point where the giants, having grown up, assume a seriousness incompatible with laughter. Their function is to allow Rabelais' verbal comedy to continue on its course. Suggests that both were created essentially "pour servir de support au comique verbal" (p. 98) and that each was provided with a particular linguistic personality. Sees the "comique verbal" of Panurge as characterized by a tendency towards caricature, logorrhea, and a mixture of elegance and vulgarity, whereas that of Frère Jean is colloquial and rustic, enhanced with picturesque expressions of popular origin, with frequent swearing, and, more rarely, with monastic jokes based on scriptural quotations and theological references. Concludes by remarking that Frère Jean remains the same throughout, whereas Panurge becomes more scholarly, more parodic.

23  LATHUILLERE, ROGER. "Les Problèmes de l'édition de Rabelais." *CAIEF* 33 (May):129–45.

Outlines the difficulties facing the prospective editor of Rabelais' complete works. Discusses the problems involved in choosing the *texte de base*, as well as "le traitement et la toilette qu'il faudra faire subir au texte": corrections, variants, spelling, punctuation, paragraph division.

24  LEWICKA, HALINA. "Le comique verbal de l'absurde dans la sottie et chez Rabelais." In *Le Comique verbal en France au XVIe siècle: Actes du*

*Colloque organisé par l'Institut d'Etudes Romanes et le Centre de Civilisation Française de l'Université de Varsovie (avril 1975).* Cahiers de Varsovie. Warsaw: Les Éditions de l'Université, pp. 55–63.

Some examples of the absurd, both linguistic and referential, drawn from Rabelais' work. Notes that folly is less all-pervasive in Rabelais than in the *sotties*.

25 MASTERS, G[EORGE] MALLARY. "Panurge's Quest: Psyche, Self, Wholeness." *A Rabelaisian Symposium. Esprit Créateur* 21, no. 1 (Spring):40–52.

Views Rabelais as a Renaissance Platonist. Reads Books III and IV from a Jungian perspective and against the backdrop of patristic texts such as Origen's homilies on the Song of Songs and Exodus, and John Chrysostome's homilies on the Epistles to the Corinthians. Considers Panurge's problem to be essentially that of a "misdirected will" (p. 48), and his quest for marriage to be a form of the quest for psychic wholeness through self-knowledge.

26 MAZOUER, CHARLES. "Le comique verbal dans le *Tiers Livre*." In *Le Comique verbal en France au XVIe siècle: Actes du Colloque organisé par l'Institut d'Etudes Romanes et le Centre de Civilisation Française de l'Université de Varsovie (avril 1975).* Cahiers de Varsovie. Warsaw: Les Éditions de l'Université, pp. 141–55.

Studies the various modalities of verbal comedy in a book where this aspect of Rabelais' art is so striking as to appear to be the author's foremost concern: "Au point qu'on peut se demander si le *Tiers Livre* ne serait que cela, un jeu comique avec le langage" (p. 141).

27 NABLOW, RALPH ARTHUR. "Was Voltaire Influenced by Rabelais in Canto V of the *Pucelle?*" *Romance Notes* 21, no. 3 (Spring):343–48.

Argues that Friar Grisbourdon's account of his adventures to the devils in hell is closer to Epistémon's visit to the underworld (*Pantagruel*, chapt. 30) than to any of the other works which have been mentioned as possible sources.

28 NASH, JERRY C. "Interpreting 'Paroles degelées': The Humanist Perspective of Rabelais and His Critics." *A Rabelaisian Symposium. Esprit Créateur* 21, no. 1 (Spring):5–11.

Finds at the heart of the episode "the humanist theme that knowledge of the past is essential and possible and that, once acquired, [it] can serve present and future" (p. 7). Rabelais' role is to awaken the past and shape the present in its light. Rabelais criticism today fulfills a similar function: "Just as Rabelais sought to preserve for his own present and future age the humanist perspective of the past,...so too do we for our own age through our critical endeavors to

1981

make Rabelais and all he represents understood and respected by modern readers" (pp. 10–11).

29 RAGLAND-SULLIVAN, MARY E[LOISE]. "Panurge and Frère Jan: Two Characters Cast from the Same Mold?" *Kentucky Romance Quarterly* 28, no. 1:53–74.

Argues for "the importance of character in Rabelais" (p. 53). Finds the four main characters worthy of interest in themselves rather than as instruments of comedy or satire. Explains the unconscious creation of the various characters in psychological terms, as an "auto-mimetic" or self-representational process, in which the author embodies in literary personages the various aspects of his psyche. Believes that such an approach can reveal "Rabelais the man behind Rabelais the artist" (p. 54). Argues that the giants become progressively less interesting as they represent more and more exclusively Rabelais' intellectual side, whereas Panurge and Frère Jan remain alive throughout, because they are endowed with emotional complexity. Finds that they not only resemble but "duplicate" each other, and that their similarities are particularly in evidence in Books III and IV.

30 REA, JOANNE E. "Joyce and 'Master François Somebody.'" *James Joyce Quarterly* 18, no. 4 (Summer):445–50.

Although Joyce's admission that he knew Rabelais' work only through Sainéan's *La Langue de Rabelais* would suffice to explain the Rabelaisian word-inventions in *Finnegans Wake*, argues that *A Portrait of the Artist as a Young Man* and *Ulysses* show direct familiarity with *Gargantua* and the *Tiers Livre* through Urquhart's Elizabethan translation.

31 RIGOLOT, FRANÇOIS [PAUL]. "La 'conjointure' du *Pantagruel*: Rabelais et la tradition médiévale." *Littérature* 41 (February):93–103.

Intertextual study of chapt. 17 of *Pantagruel* ("Comment Panurge guaignoyt les pardons et maryoit les vieilles, et des procès qu'il eut à Paris") and canto 17 of Dante's *Purgatorio*, each marking the mid-point of the work in question. Finds the two works to be conjoined by such themes as the idea of pleasure derived from doing evil. Sees in the relationship between Alcofribas Nasier and Panurge an ironic transposition of the relationship between Dante and Virgil. More generally, seeks to show that "la 'conjointure' numérologique n'est que la signature, le 'chiffre' proprement dit, d'une conjointure beaucoup plus profonde et dont rend compte, aux niveaux thématique, structurel et métalittéraire, l'intertextualité du *Purgatoire* et du *Pantagruel*" (p. 96).

32 ———. "Vraisemblance et Narrativité dans le *Pantagruel.*" *A Rabelaisian Symposium. Esprit Créateur* 21, no. 1 (Spring):53–68.

In spite of the countless ways in which Rabelais' work strains credibility, it frequently presents itself as "un discours véridique" (p. 53). Studies Rabelais' attempts to reconcile the narrator's claims and the reader's experience, to give the appearance of truth to what the reader knows to be false. In the case of *Pantagruel*, notes that the author/reader relationship is mediated, mainly in the prologue but also elsewhere, through the relationship between the narrator and his imaginary audience (the *narrataire*), and that the effort to impose the narration as *vraisemblable* takes the form of stylistic domination (mock lyricism, verbal attacks upon the implied reader). This domination weakens in the course of the novel as Panurge takes on the function of Alcofribas as narrator (at the very center of the book), and Alcofribas becomes one of the characters in the novel (in the episode of the world in Pantagruel's mouth). It disappears entirely in the last three chapters, as Rabelais takes the place of Alcofribas, the true reader replaces the imaginary *narrataire*, and the work becomes at last a joyous fiction after the initial attempt to impose it by force as truth.

33 SCREECH, M[ICHAEL] A[NDREW]. "Rabelais in Context." *A Rabelaisian Symposium. Esprit Créateur* 21, no. 1 (Spring):69–87.

In his role as teacher rather than scholar, deplores the ever-increasing difficulty of presenting Rabelais' work to students ever more ignorant of their cultural heritage. Warns against the danger of flooding the student with an erudition that does not illuminate directly the text under study, or that of projecting upon the work a past of our own making. Argues that an historical approach to Rabelais' work need not kill its comedy; suggests that on the contrary it alone can bring out its full humor and relevance.

34 SYPÑICKI, JÓZEF. "La continuation des procédés du comique verbal de Rabelais chez les burlesques: la formation des mots." In *Le Comique verbal en France au XVIe siècle: Actes du Colloque organisé par l'Institut d'Etudes Romanes et le Centre de Civilisation Française de l'Université de Varsovie (avril 1975)*. Cahiers de Varsovie. Warsaw: Les Éditions de l'Université, pp. 187–94.

Aside from specific, explicit borrowings, Rabelais' influence on the group of burlesque writers of the seventeenth century can also be seen in two forms of linguistic invention: "l'utilisation comique de la forme des lexèmes chez Rabelais et chez les auteurs burlesques et, surtout, des formations néologiques burlesques bâties à partir des modèles rabelaisiens" (p. 189). The multiplicity of examples drawn from Furtière, Scarron, Saint-Amant, and Dassouci corroborates Sainéan's opinion that Rabelais was these writers' favorite author.

1982

35 TETEL, MARCEL. "Carnival and Beyond." *A Rabelaisian Symposium. Esprit Créateur* 21, no. 1 (Spring):88–104.

Advocates an emblematic reading of Book IV, equates the voyage with the book that recounts it, and views both as imbued with the spirit of carnival, seen as a catharsis rather than "the reversal of the order with all its Marxist reverberations" which it is for Bakhtin. Suggests that the purpose of the voyage is a search for the new, the different, for a "reconciliation of present and past" (p. 93) as a basis for intellectual, spiritual, and literary renewal.

## 1982

1 BALDINGER, KURT. "Fehldatierungen zu Rabelais: Zur Bedeutung der Philologie für die Lexikologie." In *Fakten und Theorien: Festschrift für Helmut Stimm zum 65. Geburstag*, edited by Sieglinde Heinz and Ulrich Wandruszka. Tübingen: Gunter Narr, pp. 1–11.

Corrects a series of mistakes and omissions in the *Französische Etymologische Wörterbuch*.

2 BERRONG, RICHARD M. "An Exposition of Disorder: From *Pantagruel* to *Gargantua*." *Studies in Philology* 79, no. 1 (Winter):12–29.

While recognizing the striking similarities of structure and content between Books I and II, underscores equally important differences by comparing the Picrocholine War in *Gargantua* with the war between the Utopians and the Dipsodes at the end of *Pantagruel*. Sees the Picrocholine War as presented in terms of "three principal binary oppositions—*folie/raison, excès/limites, désordre/ordre*" (p. 13). Notes in the case of *folie* that both Grandgousier and Ulrich Gallet see in it an intervention of satanic forces. Relates this to the passage in Grandgousier's letter to Gargantua, in which he claims that man's "franc arbitre et propre sens" cannot be but wicked, unless it is continually guided by divine grace. Suggests that these two passages, without making man intrinsically evil, cast doubt nevertheless upon what critics frequently call Rabelais' optimism concerning human nature, as implied in the motto of the Thelemites. Endows the war episode with a cosmic dimension, and views it as an expression of a "*Weltanschauung* in which God seems to be withdrawing from the world and allowing the 'puissances souterraines du mal' to erupt and invade" (p. 20). The second and third binary oppositions refer to the direct effects of God's retreat and Satan's subsequent invasion. The second opposition, *excès/limites*, is seen as implying at least in a rudimentary form an awareness of the nature of social structure, and a belief in the importance "of the bonds that link men together in civilized intercourse," which it is one of Picrochole's chief sins to have broken. Believes that the emphasis on education in *Gargantua* is related to this danger of disintegration of social structures, because in the absence of divine grace, it is only through education that man can be shown the necessity to establish and preserve the bonds that hold together an orderly society. *Gargantua* presents a view of the world as constantly threatened by the eruption of the forces of evil, and expresses the hope that through education the social fabric can be kept intact. In so doing, it offers a systematic, theological explanation of what, in *Pantagruel*, is merely presented as a fact.

3   BLUM, CLAUDE. "Stéréotypes de l'imaginaire: le monde médiéval dans l'œuvre de Rabelais—les diables et les fous." *La Licorne* 6:227–33.

    Discusses Rabelais' conception of devils and fools as an example of the use of medieval figures by a Renaissance text fully conscious of representing a break with an antiquated mode of thought. Notes that while retaining their stereotypical figuration, the devils in Rabelais have lost their fundamental ambivalence: viewed as both terrifying and ridiculous from the thirteenth century onward, they have now entirely lost their ability to induce fear. To the extent that the devil is still terrifying, he has taken on a human face: that of Picrochole, for instance. Notes a similar change in the representation of fools (both the "fol naturel" and the "fol-bouffon"), now embodied not only in such traditional types as Dindenault and Triboulet, but also in Panurge, whose *philautie* makes of him a figure of sin. Relates this change in the representation of devils and fools to a progressive internalization of death and the beyond: "L'homme est désormais considéré comme l'origine, la source et la scène où se joue le Péché, la Mort et son au-delà" (p. 233).

4   BOOTH, WAYNE C. "Freedom of Interpretation: Bakhtin and the Challenge of Feminist Criticism." *Critical Inquiry* 9, no. 1:45–76.

    Author's "first and belated effort at feminist criticism" (p. 66). Bakhtin sought to exonerate Rabelais from the charge of antifeminism by noting that his portrayal of women fits squarely into the carnivalesque spirit of Gallic tradition, which is neither negative nor hostile, but healthily ambivalent. Agrees that the problem cannot be argued on the basis of a reading of any isolated fragment, without regard to "the quality of the response invited by the whole work" (p. 59), but ultimately rejects Bakhtin's rehabilitation: "The truth is that nowhere in Rabelais does one find any hint of an effort to imagine any woman's point of view or to incorporate women into a dialogue" (p. 65). Judges these marks of sexism to be a serious flaw, since they diminish the pleasure with which he now rereads some parts of the work. Notes also in passing another ideological limitation in Rabelais: "the author's total obliviousness to the lot of the lower orders" (p. 69), namely the servants at whose expense the Thelemites enjoy their freedom in the abbey, as well as what he takes to be Rabelais' indifference to the burning of heretics. Refuses to condone such "acts of injustice" on the grounds that they do not violate the ethical norms of Rabelais' day. But finds sexism to be an even more disturbing flaw than any of the others, because it "goes to the very heart of our picture of what it is to be human" (p. 73). Reprinted: 1983.10. See also 1988.9.

5 CAVE, TERENCE. "Panurge and Odysseus." In *Myth and Legend in French Literature: Essays in Honour of A. J. Steele*, edited by Keith Aspley, David Bellos, and Peter Sharratt. London: The Modern Humanities Research Association, pp. 47–59.

Notes the classical context—Virgilian and Homeric—in which Panurge appears in Rabelais' narrative. Panurge mirrors Odysseus (to whom he compares himself) in the dual role of protagonist and teller of stories. The chapter in which he introduces himself echoes a series of parallel chapters in the *Odyssey* dealing with the motif of the appearance of a stranger and the subsequent offer of hospitality. Views this unique example of transposition of narrative elements in Rabelais as suggesting, Plattard's assertions to the contrary notwithstanding, that Rabelais not only knew of Homer from the *Adages* of Erasmus, but that he had direct knowledge of the *Odyssey* as a narrative. As transposition of narrative elements, chapt. 9 of *Pantagruel* also offers "a rare insight into the way in which Rabelais read Homer, and into his own strategies as a narrator conscious of his readers" (p. 52). Not so much a parody as a "tropological reading," allowing Rabelais to bring out the meaning of his own text not through explicit commentary or allegorization, but by emphasizing the differences between his transposition and the original. What in Homer has a narrative function and allows the text to proceed, has in Rabelais a dramatic and heuristic function, turning the narrative into a (non-)dialogue. The comparison also underscores the active, participating role which Rabelais reserves for his reader: the recognition is effected by the reader, who also decodes the meaning of the episode. Concludes by drawing attention to the similarity between Panurge and Odysseus as "trickster-figures" conjuring up their own fictions, and pointing out that by further endowing Panurge with the capacity to express himself in a variety of languages, Rabelais transforms Homer's personification of legendary fictions into "a personification of language itself."

6 CÉARD, JEAN. "Rabelais et la matière épique." In *La Chanson de geste et le mythe carolingien: Mélanges René Louis*, vol. 2. Saint-Père-sous-Véselay: Musée Archéologique Régional, 1259–76.

Reminds us that *Pantagruel* and *Gargantua* follow the tripartite structural pattern of the "chansons de geste": "Enfances" / "Chevaleria" / "Moniage." Notes that the two books, like the "chansons de geste," form a cycle. Points out that they also resemble the medieval epic in matters of detail: genealogies at the beginning, rewards for valor in battle at the end. Reminds us of the presence in the "chansons de geste" of such giants as Loquifer, Otinel, and Rainouart, whose "tinel" foreshadows the tree with which Gargantua destroys the castle of the "gué de Vède," the mast with which Pantagruel fights Loupgarou, or the cross used by Frère Jean to welcome the assailants at the abbey of Seuillé. Notes similarities in the description of sieges and battles, but acknowledges that Rabelais does not refer to any specific "chansons de geste," which he most likely had not read. Seems rather to refer to later prose adaptations. Notes more specific similarities with *Les Quatre fils Aymon* and *Robert le Diable*. Calls attention to the striking parallel between *Gargantua*, chapt. 3 (dealing with the contradictory emotions felt by the giant at the birth of his son), and a similar scene in *Huon de Bordeaux* as well as in a chronicle by Richer, monk of Senones, recounting a miracle by St. Elizabeth. What meaning should one attach to these reminiscences? Noting that they are only passing allusions and that they are satirical only up to a point, concludes that the romances of chivalry are not in themselves the object of his satire. They are merely a part of Rabelais' more general design to protect the truth of history from, among other things, fictional narratives which lay unfounded claims to historical veracity.

7  CHARPENTIER, FRANÇOISE. "Le symbolisme de la nourriture dans le *Pantagruel*." In *Pratiques et discours alimentaires à la Renaissance: Actes du Colloque de Tours 1979*, sous la direction de J.-C. Margolin et R. Sauzet. Paris: Maisonneuve et Larose, pp. 219–31.

Studies food in its "modes d'apparition romanesque" (p. 219), its narrative function, and its meaning, insofar as it may stand for something other than itself. Notes the importance of food in the nativity scenes, and the link therein of food and generation. Notes also the importance of hunger in the first encounter with Panurge; comments on Rabelais' interest in ingestion and excretion (treated on a lyrical rather than a satirical mode), and in the physiology of nourishment. Discusses the relation between food and sexuality in the scene in which Panurge extolls the benefits of eating one's "blé en herbe," studies "le déplacement de l'érotisme à la mangeaille" at the bishop's court among the Papimanes, and above all during the "guerre des Andouilles," where food is clearly a metaphor for sex. Notes the bisexual nature of the Andouilles, and Rabelais' verbal exaltation of male sexuality, in contrast to "une pauvreté consternante de la représentation du féminin" (p. 227). Wonders whether *consumption* is not meant to replace *generation* in the Pantagruelian universe from which women are conspicuously absent and which is thereby threatened with death. Reads in that light the chapters in the manor of Messere Gaster, and suggests the possibility of a similar reading of the very last lines of Book V. "L'achèvement du voyage serait-il une entrée dans la mort?" (p. 230).

8  CHESNEY, ELIZABETH A[NNE]. *The Countervoyage of Rabelais and Ariosto: A comparative reading of Two Renaissance Mock Epics*. Durham, N.C.: Duke University Press, 232 pp.

Revised version of 1976.9. Studies the work of Rabelais and Ariosto as an exploration of the ambiguities and tensions inherent in the new values of

Renaissance humanism. Sees the similarity between the two authors "in their propensity for exploring the opposite of every truth and the other side of every argument" (p. 5). Reveals in both writers a critical reflection which places their work in the antiprogressist, antirationalistic movement of the Counter-Renaissance. Sees in the geographical realism and spiritual symbolism of the theme of the voyage a vehicle of Manippean satire rather than a lyrical expression of the Renaissance spirit of discovery. Believes that both Rabelais and Ariosto subvert the ideological function of myth by using it merely as a rhetorical device. Sees in both a paradoxical use of fantasy to unveil the unpleasant realities of their culture. Sees in their use of an essentially untrustworthy narrator—"neither reliable nor dependantly unreliable"—to reflect the Renaissance writer's cognitive crisis. Detects further signs of each author's ambivalent stance towards Renaissance idealism in their ambivalent conception of time as a welcome agent of progress but also as a traumatic agent of flux, and in their conception of art as an imperfect bridge to immortality, since it too is subject to man's forgetfulness and to the vagaries of his esthetic taste. Believes that for both writers the contradictions of the counter-voyage can only be reconciled on the thematic level in the alterity of folly, and on the level of genre in the notion of the mock epic, combining as it does the anachronistic and unworldly ideal of romance with the empirical reality of the epic poem. Despite their many differences, the works of Ariosto and of Rabelais "remain closer in affinity to each other than to works of the artists' own countrymen or contemporaries" (p. 213) because they unite within themselves almost all the diverse tendencies of their time.

9    CHOLAKIAN, ROUBEN C. *The "Moi" in the Middle Distance: A Study of the Narrative Voice in Rabelais*. Studia Humanitatis. Madrid: Ediciones José Porrúa Turanzas, 137 pp.

Studies the modalities of the narrative voice in Rabelais' first four books. Points out that in *Pantagruel* the narrator, given a *persona* and a name, is both the third-person chronicler of the giant's biography, the first-person narrator of the prologue, and also on occasion an actor in his own story; conversely, the actors in the story—Panurge, Pantagruel, Epistémon—are occasionally transformed into narrators. Notes that in *Gargantua* the "actor-narrator" is no longer an actor, although he continues to chronicle the story in the third person, and to fragment the narrative with the intrusion of short anecdotes. Points out that in the *Tiers Livre* the first-person narrator, identified for the first time with the author himself, turns storyteller in the prologue and the closing chapters, and is helped in his narrative capacity by such actor-narrators as Rondibilis and Bridoye, as well as by various members of Pantagruel's entourage and by Pantagruel himself, whereas the third-person narrative voice merely situates the chronicle in time and space. In Book IV, notes that the first-person narrator no longer views events from a distance but has become an active participant in them, that the role of the narrator-actor has become richer, and that the actors who also function as narrators now reach in that latter capacity their full potential. Compares Rabelais' narrative design to the types of literary frame used by storytellers of the period, and sees its originality "in a never-ending fragmentation which generates a multiple frame and a complex interchange between ACTORS and NARRATORS" (p. 51). Redefines the problem of characterization and psychological realism in Rabelais in terms of this relationship between actor and narrator, concedes that the characters are inconsistent when viewed as protagonists in the series of episodes making up the general plot, but argues that in any one episode such criticism is invalid: "the ACTOR-NARRATOR not only comes alive in his role as storyteller, but manages to define himself in a coherent manner" (p. 111). Brings to bear the narrator's relationship to his characters and to the narrative upon the question of the specific genre—novel or novella?—to which Rabelais' masterpiece belongs, and concludes that Rabelais' is "a highly original art form, from which, certainly, novellistic attributes are not absent, but which incorporates important characteristics of the popular novella tradition" (pp. 117–18). Appendix A identifies the major stories and their respective narrators. Appendix B offers a "Chronological Table of French Novella."

10   DEFAUX, GÉRARD. *Le Curieux, le glorieux et la sagesse du monde dans la première moitié du XVIe siècle: L'exemple de Panurge (Ulysse, Démosthène, Empédocle)*. French Forum Monographs, no. 34. Lexington, Ky.: French Forum, 196 pp.
      "Panurge ne peut se lire et se comprendre que par référence à Ulysse" (p. 43). In the first three chapters discusses the character of Ulysses as defined in Homer and his commentators, and as depicted in the compilations dating from the Middle Ages and the Renaissance. In chapt. 5 and 6, follows the theme of curiosity, from antiquity to the Renaissance, with emphasis on the dangers of erudition.

11   ———. "Rhétorique humaniste et Sceptique chrétienne dans la première moitié du XVIe siècle: Empédocle, Panurge et la 'Vana Gloria.'" *Revue d'Histoire Littéraire de la France* 82, no. 1 (January–February):3–22.
      Draws attention to three passages from *Pantagruel* hitherto unglossed by critics: Pantagruel's reference to "les adventures des gens curieux" in chapt. 9, Panurge's reference to Ulysses in the same chapter, and in the following contest between Baisecul and Humevesne, Panurge's allusion to Empedocles. Although these comparisons between Ulysses and Empedocles on the one hand, and Panurge on the other, may seem innocuous and totally unrelated, argues that they signal in fact three important consecutive moments in the evolution of Panurge's character: "D'abord *peregrinus* et *curiosus*, puis *aretalogus* et *gloriosus*, Panurge parcourt ainsi sous nos yeux un chemin qui ne doit au fond absolument rien au hasard, à la verve et à l'improvisation, mais dont les étapes et les détours lui sont dictés par la tradition culturelle

1982

humaniste et par sa rhétorique" (pp. 17–18). By transferring to Panurge the curiosity and vainglory hitherto attached to Pantagruel, Rabelais can make of the latter an embodiment of humanistic and Evangelical ideal. This interpretation confirms the author in his belief in the unity of purpose, coherence, and complexity of Rabelais' novel, and leads him to read the first version of *Pantagruel* as a humanistic parable: "Une parabole tout ensemble ironique, facétieuse et morale sur l'insondable et universelle folie de la prétendue sagesse du monde, sur la vanité, les dangers, mais aussi les attraits de ses concupiscences" (p. 20).

12  DUVAL, EDWIN [M]. "Panurge, Perplexity, and the Ironic Design of Rabelais' *Tiers Livre*." *Renaissance Quarterly* 35, no. 3 (Fall):381–400.
    Reviews the various interpretations offered hitherto of Panurge's character, stresses the importance of the issue for a proper understanding of the *Tiers Livre*, and shows how the ironic dimension of the text further complicates the problem of interpreting Panurge. "We must find an aspect of the work that is somehow independent of its textual uncertainties" (p. 382). Finds such an aspect in the composition of the book. Shows the series of consultations making up the core of the *Tiers Livre* to be structured symmetrically around the consultation with Her Trippa. Recalls how often medieval and Renaissance texts are organized around a center toward which all other episodes seem to point, and which contains the work's central truth. Notes that the focal consultation with Her Trippa is itself organized around a center, namely the injunction to know oneself. Argues that in Her Trippa's "Congnois toy" we have the pivotal point of the book, and sees in this essential tenet of Socratic wisdom the central truth to which, ironically, both Her Trippa and Panurge are equally blind. Concludes that Panurge is neither a positive character in quest of a higher truth, as Saulnier would have it in his *Dessein de Rabelais*, nor the morally neutral agent of Rabelais' verbal virtuosity discovered by a group of more recent critics, but—as M. A. Screech had often pointed out—a representation of *philautia*, wherein lies the chief obstacle to self-knowledge, and to the possibility of bringing the Pantagruelists' quest to a successful conclusion.

13  FRANÇON, MARCEL. "La date de publication de *Pantagruel A?*" *BHR* 44:617.
    After reading Screech on the subject, reiterates his conviction that *Pantagruel* was first published in the spring of 1533, whereas M. A. Screech believes it appeared, more specifically, before March 26 of that year (see 1980.38). In his reply (p. 618 and three pages of illustration), Screech points out that no conclusion can be drawn from an examination of the columns on either side of the title page.

14    ————. "*Le Cinquiesme Livre* et la construction de l'heptagone régulier."
*BAARD* 4, no.1:27–28.
    Provides an illustration of such an heptagonal figure, and argues that in
his discussion of the figure in chapt. 24 and 25 Rabelais follows Francesco
Colonna rather than Dürer.

15    GENETTE, GÉRARD. *Palimpsestes: La littérature au second degré*. Paris:
Éditions du Seuil, pp. 220–21.
    In the context of a discussion of *transtextualité*, comments briefly on the
*Gargantua–Pantagruel* as unfaithful, even "murderous" continuations, or
*hypotextes*.

16    GLAUSER, ALFRED. *Fonctions du nombre chez Rabelais*. Paris: Nizet,
238 pp.
    Studies numbers as generators of narrative ("promoteurs d'écriture," p.
8) in Rabelais' novels, and seeks to define the poetic significance of their presence. Notes that they are implied in the very notion of gigantism that underlies
Rabelais' work. Notes also their capacity to express precision as well as
vagueness, to contribute to the impression of realism as well as fantasy. In part
1, studies the function of numbers in the novels; in part 2, studies it in
Rabelais' "métalangage," that is in such "textes-commentaires" as the prologues and a few chapters and fragments in which Rabelais appears as a spectator and critic of his own works. Contains a somewhat reworked version of
two of the author's earlier articles: "La poétique du nombre chez Rabelais.
L'exemple du *Quart Livre*," and "Le Gouffre chez Rabelais considéré comme
espace scriptural" (1980.24 and 1978.15, respectively).

17    GOUMARRE, PIERRE [J]. "Autour des lunettes audio-visuelles de
Rabelais." *BAARD* 4, no. 1:23–26.
    Notes in Rabelais two references (*Tiers Livre*, chapt. 35, and *Quart
Livre*, chapt. 5) to the ability of spectacles to improve one's hearing. Points to
other passages associating vision and hearing (for example the episode of the
frozen words), and denoting, more generally, an intuition of what is now
called *synaesthesia*: "ce remueur d'idées s'est attaqué, aussi, aux problèmes
de la perception" (p. 26).

18    HOLQUIST, MICHAEL. "Bakhtin and Rabelais: Theory as Praxis."
*Boundary 2* 11, no. 1:5–19.
    "Like Rabelais, Bakhtin is throughout his book exploring the interface
between a stasis imposed from above and a desire for change from below,
between old and new, official and unofficial" (p. 11). Reads Bakhtin's book
on Rabelais in part as a critique of Stalinist culture, which explains Bakhtin's
otherwise rather puzzling idealization of common man: "Bakhtin's dream of

the folk is a utopian affront to the Stalinist image of the new man" (p. 14). The idea is developed in 1984.7.

19    LESTRINGANT, F[RANK]. "Rabelais et le récit toponymique." *Poétique* 50 (April):207–25.
      Studies the function of toponyms in episodes narrating an itinerary, such as Pantagruel's tour of the various French universities. Does not detect any link between the stages of the itinerary, but sees in each an immediate and necessary connection with the locality—the "nom de lieu"—in which it is set: "Celui-ci est expliqué, commenté, illustré par l'événement fictif qui s'y rattache" (p. 208). Discusses the matter against the background of the debate on the nature of the connection between words and things in Plato's *Cratylus*. Draws attention to similarities between Rabelais' toponymic allusions and those of Charles Estienne in the latter's *La Guide des Chemins de France*, published in 1553. Compares Rabelais' anecdotal etymologies (such as the one invented for Paris on the basis of Gargantua's urinal *pourboire* offered to the inhabitants of the capital *par rys*) with the *imagines agentes* recommended in classical treatises on memory.

20    MOREAU, FRANÇOIS. *Les Images dans l'œuvre de Rabelais*. Vol. 1, *L'Image littéraire, position du problème: Quelques définitions*. Paris: Société d'Édition d'Enseignement Supérieur, 128 pp.
      Defines the notion of literary image, and explains the methodology of its eventual application to the work of Rabelais. Will use image in its stylistic, rather than its general meaning, that is as a linguistic expression of an analogy rather than a mental representation. Draws some of his examples from Rabelais.

21    ———. *Les Images dans l'œuvre de Rabelais*. Vol. 2, *Inventaire, commentaire critique et index*. Paris: Société d'Édition d'Enseignement Supérieur, 428 pp.
      Offers an inventory of the more than four thousand images to be found in all five books of the *Gargantua–Pantagruel*. Indicates variants, sources, and meaning; quotes previous commentators or provides own comments. Lists the images in the order in which they appear (beginning with *Pantagruel*). Also provides an alphabetical index.

22    ———. *Les Images dans l'œuvre de Rabelais*. Vol. 3, *Un Aspect de l'imagination créatrice chez Rabelais: L'Emploi des images*. Paris: Société d'Édition d'Enseignement Supérieur, 189 pp.
      Last book in the series, presenting a synthesis based on the inventory making up vol. 2 (see 1982.21). In section 1, provides an inventory of the conceptual fields illustrated by the various analogical figures, classified as per-

taining to the following categories: the book, man, abstract notions, setting, and nature. Indicates the relative frequency of the images in each of the five books, their distribution among the various characters, their sources, and degree of originality. In section 2, studies the modalities of expression: forms and structures, stylistic levels, and finds in this aspect of Rabelaisian imagery the main elements of baroque esthetics. Section 3 is devoted to a study of the functions of imagery in relation to the work as fiction, and as a means of exploring language. Concludes by stressing the essentially poetic nature of Rabelais' conception of language and of his vision of the world. In an appendix, brings to bear the analysis of imagery upon the problem of the authenticity of Book V, and cautiously concludes that it is "pour l'essentiel" if not in the case of every episode, the work of Rabelais himself.

23 NEEDLER, HOWARD I. "Of Truly Gargantuan Proportions: From the Abbey of Thélème to the Androgynous Self." *University of Toronto Quarterly* 51, no. 3 (Spring):221–47.

Explores the thematic and structural similarities between *Gargantua* and Plato's *Symposium*. Sees in the Abbaye de Thélème "an ideal image of human potentiality," "an image of the pre-existence of the human soul," before its union with the body (p. 227). Argues that in Rabelais this soul is construed as androgynous (like in Plato, where Socrates and Diotima appear as two halves of a single androgynous mind), and that this androgynous character of the soul as symbolized in the Thélème episode is anticipated in the image on young Gargantua's hat: "The significance of Thélème...is suitably emblematized in the hat-medallion, which condenses what is abstracted and generalized in the architecture and the way of life that it encloses, and suggests its application to the human form" (p. 240).

24 NILLES, CAMILLA JOYCE. "Paradoxical Encomium in Rabelais." Ph.D. dissertation, University of Chicago.

Sees in the paradoxical encomium a key to the understanding of the function and meaning of ambiguity in Rabelais, and examines Rabelais' use of the conventions of the genre. Traces the historical evolution of the genre, compares the "Eloge des dettes" with two near-contemporary texts on the same subject matter, examines the remaining paradoxical encomia in the context of the books in which they appear. Divides those of Book IV into "unnatural" and "natural" praises, and sees the ambivalent praise of Gaster as a meeting of these two antithetical types. Concludes by noting that the paradoxical nature of the final episodes recalls the paradox of the prologue, and sees in this symmetry a suggestion that "the questions raised by paradox can be satisfied by paradox alone." See *Dissertation Abstracts International* 42 (1982):5141A.

1982

25  RIGOLOT, FRANÇOIS. *Le Texte de la Renaissance: Des Rhétoriqueurs à Montaigne*. Histoire des Idées et Critique Littéraire. Geneva: Librairie Droz, 284 pp.

   In the four chapters of part 3, "Le texte du discours narratif: Rabelais" (pp. 105–70), studies four different aspects of the Rabelaisan text in its specificity, as "écart par rapport à d'autres textes," and as "*synecdoque* d'un ensemble signifiant beaucoup plus vaste qui reste à déchiffrer" (p. 20). The first chapter, "Conjonction des textes: Des 'rhétoriqueurs' à Rabelais," deals with Rabelais' debt towards the "rhétoriqueurs," especially when that debt is not explicitly acknowledged, or perhaps even consciously felt, but informs his text nonetheless in a number of formal analogies (see also 1978.30). The second chapter, "Parémiologie: Poétique de la sentence et du proverbe," studies Rabelais' use of proverbs, unfrozen so to speak and given a new life, and discusses their place in the dynamics of the text (see 1977.31). In chapt. 3, "Narratologie: Vraisemblance et illusion référentielle," proposes to read *Pantagruel*, the least believable of all of Rabelais' novels, as a "quête de la vraisemblance" (p. 153). Defines *vraisemblance* in terms of *diegesis* rather than *mimesis*, as adherence to a *contract* between narrator and narratee, rather than to the reader's standard of what is plausible. Raises the question of the novel's *vraisemblance* in relation to its narrative strategies. Finds that the fundamental relationship between narrator and narratee is one of *domination*, notes the various ways in which Alcofrybas sets out to dominate the implied reader, and draws out the implications of substituting Panurge for the narrator in chapt. 17, and of allowing him to assume the rôle of principal character in the episode of the world in Pantagruel's mouth. In chapt. 4, "Numérologie: Structure du texte et mémoire intertextuelle," notes the numerous examples of medieval texts whose structure is based on numerology, reminds us that the central point of such works as *Lancelot*, *Yvain*, the *Roman de la Rose*, and the *Divine Comedy* is the locus of a major poetic event. Draws attention to the fact that the central point of both *Pantagruel* and of *Purgatorio* occurs in chapter (or canto) 17, and proposes to show that this numerological coincidence is the exterior sign of a deeper intertextual relationship on the thematic, structural, and metaliterary level. Among other connections, sees the relationship between Alcofrybas and Panurge as an ironic transposition of the relationship between Dante and Virgil, and the relationship between Panurge and Villon as mediated by the *Divine Comedy*, or more precisely by the parody of that work in Lemaire de Belges' *Epître de l'Amant Vert*. See "Vraisemblance et Narrativité dans le *Pantagruel*" (1981.32) and "La 'conjointure' du *Pantagruel*: Rabelais et la tradition médiévale" (1981.31) for a treatment of this numerological *conjointure* from a somewhat different point of view.

26  SAULNIER, V[ERDUN] L[OUIS]. *Rabelais II: Rabelais dans son enquête, Etude sur le Quart et le Cinquième Livre*. Paris: Société d'Édition d'Enseignement Supérieur, 356 pp.

1982

Posthumous study of Books IV and V from manuscripts left at the author's death, prepared for publication by Jean Céard. For episodes not treated in the manuscript, supplies excerpts of previously published articles on the subject. Considers each episode in its historical context as well as in the context of Rabelais' thought. Sees the five books as the product of a coherent, though evolving, design, both as a narrative and as an ideological text. Detects in Rabelais an essentially mythic form of thought: "Rabelais pense par grandes images animées" (p. 27). Notes that although Rabelais believes in God, he never seeks to define him: "Il y a un agnosticisme, dans sa pensée" (p. 37). Believes that if there is a truly hidden meaning in Rabelais, it should be sought in the works written around 1550 ("à l'heure des contraintes et de l'intolérance," p. 39) rather than in the first two books, published at a time when it was not nearly as necessary to hide one's thought. Book IV is thus an allegory, unlike the first three novels, and its quest owes less to geography than to symbolism. Studies the departure episode as a key to the meaning of the entire work. Argues that by choosing to have the Pantagruelists sing Psalm 114 ("In exitu Israël de Aegypto") in Marot's translation, Rabelais means us to read Book IV as a kind of exodus from the land of idolatry to a promised land. Finds the key to the Medamothi episode in the notion of *mirage* rather than in the more heavily underscored idea of opulence. Reads the exchange of letters between Gargantua and Pantagruel as Rabelais' homage to the past and its quest for truth. Stresses in chapt. 5–8 of the *Quart Livre* the characterization of Panurge and Dindenault ("deux vrais personnages de roman"); seeks to integrate the drowning scene into the moral design of the whole. Sees in the Ennasin episode "le procès du snobisme," in the isle of Cheli "la tentation du confort," in the Chiquanous a satire of the "petit monde de la justice" (p. 67), in Thohu and Bohu a reminder of human frailty. Believes that the storm at sea is as interesting from the artistic as from the ideological point of view, and that it underscores the dangers of a personal quest. Finds the Macreons episode to be remarkable chiefly for the gravity of its tone. Sees in Physis and Antiphysie an essential element of Rabelaisian mythology. The encounter with the Physétère shows the necessity of standing up to the most frightening monsters in one's quest for truth; the Andouilles, with their sectarian anticonformism represent a dangerous potential ally of the Pantagruelists; equally dangerous is the sterile idealism of the inhabitants of the isle of Ruach. The satire of religious fanaticism in the Papimanes and Papefigue episode aims at the Roman system rather than the pope himself. For the frozen words episode, Céard reproduces excerpts from Saulnier's "Le silence de Rabelais et le mythe des paroles gelées" (1953.43), suggesting that the unwritten commentary for *Rabelais dans son enquête* would have given more importance to the notion of faith in the future. Refuses to see in the Gaster episode an early form of philosophical materialism. Chapt. 22 reproduces an excerpt from "Le festin devant Chaneph, ou La Confiance dernière de Rabelais" (1954.35) arguing that Rabelais had no intention to abdicate his personal quest and rejoin the ranks of

1982

orthodox Christianity. The chapter on Ganabin reproduces excerpts from "Pantagruel au large de Ganabin" (1954.36). Summarizes, in the epilogue, the main tenets of a "catéchisme rabelaisien bien précis" revealed by a patient reading of Book IV. As for Book V, believes that an analysis of the contents ought to take precedence over the question of attribution: "Ce problème est de conclusion, non d'introduction" (p. 155). Thinks that L'Isle Sonante is not exactly Rome and papacy, but more generally the world of the clergy, and that to a certain extent the church is shown to be a victim of hypocrites who use it for their own advantage. L'Isle des Ferrements allows the author to express his trust in Nature: "Il y a un ordre de nature, auquel il faut croire, mais sans s'imaginer qu'il puisse être sans faille" (p. 175). L'Isle du Guichet and l'Isle des Apedeftes symbolize various forms of oppression; the chapters on Entéléchie denounce both excessive use of philosophy and total refusal to philosophize: "De la philosophie il faut à la fois user et se méfier" (p. 212). L'Isle d'Odes teaches a lesson in relativity; most chapters form in fact a series of lessons in the art of seeking the truth. Discusses the Lanternois episode mainly in relation to the character of Panurge. Interprets the visit to the temple of the Dive Bouteille to mean that the quest for wisdom is a personal quest for one's true self: "Et nous aboutissons à une définition de toute la sagesse par la simple conscience de soi-même" (p. 287). Interprets the word of the oracle as an exhortation to action and underscores its resemblance to the motto of the Thelemites. Throughout, stresses the thematic concordance between Book V and the preceding novels. Discusses at some length in the epilogue the problem of attribution and suggests that Book V is made up of manuscripts left by Rabelais and published posthumously by an admirer, perhaps one of his own children.

27 SHARRATT, P. "Rabelais, Ramus et Raminagrobis." *Revue d'Histoire Littéraire de la France* 82, no. 2 (March–April):263–69.

Questions the traditional identification of Raminagrobis with Jean Lemaire de Belges, and proposes Pierre Ramus as a more likely model, given the emphasis on Raminagrobis' hereticism and Panurge's claim that he must be "Marrabais," that is of dark complexion, suggesting an Italian or a Spanish origin. Ramus was indeed of such complexion, and he had been nicknamed "Marrabecus" by the uappreciative public before whom he was in the habit of performing plays.

28 TUTTLE, HEATH. "The Temporal Composition of Vocabulary: Evidence from Rabelais." *Romance Notes* 23, no. 1 (Fall):53–56.

Illustrates the rate at which words ending in *-icque* were used by Rabelais in each of the five books. In graph 1 considers only words which originated in Rabelais' lifetime, in graph 2 only those which first appeared before 1500. Notes that the two graphs trace a similar pattern.

**1983**

1   ALMEIDA, IVAN. "Un corps devenu récit." *Études de Lettres*, no. 2:7–18.
In his *Libro de Buen Amor*, Juan Ruiz had told the story of a wordless, gestural debate between the Greeks and the Romans. Notes that Rabelais uses the same idea in the Thaumaste episode (*Pantagruel*, chapt. 19), and points out the significance of the story, namely that gestures are even more polyvalent than words: "Le voir est encore plus polysémique que le dire" (p. 13).

2   AMORY, FREDERIC. "Rabelais' 'Hurricane Word-Formations' and 'Chaotic Enumerations': Lexis and Syntax." *Études Rabelaisiennes* 17:61–74.
Studies nonsyntactic and sentential word-lists for their sources as well as for their stylistic value. Whereas the former are ordered merely by alphabetization, phonological, and morphological sequencing and anaphoric repetition, the latter can either fall momentarily into the chaos characterizing nonsyntactic enumerations, or be rescued from formlessness by attempts at literary stylization through *adiectio*, in imitation of classical and medieval authors. "If at the 'degree zero' of writing and style it periodically pleased Rabelais to empty the French lexicon on the page and list words and phrases in a dictionary or an *adagia* format, he could not refrain from poetically touching up his lexical collections here and there in arranging them for display, and thus he involuntarily bridged the gap between the formlessness of his word-lists and the artfulness of the syntactical construction of his sentences" (p. 74).

3   ANTONIOLI, ROLAND. "L'Éloge du vin dans l'œuvre de Rabelais." In *L'Imaginaire du vin: Colloque pluridisciplinaire, 15–17 octobre 1981 (Centre de Recherches sur l'image et le symbole, Faculté des Lettres de Dijon)*, edited by Max Milner and Martine Chatelain. Marseilles: Éditions Jeanne Laffitte, pp. 131–40.
Emphasizes the polyvalence of wine symbolism in Rabelais. Discusses wine as a symbol of physical, Dionysian vitality (in the context of the tavern and carnival); of hidden spiritual truth (in the context of the *convivium*); and of artistic, creative inspiration.

4   BALDINGER, KURT. "M fr. *sphaceler*—ein neuer Italianismus bei Rabelais?" In *Scritti linguistici in onore di Giovan Battista Pellegrini*. Pisa: Pacini Editore, pp. 663–70.
Suggests the word may have been formed on the Italian *spazzare* or *spezzare*. Reprinted in 1990.2.

1983

5   BARAZ, MICHAEL. *Rabelais et la joie de la liberté*. Paris: Librairie José Corti, 288 pp.

Dedicated to the memory of Marcel Raymond and to his friends Jean Rousset and Jean Starobinski, which indicates the author's own methodological orientation: through the thematic study of the joy of freedom, attempts to render accessible to the reader the *experience*, both concrete and universal, which gave rise to Rabelais' work. Studies freedom as idea as well as feeling, on the level of intellect as well as imagination. Examines the various facets of the feeling of freedom, while admitting that feeling cannot really be an object of study other than in its exterior manifestation, namely in the thematics and the style of the literary work. Chapt. 1 studies Rabelais' magnifying vision, with emphasis on its poetic as well as its comic aspect, and finds him free from the data provided by the senses as well as from the conventional view of the world. Chapt. 2 studies the multiple meanings of words such as *wine* and *debts*, and notes their associations with the notion of joyous acceptance of life. Chapt. 3 considers polyvalence as a fusion of opposites: comedy and seriousness, carnivalesque spirit and arcane erudition, realistic satire and surrealistic poetry, and notes in Rabelais the liberating praise of both folly and reason, the joyous exaltation of both matter and spirit. The following two chapters discuss Rabelais' "jeu avec les choses" and the liberating power of "pure" Rabelaisian laughter. Chapt. 6 places Rabelais "dans la lignée des esprits libres," studies the artist as well as the thinker, and underscores the modern character of Rabelais' fusion of the poetic and the rational and of his emancipation from belief in the supernatural. The final chapter is centered upon an analysis of the Abbaye de Thélème ("Une utopie à la mesure de l'homme réel") as a perfect realization of the liberating fusion of opposites: aristocracy and the people (since the aristocracy of the Thelemites is of a purely spiritual nature), spirit and matter, utopia and reality. Concludes by remarking that Rabelais is not content to sound a call for inner spiritual freedom, but that he was one of the very first intellectuals to foresee the main forms that the quest for freedom would take in the realm of the practical: "le développement de la technique, l'humanisation de la société, la valorisation du monde matériel" (p. 282).

6   BÉNÉ, CHARLES. "Rabelais et l'Évangélisme militant: l'exemple du *Quart Livre*." In *Mélanges à la mémoire de Franco Simone*. Vol. IV: *Tradition et originalité dans la création littéraire*. Geneva: Éditions Slatkine, pp. 169–81.

Believes that Rabelais' adherence to Evangelicalism emerges most strikingly from a comparison of the two versions of the *Quart Livre*. Notes that the militant Evangelicalism which can already be clearly detected in the incomplete edition of 1548 is further strengthened in the 1552 edition through corrections and additions denouncing the cult of the Virgin and the veneration of saints, the misuse of confession, and the laziness and gluttony of the

Vatican clergy. Calls attention to Rabelais' interpretation of the death of Pan. Notes that several commentators have misinterpreted the passage by equating Rabelais' attitude with that of Eusebius, for whom Pan represented the pagan gods. Points out that for Rabelais, as for Guillaume Postel before him, the death of Pan is the death of Christ himself, evoked by him in a moving register of Evangelical piety. Finds most significant the changes made in Epistémon's speech to the effect that man must not await passively the help of the gods. Notes that in 1552 Rabelais speaks of God in the singular, and enjoins man to *cooperate* with God rather than *to seek to help* him. Points out that in so doing, Rabelais is distancing himself at one and the same time from both Stoicism and the Reformation, and affirming more strongly than ever his Evangelical faith.

7   BERRONG, RICHARD M[ICHAEL]. "Jean Le Maire de Belges, Dictys of Crete, and Giovanni Boccaccio: Possible sources for *Gargantua*, ch. 1." *Études Rabelaisiennes* 17:89–92.

   For the idea of the circumstances in which Alcofrybas Nasier discovered Gargantua's genealogy, Rabelais may be indebted to Dictys of Crete's *Ephemeridos* and Boccaccio's *Genealogia Deorum*, either directly or through the *Illustrations de Gaule et singularitez de Troye*.

8   ———. "*Gargantua* and the New Historiography." *University of Dayton Review* 16, no. 3 (Winter):47–54.

   Whereas the Alcofribas Nasier who tells the story of Pantagruel is a narrator of contemporary events, the same character in *Gargantua* is presented as a practitioner of the new science of historiography, doing research, consulting documents, interviewing eye-witnesses in preparation for his biography of a giant from a previous generation. Draws attention to Alcofribas' inadequacies as a historian: his numerous inconsistencies, his indifference to matters of chronology; reviews the various interpretations hitherto advanced to explain these inadequacies, and suggests that through his absent-minded historiographer Rabelais may be satirizing the excessive claims to objectivity and absolute truth of a science he in the main admires, but which, as the work of mere humans, is inherently fallible and prone to misinterpretation of documents in the absence of their historical context.

9   ———. "On the possible origin of the name 'Nephelibates' (*Quart Livre*, ch. 56)." *Études Rabelaisiennes* 17:93–94.

   Detects a similarity with "Nephelogetae," mentioned by More in his *Utopia*, which Rabelais had used as a source for place-names in his earlier works.

1983

10   BOOTH, WAYNE C. "Freedom of Interpretation: Bakhtin and the Challenge of Feminist Criticism." Chapter in *The Politics of Interpretation*. Chicago: University of Chicago Press, pp. 51–82.
Reprint of 1982.4.

11   BORGEAUD, P. "La Mort du Grand Pan." *Revue de l'Histoire des Religions* 200, no. 1 (January–March):3–39.
Credits Rabelais with popularizing the Christian view that the death of Pan in Plutarch's account represented the death of Christ, contrary to the interpretation of Eusebius, who in his *Praeparatio Evangelica* had equated Pan with the horde of demons of Greek and Roman polytheism.

12   CLARK, CAROL. *The Vulgar Rabelais*. Glasgow: Pressgang, 161 pp.
Proposes to "vindicate the popular side of Rabelais's writing" (p. 1) by exploring the popular background of his work, in narrative and dramatic literature as well as in the carnivalesque elements of social life. Summarizes the plot of all five books (although doubts that any of Book V is the work of Rabelais himself). In "The Festive World" discusses the carnivalesque atmosphere pervading the novels, the elements of mountebank rhetoric in Rabelais' style, Rabelais' debt to the comic theater (especially to the *sermons joyeux*, but also to medieval farces and *sotties* usually mentioned in that connection). Suggests that "many of the themes in Rabelais' book and many of the devices he uses in writing come from the oral reserves of popular sub-literature" (p. 122). Sees Panurge primarily as an actor playing in succession a variety of different roles: "What holds Panurge together as a fictional creation is not psychological plausibility but language" (p. 133), a kind of "rhétorique joyeuse" meant to disarm moral criticism. Argues that Rabelais' work is a fundamentally comic creation whose message is an exortation to the joyous acceptance of life. In the final pages, raises a number of problems of interpretation and concludes that instead of looking for the ever-elusive "book Rabelais wrote," we should resign ourselves to read his work in a necessarily subjective way, but with care to avoid the double pitfall of anachronism and of the illusion that we have gained a privileged access to the work's one true meaning.

13   COOPER, RICHARD. "'Maistre Gabriel Medicin de Savillan,' *Quart Livre* XXVII." *Études Rabelaisiennes* 17:115–18.
Contends that the physician in question has been incorrectly identified as Gabriel Taphenon, whereas in fact Rabelais was referring to Gabriele Gaffuri. Offers biographical information about Gaffuri, the other physician attending Langey at his death-bed.

14   ———. "Guillaume du Bellay, Rabelais and the University of Turin, 1538–1543." *Études Rabelaisiennes* 17:119–28.

Cites examples of cultural exchanges between Lyons and Turin, and discusses the effect of the invasion of 1536 upon the University of Turin, "which did not remain deserted for long" (p. 122) in spite of various difficulties. From the list of diplomas granted between 1540 and 1543 concludes that during the governorship of Langey a degree of activity was encouraged, especially in medicine.

15 DEBERRE, JEAN-CHRISTOPHE. "La généalogie du pouvoir dans les trois premiers livres de Rabelais." *Littérature* 50 (May):15–35.

Offers, from a Marxist perspective, a political and economic reading of key episodes in Rabelais' books. Behind a deceptive façade of generosity and toleration, the Rabelaisian giants are said to represent an oppressive social order grounded in a capitalistic notion of economy, and promising peace in exchange for a stifling sense of obligation to the state, resulting in total alienation of the individual. Panurge's brief administration of Salmigondin presents an antithetical societal model which underscores the dangers inherent in an authoritarian conception of political power. Both models are seen to be based on similar values and institutions, but their aims are said to be different. For Panurge, work and marriage are compatible with pleasure and happiness, and are ultimately justified insofar as they satisfy the deepest needs of the collectivity. For the giants, "ces deux termes n'ont de sens que dans la conservation jalouse d'un ordre social réglementé rigoureusement et violemment—fût-ce sur le plan symbolique—par le pouvoir" (p. 35). Whereas Rabelais sometimes clearly sides with Panurge, it cannot be said that he uncritically chooses one model over the other. In the passages dealing with either model, "l'énonciation est inséparable d'une immédiate mise en question" (p. 35).

16 DE LA GARANDIERE, M[ARIE] M[ADELEINE]. "Rabelais et Budé." In *Mélanges à la mémoire de Franco Simone*. Vol. IV: *Tradition et originalité dans la création littéraire*. Geneva: Éditions Slatkine, pp. 151–67.

Takes exception to Delaruelle's contention, expressed in "Ce que Rabelais doit à Erasme et à Budé" (1904), that Rabelais does not owe Budé anything of consequence: "Tout au contraire, nous sommes persuadée, et nous voudrions ici suggérer, malgré les difficultés de fournir démonstration en tel domaine, que Rabelais est fondamentalement *budéien*" (p. 154). Sees a close relationship in the logic and esthetics of the two authors. Finds Rabelais' second letter to Budé to be in the best Budeian vein, full of admiration (and imitation) of Budé's flamboyant style and the imaginative nature of his verbal creations. Suggests that Rabelais may have found in the style of Budé's *De Asse* a model he will adopt in his own narratives, "une logique complexe, non linéaire, qui néglige le discours propre à la raison pour obéir à la polyvalence des signes" (p. 159). Notes a similar taste for a certain obscurity, a certain enigmatic turn of expression, a propensity to play on several registers at once. Notes also certain specific borrowings: the praise of Pandects, the dispute between Thaumaste and Panurge in *Pantagruel*, the anecdote concerning Diogenes in the prologue to Book III, the definition of pantagruelism in Book IV, echoing as it does Budé's *De contemptu rerum fortuitarum*. But insists above all on Budé himself as a model for Rabelais: "Budé lui-même, comme personnage éminemment représentatif, comme cas typique, et en quelque sorte comme 'statue,' a joué un rôle essentiel dans la genèse du récit rabelaisien" (p. 161). Shows how much Gargantua's letter to Pantagruel owes to Budé's letter to his son (p. 162), how much the Rabelaisian myth of progress through paternity owes to Budé's own experience, and how much the myth of the abbey of Thélème owes to the reality of the Collège des Lecteurs Royaux created at Budé's instigation.

17  DELEGUE, YVES. "Le Pantagruélion, ou le discours de la vérité." *Réforme Humanisme Renaissance* 16 (January):18–40.

On methodological grounds, contests Saulnier's interpretation of the Pantagruélion as a tacit, non-militant form of evangelism (see 1956.11). Stresses the ways in which the presentation of the Pantagruélion differs from what precedes it in the *Tiers Livre*: it is the only episode that does not give rise to divergent interpretations; the description is put in the mouth of the author himself; it is curiously free of any erudite references: "la seule référence avouée du texte est la réalité qu'il décrit" (p. 26). Notes Rabelais' insistance on the veracity of what he is describing, the link between the name of the plant and the name of the hero, the emphasis on the plant's manifold usefulness. Argues that the plant is the book itself, the discourse that tells the truth, however subjective and relative that truth may be.

18  DUVAL, EDWIN M. "The Juge Bridoye, Pantagruelism, and the Unity of Rabelais' *Tiers Livre*." *Études Rabelaisiennes* 17:37–60.

Seeks to bring out the importance of the six chapters dealing with the judge, and the relevance of the episode for Panurge's quest. Underscores the fundamental ambiguity of the character, and suggests that recent attempts at reading a serious meaning into what had previously been held to be pure legal satire do not hold up under careful scrutiny: "Rabelais simply does not allow us to approve Bridoye's behavior on any grounds, whether legal or metaphysical" (p. 39). Suggests that here as elsewhere in Rabelais, and indeed in the works of the Renaissance in general, the meaning is not explicitly stated but must be discovered. Seeks to do so in this case by studying the place of the episode in the structural pattern of the novel. Notes that the episode is framed by the anecdotes dealing with Seigny Joan on the one hand, and the woman of Smyrna on the other. Suggests that the structure of the episode brings out the fact that Bridoye does not resemble either of the exemplary judges in the two framing anecdotes "as much as he resembles the defendants those judges are called upon to judge" (p. 48). Believes that by focusing on Bridoye as judge rather than seeing him as a defendant in a case to be judged by Trinquemalle, scholars have lost sight of the fact that "the primary issue of the episode is not the legitimacy or efficacy of Bridoye's methods at all, but...the legal dilemma he poses *as an object of judgment*" (p. 49). Sees the most significant aspect of the episode to be Pantagruel's refusal, when deferred to by Trinquemalle, to pass judgment and to prefer to lodge a plea for clemency. Finds his role as supplicant to be consonant with the main tenets of Pantagruelism as defined and practiced elsewhere in the *Tiers Livre*. Rejects the commonly held view that the *Tiers Livre* belongs primarily to Panurge. Concludes that "the most fundamental issue of the book is not to be found in Panurge's quest at all, but rather in Pantagruel's response to it" (p. 58). Sees the Bridoye episode not as a digression but as the climax of an essentially Christian epic.

19   FARRELL, MARY. "The Alchemy of Rabelais's Marrow Bone." *Modern Language Studies* 13, no. 2:97–104.
      Suggests that the marrow bone has alchemical overtones, and that Alcofribas' choice of the image of the marrow bone in the prologue to *Gargantua* is related to his profession of "abstracteur de quintessence," and to his tendency to transform the serious into the comic, and vice versa.

20   FONTAINE, MARIE MADELEINE. "Rabelais et Speroni." *Études Rabelaisiennes* 17:1–8.
      Notes thematic similarities between the chapters on the praise of debtors in the *Tiers Livre*, and Speroni's *Dialoghi* on usury and discord.

21   FRANÇON, MARCEL. "Du nom commun au nom propre." *BAARD* 4, no. 2:65–66.
      Cites two examples of a common noun used as a proper noun in Rabelais: *brésil* and *caniballes*. Continues the discussion about *caniballes* on pages 67 and 68.

22   ———. "Rabelais et la nomenclature guidonienne." *Études Rabelaisiennes* 17:95–98.
      Draws attention to two examples of Rabelais' familiarity with the system of musical notation invented by Guido d'Arrezzo.

23   GAUNA, MAX. "Healing the Evil Love: A Platonic Source for the *Tiers Livre*?" *Études Rabelaisiennes* 17:9–19.
      Contends that "certain Platonic texts, considered as primary sources for Rabelaisian inspiration, are bound to shift our perceptions of our author's purpose" in the *Tiers Livre* (p. 10). Thus the *Gorgias* and the *Sophist* suggest that Panurge does not, as has been argued, represent dialectic—which in Plato means the pursuit of truth—but rather rhetoric or sophistry. Reference to the *Laws* throws light on *philautia* or self-love as Panurge's central problem, and may explain why the notion is developed by Rabelais in the context of sex and

marriage. As for Rabelais' interest in divination and demons, it is better understood in the Platonic context of the *Symposium*, with its definition of Eros and other demons as intermediaries between men and the gods, than in the light of Christian tradition.

24 GOUMARRE, PIERRE J. "La Castration: Rabelais et Freud." *Language Quarterly* 21, no. 3–4 (Spring–Summer):5–11.

Notes that Freud had used an excerpt from the *Quart Livre* in one of his studies on the castration complex. Finds signs of such a castration complex in Panurge's disdain for women, and in his fears—particularly of being eaten and rendered impotent. Finds them also in Panurge's exhibitionism, and in his dream of being betrayed and beaten (in the owl and drum episode). Concludes that Panurge does suffer from a sexual malaise, but that the Freudian notion of a castration complex is insufficient to explain it, since it is related to a fear of women (as in Jung) rather than being a consequence of the œdipal complex.

25 HERRMANN, LÉON. "La Langue lilliputienne et Lemuel Gulliver d'après Swift." *Revue de Littérature Comparée* 225, no. 1 (January–March):95–100.

Adds to what is known of Rabelais' influence on Swift by pointing out a number of linguistic and cryptological reminiscences, notably the fact that Gulliver initially addresses the emperor of Lilliput in a variety of foreign languages, as does Panurge in his first encounter with Pantagruel.

26 HUCHON, MIREILLE. "Rabelais et les majuscules." *Études Rabelaisiennes* 17:99–113.

Notes the earliest attempts at codifying the use of capital letters. Offers a comparative study of the use of capitals in the *Tiers Livre* to test a remark by Screech to the effect that Fezandat's 1552 edition of the *Tiers Livre* makes a systematic use ("un emploi raisonné") of capital letters. Taking into account the editor's habits and the norms in use at the time, concludes that Rabelais made a coherent use of the capitals, often following common usage although without slavish compliance. But notes also that an essentially similar use of capitals is made in the first known edition of *Pantagruel*.

27 JEANNERET, MICHEL. "Alimentation, digestion, réflexion dans Rabelais." *Studi Francesi*, no. 81:405–16.

Notes that for Bakhtin and his followers the Rabelaisian feast is a celebration of abundance, an occasion to rehabilitate the body and its instinctive quest for physical pleasure in an atmosphere of joy and freedom. But argues that such an interpretation threatens to obscure the polyvalence of discourse which here as elsewhere characterizes Rabelais' text, and to overshadow the progressive devalorization of the theme, especially in the *Quart Livre*. Underscores the pages that proclaim an ideal of moderation, and shows their kinship with such dietetic treatises of the Renaissance as Ficino's *De Triplici Vita*, the Hippocratic theory of the four humors, and the theory of the spirits according to which sound intellectual activity is incompatible with overindulgence. Argues that in this area Rabelais owes as much to humanist medicine as to popular, carnivalesque tradition. "Dans le champ alimentaire comme ailleurs, Rabelais manipule des éléments hétérogènes et enrichit son texte de leur tension" (p. 416).

28 ———. "Quand la fable se met à table: Nourriture et structure narrative dans le *Quart Livre*." *Poétique* 54 (April):163–80.

Notes that allegory loses ground as Rabelais' work progresses, and that in Book IV it is only one mode of perception and exposition among many. Argues that with this displacement in the status of allegory, contraries are no longer meant to be subsumed under a higher unifying principle but are meant to coexist; that the figurative no longer annihilates the literal. Studies the relationship between the theme of food ("le thème alimentaire") and textual ambiguity in the Gaster episode (chapt. 57–62), and interprets it as putting in doubt the pertinence of allegorical decoding: both the literal and the allegorical, the stomach and technology, are meant to have equal importance. Sees the same equal value ascribed to the literal and the figurative in the episode of the feast off the island of Chaneph (chapt. 63–65). The theme of food, previously an agent of cohesion, is now associated with violence and intolerance, and acquires a dualistic structure; Pantagruel's voice, previously the unquestioned voice of wisdom, now loses its authoritative status: "Pantagruel et ses amis ont chacun voix au chapitre" (p. 178). Besides this binary oscillation between the spiritual and the material, notes the interference of other voices, other visions: that of the monstrously strange, for example, which adds to the fundamental heterogeneity of Rabelaisian narrative in the *Quart Livre*.

29 LOGAN, PAUL W. "The Grotesque in Rabelais's *Quart Livre*." Ph.D. dissertation, Michigan State University, 177 pp.

Points out that "crotesque" came into usage in France in the year which saw the publication of *Pantagruel*, that Rabelais uses the term in the *Tiers Livre*, and is thus apparently familiar with the style designated by the word: "the pictorial and decorative style which fused disparate elements into a single, ambivalent image." Believes Mikhail Bakhtin to have been the first critic to apply to Rabelais' first two books Ruskin's definition of the grotesque as an essentially ambivalent style in which both comic and fearful elements are necessary components. Extends this application to the *Quart Livre*, "perhaps the most ambivalent and grotesque of all Rabelais's works." Studies Rabelais' use of the grotesque for both comic and satiric effects throughout the book. See *Dissertation Abstracts International* 44, no. 3 (September 1983):766–A.

1983

30  McNEIL, DAVID. "The 'Choicest Morsel' of Sterne's Borrowings from Rabelais Unnoticed." *English Language Notes* 21 (September):42–44.

Believes that the reference to Toby's loves in *Tristram Shandy* as the book's "choicest morsel" echoes Panurge's words to Friar John, to the effect that by keeping his advice for last ("à bonne bouche"), in the series of consultations as to whether he should marry, Panurge was saving the best for last.

31  MORRIS, DAVID. "The Place of Jewish Law and Tradition in the Work of Rabelais." *Études Rabelaisiennes* 17:75–88.

Acknowledges an interest among Renaissance humanists in Hebrew and the Jewish Cabbala, but contends that the Christian humanists harbored many "erudite misconceptions" about the nature of Jewish law and tradition (p. 77). Despite an exceptional tolerance towards Judaism, and despite a remarkable integration of Jewish tradition into the totality of his literary work, Rabelais shares these misconceptions, mainly about the relationship between Jewish written and oral law.

32  QUINT, DAVID. "Rabelais: From Babel to Apocalypse." In *Origin and Originality in Renaissance Literature: Versions of the Source*. New Haven: Yale University Press, pp. 167–206.

Beginning with a reading of the Pantagruélion episode in Book III, considered as linking "the advancement of human learning and technology to the unfolding of salvation history" (p. 171), discusses the interdependent themes of literary creation and spiritual quest in all five books. Argues that Rabelais' text presents itself, contrary to Renaissance norms, as both a human, individual achievement and a vehicle of spiritual truth grounded in a higher authority. Believes that for Rabelais this spiritual truth cannot be apprehended apart from its incarnation in history, so that his text must not be allegorized at the expense of its literal meaning through which alone the higher spiritual truth can be intimated. Concludes that Rabelais' relativistic concept of truth and his pluralistic vision of men reconciling their differences within a pantagruelistic community "marked a moment in the history of the Renaissance thought that was not to be repeated" (p. 206).

33  SAULNIER, V[ERDUN]-[LOUIS]. *Rabelais I: Rabelais dans son enquête, La Sagesse de Gargantua, Le Dessein de Rabelais*. Paris: Société d'Édition d'Enseignement Supérieur, 224 pp.

A general study of Rabelais' thought, and an analysis of Rabelais' first three books. The first volume of a two-volume work based on manuscripts left by the author at his death and prepared for publication by Jean Céard. Volume 2, covering Books IV and V, appeared a year earlier (see 1982.26). Part 1— the first thirty-five pages—is a reworking by Saulnier himself of materials published earlier in "La philosophie de Rabelais," "Ce que Rabelais dénonce," and "Aspects et motifs de la pensée rabelaisienne" (see 1960.10,

1962.9, and 1963.20 respectively). Studies Books I and II as well as the *Pantagrueline Prognostication* of 1533, and claims that these early works already contain the essence of Rabelais' thought and express the same didactic message: a lesson of courage in the struggle against hypocrisy, a quest for textual authenticity in matters of religion, literature, and medicine, and a call for action and self-knowledge in a spirit of charity. Part 2 was meant to consist of earlier articles, some of which had not previously been published, all bearing on various aspects of "la sagesse de Gargantua." As assembled by the editor in the absence of a definitive list of texts to be included, begins with a claim for considering Rabelais not as the heir of a Gallic narrative tradition of long standing, but as the father of the French popular novel, written for the amusement of the masses (provided they could read). Chapt. 2 reproduces "Pantagruel et sa famille de mots" (1960.10), chapt. 3 is a reprint of "Rabelais maître de volonté" (1955.10), and chapt. 4 reproduces "Le formulaire rabelaisien" (1961.7). Chapt. 5 summarizes Rabelais' ideas on education, as set out in "Les idées pédagogiques de Rabelais" (1961.8), followed by a "note complémentaire" added after the original publication of the article. Chapt. 6, "Erasme et les Géants," reproduces an excerpt from the author's introduction to Pierre Michel's 1962 edition of *Pantagruel* for Le Club du Meilleur Livre, revealing behind the amusing façade of Rabelais' least philosophical work the presence, nevertheless, of serious preoccupations which make the author of *Pantagruel* a disciple of Erasmus. Chapt. 7 reprints "Le doute chez Rabelais? Un programme circonstancié: le premier *Pantagruel*" (1977.36), and argues that Gargantua's letter to Pantagruel, although *circonstanciée* (that is, determined, to an extent, by the narrative context and by Rabelais' essentially satirical design), does nevertheless express Rabelais' deepest convictions. Chapt. 8, "Une philosophie du quant-à-soi: Du *Gargantua* au *Tiers Livre*," is an excerpt from "Rabelais et le Populaire" published in *Lettres d'Humanité* in 1949. In this last chapter, argues that it is in the notion of "la paix chez soi," as it slowly develops in Rabelais' text, that one ought to seek the most fundamental element of Rabelais' thought. Defines it as the decision not to meddle in other people's affairs and not to allow them to meddle in one's own; distinguishes this *hésuchisme* from individualism and finds it to be perfectly compatible with the ideal of communal life. Uses the speech against the Papelards, at the end of *Pantagruel*, and the Abbaye de Thélème episode to support his thesis. Finds echoes of this ideal generally among the Evangelicals around 1535–40, and more specifically in the *Cymbalum Mundi* and in Marguerite de Navarre's *Comédie de Mont de Marsan*. Part 3 reproduces, with only very minor changes, the author's *Dessein de Rabelais* (see 1957.8).

34  SCHWARTZ, JEROME. "Rhetorical tensions in the liminary texts of Rabelais' *Quart Livre*." *Études Rabelaisiennes* 17:21–36.
     Compares the 1548 prologue with the epistle to Odet de Châtillon, and the latter with the 1552 prologue which precedes it in the definitive edition.

1983

Notes that the violence of the satire in the 1548 prologue is considerably toned down in those passages which find their new place in the epistle, but believes that this merely signals a change in strategy: instead of "railing against his enemies" (p. 26), Rabelais now seeks to intimidate them by invoking powerful admirers (the king, Cardinal Du Bellay). In the praise of Odet de Châtillon, its hyperbolic nature creates the "antiphrastic effect" produced by overstatement (p. 27). Considered in itself, the 1552 prologue is ironic, contradictory, and ambiguous. Taken together with the letter, it constitutes "one larger liminary text presenting two quite different attitudes and tones which both complement and undercut one another" (p. 35). Believes they need to be read as "a disjunctive structure whose contradictions or incompatibilities are indices of Rabelais' capacity to distance himself from partisan politics by means of various rhetorical disguises which, nevertheless, reveal tensions between his dependence upon the rhetoric of courtship in the context of sixteenth-century realities and the idealism of his comic vision" (p. 36).

35    SMITH, P[AUL] J. "Aspects de la rhétorique rabelaisienne." *Neophilologus* 67, no. 2 (April):175–85.
        Although it appears and presents itself as effortless and spontaneous, argues that Rabelais' work is the fruit of a conscious rhetorical strategy. Recognizes in Rabelais' claim that his work is a product of drunken delirium, a parody of the notion of *furor poeticus* and of *modestie affectée*, an oratorical device used by Erasmus and later by Montaigne. Notes that even Rabelais' verbal exuberance has its source in the rhetoric of *copia*. Finds rhetoric to be pervasive throughout the novel, and attempts to define Rabelais' concept of rhetoric and to show by the use of a few examples how it determines both the form and the content of Rabelais' work. Draws attention to the presence in the novels of a *métadiscours*, both rhetorical and stylistic, as the narrator and his characters comment on style or etymology; in examples of good and bad rhetoric (although critics may not always agree on which is which); in the parody of rhetoric—as in the Baisecul and Humevesne episode, or that which concerns Thaumaste—which betrays a lack of confidence in language in favor of other semiotic systems. Speaks of Rabelais' ambivalent conception of language as both Cratylian and Hermogenic, both arbitrary in theory and viable, "remotivated," in practice. Argues that beyond its thematic function, rhetoric also acts as a structural element shaping the work. Ends with a few "réflexions spéculatives" on the possible application to Rabelais' work of modern rhetorical concepts related to the question of narrativity: Who is speaking? To whom? How does the *narrataire* manipulate his audience? Can any of the characters be said to speak for the author? Believes that on these all important questions the reader still finds himself or herself in the throes of Panurgian perplexity.

36  STAROBINSKI, JEAN. "L'Ordre du jour." *Le Temps de la Réflexion* 4:101–25.

Studies, in a group of writers from Horace to Rousseau, the literary expression of the need to escape from the constraints of what the individual has come to see as an unsatisfactory structuring of the "manière de vivre" prevalent in society. In *Gargantua*, reads the daily curriculum under the tutelage of Thubal Holoferne as representing an unsatisfying organization of temporal space, and the episodes of Gargantua's education under Ponocrates and of life at Thélème as the two diametrically opposed alternatives at the individual's disposal in his effort to reform a defective *status quo*. Underscores the "hyperorganization" of time under Ponocrates, aimed at achieving the most effective—and ultimately the most enjoyable—use of the student's waking hours. In the Abbaye de Thélème chapters, on the other hand, notes the total suppression of temporal constraints: "La loi du temps subit une décompression complète; la vie se déroule selon le rhythme paradisiaque de l'alternance impromptue, qui fait de chaque instant le commencement d'un nouveau divertissement" (p. 112). Sees in these two examples of reformed existence the anthropological paradigm underlying all specific attempts, at various moments in human history, to change "l'ordre du jour" and to make it conform to one's more-or-less utopian aspirations.

37  STONE, DONALD, Jr. "Ethical Patterns in *Gargantua*." *French Review* 57, no. 1 (October):10–13.

Suggests that the apparently incongruous enthusiasm of Grandgousier at his son's invention of a *torche-cul* (in chapt. 13), and the somewhat puzzling content of Eudémon's rhetorical praise of Gargantua in the following chapter, become more understandable when these episodes are viewed not only in terms of comedy and humanist propaganda, but also as narrative illustrations of Erasmus' pedagogical ideas, as set out in *De pueris statim ac liberaliter instituendis*.

38  TOURNON, ANDRÉ. "De l'interprétation des 'motz de gueule': Note sur les chapitres LV–LVI du *Quart Livre du Pantagruel*." In *Hommage à F. Meyer*. Aix: Publications de l'Université de Provence, pp. 145–53.

In the frozen words episode, the "mots de gueule" in question designate the kind of cordial insults hurled at Rabelais' readers by the narrator in the prologues, or by Frère Jean at Panurge throughout the novels, and singled out by Bakhtin as examples of the vocabulary of the marketplace. Signifying contempt but expressing affection, they presuppose the type of tolerant, well-meaning interpretation which characterizes the true Pantagruelists as they seek out the spirit behind the letter. Sees in these "mots de gueule" and their Pantagruelistic interpretation an example of the way in which Rabelais means us to read his text. Suggests that what intonation and mimickry do to insure

1984

the intended interpretation in oral communication, is achieved in the written text by a metalinguistic stratification of Rabelais' message. Argues that this message resides not only in the serious and learned pronouncements voiced by the giants, but also—perhaps mostly—in the playful, poetic, enigmatic pages associated with Panurge and Frère Jean: "le sens réside aussi, et peut-être surtout, dans ces fariboles cautionnées par la sympathie et le plaisir" (p. 151).

39  VASSAL, PIERRE. "De l'alme, inclyte et celebre academie que l'on vocite Lutece." *BAARD* 4, no. 2:71–72.
    Offers linguistic comments on the Ecolier Limousin's allusion to Paris.

40  WALTER, PHILIPPE. "*Homo viator*, ou le sens de la quête chez Rabelais." *BAARD* 4, no. 2:73–74.
    "Le monde a-t-il un sens? Le langage contient-il une vérité?" Interprets Panurge's quest as, in fact, Pantargruel's and Rabelais' own search for meaning, "une quête des signes."

41  WEINBERG, FLORENCE M[AY]. "Fischart's *Geschichtklitterung*: A Questionable Reception of *Gargantua*." *Sixteenth-Century Journal* 13:23–35.
    Studies Fischart's adaptation of *Gargantua* as an example of "questionable reception": finds it to be true to the letter, but to betray the spirit of Rabelais' text.

## 1984

1  BALDINGER, KURT. "Mißverstandener Rabelais: *Aller long comme un vouge* und die *cuideurs des vendanges* (*Gargantua*, 25)." *Romanistische Zeitschrift für Literaturgeschichte* 8:1–17.
    Attracts attention to the variant *aller/dasler* and its scatological meaning (*pisser abondamment*). Believes the second expression to be a play on words and to signify "those who delude themselves." Reprinted in 1990.2.

2  BARAZ, MICHAEL. "Un texte polyvalent: le prologue de *Gargantua*." In *Mélanges sur la littérature de la Renaissance à la mémoire de V.-L. Saulnier*. THR, no. 202. Geneva: Librairie Droz, pp. 527–35.
    Spitzer had suggested that Rabelais' advice to the reader to seek a "substantifique mouelle" in his text smacks of parody of medieval poetics. While accepting this idea, questions Spitzer's conclusion, namely that the prologue as well as the rest of the work is essentially a free play of ideas. Claims that the work is anti-intellectual only in that it rejects what the author calls "l'intelligence prosaïque." Rabelais is neither exclusively a thinker nor a poet: "une imagination purement ludique coexiste dans toute son œuvre avec une pensée

cohérente, profonde et souvent inspirée" (p. 529). The apparent contradiction between the two parts of the prologue disappears when the latter is read not as a one-dimensional rational text, but as an elaborate and polyvalent "jeu d'idées."

3   BÉNÉ, CHARLES. "L'édition Nourry (1532) est-elle l'édition originale du *Pantagruel*?" In *La littérature de la Renaissance: Mélanges offerts à Henri Weber*, edited by Marguerite Soulié. Introduction by Robert Aulotte. Bibliothèque Franco Simone, no. 13. Geneva: Éditions Slatkine, pp. 49–58.

Notes that despite certain details pointing to an opposite conclusion, Nourry's is indeed, without any doubt, the oldest—and the most beautiful—edition of *Pantagruel* known today. But points out that material and textual considerations suggest the possibility that François Juste, who was already Rabelais' editor in 1532 for the *Pantagrueline Prognostication pour 1533*, and who was to publish Rabelais' works right through 1542, had published the very first edition of *Pantagruel*, of which Nourry subsequently brought out a pirated version, carefully edited and elegantly printed for a wealthier, more discriminating public.

4   ———. "Rabelais et l'art épistolaire dans le *Pantagruel*." *Langue et Littérature: Hommage à Yves Le Hir. Recherches et Travaux*, no. 26:114.

Calls attention to the four examples of epistolary art to be found in Rabelais' first four books, only one of which—the famous letter from Gargantua to Pantagruel—had hitherto been an object of critical scrutiny. Stresses Rabelais' debt to Cicero, Seneca, Erasmus, and above all to the Epistles of Saint Paul, whose structure Rabelais seems to have adopted as a model.

5   CHAKER, JAMIL. *Sémiotique narrative de l'œuvre de François Rabelais: Récit–Symbole–Imaginaire*. Préface de Jean Larmat. Sixième série: Philosophie-Littérature, no. 24. Tunis: Publications de l'Université de Tunis, 398 pp.

Interdisciplinary study of characters and episodes in Rabelais' first four books in the light of Greimas' semiotics and Lacan's distinction between the symbolic and the imaginary. Seeks to describe Rabelais' work with the tools of contemporary narratology, and show how the manifestations of reality in Rabelais are affected, how they are "déformées sous les actions multipliées des deux univers symbolique et imaginaire" (p. 28). Substitutes the notion of *cycle* for that of *narrative structure*, and distinguishes three such cycles: those of Gargantua, Pantagruel, and Panurge. With the terminology of Gilbert Durand's *Structures anthropologiques de l'imaginaire*, studies the semiology of the human body and of the surrounding natural world, underscoring the symbolic relationships between the two. Proceeds to a semiotic analysis of artificial and meta-semiotic objects (the latter so called because "ils figurent la problématique du sens," p. 127). Interprets the image of Diogenes' tub as signifying that, from Book III on, "l'écriture n'est plus asservie à une instrumentalité quelconque. [Elle] se déroule désormais à la surface, langage du jeu et jeu du langage" (p. 148). In the section on "Sémiotique de la manifestation narrative," develops a semiotic of Rabelais' narrative discourse; studies the relationship between the author and his work, narrative time, the presence of the narrator, the narrator's anaphorical function, the fragmented nature of his discourse, his changing status from one book to the other. In his investigation of the relationship between the narrative discourse and the narrative itself ("diégèse"), studies the distortions of the statement (omission, expansion, and contraction), interaction between discourse and narrative (between "discours" and "récit"). In the section on "L'Auto-dynamisme de l'énoncé," studies how discourse engenders the main components of narrative: events, characters, meaning, and how it leads to a ludic treatment of myth. Studies the position of each cycle in the economy of the entire work, emphasizes the importance of genealogy in the first cycle, of the father/son relation in the symbolic framework of the novels. In "L'Imaginaire des personnages," shows that Panurge lacks any sense of collectivity, on both the social and the linguistic level, and finds him guilty of "subversion du langage" (p. 302). Notes the significance of the substitution of Frère Jean for Panurge in *Gargantua*; finds them to be fundamentally different from each other: whereas Panurge exists only as a "sujet parlant" (p. 320), Frère Jean "a pris le parti de la praxis, de la conquête et du faire" (p. 319). Finds them both to be ludic characters to a varying degree, as are also the giants (at the moment of disjunction from the father). In a final chapter, "Problématique du signifiant et de la littérature," studies the work as verbal creation in the light of concepts borrowed from psychoanalysis and anthropology. With the exception of *Gargantua*, sees in Rabelais' work an eclipse of the referent in favor of discourse and narrativity, "c'est-à-dire du linguistique, de la fonction poétique" (p. 382).

6    CLARK, CAROL. "*Stultorum Numerus Infinitus*: Attitudes to Folly in the Sixteenth Century and in Rabelais." In *Rabelais in Glasgow: Proceedings of the Colloquium held at the University of Glasgow in December 1983*, edited and published by James A. Coleman and Christine Scollen-Jimack. Glasgow: University of Glasgow Printing Unit, pp. 113–24.

Notes that the quotation from Ecclesiastes regarding the existence of an infinite number of fools was one of the most widely known biblical texts in Rabelais' day. Considers his treatment of the theme of folly against the background of writings that speak of it censoriously (Brant), with ambiguous irony (Erasmus), or with enthusiastic approval (the burlesque preachers of the *sermons joyeux*). Suggests that Rabelais' attitude clearly does not lie at the censorious, punitive end of the spectrum. Notes that Panurge is "the most obvious of the fools on display," but that to some extent all his characters, the narrator, and the implied reader as well, illustrate the truth of the biblical quotation.

7   CLARK, KATERINA, and HOLQUIST, MICHAEL. "Rabelais and His World." Chapt. 14 in *Mikhail Bakhtin*. Cambridge: Harvard University Press, pp. 295–320.

Discusses Bakhtin's work on Rabelais as an example of political propaganda under the guise of literary scholarship. Places the book in the political and intellectual context in which it was written. Believes that the work's political dimension accounts for Bakhtin's idealization of the people, presented as "instinctively anti-absolutist, pro-universalist, and anti-war" (p. 311). Also stresses Bakhtin's appreciation for Rabelais' linguistic innovations, in particular for his successful and daring attempt to raise the vernacular to the dignity of literary language. See also 1982.18.

8   COLEMAN, DOROTHY GABE. "Language in the *Tiers Livre*." In *Rabelais in Glasgow: Proceedings of the Colloquium held at the University of Glasgow in December 1983*, edited and published by James A. Coleman and Christine Scollen-Jimack. Glasgow: Glasgow University Printing Unit, pp. 39–53.

Believes the essential task of Rabelais criticism to be the study of Rabelais' use of language to obtain a "total, complex, emotional response" in the reader (p. 39). Notes the changes of tone in the prologues, in turn serious, light-hearted, violent, mocking, scoffing. Finds the Pantagruel of Book III "unmistakably comic" (p. 45), and sees in Panurge and Pantagruel "parodies of the traditional epic couple." Concludes with remarks on Panurge's language and behavior; argues that it is in Panurge "that we see linguistic comedy at its best" (p. 50). Suggests that if the *Tiers Livre* is still readable today, it is mainly due to Panurge's character, and that in creating Panurge Rabelais showed himself a worthy predecessor of Molière.

9   COMPAROT, ANDRÉE. "Rabelais ou la quête du macrocosme." *BAARD* 4, no. 3:92–104.

Discusses the praise of debts and the Pantagruélion in the light of a possible influence upon Rabelais of the Padovan school of Averroistic philosophy, with references to Pomponazzi's *De Incantationibus*, Sperone Speroni's *Dialoghi*, and the works of Cornelius Agrippa. Sees in the *Tiers Livre* a successful attempt to impose an esthetic of moderation consonant with Rabelais' ideal of world harmony.

10   COOPER, RICHARD. "Rabelais' Neo-Latin Writings." In *Neo-Latin and the Vernacular in Renaissance France*, edited by Grahame Castor and Terence Cave. Oxford: Oxford University Press, pp. 49–70.

Notes that Rabelais' neo-Latin works have been comparatively neglected by scholars. Classifies them into categories: personal and dedicatory letters, poems, and lost works. Studies each category, insists on the rhetoric of the letters to Tiraqueau and Du Bellay, discusses briefly the ideas contained in the letters, and provides an analysis of the only two poems in Latin that have survived. "Although no more than a pale shadow of his French works, Rabelais's neo-Latin writings provide a number of points of comparison with them, whether in themes and content, in stylistic inventiveness, or in hints of irony and badinage" (p. 67). Promises a new critical edition of Rabelais' Latin works, together with the Greek and minor French writings.

11    CORNILLIAT, FRANÇOIS. "L'Autre géant: les *Chroniques Gargantuines* et leur intertexte." *Littérature* 55 (October):85–97.
       Interested in the relationship between the various  chronicles, rather than in the relationship of these chronicles to Rabelais' text.

12    DEMERSON, GUY. "Tradition rhétorique et création littéraire." *Etudes de lettres*, no. 2 (April–June):3–23.
       Studies the function of classical rhetoric in Rabelais. Finds it to be above all ornamental rather than persuasive. Claims that Panurge's rhetoric does not persuade because it is excessively obvious and does not take into account the nature of his audience. Finds that rhetoric is used to the detriment of ideas as well as to the detriment of its own credibility. Argues that Rabelais uses it to underscore the psychological vacuity of some of his characters: "Quant aux personnages du roman, on peut dire que c'est leur type d'éloquence qui leur tient lieu de personnalité" (p. 10). Denies that Gargantua's encounter with Eudémon (*Gargantua*, chapt. 15) is tinged with irony. Sees it as an allegory of good rhetoric, which ennobles, disciplines the mind through mastery of one's language: "Maîtriser son langage, c'est s'humaniser, mettre en ordre le monde en surmontant l'immonde" (p. 14). Believes the same could be said of Gallet's harangue before Picrochole (*Gargantua*, chapt. 31), and Pantagruel's prayer (*Pantagruel*, chapt. 29). Claims that rhetoric seeks to draw the reader into the work rather than to convince. Notes that for some critics (such as Bakhtin), eloquence bears witness to the author's sincerity, whereas for others (such as J. Brault), it is a sure sign that Rabelais mocks what he is talking about. Claims that it is neither, since as in Plato rhetoric is not about truth but about illusion: "L'étude de la rhétorique de Rabelais montre qu'elle n'est ni une sophistique ni une dialectique mais un jeu, et une *allusio*, appel au jeu, en alternance avec les évocations sérieuses d'une histoire brutale ou glorieuse" (p. 19).

13    DUVAL, EDWIN M. "Pantagruel's Genealogy and the Redemptive Design of Rabelais's *Pantagruel*." *PMLA* 99:162–78.
       Argues that over and above whatever coherence *Pantagruel* may be shown to possess on the thematic, stylistic, or philosophical plane, the work also exhibits an "overarching design" outlined in the first chapter ("De l'origine et antiquité du grand Pantagruel"), fulfilled at the end, and which must be grasped before the individual episodes can be properly understood. Discusses

the controversies to which the chapter on Pantagruel's genealogy has given rise. Notes that the number of generations parallels that of Christ's genealogy in Matthew, if one counts (as Matthew does not) starting from Adam. Argues that this points to a "deliberate and carefully worked out analogy" (p. 164) between Pantagruel and the Messiah. Notes that Rabelais' account of the transformation of Chalbroth, Pantagruel's ancestor, from ordinary man to giant parallels the biblical account of the Fall, and concludes that Pantagruel must have been meant to represent "a *type* of the Christian Messiah" (p. 165): a redeemer of an Original Sin that did not consist in the willful tasting of the fruit of knowledge but in the unwitting contamination by fratricide blood. Notes that the messianic role thus given to Pantagruel is underscored by a number of allusions linking Rabelais' hero with Christ throughout an otherwise burlesque, and even obscene account of his exploits. Concludes that Pantagruel's victory over the Dipsodes should be read as a fulfillment of the redemptive promise made by the narrator at the outset, "not as a burlesque adventure unrelated to the others, but as the consummation of the typological design of the book" (p. 168). Believes the specific redemptive act to be the duel with Loup Garou, associated in the mind of Rabelais' contemporary readers with the figure of Cain. Interprets the duel as "the redemptive eradication of anti*caritas*" (p. 173), in the name of the brotherly love proclaimed in the second article of the "Great Commandment" of the New Testament, which is shown by the author to echo throughout the book, often in the most unexpected contexts.

14   FRECCERO, CARLA ANN. "The Books of Rabelais: Genealogy and the Failed Quest." Ph.D. dissertation, Yale University, 277 pp.
     Studies genealogy as both a thematic and a structural component of Rabelais' work. Sees it not only in the biological relationship between father and son, but also in questions of literary inheritance, as well as in the structural problem of narrative sequence. Detects a movement towards the past "as an authoritative and authenticating origin and the simultaneous challenge to that past, the 'modernist' claim to autonomy." The quest for the Word of the Holy Bottle "transforms the genealogical problem into a question of teleology, expressed in narrative terms," and is by its very nature a failed quest. Shows in the concluding chapter how Rabelais' text "allegorizes this failure," and suggests that it is precisely this failure that "clears the way for the future of narrative in the novel." See *Dissertation Abstracts International* 46 (1985):1642–A.

15   FONTAINE, MARIE MADELEINE. "Quaresmeprenant: l'image littéraire et la contestation de l'analogie médicale." In *Rabelais in Glasgow: Proceedings of the Colloquium held at the University of Glasgow in December 1983*, edit-

ed and published by James A. Coleman and Christine M. Scollen-Jimack. Glasgow: Glasgow University Printing Unit, pp. 87–112.

Takes issue with recent critics who dismiss the chapters on the anatomy of Quaresmeprenant as devoid of meaning, and considers the lists and comparisons in chapt. 29 through 32 of the *Quart Livre* in the light of Rabelais' medical references and in the context of contemporary medical debate. Claims that neither the order nor the vocabulary of the anatomical lists are as haphazard and unsystematic as has been claimed, and that both conform to an acceptable inner logic. Shows that Rabelais is fully aware of the "querelle des médecins" raging with particular violence in the years 1548–52 between the supporters and detractors of Galien. Notes that in the *Quart Livre* Rabelais refers to Galien more frequently than ever, often approvingly, but that he does not hesitate on occasion to exploit for comic purposes Galien's purported "errors." Argues that Rabelais' analogies between the parts of the body and a range of miscellaneous objects they are claimed to resemble correspond closely to what one finds in Galien or Chauliac, and that their use is meant to underscore through laughter the absurdity of the analogical method in the medical sciences of Rabelais' time. Notes the gradual substitution of verbal analogies by references to geometric forms in Vesalius, and by illustrations in such contemporary *Anatomies* as those of Guido Guidi or Charles Estienne, leading at last to a global perception of the human body. Sees a similar denunciation of comparisons and analogies in favor of a global perception of the body in Rabelais' use of the literary image. "En abusant de l'image, il la rend inapte à toute description, qu'elle soit médicale ou littéraire, mais il n'en détruit pas pour autant—bien au contraire!—les possibilités de représentation" (p. 106). Refers to Arcimboldo's portraits, or better still to Braccelli's *Bizarrie*, drawn in the second half of the century, as further illustrations of this effort to arrive at a global perception of the body.

16  GLIDDEN, H. H. "From History to Chronicle: Rabelais Rewriting Herodotus." *Illinois Classical Studies* 9:197–214.

Although Rabelais had made very few direct borrowings from Herodotus, suggests that he did draw heavily from the *Histories* in more subtle, more imaginative ways. Argues for "an affinity of imagination" between the two writers.

17  JEANNERET, MICHEL. "'Ma patrie est une citrouille': Thèmes alimentaires dans Rabelais et Folengo." *Etudes de lettres*, no. 2 (April–June):25–44.

Intertextual study of the ethical as well as the poetic implications of the celebration of food in Rabelais' first two books and in Folengo's *Baldus*. Notes the association throughout Folengo's poem of the pleasure of eating with the pleasure of verbal creation. Also notes the emphasis on food preparation rather than consumption: on transformation of nature into culture. Associates the manipulation of foodstuffs with the manipulation of language in the creation of his macaronic Latin ("latin de cuisine"): "manger et parler entretiennent un rapport de solidarité, de similarité" for Folengo as well as Rabelais (p. 29). Reminds us that Rabelais had read Folengo, and that the episodes of Panurge's sheep and of the storm at sea are imitated from *Baldus*. Studies the affinities between the two writers. Notes a similar use of the alimentary theme as an "overture" to their respective works, a similar association of feasting with the theme of origins, of eating with procreation. Points out that not only the giants but also their favorite companions on the human scale (Frère Jean and Panurge) make their entrance in an alimentary context: the defense of the "service du vin" and the tyranny of hunger. Notes that the birth of the individual and the creation of links with the collectivity are both associated with the theme of food. Thus Pantagruel's initial social act is to sit down to a feast and share a meal with his adult companions: "la nourriture est un thème inaugural en ce sens qu'elle prépare le héros à tirer le meilleur parti des choses et l'installe de plein-pied avec les hommes et les événements. Manger et boire, c'est faire symboliquement l'apprentissage du monde, c'est libérer un appétit, une force de désir, qui dynamisent toute la suite" (p. 34). Detects the same inaugural role of the "thème alimentaire" in the prologues, where reading is redefined as an essentially convivial, symposial activity, and where writing is seen as belonging to the same referential register as drinking and eating, in a classical as well as a popular context—that of Plato's *Symposium* and that of the country fair. Underscores the ambivalence of the theme, and claims that it allows Rabelais to free himself from the antithetical dualism of the material and the spiritual, the trivial and the sublime, in which the mock-heroic traditionally confines the writer. Concludes by suggesting that the alimentary theme allows Rabelais to propose a happier version of the story of creation, with its absence of any reference to Original Sin, and its emphasis on the realization of man's highest potential in an atmosphere of happy conviviality.

18   ———. "Polyphonie de Rabelais: Ambivalence, antithèse et ambiguïté." *Littérature* 55 (October):98–111.

Both Victor Hugo (in a chapter of his *William Shakespeare*) and Mikhail Bakhtin have noted the importance given by Rabelais to the lower body, and its treatment in the comic perspective of grotesque realism. But Hugo views this emphasis on the bodily functions in the light of the traditional opposition between spirit and matter, and sees this as a daring acknowledgement by Rabelais of the material, inferior, and essentially evil side of human nature: "Tout le discours de Hugo sur Rabelais est accroché à une échelle de valeurs résolument spiritualiste, qui rejette la tripe, si séduisante soit-elle dans l'ordre du mal" (p. 99). For Bakhtin, on the other hand, the grotesque elements in Rabelais are not negative but ambivalent: "Ils ne sont ni bas ni hauts, mais l'un et l'autre à la fois, principes de négation *et* d'affirmation, de mort *et* de vie. Ce que la morale censure, ils le régénèrent et le recyclent dans le processus positif des forces naturelles" (p. 100). Suggests that in one's search for the moral meaning of the text, Hugo's notion of antithesis is most fruitful in connection with Books III and IV, whereas Bakhtin's principle of ambivalence works best when brought to bear on *Pantagruel* and *Gargantua*. Illustrates this thesis by an analysis of the first chapter of *Pantagruel* and the last chapter of Book IV. Claims that yet another category, that of ambiguity, is required to account for those passages which are generically and tonally heterogeneous, those in which stylistic virtuosity takes precedence over meaning, or the numerous episodes which to this day remain incomprehensible.

19   KIDD, JOHN. "Joyce, Rabelais and Plutarch: The Deaths of Parnell and Pan." *James Joyce Quarterly* 21, no. 3 (Spring):279–81.
       Believes that the allusion in *A Portrait of the Artist as a Young Man* to the death of Pan, in connection with Parnell's death report, points directly to Plutarch's *Morals*, "excluding Pantagruel's version from the flow of influence" (p. 280). See 1981.30.

20   KRITZMAN, LAWRENCE D. "Rabelais in Papimania: Power and the Rule of Law." *Romanic Review* 75:25–34.
       Studies the Papimanes episode in the *Quart Livre* as a satire of the "unequivocally repressive policies of the Papal order" (p. 25). Does so in the light of the Gallican crisis of 1551–52, during which the Vatican is attacked, more specifically, for "the power of decretaline law to subtly draw gold out of France and direct it to the papal coffers in Rome" (p. 25). Notes that Rabelais' use of satire may be considered as going beyond "the traditional view of satire as purely moralistic literature" (p. 27), since Rabelais both satirizes and attacks. Believes that Rabelais' book also "demonstrates how writing functions as an integral part of the social process of incorporation and rule; it serves power by subjugating individuals to a supra-personal discipline or authority" (p. 32).

21   LARMAT, JEAN. "Du *Quart Livre de Pantagruel* de 1548 au *Quart Livre* de 1552: De l'ébauche au chef-d'œuvre." In *Mélanges sur la littérature de la Renaissance à la mémoire de V.-L. Saulnier*. THR, no. 202. Geneva: Librairie Droz, pp. 537–46.
       Notes, from one edition to the other, a greater sense of structural symmetry, a heightening in the violence of religious satire, a greater place given to erudition, a wider vocabulary, a more daring disarticulation of syntax, a greater variety of narrative modes, an emphasis on the two key motifs of food and danger, on the notion of voyage as initiation, and generally an ever more evident progress toward artistic perfection.

22   LESTRINGANT, FRANK. "La famille des 'tempêtes en mer': Essai de généalogie, (Rabelais, Thevet et quelques autres)." *Etudes de lettres*, no. 2 (April–June):45–62.

In analyzing the motif of the storm at sea, is less interested in Rabelais' predecessors, who have already received critical attention, than in writers such as Bertrand de La Borderie, Jacques Colin, and André Thevet, who wrote more or less at the time when Rabelais published his *Quart Livre*. Notes in these "collateral" works the convergence of two traditions: the courtly habit of assimilating the journey at sea to the experience of love, and the Evangelical tendency to view the perils of such a journey as the cornerstone of true faith. Sees these collateral works as originating in the *Naufragium* of Erasmus and culminating in an authentic "relation de voyage" with Thevet's *Cosmographie de Levant*. Sees La Borderie's *Discours du voyage de Constantinople* and Rabelais' *Quart Livre* as channeling the Erasmian message in the direction of Thevet's *Cosmographie*. Underscores the moralizing tendency of all these accounts, their advocacy of constancy in love (Chappuy's *Epistre d'une navigation* and Colin's *Conformité de l'Amour au Navigage*), and submission to God and faith in Providence (La Borderie and Thevet). Notes similarities between the *Cosmographie* and Rabelais' Book IV: both transcend the selfish plane of love poetry and rise to a spiritual plane of moral and theological reflection.

23   LEVI, A. H. T. "Rabelais and Ficino." In *Rabelais in Glasgow: Proceedings of the Colloquium held at the University of Glasgow in December 1983*, edited and published by James A. Coleman and Christine Scollen-Jimack. Glagow: Glasgow University Printing Unit, pp. 71–85.

Argues that it is from Ficino—via Erasmus—that Rabelais derived his belief in man's free will "in the fullest sense," and in man's ability "to rely on his own instincts as a guide to virtue" (p. 72) if acquired at birth and developed in a suitable environment. Notes that these insights of the Neoplatonist tradition, as expounded in the Abbaye de Thélème episode and as implied in the ethic of the *Tiers Livre*, are presented in a "literary register" rather than in the form of a theological debate, which probably accounts for Rabelais' ability to express his convictions without laying himself open to the charge of heresy.

24   MARI, PIERRE. "Une politique humaniste de la parole: L'interlocution rabelaisienne." *Etudes de lettres*, no. 2 (April–June):63–72.

Studies the problematics of communication in Rabelais' first two books, focusing mainly on two episodes: the Ecolier Limousin and the Abbaye de Thélème. Sees an evolution, from interlocution as verbal extravagance and source of incomprehension in *Pantagruel*, to "une régulation de la parole," whereby verbal exchange is brought under control and made to conform more or less closely to the serenity of humanistic dialog. But notes also, in the Picrocholine War episodes, a consciousness of the limits of language: "face à Picrochole, il n'est d'autre interlocution que celle du bâton" (p. 70). Sees it even more clearly in the Abbaye de Thélème, where the ability to anticipate the reaction to one's discourse robs the process of interlocution of its essential vitality, and underscores thereby the danger of sclerosis which threatens humanistic discourse.

25  MAYER, C.-A. *Lucien de Samosate et la Renaissance Française*. La Renaissance Française, no. 3. Geneva: Éditions Slatkine.

   In chapt. 5, entirely devoted to Rabelais, sees the latter as the most important of Lucian's disciples. Points out that Rabelais had been recognized as such for centuries. Notes that Lucian's influence had been questioned recently (see 1978.24); rejects such a view as—at the very least—unfounded. Reprints the list of borrowings as established by Plattard, expands it, summarizes Lucien Febvre's arguments against believing that Rabelais was an atheist, and categorically rejects his logic and his conclusions. Argues that Rabelais' satirical outbursts against monks and monastic life cannot be brushed off, as they are by Febvre, as inconsequential *gamineries* devoid of serious critical intention. Believes that Rabelais mocks not only the Church but also fundamental episodes of the New as well as the Old Testament: "il est impossible de faire de lui un catholique comme il est impossible de faire de lui un protestant" (p. 152). As for Rabelais' so-called Evangelical passages, argues that many of them are satirical, and explains the rest by Rabelais' political decision to opt for the lesser of two evils. Sees in the Evangelical propaganda at the time of the Renaissance "une machine de guerre" rather than the expression of true conviction. Alleges Dolet and Barthélémy Aneau as examples of writers who used Protestantism as a subterfuge. Sees the clearest proof of Rabelais' atheism in his irreverent attitude towards the notion of Providence in *Gargantua*, chapt. 27, a passage based on Lucian's *Jupiter tragoedus*. Argues that we have in these few lines "la source vive" (p. 163) of Rabelais' religious thought.

26  MORRISON, IAN. "Pleading, Deciding, and Judging in Rabelais." In *Rabelais in Glasgow: Proceedings of the Colloquium held at the University of Glasgow in December 1983*, edited and published by James A. Coleman and Christine Scollen-Jimack. Glasgow: Glagow University Printing Unit, pp. 55–70.

   Janotus de Bragmardo's highly rhetorical plea for the return of the bells of Notre-Dame (*Gargantua*, chapt. 17–19) and Ulrich Gallet's eloquent *harangues* to Picrochole (*Gargantua*, chapt. 28–32) in favor of peace meet with failure in their attempt at persuasion, whereas Couillatris' verbally clumsy appeal to Jupiter for the return of his axe (*Quart Livre*, prologue) is rewarded, "despite the execrable rhetorical performance of the pleader" (p. 61). In a second group of episodes, of a forensic nature, Pantagruel suggests that the legal dilemma of the woman of Smyrna (*Tiers Livre*, chapt. 44) should have been solved by recourse to lottery, and clearly sides with Bridoye and his recourse to dice in deciding the cases brought before him. Both instances imply Rabelais' "keen sense of the inadequacy of the mind to resolve problems of legal judgment" (p. 63). The case of Baisecul and Humevesne in *Pantagruel* and the anecdote of Seigny Joan paying for the smoke of a roast with the sound of his money may seem to imply the opposite, but in fact provide added proof of the inadequacy of man's power of judgment. Suggests that these two series of paradoxical episodes are best viewed as "counterweights" to the importance given to rhetoric in Rabelais' educational program, and to Rabelais' optimistic belief in the ability of the good king to make just laws and administer sound justice.

27  NILLES, CAMILLA. "The Economy of Owing." *Etudes de Lettres*, no. 2 (April–June):73–88.

Calls attention to the ambiguity of the episode, in which Panurge's dazzling rhetorical evocation of a universe held together by the principle of mutual exchange gives the appearance of "a very real humanist ideal" to what is at the same time "a blatant example of bad faith" (pp. 73–74). Notes that Pantagruel condemns Panurge's intention while admiring his rhetoric, and that the reader, in his search for an "unequivocal meaning," is tempted to choose "between the point of view of Pantagruel, the ideal humanist prince, and that of Panurge, the linguistic prestidigitator" (p. 74). Argues that both attitudes are unwarranted by the text. In an attempt to restore the "integrity" of the episode, studies the two chapters contrasting the world of debtors and creditors on the one hand, and the world devoid of debts on the other; uncovers beneath the binary oppositions of their thematic and formal organization a network of recurring structures—chiasmus, circularity—which allows the text to achieve oneness "by embracing contradiction and thereby preserving it" (p. 80). Brings out this aspect of Rabelais' treatment of the episode by contrasting it with a Latin adaptation written by a certain Robert Turner some thirty years after the publication of the *Tiers Livre*. Shows how Turner sacrifices the ambiguity of the original text to a conventionally Christian moral message, whereas "Rabelais transforms the tension produced by the co-existence of irreconcilables into a creative force, exalts contradiction and uses paradox as the foundation, motivation and expression of his universe" (p. 86).

28  NORTON, GLYN P. *The Ideology and Language of Translation in Renaissance France and their Humanistic Antecedents*. Geneva: Librairie Droz, 361 pp.

On pages 261–64, comments on chapt. 38–40 of the *Cinquiesme Livre*, in which the Pantagruelists stop to admire six mosaic panels depicting Bacchus' victory over the Indians, and reflect on the ability of art to create the illusion of reality. Notes the substitution of "parolles" to "echo" in the 1564 edition of the complete *Cinquiesme Livre*; finds it significant "because it enriches the linguistic and scriptural dimension of the entire scene" (p. 263) and because it sheds some light on the distinction between the concepts of *energeia* and *enargea* in the context of the theories of translation in the Renaissance. See 1979.21.

29   PARKIN, JOHN. "Rough Justice in Rabelais." In *Rabelais in Glasgow: Proceedings of the Colloquium held at the University of Glasgow in December 1983*, edited and published by James A. Coleman and Christine Scollen-Jimack. Glasgow: Glasgow University Printing Unit, pp. 125–43.

Despite the obvious relish with which Rabelais' characters mete out disproportionately cruel punishment throughout his novels, Rabelais does believe in a "transcendent moral order" and in the ability of human justice to be inspired in its institutional practices by "the sublime justice of God" (p. 125). Draws on Bakhtin's notion of the carnivalesque spirit in Rabelais to account for this apparent contradiction. More specifically, argues that Panurge's mistreatment of the "haulte dame de Paris" and of Dindenault should be viewed as instances of "ritual punishment of carnival" rather than disquieting manifestations of a sadistic personality. Claims that in such episodes Panurge does not act as an individual character, but merely plays a temporary role entrusted to him by the author so that he may enact, in a typically carnivalesque atmosphere and in a typically carnivalesque situation, a ritual punishment whose violence (as both destructive and regenerative, at once socializing and ostracizing) is sanctioned by the inverted morality of carnival.

30   POT, OLIVIER. "La mélancolie de Panurge." *Etudes de Lettres*, no. 2 (April–June):89–114.

With references to a lithograph by Martin van Heemskerck representing the various activities of "the children of Saturn" and to Burton's *Anatomy of Melancholy*, proposes a typological reading of Panurge as a literary representation of the melancholy type. Sees as typically Saturnian such features of Panurge's character as his obsession with food, his attraction to the earthy (and his concomitant hydrophobia), his superstition and his attraction to the demonic, his cleverness, his malice, his curiosity, and his chronic irresolution. Believes that this typological reading accounts for every facet of Panurge's behavior, that it brings out the character's inner coherence, and that the "excentrique" and individualistic component of Panurge's melancholy personality has important repercussions on the level of narrative strategy as well, since it provides the "problématique" necessary to raise Rabelais' text above the level of the *topos* and *exemplum* to the status of a true novel.

31 PRESCOTT, ANN LAKE. "The Stuart Masque and Pantagruel's Dreams." *ELH* 51, no. 3 (Fall):407–30.

The reference is to *Les Songes drolatiques de Pantagruel*, which at their publication in England by Richard Breton were said on the title page to be "de l'invention de maistre François Rabelais: et derniere œuvre d'iceluy, pour la recreation des bons esprits," and which until early in this century continued to be attributed to Rabelais.

32 RASSON, LUC. "Rabelais et la maîtrise: l'exemple du *Tiers Livre*." *Revue Belge de Philologie et d'Histoire* 62, no. 3:493–503.

Notes that the shift from narrative to discourse in the *Tiers Livre* parallels a loss of self-confidence on the part of the narrator (and of Panurge who replaces him in chapt. 2), and of confidence in the value of what he will have to say. Argues that the presence of Pantagruel, the notion of Pantagruelism, and the Pantagruelion episode at the end of the book have a reassuring, equilibrating function, insofar as they represent the elements of mastery necessary to counterbalance the "crisis" of ambiguity and self-doubt characterizing the prologue and the praise of debts. "Ce n'est que dans l'intéraction féconde de la crise et de la maîtrise, des forces centrifuges et centripètes que le texte de Rabelais peut se concevoir" (p. 503).

33 SCREECH, M[ICHAEL] A[NDREW]. "Celio Calcagnini and Rabelaisian Sympathy." In *Neo-Latin and the Vernacular in Renaissance France*, edited by Grahame Castor and Terence Cave. Oxford: Oxford University Press, pp. 26–48.

Although Calcagnini's influence had hitherto not passed unnoticed, believes it has been vastly underestimated. Notes that Rabelais refers in both the *Tiers* and the *Quart Livres* to the prophetic ventriloquist Jacoba Rhodigina, who exercized her art of "Gastromantie" at Ferrara, and that he associates her with Calcagnini "in some undefined way" (p. 28). Believes that Rabelais had seen Calcagnini at least once in Ferrara, and that he had read all sixty-four works contained in the 1554 edition of Calcagnini's *Opera*. Sees Calcagnini's influence on Rabelais in matters of detailed erudition as well as in Rabelais' conception of his work. Notes the similarity between the Pantagruelion episode and Calcagnini's apologue entitled *Linelaeon*, in which flax is also presented as a potential source of wealth, but above all ascribes to Calcagnini's influence the all-important part played by myths in the *Quart Livre*, with Rabelais' most obvious debt coming in the episode of Physis and Antiphysie where Rabelais exploits Calcagnini's concept of *sympathia rerum*, and in the chapter on the manner of "hausser le temps." "When Rabelais was creating major parts of the *Quart Livre*, he had his *Opera Calcagnini* on his desk" (p. 31).

1984

34    ———. "Printers' Helps—and Fruitful Errors." *Etudes de Lettres*, no. 2 (April–June):115–121.

Offers a few observations gathered in the course of preparing, with a group of collaborators, the forthcoming *New Rabelais Bibliography* (1987.15). Suggests that much light can be thrown on a work such as Rabelais' chronicles by bibliographical knowledge alone. As a case in point, notes the misunderstandings arising from such material obstacles as the inability of some printers to do justice to Rabelais' Greek quotations in the absence of Greek type; the unintentionally comic effect resulting from the decision by the printer to ignore sense and context, and to delay the drawing of the bottle promised by the text of the *Cinquiesme Livre* (chapt. 44) until such time as was practical in terms of *mise en page*; and the providential effect on Rabelais' reputation, in Calvinistically-inclined England, of the omission by the French printers of the reference to *Demoniacles Calvins* in chapt. 32 of the *Quart Livre*.

35    SCHLIFER, CATHY. "Contextual Misogyny in the *Tiers Livre*." *Chimères* 17, no. 2 (Spring):53–67.

"Rather than assuming misogyny as an underlying ideology in this Rabelaisian chronicle, one can quite easily see in it a simple continuation of prevailing literary practice" (p. 55). Points out that Rabelais is writing within an antifeminist tradition, that within his novel the misogynist comments are spoken by characters who need not necessarily be considered as expressing Rabelais' position, that men are not entirely spared, and women not always shown in an unfavorable light. Argues that Rabelais' intention is "to debate the extremes of the question at hand and to harmonize them" (p. 64), and that the dedication of the book to the spirit of Marguerite de Navarre should be taken as a sincere tribute to a woman who shared Rabelais' own interest in exploring the relations between the sexes.

36    SMITH, PAUL. "Le Prologue du *Pantagruel*: Une lecture." *Neophilologus* 68, no. 2:161–69.

Commenting on Deborah N. Losse's *Rhetoric at Play: Rabelais and Satirical Eulogy* (1980.31), discusses the impact of rhetoric, be it *ironisée*, on Rabelais' first prologue. Argues that it is no less rhetorical for looking more improvised, more popular, less learned, for this apparent spontaneity has its own rhetorical tradition. Notes that the nine paragraphs form a whole, conscientiously structured according to the rules of *dispositio*, and that each of the three parts into which it can be divided parodies one of the elements of the literary *exorde*: a flattering greeting to the reader, a flattering appraisal of the book, and finally the text's authentification. Claims that the entire prologue can be summarized in one sentence: "Cher lecteur (paragraph 1), ce livre sans pareil (paragraphs 2–7) est conforme à la vérité (paragraphs 8–9)" (p. 168).

37  SOZZI, LIONELLO. "Physis et Antiphysie, ou de l'arbre inversé." *Etudes de Lettres*, no. 2 (April–June):123–33.

Beyond Calcagnini's *Gigantes*, to which Jean Plattard had long ago attracted attention as a source of the Physis and Antiphysie episode in the *Quart Livre*, detects a double Platonic reference: to the passage on the Androgyne in the *Symposium*, and to the image of man as an inverted tree in the *Timeus*. Points out that in both ancient and Christian philosophy, this latter image is imbued with a religious and moral significance, and is used to emphasize man's fundamental dignity and his celestial essence. Argues that Antiphysie hides her monstrosity by seemingly adhering to the human ideal implicit in these two highly positive images of man, while in fact it blatantly betrays both that ideal and the true laws of nature.

38  SUTHERLAND, GEORGE. "The Rabelaisian See-Saw: Some Remarks on the Enigma of Thélème." In *Rabelais in Glasgow: Proceedings of the Colloquium held at the University of Glasgow in December 1983*, edited and published by James A. Coleman and Christine Scollen-Jimack. Glasgow: Glasgow University Printing Unit, pp. 13–38.

Through a close reading of the dialog between Gargantua and Frère Jean as to the possible meaning of the *Enigme en prophétie*, argues that Gargantua's sigh ("Gargantua souspira profondément") and his interpretation (namely that the subject of the poem is "le decours et maintien de verité divine") does not refer to the plight of contemporary Evangelicals or to their mission, so that it cannot be said to allude to the Affaire des Placards, and is thus of no help (as has sometimes been claimed) in dating the text. Points out that of the two proposed solutions, it is Frère Jean's that is given most importance: not only is he made to have the last words, but those last words are expanded from fifty-five in the first edition to 152 in the last edition, "revue et corrigée" by Rabelais himself. The character who utters them had previously built up by his behavior "a huge *crédit* of good will" (p. 27); his optimistic interpretation of the horrors mentioned in the Enigma as a game of tennis— "sublime metaphor"—deserves to be taken no less seriously than Gargantua's own reaction, and seen for what it really is, namely "an allegorical transposition of the Enigma in the spirit of the New Testament, as Gargantua's solution is in the spirit and in the letter of the Old" (p. 28). Seeks to place the last page of *Gargantua* "where alone it belongs, i.e. with all the others" (p. 38n.35). Believes the last group of chapters to be derived from Matthew, chapt. 25, and linked together by the theme of judgment and election; in that light, sees Gargantua and Frère Jean as two characters both deserving of Rabelais' Heaven. Argues that by claiming to have found the Enigma in the foundations of the abbey, Rabelais meant to undermine *in extremis* the seriousness we may be tempted to attach to the episode of the Abbaye de Thélème, seen here as a *leurre*, a *piège*, as "Rabelais' way down to Hell" (p. 26).

1984

39 TOURNON, ANDRÉ. "Vérité de l'erreur: le 'Lanternoys.'" In *La littérature de la Renaissance: Mélanges offerts à Henri Weber*. Geneva: Éditions Slatkine, pp. 59–72.

Notes that chapt. 47 marks a turning point in Book III. After having passively expected from others a solution to his dilemma, Panurge takes matters in hand and decides to stop by the "pays de Lanternoys"—whose language he claims to understand—to pick up a lantern that will guide the travellers in their journey to the Dive Bouteille. Here as elsewhere throughout the *Tiers Livre*, Panurge is an embodiment of error and folly, in contrast to the wisdom of Pantagruel. But this aberrant way of thinking and behaving is an inspired kind of folly, which refuses to listen to wisdom when it predicts disappointment, and seeks refuge in poetic fiction. Argues that the "rhétorique de l'enthousiasme" Rabelais lends to Panurge is not meant to discredit wisdom, but to point to an even higher spiritual plane: "cette folie qui s'escrime en vain tant qu'elle argumente *contre* la raison ne prend force que lorsqu'elle va *au-delà*" (pp. 69–70). Believes that not only the character of Panurge, but all the forms of "error" that inform the book, are meant to underscore the limits of conventional wisdom. "Si Rabelais adopte et pousse à ses dernières limites l'expression paradoxale, mythique et ludique, c'est parce que les problèmes qu'il entrevoit ne peuvent être résolus, ni même formulés exactement, dans le langage philosophique de son temps" (p. 70). Sees Rabelaisian folly as the paradoxical expression of an ethic of joy and freedom which cannot be confined within the parameters of sixteenth-century thought.

40 TRIPET, ARNAUD. "Le Prologue de *Gargantua*: Problèmes d'interprétation." *Etudes de Lettres*, no. 2 (April–June):135–50.

Should we take Rabelais seriously when he invites us, in the first part of the prologue to *Gargantua*, to seek a serious meaning behind the comic aspects of his novel? Does not think so. Not, as is frequently alleged, because Rabelais goes back in the second part on what he had intimated in the first, but because the first part itself—the reference to Socrates notwithstanding—is in essence a comic encomium. Argues that the second phase of Rabelais' argument merely underscores, by its intentional incoherence, the comic dimension of the first phase, thus illustrating once again what the author believes to be a feature of Rabelais' comic style, namely his "comique en deux temps." Suggests that Rabelais' adherence to the traditional structure of the prologue as a genre further reinforces his fundamentally comic purpose, that the opposition between *comique* and *sérieux* exists in the text as part of a network of "complementarity," and that the decision to favor one or the other of these complementary notions is the privilege, and the responsibility, of the reader.

41    WALTER, PHILIPPE. "La peur, le sel et la soif." *BAARD* 4, no. 3:89–91.
        Insists upon the dark side of the Renaissance as an age of fear. "L'idéal
qui tente de se définir dans le *Tiers Livre* et le *Quart Livre* est l'expression
d'un désir et d'un espoir nés en face de la peur du gouffre" (p. 90).

42    WEINBERG, FLORENCE M[AY]. "Platonic and Pauline Ideals in Comic
        Dress: 'Comment on vestit Gargantua.'" *Illinois Classical Studies* 9:183–95.
        Behind the grotesque exaggeration of the chapter, reads a Platonic and
Pauline message. Notes the presence of a blue pelican plume as Gargantua's
hat-feather, suggesting "Christ's redemptive sacrifice" (p. 186) according to
medieval Church symbolism. Finds Fischart's treatment of the androgyne figure in his adaptation of *Gargantua*, and the androgyne as depicted in
Holtzwart's *Emblematum Tyrocinia*, to be helpful in our understanding of
Rabelais' androgyne as "a symbol of perfect marriage" (p. 188). Finds equally emblematic of the giant's spiritual qualities the medallion on his hat, the
golden chain around his neck, and his three rings. Argues that the significance
of the chapter lies in these details of Gargantua's clothing, and brings out their
ancient and Christian symbolism: "they amount to a semiotic system of 'body
language' that provides a key to the character, ideals and intentions of his paradigm for a perfect ruler, the young Gargantua" (p. 195).

## 1985

1    BEAULIEU, JEAN PHILIPPE. "La description de la nouveauté dans les réc-
     its de voyage de Cartier et de Rabelais." *Renaissance and Reformation/
     Renaissance et Réforme* 9, no. 2:104–10.
        Notes that the *Brief Récit* of 1545 attributed to Cartier emphasizes the
new information contained therein, whereas the emphasis in Rabelais' *Quart
Livre* is on the mode of presentation: "les descriptions du *Brief Récit* s'articu-
lent comme des définitions qui tentent de cerner la nature de l'objet décrit au
moyen d'une diversification des éléments informatifs, alors que les descriptions
du *Quart Livre* esquissent une image globale de l'objet décrit en utilisant un
minimum de renseignements qu'elles mettent cependant en évidence par des
procédés rhétoriques" (p. 105). In the *Brief Récit*, the experientially verifiable
description is related to the new analytico-referential discourse as it was to be
soon formulated by Francis Bacon, whereas Rabelais' imaginary descriptions
are more closely related to the medieval epistemological tradition.

2    BERLIOZ, MARC. *Rabelais restitué*. Vol. 2, *Gargantua: Tome I, Du
     Prologue au chapitre XXIV*. Paris: Didier Erudition, 743 pp.
        Second volume of commentaries seeking to recover the meaning of
Rabelais' text in a spirit of unfettered enquiry, mainly by recourse to lexicog-

raphy. In contrast to most critical editions, deals with *Gargantua* after having previously commented upon *Pantagruel* (see 1979.3); is convinced of the futility of any attempt to understand a work without taking into account "la chronologie de l'écriture" (p. vii). Works on facsimiles of the 1534 edition, augmented by the two leaves supplied in 1535, and the facsimile of the "definitive" edition. Discusses the interpretations offered by the authors of the standard critical editions (Boulenger, Guilbaud, Plattard, Jourda, Michel, Demerson, and Gaignebet) and finds them often to repeat the opinions of Lefranc. In his discussion of the prologue, refuses to have recourse to esoteric interpretations, since in his search for the meaning of the book the reader is enjoined to "ouvrir la boîte," that is to find the meaning in the work itself, without recourse to outside considerations. Does not believe that the second phase of Rabelais' argument in the prologue invalidates the original injunction to seek a higher meaning, since it bears only on the authorial intention and not on the absence or presence of an allegorical meaning *per se*. But is led by philological considerations to conclude that Rabelais' references to the hidden mysteries buried under the amusing façade of his novel are merely antiphrastic: "Il paraît donc indiscutable que la promesse des révélations touchant la religion, l'état politique et la vie économique sont de ces billes vezees qu'il ne faut pas prendre au sérieux" (p. 13). Believes the marrow is a "matière à rire," be it a higher form of laughter: "un comique réservé à l'usage des initiés" (p. 20). Insists on the primacy of *Pantagruel* in the order in which Rabelais' text should be read (and printed), since for him the meaning of *Gargantua* emerges clearly only when any given passage is compared with the corresponding passage of *Pantagruel* (for example the two genealogies of the hero). Refuses to believe that the *Fanfreluches antidotées*, or any other text in Rabelais or any other author of the sixteenth century, are consciously, willfully meaningless; sees in them an erotic (even a pornographic) significance. Believes the poem to be a cryptogram rather than an enigma. Finds the debate on eleven-month pregnancies and Gargantua's strange nativity to be merely facetious. Subjects the "Propos des bien-ivres" to a lexicographic commentary of over seventy pages (pp. 110–83). In Gargantua's emblem sees (with Plattard and against most other commentators) a licentious interpretation of Saint Paul's "sentence" about charity not seeking its own advantage; finds the chapter on the colors of Gargantua's livery to be merely "circumstantial," the result of a (failed) attempt to secure for himself the "charge de rédacteur du livre des Emblèmes." Discusses the meaning of the proverbs which make up nearly the entire chapter on Gargantua's "adolescence" (pp. 254–318). Believes that for not seeing the sexual allusion in *chevaucher*, most commentators (but not Screech) misunderstand much of the chapter on the "chevaux factices de Gargantua." Comparing the chapter on Gargantua's instruction by a "sophiste" in Latin letters (chapt. 14) in the 1534 edition and in that of 1542 (where *sophiste* replaces *théologien*), suggests that far from attenuating his criticism of the Sorbonne in the latter text, as is habitually believed, Rabelais may in fact have sharpened his attack. In the following chapter, strongly doubts that Eudemon was for Rabelais what he is for most commentators, namely an ideal product of Renaissance education. Proposes an erotic interpretation of the games Rabelais has Gargantua play (chapt. 22), and suggests that most of them were fictitious, invented "pour les besoins de la cause": for their erotic double entendre. Finds chapt. 23 (on Rabelais instructed by Ponocrates) as exceptionally boring to read as it must have been for Rabelais to write. Wonders whether Rabelais was as interested in education as we have been led to believe, and whether what he says about it is not "un tantinet antiphrastique" (p. 743).

3   BERRONG, RICHARD [MICHAEL]. *Every Man for Himself: Social Order and its Dissolution in Rabelais*. Stanford French and Italian Studies, no. 38. Saratoga, Calif.: Anma Libri, 113 pp.

Presents Rabelais' Books II, III, and IV as reflecting the disintegration of social order in the early sixteenth century. Whereas the Dipsodian War in *Pantagruel* was merely depicted as an invasion, notes that the Picrocholine War in *Gargantua* is presented as a disruption of social bonds, with education as the one weapon that allows man to keep the satanic forces of folly, disorder, and excess at bay. Points out that despite the absence of any war episodes, the *Tiers Livre* continues to be concerned with the ever more insidious danger of social disorder, as Pantagruel struggles to subdue the forces of disruption now represented by Panurge, through whom Satan threatens to undo the very fabric of society. In the *Quart Livre*, notes a similar preoccupation with disintegrating social order, but detects an increasing pessimism as to the possibility of avoiding catastrophe, in the light of the growing religious tensions in the aftermath of the Reformation, and perhaps a premonition of a return to ancient chaos as God withdraws from a world in which man increasingly withdraws into himself, in pursuit of his own individual interest. Does not believe that any valid observations can be drawn from the *Cinquiesme Livre*, and suggests by way of a general conclusion, that "early sixteenth-century French thinkers did not devote themselves primarily to the glorification of the individual, but rather were concerned above all with the continued functioning of society as a whole" (p. 88). In an appendix, suggests that Rabelais meant his books to serve as a source of spiritual strength in the face of a hostile, disintegrating world: to provide comfort rather than to heal. See also 1981.6 and 1982.2 for earlier versions of chapt. 1 and 3.

4   ———. "The Evolving Attitude toward Material Wealth in Rabelais's *Oeuvres*." *Stanford French Review* 9, no. 3 (Winter):301–19.

Notes that in *Pantagruel* Rabelais had been generally indifferent towards material possessions, whereas in *Gargantua* he shows a new respect for material wealth, insisting for example on the redemptive value of generosity. Sees this respect as further intensified in the *Tiers Livre*, with its emphasis on the valorization of money, of efforts to save for the future, and of work as a means of acquiring wealth. "One now is, in part, what one owns" (p. 312). Points out that in the *Quart Livre*, excessive preoccupation with wealth is seen as degrading, and that Rabelais seems to extend his ideal of *médiocrité* to this area as well. Explains this evolution in attitude towards money and possessions by the influence of his intended audience, as Rabelais progressively distances himself from popular culture and comes to espouse the values of the bourgeoisie for whom he writes *Gargantua* and the *Tiers Livre*, before becoming aware, in Book IV, of the dangers represented by the obsessive concern for wealth within the ranks of the upper classes.

5 ———. "Finding Antifeminism in Rabelais; or, A Response to Wayne Booth's Call for an Ethical Criticism." *Critical Inquiry* 11, no. 4:687–96.

In "Freedom of Interpretation: Bakhtin and the Challenge of Feminist Criticism" (1982.4), Booth felt justified in accusing Rabelais of sexism on the grounds that he treats women as inherently inferior to men, that he addresses himself only to male readers, and that there is no evidence of a feminine point of view anywhere in his novels. Challenges this accusation. Argues that in the prologue to *Pantagruel* "Rabelais is not really portraying women as excluded from his audience" (p. 690), that Gargamelle's entrance into labor at the beginning of *Gargantua* shows "more than a hint of an effort to imagine a woman's point of view" (p. 691), and that the examples upon which Booth bases his claim that Rabelais ridicules women *as* women (Rondibilis' opinion, the place of women in the Abbey of Thélème, and the trick played by Panurge on the great lady from Paris) do not support his view when read against the background of the work as a whole.

6 ———. "The Presence and Exclusion of Popular Culture in *Pantagruel* and *Gargantua* (or, Bakhtin's Rabelais Revisited)." *Études Rabelaisiennes* 18:19–56.

Challenges Bakhtin's thesis that popular culture is of paramount importance in Rabelais' narratives, that it is totally incompatible with learned culture, and that Rabelais uses it mainly as a weapon in his revolutionary struggle against the establishment. Admits the presence of elements of popular culture in *Pantagruel*, but argues that they coexist with learned, official culture on an equal footing, before being "methodically and systematically excluded from *Gargantua*" (p. 39). Notes that this change parallels the rejection of the values of popular culture among the clergy and the upper classes. Explains it, in Rabelais' case, not by any decision to "sell out" to the establishment but by the refusal of the learned public—his intended audience—to take seriously, because of its emphasis on popular culture, the *substantifique moelle* of his first narrative. Further developed and extended to Rabelais' whole narrative output in 1986.4.

7   BOOTH, WAYNE C. "Reply to Richard Berrong." *Critical Inquiry* 11, no. 4:697–701.

To the extent that Berrong's disagreement with the author (see 1985.5) is about Rabelais rather than about their conception of ethical criticism, rejects his arguments and argues for the validity of his own reading of the passages cited in the dispute: women are not truly invited to read Rabelais' novel; Gargamelle's exchange with Grandgousier just before the birth of Gargantua, when read in its entirety, is not narrated from a woman's point of view; and the Parisian lady upon whom Panurge takes his revenge is not ridiculed (like many a man in Rabelais' novels) because she is of high degree, but because, by refusing Panurge's advances, she violated "her stereotype *as* woman-who-should-be-available, just as Gargamelle finally *validates* the male reader's stereotypes by taking back her curse against the blessed penis" (pp. 698–99).

8   DEFAUX, GÉRARD. "D'un problème l'autre: Herméneutique de l'altior sensus' et 'captatio lectoris' dans le Prologue de *Gargantua*." *Revue d'Histoire Littéraire de la France* 85 (March–April):195–216.

Views post-structuralist criticism of Rabelais as fundamentally wrong-headed in its adoption of an anti-humanistic approach to an essentially humanistic work. Warns against the fashionable tendency to equate Rabelais' fascination with the problems of language with the deconstructionists' emphasis on the inadequacies of linguistic discourse. On the basis of a semantic argument concerning the meaning of the key phrase "combien que" at a pivotal point in the prologue, denies the presence of a structural duality in the text. Together with the notion of the text's "plurality," rejects the view that the problem it raises is that of allegorical reading: "le problème qui mobilise Rabelais dans son Prologue n'est pas, comme nous le voudrions, un problème essentiellement théorique et réflexif, mais, plus modestement, un problème de réception littéraire." Rabelais' aim is not to contest the validity of allegorical interpretation, but to gain for *Gargantua*, after the popular success of *Pantagruel*, a more cultivated readership by underscoring the fact that laughter and seriousness are not mutually exclusive. Insofar as it raises the problem of hermeneutics, the prologue merely reminds us that a text means more than its author meant it to mean: "Un texte est...infiniment plus que la pensée consciente de son auteur." Rabelais' hermeneutics are also characterised by a moral dimension: the search for the total meaning of a work—both conscious and unconscious—must be carried out in the spirit of evangelical benevolence.

9   DE WEER-D'HOOGHE, MARIA SYLVIA. "Homo Legens: Reader-oriented criticism and Rabelais." Ph.D. dissertation, Washington University, 436 pp.

Insofar as Rabelais' text frequently calls attention to the problems of reading, finds it "a suitable medium for testing reader-centered criticism." Studies the text against the background of theories of reception and response

1985

as developed by Jauss and Iser. The presence of an implied author and an implied reader (the Homo Legens of the title) in Rabelais ensures "the mandatory fictional author reader contract," and the Homo Legens underscores "a threefold concern in Rabelais' Prologues: the conflicting low-and-high-level reader's expectations, the writer's paradoxical situation between tradition and avant-garde, and the true/false status of fiction." See *Dissertation Abstracts International* 47 (1986):1961–A.

10   DUPÈDE, JEAN. "La date de la mort de Rabelais (suite)." *Études Rabelaisiennes* 18:175–76.

   Quotes a legal document implying that Rabelais was already dead by March 14, 1552 (old style), that his death occurred shortly before that date, that his brother and sole heir was a certain Jamet Rabelais, a merchant settled at Chinon, and that in the last years of his life Rabelais probably belonged to the *entourage* of Antoine Sanguin, bishop of Orléans. See also 1980.19.

11   DUVAL, EDWIN M. "Interpretation and the 'doctrine absconce' of Rabelais's Prologue to *Gargantua*." *Études Rabelaisiennes* 18:1–17.

   Challenges the prevalent assumption that the prologue consists of two antithetical, contradictory statements concerning the validity of allegorical interpretation. By subjecting the passage marking the purported "turning point" of the argument to "the most elementary kind of textual exegesis" (p. 2), sets out to prove that the second phase of the argument, far from contradicting the first, in fact confirms it, and that far from discouraging the reader from seeking an *altior sensus* in the ensuing chronicle, as he had been adjoined to do, it merely "justifies and confirms the charge" (p. 5). Furthermore, believes that the prologue is not so much about the validity of seeking a higher, allegorical significance behind the literal meaning of any given text, as it is about authorial intention and its irrelevance to the value of a literary work. "The implicit argument is that higher truth and wisdom in literature is not the product of conscious design and hard labor, but of effortless inspiration" (p. 5). Concludes by suggesting that Rabelais' main purpose is less to convince the reader of the presence of a higher meaning behind the frivolous title and subject matter of his book, than to bring him to read it in a spirit of *caritas*: to persuade him to seek with Pantagruelistic benevolence and good faith the book's Pantagruelistic message.

12   FRANÇON, MARCEL. "Derniers mots sur la nomenclature guidonienne et la littérature." *Études Rabelaisiennes* 18:173.

   Notes three further examples of Guidonian nomenclature in *Pantagruel* and the *Tiers Livre*.

13   FRECCERO, CARLA [ANN]. "Damning haughty dames: Panurge and the Haulte Dame de Paris (*Pantagruel*, 14)." *Journal of Medieval and Renaissance Studies* 15, no. 1:57–67.

Finds it surprising that this important chapter should not have been discussed more frequently in the context of the debate concerning Rabelais' attitude towards women. Believes that until now the episode has received an exclusively masculine reading, emerging as an essentially comic text: the reader identifies with Panurge (as well as with the narrator), and laughs at the lady's discomfiture and the hypocrisy of her profession of virtue. Argues that for the female reader, on the other hand, "Panurge's revenge upon the 'haulte dame de Paris' testifies to the triumph of her resistance" (p. 65). Sees Panurge's rhetoric as a substitute for impotence, and proposes a reading in which an "effeminized," "somewhat androgynous" Panurge, having seduced Pantagruel, proceeds to work with his companion "to forcibly exclude the woman from the courtship phase of this romance" (p. 64) and to exclude her from Rabelais' text.

14   ——. "Rabelais's 'Abbaye de Thélème': Utopia as Supplement." *Esprit Créateur* 25, no. 1 (Spring):73–87.

Studies the episode as it relates, thematically and narratively, to the first two books, as well as in its political dimension as a utopia, that is "the textualization of a spacial construction." As such, argues that Thélème "renders *visible* ideological contradictions that work to deconstruct its architecture and to open it up to (historical) forces that it seeks to resist through metaphorization" (p. 73). In part 1 stresses the shift in focus "from Frère Jean (who disappears in the ensuing chapters) to Gargantua as founder and legislator of the abbey" (p. 76), and sees signs of filial rebellion in the relationship between Rabelais' two giants. In part 2 discusses Thélème "as a political *figure* rather than merely an *ideal* representation" (p. 78). Notes that Rabelais begins by giving his abbey a set of referents in society, but that this specificity is immediately "neutralized": "Theleme is not another world, another kind of organization; rather, chapter L creates a binary relation, the monastery and its opposite, such that the process at work becomes one of the neutralization of a given ideology, rather than the independent, 'positive' ideological construction of an ideal world" (p. 79). Stresses the "non-coincidences of the narrational passages with the descriptions of the place" (pp. 79–80), and notes that "the conflicting ideologies of monastic and courtly institutions are juxtaposed and 'neutralized,' but not reconciled or synthesized into a harmonious discourse" (p. 81). Sees also contradictions in the area of political authority and economic activity, wonders whether they should be put down to "sloppiness or imaginative failure," agrees with Louis Marin that utopia serves an essentially critical function, and underscores the failure of the Thélème episode as the expression of a coherent social, political, and economic system.

1985

15  GILROY, JAMES P. "Rabelais, the Good Doctor: Health and Sanity in the *Quart Livre*." *European Studies Journal* 2, no. 1:27–34.

Believes that the health of which Rabelais writes in the prologue to the *Quart Livre* is that of the soul as well as that of the body, that throughout the book "soundness of body and mind occupies Rabelais's thoughts with an almost obsessive urgency" (p. 32), that such monsters as Quaresmeprenant, Bringuenarilles, and Gaster represent "aberrations from the principles of healthiness and sanity" (p. 29), and that only in the island of Ruach episode are medical themes "entirely lacking in any sort of practical or ideological significance" and are made an object of ironic self-parody.

16  GOUMARRE, PIERRE [J.]. "Rabelais: Le Panurge du songe." *Les Lettres Romanes* 39, no. 3:157–66.

Reviews the positions of earlier critics on Pantagruel's and Panurge's interpretation of Panurge's dream in the *Tiers Livre* (chapt. 14): those who believe that Rabelais sides with Pantagruel (see 1960.1), or that he sides with both (see 1974.22), or yet again those who believe that Rabelais is too lucid to side with either (see 1970.16). Notes that some believe Pantagruel's interpretation to be Jungian (see 1960.1), or Freudian (see 1967.12), or that of a disciple of Saint Thomas Aquinas (see 1976.7). Brings out the contradictions and incompatibility of these views, finds them all wanting, and offers his own. Reminds us that the dream in question is not really Panurge's but a dream imagined by Rabelais, in other words a literary text in a specific context. Points out that Pantagruel's ability to show that the symbols in the dream confirm the other predictions is of strictly literary significance: "cela prouve non pas que le géant connaît son métier d'analyste, mais que Rabelais connaît son métier d'écrivain" (p. 161). Argues that the interpretations are dictated by the antithetical structure of the *Tiers Livre*: "Autant Pantagruel est condamné à voir dans chaque signe un mauvais augure, autant Panurge est condamné à y voir un bon présage" (p. 162). Rejects as pure whimsy the various psychoanalytic interpretations. Sees the interest of the episode as revealing Panurge in an altogether unexpected light: newly humble, he has lost his aggressivity towards women, and shows an unsuspected appreciation of a woman's beauty and tenderness: "Le rêve fait de ce séducteur un amoureux, qui s'épanouit dans une relation à la fois sentimentale et érotique" (p. 165), until by planting horns in Panurge's head the woman shatters his dream and transforms him back into himself. Sees the deepest significance of the dream in what it may be saying about Rabelais himself as a possible victim of a woman's scorn, and in suggesting that the misogyny of Panurge and of Rabelais is but a form of revenge.

17  HANSEN, BJORN BREDAL. *La peur, le rire et la sagesse: Essai sur Rabelais et Montaigne*. Revue Romane, no. 28. Copenhagen: L'Institut d'Etudes Romanes de l'Université de Copenhague, 157 pp.

In the wake of Jean Delumeau's *La Peur en Occident*, sees the Renaissance as an age of insecurity, and offers a comparative reading of the two authors centered on the theme of fear. Studies fear of the sea in Rabelais and fear of war in Montaigne, and views Rabelais' laughter and Montaigne's *sagesse* as two fundamentally different answers to the pervading presence of fear in themselves and in the world as they see it. Argues that Rabelais' response to fear lies in the transcendence of the self: "La peur est vaincue, non par l'individu, mais par l'homme, par le peuple" (p. 143). Whereas in Montaigne, fear is conquered by an individual, solitary effort of self-mastery.

18  HORNIK, HENRY. *On Change in Literature: Studies on French Renaissance, Theory and Idealism.* Geneva: Éditions Slatkine, pp. 57–77.
      Contains reprints of "Time and Periodization in French Renaissance Literature: Rabelais and Montaigne" and "Rabelais and Idealism" (see 1969.11 and 12).

19  HUMPHRIES, JEFFERSON. "The Rabelaisian *Matrice.*" *Romanic Review* 76:251–70.
      Rabelais' text is elaborated in the *matrice* (or womb) of language, "both woman and language being an emblem for each other's procreative excessiveness" (p. 265). Notes that the various images to which Rabelais compares his text in the prologue to *Gargantua*, the nativity scenes at the beginning of his first two books, the episode of the frozen words, and that of the Divine Bottle are most often seen as representations of "the Rabelaisian dialectic of consumption, each container always leading to another, each content turning out to be another container, another means to an end which is a means" (p. 262). Argues that this dialectic is also the dialectic of reading (the "intellectual analogue" of bodily consumption), and that such metaphors for reading suggest Rabelais' consciousness of the futility of any attempt to grasp a text's definitive meaning. It is thus wrongheaded to identify the act of reading with the quest for an immutable "substantifique moelle." Such a "substantifique moelle" does not exist. "The primary text and the critical commentary are a chiasmus and a tautology in which each is the possibility of the other, of a certain reading or hallucination of the other; each is both container and content" (p. 269). The quest for meaning is of its very nature open-ended: "The text itself seems to imply that so long as it is a text—so long, that is, as it is read and studied—it is still in progress, unfinished" (p. 270). Reprinted in 1986.24.

20  KIDD, JOHN. "The Mallow Concert at Maryborough." *James Joyce Quarterly* 22, no. 3 (Spring):323–25.
      Wonders whether the reference to the concert at Mallow which Molly attends in *Ulysses* may not have been suggested by the herb *mallow*, in Urquhart's translation of the Pantagruélion episode, so called because it *mollifies*.

1985

21   LA CHARITÉ, RAYMOND C. "Lecteurs et lectures dans le prologue de *Gargantua.*" *French Forum* 10, no. 3 (September):261–70.

Argues that the prologue to *Gargantua* was conceived with the intention to derail ("brouiller et faire dévier") any possible interpretation. Examines its textual strategy and its ironic structure. Compared with the prologue to *Pantagruel*, finds it to be addressed to a more sophisticated reader by a more sophisticated narrator. Through an allusive reading of the text, argues that Socrates' role is pervasive throughout the text, even though he is mentioned only at the outset; and that he is used to legitimate Rabelais' original conception of his book as inviting a multiplicity of readings. "En plus de toutes les résonances ironiques et dramatiques qu'il évoque, son nom signifie immédiatement l'abandon de modèles déjà utilisés et l'introduction d'une réflexion compliquée et dynamique sur les rapports de la création et de l'interprétation et les fins de la littérature" (p. 265).

22   LAZARD, MADELEINE. *Images littéraires de la femme à la Renaissance.* Paris: Presses Universitaires de France, 239 pp.

Briefly discusses Rondibilis' physiological views of women (pp. 20–23), the general conception of woman in the *Tiers Livre* (pp. 139–43), and the Sibyl of Panzoust as a "sorcière de village" (pp. 220–21).

23   LEWIS, JOHN. "Towards a chronology of the *Chroniques gargantuines.*" *Études Rabelaisiennes* 18:83–101.

Lists the seven chronicles in the order in which they are thought to have appeared, points out the arbitrariness of the accepted chronology, questions the "unorthodox theory of filiation" proposed by Marcel Françon (see 1954.11), and proposes his own "stemma of literary dependence" (p. 87). Sees *La grande et merveilleuse vie [...] de Gargantua* (1527–31), and *Les Grandes et inestimables Croniques* (1532) as being at the source of two distinct branches of the legend which merge in *Les Croniques admirables*, published sometime before *Pantagruel* since it borrows three chapters from Rabelais' first novel.

24   MORRIS, EDWARD. "Rabelais, Romances, Reading, Righting Names." In *Romance: Generic Transformation from Chrétien de Troyes to Cervantes*, edited by Kevin and Maria Brownlee. Hanover, N.H.: University Press of New England, pp. 155–77.

Reflects on the relationship between Rabelais' books, the Arthurian romances, and the Gargantuine chronicles. Remarks on the tripartite structure of *Pantagruel*, notes the absence of the fourth part of traditional romances (the one dealing with the hero's marriage), and provides a close reading of chapt. 16, in which Pantagruel leaves Paris upon hearing that the Dipsodes are invading the land of the Amaurots and that his father has been "translated" to the Isles of the Blessed. Notes the allusions to Genesis and to the *Aeneid* in connection with the themes of disappearance and disloyalty treated in the chapter, and perhaps to Marot (Clément or Jean, son or father) in connection with Marotus du Lac, who had explained in the *Chronicles of the Kings of Canarre* why leagues are shorter in France than elsewhere. Points out how much of the chapter (and how much of Rabelais' book itself) is about writing and reading: Marotus' fable, the period of waiting for the wind (of inspiration?) before undertaking the journey from Rouen to Utopia, the puzzling message from the mysterious lady whom Pantagruel had left behind. With the help of Jakobson and Geoffroy Tory, suggests a possible meaning for the name of Pantagruel as written (without vowels) by the lady.

25 PARKIN, JOHN. "Comic Modality in Rabelais: Baisecul, Humevesne, Thaumaste." *Études Rabelaisiennes* 18:57–82.

After Bakhtin, distinguishes parodic and satirical laughter in Rabelais, reacts against Bakhtin's "tendency towards a reductive, parodic reading of Rabelais such as leads him to downgrade the importance of his satirical message" (p. 59), and applies the "dichotomy of satire and parody" to the two episodes mentioned in the title, in the hope of arriving at "a fuller reading than has yet been achieved" (p. 70) by critics who have tended to oversimplify "the rich ambiguity" of these Rabelaisian texts.

26 PEACH, T. "Boccace, Panurge-Poireau et Ronsard." *Études Rabelaisiennes* 18:177–78.

Suggests that when Rabelais has Panurge compare himself to leeks ("es quelz nous voyons la teste blanche et la queue verde, droicte et viguoureuse," *Tiers Livre*, chapt. 28) in the passage in which he argues before Frère Jean that it would be unwarranted to conclude to a lack of sexual vigor from the white hair on his head, he is borrowing the image from Boccacio, perhaps in Antoine Maçon's 1545 translation.

27 RIGOLOT, FRANÇOIS [PAUL]. "*Leda and the Swan*: Rabelais's Parody of Michelangelo." *Renaissance Quarterly* 38, no. 4 (Winter):688–700.

Michelagelo's *Leda and the Swan*, subsequently destroyed and known to us today only through Cornelius Bos' engraving, was exhibited in Lyons, with great success, in the early 1530s. Contends that the picture may well have aroused Rabelais' imagination by its eroticism, and that it may have suggested to him the "torchecul" episode of *Gargantua* (chapt. 12 of the *edition princeps*) as a parody, in a carnivalesque mode, of the Ovidian theme of Michelagelo's painting. Notes the various elements in Rabelais' text that recall the picture, points out that certain aspects of the painting are foreshadowed in the *Fanfreluches antidotées* preceding the "torchecul" episode, and suggests that under these circumstances the episode "can no longer be viewed as a naïve scatological joke or as a surrealistic *tour de force*" (p. 700).

1985

28    RYAN, LAWRENCE V. "Panurge and the Faustian Dilemma." *Stanford Literary Review* 2, no. 2 (Fall):147–63.

Compares Panurge to Faust in Marlowe's *Doctor Faustus*. Without claiming any direct influence of Rabelais on Marlowe's play, argues that the "Faustian dilemma" of rejecting official sources of knowledge (law, medicine, philosophy, and theology) and turning to magic in one's search for absolute truth is already prefigured in Panurge's predicament as presented in the *Tiers Livre*. Notes a number of other parallels: both heroes' desire to get married, their *philautia*, their lack of self-knowledge. Concedes that Marlowe may have found most of his material in the *Faustbuch* or in Cornelius Agrippa's *De incertitudine et vanitate scientiarum et artiorum*, but argues that Rabelais' *Tiers Livre* is the closest analogue to the *Tragical History of Dr. Faustus*.

29    SMITH, PAUL. "Ambroise Paré lecteur de Rabelais." *Études Rabelaisiennes* 18:163–71.

Although Ambroise Paré has not hitherto been counted among Rabelais' readers, points out three borrowings from the *Quart Livre*—"l'un certain, les deux autres probables" (p. 163)—in Paré's *Le discours de la licorne, Des monstres et prodiges,* and *Des animaux et de l'excellence de l'homme.*

30    TORNITORE, TONINO. "Interpretazioni novecentesche dell'episodio delle *Parolles Gelées.*" *Études Rabelaisiennes* 18:179–204.

Offers a critical survey of major twentieth-century interpretations of the frozen words episode, from Plattard, through Folkierski, Guiton, Saulnier, and Spitzer, to such recent commentators as Glauser and Rigolot, and three purported representatives of *la nouvelle critique*: Paris, Pouilloux, and Jeanneret. Finds them all wanting, and briefly proposes his own double conclusion, which he claims to follow directly from a comparison of Rabelais' sources and an awareness of the importance and novelty of his variants. Believes that through the episode of the *parolles gelées*, Rabelais is criticizing both the Platonic theory of language and its Christianized version as presented in Ficino. Claims that by casting doubt on any necessary connection between signifier and signified, Rabelais discredits in particular the biblical hypothesis of the divine origin of language and undermines the Church's claim to a privileged reading of the Book of the World.

31    ZEGURA, ELIZABETH CHESNEY. "Toward a Feminist Reading of Rabelais." *Journal of Medieval and Renaissance Studies* 15, no. 1:125–34.

"Far from solving the riddle of Rabelais' misogyny, male logic and learning have proved only, much like Trouillogan, that the Gallic monk was either antifeminist or 'truly feminist,' 'ne l'un ne l'aultre,' or 'tous les deux ensemblement'" (p. 125). Proposes to attack the problem of reconciling Book III's unflattering portrayal of women with their egalitarian treatment in the

336

Abbaye de Thélème from a woman's perspective. Following up a suggestion by Christine de Pisan in reference to another misogynist text, proceeds to read Rabelais antiphrastically; sees herself authorized to do so by the author himself, and contends that "Rabelais has woven the possibility of this reversed feminist reading into the fabric of the text, equating sexuality with textuality, and using the cuckolding woman as a metaphor for the unfaithful reader" (p. 126). From this perspective, Rabelais' "stereotypical misogyny" emerges as "a specular satire of men," and his novel as a text which questions the basic tenets of phallocentric antifeminism.

## 1986

1  AERCKE, K. P. "Un passeport belge pour Panurge-Tijl." *Revue Belge de Philologie et d'Histoire* 64, no. 3:514–19.

Discusses Edmond Picard's *Au Pays des Bilingues* (1923), which combines the Latin Panurge and the Germanic Till Eulenspiegel of the sixteenth-century *Volksbuch* into a character embodying the Belgian predicament ("le problème belge").

2  BALDINGER, KURT. "François Rabelais: Son importance pour l'histoire du vocabulaire français." In *Le Moyen Français: Actes du Ve Colloque International sur le Moyen Français, Milan 6–8 mai 1985*, vol. 2. Milan: Pubblicazioni della Università Cattolica del Sacro Cuore, pp. 163–79.

Deplores that studies of Rabelais' vocabulary should be at a standstill since Sainéan's *La Langue de Rabelais* (1923). Outlines the work that remains to be done in the area of etymology, regionalisms, chronology, and semantics. "Il faut reprendre Rabelais d'un bout à l'autre, presque mot par mot" (p. 165). Reprinted in 1990.2.

3  BATANY, JEAN. "Jean de Meun et Rabelais." *BAARD* 4, no. 5:161–62.

Sees in the two authors the same tendency to digress and the same love of nature.

4  BERRONG, RICHARD [MICHAEL]. *Rabelais and Bakhtin: Popular culture in "Gargantua" and "Pantagruel"*. Lincoln: University of Nebraska Press, 156 pp.

Tests Bakhtin's claim that Rabelais' novels are a faithful reflection of popular culture, that therein lies their essential significance, and that the language and imagery of the marketplace are the most effective weapons in Rabelais' struggle against the oppressive hold of official culture. Follows such historians as Peter Burke (*Popular Culture in Early Modern Europe*) in pointing out that at the beginning of the sixteenth century the opposition between popular and official culture was not nearly as clear cut as Bakhtin assumed it to be (and as it would in fact tend to become later in the century). Believes that Bakhtin's assertion applies more accurately to Rabelais' first two books than to Books III and IV, but that even in *Pantagruel* popular and learned culture are given equal importance, and that from *Gargantua* onward "there begins a systematic and radical exclusion of popular culture" (p. 21). Relates this "progressive devaluation and exclusion" of popular culture to its rejection by the Church and the aristocratic elite, and, on the biographical level, to Rabelais' experience of "the politically and socially great" in the entourage of Jean du Bellay, his discovery of the Italian Renaissance, as well as his desire to be taken seriously by the learned audience for whom he was writing. Argues that Books III and IV continue to downplay the popular elements in favor of learned culture. Reminds us that Book III was published by Chrestien Wechel (an editor of scholarly works), that it was dedicated to Marguerite de Navarre, that it was signed with his own name (followed by the title Doctor of Medicine), that it contains a greater number of references to antiquity and a corresponding absence of references to the material lower bodily stratum. Argues against the presence in Book III of an anti-capitalistic economic ideology of the rising middle class as claimed by Jean Paris and other Marxist critics. Concedes that Book IV is somewhat more "popular" than its predecessor, but not as much so as *Pantagruel* or the first part of *Gargantua*. Admits that references to excrement are frequent, but sees no criticism of figures of authority, little mention of sex, and no evocation of the land of Cockaigne, although several episodes of *Les Navigations de Panurge*, which served as a model, are based upon this popular-culture image. Also notes that the banquet scenes lack the popular, democratic aspect found elsewhere, and that Panurge's role is downgraded. Argues that Rabelais seems to "distrust and devalue popular culture" throughout that book (p. 101). In part 3 studies Bakhtin's *Rabelais and His World* (1968.1) in the political context in which it was written, as well as in relation to the concept of dialogism as developed by Bakhtin in his *Dostoyevsky*. Although finds it to be weak as a literary study, believes *Rabelais and His World* to be a courageous "allegorical work of political criticism and theory" (p. 109) in reaction to the tenets of socialist realism. Underscoring Rabelais' allusions to Thomas More's *Utopia*, concludes by suggesting the possibility of a "pluralistic" reading of *Pantagruel*.

5   BOWEN, BARBARA C. "Rabelais and the Rhetorical Joke Tradition." In *Rabelais's Incomparable Book: Essays on his art*, edited by Raymond C. La Charité. Lexington, Ky.: French Forum, pp. 213–25.
      Although there are traces of joke collections in Rabelais' work, notes that most of them occur in non-comic contexts. Traditional jokes, when present, are used to make a serious point, "as *exempla* rather than as gags or persuasive humor" (p. 221). In fact, observes that Rabelais does not put them to any of the uses—recreational, oratorical, or civilizing—encountered in the rhetorical joke tradition. "In his fictional world jokes do not heal the sick,

function as rhetorical weapons, provide comic relief, or define the urbane Ideal Prince" (p. 223). Which does not prevent Rabelais' comedy from being "infinitely rich, ambiguous, and surprising."

6  CALDARI, FRANCA BEVILACQUA. "François Rabelais a Roma." *Studi Romani* 34, no. 1–2 (January–June):40–60.

"[I]l rapporto di Rabelais con il suo illuminato mecenate non fu mai di dipendenza, ma di reciproca stima e collaborazione" (p. 44). Evokes in some detail Rabelais' three sojourns in Rome as a member of Jean du Bellay's *entourage*. Alongside the personal reasons for Rabelais' presence in Rome and his professional functions as secretary and physician, stresses his political role, and the broad scope of knowledge ("la sua immensa erudizione, la sua vasta esperienza in tutti i campi allora noti, in particolare in teologia e in giurisprudenza," p. 41) which made Rabelais so useful to his protector in the latter's diplomatic missions.

7  CAVE, TERENCE. "Reading Rabelais: Variations on the Rock of Virtue." In *Literary Theory/Renaissance Texts*, edited by Patricia Parker and David Quint. Baltimore: Johns Hopkins University Press, pp. 78–95.

Charting a middle course between a historical, "positivistic" approach which does not take into sufficient account the specificity of the particular text under study, and a modern critical reading which does not pay sufficient attention to the historical data which impose limits to the possible meanings of the text, offers an intertextual reading of the Gaster episode (*Quart Livre*, chapt. 57–62). Studies the pattern of references to somewhat similar episodes in Rabelais' own work, as well as to Hesiod's description of the "manoir de Areté" and to Lemaire de Belges in his *Concorde des deux langages*. Stresses the thematic and ethical instability of Rabelais' text, the manifold and provisional nature of its implications, the superposition of a variety of textual echoes. Sees in Rabelais' treatment of the ancient *topos* a strategy whose effect is "to prevent *any* moral injunction, however venerable, from establishing itself as an interpretative key" (p. 86). Summarizes four previous readings (those of Marichal, Screech, Jeanneret, and Rigolot), acknowledges the presence in the text of a number of "evangelical humanist topics" and of a reflection on the problem of language, but insists on the specific configuration these elements acquire in Rabelais's text, which point to the text's plurality of meanings, although within "strict limits." "Like Pantagruel and his crew, we are committed to a voyage for which no completely reliable map will ever be drawn" (p. 92).

8  CAVE, TERENCE, MICHEL JEANNERET, and FRANÇOIS RIGOLOT. "Sur la prétendue transparence de Rabelais." *Revue d'Histoire Littéraire de la France* 86, no. 4 (July–August):709–16.

In reaction to Gérard Defaux (see 1985.8) and Edwin Duval (see

1986

1985.11), the authors reaffirm their belief in the polyvalence and ambiguity of both the prologue in question and of Rabelais' entire work. Insist that the prologue does not prescribe unequivocally the search for a "substantifique moelle" in *Gargantua*; even if it had so prescribed, the prescription would not necessarily be valid for Rabelais' work as a whole. "Toute lecture qui prétend dégager un sens 'univoque' et 'transparent' omet de rendre compte du choix d'une forme et d'une langue toujours en excès par rapport à ce qui serait requis pour communiquer un tel sens" (pp. 713–14).

9   CHARPENTIER, FRANÇOISE. "Un Royaume qui perdure sans femmes." In *Rabelais's Incomparable Book: Essays on his art*, edited by Raymond C. La Charité. Lexington, Ky.: French Forum, pp. 195–209.
    From an anthropological perspective, underscores the paradoxical nature of Rabelais' effort to create, through generation in the framework of the family—and thus presumably through the collaboration of both sexes—a new world from which women are to all intents and purposes absent. In the context of the family cell, women matter only at conception and at birth, as partners in the act of procreation. In the context of sexuality, they are present as objects of desire, but only "dans les registres de l'obscène, de l'agressivité et d'un mépris évident de l'autre sexe" (p. 200). In the case of Panurge, moreover, a vehemently professed erotic ardor hides, in fact, a fear of sex. Believes that this fear of women and of sexuality, perceptible throughout the novel, explains to a large extent Rabelais' misogyny. Notes that the female inhabitants of Thélème lack any trace of particularization, and that the lady courted and abandoned by Pantagruel similarly lacks reality. The "haulte dame de Paris" who rejects Panurge's advances turns out to be "une pimbêche hypocrite" (p. 205), a bitch in heat. Only when old and degraded are women described at any length, in sordidly realistic detail. In the Rondibilis episode, believes Rabelais to be even more misogynous than Plato in the *Timæus*. "Il est difficile de rêver un bilan plus négatif" (p. 207). Only the requirements of fictional logic ("la logique narrative") save the world from extinction in the temple of Badbuc, by inciting Panurge and his companions, under the beneficial influence of the temperate use of wine, to marry and thus ensure the survival of the species.

10  DEFAUX, GÉRARD. "A propos de paroles gelées et dégelées (*Quart Livre* 55–56): 'plus hault sens' ou 'lectures plurielles'?" In *Rabelais's Incomparable Book: Essays on his art*, edited by Raymond C. La Charité. Lexington, Ky.: French Forum, pp. 155–77.
    Argues that from its very start the *Quart Livre* reveals Rabelais' intention to carry meaning. "Par delà la pluralité de ses voix, la diversité de ses modes scripturaires, le *Quart Livre* est un livre qui juge et qui condamne. Un livre qui est constat, et refus" (p. 162). Rejects Jeanneret's interpretation of the episode as denouncing, through the character of Pantagruel, all "reduc-

tive" critical attempts to immobilize the text by ascribing to it a fixed meaning. Nor is the episode, as Jeanneret and others would have it, essentially about interpretation, but about linguistics and epistemology. To the extent that it *is* about interpretation, it is not Pantagruel but Panurge who is the exemplary figure, with his insistence on literal meaning. Seeking the spirit without having previously taken into account the letter, Pantagruel the idealist is inadequate to the task of interpreting the frozen sounds and voices: "un piètre interprète" (p. 170). Argues that through his myth Rabelais does not proclaim the polyvalence of words, but rather the necessity to ascribe to them a specific, literal sense before launching on the quest for their higher meaning. Finds the shift from chapt. 55 to chapt. 56 to be particularly significant in that respect. "Loin de prôner la liberté de l'interprète, de vanter la grandeur et les vertus de la 'polyvalence,' le texte en question opère en fait sous nos yeux, des 'paroles dégelées' aux 'paroles gelées,' *une réduction progressive des possibilités de sens*" (p. 171).

11    ————. "Sur la prétendue pluralité du prologue de *Gargantua*: Réponse d'un positiviste naïf à trois illustres et très chevalereux champions." *Revue d'Histoire Littéraire de la France* 86, no. 4 (July–August):716–22.
         In response to "Sur la prétendue transparence de Rabelais" (1986.8), counters that his claim of "transparence" does not apply to Rabelais' work as a whole, but only to the prologue to *Gargantua*, and that on that score his conviction remains unshaken. Suggests that the modern critics' insistence upon the polyvalence of Rabelais' text stems from their adherence to the fashionable tenets of post-structuralist criticism rather than from a careful reading of Rabelais.

12    DEMERSON, GUY. *Rabelais.* Collection Phares. Paris: Balland, 404 pp.
         Discusses Rabelais both as a witness and a judge of his time. Views his practice of medicine, his knowledge of law, and his political ideas as extensions of his humanism. Believes with such critics as Febvre and Screech that Rabelais' satire of religious practices, dogmas, and theologians is carried out in the name of an Erasmian evangelism. "Les citations de l'écriture sont, chez Rabelais, trop fréquentes, les allusions aux problèmes qui déchiraient les théologiens de son époque trop précises, pour qu'on ignore le sens religieux de cette œuvre comique" (p. 86). Underscores the scope of Rabelais' scientific curiosity, and the variety of methodological approaches in his quest for scientific truth; discusses the place given to the arts of the trivium and quadrivium in his pedagogy. Proceeds to an analysis of each of the five books, based on the results of current research (summarized in an "anthologie critique" which follows the analyses). Makes a point of beginning with *Gargantua*, which in the 1547 edition, and thus presumably in accordance with Rabelais' wishes, is the first book in the series. Notes how problematic is the question of its dating (1534 or 1535?). Claims to see in

*Gargantua* an example of composition "en inclusion," whereby the second part of the book becomes a thematic mirror-image of the first, around a central point, which the author takes to be chapt. 41 and 42, considered as the "clé de voûte" of the entire edifice. Finds the book to have an essentially communal character in its presentation of "petits groupes humains unis dans la joie" (p. 152). In the case of *Pantagruel*, again notes our uncertainty as to the date of composition and publication. Points out that it owes less to the *Chroniques* than does *Gargantua*. Notes structurally symmetrical patterns which make him believe that the book, like *Gargantua* (and also the *Tiers Livre*), is constructed "en inclusion." Finds a "moelle épistémologique" even in this earliest of Rabelais' novels (p. 176). In the prologue to the *Tiers Livre*, sees a reading contract between the author and the reader, whereby the book is to be read in the spirit of Pantagruelism, that is a spirit of good will. Accepts with some modifications Duval's analysis of the work's structure (see 1983.18). Sees the question of women as part of the larger question of marriage as debated by Rabelais' contemporaries, but treated here on a fictional plane, "dans l'univers autonome de la littérature" (p. 237). Notes changes in the two main characters: Pantagruel has grown more serious, Panurge more melancholy and superstitious. Considers the *Quart Livre* to be Rabelais' masterpiece, and studies it above all as a "roman de la vie sociale," while conceding that it is also "le roman des paroles et des voix" (p. 281). Notes that Pantagruel becomes ever more serene, and Panurge ever more cowardly, even bestial, whereas Frère Jan remains his old self. Notes also the emergence of the narrator as a character, a participant in the fiction. In the case of the *Cinquiesme Livre*, finds the structure to be more simplistic and lacking in dynamic thrust, the characters to be as alive as before, and the style as full of verve. But admits that such considerations are inconclusive and cannot be used to resolve the problem of the book's authenticity. Discusses the various arguments previously advanced in the matter. Finds it likely, with Mireille Huchon (see 1981.17), that Book V is made up of manuscripts by Rabelais but destined for other uses. Warns against excessively mystical interpretations of the book, which would not be in keeping with the rest of Rabelais' work. In the final section ("L'œuvre et le temps") rapidly surveys Rabelais' cultural impact, traces signs of his presence in innumerable adaptations, translations, and imitations, from the tales of Noël du Fail and La Fontaine to the dramatic adaptations of Jean-Louis Barrault and beyond. Follows the progressive emergence of a "mythe de Rabelais" in the popular imagination as well as in the minds of highly cultured readers (La Bruyère, Chateaubriand, Hugo). Concludes by tracing the novels' reception, at first as works of literature and entertainment (Montaigne's "livres simplement plaisants"), then as allegorical texts made to refer in turn to historical events, religious heresies, or—most recently—to a more or less prophetic, more or less pre-revolutionary system of thought.

1986

13   DOMINGUEZ, ANTONIO. "La aventura humana de *Pantagruel.*" *Queste* 3:101–12.

With frequent references to Gilbert Durand's *Les Structures anthropologiques de l'imaginaire*, offers a symbolic reading of Pantagruel's journey on the two coexisting planes of reality and myth as, among other possible readings, "un viaje iniciático" (p. 111) of a man who has shed for the occasion his gigantic stature and opted for a "dimensión humana" (p. 102). Believes that this adventure transcends the individual and becomes the collective journey of mankind. Notes that the journey is a series of encounters with monsters (often associated with the sea, often female in shape), from which the hero emerges victorious thanks to his recourse to common sense ("una arma típicamente humana"). Sees the adventure as a struggle with certain aspects of contemporary reality ("los rostros del tiempo"), the perils of femininity and water. Studies the symbolism of ascension and descent, darkness and light, and equates the symbols of verticality and ascent with man's recovery of the power he had lost at the time of the Fall. At the end of the journey, sees Pantagruel emerging as a new man, whom Rabelais fails to describe in detail, but who defines himself essentially through his discovery of the importance of knowledge.

14   DUVAL, EDWIN M. "The Medieval Curriculum, the Scholastic University, and Gargantua's Program of Studies (*Pantagruel*, 8)." In *Rabelais's Incomparable Book: Essays on his art*, edited by Raymond C. La Charité. Lexington, Ky.: French Forum, pp. 30–44.

Despite an initial impression of disorder, the program of studies outlined in *Pantagruel*, chapt. 8, adheres to the structure of the canonical medieval curriculum. Its details, however, "modify and transform the structure that subtends them" in crucial ways, and it is in "these deliberate departures from the implicit norm, and not in the words, ideas, themes and sources of the text itself, that the significance and most profound meaning of the program are to be found" (p. 31). These departures underscore the shift from the corrupt medieval Latin to the languages which offer direct access to the Bible on the level of grammar, from *inventio* and *dispositio* to *elocutio* on the level of rhetoric, from dialectic to history. In short, they emphasize a shift from what was taught in the trivium and quadrivium at the Faculty of Arts in Paris, to the innovative teaching of the humanists under the same headings. Omission of any reference to canon law, association of natural science with medicine, and Rabelais' implicit redefinition of theology at the end of the program are seen as further signs of a basic reorientation on the professional level of the curriculum. "Just as the ideal Christian community in *Gargantua* is the ironic result of a deliberate, systematic inversion of the rules and characteristics of the traditional monastery, so the ideal education in *Pantagruel* is the ironic result of a deliberate, systematic inversion of each and every discipline of the traditional medieval curriculum" (p. 39). As such, it is not, as is sometimes thought, an extraneous chapter, but forms "an integral, necessary, and particularly brilliant part" (p. 41) of the series of episodes that satirize medieval learning.

15  FRANÇON, MARCEL. "A propos de *Pantagruel* et de la comète de Halley." *BAARD* 4, no. 5:156.

Believes that the comet did appear in 1531, as mentioned in the *Pantagrueline Prognostication* of 1533.

16  FRECCERO, CARLA [ANN]. "The 'Instance' of the Letter: Woman in the text of Rabelais." In *Rabelais's Incomparable Book: Essays on his art*, edited by Raymond C. La Charité. Lexington, Ky.: French Forum, pp. 45–55.

Feminist and intertextual reading of chapt. 21, 22, and 24 of *Pantagruel* dealing with Panurge's and Pantagruel's treatment of two Parisian ladies, in the light of a story in Masuccio Salernitano's *Il Novellino*, Derrida's notion of *écriture* as an "opération féministe," and "two metaphors of writing as resistance" (p. 50) in the ring episode of *Pantagruel*. Claims that in Rabelais' first book woman "is the body in and of the text. As such she makes her appearance and is threatened with defacement, a defacement that is also an attempted erasure whose literalization is a transformation into letters. As letter, she is the blank page that marks the erasure of an immemorial inscription; as inscription, she is the message of unconscious desire. The enigma that is woman in the text of Rabelais is also the condition of the possibility for writing; it inscribes Rabelais in a textual quest, a quest that is the impossibility of closure or the in-corporation of that otherness" (p. 53).

17  ———. "The Other and the Same: The Image of the Hermaphrodite in Rabelais." In *Rewriting the Renaissance: The Discourse of Sexual Difference in Early Renaissance Europe*, edited by Margaret W. Ferguson, Maureen Quillian, and Nancy J. Vickers. Chicago: University of Chicago Press, pp. 145–58.

Observes that Gargantua's image (*Gargantua*, chapt. 7) is most often seen as an example of Renaissance syncretism, with its reconciliation of paganism and Christianity, and its synthesis, in the figure of the *androgyne*, of the male and female principle into a symbol of human wholeness. Challenges this interpretation in the light of the story of Hermaphroditus in Ovid's *Metamorphoses*, of the homosexual register of the vocabulary used by Rabelais, and of certain telling changes brought by Rabelais to the myth of the *androgyne* as told by Aristophanes in Plato's *Symposium*. Proposes an "androcentric" reading of the text, in line with a perceived exclusion of women from Rabelais' fictional world. Argues that by excluding the feminine from Plato's composite figure Rabelais has depicted "a double-headed monster," and notes that in spite of its evident androcentricity the episode has enlisted "the blind complicity of its (masculine) interpreters, who find in the image of Rabelais's hermaphrodite a symbol of human totality" (p. 158).

18    GAIGNEBET, CLAUDE. *A plus hault sens: L'ésotérisme spirituel et charnel de Rabelais.* 2 vols. Paris: Maisonneuve et Larose, 473 and 584 pp.

In a forty-seven page "Pro-loge," claims to have solved the enigma presented by the fact that on the last page of the manuscript of Rabelais' *Cinquiesme Livre* the Egyptian word for God is left blank. In the 1562 edition, the blank is merely suppressed. Argues it should have been filled with the word *Amon*, which Plutarch claims to be the Egyptian name for Jupiter (see also 1988.26). Presents the book itself as the fruit of twenty years of "recherches dispersées," originating in part from his interest in the obscene folklore of children. Interprets the prologue to *Gargantua* as legitimating the reader's quest for a hidden meaning; claims that the second part does not contradict the first. Rejects with equal vigor Lefranc's attempt at reading a "pensée secrète" into Rabelais (by pointing out that there is nothing secret in that thought as Lefranc understands it), and Febvre's effort to prove Lefranc wrong by an appeal to historical sociology (whose presuppositions are debatable at best). Will uncover the work's truly hidden meaning through an allegorical reading of a number of enigmatic passages, using the very method used by Rabelais himself to hide it: "Les techniques de lecture que nous appliquerons au texte doivent...tout aux méthodes dont Rabelais même use dans son œuvre. Le jeu de mots, le calembour, le symbole y tiennent une place centrale" (p. 10). Notes that signs (semiology) and their possible interpretation (semantics) are for Rabelais a constant object of preoccupation. Notes the instances of signs deciphered in accordance with each character's personality or situation. Believes that Rabelais himself intervenes and insists that the meaning of signs is not arbitrary. Lists, for each of the five books, the episodes dealing with such signs and reviews their proposed interpretations, as well as the enigmas for which Rabelais offers no key. In part 1 proposes an allegorical reading of the first six chapters of *Gargantua* (the hero's birth and the *Fanfreluches antidotées*). Sees in the 112 lines of the poem specific allusions to the most important episodes of the novel. Takes note of the various interpretations of the *Fanfreluches* proposed since Bernier (1697). Calculates Gargantua's date of birth to be February 3, and claims that in this date lies the secret of the work's higher, hidden meaning. Notes that February 3 is also Mardi Gras and Saint Blasius' day. Compares the components of the devotional ritual for Saint Blasius with the circumstances of Gargantua's birth. Notes that Saint Blasius is associated with the diseases of the throat, and relates this to Rabelais' interest in the throat as manifested in the etymology of so many of his heroes. Wonders whether Rabelais' decision to hide the significance of Gargantua's birth denotes his affiliation with the esoteric tradition. Seeks to revive the thesis, put forth by Péladan in 1905, and later taken up by Probst-Biraben, of Rabelais' connection with Freemasonry. Claims that equating Saint Blasius with Gargantua allows one to clarify certain mysterious lines of the *Fanfreluches*. Reads in lines 73–74 an allusion to the date of birth of Pantagruel, taken to be July 25. In part 2, dates the journey to the Dive Bouteille as beginning in early June and ending in late July, and notes Rabelais' interest in astrological considerations and in the saints associated with the canicular months. Concludes that it is not a trip around the world but a journey in time, corresponding to the trajectory of the sun on the ecliptic. Places Pantagruel in the biblical tradition: equates him with Elie, "c'est-à-dire au prophète et au saint commun à trois religions, au maître secret des libertins spirituels de la Renaissance, des cabbalistes et des alchimistes" (p. 339); with Samson; and with Boaz and Iakin, the two pillars of the Temple of Jerusalem. Considers the most significant part of Rabelais' work to be a commentary on the name of the two pillars, and compares Rabelais' text to Postel's unpublished work on the same subject. Notes that Rabelais uses the expression "mythologies galliques" for the first time in the *Pantagrueline prognostication* of 1533, and finds his position on these matters to lie exactly half-way between that of Lemaire de Belges and that of Postel, between "historical" and mystical gallicanism. In the last section of part 3, "La religion de Rabelais," believes he has shown the preponderance of the esoteric symbols of Freemasonry throughout Rabelais' work, and concludes that Rabelais is neither a good Christian, nor an Evangelical, nor an atheist. "Comme celle de Plutarque ou de Porphyre, la religion de Rabelais est un ensemble complexe où les conceptions relatives au monde (cosmogonie), à l'homme (anthropologie), à leurs âmes, aux rites et au calendrier (héortologie), s'expliquent mutuellement à travers des récits concernant des personnages divins (mythologie)" (p. 447). Identifies Pantagruel with Christ, sees in Rabelais' purpose a messianic design, compares his religious syncretism with the *Timæus*, and provides an esoteric interpretation of Thélème and the Temple de la Dive Bouteille as both the source and the death of the world. The second volume contains an extensive iconography, twenty appendices ("Annexes"), and notes.

19  GOUMARRE, PIERRE [J.]. "Rabelais: Misogynie et misogamie." *Littératures* 15 (Fall):59–71.

"Rabelais a bien été, comme le pensait Lefranc, le grand contempteur du sexe féminin" (p. 65). Catalogues five different types of answers provided by twentieth-century critics to the question of Rabelais' attitude toward women and marriage, and notes that only for Lefranc is Rabelais a thoroughgoing antifeminist. Studies one by one the two series of chapters (16 through 19, and 30 through 35) in which Rabelais raises the question in the *Tiers Livre*, and sides with Lefranc against those who felt entitled to pass a more mitigated verdict. Dismisses the positive statements of Panurge, Hippothadée, and Rondibilis on the grounds that they cannot be taken seriously. "Quant à Pantagruel, s'il n'attaque pas les femmes, il ne les défend pas non plus" (p.

65). Argues that in raising the question of women Rabelais does not seek to take sides in the Querelle des Femmes. Rather than express an ideological conviction, he satisfies a psychological need to denigrate women. On the question of marriage, contests Screech's contention that both *Pantagruel* and the *Tiers Livre* are manifestos in favor of marriage. Observes that one can speak ill of women and well of marriage—or vice versa—but argues that in Rabelais "misogynie et misogamie font bon ménage" (p. 67). Does not believe that any of Rabelais' characters are made for married life. Even more than the tendency to speak ill of women, finds disturbing Rabelais' habit of getting rid of them in his text: "Dans l'univers qu'il a créé, la femme, en tant qu'être humain, est *de trop*." Only of the Thélème episode is none of this true, but "Thélème est l'endroit le moins rabelaisien de l'œuvre" (p. 70). Everywhere else, Rabelais' fictional universe reflects the mental world of an out and out misogynist.

20  GRAY, FLOYD. "Rabelais's First Readers." In *Rabelais's Incomparable Book: Essays on his art*, edited by Raymond C. La Charité. Lexington, Ky.: French Forum, pp. 15–29.

"For whom did Rabelais write, and who actually read him?" (p. 24). Distinguishes the popular, largely illiterate audience addressed by Alcofrybas in the prologue to *Pantagruel* from the "actual reader" of Rabelais' text: "While *Pantagruel* exploits various aspects of popular culture for much of its humor and some of its satire, it was conceived for a public which, if not precisely humanist, would have been prepared to distinguish the cultural difference between itself and the one the prologue portrays" (p. 23). Compares Rabelais' book with the *Grandes Chronicques* in order to emphasize differences rather than suggest similarities. Concludes that what makes *Pantagruel* an incomparable book is the fact that it "represents a new mode of writing and requires a new mode of reading" (p. 26).

21  GREENE, THOMAS M. "The Hair of the Dog that Bit You: Rabelais' Thirst." In *Rabelais's Incomparable Book: Essays on his art*, edited by Raymond C. La Charité. Lexington, Ky.: French Forum, pp. 181–94.

Acknowledges that the theme of thirst is all-pervasive in Rabelais, and that as such it has often been discussed by critics, but suggests that its essentially negative implications have not always been sufficiently recognized. As lack, need, privation, the theme of thirst in all its forms—"economic, moral, sexual, social, intellectual, spiritual, semiotic" (p. 190)—defines the essential element of the human condition; and the concomitant notion of replenishment—enrichment—appears in Rabelais as "the quintessential human act" (p. 186), and the highest function of the Rabelaisian text. Sees in Messer Gaster the archetype of this fundamental lack and of the praiseworthy desire to fill it, and the monstrous Quaresmeprenant as an incarnation of "that enduring will to privation which has appeared so often in human history and has been institutionalized by Christianity" (p. 187). Argues that the *Tiers Livre* presents the restorative communication between writer and reader through the medium of the text as fraught with difficulties: signifiers do not signify clearly; symbols "leak significance" (p. 189), they require the hazardous act of interpretation: "man understands and communicates through codes admitting of probabilities but not of certainties" (p. 188). But this epistemological and semiotic insufficiency can be remedied. The text can fulfill its function by satisfying at least in part the reader's thirst for understanding, on condition that the reader's quest for meaning be carried out in a spirit of *médiocrité*, with full realization that the writer cannot provide absolute certainty, absolute knowledge, and that the text requires, in order to yield its replenishing message, the imaginative participation of the Pantagruelistic decoder. The latter's function it is to "fill up the vacancies of significance that punctuate the text" (p. 190).

22 ———. *The Vulnerable Text: Essays on Renaissance Literature.* New York: Columbia University Press, pp. 79–98.
  Reprint of 1986.21.

23 HUCHON, MIREILLE. "Rabelais et les genres d'escrire." In *Rabelais's Incomparable Book: Essays on his art*, edited by Raymond C. La Charité. Lexington, Ky.: French Forum, pp. 226–47.
  The significant number of references to poetic terms in the *Briefve declaration* leads the author to examine Rabelais' discourse on literary genres, as well as "les traces d'un éventuel art poétique" (p. 227) in his fiction. Notes that Rabelais' interest in the theoretical problems raised by the various literary genres is attested by his introduction of such terms as *catastrophe*, which he was the first to use in French, and his reference to *tragicque comedie*, of which he offered the very first example with the Chiquanous episode. Attracts attention to the numerous theatrical metaphors in Books III and IV, and to two chapters devoted to the etymology of two new poetic forms: the sonnet and the ode. Reminds us of Rabelais' reputation as a poet among his contemporaries. Believes that his poetic practice, at various points in his novel, reveals an evolution which parallels that of the other poets of his day. "Du *Pantagruel* au *Quart Livre*, on passe donc d'une poésie de l'inscription à une poésie de l'imitation antique et du chant" (p. 239). The *Cinquiesme Livre* marks an intermediate stage, consistent with the author's view, as expressed in *Rabelais grammairien*, that the final book is made up of drafts either contemporary or predating the text of Books III and IV.

24 HUMPHRIES, JEFFERSON. *Losing The Text: Readings in Literary Desire.* Athens: University of Georgia Press, pp. 108–37.
  Reprint of 1985.19.

25   JEANNERET, MICHEL. "*Gargantua* 4–24: L'Uniforme et le discontinu." In *Rabelais's Incomparable Book: Essays on his art*, edited by Raymond C. La Charité. Lexington, Ky.: French Forum, pp. 87–101.

Another of the author's studies of the "thème alimentaire," with emphasis on methodological implications. Believes that in interpreting Rabelais, the search for meaning and attention to forms should go hand in hand: "Conflictuelles, les deux méthodes sont pourtant pertinentes et compensent mutuellement leurs excès: la première empêche la seconde de verser dans le formalisme et la vaporisation du sens; la seconde déjoue les tentations réductrices et niveleuses de la première" (p. 88). Notes that the three phases of Gargantua's relation to food—"gloutonnerie joyeuse et légitime, gloutonnerie coupable, frugalité" (p. 87)—create a double axis: that of individual development (in which instinctual behaviour must give way, under the pressure of the collectivity, to the bridling of one's animal tendencies), and that of the successive stages of man's mythic destiny (the pre-moral stage before the Fall, followed by the emergence of evil, and the recapturing of happiness through an effort of will and intelligence). Notes also that Gargantua's regimen under Ponocrates is based on the theory of humors and spirits known to the humanists of the period. But warns against the temptation to see in these conclusions Rabelais' last word, so to speak, on the question of the optimal management of our daily life. For the Thélème episode contradicts in very important ways the program proposed by Ponocrates in *Gargantua*, chapt. 4–24. Suggests that ideological coherence in Rabelais can only be demonstrated in the context of short sequences, and that any attempt to generalize from these to the work as a whole is doomed to failure. For the Rabelaisian text is essentially heterogeneous, polyphonic, juxtaposing different stylistic registers, different visions of the world. "S'il reste à la critique rabelaisienne des progrès à faire, c'est en reconnaissant ces forces de rupture et en les intégrant au travail d'interprétation" (p. 99).

26   JOANNET, GINETTE. "En relisant quelques pages de Rabelais." *Bulletin de la Société de Mythologie Française*, no. 143 (October–December):56–63.

Seeks in numerology the hidden meaning of certain episodes of the novel. Thus believes that in the storm at sea episode of Book IV Rabelais reveals his date of birth, namely 1483, since Panurge repeats once in chapt. 21, four times in chapt. 20, eight times in chapt. 19, and three times in chapt. 18 the cry "je naye!" which may well stand for "je [me] noie," but also for "je nais." As for Thélème, believes it to be essentially a temporal rather than an architectural structure, since nearly every number mentioned in chapt. 53 through 58 of *Gargantua* is either 6 or a multiple of that number, and since these numbers serve to measure time. Sees in the abbey, if one includes the basement as well as the five stories above ground, an embodiment of the history of mankind, from the Deluge to the Renaissance. Numerological considerations also lead the author to suggest that *Gargantua* may well have been written—and even published—in 1532, contrary to prevailing opinion.

27  KRITZMAN, LAWRENCE D. "Rabelais' Comedy of Cruelty: A Psycho-Allegorical Reading of the Chiquanous Episode." In *Rabelais's Incomparable Book: Essays on his art*, edited by Raymond C. La Charité. Lexington, Ky.: French Forum, pp. 141–54.

Admits that the episode, as well as the "digressive text" involving Villon, are directed to a large extent against "provocative figures of censorship" (p. 142). But argues that alongside the satire of abusive authority, Rabelais' narrative also enacts a "symbolic unconscious" of repressed sado-masochistic fantasies of revenge through projection of reality into theatrical fiction. "The Rabelaisian text...transcribes a sadistic tendency to destroy an aggressor through the enactment of a comic allegory in which latent hostility is sublimated and yet unconsciously adheres to the ideological imperatives that dictate the power of repression" (p. 152).

28  KUSHNER, EVA. "Gesture in the Work of Rabelais." *Renaissance and Reformation/Renaissance et Réforme* 10, no. 1:67–77.

Studies the function of gesture in Rabelais' text against the background of gestural representation in the context of the Renaissance as well as in the light of modern semiotic theory. Draws attention to "the extent to which stylistically, thought in the Rabelaisian text is translated in terms of action" (p. 68). Notes the predominance in Rabelais of the gesture of violence, his emphasis on gesture as a means of underscoring the inadequacies of verbal communication, and as a way of encoding thoughts which the climate of the day does not allow him to express directly. Stresses "the modernity of Rabelais in terms of the almost obvious applicability of semiotic inquiry to his worlds," but also the ultimate "inability of semiotics itself to account for his humanistic treatment of meaning" (p. 67).

29  LA CHARITÉ, RAYMOND C. "Rabelais, 'sans pair, incomparable et sans parragon.'" In *Rabelais's Incomparable Book: Essays on his art*, edited by Raymond C. La Charité. Lexington, Ky.: French Forum, pp. 9–12.

Introduction to the collection of essays, emphasizing Rabelais' "understanding of textuality as process rather than end product" (p. 11). Finds throughout Rabelais' work an unmistakable awareness of an aspect of literary activity which only recently has attracted critical attention: "Long before the jargonistic conundrums of our day, Rabelais knew that reading is more than mere interpretation and that, indeed, reading à la Rabelais—as his readers are told repeatedly—calls into question the very activity itself" (p. 11).

30 ————. "Rabelais and the Silenic Text: The Prologue to *Gargantua*." In *Rabelais's Incomparable Book: Essays on his art*, edited by Raymond C. La Charité. Lexington, Ky.: French Forum, pp. 72–86.

Intertextual reading of the prologue, comparing the figure of Socrates as it emerges from Plato's account in the *Symposium*, with the corresponding passage in Erasmus' *Sileni Alcibiadis* and Alcofribas Nasier's version. Finds in the Silenic image a metaphor for reading. Suggests that the image of "text-as-onion" comes closer than that of "text-as-bone-marrow" to Rabelais' conception of literary interpretation: the text is revealed in the very peeling of its various layers. But the reader can never be certain of the validity of his interpretation, for the all-pervasive presence of irony makes Rabelais' book an "ungraspable text" (p. 84).

31 LAZARD, MADELEINE. "La Satire dans *Gargantua*." In *La Satire au temps de la Renaissance*, edited by M. T. Jones-Davies. Université de Paris–Sorbonne, Centre de Recherches sur la Renaissance, no. 11. Paris: Touzot, pp. 81–96.

Notes the presence of satire in Rabelais' "facétie verbale." Measures its degrees of violence; finds it to be moderate in the case of doctors and certain monks, aggressive when aimed at astrologers, alchemists, theologians, and tyrannical monarchs, and vindictive in the attack upon personal enemies. Points out that in his denunciation of vices as particular examples of universal folly, Rabelais' satire is more good-humored in *Gargantua* than it will become later in the *Quart Livre*, and argues that at all times it is incidental rather than systematic: "Le roman ne tourne jamais au pamphlet" (p. 95).

32 LIMBRICK, ELAINE. "Perspective in French Renaissance Prose." In *Crossroads and Perspectives: French Literature of the Renaissance, Studies in honor of Victor E. Graham*, edited by Catherine M. Grisé and C. D. E. Tolton. Geneva: Librairie Droz, pp. 143–53.

Compares Leonardo da Vinci's approach to painting with Rabelais' approach to literature, stresses its encyclopedic nature, its "multi-dimensional perspective" (p. 147). Finds similarities between the visual ordering of printed discourse and the discovery of linear perspective in art. Believes that the change from oral to written tradition allows a writer like Rabelais to "order his work logically and chronologically" (p. 149), and to multiply points of view and bring different perspectives upon the narrative. Later, growing emphasis on scientific observation will further transform the artist's perception of both external reality and his own inner world, and lead to the replacement of the kind of all-encompassing vision exemplified in Rabelais by the "narrower, single subject, introspective vision of Montaigne and his successors" (p. 145).

1986

33   LOSSE, DEBORAH N. "Rabelaisian Paradox: Where the Fantastic and the Carnivalesque Intersect." *Romanic Review* 77:322–29.
    Although not incompatible at first glance, "the carnivalesque, as defined by M. Bakhtin, and the fantastic, as defined by Tzvetan Todorov" are in fact "two mutually exclusive forces" (p. 322). Finds in such examples of satirical eulogy as Dindenault's praise of his sheep, the praise of debtors, of Quaresmeprenant, and the Pantagruélion some of the features of the folkloric time-space as defined by Bakhtin, where "the most extraordinary and hetero-geneous elements are juxtaposed" (p. 323) in sequences that are essentially unhierarchical in nature. But when an episode such as that of the Pantagruélion takes us at the end into the realm of the fantastic, it introduces an element that is incompatible with the carnivalesque, since it presupposes "a hierarchy based on the sharing of the spacio-temporal world of the text by human and supernatural forces" (p. 329). At such admittedly infrequent moments, "it diverts our attention from the focus of Rabelais' fictional uni-verse—man himself, the proper domain of the carnival" (p. 329).

34   MARIN, LOUIS. *La parole mangée et autres essais théologico-politiques.* Paris: Méridiens Klincksieck, pp. 89–120.
    Reprint of 1976.20.

35   McKINNEY, KITZIE. "Diversions of Transformation in *Pantagruel*'s Medlar Myth." *French Review* 59, no. 4 (March):546–52.
    Argues that the thematic, rhetorical, and intertextual transformations in the medlar ("mesles") episode in chapt. 1 of *Pantagruel* "sabotage" in advance the recent attempts to read it as a symbol of spiritual redemption: "the medlar myth refuses spiritual transcendence" (p. 551), and remains in so doing a deeply disconcerting text, although it does provide the reader with an opportunity to "share in the changing pleasures and ambiguities of creation" (p. 552).

36   RANDALL, CATHARINE. "Le Cocuage hypothétique de Panurge: Le monde à l'envers dans le *Tiers Livre*." *Constructions*:77–86.
    Sees in Panurge' hypothetical cuckoldry an instance of the *mundus inversus* and a metaphor for Rabelais' conception of the individual, "désaxé" in a society moving toward capitalism. Believes that the appearance of Panurge in Book III marks "un renversement du personnage qu'il avait été dans *Pantagruel*" (p. 79), and relates this "renversement" to the carnivalesque spirit of regeneration.

37   REA, JOANNE. "A Few Observations on Plutarch and Rabelais in *A Portrait*." *James Joyce Quarterly* 23, no. 3 (Spring):357–59.

Kidd's remarks on the subject notwithstanding (see 1984.19), argues that the Parnell episode in *A Portrait of the Artist as a Young Man* owes more to Rabelais than to Plutarch.

38 ———. "Joyce and Rabelais: Mallow, Marrow, and Molly." *Names* 34, no. 4 (December):430–32.

Sees a link between the "mallow" (in French, *maulve*) used by Gargantua in Urquhart's translation of the *torchecul* episode, and a passage in *Ulysses*: "Imagistically and auditorially both, the mallow Gargantua uses to wipe his rump evokes the 'smellow melons' of Molly's 'melonous rump' which Bloom kisses in *U* 374" (p. 430). Notes the near homophony of *moelle* (marrow) with *molle* and with Molly's name. Drawing on John S. Farmer's *Vocabula Amatoria* (1966), suggests that *moelle* was synonymous with *semen* in the French of Rabelais, and links these sexual connotations with Molly's erotic fantasies around the image of the dog sucking a marrowbone.

39 REGOSIN, RICHARD L. "The Ins(ides) and Outs(ides) of Reading: Plural Discourse and the Question of Interpretation in Rabelais." In *Rabelais's Incomparable Book: Essays on his art,* edited by Raymond C. La Charité. Lexington, Ky.: French Forum, pp. 59–71.

Applying to Rabelais Bakhtin's notion of multiple discourse, argues that a valid interpretation of his work transcends the polarity between the exterior and the interior suggested by the prologue to *Gargantua*. The plurality of voices and points of view with which Rabelais endows his narrator challenges "the foundations of accepted hermeneutic practice, the binary opposition of outside and inside" (p. 70). For the hierarchy of levels which had hitherto characterized "authoritative writing," Rabelais substitutes in the prologue itself "a strikingly decentered text which juxtaposes without priority or order multiple voices, that is, multiple authorities, each vying to be heard" (p. 70). The challenge to the inside-outside polarity is seen to have also a political dimension: "By putting in question the traditional model of reading, the prologue undermines the basis on which all forms of power are based, the dynamics of opposition in which each side struggles to control, repress, and eliminate the other" (p. 70).

40 REY-FLAUD, BERNADETTE. "Quand Rabelais interroge la farce: Les moutons de Panurge et l'épilogue du *Pathelin*." *Littératures* 15 (Fall):7–18.

Argues that Rabelais "subverts" the material he borrows from the farce, and that in so doing he brings out its most fundamental significance, namely that it is essentially about language. By emphasizing the often neglected final episode, Rabelais is seen to shift the focus from the psychology of the deceiver and his victim to the level of language, and to underscore its destructive power over the speaker when it is used for its own sake, independently of the

1986

*destinataire* without whom language is deprived of its indispensible "point d'appui."

41  RIGOLOT, FRANÇOIS [PAUL]. "'Enigme' et 'Prophétie': Les Langages de l'hermétisme chez Rabelais." *Oeuvres et Critiques* 11, no. 1:37–47.
Attempts to characterize Rabelais' hermeticism by studying the language of the prologue to *Gargantua*, in which the author invites the reader to seek a higher meaning in what may appear at first glance like an anodyne work. Notes the false erudition and heavy-handed use of hyperbole which tend to invalidate Rabelais' promise of a glimpse into the higher mysteries of existence. But argues that the ambiguity of the  prologue does not necessarily indicate that the invitation should not be taken seriously: it merely echoes the ambiguous attitude of Renaissance humanists towards the hermetic tradition. Sees in the initial *Fanfreluches antidotées* and the final *Enigme en prophétie* the two essential types of hermetic discourse: in the first instance, a seemingly obscure, unintelligible text which appears to call for a decoding into simple, intelligible language; in the second, a seemingly simple text, but whose apparent simplicity conceals a higher, hidden message. Argues that Rabelaisian satire of certain forms of hermetic thought notwithstanding, Rabelais finds in hermeticism a fruitful subject of reflection, and that he endows hermetic language with a deeply poetic role in his quest for a glimpse into the ultimate mysteries of the human condition.

42  ———. "Rabelais et la scolastique: Une affaire de canards (*Gargantua* 12)." In *Rabelais's Incomparable Book: Essays on his art*, edited by Raymond C. La Charité. Lexington, Ky.: French Forum, pp. 102–23.
Views the "torchecul" episode, generally neglected by critics as excessively distasteful, as part of a conscious didactic design. The added reference to Duns Scotus in the second edition, besides providing a generally comic effect, may have been suggested by the similarity between the philosopher's name and the "oyzon bien *dumenté*" put to such imaginative use by the young Gargantua (*dumenté* being derived from *dum* or *dun* signifying *duvet* in the dialects of the Western provinces since the Middle Ages). Since there may also be an onomastic link between William of *Occam* and the word *oyzon* (p. 109), suggests that the whole episode may be seen as a satirical allegory of the nominalistic as well as the realistic wings of medieval Scholasticism, and as a thickly veiled attack on the Sorbonne as the upholder of its traditions.

43  SAROCCHI, J. *Rabelais et l'instance paternelle*. Paris: Éditions A.-G. Nizet, 110 pp.
Reacts against the tendency to minimize the thematic importance of Rabelais' work, and underscores the presence of the relationship between father and son implicit in the major theme of transmission of knowledge and

power: "le problème de l'héritier y est axial" (p. 29). Admits that in *Pantagruel* the theme of paternity is only vaguely sketched (with the important exception of Gargantua's letter), and that from Book III onward it recedes into the background. But shows that in *Gargantua* it informs the whole text, and argues that its pervading presence makes of *Gargantua* the pivotal work of the entire cycle: "*Gargantua* est *le* roman de Rabelais, parce que s'y trouve réglée la question du père" (p. 30). Notes that in the first two chapters of *Pantagruel* the genealogical theme is treated in a satirical mode, although in chapt. 3, depicting Gargantua's joy at the birth of his son, the text acquires an unmistakable depth of human emotion, and in Gargantua's letter to Pantagruel the father assumes an epistolary presence which cannot be entirely ignored. But points out that it is in *Gargantua* that the role of the father, significantly amplified, becomes truly focal, acquires an autobiographical resonance, and endows Rabelaisian laughter with its characteristic warmth: "le rire de *Gargantua* est comme ensoleillé par la référence paternelle" (pp. 47–48). Sees in the "torchecul" episode "un moment décisif, l'acte par lequel la fiction rabelaisienne instaure le libre rapport entre père et fils" (p. 53). Finds in Grandgousier's piety the surest guarantee of Rabelais' own religious faith. Notes with some surprise that the death of Rabelais' father, the birth and death of his son Théodule, as well as the subsequent birth of his two other children during the years that separate Book II from its sequel do not seem to have affected the father-son theme in the *Tiers Livre*. Rejects the Marxist interpretation of the relationship between Pantagruel and Panurge in terms of a class struggle between master and servant. Remarks on the unexpected return of the father in chapt. 35, in the midst of the debate on marriage, where his majesty and the respect he inspires contrast him with the younger characters. Notes that the quest of Book IV receives Gargantua's blessing, and offers a theological interpretation of chapt. 3, inaugurating the epistolary exchanges between Gargantua and Pantagruel: notes that their communication becomes a kind of sacramental link between father and son through the intermediary of the carrier pigeon, "virtuel symbole de l'Esprit" (p. 91). Concludes by militating in favor of the unfashionable view that literary works are not self-generated but the product of an author's efforts, and that the act of reading is to a large extent a quest for meaning.

44   SMITH, PAUL J. "Medamothi: Peinture et rhétorique (Rabelais, *Quart Livre*, Chap. 2)." *Neophilologus* 70, no. 1:1–12.

   Expresses surprise at the critics' lack of interest in the paintings the Pantagruelists buy on the island of Medamothi. Notes their *impossible* character (the subjects cannot be represented in any medium but that of words), with the exception of the tapestries purchased by Pantagruel. Shows that the subject of each work of art is in character with the personality of the buyer. Sees behind Frère Jean's picture the esthetics of direct imitation (naturalism, decorum, expressivity); behind that of Panurge, the esthetics of mannerism; whereas Pantagruel's tapestries are examples of "imitation *idéalisante*" (p. 7), representing nature as it ought to be, and perhaps reflecting Rabelais' own esthetic ideal in painting. Notes corresponding forms of rhetoric in the description of the paintings: the mannerism of Panurge's painting is equated with a rhetoric of sophistry and excess; the direct naturalism of Frère Jean's with clarity and common sense; whereas Pantagruel's dialectical esthetics synthesize both extremes and embody the ideal of *mediocritas aurea*. "Tout comme il réunit le naturalisme et le maniérisme dans sa conception préclassique de la belle nature, il combine, parallèlement, les deux formes contraires d'asianisme et d'atticisme dans l'idéal érasmien du *breviter et copiose dicere*" (p. 8). Compares his analysis to that of other critics who have sought to relate the characters to rhetorical forms, and notes that most see things in terms of a binary opposition between Pantagruel and Panurge. Suggests that one is on firmer ground when one sees the distinctions in terms of a "trialisme dialectique," with Pantagruel representing, at least in the *Quart Livre*, a synthesis between the extremes represented by Panurge and Frère Jean.

45 STONE, DONALD [Jr.]. "Wrestling with the Humanists: Gargantua's Device." *Philological Quarterly* 65, no. 4 (Fall):423–32.

Is the description of Gargantua's device as ambiguous as some critics would have it? Is it meant to tease and confuse? In reaction to certain interpretations of the passage as a "plural" text, argues that the difference between Plato's and Rabelais' androgyne has been exaggerated, that the "deux culs" with which Rabelais endows his androgyne are not necessarily comic or shocking, that in fact Rabelais' text underplays the erotic value of the Platonic image, that the movement from *eros* to *agape* (that is from Plato to Saint Paul) is not an example of *coincidentia oppositorum* but an attempt to inflect Plato in the direction of Christian thought, and that "Rabelais's Christian recasting of the Platonic androgyne" results in a remarkably coherent interpretation that reflects contemporary humanist thinking about marriage.

46 TETEL, MARCEL. "Rabelais et Lucien: De deux rhétoriques." In *Rabelais's Incomparable Book: Essays on his art*, edited by Raymond C. La Charité. Lexington, Ky.: French Forum, pp. 127–38.

The anecdote of Alexander and the merchant in the Sibylle de Panzoust episode, and its source (left unacknowledged) in Lucian's *Master of Rhetoric*, suggest that rhetoric—more specifically, the relationship between the rhetoric of *copia* and that of *œconomia*—is at the heart of the passage. Argues that this gives a new meaning not only to the episode itself, but to the neighboring chapters as well, and indeed to the whole of the *Tiers Livre*. "Si l'intertexte lucianique révèle dans l'épisode de la sibylle de Panzoust un discours sur la rhétorique, il se peut qu'il fournisse également à la sibylle une identité jusqu'à présent non soupçonnée." Is she not Dame Rhétorique herself?

47  TIEFENBRUN, SUSAN W. "The Secret of Irony: Apollo and Isis in Rabelais." *Oeuvres et Critiques* 11, no. 1:21–35.

Examines irony in Rabelais as a by-product of hermeticism, and discusses "potential effects of irony on the implied author and reader in the light of psychoanalytic theory" (p. 21). Locates irony in the contradiction between the surface meaning of the text (Apollo) and its deeper levels (Isis), and suggests that in Rabelais it expresses itself through such indirect forms of satire as understatement, oxymoron, polyvalence, exaggeration, and puns. Discusses the problems inherent in the detection of irony in general, and finds them to be compounded in Rabelais by the difficulty of identifying the voice of the writing subject. In a Freudian perspective, sees the function of irony—in Rabelais as elsewhere—as socializing repressed thought and eliciting in the reader the pleasure of discovery of the work's hidden meanings.

48  WEINBERG, FLORENCE M[AY]. *Gargantua in a Convex Mirror: Fischart's View of Rabelais.* Studies in the Humanities. Literature–Politics–Society, no. 2. New York, Bern, and Frankfurt: Peter Lang, 200 pp.

Deplores the nationalist bias and linguistic limitations of French and German scholars who have hitherto studied Fischart. "As an American specialist on Rabelais, who is familiar with both languages and who has no nationalist prejudice" (p. x), undertakes to compare Fischart's translation (or rather adaptation) of *Gargantua* with the original, to examine the changes made by Fischart to Rabelais' text, to evaluate Fischart's success as a translator, and to show "how much his vast additions can tell us about his own period and intellectual climate" (p. ix). Notes that Fischart blurs "almost anything that could be considered esoteric or hermetic" in Rabelais' text (p. 2), that he deletes or distorts Rabelais' allusions to Evangelicalism, and that he inflates the passages dealing with indulging in food and drink. In chapt. 1 (a reprint of 1983.41), outlines the ways in which Fischart's text differs from the original (embroideries, omissions, and "additions independent of the underlying text," p. 11). In chapt. 4, shows how Fischart denatures Rabelais' Evangelicalism (notably by transforming the character of Frère Jean into "a caricature of bigoted Roman Catholicism" (p. 97). In chapt. 5, brings out the shadowy side of Fischart's religion (anti-Semitism, witchcraft, necrophilia). Defines, in the following two chapters, Fischart's "humanism" as it emerges from his ambiguous attitude towards the most clearly humanistic passages in Rabelais, and exposes him as a product of his own time and place.

## 1987

1   BALDINGER, KURT. *"Air et envie (Gargantua*, 50): Die Rabelais-Exegese als Opfer einer Homographie." In *Romania ingeniosa: Festschrift für Prof. Dr. Gerold Hilty zum 60. Geburstag*. New York, Bern, Frankfurt, and Paris: Peter Lang, pp. 115–23.

Instead of *air*, believes one should read *aïr*. Relates the term to *ira*, and consequently translates as *anger*. Reprinted in 1990.2.

2   BEDOUELLE, GUY-THOMAS. "L'Humanisme chrétien de Rabelais." *Revue Thomiste* 87, no. 1 (January–March):117–27.

By way of a commentary upon M. A. Screech's *Rabelais* (1979.23), seeks to provide—as the book itself does not—a systematized account of the humanistic and Evangelical dimension of Rabelais' work. Stresses the omnipresence of the Bible (in the dual registers of the serious and the comic), discusses Rabelais' attempt to syncretize the classical and the Christian ideal, underscores the moral and spiritual component of his new pedagogy, the link he establishes between *connaître* and *savoir vivre*. Finds further manifestations of Rabelais' Christian humanism in his notion of authentic prayer, in the element of synergism in his position on the question of free will, in his denunciation of *philautia* and his exaltation of Christian folly, as well as in his awareness of the dual nature—both spiritual and animal—of man. Sees the abbey of Thélème as combining the humanist dream of restoring Plato's Academy and the Evangelicalists' efforts to reform monastic life, and reads the episode on the death of Pan as the culmination of Rabelais' spiritual itinerary: "Du *Pantagruel* au *Quart Livre*, on passe ainsi, dans la trajectoire de toute une carrière littéraire, de la vie théologale recommandée par Gargantua à son jeune fils en l'engageant à 'foy formée de charité' à Celui qui en est la source redécouverte en sa mort: le Christ" (p. 126).

3   BOYER, ALAIN-MICHEL. "Les Architectures du lisible: Quelques réflexions autour de l'almanach pour 1541 de Rabelais." *Textes et Langages* 14:1–27.

In the context of a discussion bearing on the cultural significance of almanacs in general, studies the physical layout of the remaining fragments of Rabelais' almanac for 1541. Finds in them a confirmation of Foucault's ideas on the four figures of analogy which inform, according to the *Archéologie du savoir*, the *épistéme* of the Renaissance.

4   BURRELL, PAUL. "Rabelais's Debts to the Medieval World." *Studies in Medievalism* 3, no. 1 (Fall):77–82.

Reads chapt. 10–13 of *Pantagruel* (the giant's attempt to settle the dispute between Baisecul and Humevesne) and chapt. 17–20 of *Gargantua* (Janotus pleading for the return of the bells of Notre-Dame) as "examples of how Rabelais portrays the late medieval world as having allowed and encouraged the loss of essential legal knowledge and fundamental truths of Christianity by failing to conserve the underlying purpose of these institutions" (p. 81).

5  DEFAUX, GÉRARD. *Marot, Rabelais, Montaigne: L'écriture comme présence*. Paris: Champion; Geneva: Slatkine, pp. 101–42.

Chapt. 2, "Rabelais herméneute: De la lettre à l'esprit," argues on the basis of a re-reading of the prologue to *Gargantua* and the episode of the frozen words that Rabelais does not share the deconstructionists' rejection of language as a trustworthy vehicle of thought, or their contention that he leaves entirely to his reader the responsibility to provide his work with a higher, hidden meaning. For the most part, the chapter reiterates the author's convictions as previously presented in 1985.8.

6  DESROSIERS-BONIN, DIANE. "Macrobe et les âmes héroïques (Rabelais, *Quart Livre*, chapitres 25 à 28)." *Renaissance and Reformation/Renaissance et Réforme* 15, no. 3:211–21.

Sees in Rabelais' Macrobe a reference to the Latin author Macrobius, the famous commentator of Cicero's *Somnium Scipionis*, from whom Rabelais may have borrowed the theme of man's salvation through the exercise of civic duties (*virtus*), as exemplified by the life and death of Guillaume du Bellay.

7  FONTAINE, MARIE MADELEINE. "Le jeu de paume comme modèle des échanges: Quelques règles de la sociabilité à la Renaissance." In *Sociabilité, Pouvoirs et Société: Actes du Colloque de Rouen, 24/26 Novembre 1983*. Rouen: Publications de l'Université de Rouen, pp. 143–53.

Notes that the *jeu de paume* has been allegorized ("moralisé") from the very first appearance of the game in the Middle Ages and has been made to serve as an allegorical model of whatever activity seems to have been the most important at the time. Sees in Frère Jean's interpretation of the *Enigme* at the end of *Gargantua* an interesting reversal of the common practice of allegorizing, a rare attempt to look at the game for its own sake.

8  GENETTE, GÉRARD. *Seuils*. Paris: Éditions du Seuil, pp. 197–206.

Alludes to the extreme ambiguity of Rabelais' prologue to *Gargantua* and presents it as the first modern preface.

9  HANSEN, MICHEL. "La figure du monstre dans le *Pantagruel* de Rabelais." *Réforme, Humanisme, Renaissance*, no. 24 (June):25–45.

Studies the grotesque in Rabelais' novel through the fictional representation of the monstrous. Stresses the double ambivalence of the concept: the monster as a sign (to be deciphered), as well as a presence (to be acknowledged), as something frightening as well as admirable. Notes the presence of the monstrous throughout the novel in four successive forms: as norm in the grotesque universe of the chapters on Pantagruel's origin, birth, and feeding; as a cultural, and above all a linguistic phenomenon in the chapters on the giant's education and his intellectual exploits; as a political phenomenon in the chapters on the invasion of Utopia by monstrous giants; and finally, in chapt. 30–34, as a set of variations on the theme of the other world. Points out that in all these instances monstrosity is internalized, viewed by Rabelais as an internal threat, "un fait psychologique, moral ou éthique" (p. 33), an evil within man himself. Stresses the paradoxical nature of Pantagruel, monstrous by his origin, but a philosopher-prince by upbringing, and charged with the messianic role of freeing the world of its monsters. Sees him as a "dominateur des altérés" in that he will triumph over the most dangerous monsters of all, those who *alter* religion and justice. Notes that Pantagruel's transformation from monster to philosopher-prince coincides with the arrival of Panurge, who takes upon himself what is grotesque in the giant, allowing the latter to become at last the mouthpiece of Renaissance humanism. Argues that both are charged with the task of revealing the presence of the monstrous: Pantagruel in his defense of humanism against ignorance, injustice, and super-stition, Panurge in pointing out the dangers of monstrosity in humanism itself (for example in the dangers inherent in the misuse of rhetoric). "De fait s'établit entre ces deux figures antithétiques un jeu dialectique par lequel cha-cun montre le monstrueux de l'autre" (pp. 40–41). Compares their friendship to the figure of the androgyne, "ce monstre qui est la perfection." Insists that for Rabelais it is only through the monstrous that monstrosity can be tran-scended. Suggests that therein lies the explanation of the ambiguous nature of *Pantagruel*, the resolution of the seeming contradiction between its grotesque esthetics and its humanistic ideology, as it attempts to reach its paradoxical goal: "chercher et dire l'Homme, la Culture et la Vérité par les voies mêmes de l'invraisemblable, de l'informe et du monstre" (p. 43).

10  JEANNERET, MICHEL. *Des mots et des mets: Banquets et propos de table à la Renaissance*. Paris: Librairie José Corti, 291 pp.

Uses Rabelais' text throughout the book as an example in his discussion of the communal partaking of food as a social institution and a cultural sign. Uses it also to illustrate the Platonic notion of the banquet as reconciling in the acts of eating, drinking, and speaking, the pleasures of the body and those of the mind. In "Le déjeuner sur l'herbe" (pp. 23–31) discusses Rabelais' set-ting of the nativity of Pantagruel and Gargantua against the background of a country "Kermesse," in an atmosphere of conviviality and communion with the natural forces of abundance and fertility. Argues that in the overture to the first two books Rabelais rewrites the story of Creation in a Garden of Eden where man is enjoined rather than forbidden to partake of the fruit of the tree of knowledge and of life. In "Des mots pleins la bouche" (pp. 92–100), examines Rabelais' transposition of table talk into literature in a spirit of fantasy and inventiveness, and comments on the richness and variety of the convivial discourse at the Rabelaisian feast. Notes the linguistic virtuosity of the prologues (pp. 112–16), discusses food as image of the literary work (pp. 119–23), and brings out in "Normaliser le récit" (pp. 258–63) "l'assiette référentielle des récits" which the reader can detect beyond Rabelais' linguistic and formal games.

11 MARSHALL, F. W. "The Allegory of Rabelais' *Gargantua*." *Australian Journal of French Studies* 24, no. 2 (May–August):115–54.

Having argued (see 1987.12) that the prologue to *Gargantua* prescribes an allegorical reading of the novel, and that according to the prologue "[t]he book is about Religion, the State and the Individual" (p. 115), attempts a systematic allegorization in the light of the rules of biblical exegesis. Sees the giants as models of the perfect Church, and Frère Jean as representing the Church on earth, "the symbol of traditional ecclesiastical structures and practices" (p. 128). Brings out the Christian resonance of a group of major symbols, seeks confirmation of the allegory in the individual chapters of the book, and defends his reading as providing Rabelais' work with an increased coherence on the level of ideas.

12 ———. "Worrying the Bone Again: The Structure and Significance of the Prologue to *Gargantua*." *Australian Journal of French Studies* 24, no. 1 (January–April):3–22.

"The Prologue to Gargantua states that the book is to be read allegorically. The evidence is unequivocal" (p. 3). Sees in the prologue an (admittedly) enigmatic "statement of method and intention" (p. 18) rather than a mystifying riddle intended to mislead. Rejects recent attempts to see the second part of the prologue as denying the validity of the first, or as seeking *captatio benevolentiae* rather than suggesting a mode of interpretation. Argues that Rabelais means his work to be read as an allegory in the mode of biblical (and not mythological, or poetic) exegesis, that is an allegory whose meaning is not supplied by the reader but is deliberately placed in the text by the author, in this case for reasons related to the climate of religious intolerance prevalent in Rabelais' day. Believes that the main theme of the prologue is the transmission of divine wisdom through Socrates, Erasmus, and Rabelais, and that the work as a whole does reveal, as Rabelais promises in the prologue, the mysteries of religion as well as those which pertain to "l'estat politicq et vie œconomique," understood as "the proper ordering (*œconomia*) of the Church, the State and the private life within the context of the Christian dispensation (*œconomis dei*)" (p. 16).

1987

13  McKINLEY, MARY B. "Bakhtin and the World of Rabelais Criticism."
    *Degré Second* 11 (September):83–88.
    Centered on Richard Berrong's *Rabelais and Bakhtin* (see 1986.4),
    notes the excessive polarization between those critics who see Rabelais' work
    as a product of its cultural context and those for whom it is essentially "a
    product of linguistic creativity" (p. 83). Suggests that historicists, such as
    Berrong, tend to underestimate Bakhtin's contribution to Rabelais criticism by
    overemphasizing the limitations of Bakhtin's understanding of popular
    culture.

14  MORRISON, IAN R. "Le Chapitre 8 de *Pantagruel*, remarques sur des inter-
    prétations récentes." *Studi Francesi* 31, no. 91:63–70.
    G. J. Brault (see 1966.2) had studied Gargantua's letter to his son in the
    context of the rest of the book and concluded that it was not, as had been com-
    monly held, a paean to the Renaissance but, on the contrary, a parody of its
    excessive ambitions. Finds some of Brault's conclusions (as well as those of
    Defaux in *Pantagruel et les Sophistes*, see 1973.3) to be questionable. Argues
    that Pantagruel is not quite the fool he is made out to be, that the two sur-
    rounding chapters are not as exclusively satirical as Brault thought they were,
    that the comparisons used by Gargantua in his letter are not as self-evidently
    absurd as Brault had claimed, and that the exaggerated nature of the objec-
    tives in Gargantua's educational program are not necessarily ridiculous, since
    they have to do with aspirations and not with what Gargantua believes can be
    accomplished in reality. Does not believe that Rabelais is mocking
    Gargantua's excessive intellectual pretensions: "au contaire, il convient de
    reconnaître à Gargantua le mérite d'équilibrer par la lucidité l'enthousiasme
    qui anime sa lettre." Suggests that Rabelais' occasional jibes at Gargantua and
    Pantagruel are not meant to discredit his giants, and that the letter as a whole
    remains an essentially serious document.

15  RAWLES, STEPHEN, and SCREECH, M. A. *A New Rabelais Bibliography:
    Editions of Rabelais before 1626*, with the collaboration of Sally Burch North
    and Anne Reeve, and incorporating preliminary work done by and with
    Gwyneth Wilkie. Geneva: Librairie Droz, 691 pp.
    Lists "every copy of every known work of Rabelais, and of every work
    edited by Rabelais and printed or dated before 1626 (p. xi). Based on Plan's
    *Bibliography rabelaisienne* of 1904. Includes the *Cinquiesme Livre* and such
    apocryphal works as the *Grandes Chroniques* and the *Disciple de Pantagruel*.
    Mostly based on an examination of actual copies; the descriptions "present
    the maximum possible useful and relevant information about each edition, in
    a format intelligible to most users" (p. 2). Title pages reproduced as illustra-
    tions.

16 ROLOFF, VOLKER. "Mittelalterische Farcenkomic bei Rabelais und im Lazarillo de Tormes." *Zeitschrift für Romanische Phililogie* 103, no. 1–2:49–67.

Studies the integration of themes and techniques of medieval farce into the narrative framework of Rabelais' novels, with emphasis on the Basché and Dindenault episodes of Book IV and the scene with the Ecolier Limousin in Book I. Views Lazarillo and Panurge as literary representations of carnivalesque laughter.

17 SMITH, PAUL J. "Description et zoologie chez Rabelais." In *Description–Ecriture–Peinture*, edited by Y. Went-Daoust. Cahiers de recherche des instituts néerlandais de langue et littérature françaises, no. 17. Gronigen: Department of French, University of Gronigen, pp. 1–20.

Attempts a typology of description in Rabelais' works by studying a number of zoological passages. Detects a parodic intention behind Rabelais' predilection for zoological lists; claims that they mock scientific knowledge, "produit néfaste de la curiosité humaine" (p. 6). Finds them to lack an organizing principle, and thus to have the unsettling effect of challenging the accepted and reassuring vision of reality. Emphasizes their pictorial quality, and briefly comments on the relationship between Rabelaisian literary esthetics and the pictorial esthetics of Bosch and Brueghel. Argues that Foucault's notion of universal analogy as characterizing the *épistéme* of the Renaissance is only partially corroborated by Rabelais' work, and that in most cases Rabelais is questioning the reassuring character of these analogies, especially in the case of Quaresmeprenant. "Au lieu d'expliquer, l'opération comparative brouille les pistes" (p. 10). Nor is description always aiming at representation. In the case of Quaresmeprenant, of the flying pig and other monsters in the *Quart Livre*, zoological description is self-referential: "Selon nous, Quaresmeprenant est justement irréprésentable, inconcevable même" (p. 14).

18 ———. *Voyage et écriture: Etude sur le "Quart Livre" de Rabelais.* Études Rabelaisiennes, no. 19. THR, no. 217. Geneva: Librairie Droz, 226 pp.

Notes that the book, perhaps because of its episodic nature, had not yet given rise to a single monograph. Studies the journey in the *Quart Livre* as a reading (with commentary) of the book of the world. Notes the verbal basis of most episodes, such as the expression "parler en l'air" in the case of the frozen words. Behind the work's apparent incoherence, finds "une vision structurante" (p. 14) holding the episodes together. In the first of the four parts into which the study is divided, discusses the book's "avant-textes," that is passages in the preceding novels that throw light on Book IV: the Lucian tone of the final chapters of *Pantagruel*, the complementarity of Panurge's and Pantagruel's quest in the final chapters of the *Tiers Livre*. In part 2, brings out the thematic constants imposed by literary conventions, with emphasis on their modifications in Rabelais' text. Part 3 is entirely devoted to a reading of the Medamothi episode as an indicator of Rabelais' esthetics and his rhetoric. In part 4, studies the final episode of the *Quart Livre*, and argues that it is much less arbitrary than is commonly thought. Reads it as a highly significant apex of the entire work, "mettant en scène, sous la thématique sacramentale du baptême et de l'eucharistie, la phase décisive de la quête panurgienne" (p. 15). Stresses the ambivalence of the book, perhaps truly mysterious, perhaps merely mystifying, ultimately leaving the reader and the characters themselves in the same uneasy quandry before the puzzling signs that beckon throughout Books III and IV. See also 1985.29 and 1986.44.

19   TOURNON, ANDRÉ. "Ce qui devait se dire en utopien (*Pantagruel*, IX)." In *Croisements culturels. Michigan Romance Studies* 7:115–35.
　　Studies the plurilingualism of Panurge's discourse, and reflects on the possible meaning of the episode in which Panurge introduces himself in several languages. By comparing this episode to that of the Ecolier Limousin, calls attention to an interesting paradox: for answering in a corrupted form of Latin, the young scholar attracts upon himself Rabelais' scorn and ridicule, whereas for refusing to answer altogether, Panurge is rewarded with Pantagruel's help and friendship. Moreover, when Panurge finally responds in perfect Latin, his answer falls into a void, whereas both French and Utopian, although diametrically opposed in that one language is perfectly transparent and the other perfectly opaque, are made to serve as a basis for a meaningful dialogue. Explains the paradox by pointing out that both French and Latin and Utopian possess in common a quality which Latin lacks, namely that of being a mode of reciprocal recognition and communication, over and above whatever specific information they may be able to convey. "Voilà pourquoi la langue la plus insolite, l'utopien, comme la moins insolite, le français, permet le dialogue: elle postule, comme sa seule chance de sens, la proximité humaine que vérifient ensuite les claires paroles," (p. 127). Interprets in a similar sense the lawsuit between Baisecul and Humevesne, the episode "de modis significandi" and the gestural disputation between Thaumaste and Panurge: in spite of its apparent absurdity, each episode reveals its meaning to the reader of good will, for it requires for its understanding an act of faith rather than merely linguistic recognition. Suggests that this casts a new light on the character of Panurge and on the playing with languages: both are meant to be interpreted in the spirit of Pantagruélisme, that is in a spirit of charity transcending reason.

20   ———. "L'abbé de Thélème." In *Saggi e Ricerche di Litteratura Francese* 26. Rome: Bulzoni, pp. 201–20.
　　"Sans Frère Jan, pas de Thélème; à Thélème pas de Frère Jan. Qu'est-ce à dire?" (p. 201). In opposition to prevalent critical opinion, argues in favor of

the logical coherence of the Thélème episode, both in relation to Frère Jan upon whose *devis* the abbey was built, and to the novel as a whole. Seeks to prove that there is nothing artificial in its articulation with the rest of the narrative, and that, as in the case of the other rewards offered by Gargantua to those who helped him achieve victory, the reward is here perfectly appropriate to the personality of the receiver. Shows that Frère Jan plays here the role he has played in the rest of the novel (and that Panurge had played throughout *Pantagruel*): that of the "trouble-sagesse" (p. 205) who through his streak of madness wins the reader's sympathy without losing his status as a positive hero. "Placée sous le patronage de Frère Jan en même temps que sous la protection de Gargantua, Thélème sera une utopie dialogique" (p. 207) whose rule, the celebrated "Fay ce que vouldras," is contained implicitly in the actions of both Gargantua and Frère Jan before being expressed in its canonical form in the closing chapters of the narrative. Justifies Frère Jan's absence from the abbey by pointing out that both he and Gargantua, as men of the present, are merely the *founders* of the future abbey and not its residents. ("Moïse non plus n'a pas pénétré dans la terre promise," p. 217.) Concludes by arguing that Frère Jan's and Gargantua's interpretations of the *Énigme en prophetie* are equally valid and equally incomplete, and that the meaning of the riddle, as that of the entire Thélème episode, is *dialogical*, "produit par composition des perspectives antagonistes" (p. 219).

## 1988

1 ANTONIOLI, ROLAND. "La matière de Bretagne dans Pantagruel." In *Rabelais en son demi-millénaire: Actes du Colloque International de Tours (24–29 Septembre 1984)*, edited by Jean Céard et Jean-Claude Margolin. Études Rabelaisiennes, no. 21. Geneva: Librairie Droz, pp. 77–86.

Believes that the *Grandes et inestimables cronicques* and its related legends play a more important role in *Pantagruel* than had been thought. Inquires into the reasons for its relevance in 1532 and its function within Rabelais' narrative. Direct allusions are few, but the borrowings and their transformation are not without significance: "Car ce que Rabelais emprunte à la matière de Bretagne n'est pas seulement l'énormité d'un héros qui la perdra par la suite. C'est le merveilleux populaire d'une force maléfique et primitive, sauvage et destructrice, mais retournée par la volonté divine, et devenue sur l'enclume de Merlin un homme nouveau, pouvoir indestructible et bienfaisant, au service de la justice et de la foi" (p. 82).

2 ARAKI, SHOTARO. "Les contributions aux études rabelaisiennes d'un humaniste japonais: Kazuo Watanabe." In *Rabelais en son demi-millénaire: Actes du Colloque International de Tours (24–29 Septembre 1984)*, edited by

1988

Jean Céard et Jean-Claude Margolin. Études Rabelaisiennes, no. 21. Geneva: Librairie Droz, pp. 381–87.

An overview of the career of the Japanese scholar and translator by one of his disciples, with emphasis on Watanabe's translation of *Gargantua*. Bibliography of his work on Rabelais, humanism, and the Renaissance.

3   ARON, EMILE. "Ce que Rabelais doit à la médecine et ce que la médecine lui doit." In *Rabelais en son demi-millénaire: Actes du Colloque International de Tours (24–29 Septembre 1984)*, edited by Jean Céard et Jean-Claude Margolin. Études Rabelaisiennes, no. 21. Geneva: Librairie Droz, pp. 87–95.

Owes more to it than it owes to him. Whereas medicine was a great source of inspiration for Rabelais, Rabelais had no influence upon its course: "Rabelais n'est cité dans aucune publication médicale sérieuse du XVIe siècle à nos jours" (p. 89). Rabelais' reputation as a great physician is attested only by Dolet: "Ainsi un éloge de circonstance a inspiré tous les biographes quant à la réputation médicale de Rabelais, comme des moutons de Panurge!" (p. 89).

4   BAILBÉ, JACQUES. "Picrochole en fuite: Autour du chapitre 47 de *Gargantua*." In *Prose et Prosateurs de la Renaissance: Mélanges offerts à Robert Aulotte*. Paris: SEDES, pp. 85–92.

Studies the brief confrontation between Gargantua and Picrochole in the chapter in question, just before the famous "concion de Gargantua aux vaincus." Emphasizes the extent to which the passage brings out, "dans une sorte de diagnostic clinique" (p. 86), Picrochole's choleric temper and the various aspects of his tyrannical madness, including a propensity to day-dream and lose sight of reality. Notes the use of narrative and comic techniques borrowed from the farce and the popular tale in the carnivalesque dethroning of the tyrant. Mentions similarities in the treatment of Anarche in *Pantagruel* and Panurge in the *Tiers Livre*: all are shown as seduced by Satan and abandoned to the dubious guidance of their free will. Thus presents the Picrocholine War as a conflict, in miniature, between Good and Evil, between Satan and God. Points out that some qualities in Picrochole ("Il est instruit, il est proche de son peuple," p. 90) earn him a certain amount of commiseration, and concludes by stressing the thematic and stylistic connections between the episode and the rest of the novel.

5   BALDINGER, KURT. "*Gargantua*, Nouvelles recherches lexicographiques." In *Rabelais en son demi-millénaire: Actes du Colloque International de Tours (24–29 Septembre 1984)*, edited by Jean Céard et Jean-Claude Margolin. Études Rabelaisiennes, no. 21. Geneva: Librairie Droz, pp. 49–58.

Emphasizes the importance of a philological basis as preliminary to any sound literary interpretation. Attracts attention to numerous errors in the

1988

*Französisches Etymologisches Wörterbuch* concerning Rabelais' vocabulary. Offers lexicographical remarks about fifteen terms found in *Gargantua*, and groups them under three headings: "jeux de mots," "problèmes sémantiques et étymologiques," and "régionalismes." Contains a bibliography of the author's articles on Rabelais. Reprinted in 1990.2.

6  BAUSCHATZ, CATHLEEN M. "'Une description du jeu de paulme soulz obscures parolles': The Portrayal of Reading in *Pantagruel* and *Gargantua*." *Études Rabelaisiennes* 22:57–76.

Believes that the importance of the prologue to *Gargantua* as a text in which Rabelais expresses his ideas about reading can only be judged adequately when the prologue is placed "in the context of the many other statements about reading in the *Pantagruel* and *Gargantua*" (p. 57). From the perspective of reader-oriented criticism, finds that Rabelais presents the act of reading, in the first two books, as either passive and reactive, or active and interpretive. Passive, reactive reading predominates in *Pantagruel*, and is recommended for its therapeutic value, as a source of belief, or as pure entertainment. Active, interpretive reading also appears on occasion in the first two books, mostly in an ambivalent or squarely negative light as hostile exegesis, "lecture calumnie." Offers an analysis of the prologue to *Gargantua* in the context of the tension between the active and the passive view of reading, the one centered on the author, the other on the reader. Sees the analogy with the "Silènes" and the "os médullaire" as assuming a "receptive, reverent attitude on the part of the reader" in his or her search for the text's higher meaning, for "the author-designed truth contained therein" (p. 69). Considers "the turning point" in the prologue from the reader's point of view (rather than the author's point of view adopted by Duval and Dufaux in their interpretations), and sees it as promoting, almost for the first time in Rabelais, an "active but positive, informed interpretative reading" (p. 71). In the episode of the *Énigme* preserved in the foundation of the Abbaye, argues that Gargantua's reading is author/authority centered, an activity whose aim is to discover a meaning "placed in the text by the author" (p. 73), whereas Frère Jean's is a reader-centered interpretation, a possible source of hostility or at least disagreement between writer and reader, but an inspired reading, which pleases as it instructs. Further suggests that, like Montaigne, Rabelais may be using the tennis game as a metaphor for reading, turning the potentially adversarial relationship between author and reader into one that is both playful and productive. Concludes that Rabelais' view of reading, conditioned as it is by the fact that he sees scriptural, evangelical reading as the model for all good reading, is still essentially medieval, but that his view of writing "comes closer to a modern, language and text-centered view of communication" (p. 75).

1988

7   BERRONG, RICHARD M[ICHAEL]. "*Non est solum Sophista quis loquitur*:
    Further thoughts on Rabelais's Presentation of Linguistic Mastery in
    *Gargantua*." *Études Rabelaisiennes* 22:27–42.
        Offers reflections suggested by Gérard Defaux's "Rabelais et son
    masque comique: *Sophista loquitur*" (see 1974.8), especially the idea that
    paradox and ambiguity in *Gargantua* are related to the personality of the nar-
    rator, that there is in that respect a striking similarity between the narrator of
    *Gargantua* and the Panurge of Rabelais' Book I, and that sophistry can be
    equated with the art of fiction in Rabelais' "poetics of the narrative" (p. 31).
    Contrasts these poetics with those of Lemaire de Belges as they emerge from
    the story of Paris, Oeunone, and Helen of Troy in *Illustrations de Gaule et
    Singularités de Troye*. Points out that whereas that episode, viewed by itself,
    suggests "a very one-sided, negative view of eloquence," the *Illustrations* as
    a whole indicate "a real fascination with the artful, aesthetic deployment of
    words" (p. 38). Sees this ambivalence as resulting from Lemaire's awareness
    of the dangers of eloquence but also of its power, which he does not hesitate
    to use in order to mask the weakness of the historical arguments he musters
    for his thesis of the Trojan origins of France. Points to the "positive presenta-
    tion of eloquence in *Gargantua*" (p. 40) although concedes that it is nowhere
    shown to be as effective as Panurge's and Alcofrybas' sophistry. "Though as
    he had demonstrated quite clearly in *Pantagruel* he was fully aware of the
    dangers of 'l'utilisation sophistique du savoir,' Rabelais would seem to have
    returned to this topic in *Gargantua* in part to argue that this 'utilisation
    sophistique,' though potentially dangerous, was nevertheless a valuable and
    perhaps even essential tool in literary creation" (p. 41).

8   BONNARD, H. "Etude de langue d'un passage de *Gargantua*."
    *L'Information grammaticale* 39 (October):18–22.
        Study of the poem above the portal of Thélème. Notes on spelling, mor-
    phology, syntax, and vocabulary. Claims to discover in the poem, which
    belongs to a type known as *cri*, the main features of Rabelaisian verve.

9   BOOTH, WAYNE C. "Rabelais and Feminist Criticism." In *The Company
    We Keep: An Ethics of Fiction*. Berkeley and Los Angeles: University of
    California Press, pp. 383–418.
        A version of 1982.4 (see also 1983.10). Finds feminist criticism, as a
    form of doctrinal, ethical criticism to be "the most original and important
    movement on the current scene, even more transformative than the decon-
    structionists" (p. 388). Believes that *Gargantua* and *Pantagruel* treat women
    as inherently inferior to men, and that by writing these novels Rabelais com-
    mitted "an act of injustice" and introduced "a serious flaw" into his master-
    piece. Does not base his judgment on the numerous anti-feminist statements
    made in the course of the book by such characters as Panurge or Rondibilis,

since such statements "work only against the speakers" (p. 397). Finds the books to be sexist in their general outlook, in the kind of exclusively masculine laughter they evoke. Notes that the female reader is excluded, with the possible exception of Marguerite de Navarre, and that even in such a supposedly egalitarian episode as that of the abbey of Thélème, women are not the equals of men. "Rabelais is unjust to women not simply in the superficial ways that the traditions have claimed but, to some degree, in much of his central imaginative act" (p. 408).

10   BOWEN, BARBARA C. "Rire est le propre de l'homme." In *Rabelais en son demi-millénaire: Actes du Colloque International de Tours (24–29 Septembre 1984)*, edited by Jean Céard et Jean-Claude Margolin. Études Rabelaisiennes, no. 21. Geneva: Librairie Droz, pp. 185–90.
      Notes the scarcity of attempts to define Rabelais' laughter, as if laughter were a universal language, and thus easily understandable. "Malheureusement ce n'est pas le cas, le rire à la Renaissance se rattachant à des contextes et à des traditions intellectuelles qui nous sont complètement étrangers" (p. 185). Briefly places Rabelaisian laughter in the context of Scholastic debate (Is laughter essential to man, or is it merely one of man's characteristics?), medical theories (Is laughter always therapeutic, or is there also evil laughter, *immodicus risus*?), and rhetoric (laughter as a tool to win over one's public and defeat one's adversary). Points out in conclusion that Rabelais' characters, surprisingly, hardly ever laugh. Suggests that for Rabelais it is not laughter but *joy* that is "le propre de l'homme": "pour Rabelais le rire, bon ou mauvais, n'est pas indispensable à la condition humaine; ce qui l'est, ce qui devrait constituer le *proprium hominis*, c'est la joie chrétienne" (p. 190).

11   CAVE, TERENCE. "Transformations d'un *topos* utopique: Gaster et le rocher de Vertu." In *Rabelais en son demi-millénaire: Actes du Colloque International de Tours (24–29 Septembre 1984)*, edited by Jean Céard et Jean-Claude Margolin. Études Rabelaisiennes, no. 21. Geneva: Librairie Droz, pp. 319–25.
      Examines briefly one by one the various transformations which the *topos* of the rock of Virtue undergoes at the beginning of the Gaster episode in Book IV, and shows to what extent the polysemy of the text forces us to rethink at every stage our allegorical interpretation of the episode: "le texte marque avec une netteté étonnante que les intentions peuvent très bien être multiples et versatiles, qu'elles peuvent même se contredire, ou déboucher sur une perspective étrangère à celle qui était prévue au premier abord" (p. 325). See 1986.8.

12   CÉARD, JEAN. "Rabelais, lecteur et juge des romans de chevalerie." In *Rabelais en son demi-millénaire: Actes du Colloque International de Tours*

1988

*(24–29 Septembre 1984)*, edited by Jean Céard et Jean-Claude Margolin. Études Rabelaisiennes, no. 21. Geneva: Librairie Droz, pp. 237–48.

Of the many passages in Rabelais' work that parody the romances of chivalry, the most significant ones challenge both the structure and the meaning of the genre. The genealogy of Pantagruel contains several Saracens, defeated by epic heroes of national history. In Epistémon's descent into the underworld, these heroes are shown to have a status far inferior to their prestige in our imagination: "les premiers de chez nous sont là-bas les derniers" (p. 242). In the episode of the duel between Pantagruel and Loupgarou, Pantagruel's humble prayer emphasizes the pride and self-righteousness usually displayed by the epic knight in similar circumstances, whereas it is Loupgarou's prayer to his God Mahon that is reminiscent of the typical knight's plea for God's help. The cruel deeds perpetrated by knights for renown and glory, and dignified in the romances of chivalry with the name of *prowess* are denounced by Rabelais as "briguanteries et mechancetez" (quoted p. 245). Similarly, Rabelais distorts the structure of the romances of chivalry to reflect his own ideology. Thus the Abbaye de Thélème episode can be considered as a *Moniage Gargantua*, but what in the romances is the end of a life is here only a beginning. Under the impact of parody, the romances of chivalry are "deconstructed." Their subsisting fragments, integrated into new structures, acquire a totally new function and meaning.

13  CHARITOS, STÉPHANE A. "Un monstre du rire et un rire monstrueux: Directions pour une étude sur François Rabelais et Georges Bataille." *Romance Notes* 28, no. 3 (Spring):217–25.

"Une approche de Rabelais ne peut jamais être totale si elle néglige le discours de la gratuité, c'est-à-dire le discours ludique qui est l'intégralité du texte" (p. 223). In the light of Bataille's analysis of the concepts of work and knowledge, contends that the premise that Rabelais' books have a meaning, and that the reader's task is to search for that meaning, results in "censuring" that part of the text that is not knowledge, namely laughter and obscenity. Believes that to appreciate it in its totality, one must submit to the text's "transgressions" against truth and beauty as well as to its search for positive values.

14  CHARPENTIER, FRANÇOISE. "Une éducation de prince: *Gargantua*, chapitre XI." In *Rabelais en son demi-millénaire: Actes du Colloque International de Tours (24–29 Septembre 1984)*, edited by Jean Céard et Jean-Claude Margolin. Études Rabelaisiennes, no. 21. Geneva: Librairie Droz, pp. 103–08.

Reads the chapter—on childhood and not, as the title would have it, on adolescence—in the light of Erasmus on the one hand, and Freud on the other. Rabelais here goes against Erasmian precepts, which would civilize, domesticate the instincts of the child, by giving them free rein. In chapters on pedagogy, Rabelais shows his modernity in relation to his contemporaries; in this passage, he gives proof of a modernity that leaves his contemporaries far behind and prefigures our own ways of thinking: "les notions de la psychanalyse se révèlent opératoires pour la lecture de ce passage" (p. 108).

15  COLEMAN, DOROTHY [GABE]. "L'Evolution de l'art de Rabelais d'après les variantes du *Tiers Livre*." In *Rabelais en son demi-millénaire: Actes du Colloque International de Tours (24–29 Septembre 1984)*, edited by Jean Céard et Jean-Claude Margolin. Études Rabelaisiennes, no. 21. Geneva: Librairie Droz, pp. 59–65.

Claims that a comparison of the Wechel edition of 1546 with Fezandat's edition of 1552 enables one to "saisir sur le vif la méthode de composition de Rabelais" (p. 59). Believes that Rabelais' additions are made for comic and esthetic effect rather than for didactic clarification.

16  COOPER, RICHARD. "'Charmant mais très obscène': Some French Eighteenth-Century Readings of Rabelais." In *Enlightenment Essays in Memory of Robert Shackleton*, edited by Giles Barber and C. P. Courtney. Oxford: The Voltaire Foundation, At the Taylor Institution, pp. 39–60.

Notes the absence of any full-scale investigation of the various attitudes towards Rabelais and his work in the age of Enlightenment. Points out that some judgments were uncompromisingly hostile both to the man (seen as a womanizing drunkard) and to his novels (taken to be obscene, incoherent, and boring, attractive only to those who prided themselves on their *libertinage*). But finds other critics ready to explain away the licentiousness as a feature of Renaissance sensibility, the obscurity as a necessary stratagem to hide his daring thought, the unfavorable assessment of the man as a result of baseless legends and confusion between the author and his characters. Notes also some vigorous attempts to rehabilitate the works on the strength of their satirical wit and their erudition. Stresses the lucid admiration of Diderot. Traces the first efforts to bring out the *substantifique mouelle* by reading the work as a *roman à clef* (Voltaire) or as an allegory (Le Motteux), or by seeing in Rabelais "a kind of *philosophe avant la lettre*" (p. 49) on the grounds of his anticlericalism (Voltaire) or what was regarded as his opposition to the ancien régime (Guinguené). Points to the existence of numerous editions, published mostly in Amsterdam or Geneva; notes the rediscovery of the *Sciomachie* and the emergence of scholarly concerns on the part of Daniel Huet, bishop of Avranches, Jean Bouhier, and above all Le Duchat, whose extremely successful edition would not be equalled until that of Marty-Laveaux. Cites a number of modernized or expurgated editions (abbé de Marsy, abbé Pérau), and the "predigested synopsis" offered by the *Bibliothèque universelle des romans*. Besides Voltaire and Diderot, counts among Rabelais' readers Montesquieu, the duc de La Vallière, and Fontenelle. Documents the "cult of

Rabelaisian pastiche" (p. 55), and notes a number of works written in Rabelais' name.

17 ————. "Rabelais et l'Église." In *Rabelais en son demi-millénaire: Actes du Colloque International de Tours (24–29 Septembre 1984)*, edited by Jean Céard et Jean-Claude Margolin. Études Rabelaisiennes, no. 21. Geneva: Librairie Droz, pp. 111–18.

Discusses five documents, hitherto unknown or unpublished, which throw new light on Rabelais' relations with the Church. The *Registri Sanctæ Pænitentiariæ* of the Vatican, recently opened to scholars, contain the "supplique" addressed by Pierre Lamy and dated March 10, 1524, for authorization to leave the Franciscan abbey of Fontenay-le-Comte and to join the Benedictine order. The authorization was granted. Rabelais may have addressed a similar request at the same time, and the latter may also have been granted. Why had he not done so again in 1527, but chosen instead the way of apostasy? Has also discovered, in the Vatican's *Brevia lateranenses*, the original of the absolution granted to Rabelais by Paul III, authorizing Rabelais among other things to practice medicine and "le permis de posséder des bénéfices" (p. 115). Concludes from another document, mentioned by Cruchet in 1959 but the original of which cannot be traced, that Rabelais was "curé de Saint-Christophe-du-Jambet" in 1549, six years earlier than had been thought. Also contains references to two documents concerning the "cure de Meudon." Transcription of three of these documents on pp. 119–20.

18 CUSSET, MONIQUE D. "Mythe et histoire: La mythologie du pouvoir et de la transgression dans l'œuvre de Rabelais." Ph.D. dissertation, University of Southern California.

In the first part, discusses political theories and practice in France under Charles V and Francis I. Gives the history of the Franciscan Order. Believes that the ideas of Joachim de Fiore and the Franciscans "pervade Rabelais' work." The second analyzes Rabelais' syncretic use of Greek and Christian myths. Studies the function of myth as "regeneration through integration of opposed principles" and as a basis for Rabelais' numerous cosmogonies. Claims that Panurge's transgressions are "cancelled through language: the author's anecdotes allow for a permutation of elements in the stories which erases transgressivity." This leads to Panurge's regeneration and "androginisation" in Book V. Concludes by arguing that Rabelais follows "the Platonic model" of mythic expression of destruction and renewal. "Myth represents an effort to disengage history from its vicious cyclic orientation and to engage history on its way to *metabolé* and the ideal linear pattern." See *Dissertation Abstracts International* 49 (1989):3715A.

19 DEFAUX, GÉRARD. "Vers une définition de l'herméneutique rabelaisienne: Pantagruel, l'esprit, la lettre et les paroles gelées." In *Rabelais en son demi-*

*millénaire: Actes du Colloque International de Tours (24–29 Septembre 1984)*, edited by Jean Céard et Jean-Claude Margolin. Études Rabelaisiennes, no. 21. Geneva: Librairie Droz, pp. 327–37.

Seeks to dispose of Michel Jeanneret's contention, developed in an article on chapt. 55–56 of the *Quart Livre*, that Rabelais uses the contrast in attitude between Pantagruel (who is right) and the other travelers (who are wrong) in the face of the "paroles gelées," to propound an ideal theory of language, according to which words convey latent realities that go well beyond their common, immediate meaning, and to proclaim the vanity of univocal, historical interpretations. Contends in turn that the episode is not primarily about hermeneutics but about linguistics and epistemology, and that to the extent that it can be read as being at all about interpretation, it clearly contradicts Jeanneret's thesis. Pantagruel is not right, and his companions are not wrong. Pantagruel, in Book IV, remains in large measure an exemplary character, but as an interpreter of truth he is no longer infallible: "S'il a correctement lu ce qui se cache derrière la mort du grand Pan, il se trompe en revanche totalement dans sa tentative d'explication du phénomène des paroles gelées" (p. 332). Supremely at ease in the world of the spirit, he is powerless to understand the corrupted world of matter. He is thus not, as Jeanneret had implied, Rabelais' mouthpiece. Pantagruel's companions, on the other hand, are not to be dismissed as inadequate interpreters, since it is Panurge who, by suggesting a parallel with Moses on Mount Sinaï, unveils the significance of the episode. As for the passage from chapt. 55 to chapt. 56, that is from "paroles gelées" to "paroles dégelées," it does signify, as Jeanneret points out, a progressive reduction of the possibilities of meaning, but that reduction is not, as Jeanneret would have it, condemned by Rabelais. On the contrary, it is given a positive value, and is meant to illustrate Rabelais' conviction that before interpreting any word "à plus haut sens," we must be careful to understand its literal meaning. Jeanneret notwithstanding, it is only when the word is frozen—that is, when it is clearly explained and given a definite meaning—that it becomes for Rabelais "la parole idéale." "Le 'plus hault sens,' et les richesses inestimables dont il est porteur, ne sont accessibles qu'à ceux qui ont d'abord su se rendre maîtres du sens littéral" (p. 337). Insofar as the episode is about hermeneutics, the Rabelaisian myth of the frozen words does not proclaim the superiority of polyvalent over univocal interpretation, but the primacy of literal over "higher" meaning.

20  DE GRÈVE, MARCEL. "Actualité de Rabelais." In *Rabelais en son demi-millénaire: Actes du Colloque International de Tours (24–29 Septembre 1984)*, edited by Jean Céard et Jean-Claude Margolin. Études Rabelaisiennes, no. 21. Geneva: Librairie Droz, pp. 389–400.

The Renaissance was not only a re-birth, but a birth: "une véritable 'naissance,' dans la mesure où elle annonce, où elle introduit un monde nouveau, c'est-à-dire le monde moderne, notre monde à nous" (p. 389). Surveys

1988

the ways in which Rabelais has been read since the publication of his work, and notes that he has always been considered to be relevant. Believes that in most of his ideas Rabelais is not only ahead of his time but also of ours: "certaines de ses considérations ne seront, si tout va bien, comprises et réalisées que dans un siècle ou deux dans le meilleur des cas" (p. 391). Finds Rabelais' work to be relevant in its message, its paradoxical form, and its "remise en question du langage" (p. 396).

21  DE DIÉGUEZ, MANUEL. "Un aspect de la théologie de Rabelais: Le chapitre 38 du *Gargantua*." In *Rabelais en son demi-millénaire: Actes du Colloque International de Tours (24–29 Septembre 1984)*, edited by Jean Céard et Jean-Claude Margolin. Études Rabelaisiennes, no. 21. Geneva: Librairie Droz, pp. 347–53.
    Presents an anguished view of the Renaissance as the dawn of nihilism in the Western world. "Comment Gargantua mangea en salade six pèlerins," before *Gulliver's Travels* and *Micromégas*, seen as the expression of a tragic view of man lost in a world governed by a God totally unmindful of his creatures. "Toute la scène se déroule à des années-lumières de l'optimisme de la Renaissance et de la superficialité de sa philosophie du bonheur telle qu'elle sera illustrée par les Thélémites" (p. 349). Like all great writers, Rabelais gives meaning, through literary form, to the meaninglessness of life: "Le sens est toujours une conquête de l'imagination" (p. 351).

21  DEMERSON, GUY. "Paradigmes épiques chez Rabelais." In *Rabelais en son demi-millénaire: Actes du Colloque International de Tours (24–29 Septembre 1984)*, edited by Jean Céard et Jean-Claude Margolin. Études Rabelaisiennes, no. 21. Geneva: Librairie Droz, pp. 225–36.
    Although Rabelais' work can be read as a parody of the Homeric and Virgilian epic, it is not a satire of the genre so much as a reflection upon it. Through parody, Rabelais expresses his distrust of epic values, and more specifically his condemnation of pagan violence in the name of a new, Christian epic. Shows that Rabelais' work is organized around certain traditional epic themes: the exotic odyssey, the nostalgic return to a familiar universe of everyday reality, the defense of national values, and above all the notion of an essentially epic hero, with his steadfast character, his faith in the divine, and his belief in its intervention in human affairs, his willingness to sacrifice his individuality in order to stand as a representative of his people. Whereas Panurge and Frère Jean, with their skepticism, their individuality, their lack of roots, are essentially heroes of fiction ("des héros de roman"), Pantagruel and Gargantua provide Rabelais' hybrid work with an epic dimension. "L'œuvre composite de Rabelais comporte des marques qui la réfèrent à un roman ridicule, mais les indices qui incitent à briser l'os et à inventer un sens rapportent le récit à une histoire épique et à un merveilleux croyable" (p.

235). Contains a short bibliography on the epic as a genre, and on Rabelais' work as related to it.

23   DE ROCHER, GREGORY. "Vers un nouvel humour rabelaisien." In *Rabelais en son demi-millénaire: Actes du Colloque International de Tours (24–29 Septembre 1984)*, edited by Jean Céard et Jean-Claude Margolin. Études Rabelaisiennes, no. 21. Geneva: Librairie Droz, pp. 301–08.

With the help of Freud, Lacan, Julia Kristeva, and Robert Rodgers, redefines laughter (somewhat tongue-in-check?) in psychoanalytic terms, and assimilates the process of reading Rabelais' masterpiece to the child's discovery of the surrounding world: same initial stage of unawareness (*risus sine re*), same constitution of the subject's identity in the mirror stage (its analogue in Rabelais being the moment of self-identification with the reader as portrayed in the prologues), same threat of castration at the hand of the law (here in the shape of Rabelaisian criticism, personified for the occasion by M. A. Screech and his frequent warnings not to hasten to read as comic what may very well have been meant in earnest). The obscenities contained in the images, metaphors, plays on words are largely manifestations of the unconscious rising to the level of consciousness; as expressions of the forbidden they are cathartic for the author, and equally therapeutic for the reader to the extent that they elicit the visceral reaction of laughter: "avec des théoriciens du fait psychanalitique comme Lacan et du fait littéraire comme Rodgers, la psychanalyse et la poésie redeviennent des phénomènes à charactère physiologique" (p. 308), and laughter reassumes the therapeutic function which it already had 450 years ago for Rabelais.

24   DUVAL, EDWIN. "La messe, la Cène, et le voyage sans fin du *Quart Livre*." In *Rabelais en son demi-millénaire: Actes du Colloque International de Tours (24–29 Septembre 1984)*, edited by Jean Céard et Jean-Claude Margolin. Études Rabelaisiennes, no. 21. Geneva: Librairie Droz, pp. 131–41.

Analysis of four episodes from Book IV (dealing with "l'isle Farouche," the island of Ruach, the "Papimanes," and Messer Gaster), which the author reads as a satire of the Catholic Mass, and more specifically the Eucharist, a topical subject debated at the time at the Council of Trent. Like such other Christian reformers as Erasmus and Calvin, Rabelais denounces in these episodes the excessive emphasis on ceremony, the belief in the Eucharist as a true sacrifice, and the doctrine of the "présence réelle," insofar as it leads to the idolatry of matter in the form of bread and wine. The assembly of Pantagruel and his companions on board the Thalamège represents Rabelais' own conception of the nature of Mass: "dans cette assemblée eucharistique authentiquement chrétienne tous les 'abus' de la messe...sont systématiquement corrigés" (p. 139). If the book does not end, it is because the quest is literally unending: "la vérité et le salut ne sauraient être un but à atteindre au

1988

terme d'un voyage qui n'a d'autre fin que la continuelle mise en œuvre de l'Évangile" (p. 141).

25  FRAME, DONALD M. "Notes on Rabelais by a recent translator." *Études Rabelaisiennes* 22:173–80.

Points out certain textual inconsistencies in Books III and IV (mainly centered around the intermittent presence of Alcofribas Nasier in the latter book). To the usual arguments brought forth to explain the long interval between the publication of the first two books and the *Tiers Livre*, adds Rabelais' hesitation, mentioned on two occasions in Book III, to offer to the public something very different from his previous novels. Sees a possible trace of self-mockery in the relation between this hesitation on his part, and Panurge's inability to make up his mind about marriage.

26  GAIGNEBET, CLAUDE. "Sur un mot en / / du *Cinquième Livre*." In *Rabelais en son demi-millénaire: Actes du Colloque International de Tours (24–29 Septembre 1984)*, edited by Jean Céard et Jean-Claude Margolin. Études Rabelaisiennes, no. 21. Geneva: Librairie Droz, pp. 29–36.

The blank left by Rabelais on the last page of the manuscript was erroneously filled in with the word *l'abscond* in the 1562 edition. What was left blank was in fact the name of the god *Amon*. See also 1986.18.

27  GENDRE, ANDRÉ. "Le vin dans *Gargantua*." In *Rabelais en son demi-millénaire: Actes du Colloque International de Tours (24–29 Septembre 1984)*, edited by Jean Céard et Jean-Claude Margolin. Études Rabelaisiennes, no. 21. Geneva: Librairie Droz, pp. 175–83.

Focuses on six episodes in which wine plays a particularly important role. Studies the literal meaning of wine (its "réalisme référentiel"), as well as its "valeurs associatives." Alluding to the symbolic interpretations of Weinberg and of Screech, stops short of seeing in wine as treated in the first two books "une parabole établie": "La 'christianité' bachique est en puissance dans *Gargantua*: quand le texte rabelaisien s'émondera et deviendra plus sage, comme le héros dont il raconte la vie, la parabole y aura sa place. Nous serons alors au *Tiers* ou au *Quart Livre*."

28  GHARBI, BRAHIM. "En lisant Rabelais: Quelques exégèses classiques." *L'Information littéraire*, no. 3–4 (October–November):8–10.

Compares various episodes in Rabelais with texts of Homer, Hesiod, and Plato. Finds Gargantua's uprooting of the tree at the castle of the Gué de Vède reminiscent of Heracles fighting the Centaurs, and Gargantua's miraculous birth similar to the birth of Athena from Jupiter's forehead. Draws attention to similarities with Plautus and Virgil, the Bible, Villon, Montaigne, and Boileau.

29   GILMAN, PETER L., and ABRAHAM C. KELLER. "Who is Pantagruel?"
*Études Rabelaisiennes* 22:77–100.
     The authors argue that Pantagruel is none other than Hercules himself.
Point out that what Rabelais says of the *Grandes et inestimables Chronicques*
in the prologue to *Pantagruel* is patently false of that little book, but that it
applies perfectly to Lemaire de Belges' *Illustrations de Gaule et Singularités
de Troye*, which Rabelais may well have been intending to mock. Cite among
Rabelais' possible motives his antipapal stance and his dislike of Charles V as
perhaps fueling his desire to ridicule a work based on forgeries sanctioned by
the Vatican and praising France's greatest enemy at the time, and thus to
"destroy the credibility of a potentially dangerous book" (p. 88). To account
for Rabelais' puzzling transformation of a little devil into a gigantic prince as
the hero of his first book, suggest that we reject Rabelais' own patently inadequate etymological explanation, and see *gruel* as an altered form of *Ergul*, or
Hercule, so that "Pantagruel" means "Tout Hercule," one of the giants in
Lemaire de Belges and "the most celebrated prince in sixteenth-century
French literature" (p. 90). Argue that Rabelais himself provided clues to this
identification in the prologue and the first two chapters of *Pantagruel*, draw
parallels between the two heroes, find a "mock-Amazonian" flavor in the
Andouilles episode of Book IV, and note that Rabelais proposes in the prologue to that book that Odet de Coligny be his "Hercule Galloys." Conclude
by suggesting that Rabelais' greatest debt to Lucian is Pantagruel himself, as
a reincarnation, through Lemaire, of his Gallic Hercules.

30   GOUZÉ, ANDRÉ. "Rabelais et l'anatomie." In *Rabelais en son demi-millénaire: Actes du Colloque International de Tours (24–29 Septembre 1984)*,
edited by Jean Céard et Jean-Claude Margolin. Études Rabelaisiennes, no. 21.
Geneva: Librairie Droz, pp. 97–101.
     Claims that Rabelais' anatomical comparisons in the Quaresmeprenant
episode and his detailed account of the wounds inflicted by Frère Jean at the
abbey of Seuillé are those of a great anatomist.

31   GREENE, THOMAS M. "The Unity of the *Tiers Livre*." In *Rabelais en son
demi-millénaire: Actes du Colloque International de Tours (24–29 Septembre
1984)*, edited by Jean Céard et Jean-Claude Margolin. Études Rabelaisiennes,
no. 21. Geneva: Librairie Droz, pp. 293–99.
     Finds Rabelais' book so complex and mysterious as to wonder whether
"it can truly be read at all" (p. 293). Believes this to be particularly true of the
*Tiers Livre*, where the difficulty of seeing the connection with the preceding
volumes is compounded by the apparent lack of connection between the various sections of the work itself. In the first two books, feudal patterns are
replaced by an often joyous improvisation of new values. The *désinvolture*
with which Panurge, "lacking a ceremonial identity and cheerfully peripheral
to a structured society" (p. 294), "improvises" in *Pantagruel* gives way in

1988

Book III to a paralyzing anguish. The source of Panurge's anxiety lies in his new awareness of his vulnerability in the face of the conflicts inherent in human life as he contemplates the prospect, through marriage, of taking his place in the social order. The apparently disconnected sections of the book—the *encomium* of war in the prologue, that of debts in the early pages, the consultation with authorities—represent the various aspects of this conflict. The Pantagruélion, symbolizing Pantagruelism as embodied in the hero, represents Rabelais' solution, namely the courage to face the conflicts of existence in a spirit of hope and serenity, and the ability to emerge purified from the engagement in the struggles of life, just as the plant is purified through contact with fire. It is in this notion of courage that the author finds "the binding element" of a book so difficult to apprehend that the best hope it can offer to the reader engaged in the struggle for its meaning is "a partial flickering of clearer understanding" (p. 299).

32 HALLYN, FERNAND. "Le paradoxe de la souveraineté." In *Rabelais en son demi-millénaire: Actes du Colloque International de Tours (24–29 Septembre 1984)*, edited by Jean Céard et Jean-Claude Margolin. Études Rabelaisiennes, no. 21. Geneva: Librairie Droz, pp. 339–45.

The medieval author writes with symbols; the Renaissance author writes with signs. The "sovereignty" in question is the freedom with which the Renaissance writer, and Rabelais in particular, endows his signs with the meaning of his choice and creates "le discours perspectiviste" wherein the perspective is set by the author himself, in contrast with the medieval text whose meaning is predetermined by the symbolic nature of the author's discourse. The prologue to *Gargantua*, of which it is impossible to assert that it is a metatext (meant to explain the text from without, so to speak) or that, on the contrary, it is part of the fiction, suggests that the reader is meant to exercise the same sovereign freedom in the interpretation of what is thus conceived as a polyvalent work: "Si le narrateur crée des sens, souverainement, dans son discours à lui, le lecteur peut en faire autant—attribuer souverainement des sens aux signes" (p. 345).

33 HAUSMANN, FRANK-RUTGER. "Comment doit-on lire l'épisode de l'Isle des Papefigues (*Quart Livre*, 45–47)?" In *Rabelais en son demi-millénaire: Actes du Colloque International de Tours (24–29 Septembre 1984)*, edited by Jean Céard et Jean-Claude Margolin. Études Rabelaisiennes, no. 21. Geneva: Librairie Droz, pp. 121–29.

Suggests that the episode should be read on many levels: as a fictional development of the various lexicological possibilities of the expression "faire la figue"; as proof of Rabelais' interest in fairy tales; and as an ideological commentary on religious, economic, and political matters.

34  HENRY, GILLES. *Rabelais*. Paris: Librairie Académique Perrin, 308 pp.
General study, interweaving Rabelais' life and thought. "Son érudition et son esprit inventif étant sans bornes, il crée des mondes fantastiques avec une fécondité intarrissable, mais en s'appuyant sur des connaissances et une pensée qui leur donnent du poids et de la portée" (p. 14). Does not believe that the recent studies on the question of the authenticity of Book V provide a definitive solution to the problem.

35  HUCHON, MIREILLE. "Archéologie du Ve Livre." In *Rabelais en son demi-millénaire: Actes du Colloque International de Tours (24–29 Septembre 1984)*, edited by Jean Céard et Jean-Claude Margolin. Études Rabelaisiennes, no. 21. Geneva: Librairie Droz, pp. 19–28.
An analysis of chapt. 26, 27, and 28 making up the "Celtic" episode of the Fredons, a part of the "navigation française symbolique destinée à conduire les compagnons vers la Dive Bouteille à Chinon" (p. 19). Believes the episode to have been intended originally for Book IV, but to have been discarded by Rabelais in favor of the voyage to the New World as we have it, and used by the editors of Book V. Brings out the geographical, psychological, and religious associations between Fredons and Bretons. Among other things, sees the episode as a satire of confession.

36  ———. "Pour une histoire de la ponctuation: 1532–1553, Les variations des éditions des premiers livres de Rabelais." *Nouvelle Revue du XVIe siècle* 6:15–28.
Argues that the editions of Rabelais' works published in his lifetime form a particularly important phase in the history of the emerging vernacular—its grammar, vocabulary, spelling, and punctuation—since they coincide with a period of twenty years when the vernacular underwent fundamental changes in these areas, and since Rabelais himself, as the author had shown in her *Rabelais grammairien* (see 1981.17), had developed an elaborate system of grammar and spelling. Extends her study to include all works and all editions published during Rabelais' lifetime, and notes variations affecting 17,011 signs in thirty-five editions of the first four novels as well as the *Pantagrueline prognostication*. Concludes that most differences have to do with the use of the comma, whereas the limits of the sentence are hardly affected from one edition to the next. This seems to suggest that the Rabelaisian sentence was clearly delineated and perceived as such by the contemporary reader, and that modern editions ought to take this phenomenon into account as an important element of the text. Provides in an appendix the "taux de divergences de ponctuation" for each edition in relation to the edition which it reproduces.

1988

37 ———. "Variations rabelaisiennes sur l'imposition du nom." In *Prose et prosateurs de la Renaissance: Mélanges offerts à Robert Aulotte*. Paris: SEDES, pp. 93–100.

Attracts attention to passages indicating Rabelais' interest in proper nouns and their etymology, and to his syncretic attempt to reconcile the Aristotelian belief that the imposition of names is arbitrary and conventional with Plato's theory that they are images of the things they designate. Notes that the advisability of adapting ancient names to French usage was a matter of contemporary debate (Du Bellay was for, Montaigne will be against). Points out that in the corrected 1534 edition of *Pantagruel* Rabelais transposed the Latin names ending in *-us*, making use of the new accents (Sisyphus becoming *Sisyphé*, Darius becoming *Dariè*), but that in the 1542 edition he went back to Latin endings. In *Gargantua*, notes that the "Gargantuistes" all bear Greek names which faithfully reflect the character's function, and shows that in the *Tiers Livre* the "imposition" of names is more varied, less systematic, while in the *Quart Livre* Rabelais goes back to the tradition of the "significant" name of Greek origin, and retains proper nouns in their original form. Concludes that there was a tension in Rabelais between the desire to unify the French language by transforming foreign names, and to reject such modifications as presenting an even greater danger of linguistic corruption. Rabelais hesitates between the two positions, but in the end he opts for the conservation of foreign names in their original spelling.

38 ISHIGAMI-IAGOLNITZER, MICHICO. "François Rabelais et l'esprit franciscain: Peut-on être à la fois humaniste et franciscain?" *Études Rabelaisiennes* 22:151–71.

To the question posed by the article's subtitle, answers "yes" and "no." Insofar as humanism implies intellectual curiosity, a critical mind, hedonistic tendencies, a positive view of laughter, and a need to develop one's full potential in an atmosphere of freedom, finds it to be incompatible with the Franciscan ideal. But stresses, on the other hand, what Rabelais shared with Saint Francis: the belief in a "pure" form of Christianity based on the teachings of Christ, distrust of theologians, hatred of hypocrisy, a strong feeling of human brotherhood, and a harmonious and cosmic vision of the world.

39 JEANNERET, MICHEL. "Parler en mangeant: Rabelais et la tradition symposiaque." In *Rabelais en son demi-millénaire: Actes du Colloque International de Tours (24–29 Septembre 1984)*, edited by Jean Céard et Jean-Claude Margolin. Études Rabelaisiennes, no. 21. Geneva: Librairie Droz, pp. 275–81.

Distinguishes four types of literary banquet: "le banquet philosophique," of which Plato's *Symposium* offers the most illustrious example, and which Rabelais "subverts" in the symposium of the *Tiers Livre*; "le banquet encyclopédique" of the type described by Plutarch in his *Symposiaka*, and echoed in the pedagogical system of Ponocrates, with its meals accompanied by readings and discussions; "le banquet narratif," as in the episode of Ulysses at Alkinoos's table in Homer, and in the Villon episode in Rabelais' Book IV; and "le banquet farcesque ou burlesque," of which Rabelais offers the first literary example in the scene describing Frère Jean at Grandgousier's table. Notes the presence of similar banquets in Erasmus. In Rabelais, shows that the paradigm of the *convivium* functions on the narrative level throughout the novel, where it is related to the presence of each individual protagonist and creates a social link between the members of the group of friends. Most interestingly, it functions also in the context of the relations between the author and his public. Here, the effect is to transform the traditionally silent and solitary act of reading into a form of social communication: "Comme dans les banquets, la narration serait un acte de parole dans un milieu concret, un plaisir social et sensoriel, où le corps serait engagé, où le contact à autrui se jouerait dans la circulation des voix et de l'échange des nourritures" (p. 281). The author sees in this conception of narrative one aspect of a more general design, consisting in an attempt to "naturalize," to "authenticate" literature by associating it with the activities of everyday life. Concludes by stressing the paradoxical nature of the enterprise, since Rabelais seeks to achieve this assimilation of literature to life by strictly literary means: "Le texte symposiaque nie sa textualité cependant qu'il l'exhibe" (p. 281).

40  LA CHARITÉ, RAYMOND C. "Lecteurs et lectures dans le Prologue du *Gargantua*." In *Rabelais en son demi-millénaire: Actes du Colloque International de Tours (24–29 Septembre 1984)*, edited by Jean Céard et Jean-Claude Margolin. Études Rabelaisiennes, no. 21. Geneva: Librairie Droz, pp. 285–92.

　　Considers the prologue—"à la fois texte et analyse de texte" (p. 292)—as having been purposely constructed in order to render impossible any attempt at a single, definitive interpretation. Sets out to examine its textual strategy "en fonction des lectures et des lecteurs qui le constituent" (p. 286). Among these "lecteurs" is Alcofribas Nasier himself, and Socrates (although the text does not identify him specifically as a reader). Concludes that the dynamics of the prologue, the aim of which is to insure a plurality of non-hostile interpretations, is grounded in Rabelais' ingenious use of textual allusions to a variety of readers and readings. "Le jeu textuel fait ressortir les démarches que la lecture critique doit effectuer et la met simultanément en pratique comme partie essentielle de la création" (p. 292).

41  LANGER, ULRICH G. "Merit in Courtly Literature: Castiglione, Rabelais, Marguerite de Navarre, and Le Caron." *Renaissance Quarterly* 41, no. 2 (Summer):218–41.

　　Makes a brief reference to the Abbaye de Thélème episode as a courtly utopia in miniature. Seeks to apply to the episode the Scholastic distinction between "meritum de congruo" and "meritum ex condigno," used in theological discussions concerning the relationship between man's charitable works, and God's faith and grace as rewards for such actions. "The building of the abbey is to the courtier's service what faith and grace are to charitable works" (p. 234). Since Gargantua's gift is in no direct way related to Frère Jean's merit, his reward depends totally on his own generosity, and that generosity is itself rewarded as an act of charity. Hence the abbey episode offers an example of "condign merit."

42 LARMAT, JEAN. "Variations sur des motifs rabelaisiens chez Noël du Fail." In *Rabelais en son demi-milléna ire: Actes du Colloque International de Tours (24–29 Septembre 1984)*, edited by Jean Céard et Jean-Claude Margolin. Études Rabelaisiennes, no. 21. Geneva: Librairie Droz, pp. 365–72.

 Etienne Pasquier had called the author of *Propos rustiques* "un singe." Seeks to show that the Rabelaisian motifs in du Fail's works are enlivened with personal touches and are thus variations rather than servile imitations: "Il n'est pas un singe, mais un disciple et un émule de Rabelais, sans lequel il n'aurait jamais écrit de *Propos rustiques* ni de *Baliverneries* et à qui il doit ce qu'il a de meilleur" (p. 372).

43 LAUVERGNAT-GAGNIERE, CHRISTIANE. *Lucien de Samosate et le lucianisme en France au XVIe siècle: Athéisme et polémique*. THR, no. 227. Geneva: Librairie Droz, 434 pp.

 Discusses in chapt. 7 (pp. 235–61) the question of Lucian's influence on Rabelais. Studies Rabelais' borrowings in the first four books, in particular the relationship between Picrochole and Lucian's Samippus, the world in Pantagruel's mouth in relation to a similar exploration inside the body of a whale in Lucian's *True History*, and Épistémon's visit to the underworld, in which Lefranc had seen the clearest proof of Lucian's influence on what he took to be Rabelais' atheism. In each case underscores the differences in Rabelais' treatment of Lucian's themes, and finds Rabelais to be attracted by the characteristic turn of Lucian's imagination and style rather than the nature of his ideas. Even here, however, stresses the differences between the two authors, and finds Lucian to be more respectful of classical rhetoric, less "Dionysian," and inferior in matters of literary creativity. All in all finds the label of "Lucien français" to be justifiable, so long as it is not seen as "un indice de l'incroyance de Rabelais" (p. 258).

44 ———. "Le Portrait dans l'œuvre de Rabelais." In *Le Portrait littéraire*, edited by K. Kupisz, G.-A. Pérouse, and J.-Y. Debreuille. Lyons: Presses Universitaires de Lyon, pp. 43–50.

 Notes the scarcity of literary portraits in sixteenth-century French fiction. Points out that even in Rabelais, Panurge and Frère Jean are the only characters to have a right to a physical and psychological portrait, or at least a sketch. Argues that generally Rabelais manages to bring his characters to life by other means: by the evocative power of their names, by their actions ("leurs actes disent ce qu'ils sont" p.48), and above all by what they are made to say: "on les voit avant tout parce qu'on les entend" (p. 49). In short, by means more appropriate to the theater than to the novel.

45 ———. "Rabelais personnage de dialogue." In *Prose et prosateurs de la Renaissance: Mélanges offerts à Robert Aulotte*. Paris: SEDES, pp. 101–07.

A few years after Rabelais' death, Le Caron revived him as a character in one of his dialogues. In a style reminiscent of his prologues, Rabelais is made to develop a vaguely Epicurean defense of pleasure, with allusions to Plato and Demosthenes, and to define the highest Good as that pleasure which comes from the discovery of Truth. Wonders about Le Caron's motive for introducing Rabelais into the discussion; and suggests that in so doing Le Caron may have meant to express his conviction that Rabelais was not a mere *amuseur*, and to defend him against attacks which began in the last years of his life and which even his death had failed to stop.

46 LAZARD, MADELEINE. "Perceval et Gargantua: Deux apprentissages." In *Prose et prosateurs de la Renaissance: Mélanges offerts à Robert Aulotte*. Paris: SEDES, pp. 77–83.

Notes that *Perceval* and *Gargantua*, although neither can be reduced to a mere "manuel de pédagogie," give the same considerable importance to the matter of their hero's "formation." Acknowledges that Rabelais means to be innovative, and to raise Gargantua to unprecedented heights of wisdom and knowledge, whereas Chrétien is content to have Perceval embody ("tout en le dépassant") the aristocratic ideals of King Arthur's court. But claims to detect similarities in the starting point of both novels and in the three phases of their heroes' development: early upbringing and education, the experience of love, and awakening to spiritual realities. "Marqués par l'idéologie particulière de leur époque, le héros de Chrétien et celui de Rabelais suivent ainsi un itinéraire qui offre *mutatis mutandis* bien des jalons semblables" (pp. 81–82).

47 LESTRINGANT, FRANK. "L'Insulaire de Rabelais, ou la fiction en archipel: (Pour une lecture topographique du *Quart Livre*)." In *Rabelais en son demi-millénaire: Actes du Colloque International de Tours (24–29 Septembre 1984)*, edited by Jean Céard et Jean-Claude Margolin. Études Rabelaisiennes, no. 21. Geneva: Librairie Droz, pp. 249–74.

Four-part topological study of Book IV. In the introduction, draws out the implications of the fact that the *Quart Livre* is an *insulaire*, that it narrates a voyage from island to island instead of being a traditional journey on land: "La liste d'îles radicalise la discontinuité de l'itinéraire" (p. 250). Underscores the aleatory nature of that itinerary, and the extent to which it throws a new light on the question of the book's lack of closure. Studies the topography of

1988

the Ennasins' episode, stressing the relationship between the shape of their island and their physical shape, and bringing out the relevance of this relationship to the meaning of the episode. In the last three sub-sections, suggests that what has hitherto been taken to be a westward journey inspired by Jacques Cartier's discovery of Canada is in fact, to a large extent, an Aegean Odyssey. "En d'autres termes, l'Atlantique finit par ressembler à s'y méprendre à la Méditerrannée des *Insulaires* catalans ou vénitiens" (p. 260). This further underscores the incoherence of the itinerary: "Mais il n'est aucune raison non plus pour rechercher dans l'Insulaire du *Quart Livre* quelque cohérence d'ordre référentiel ou géographique que ce soit" (p. 266).

48    LEWIS, JOHN. "Quelques aspects de la littérature para-rabelaisienne d'avant 1562." In *Rabelais en son demi-millénaire: Actes du Colloque International de Tours (24–29 Septembre 1984)*, edited by Jean Céard et Jean-Claude Margolin. Études Rabelaisiennes, no. 21. Geneva: Librairie Droz, pp. 357–64.
     Discusses four of the seven anonymous *Chroniques gargantuines* written before and after *Pantagruel*. Questioning the views of Marcel Françon on the matter, argues for "la filiation orthodoxe des textes" (p. 359), according to which *La grande et merveilleuse vie du puissant et redouté roy Gargantua* (1527–31) and *Les grandes et inestimables Cronicques* (1532) were amalgamated into *Cronicques du roy Gargantua* (1533). The latter, and *Les croniques admirables du puissant roy Gargantua*, were both written after *Pantagruel*, and bear witness to the immediate success of that book. As for the anonymous *Disciple de Pantagruel*, and Habert's *Songe de Pantagruel*, they too draw on Rabelais' book, but are in turn used by Rabelais in the *Tiers* and *Quart Livres*.

49    ———. "Rabelais and the *Disciple de Pantagruel*." *Études Rabelaisiennes* 22:101–22.
     Notes the influence of Rabelais' *Pantagruel* on the *Disciple*, and reciprocally the influence of the latter on the two versions of the *Quart Livre*, wherein what Rabelais borrows is transformed into comic and philosophical fiction that far surpasses the quality of the original. Compares closely the borrowings from *Le Disciple de Pantagruel* in Books IV and V, comments on Dolet's "pirating of *Pantagruel* and *Gargantua*" (p. 116) in his edition of the *Disciple*, and by the Dugort brothers in theirs, and notes a second wave of borrowings after Rabelais' death.

50    MASTERS, GEORGE MALLARY. "Séance du 17 décembre 1984: L'Humanisme à Montpellier à l'époque de Rabelais, Rondelet, Rabelais et Guillaume Pellicier; Séance du 30 juin 1986: Rabelais à Montpellier." *Bulletin de l'Académie des Sciences et Lettres de Montpellier*, suppl. vol.:1–30.
     In the second of the two papers, evokes briefly what we know of Rabelais' sojourns in Montpellier from archives and university registers.

Supplements this meager information with details drawn from Rabelais' work, most notably the consultation with Rondibilis, seen as both a satire and a panegyric of Rondelet. Also quotes from three letters addressed to Rabelais from Venice by Guillaume Pellicier, alluding, among other things, to the friendly relations between Rabelais, Rondelet and Pellicier himself, and their common interest in botany. Argues for taking seriously the humanist behind the comic writer: "Refuser au texte de Rabelais une signification humaniste, c'est refuser à la satire son vrai sens." (p. 28)

51   MOREAU, FRANÇOIS. "La bibliothèque de Saint-Victor (*Pantagruel*, VII)." *Littératures* 19 (Fall):37–42.

Recalls Rabelais' predilection for lists and deplores the lack of studies of this aspect of his work. Points out that from around forty books, the catalogue grew to nearly one hundred more in the subsequent editions. Notes that it was an existing library, located on a site which is now that of the Université Paris VI and VII. Follows its history, and points out that most of its manuscripts are now at the British Museum. Believes that Rabelais had a specific book in mind for just about every title in his whimsical catalogue, and that it represents an accumulation of useless knowledge, like the knowledge of the Ecolier Limousin in the immediately preceding chapter. Finds significant the absence of any reference to the Old Testament or the Gospels, or to a single of Paul's Epistles. Concludes that all the aspects of the chapter point to the same inten tion: "dénoncer une dévotion tout extérieure et quasi mécanique...fondée sur la lecture appauvrissante de textes de seconde main, alors qu'est ignorée la seule connaissance vraiment capable de nourrir le cœur—celle des Ecritures" (p. 40).

52   MORRISON, IAN R. "Aspects du dialogue dans *Pantagruel*." *Études Rabelaisiennes* 22:123–35.

Attempts a general study of the dialogues in Book I, with the exception of those that are incomprehensible to the reader, such as the Baisecul-Humevesne episode. Divides them into categories, as "dramatic" or "non-dramatic," depending on the degree of interaction between the participants; stylized or not; and functional or non-functional, depending on their relationship to the rest of the novel. Lists the dialogues and the category to which they belong. Analyzes several samples from a literary rather than an ideological or linguistic point of view, and concludes that they are "multiformes" and remarkable for the variety of their characteristics.

53   ———. "Remarques sur les pronoms allocutifs chez Rabelais." *Zeitschrift für Romanische Philologie* 104, no. 1–2:1–11.

Shows that the choice of pronouns (between *tu* and *vous*) is linked in Rabelais with the interlocutors' rank (within the family unit, within a given professional or institutional group, within the social hierarchy). Argues that the rare exceptions to this rule are motivated by linguistic or literary consider-

1988

ations: "l'usage de Rabelais atteste à la fois le respect des normes...et aussi le sens de la valeur expressive des écarts par rapport aux normes" (p. 11).


54 NASH, JERRY C. "Rabelais et Epictète: Une nouvelle hypothèse." In *Rabelais en son demi-millénaire: Actes du Colloque International de Tours (24–29 Septembre 1984)*, edited by Jean Céard et Jean-Claude Margolin. Études Rabelaisiennes, no. 21. Geneva: Librairie Droz, pp. 193–201.

Sees in the serious, philosophical parts of Rabelais' work the same preoccupations as those of Epictetus in his *Discourses*: the same opposition between wisdom (*formation*) and knowledge (*information*), the same emphasis on the former, and on man's freedom to will what is virtuous and to act accordingly.


55 NICHOLS, FRED J. "Generating the Unwritten Text: The Case of Rabelais." *Esprit Créateur* 28, no. 1 (Spring):7–17.

Reflects on the significance of the "(non)existence" of texts either promised by Rabelais and never written (such as the future adventures of Panurge and Pantagruel mentioned at the end of the Book I), or "known to the narrator but unaccessible to us" (p. 8), as for instance most of the books that make up the library of the Monastery of Saint Victor, or the *Histoire des Gorgias* written by Alcofrybas Nasier after his sojourn in Pantagruel's mouth. Notes the progressive scarcity of these unwritten texts as the existing text grows longer. "What we have been looking at here is a complex series of displacements, and I would argue that generation in Rabelais always implies the eclipsing that displacement entails" (p. 16).


56 NILLES, CAMILLA J. "Solution and Dissolution in the Closure to the *Quart Livre*." *Essays in Literature* 15, no. 1 (Spring):131–40.

Explores "the interaction of the forces of cohesion and disjunction" (p. 131) in the concluding chapters of the *Quart Livre*, as an example of the "irresolution" characterizing the entire work. Brings out the importance of the list of prodigies at the end of the Gaster episode, and argues that it introduces "a new spiritual reality" into the "strictly material" kingdom of Gaster. Sees the list as a pivotal moment in the text, underscoring Gaster's materiality and preparing the reader for the at once material and spiritual "solution" to the riddle of life provided by Pantagruel during the feast off the coast of Chaneph and Ganabin. But notes that the solution does not bring final satisfaction and fulfillment, and that at the very end both the reader and the crew aboard the Thalamège are left "at sea," in a work that hesitates to come to closure and perpetually defers the attainment of truth, focusing instead on the dynamic and creative process of its discovery.

57   NUTTON, VIVIAN. "Rabelais's copy of Galen." *Études Rabelaisiennes* 22:181–87.

Draws attention to the five volumes of the 1525 Aldine edition of Galen that belonged to Rabelais and are now at the University Library in Sheffield. Points out that most of the annotations are not by Rabelais, briefly discusses some of them, bolsters Screech's contention that the medical satire in the *Tiers Livre* echoes Rabelais' confrontation with Galen, and finds reasons to admire Rabelais' skills as a medical philologist: "Rabelais' medicine was, in its way, as up to date as his satire" (p. 187).

58   OGINO, ANNA. "Le comique et le cosmique dans l'œuvre de Rabelais: L'Éloge des dettes (*Le Tiers Livre*, ch. iii–ch. iv)." *Etudes de langue et littéra ture françaises* 52 (March):13–28.

Among the various episodes dealing with paradoxical praise, singles out for analysis the praise of debtors as being the only one to be grounded in contemporary cosmological theory. Defines the notions of the cosmic and the comic in terms applicable both to Rabelais and to the Renaissance in general, and sees in them the two key notions of Rabelaisian dynamics. Reacting against recent tendencies, defines the comic in terms of content as well as form. Considers the cosmic in terms of its literary effects rather than in terms of cosmological theories. Traces the history of the paradoxical *encomium*, notes the interpenetration of the comic and the cosmic throughout the *Tiers Livre*, and sees in the antithetical juxtaposition of chapt. 3 (laudatory) and chapt. 4 (critical) the essential reality of the Rabelaisian text. Studies debts as an economic and social phenomenon, noting that the publication of Rabelais' book is nearly contemporary with that of Calvin's letter on usury (1545). Also studies their symbolism, and compares the episode with the *Querela Pacis* of Erasmus and with Speroni's *Dialogues*. Concludes that in its serious dimensions, the episode raises one among many existential questions debated throughout the book, and that it is treated from a Christian rather than a Neoplatonist perspective.

59   PARKIN, JOHN. "Rabelais and Henry Miller." *Arcadia* 3:276–95.

Reminds us that Rabelais was one of very few writers venerated by Miller as a "counter-cultural talisman" (p. 277). Notes that they share the same enemies, the same isolation in a hostile culture, a similar conception of laughter as therapy, and a similarly serious message couched in a rhetoric at odds with itself ("for Rabelais the rhetoric of Christian Humanism, for Miller that of rebellious anarchism," p. 279). Finds in their work a similar "dialectic of negative desecration and positive recreation" (p. 281), a similar fusion of erudition and popular culture, and a similar love of language, coupled with an awareness that truth lies beyond it. Finds them alike in their anticapitalism, their equation of folly with wisdom, their propensity to carnivalize reality. Argues that in both writers obscenity is "an aspect of a collective freedom which bursts through other channels as well" (p. 289), and that both have a tendency to seek refuge in a utopia—Thélème, Big Sur—which "cannot stand up to intellectual scrutiny" (p. 294). But notes that Rabelais' essentially ironic attitude towards his work finds no echo in Miller.

60   POT, OLIVIER. "Ronsard et Panurge à Ganabim." *Études Rabelaisiennes* 22:7–26.
   Offers a literary interpretation of the Ganabim episode, by reading it as a parody of poetic language aiming specifically at the intensely lyric style of Ronsard's *Odes pindariques*. Suggests that this may in turn account for Ronsard's animosity towards Rabelais in his famous "Epitaphe." Concludes by suggesting that the choice of Ronsard's *Odes* as the object of his parody may also correspond to an intention to emphasize the etymology of the term, since parody is *par-odê*, "parabole de l'*ode*, contre-point ou contre-chant" (p. 26).

61   POUTINGON, GÉRARD MILHE. "Frayeur et syderation magnétiques chez Rabelais." *Études Rabelaisiennes* 22:137–50.
   Notes how often paralyzing fear (*sidération* in modern French) is related in Rabelais to magnetic action: the fascination of the Pantagruelists at the sight of Quinte Essence, the "altération" caused by Pantagruel upon his enemies, the fright caused by sudden sounds, the punishment of Picrochole and Anarche, the fear of thunder or other prophetic signs of celestial origin. Through self-mastery the Pantagruelists (though not such tyrants as Picrochole and Anarche) conquer that fear and achieve the mediating virtue of *médiocrité* leading to moral and philosophical truth. "Pénétré de cette Vérité, le pantagruéliste évite les écueils de la 'syderation' et la transmue en réalité quintessentielle" (p. 150). Wonders to what extent Rabelais can be said to be serious (despite his occasionally mocking references to alchemy), when he puts moral and philosophical problems in such alchemical terms.

62   RAGLAND-SULLIVAN, ELLIE. "The Myth of *Sustantificque Mouelle*: A Lacanian Perspective on Rabelais's Use of Language." *Literature and Psychology* 34, no. 3:1–21.
   Sees the ambiguity of Rabelais' language "as an end in itself," rather than "an obstacle to be overcome," or an intentional, conscious attempt to destroy meaning. Believes that Rabelais' work illustrates Lacan's contention that we are objects of language rather than its masters. Argues that "Rabelais dramatized what Lacan has only in recent decades explained, namely that 'there is no universe of discourse or thought, no one system of language, no meta-language. There is only language in its multiform links to images, desire and the body'" (p. 10). Reads the episode of the frozen words as "a literary anticipation of Lacan's theory that conscious and unconscious are finally inseparable" (p. 11), and claims that the *sustantificque mouelle* we are invited

to seek does not represent "a deep truth to be dug out," but language itself, "an irreducible symbol of the truths that are half-spoken" (p. 19).

63    RAWLES, STEPHEN. "La typographie de Rabelais: Réflexions bibli-ographiques sur des éditions faussement attribuées." In *Rabelais en son demi-millénaire: Actes du Colloque International de Tours (24–29 Septembre 1984)*, edited by Jean Céard et Jean-Claude Margolin. Études Rabelaisiennes, no. 21. Geneva: Librairie Droz, pp. 37–48.

Regroups conclusions by different scholars about the earliest editions (1537 and 1538) of *Gargantua* and *Pantagruel* set in roman type. Neither was published by Janot, as had been thought previously, but by Denis de Harsy in Lyons. Rabelais had used him temporarily, before entrusting his "definitive edition" back to François Juste. The editions in gothic type seek to look deliberately anachronistic, for stylistic reasons.

64    RIGOLOT, FRANÇOIS [PAUL]. "L'affaire du 'torchecul': Michel-Ange et l'emblème de la charité." In *Rabelais en son demi-millénaire: Actes du Colloque International de Tours (24–29 Septembre 1984)*, edited by Jean Céard et Jean-Claude Margolin. Études Rabelaisiennes, no. 21. Geneva: Librairie Droz, pp. 213–24.

Even the most whimsical episode in Rabelais' work is in fact grounded in the writer's experience. In the case of the "torchecul" episode, suggests that Rabelais' flight of fancy was triggered by Michelangelo's now lost "Leda and the Swan," exhibited in Lyons at the time of Rabelais' arrival in that city. By a process of devaluation from high to low culture (of which, ironically, only the highly cultured reader of Rabelais could be aware), "la femme au cygne devient le gamin à l'oison" (p. 215). Rabelais had prepared the reader for this assimilation by proleptic allusions to the myth in the *Fanfreluches antidotées* as well as in the chapter on the hero's birth, especially in the 1552 edition: "Tout se passe comme si, en se relisant, Rabelais avait voulu réinscrire dans son texte, au chapitre de la naissance du héros, le mythe dont il allait parodier la splendide représentation" (p. 220). Furthermore, suggests a connection between the Michelangelo-inspired emblem of the Aumône-Générale of Lyons representing charity as a woman seated under the image of a pelican, with the emblem on Gargantua's hat. "Qui eût cru que Michel-Ange, l'Aumône-Générale et Gargantua aient pu avoir quelque chose en commun? Les faits sont pourtant là: l'argument néoplatonicien du tableau italien devait servir de repoussoir au syncrétisme platonico-évangélique de la *Caritas* rabelaisienne" (p. 219). See also 1985.27.

65    RIGOLOT, FRANÇOIS, and SANDRA SIDER. "Fonctions de l'écriture emblématique chez Rabelais." *Esprit Créateur* 28, no. 2 (Summer):36–47.

Recall the vogue of Horapollo's *Hieroglyphics*, which were read in the sixteenth century as pre-Christian symbols. Distinguish between two types of

1988

emblematic episodes in Rabelais: those which, like Gargantua's medallion, require an allegorical mode of reading leading to the apprehension of moral truths as foundations of a new social harmony; and those which, like the description of the temple of the Divine Bottle, are to be read like hieroglyphs, and lead to the contemplation of mystic truths. See in the dual nature of the emblematic episodes, and in the two different modes of reading they entail, a manifestation of Rabelais' dual and paradoxical view of reality.

66  SCHRADER, LUDWIG. "Panurge: Théories récentes–observations méthodoligiques–conséquences possibles." In *Rabelais en son demi-millénaire: Actes du Colloque International de Tours (24–29 Septembre 1984)*, edited by Jean Céard et Jean-Claude Margolin. Études Rabelaisiennes, no. 21. Geneva: Librairie Droz, pp. 145–56.

Reviews the various interpretations given of Panurge since Mario Roques' seminal article on the subject (see 1953.42), and classifies them according to each scholar's methodological approach: archetypal (comparisons with Mercury, Ulysses, Renart, the picaresque hero), psychological (a melancholy type, a child), linguistic (modern man in search of meaning, sophist), historical (Panurge in relation to Evangelicalism), comparative (Panurge compared to Falstaff, to other characters in Rabelais). Also takes into account the studies of Panurge as he appears in the episodes in which he is the main character: chiefly his first appearance in *Pantagruel* (chapt. 9), and his attitude throughout the *Tiers Livre*. Concludes that Panurge emerges as an essentially coherent, albeit ambiguous, character. Notes an increasing tendency towards historical interpretations. Contains a bibliography of studies on Panurge from 1953 to 1984.

67  SCREECH, M[ICHAEL] A[NDREW]. "Histoire des idées et histoire du livre: Une optique personnelle et une profession de foi." In *Le Livre dans l'Europe de la Renaissance: Actes du XXVIIIe Colloque international d'Études humanistes de Tours*, edited by Pierre Aquilon, Henri-Jean Martin, and François Dupuygrenet Desrousilles. [N.p.]: Promodis, pp. 553–66.

In the context of a discussion on the importance of the material side of bibliographical studies ("bibliographie matérielle"), comments on the frame surrounding the title in Claude Nourry's first edition of *Pantagruel*. Notes that this frame had been used by other printers for their scholarly editions of law books. Argues that this material sign reveals Rabelais' satirical intentions, and that it indicates the kind of reader Rabelais had in mind when writing his ostensibly popular work. Points out that Rabelais' text becomes progressively more obscene as printing errors accumulate over the years, transforming for instance *d'Hivernie* into *de Brenie* ("*bren* ayant alors le sens de *merde*," p. 560).

1988

68    ———. *Looking at Rabelais*. Oxford: Clarendon Press, 24 pp.
Discusses various aspects of the preparation of *A New Rabelais Bibliography*: the visual clues for dating the editions, the information provided by woodcuts, the liberties taken by the printers with the text after Rabelais' death. With illustrations. The Zaharoff Lecture for 1987–88.

69    ———. "Sagesse de Rabelais: Rabelais et les 'bons christians.'" In *Rabelais en son demi-millénaire: Actes du Colloque International de Tours (24–29 Septembre 1984)*, edited by Jean Céard et Jean-Claude Margolin. Études Rabelaisiennes, no. 21. Geneva: Librairie Droz, pp. 9–15.
Introduction to the collected papers. Defines Rabelais' laughter as that of Saint Jerome and Erasmus, an ironic laughter tempered with Christian charity. "Le rire de Rabelais est un rire sain et moral" (p. 15): it condemns, but it also redeems and forgives.

70    SOZZI, LIONELLO. "Quelques aspects de la notion de 'dignitas hominis' dans l'œuvre de Rabelais." In *Rabelais en son demi-millénaire: Actes du Colloque International de Tours (24–29 Septembre 1984)*, edited by Jean Céard et Jean-Claude Margolin. Études Rabelaisiennes, no. 21. Geneva: Librairie Droz, pp. 167–74.
Denies the recent contention that the "mouvement vers le bas" is the most distinctive characteristic of Rabelais' work. Despite apparent attempts to degrade the notion of "dignitas" and the idealistic posture it implies, Rabelais shares the humanists' belief in man's dignity as manifested in action and in the cultivation of spiritual values: "malgré tout ce que l'on a dit sur la présence du réel, de la matière, du corps dans l'œuvre de Rabelais, il est de toute évidence que l'idéal de Rabelais, c'est parfois aussi le détachement de la matière, voire son mépris" (p. 171). In Gargantua's letter to his son, in the episode of the abbey of Thélème, finds echoes of the humanists' aspiration towards honor, virtue, and knowledge.

71    SPILLEBOUT, GABRIEL. "Le Réalisme chinonais." In *Rabelais en son demi-millénaire: Actes du Colloque International de Tours (24–29 Septembre 1984)*, edited by Jean Céard et Jean-Claude Margolin. Études Rabelaisiennes, no. 21. Geneva: Librairie Droz, pp. 69–75.
Names of places and of people, details of daily life are constantly transformed in Rabelais' work. But there is nothing irrational or unreal about this transformation. Rabelais' reality parallels that of the Chinonais as well as being a comic version of that reality. Our knowledge of some historical characters leads us to believe in the historical reality of others.

1988

72  TAZBIR, JANUSZ. "Jeszcze o znajomosci Rabelais'go w Polsce" (More on the knowledge of Rabelais in Poland). *Pamietnik Literacki* 79, no. 2:205–23.
    Completes and updates the surveys by W. Weintraub (1936 and 1977) of references to Rabelais' works among Polish writers and translators. Notes that Rabelais ignores Poland, whereas Montaigne makes several references to it. Deplores that whereas Polish readers unfamiliar with French can read *Pantagruel* and *Gargantua* in Boya's translation, no French reader unfamiliar with Polish can savor a text such as Rej's pastiche on the imaginary meeting between Pantagruel and a young man who wanted to speak beautiful and erudite Polish. (The text of the pastiche is quoted on pp. 222–23.)

73  TETEL, MARCEL. "Rabelais et Folengo: *De Patria Diabolorum.*" In *Rabelais en son demi-millénaire: Actes du Colloque International de Tours (24–29 Septembre 1984)*, edited by Jean Céard et Jean-Claude Margolin. Études Rabelaisiennes, no. 21. Geneva: Librairie Droz, pp. 203–11.
    Twice in his work, Rabelais alludes to an imaginary book by Merlin Coccaie entitled *De patria diabolorum*, which the latter claims to have published. Although strictly speaking no work bearing this title exists, Folengo may be said to have written it, since *De patria diabolorum* could very well have served as a title for his *Baldus*: "En fait, Merlin Coccaie a bien composé un ouvrage intitulé *De patria diabolorum*, tout comme Rabelais a, effectivement, publié *De la Dignité des Braguettes*, un des titres que l'on pourrait donner à l'œuvre rabelaisienne" (p. 203). The last canto of *Baldus* is devoted to a descent in hell, on the model of the sixth canto of the *Aeneid*. Compares *Baldus* to the *Aeneid*, and *Pantagruel* to *Baldus*: "Bien que les textes de Folengo et de Rabelais exigent parfois une lecture allégorique, parfois une lecture emblématique que médiatise un langage volontairement déformé et déformateur, le texte de Folengo généralement est plus transparent et se charge de moins de virtualité plurielle, de moins de juxtaposition de plusieurs couches de significations, que le texte de Rabelais" (p. 209).

74  TORNITORE, TONINO. "Parole gelate prima e dopo Rabelais: Fortuna di un topos." *Études Rabelaisiennes* 22:43–55.
    Notes that the classical sources of the theme, from Antiphano's parable in Plutarch to the story of the fur merchant narrated by Castiglione in the *Libro del Cortegiano*, have received sufficient attention in the past. Investigates here the presence of the myth in popular literature rather than in "alta cultura"; finds them to be relatively few and probably unknown to Rabelais. Traces the recurrences of the theme to the present, and argues that most frequently their source is to be sought in Rabelais (see 1985.30).

75  TOURNON, ANDRÉ. "Le Paradoxe ménippéen dans l'œuvre de Rabelais." In *Rabelais en son demi-millénaire: Actes du Colloque International de Tours*

1988

*(24–29 Septembre 1984)*, edited by Jean Céard et Jean-Claude Margolin. Études Rabelaisiennes, no. 21. Geneva: Librairie Droz, pp. 309–17.

By its hybrid character, Menippean satire as practiced by Lucian and the humanist writers of the Renaissance lends itself particularly well to the expression of paradoxical themes. A Menippean text is not a haphazard juxtaposition of fantasy and didacticism: "car le genre requiert un travail de combinaison qui rende indissociables ces éléments et ces aspects hétéroclites, et les fasse réagir les uns sur les autres" (p. 310). Studies these effects of interaction between the playful and the serious elements in the 1552 prologue to Book IV, with emphasis on the paradoxical nature of the deliberation whereby Couillatris is granted his wish, and the intervention of Priapus.

76  TSUQUIASHI-DADDESIO, EVA. "Le Bruissement silencieux de la graphie dans *Les Fanfreluches antidotées*." *Esprit Créateur* 28, no. 2 (Summer): 48–57.

Notes the lack of interest shown by critics for the poem, seen as unimportant and less than felicitous. "Nous proposons qu'il s'agit, au contraire, d'un moment fécond et essentiel pour la compréhension de l'œuvre dans laquelle il est inséré et que l'hermétisme récalcitrant qu'on lui reproche tient à un dessein précis: celui de matérialiser dans le language un moment purement graphique, silencieux, prégnant de virtualités dont l'organisation fait plutôt appel à une perception visuelle qu'à la perception d'un discours purement phonique exigée par la suite linéaire" (p. 48). Studies the graphic aspect of the poem, distinguishes an inner pattern of repetition and inversion of selected consonants and vowels within each stanza, relates it to Tory's theory of the origin of typographical letters in *Champ fleury*, and sees in the juxtaposition of the poem with the first chapter on the genealogy of the giant, an example of the characteristic relation in Rabelais' narrative between the text and its enigmatic, cryptic meaning.

77  WALTER, PHILIPPE. "Le sel, la poêle et le géant." *Études Rabelaisiennes* 22:189–201.

Rabelais is believed to have sought political refuge in Metz after the condemnation of the *Tiers Livre* by the Sorbonne. Argues that Rabelais may have also been attracted to the city by its carnivalesque festivities surrounding a group of giants and above all a certain "saint Gorgon, dont le nom suggère un évident rapprochement avec celui de Gargantua" (p. 190). Identifies "Bramont en Lorraine" (*Pantagruel*, chapt. 4) with the town of Bâmont located near a salt mine in the Vosges, and suggests that the most fruitful research on Rabelais may well lie in the area of Gallic mythology surrounding the Rabelaisian giants.

78  WEBER, HENRI. "Eléments structurels de quelques mythes rabelaisiens." In *Rabelais en son demi-millénaire: Actes du Colloque International de Tours*

1989

*(24–29 Septembre 1984)*, edited by Jean Céard et Jean-Claude Margolin. Études Rabelaisiennes, no. 21. Geneva: Librairie Droz, pp. 157–65.

Analyzes the structural elements of the type of myth most often found in Rabelais, namely the Odyssean or Lucianesque myth based on the description of a country, a character, or a people of strange appearance and behavior. These myths imply a reversal of habitual notions, and are developed according to scientific or rhetorical categories of description, combined with the process of accumulation, the most typical form of which in Rabelais is the "kyrielle." To these characteristics is added "un dernier élément inséparable du mythe rabelaisien: la glose" (p. 164), whose origin is to be found in the humanistic tradition.

79  WEINBERG, FLORENCE M[AY]. "Thélème selon Fischart: Omissions fécondes." In *Rabelais en son demi-millénaire: Actes du Colloque International de Tours (24–29 Septembre 1984)*, edited by Jean Céard et Jean-Claude Margolin. Études Rabelaisiennes, no. 21. Geneva: Librairie Droz, pp. 373–79.

Explains the omissions and interpolations in Fischart's adaptation of *Gargantua* as due to the fact that Rabelais and Fischart wrote with different purposes in mind. Suggests that Fischart's aim was principally to entertain the reader, whereas Rabelais also sought to express his religious and ethical views. Shows that Fischart omits all passages where Rabelais expresses a religious opinion: "il ne veut pas courir le risque de déplaire aux autorités" (p. 374). Studies Fischart's version of the Thélème episode as typical of his attitude towards the religious passages in Rabelais' entire work, and notes that the German translator tends to minimize (where he does not frankly misunderstand it), the complexity of Rabelais' thought. Finds Fischart's omissions and misunderstandings to be fruitful in that they call the reader's attention to certain neglected passages in Rabelais, and lead to new perspectives on the meaning of the text.

## 1989

1  BAUSCHATZ, CATHLEEN M. "From 'estudier et profiter' to 'instruire et plaire': Didacticism in Rabelais's *Pantagruel* and *Gargantua*." *Modern Language Studies* 19, no. 1 (Winter):37–49.

Examines "the passages describing educational or didactic reading" (p. 37) in the prologues and the Abbaye de Thélème episode as well as in the more directly "educational" chapters; is struck by the constant juxtaposition of the verbs *estudier* and *profiter*; notes that by the time we reach the Abbaye de Thélème episode, *estudier et profiter* have been replaced by *instruire et plaire* as Rabelais' "dominant didactic aesthetic" (p. 43). Believes that

1989

Rabelais seeks to establish a similarity between the relationship of the writer/reader on the one hand, and of the teacher/student on the other. Argues that despite the apparent emphasis on an active role for both student and reader, Rabelais/Alcofribas almost always gives to the teacher and the writer the final word in the process of learning and interpretation.

2  BERLAN, FRANÇOISE. "Principe d'équivalence et binarité dans la Harangue d'Ulrich Gallet à Picrochole." *L'Information grammaticale* 41 (March):32–38.

Studies this "morceau d'éloquence judiciaire" not as a pastiche of Ciceronian rhetoric, but as an example of the use of semantic and syntactic binarity. Sees the latter as the main unifying principle of the passage.

3  BLUM, CLAUDE. *La représentation de la mort dans la littérature française de la Renaissance.* Vol. 1, *D'Hélinant de Froidmont à Ronsard.* 2d ed. Paris: Librairie Honoré Champion, 518 pp.

In part 2 ("Mort humaine et mort universelle"), devotes pp. 345–415 to Rabelais. Argues that Rabelais humanizes death and makes it possible for future generations to think of it as a natural phenomenon. But warns that Rabelais' representation of death should not be equated with that of later naturalists: "Nous sommes là, plutôt, en présence d'un témoignage privilégié de la transformation d'une mentalité, transformation lente, complexe, sans ruptures brutales et définitives, où la figuration de certaines interrogations précède de beaucoup leur prise de conscience" (p. 346). Stresses the Evangelical roots of Rabelais' reflection on death, but notes the preeminence of the terrestrial and the humanization of the hereafter, in his conception of the Devil, the devils, sin and madness: the devil acquires a human appearance; sin, death, and madness become carnivalesque figures. Studies the episode of Epistémon's resurrection as bringing together the scattered elements of Rabelais' attitude towards death. Finds that Rabelais is underscoring the illusory, contradictory, literary character of the episode at the expense of its "truth." Shows that in Epistémon's account of what he saw on his journey Rabelais reinforces the terrestrial, human meaning given to his death. Sees a similar treatment of the theme of death in the Raminagrobis episode of Book III, and in the account of the death of Langey in Book IV. Argues that the undoubted spiritual background of this terrestrial, humanized, internalized representation of death is enlarged to enclose not only the individual but society, nature, and the whole cosmos. Argues that Rabelais endows the antithetical notions of life and death, health and disease, with a new ambivalence based on the notion of exchange (as in the birth of Pantagruel or the praise of debts in the *Tiers Livre*). Studies Rabelaisian laughter as a reaction to death, and reaffirms his interpretation of Rabelais' conception of death as ultimately steeped in a sense of the divine origin of man and nature.

1989

4  DEMERSON, GUY. "Le 'Prologe' exemplaire du *Gargantua*: Le Littéraire et ses retranchements." *Versants*:35–57.

In the wake of some recent studies on the subject, argues that the main function of the prologue is not to recommend any particular interpretation of *Gargantua*, but to enter into a contract with the reader ("un pacte de lecture"), to create between the reader and the author a climate of intimacy and tolerance favorable to the proper reception of the ensuing novel: to propose "un mode d'emploi," rather than to unveil the work's meaning. Suggests that to understand the prologue is to have by the same token grasped its fundamental message: "la bienveillance requise pour entrer dans le royaume du Livre est déjà une adhésion au Pantagruélisme" (p. 52). Thinks that the thematic structure of the prologue mirrors that of the work itself: "le Prologe est un analogue: il enseigne un mode d'approche valable pour l'œuvre entière" (p. 37). Points out, after Rigolot (see 1972.29), that the liminary *Dizains* act as "coups d'essay," as preliminary exercises meant to test the reader's competence. Notes, as most others have not, that the celebrated passage about the dog and its bone insists on the *explication* of the text as a prerequisite for its interpretation (since Rabelais enjoins us to "fleurer, sentir et estimer ces beaux livres de haulte gresse" before seeking to get to their "substantificque mouelle"). Believes that for Rabelais the meaning of his work—perhaps of any work—is not to be found within the text itself, but is a product of the act of reading, and that his main intention in the prologue is to teach us to read not like "un fanatique, ni un allégoriste farfelu, ni un obsédé" (p. 52), but like a poet, recreating the work and assuming responsibility for our interpretation.

5  ESCLAPEZ, RAYMOND. "La parodie des *Antiquités* chez Rabelais." *Nouvelle Revue du XVIe siècle* 7:25–36.

Notes that the theme of origins—of the hero, of nations, of cities—is always treated by Rabelais in a parodic vein, from the very first chapter of *Pantagruel* onwards. Argues that when Rabelais appears to find etymological connections between the Gauls and Noé, between Chinon and Caïn, he is in fact mocking the etymological mania so widespread among his contemporaries, especially Postel. "S'enquérir de l'origine, c'est presque automatiquement s'exposer au ridicule; armé de l'appareil érudit des étymologies grecques, latines, hébraïques, on peut faire dire aux noms propres tout et n'importe quoi" (p. 36).

6  GORDON, ALEX. L. "Rabelais en anglais: Bonheurs et malheurs de la traduction." In *L'Europe de la Renaissance: Cultures et Civilisations, Mélanges offerts à Marie-Thérèse Jones-Davies*. Paris: Jean Touzot, pp. 463–75.

In matters of tone, vocabulary, and sonority, compares three translations of *Gargantua*: that of Urquhart (1653), and the modern translations of Jacques Le Clercq (1936) and J. M. Cohen (1955). Of the twentieth-century translators, finds Le Clercq to be more faithful to the spirit of Rabelais' text, and Cohen more faithful to the letter.

7  GOSSELIN, LAURENT. "Rabelais: Une ontologie de la contingence." *Cahiers Textuel* 34/44, no. 4–5:33–39.

Believes Rabelais' novels to have been written from the point of view of Ockhamian nominalism carried to its ultimate consequences. Explains the coexistence of realism (the representation of the reality of the world around us) and of the fantastic (the gigantic, the monstrous) in Rabelais as a consequence of Rabelais' need, as a nominalist, to reject classical modes of discourse, and to invent instead a form of discourse capable of expressing both the contingency of the real and the reality of the contingent. Singles out three characteristics of Rabelais' text: its lack of referential coherence (whereby an object changes in size, for instance, from one chapter to the next), its constant oscillations between one linguistic register and another, as well as the incoherence ("la polyphonie") of its ideology, and explains them as so many direct consequences of the "contingence énonciative" of Rabelais' discourse. Briefly studies this contingency in two episodes: Gargantua's invention of the "torchecul" and Panurge's quest in the *Tiers Livre*.

8  HUCHON, MIREILLE. "Définition et interprétation dans le *Gargantua*." *Cahiers Textuel* 34/44, no.4–5.21–28.

Notes in *Gargantua* the frequency of syntactical patterns expressing equivalence, and studies them as examples of *définition*, on the one hand, and *interprétation* (in the rhetorical sense of the word) on the other. Refers to the definitions of these terms in Aristotle, in Fabri's *Grant et vray art de pleine rhetorique* (1521), and in Ramus' *Dialectique*. Sees in *Gargantua* "une véritable rhétorique de l'équivalence où se trouve privilégiée l'interprétation" (p. 27), and suggests that the use to which these essentially rhetorical or logical notions are put in a literary work might prove a subject of fruitful investigation.

9  ———. "Le langaige de Frère Jean dans *Gargantua*." *L'Information grammaticale* 41 (March):28–31.

At first reading, such linguistic constants as abundance of swearwords, or recourse to clerical Latin seem to characterize Frère Jean's speech, but in fact these traits are also present in the speech of other characters. The transcription of a wide variety of oral devices is also "focalized" on the character of Frère Jean, but here again these devices are shared by others. What is exclusively his is a series of terms listed on p. 29. But what above all characterizes the language of Frère Jean is his predilection for rhetorical devices. His speech offers examples of a variety of devices defined by Fabri in his *Grant et vray art de pleine Rhetorique*. "Ainsi plus qu'une parole débridée, qui se donne libre cours dans les propos de table, mais qui apparaît surtout en fait

1989

comme transcription littéraire de la langue parlée par des procédés conven-
tionnels, ce sont bien les accumulations de procédés, les couleurs de rhétorique et leur variété qui caractérisent le langage de Frère Jean qui se veut
efficace et persuasif" (p. 31). Goes so far as to suggest that the monk is an
example of the perfect orator described by Cicero in *De oratore*.

10 JEANNERET, MICHEL. "La lecture en question: Sur quelques prologues
comiques du seizième siècle." *French Forum* 14, no. 3 (September):279–89.
    Discusses the prologue to *Gargantua* as one of various examples of
comic prologues which, in contrast to the canonical prefaces to narratives of a
serious nature, acknowledge the inability of the preface to impose any particular interpretation, and encourage the reader's participation in the search for
the meaning of the author's work.

11 LAJARTE, PHILIPPE DE. "Le champ ludique et l'interprétation de l'œuvre
de Rabelais (d'après le *Gargantua* et le *Pantagruel*." *Cahiers Textuel* 34/44,
no. 4–5:61–67.
    Distinguishes five levels of discourse ("champs discursifs") in Rabelais'
text: referential (pertaining to the real world or to realistic fiction), intertextual, axiological (gravitating around the positive pole of ideological assertion
and the negative pole of satire and parody), hermeneutic, and playful
("ludique"). Seeks to define the nature and functions of the "champ ludique."
Warns that the latter is not to be equated with the comic or with sophistry; nor
should it be thought of as merely verbal or formal. Argues that playfulness in
Rabelais is not gratuitous, and that its presence does not annihilate the ideological significance of Rabelais' text. Notes that it does not exist in isolation,
but alters the autonomy of the other four levels of discourse. Believes that the
"champ ludique" manifests itself primarily in a coexistence between those
episodes that can be read with the help of a humanistic grid, and those that do
not lend themselves in any way to a humanistic interpretation. Claims that the
"champ ludique" takes on three main forms: hyperbole, reversal of certain
fundamental humanistic values, and play on meaning, whereby meaning is
either suspended (as in the "Fanfreluches antidotées") or subverted into non-
meaning (as in the lawsuit between Baisecul and Humevesne). Underscores
the relationship between these forms of playfulness, which are viewed as
three facets of one and the same activity: "Le jeu rabelaisien est un jeu de
nature indissociablement sémiotique, ontologique et axiologique" (p. 63).
Believes that the function of this activity is to underscore the union of  opposites as illustrated throughout Rabelais' text and proclaimed in the prologue to
*Gargantua*. Claims that the higher meaning to which the prologue refers is,
paradoxically, the playful dimension of the work, emblematized in the symbolism of wine: "c'est dans les réalités universellement considérées comme les
plus basses que le lecteur de Rabelais devra chercher les vérités les plus

hautes" (p. 64). Consequently, rejects as equally wrongheaded the types of didactic interpretations—be they humanistic or esoteric—that fail to take into account the playful element in Rabelais, and those that claim that the presence of this playful element in otherwise seemingly serious episodes robs them of all ideological significance.

12  LAUVERGNAT-GAGNIERE, CHRISTIANE. "*Pantagruel, Gargantua*, et les Chroniques." *Cahiers Textuel* 34/44, no. 4–5:29–32.
        Draws attention to the forthcoming edition of the *Chroniques Gargantuines*, and to its introduction which seeks to show the relationship between these chronicles and Rabelais' novel. Offers a brief analysis of a number of episodes in Rabelais' first two books which owe some debt to the *Chroniques*, and insists on the differences between Rabelais' version of the events and what can be found in the anonymous text. Points out that the giant of the chronicles is an essentially solitary creature characterized chiefly by his size, whereas Rabelais' giants, surrounded by human companions, are also endowed with intellectual and moral qualities which transform them into Rabelais' contemporaries.

13  LESTRINGANT, FRANK. "Dans la bouche des géants. (*Pantagruel*, 32; *Gargantua*, 38)." *Cahiers Textuel* 34/44, no. 4–5:43–52.
        Compares the episode of the world in Pantagruel's mouth with the parallel chapter in which six pilgrims are ingested by Gargantua "en salade." Notes that the former, echoing as it does the new world of the great discoveries, is usually considered to be more innovative and richer in significance, even though as a whole *Pantagruel* is most often viewed as a mere draft ("une esquisse") of *Gargantua*. But suggests that the pilgrims' episode, when studied in itself, that is independently of the evangelistic message which it is made to illustrate seven chapters later, proves to be at least equal in ideological significance. Making use of a distinction first proposed by Michel Korinman, notes that the horizontal itinerary described in *Pantagruel*, chapt. 32, offers an example of *itinérance*, a journey in the course of which nothing can be said to have happened, and during which the traveller merely registers the landscape around him without being in any way transformed by it, whereas the vertical odyssey of *Gargantua*, chapt. 38, is a *pérégrination*, in which the participants are subjected to a series of vicissitudes leading to spiritual illumination. Concludes that the *Gargantua* episode is equal to that of *Pantagruel* in the dignity of its symbolism and its evocative power. If the author's *itinérance* in the world of Pantagruel's mouth suggests a lesson in geographical relativism, the pilgrims' *pérégrination* in *Gargantua* contains, for its part, a meditation on human destiny, and a warning against wars of aggression and the vanity of seeking to transcend the limits of the human condition by inquiring into the mysteries of a future whose secrets belong to God alone.

1989

14  MARSHALL, F. W. "The Great Allegory." *Australian Journal of French Studies* 26, no. 1 (January–April):12–51.

Third in a series of articles presenting Rabelais' work as an allegory in the mode of biblical exegesis. Less systematically, less exhaustively than in the case of *Gargantua* (see 1987.11 and 12), applies the method of allegorical reading to Books III and IV. Offers a series of notes as "reference points for later detailed studies of sections and topics" (p. 14). Believes the two books to be essentially about concern for humanity, about the need to recognize and accept human imperfection, and about tolerance and moderation as a proposed corrective.

15  MATORÉ, GEORGES. "*Gargantua*: Remarques sur le vocabulaire du Temps." *L'Information grammaticale* 40 (January):16–17.

Brief lexicological study pointing out that the characters have a very approximate sense of the passage of time, that Rabelais' emphasis on memorization as a pedagogical device shows "un vif respect pour ce qui a acquis grâce au temps un caractère trompeur de perennité" (p. 17), that a clearly regulated schedule in the ideal educational system of Ponocrates coexists with a totally unstructured, yet equally ideal education at Thélème, that the desire to cram as much knowledge as possible into a limited interval of time presupposes that the latter is infinitely extensible, that the text signals a definite valorization of leisure—games, sports—and of work as creative rather than professional activity. Presented as potentially helpful data for the hitherto neglected study of temporality during the Renaissance, when the notion of time undergoes complex changes, whose main features are fragmentation and neglect of the future in favor of the present, in contrast with the conception of time as progressive and uninterrupted.

16  MÉNAGER, DANIEL. "La stratégie des titres dans *Gargantua* et *Pantagruel*." *Cahiers Textuel* 34/44, no. 4–5:13–19.

Rabelais' contemporaries do not seem to have paid much attention to titles. Most titles inform the reader on the nature of the text about to be discovered, the genre to which it belongs—"Sonnets," "Odes," "Discours"—rather than the subject-matters treated therein. Judging by an episode such as that of the Saint Victor Library, Rabelais, for his part, seems to have taken pleasure in inventing titles, although those he chose for his own works are curiously lackluster. Compares the first two books in that regard and finds *Gargantua* significantly more interesting than *Pantagruel*. Studies also Rabelais' "intertitres," or chapter headings. Notes that they are sometimes brief, sometimes "interminables." Many are made up of binary groups. Most are informative, sometimes to the point of giving away the story; some suggest the narrator's attitude to the events about to be related; others contain a message to the reader. Some are consciously puzzling, and meant to awaken the reader's curiosity; others still are consciously disconcerting. Some are in sharp contrast to the episode they introduce: the richer and more significant the episode, the shorter and more matter-of-fact the heading, as in the series of chapters on the Abbaye de Thélème. In none, however, does Rabelais show as much freedom in relation to the subject-matter as Montaigne will show fifty years later: "ils n'appartiennent qu'à moitié à l'auteur" (p. 18).

17 ———. *Rabelais en toutes lettres.* Paris: Bordas, 191 pp.
    Presents a general survey of Rabelais' life and of all five books of his novel. Believes that the work cannot be understood unless it is set against the background of Renaissance humanism, but that it is also an adventure in creative writing, occasionally leading the author beyond the confines of humanistic thought. Makes frequent references to the most recent critical studies. The penultimate chapter, "Les mots et le monde," underscores the plurality of styles and tonalities, brings out the relationship between the oral and the written aspects of the work, between action and discourse, description and lists, and stresses Rabelais' consciousness of the power and the limitations of language, as well as the main characteristics of his comic vision of the world.

18 NILLES, CAMILLA J. "Revisions of Redemption: Rabelais's Medlar, *Braguette* and Pantagruelion Myths." *Renaissance and Reformation/ Renaissance et Réforme*, n.s., 13, no. 4 (Fall):357–70.
    Reacting to a recent tendency to link the theme of redemption with Christian doctrine, explores these myths in the light of the natural subtext provided by Rabelais' knowledge of the human body and curative plants, and shows redemption in Rabelais to be a specifically human activity. Argues that the medlar myth in the first chapter of *Pantagruel* is a "dramatic reversal" of the biblical account on which it was modelled, in which "the spiritual gives way to the material" (p. 358); that in the story of the *braguette*'s origin, redemption through divine grace is replaced by the discovery of a clever use for fig leaves; and that in his praise of the Pantagruélion, the same comic substitutions take place once again, although here "the transitions from one level of reality to the next are fully articulated" (p. 361), and the various levels are seen to be linked in the same continuum: from the vegetal through the human to the divine.

19 POUILLOUX, JEAN-YVES. "Questions de lecture." *Cahiers Textuel* 34/44, no. 4–5:7–12.
    Underscores the complexity of Rabelais' text and the difficulty of reaching a conclusion as to its meaning. Argues that references to important texts and allusions to important historical events offer no guarantee of seriousness of purpose. Believes that the customary division of Rabelais' text into serious and comic episodes is wrongheaded, for there is constant contamination of one by the other. This reciprocal subversion of seriousness and comedy often stems from the narrative context in which any given text is inserted, as when,

for example, the apparent seriousness of Gargantua's letter on education is put into question by the immediately following chapters which clearly show that Pantagruel has not paid any heed to his father's high-minded advice. Points out that Rabelais' text can also be subverted by the mode of its formulation. Thus passages which are frequently taken to be earnest expressions of humanistic ideology—such as Gallet's and Gargantua's political speeches in the context of the Picrocholine War—contain elements of parody and may point to ironic intentions. But the presence of irony does not necessarily imply an attitude of cynicism. In fact, no single, univocal reading can do justice to Rabelais' multifaceted text: an intelligent reading does not confine itself to any single fixed interpretation, but oscillates ceaselessly from one meaning to its opposite, in keeping with the paradoxical logic of the text.

20  PRESCOTT, ANNE LAKE. "Reshaping Gargantua." In *L'Europe de la Renaissance: Cultures et Civilisations, Mélanges offerts à Marie-Thérèse Jones-Davies*. Paris: Touzot, pp. 477–91.

In the wake of studies by Huntingdon Brown and Marcel de Grève on Rabelais' reception in England, notes a number of allusions in English sixteenth- and seventeenth-century texts to a giant named Gargantua, whose characteristics, borrowed for the most part from the giant of folklore, account for the deformation undergone by Rabelais' utopian king and by the author himself in the mind of the English public.

21  RENAUD, MICHEL. "Le scatologique dans l'œuvre de Rabelais: De l'invective à la jubilation." *Cahiers Textuel* 34/44, no. 4–5:53–59.

"Rabelais peut-il choquer le lecteur d'aujourd'hui, offusquer ses pudeurs en matière de langage?" (p. 53). Suggests that Rabelais' obscenity is more shocking to the modern reader for its scatology than its eroticism, and that the reader finds it objectionable not so much in itself but because he or she finds it incompatible with the dignity of a great literary work. Distinguishes what is scatological from what is merely the language of the marketplace (see Bakhtin, 1968.1). Notes that excremental allusions frequently occur in a polemical context, in satirical passages where the author expresses his hostility to the ideas or intellectual attitude embodied by a particular character. Elsewhere, finds that scatological allusions are marked by a spirit of jubilance, a poetic enthusiasm that signals the joyful acceptance of natural functions as an integral part of the human condition. Believes that the scatological dimension of Rabelais' work is all the more disconcerting since from the seventeenth century onward scatology finds refuge only in relatively minor works. Perverse in the works of the marquis de Sade, disquietingly murky in that of Georges Bataille and Michel Tournier, it has lost its Rabelaisian vigor and virulance to become, instead, an expression of neurosis and metaphysical despair. "Le scatologique ne nous est acceptable que s'il est tragique, douloureux, prétexte à discours philosophiques, et non dévoilement de l'être à travers la matière"(p. 58).

22   RIGOLOT, FRANÇOIS [PAUL]. "Rabelais' Laurel for Glory: A Further Study of the 'Pantagruelion.'" *Renaissance Quarterly* 42, no. 1 (Spring): 60–77.

Noting that the plant is said by Rabelais' narrator to be always green, proposes "a reading of the Pantagruelion as a possible enigmatic transposition of the laurel" (p. 64), to which there are several references in the text. The "parodistic allusions to the 'laurels' of poetic glory" (p. 77) underscore the very different symbolism of Rabelais' plant, which guarantees immortality through productive endeavor rather than through the glory to be derived from the literary expression of Petrarchan love. "Just as the 'Praise of Debts' has been interpreted as a parody of the neo-Platonic philosophy of love, the praise of Pantagruel's plant could be viewed as a parody of the neo-Petrarchan emblematic tradition" (p. 77).

23   STEPHENS, WALTER. *Giants in Those Days: Folklore, Ancient History, and Nationalism*. Lincoln: University of Nebraska Press, 456 pp.

Believes that what has been written on Rabelais' giants is "fundamentally wrong." Seeks to trace "a cultural history of the concept of the Giant, from Old Testament times to the early modern period," and study Rabelais' giants against the background of this cultural tradition. The theory that Rabelais' good giants have their source in popular culture was first promoted by Paul Sébillot in the latter part of the nineteenth century; it was later popularized by Abel Lefranc, and has been most recently revived by Jean Larmat and Mikhail Bakhtin. Believes this idea to be the product of unscientific, wishful thinking: "a figment of the patriotic imagination" (p. 5) as far as the French folklorists are concerned, and, in the case of Bakhtin, a product of an essentially circular reasoning, since his analysis of folk culture relies almost entirely on what he finds in Rabelais' text. Examines the evolution of the giant from biblical times to the Middle Ages, as an object of the science of gigantology as well as a symbol of all that was contrary to the religious and cultural ideals prevalent at any given time. In chapt. 3 and 4 studies the emergence of a positive concept of the giant. Sees its origin in the debates on national precedence launched by Annius of Viterbo in his forged pro-Italian *Chronicles of the Giants since Noah and the Flood*, and adapted to further the cause of Gallic nationalism by Jean Lemaire de Belges in his *Illustrations de Gaule et singulaitez de Troye*. In chapt. 5 through 7, dealing most directly with Rabelais, presents Rabelaisian giants as "parodies of the nationalistic Giants of French cultural polemics," owing very little to folkloric sources, and progressively turning into symbols of moral and intellectual superiority as Alcofrybas Nasier and Panurge are made to assume the foolish dimension with which the giants had originally been endowed. In his study of *Pantagruel* (chapt. 6), attracts attention to traces of Annian influence in Alcofrybas' account of the genealogy of the giants, and to the Annian aspects of Panurge's sophistry. Notes a similar influence of Annius and Lemaire de Belges in Gargantua's genealogy, and in Alcofrybas' account of the circumstances in which the document was found.

24 TOURNON, ANDRÉ. "'Plus haut sens' ou 'sens agile'?" *Cahiers Textuel* 34/44, no. 4–5:69–78.

Examines the "Fanfreluches antidotées" and the "Enigme trouvée ès fondements de l'Abbaye des Thélémites" as two episodes which confirm most clearly the narrator's promise of a higher meaning in the prologue to *Gargantua*. Claims these episodes require two different types of interpretation, between which the reader is invited to choose. Notes that the first text is only a fragment, so that the poem cannot by its very nature be decoded in its entirety. Whereas this first text can be said to have insufficient meaning, the second is presented as open to two possible interpretations, namely Gargantua's higher meaning ("le maintien et décours de vérité divine") and Frère Jean's prosaic one ("la description du jeu de paume"). Notes that far from being in any way hidden, Gargantua's higher meaning is in fact the more obvious of the two. Claims that the equivocal nature of the context leads the reader to give to the literal "description du jeu de paume" an anagogical interpretation, and to create through this back-and-forth movement between the literal and the anagogical the "sens agile" referred to in the inscription over the portals of Thélème, produced by the vivifying influence of the spirit over the letter. Provides a synoptic reading "en sens agile" of the serious and seemingly explicit passage dealing with Gargantua's education, and of the trivial tale of the lion, the fox, and the old woman as told by Panurge in connection with the building of walls around Paris. Rejects as unduly reductive readings that do not take into account the synoptic process inherent in interpretations "à sens agile," whether they view Rabelais from the perspective of the *altior sensus* of Erasmian evangelism (Screech and Defaux), or exclusively in terms of carnivalesque discourse (Bakhtin). Concludes by suggesting that Rabelais' use of Menippean language has no equivalent in the writings of the time, with the notable exception of those whom Calvin denounces as "libertins qui se nomment spirituels," and among whom one could include Maguerite de Navarre.

25 TRIPET, ARNAUD. "Aux abords du prologue." *Versants*:7–20.

In the context of a discussion of the various functions of prefatory texts, uses the prologue to *Pantagruel* as an example of a liminary text designed by its author to insist on the legitimacy of his work by placing it within the framework of tradition (in this case, that of the *Grandes et inestimables*

*Chronicques*), but also to underscore the novelty (here the superiority) of his enterprise.

## 1990

1   BAKER, MARY J. "Narration in *Pantagruel.*" *Romanic Review* 82, no. 3:312–19.
  The critical questioning of Panurge by Alcofribas in chapt. 17 illustrates "an author's dramatic disillusionment with one of his characters" (p. 316) and anticipates "the decline in prestige later suffered by Panurge" (p. 317). Alcofribas' dialogue with Pantagruel in chapt. 32 ("The World in Pantagruel's Mouth") illustrates the mutual interdependence of the author and his characters, Rabelais' ability to live within as well as without his literary creation. Argues that the function ascribed to Alcofribas—at once "mock author," narrator and character—bears witness to Rabelais' "prescient understanding of narrative" (p. 318), and to his desire to seek "a harmonious relationship with his reader" through the mediating concept of a "mock author" who is also a narrator and a character in his own fiction, and a "characterized reader" whom Alcofribas is ostensibly addressing.

2   BALDINGER, KURT. *Études autour de Rabelais*. Études Rabelaisiennes, no. 23. THR, no. 238. Geneva: Librairie Droz, 293 pp.
  Contains, most often with addenda, a number of lexicological studies originally published elsewhere. Begins with "François Rabelais: Son importance pour l'histoire du vocabulaire français" (see 1986.2). "Splendeur et misère des glossaires: A propos de nouvelles recherches rabelaisiennes" enumerates the weaknesses of most glossaries, with numerous examples of misreadings and false meanings (the study also appears in *Actes du VIe Colloque International sur le Moyen Français*, "sous presse"). Collection includes: "*Gargantua*, nouvelles recherches lexicologiques" (see 1988.5); "Fehldatierungen zu Rabelais: Zur Bedeutung der Philologie für die Lexicologie" (see 1982.1); "Beiträge zum Glossar der Pantagrueline prognostication" (see 1976.3); "Rabelais' Späße und die Humorlosigkeit der Lexikographen" (see 1977.2); "M fr. *aubeliere*, mot créé par Rabelais" (see 1978.3); "*Premier*, terme de jeu de paume méconnu dans Rabelais" (see 1978.4); "*Stupide* bei Rabelais: *Faux-amis* in der Übersetzung" (see 1981.1); "Mißverstandener Rabelais: *Aller long comme un vouge* und die *cuideurs des vendanges* (*Gargantua*, 25)" (see 1984.1); and "*Air et envie* (*Gargantua*, 50): Die Rabelais-Exegese als Opfer einer Homographie" (see 1987.1). "Des Marais de Camarina en Sicile jusqu'aux halles sacrées de la Sorbonne" (pp. 121–24) bears on two references to Camarina in Rabelais, showing that the latter was aware of the reputation of that city as a foul-smelling place. "Les

1990

romipetes dans les Devinettes" (pp. 125–30) first appeared in *De la plume à l'ordinateur: Études de philologie et de linguistique offerts à Hélène Naïs* (*Verbum*, Revue de linguistique publiée par l'Université de Nancy II, 1985). It notes the use of *romipetes* in the prologue to Book IV.

3   BERLIOZ, MARC. *Rabelais restitué*. Vol. 3, *Gargantua: Tome II, Du chapitre XXV à la fin*. Paris: Didier Érudition, 646 pp.

Third in a series of lexicological commentaries questioning the conventional readings of Rabelais' work and proposing new interpretations (see 1979.3 and 1985.2). Believes Lefranc's identification of the participants in the Picrocholine War with real inhabitants of the Chinonais to be totally devoid of literary interest. Questions not only the authority of commentators, but of their sources as well (for example Sainéan or Cotgrave's dictionary). Except for Picrochole, believes that the names of all the captains mentioned in the episode are "burlesques." In contrast to all previous commentators for whom *entommeures* equals *hachis*, proposes to see in Frère Jean des Entommeures "celui qui entame, celui qui met la main à quelque chose," in other words "he who does not hesitate to take action," an equivalent of "Frère Jean des entreprises" (p. 63). In the case of Grandgousier's letter to Gargantua, sees a parody of humanistic pedantry in what is for most commentators a moving example of humanistic eloquence. Questions the traditional identification of Picrochole with Charles V. Disputes Screech's contention that the scene between Picrochole and his "gouverneurs" owes anything to Lucian. Finds evidence of parody and satire in Gargantua's discourse to the "vaincus" (chapt. 50), where others see nothing but humanistic idealism; suggests the chapter may have been written by Rabelais (perhaps at the instigation of his protector) to warn the king against excessive magnanimity towards the enemy. Rejects the view that the Abbaye de Thélème episode was not written as an integral part of the novel. Questions the religious significance with which most scholars (Screech in particular) burden the episode; sees no reason to seek the etymology of Thélème in the Greek of the New Testament rather than the Old, and thus to endow the word with Evangelical overtones. Believes the abbey is so called because the Thelemites are there of their own free will ("de bon gré"); since the entrance age coincides with puberty, sees the sojourn as an initiation to sexuality. Does not see how the commentary following upon the Thelemites' motto amounts to a rejection of Original Sin and hence of the Christian religion. But points out that by subordinating the will of the individual to that of the community, Rabelais makes of Thélème a self-contradictory, and thus an insignificant notion: "la conception de l'Abbaye de Thélème ne peut avoir de réalité, même utopique, attendu qu'elle porte en elle sa négation" (p. 611). Does not see in the *Enigme en prophétie* any reference—premonitory or otherwise—to the Affaire des Placards. Offers of the poem an erotic interpretation.

4  BON, FRANÇOIS. *La Folie Rabelais: L'invention du "Pantagruel."* Paris: Les Éditions de Minuit, 255 pp.

An enthusiastic *lecture commentée* of *Pantagruel* with emphasis on Rabelais' language and the place of madness in his work. In the preliminary pages attracts attention to Flaubert's fascination with Rabelais, and insists at some length on comparisons with Dürer. Finds Gargantua's letter to his son "[un texte] stupéfiant par la force des idées qui s'y superposent" (p. 108), and considers the final chapter of the book as perhaps "le plus beau texte de la langue française." Concludes by stressing the necessity to read the novels in the order in which they were written, and thus to give to *Pantagruel* pride of place as the indispensible introduction to Rabelais' fictional world.

5  CAMPBELL, KIM. "Of Horse Fish and Frozen Words." *Renaissance and Reformation/Renaissance et Réforme* 26, no. 3:183–92.

Considers the episode of the frozen words in the light of Renaissance travel journalism, and in particular Jacques Cartier's accounts of his discovery of North America. In connection with Cartier's difficulty in naming a walrus ("poissons qui ont forme de chevaulx"), argues that the necessity to name the unknown in terms of the known brought about a new consciousness of "the fragility of the bond between signifier and signified" (p. 183) and led to a "disruption of language" at the time of the Renaissance. In the frozen words episode, sees Rabelais' synesthetic description of sounds in terms of colors as signalling his awareness of the phenomenon of linguistic disruption, and views the episode as representing an imaginary, poetic solution to the problem.

6  DAVIS, NATALIE ZEMON. "Rabelais among the Censors (1940s, 1540s)." *Representations*, no. 32 (Fall):1–32.

On the basis of unpublished correspondence and interviews, reconstructs the circumstances in which Lucien Febvre brought out his book on the problem of unbelief in the sixteenth century. Draws parallels between the publication of *Le Problème de l'incroyance au XVIe siècle, La Religion de Rabelais* during the German occupation, and that of Rabelais' *Tiers* and *Quart Livres* at a time when the Sorbonne and the Parlement de Paris had joined forces in the face of growing Protestantism and established a rigorous system of censorship designed to stamp out heretical books. Detects in both authors a similar intention to take a stand, over and beyond the immediate purpose of their work, against the forces of intellectual oppression by the censors of their respective periods. Among the differences, notes the absence of open allusions to Judaism and to Jews in Febvre's book, and stresses by contrast the very significant presence of Judaism in the *Quart Livre*. Believes Rabelais' knowledge of Hebrew and Jewish thought and customs to have been more extensive than has sometimes been alleged. Reminds us of the numerous Hebrew names and words in Rabelais' last authenticated work. Notes that the oracle of La Dive

1990

Badbuc is that of the Jewish Purim prophet, about whom Rabelais may have learned from books by Provençal rabbis, from Marranos during his medical studies in Montpellier, or from his own sojourns in Rome, where Jews celebrated the feast of Purim; specifies that *ruach*, as in Isle de Ruach, is not only a Hebrew word meaning wind or spirit, as the glossary to the *Quart Livre* has it, but one of the three souls that men are said to possess according to popular Jewish belief; and suggests, more generally, that Jews are present in Rabelais' work not only as allegories or symbols, but also "in their own name," "worth observing and listening to as people" (p. 19).

7   DIANÉ, ALIOUNE. "Rabelais et Montaigne: De la chronologie gigantale à l'essai infini, Réécriture kaléidoscopique d'un parcours." In *Montaigne penseur et philosophe: Actes du Congès de Dakar (Mars 1988)*, edited by Claude Blum. Paris: Honoré Champion, pp. 101–12.

Finds parallels between Rabelais' *Tiers Livre* and Montaigne's *Essais* (especially *Du Repentir* and *De la Vanité*). Reads both as a quest (for truth in the first case, for the self in the second). Sees Panurge's consultations and Montaigne's additions to his text as the various episodes of an intellectual journey the significance of which lies less in the attainment of its goal (in both cases uncertain, ambiguous, illusory) than in its method of inquiry. Insofar as Rabelais' and Montaigne's journeys differ, they do so mainly because the reality reflected in the authors' kaleidoscopic texts has changed: the world of the *Tiers Livre* still retains something of the enthusiastic optimism of Rabelais' earlier works; that of the *Essais* is a world threatened with imminent disintegration.

8   HÖFLER, MANFRED. "Fr. *croquignole* 'petite pâtisserie croquante': Probleme der Textüberlieferung und Interpretation bei Rabelais und die historische Lexikographie." *Zeitschrift für Romanische Philologie* 106, no. 1–2:140–42.

Pinpoints the first occurrence of the term in Rabelais. Notes that the "corquignoles savoreuses" in a later edition of *Cinquiesme Livre* ("Comment furent les dames Lanternes servies a soupper") is a distortion of the "croquignoles" mentioned in chapt. 7 of *Pantagruel*.

9   JORDAN, CONSTANCE. *Renaissance Feminism: Literary Texts and Political Models*. Ithaca: Cornell University Press, 319 pp.

Sees many good reasons for subscribing to Rabelais' reputation as a misogynist, and acknowledges in Panurge "the curious mixture of moral vulgarity and philosophical sophistication of so much contemporary clerical writing on women" (p. 191). Yet hesitates to tax Rabelais with anti-feminism, and notes that Panurge's dilemma in Book III, based as it is on his sexual anxiety, is more prejudicial to his own case than to the case of the woman he may or may not marry. Extending the notion of debt in Panurge's encomium to the sexual exchange involved in marriage, shows Rabelais to provide "a feminist critique of the transactional element in marriage" (p. 196) during Panurge's consultation with Frère Jean on the subject, when the latter extolls with facetious logic the advantages of cuckoldry. Notes also Rabelais' "critique of contemporary marriage doctrine" (p. 198) in the allusion to Hans Carvel's ring and his wife's refusal to be treated as a sexual object. Shows Rabelais' position on the question of *potestas patris* to be equally at odds with contemporary opinion, and argues that his condemnation of clandestine marriage hides a violent disapproval of the abusive power of the father over his marriageable children.

10  KINSER, SAMUEL. *Rabelais' Carnival: Text, Context, Metatext*. Berkeley and Los Angeles: University of California Press, 293 pp.
    Four-part study of Rabelais' novels (with emphasis on Book IV) against the backdrop of Rabelais criticism since the 1960s, especially Bakhtin and his assertion that Rabelais' work is imbued with the spirit of carnival. Distinguishes two meanings of "carnivalesque": the narrow meaning pertaining to pre-Lenten festivity (of which Bakhtin says very little), and the meaning that "refers to a more general category of festivities characterized by glittering spectacle and fantasy" (p. xi, note). In part 1 ("Text/Context") studies the Pantagruelists' encounter with Quaresmeprenant in Book IV as crucial to Bakhtin's thesis (although Bakhtin himself deals with it only in passing). Underscores its paradoxical nature. Points out that Quaresmeprenant "meant Carnival in the sixteenth century" (p. 13), although etymologically it means "taking Lent." Believes that the episode largely "dissolves the traditional difference between Carnival and Lent," whereas critics tend to think that Rabelais "equivocates between the two calendrical moments." Believes the misinterpretations to be due to the fact that the context of the episode "has been wrongly defined" (p. 14). Analyzes the "paratextual frame of the text" (p. 46) as part of the context, and sees the Quaresmeprenant episode as belonging to a subgenre, both artistic and literary, depicting the differences between carnival and Lent as a conflict between personifications of the two occasions. Studies the ways in which the episode in Rabelais deviates from the traditional pattern followed in the literary versions of the carnival-Lent allegory. Studies closely the anatomical descriptions of Quaresmeprenant and the etymology of his name. Finds appealing Leo Spitzer's suggestion that *-prenant* comes from *praegnans*, "full of something imminent," and not from *prehendere*, "to take hold of": "What if Rabelais was thinking of Quaresmeprenant not as a fixed and determined object in the Christian calendar, but as a transition period? What if his purpose was to pry loose this personification from its medieval allegorical web of equivalences and oppositions and to offer instead a sense of what happens psychologically as Lent takes hold of the Christian soul?" (p. 84). Concludes that Quaresmeprenant is ambivalent rather than ambiguous, that he represents neither carnival nor Lent, "but the inversive logic that binds them together" (p. 84). Offers a similar analysis of the

encounter with the Andouilles, and argues that here again Rabelais is not denouncing either carnival or Lent, but that the comic underpinning of the episode suggests an affable acceptance of both institutions, "even with their tendency to encourage excess" (p. 122). Traces subsequent misreadings of the episode to the fact that its sociological context came to be disregarded, and that it came to be read as a weapon of Protestant propaganda. Believes that in the seventeenth century the text came to be "normalized," not as carnivalesque ebullience, let alone as multidimensional morality, but as "irreligious excess" (p. 130). Studies the metatexts created by critics around the texts themselves as attempts at obfuscation of meaning. Argues that contemporary formalistic and semiotic criticism, with its emphasis on the work's literariness, is as reductive as preceding historical and philosophical perspectives insofar as it confines itself to the surface of the text. After the methodological considerations of part 3, returns to the analysis of Quaresmeprenant and finds him monstrous above all because of his inability to partake in the kind of communality which otherwise defines the social world of Rabelais' characters. Speaks of Quaresmenprenant as "the only *practicing* individualist in Rabelais' books" (p. 189). Notes a change in the relations between author and reader in the 1552 version of Book IV, in that Rabelais now appeals specifically to readers of good will, and correlates this change with the introduction of a new element of satire, namely the "countertextual mockery" which extends to Pantagruelism itself. Notes a decline in Rabelais' idealism in the face of attacks from his detractors, and shows its effect on his new definition of Pantagruelism, which is no longer synonymous with conviviality but is "an individual's mode of resistance to life's troubles" (p. 242). The community addressed is now only the community of well-wishers, and mockery, hitherto used only as a defensive shield, becomes a weapon. Traces the hostility of the seventeenth and eighteenth centuries towards Rabelais largely to a shift in the direction of regulation and individualism and away from the communalism and freedom evident in Rabelais' fiction and present in contemporary reality. Believes that Bakhtin's carnivalesque interpretation, although useful in emphasizing the popular side of Rabelais' metatext, is nonetheless a distortion of his work insofar as it views it as subverting official norms: "Rabelais' procedures are less carnivalesque than communal and less festively inversive than mockingly masked" (p. 249). Suggests in conclusion that "spiritualist organicism" describes Rabelais' characteristic worldview more accurately than such adjectives as "populist" and "carnivalesque." Four appendices and an extensive bibliography.

11    KITTAY, JEFFREY. "On Notation." *Language and Communication* 10, no. 2:149–65.
       Uses the list of games in *Gargantua*, chapt. 24, to illustrate a number of theoretical remarks on the concept of notation. Discusses the particular semiotic process at work in such a list, and underscores its unexpected character

within the novel of which it is a part. Argues that it is only one instance of the ways in which Rabelais makes his novel burst out at the seams, as part of "an attack upon the status of select 'container' that the book held at the time" (p. 160). And as part, alongside such experimental passages as "Les propos des bien yvres," or the exact transcription of the monks' prayer at the abbey of Seuillé, of Rabelais' reflection on the relationship between discourse and knowledge.

12   LA CHARITÉ, RAYMOND C. "Par où commencer? Histoire et récit dans le *Pantagruel* de Rabelais." In *Le Signe et le Texte: Études sur l'écriture au XVIe siècle en France*, edited by Lawrence D. Kritzman. Lexington, Ky.: French Forum, pp. 79–89.

Studies *Pantagruel* in the light of "historical" events used in its narrative and acting as its frame. Notes that Rabelais begins by anchoring his fiction in biblical history (since Pantagruel's genealogy has its roots in Genesis), and that biblical history in turn determines the work's narrative development. But shows that Rabelais reworks Genesis, offers his own version of the Fall, and uses it as a metaphor for original textual production. "La procréation humaine et la génération textuelle vont de pair" (p. 87).

13   LANGER, ULRICH. *Divine and Poetic Freedom in the Renaissance: Nominalist Theology and Literature in France and Italy*. Princeton. Princeton University Press, 215 pp.

Argues that the distinctions governing divine will in the context of scholastic nominalist theology "are a model for the way in which literary characters come to a decision in the novels of Rabelais" (p. 4). In chapt. 1 ("The Free Reader: Hypothetical Necessity in Fiction"), studies the many representations of the reader in Rabelais' prologues, and Rabelais' efforts to predetermine the reader's reaction to the text by limiting the reader's freedom. In chapt. 2 ("Free Reward: Merit in Courtly Literature"), comments on the Picrocholine War and the Abbaye de Thélème as "illustrations of generosity and congruous merit" (p. 76), which he also sees in Pantagruel's extension of friendship toward Panurge. In chapt. 3 ("The Free Creator: Causality and Beginnings"), studies the prologues (especially in the case of Book III) as statements of the author's autonomy, *prima causa efficiens* of his fictional world. Comments most extensively on Rabelais in chapt. 4, devoted entirely to "will and its objects" in Rabelais' fiction. Studies the Abbaye de Thélème episode in the light of "the theological complex informing the concept of will" (p. 127). Notes the tendency among the late Scholastics "to privilege the autonomy of the will" (p. 135), and analyzes Gargantua's dilemma upon the birth of his son (*Pantagruel*, chapt. 3) and Pantagruel's choice of Panurge as exercises of autonomous will, independent of the knowledge of its object as final cause. Similarly, sees in Panurge's dilemma in Book III an indirect influence of the Scholastic notion of priority of will over knowledge, emphasizing the irrational nature of decision making. Finds the consultation with Hippothadée particularly significant in that regard: "The radical conditionality of Hippothadée's statements demonstrates the irrelevance of advice to an autonomous will, and the permanent gap between the autonomous will of Pantagruel and the dependent will of Panurge" (p. 146). Notes the same dependence in the case of Picrochole, whereas the Thelemites provide the most extreme illustration of autonomous will. Points out that the latter is by its very nature both non-individual and non-representable, since it is identical in every member of the group. Ascribes to the autonomy of the Thelemites' will the lack of narrative interest of the Abbaye de Thélème episode. "Rabelais' utopian abbey of will in its very lack of interest is an incarnation of divine will in human individuals" (p. 148).

14   LAVATORI, GERARD PONZIANO. "Language and Money in Rabelais." Ph.D. dissertation, Brown University, 313 pp.

Studies linguistic and economic exchanges in Rabelais' first four books, in the light of contemporary notions of communicative action (Jurgen Habermas) and cooperation (Grice), and in relation to the socio-economic foundations of the French Renaissance. Argues for the existence of "important similarities in the ways the novels' characters manipulate both language and money." See *Dissertation Abstracts International* 51 (1991):2764A.

15   MONAS, SIDNEY. "Literature, Medicine, and the Celebration of the Body in Rabelais, Tolstoy, and Joyce." In *The Body and the Text: Comparative Essays in Literature and Medicine*, edited by Bruce Clarke and Wendell Aycock. Lubbock: Texas Tech University Press, pp. 57–75.

Touches upon Rabelais' medical experience, relates it to his treatment of the body as one with the soul, and comments, after Bakhtin, upon Rabelais' "translation" of the spirit of carnival into literature. Views this achievement as laying "the cornerstone for that most carnivalistic of literary genres, the novel" (p. 64). Ascribes Joyce's "celebration of the ensouled body" (p. 69) in *Ulysses* to Rabelais' influence upon him.

16   PARKIN, JOHN. *Henry Miller, the Modern Rabelais*. Lewiston, N.Y.: Mellen, 279 pp.

Expanded version of 1988.59. Documents Miller's "intuitive and paradoxical readings of Rabelais" (p. 65), and discusses the authors' common-ground in chapters on style and composition ("Word Lists"), food and drink ("The Holy Bottle"), grotesque scenes and carnival language, "Laughter," "Liberation Ideology" (though not a coherent system of thought), "Polystylism" (stylistic interplay of a variety of registers, rather than the presence of an authentic authorial voice), and "Self-transcendence."

17   RIGGS, LARRY W. "Critiques of Technique: The Literary Subversion of Mastery in Rabelais, Molière, Laclos and Sand." *Selecta* 11:18–24.

Equates Panurge's quest for an authoritative answer to his doubts about marriage with the reader's quest for a definitive interpretation of Rabelais' text. Argues that in thus seeking a clear, unequivocal message, both Panurge and the reader are guilty of over-simplification, and deprive themselves of the playful pleasure of ambiguous experience. Draws a parallel between Panurge's attitude towards marriage in the *Tiers Livre* and that of Molière's *ridicules*, and argues that both Rabelais and Molière are determined to resist the trend "toward consolidation of cultural hegemony in and through discourse" (p. 20).

18   SCHWARTZ, JEROME. *Irony and Ideology in Rabelais: Structures of Subversion.* Cambridge: Cambridge University Press, 251 pp.

Rejecting the notion of irony as implying authorial intention, studies the first four books of Rabelais as "a space where texts confront one another, where speech, language and writing collide, where the multiple discourses of sixteenth-century society—classical, Christian, biblical, legal, medical, humanist, popular—inscribe the traces of an interdiscursive space of social and ideological conflict" (p. 2). Refuses to choose between the historical and the esthetic approach. Finds them to be "fundamentally opposed," yet "necessarily complementary and reciprocally corrective" (p. 1). Disputes Bakhtin's view that carnivalesque laughter is the only element of subversion in the novel: "Indeed, much that is subversive in Rabelais is not popular, but erudite, evangelical and humanist" (p. 2). Finds more helpful Bakhtin's theory of the dialogic functioning of language in the text, seen as "composed of plural, competing voices" asserting its internal tensions. Drawing on a variety of critical approaches, seeks to bring out the ideology of an essentially ironic work as it emerges from the tensions produced in the text by the ironic coexistence of discourse and counter-discourse in a number of particularly problematic chapters or episodes. Far from reading into the prologue to *Pantagruel* a parody of the Church, as Bakhtin and others had done, sees it merely as proclaiming, in its constant undercuttings and contradictions, "the freedom of writing and the freedom of reading" (p. 15). Against those who read Gargantua's letter to his son as propaganda for the new learning, or, conversely, as a parody of humanistic concerns, affirms the seriousness of the text as an ideological statement as well as a reflection upon the nature of textual rhetoric. Argues that the incongruity of the juxtaposition of the letter with the ensuing encounter between Pantagruel and Panurge does not invalidate the ideology of the letter, but explores "Pantagruel's unacknowledged desire to liberate himself from the Law of the Father" (p. 29). Generally, finds the subversive counter-discourse in *Pantagruel* to have been placed in Panurge's mouth, and studies "Panurgian discourse" as a "negative, socially marginal, subversive, obscene and scatological counter-discourse that is opposed" to the discourses

1990

of the giants (p. 38). In *Gargantua*, argues that the problematic episodes under discussion perform, each in its own way, the "subversive overlapping of antagonistic discourses" (p. 89). Does not see the prologue as a defense of allegorical interpretation but as an appeal to the reader to respond actively and critically to the text. Argues that the birth of Gargantua further "desanctifies" the written word. In the episode of Gargantua's "devise," finds that image and text subvert one another, and show Rabelais as uncommitted on the question of the relation between *eros* and *agape*. Argues that the chapters dealing with color symbolism cannot be said to plead conclusively for natural symbolism, since "the case against arbitrariness is ironically undermined through the use of appeals to arbitrary authority" (p. 70). The chapters on Gargantua's education do not clearly proclaim the superiority of the new pedagogy over the old, but reveal a similar subversion of a discourse by the very ideological discourse it purports to reject. The Picrocholine War, although not ambiguous on the plane of moral values, is decidedly ambiguous on the level of political allegory: the imperfect analogy between Gargantua and Francis I suggests that Rabelais' purpose is not so much to flatter the king by sanctioning his policies but rather to hint as subtly as possible at the gulf that separates the actual king from his idealized model. The rest of the novel is submitted to a similar inter-discursive analysis, tending to prove that everywhere irony deconstructs the apparent ideological content of the text. In the praise of debts and the consultations of Book III as well as in the apparent praise of the Pantagruélion, the polyvalent text is shown to bear within itself its own condemnation. In the *Quart Livre*, points out that Panurge is given once again the function of producing the counter-discourse which puts into question the optimism towards which the dialectic of the book was leading. Concludes by suggesting that the recourse to the interplay between ideology and irony may have been Rabelais' "chief means of distancing himself not only from the ideology of his protectors and patrons, but also from the philosophical, theological and epistemological paradigm of medieval discourse" (p. 200). Extensive bibliography.

19   TOMARKEN, ANNETTE H. *The Smile of Truth: The French Satirical Eulogy and Its Antecedents*. Princeton: Princeton University Press, 354 pp.
    Briefly discusses Rabelais' "Eloge des dettes" in chapt. 5 ("The Vice Eulogy in France"). Scattered references to Rabelais throughout the study.

20   WALLACE, NATHANIEL OWEN. "Religious Folly and Hermeneutic Prudence in Rabelais's Narratives and Wu Ch'êng-ên's *Hsi-yu chi*." In *Proceedings of the XIIth Congress of the International Comparative Literature Association, Munich 1988*. Vol. 2, *Space and Boundaries in Literature*, edited by Roger Bauer *et al*. Munich: Iudicium Verlag, pp. 449–54.
    Interprets Frère Jean's defense of the abbey of Seuillé during the Picrocholine War and the founding of the abbey of Thélème as examples of

religious folly, and argues that this notion of religious folly "provides a hermeneutic safety-net that can prevent a number of episodes in Rabelais from collapsing into farce or scatology" (p. 451).

21    WEINBERG, FLORENCE M[AY]. "Written on the Leaves: Rabelais and the Sibylline Tradition." *Renaissance Quarterly* 43, no. 4 (Winter):709–30.
       Examines at length the episode of the Sibylle de Panzoust in itself, as well as in the context of Rabelais' general treatment of women and that of the series of consultations making up the bulk of the *Tiers Livre*. Points out that the Sibylle is portrayed more concretely, with greater realism, than is customary with Rabelais where women are concerned. Suggests that by making her a spinner Rabelais "dignifies her by association" with the traditional Western archetype of woman as creator. Underscores the mixture of mythic symbolism and folk superstition surrounding the Sibyl and her actions as she sets about to forecast the future. Notes the symbolism of numbers running through the chapter, and sees in it an indication of the Sibyl's "divine inspiration, her spirituality, despite her burlesque behavior and grotesque outer appearance" (p. 726). Does not believe that the parodic and grotesque aspect of the episode necessarily invalidates any attempt to read a serious message into the Sibyl's prophecy. Argues that the satire in the episode is aimed at Panurge's reaction to the old woman and not to the woman herself. Agrees with Céard that she "was meant to portray a legitimate source of divine knowledge" (p. 729), and suggests in conclusion that as an amalgam of the grotesque and the divine she stands as "a typically Rabelaisian syncretic creation," "a feminine version of the Silenus," an unlikely but nevertheless genuine mouthpiece of wisdom.

# Author Index

Aercke, K. P., 1986.1
Alberti, G., 1959.1
Alcofry, Étienne, 1972.1
Almeida, Ivan, 1983.1
Amory, Frederic, 1983.2
Anon., 1954.1
Antonioli, Roland, 1976.1; 1978.1–2;
    1980.1; 1983.3; 1988.1
Araki, Shotaro, 1988.2
Aron, Émile, 1988.3
Aronson, Nicole Habatjou, 1970.1; 1972.2
Arveiller, R., 1964.1
Astruc, Pierre, 1953.1
Auerbach, Erich, 1950.1; 1953.2; 1957.1;
    1964.2
Aulard, Marie-Louise (pseud.?), 1954.2
Aury, Gabriel, 1959.2

Babcock-Abrahams, Barbara, 1974.1
Bady, René, 1972.3
Bailbé, Jacques, 1959.3; 1988.4
Baillot, A.-F., 1967.1
Baker, Mary J., 1990.2
Baker, Paul V., 1977.1
Bakhtin, Mikhail, 1965.1; 1968.1–2;
    1970.2; 1974.2; 1979.1
Baldinger, Kurt, 1976.2–3; 1977.2;
    1978.3–4; 1981.1; 1982.1; 1983.4;
    1984.1; 1986.2; 1987.1; 1988.5;
    1990.2
Bambeck, Manfred, 1956.1; 1973.2
Bar, Francis, 1981.2
Baraz, Michael, 1972.4; 1980.2; 1983.5;
    1984.2
Barrault, Jean-Louis, 1968.3–4
Bart, B. F., 1950.2
Bastiaensen, Michel, 1968.5; 1974.3
Batany, Jean, 1981.3; 1986.3
Bauschatz, Cathleen M., 1988.6; 1989.1

Beaujour, Michel, 1969.1
Beaulieu, Jean Philippe, 1985.1
Beck, William John, 1970.3; 1980.3
Bedouelle, Guy-Thomas, 1987.2
Bellenger, Yvonne, 1980.4
Béné, Charles, 1961.1; 1964.3; 1973.2;
    1979.2; 1981.4; 1984.3–4
Benot, Yves, 1953.3
Benson, Edward George, Jr., 1971.1;
    1976.4; 1980.5
Berk, Philip Robert, 1969.2
Berlan, Françoise, 1989.2
Berlioz, Jean-Paul, 1980.6
Berlioz, Marc, 1979.3; 1985.2; 1990.3
Bernard, Claudie E., 1981.5
Berrong, Richard M., 1977.3–4; 1978.5;
    1979.4–5; 1980.7; 1981.6; 1982.2;
    1983.6–9; 1985.3–6; 1986.4;
    1988.7
Berry, Alice Fiala, 1973.1; 1975.1;
    1977.5; 1979.6; 1980.8
Bertalot, Enrico U., 1964.4
Berthoud, Gabrielle, 1953.4
Bichon, Jean, 1967.2; 1980.9
Billacois, François, 1980.10
Blum, Claude, 1982.3; 1989.3
Bolgar, R. R., 1954.3
Bon, François, 1990.4
Bonfantini, Mario, 1959.4
Bonnard, H., 1988.8
Booth, Wayne C., 1982.4; 1983.10;
    1985.7; 1988.9
Borgeaud, P., 1983.11
Bossuat, Robert, 1963.1
Boucher, A., 1957.2; 1966.1; 1967.3;
    1972.5; 1976.5
Bowen, Barbara C., 1968.6; 1972.6;
    1976.6; 1981.7–8; 1986.5; 1988.10
Boyer, Alain-Michel, 1987.3

417

# Subject Index

The entries are arranged in alphabetical order, without any attempt to group them into more general categories, which might have proved more confusing than helpful. Studies focused on a particular episode or a particular book are listed twice, alphabetically and again under the episode or the book in question. For the purpose of localizing the various entries, the five books of the Rabelaisian chronicles are designated as P (Pantagruel), G (Gargantua), TL (Tiers Livre), QL (Quart Livre), and CL (Cinquième Livre).

Abbaye de Thélème (G, 53–58), 1952.7;
    1953.12; 1954.42; 1958.7; 1959.21;
    1963.27; 1966.11; 1982.23; 1987.5;
    1988.41
    as illusion, 1984.38
    as new Academy, 1971.32
    as the New Jerusalem, 1977.27
    as reflection of new economic order,
    1978.29
    as self-contradictory concept, 1985.14;
    1990.3
    as utopia, 1976.20
    geographical site, 1962.2
    Loyola's Jésuitières and, 1980.10
    paradoxical aspects, 1966.3
    place in the narrative, 1969.22;
    1971.29
    poem above the portal of, 1988.8
    realism and fantasy in, 1971.30
    stoic elements in, 1956.14
    thematic reading of episode, 1959.21
absolutism, 1953.19; 1981.5
the absurd, 1972.20
Acadia, 1971.20
Aesop, 1967.20; 1970.13
Affaire des Placards
    Abbaye de Thélème and, 1969.22
    date of publication of G and, 1971.8;
    1972.13; 1974.7, 32; 1976.34
Africa, 1975.13
aggression, 1971.16
Agrippa, Cornelius, 1984.9
alchemy, 1973.17
Alciati, Andrea, 1963.3; 1969.20
Alexandria, 1956.4

Alibantes (P, 2), 1956.18; 1966.6; 1972.17
allegorical interpretation, 1976.18;
    1978.27. See also altior sensus
allegorization, 1979.7; 1987.11
allegory
    in QL, 1982.26
    in TL and QL, 1989.14
Alliances, l'isle des (QL, 9), 1952.7
    as a rhetorical system, 1978.35
Almanacs, 1959.29; 1974.31; 1987.3
altior sensus, 1976.18; 1986.18. See also
    allegorical interpretation; marrow
    bone; sustantificque mouelle
America (R. studies in), 1954.43
ambiguity, 1965.8; 1972.6; 1974.18;
    1976.22; 1977.41; 1983.28; 1984.18
ambivalence, 1968.1; 1984.18
Amboise, Michel d', 1967.20
Amon, 1986.18; 1988.26
Ampère, Jean-Jacques, 1953.45
Amy, Pierre, 1959.27; 1965.2
anagrams, 1953.49
analogy, 1977.15
anatomical descriptions, 1954.22;
    1987.17; 1988.30
Andouilles (QL, 35–42)
    bisexuality, 1980.12
    general study of the episode, 1953.27;
    1954.9; 1981.7–8
    problematics of language and, 1980.12
androgyne, 1953.6; 1977.37; 1978.33;
    1984.42; 1986.17
animals, 1959.24; 1987.17
antifeminism, 1958.7; 1970.15; 1976.8;
    1985.5, 7; 1988.9

Neoplatonism, 1953.33; 1971.14
Nephelibates (QL, 56), 1983.9
Netherlands, 1955.2–3
the New World, 1977.32
Niceron, Jean-Pierre, 1970.7
nihilism, 1988.21
nominalism, 1989.7
nonsense, 1981.14
Northern provinces, 1956.12
notation, 1990.11
Nourry, Claude, 1988.67
numerology, 1950.7; 1959.15; 1968.19;
    1970.4; 1971.11; 1978.39; 1980.24;
    1982.16, 25; 1986.26

obscenity, 1956.17; 1968.22. See also
    scatology
occult tradition, 1954.28; 1973.17
Odysseus, 1982.5, 11. See also Ulysses
Olaus Magnus, 1965.21
Old Testament (in QL), 1977.5
onomastics, 1970.19; 1974.18; 1977.30;
    1985.24
optimism, 1968.26
orality, 1968.6; 1976.17
originality, of R.'s thought, 1953.18
origins, search for, 1977.3
the owl and the drum (TL, 14), 1974.22;
    1976.7
Ozell, translation of R., 1978.8

Pacorus, Panurge and, 1980.13
paintings. See Medamothi
Pan, 1955.12; 1961.6; 1983.11
Panigon (QL, 10), 1953.24
Pantagruel
    coherence of, 1974.21; 1977.24
    commentary on, 1979.3
    editions of, 1964.3; 1980.38; 1982.13;
        1984.3
    general study of, 1990.4
    narrative in, 1990.12
    structure of, 1968.7; 1978.22; 1981.31
Pantagruel
    as comic character, 1980.18
    as embodiment of Christian humanism,
        1977.13
    as embodiment of sophistry, 1973.3;
        1977.13
    as Gallic Hercules, 1988.29
    as Messiah, 1984.13
    as Pico della Mirandola, 1977.12;
        1978.10
    demonic nature of, 1975.10; 1980.30
    derivatives of the name, 1960.10

in QL and CL, 1953.29
quest of, 1986.13
relationship with Panurge, 1977.30
Pantagrueline Prognostication, 1955.5;
    1974.31; 1983.33
    lexicological notes on, 1976.3
Pantagruélion, 1956.11; 1963.13;
    1968.23; 1969.4; 1971.23; 1977.16;
    1981.5; 1983.17; 1989.22
Pantagruelism, 1953.41; 1959.12; 1962.1;
    1968.23; 1981.5; 1983.18
Panurge, 1950.9; 1953.31; 1981.22;
    1985.13
    ambiguity of, 1973.9
    as comic character, 1959.15
    as courtier, 1976.13
    as Faust, 1985.28
    as modern character, 1955.7
    as picaro, 1978.31; 1979.28
    as Rabelais, 1953.32
    as satirical device, 1967.18
    as sophist, 1973.3; 1974.6
    as subversive character, 1990.18
    coherence/inconsistency of, 1953.42;
        1968.17; 1986.36
    demonic ancestry and nature of,
        1972.18; 1975.10; 1980.30
    encounter with Pantagruel, 1978.36
    Eulenspiegel and, 1985.1
    Falstaff and, 1959.16
    function in the novel, 1978.14
    Hamlet and, 1971.26
    Hermes and, 1958.6
    in TL, 1977.33
    meaning of name, 1980.13
    meaning of his quest, 1983.40
    obscenity and, 1956.17
    Odysseus and, 1982.5; 1982.10–11
    philautia and, 1958.7; 1982.12
    political dimension, 1976.10
    psychoanalytic approach to, 1972.26;
        1976.26–27; 1981.25, 29
    recent interpretations, 1988.66
    relationship with Pantagruel, 1976.29;
        1977.29
Panurge's dream (TL, 14), 1967.12; 1985.16
Panurge's languages (P, 9), 1965.6
Panurge's sheep, 1986.40
the Papefigues episode (QL, 45–47),
    1988.33
the Papimanes episode (QL), 1981.3
    as satire of Papal repression, 1984.20
paradox, 1966.3; 1970.18; 1972.6;
    1976.11; 1979.19; 1982.24;
    1986.33; 1988.75

words
    as objects, 1975.18;
    generative power of, 1977.23
    things and, 1981.13
the world in Pantagruel's mouth (*P*, 32),
    1950.1; 1978.15; 1989.13

writing, as theme, 1978.15; 1985.24

Xenophon, 1980.3

zoological descriptions, 1987.17. *See also*
    animals